AMERICAN VANGUARD

AMERICAN VANGUARD

THE UNITED AUTO WORKERS DURING THE REUTHER YEARS, 1935–1970

John Barnard

Wayne State University Press   Detroit

Published with the assistance of the Walter and May Reuther Memorial Fund

Manufactured in the United States of America.
07 06 05 04   5 4 3 2 1

Library of Congress Cataloging-in-Publication Data

Barnard, John, 1932– *MBC – JOHNSON*
   American vanguard : the United Auto Workers during the Reuther years,
1935–1970 / John Barnard.
      p. cm.
   ISBN 0-8143-2947-0 (cloth : alk. paper)
   1. International Union, United Automobile Workers of America (CIO)—History.
2. Automobile industry and trade—United States—History.   I. Title.
   HD6515.A82I584 2003
   331.88'1292'0973—dc22

2003017663

49.95

We are the vanguard in America
in that great crusade to build a better world.

WALTER P. REUTHER

From his acceptance speech on the occasion of his reelection
as president of the United Auto Workers in 1947

CONTENTS

ILLUSTRATIONS

ACKNOWLEDGMENTS

IT IS A PLEASURE TO ACKNOWLEDGE THE MANY DEBTS I HAVE incurred in writing this book. Irving Bluestone, a UAW member and former vice president, invited me to undertake this study and always offered encouragement and assistance. Leonard Woodcock and Douglas Fraser, two former UAW presidents, were equally supportive, and Owen Bieber, president of the union when I began my research, offered an unrestricted grant that allowed me to devote a portion of my working time to the project for a period of four years. Although these former UAW officers have supported the project in word and deed, this study is not in any sense an "authorized" or "official" history. It has not been reviewed or approved by the UAW, nor should it be taken to represent the views of anyone except myself. Responsibility for the text is entirely mine.

As an additional disclosure, readers are entitled to know that for nearly thirty years of my academic employment I was a member of a union (not the UAW) and a participant in its activities, both in the rank and file and as an elected officer.

Most of the research for this study was conducted at the Archives of Labor and Urban Affairs, located in the Walter P. Reuther Library, Wayne State University. I am greatly indebted to Dr. Philip P. Mason, the founding director of the Archives, to Warner Pflug, its former associate director, and to its interim director Michael O. Smith. During the several years of research many members of the Archives staff cheerfully and with the utmost professional competence made materials from the collections available to me. They include Alberta Asmar, Pat Bartkowski, Raymond Boryczka, Carrolyn Davis, Tom Featherstone, William Gulley, Louis Jones, William LeFevre, Margery Long, Cathy Short Lyles, Margaret Raucher, and Kathy Schmeling. To all of the Archive's past and present staff, my sincere thanks and best wishes. Association and friendship with them has been a pleasure.

I would also like to thank my colleagues in the Department of History and in the administration of Oakland University for their cooperation in arranging leaves of absence from my teaching duties there.

This study does not represent the first attempt to write a general history of the UAW and I have greatly benefited from the work of one who went before. With UAW encouragement and cooperation, John "Jack" Herling, a distinguished labor journalist, proposed to write such a history in the 1970s; he prepared for the task by interviewing dozens of UAW officers and union members. Unfortunately, he did not live to complete his study but transcripts of his interviews, made available to me by the UAW and now deposited in the Archives, have been a valuable resource. I hope he would be pleased with this result.

For this work I have drawn freely on the research and writing of others. Interviews conducted by Jack W. Skeels in the 1960s with UAW officers and activists have been especially helpful. Among scholarly authors I am particularly indebted to Professor Sidney A. Fine of the University of Michigan and several of his doctoral students, including Kevin Boyle, Nancy Gabin, and Martin Halpern, for their writings on UAW subjects. Citations to the studies of these and other authors will be found in the endnotes and the bibliographical note. I thank them all. Without their work this book could not have been written.

All or portions of the text were read and commented on by several colleagues. Their number includes Steve Babson, Irving Bluestone, Douglas Fraser, and William S. McIlrath. They were joined by anonymous readers enlisted by the Wayne State University Press. Their suggestions have been most helpful in improving the text. For errors that remain, I alone am responsible.

I welcome readers' comments on the events discussed in this book. I may be reached by e-mail at: VJB11@earthlink.net.

INTRODUCTION

"THE HISTORY OF THIS UNION IS SO REMARKABLE AND SO wonderful, and it is getting lost." The words are Leonard Woodcock's, in remarks made to United Auto Workers officers and other members of its International Executive Board shortly after he became the union's president. Even before Woodcock spoke the UAW had taken a major step to protect its story from loss by designating Wayne State University as the official repository of its records, pledging that inactive files would become available for research there ten years after their date of origin. The university established the Archives of Labor and Urban Affairs to house the UAW collections and such research materials as might be placed there by other unions and metropolitan Detroit community organizations. The union funded the construction of a model archives facility, the Walter P. Reuther Library, on the Wayne campus. Without this UAW commitment to historical scholarship neither this study nor the many others that have drawn on the records in this archive would have been possible.[1]

Embedded in the UAW's history are both fulfillment and frustration, victories and defeats. The industrial union movement, in which the UAW was a pioneer and an inspiration, gained its momentum from the Great Depression and the New Deal of the 1930s. Once the union won recognition as the workers' representative in dealing with the auto manufacturers, it sought to better the lives of its members and their families through reforming working conditions, enhancing economic security, and raising wages. Auto workers transformed their relationships with their work and the factory. Acting in solidarity, they affirmed and enhanced their sense of their humanity as they created, participated in, and controlled a powerful, effective, democratic organization. The union offered new opportunities for self-expression and growth, and eventually opened the way to a substantial measure of the promise, security, and material standards of middle-class American life. Although the work was and remains physically demanding, in compensation, in job protection, and in gaining a voice in shaping their working conditions and their future, auto workers advanced through the instrumentality of the UAW. A factory floor regime once notorious for unbalanced distribution and exercise of power conceded respect to those who labored there and acknowledged their human dignity.

In formulating its mission the UAW looked beyond the workplace and the immediate interests of its members to the larger society. It sought to establish an American social democracy in which all citizens had a fair chance to better their economic and social status, receive equal treatment, and enjoy a secure livelihood through a private economy that provided jobs and produced goods needed by all. A comprehensive array of public policies would guarantee to each citizen a good education, adequate housing, health care, and protection against loss of income through unemployment or retirement.

The union's ambitious goals in the workplace and in the broader society could be attained only through unremitting effort and struggle. In its early years the UAW had to overcome internal divisions of ideology, ethnicity, race, and culture to forge a consensus in respect to its direction and leadership. In its daily activities, it confronted some of the world's largest and most powerful corporations, which would not accept restraints on their behavior or surrender any portion of their privileges without a contest. Securing the public policies it favored brought the union into conflict with hostile interests entrenched in the political system. In order to understand and assess the UAW's story, it is essential to keep in mind the complex set of historical, political, legal, economic, industrial, social, cultural, and ideological contexts in which it was placed and had to work out its destiny. To a degree the boundaries of these contexts could be redrawn and their content reshaped, but their deeply rooted substance set limits to what was possible.

CHAPTER 1

"Hurry up!"

The Auto Industry before the Union

WHEN THE UNITED AUTOMOBILE WORKERS (UAW) WAS founded in 1935 the American auto industry was already a generation old and Americans were known around the world as a people on wheels. Born at the turn of the century, the industry roared at breakneck speed through three decades of headlong growth, providing millions of cars for Americans and huge profits for the successful manufacturers, only to see growth and profits shrink and disappear when the economy suddenly and severely collapsed in 1929. The automobile had quickly become, next to a home, the American family's most costly and prized possession. In this unfolding saga of invention and industrial development, with the new options for transportation and displays of affluence they made possible, a union of auto workers had played no part. The spark that ignited the workers' resolve to speak as one in support of their common interests was struck when the Great Depression's hardships and insecurities undermined an uneasy equilibrium in the industry's labor relations. A new balance of political forces, engendered by the depression, created the context in which a definition and assertion of auto workers' interests and rights became possible and necessary.[1]

The UAW's first convention met in 1935 in Detroit, Michigan, the capital of American auto production, under the auspices of the American Federation of Labor (AFL), then the nation's only significant national trade union organization. Most of the unions comprising the AFL were craft-based, each representing workers in a skilled trade—carpenters, machinists, electricians, and the like—but a few—for example, the United Mine Workers and the Amalgamated Clothing Workers—were industrial unions that sought to organize all of an industry's workers regardless of the task each person performed. John L. Lewis, president of the United Mine Workers, would soon seize the opportunity offered by the Great Depression to bring the millions of factory hands in the core industries of auto, steel, agricultural implements, rubber, electrical equipment, and chemicals into industrial unions, affiliated with a new labor body, the Committee for (later Congress of) Industrial Organizations (CIO). Industrial workers, inspired by a vision of a "new deal" in the workplace as well as in politics, prepared to challenge the owners and managers of capital for control of their working lives.[2]

The UAW as founded in 1935 was not an autonomous organization. Issued only a probationary charter by the AFL, its officers were appointed and its policies shaped by AFL president William Green. Auto workers soon rebelled against the timid leadership of Francis Dillon, Green's appointee as UAW president, an outsider without autoworker experience. In less than a year, in April 1936, a second UAW convention meeting in South Bend, Indiana, dismissed Dillon and refounded the union as a self-governing affiliate of the AFL. Free to set their union's course, the delegates elected officers from within their ranks and joined other industrial unions from the coal mining, steel, rubber, electrical equipment, and clothing industries in the CIO, an affiliation that soon led to the UAW's expulsion from the AFL. The UAW remained in the CIO until the merger of the two labor federations as the AFL-CIO in 1955. Within the union, a three-tiered structure was established. The International Union's officers were at the top; a second layer consisted of geographically defined regions, each headed by an elected director who was also a member of the union's executive board; and at the base were the local unions chartered by the International and situated in the dozens, and later hundreds and even thousands, of workplaces.[3]

The two hundred and sixteen delegates who gathered in South Bend in 1936 represented only a small fraction of the industry's workers, although they expressed the aspirations of many. Very few came from the plants of auto manufacturing's "Big Three," the General Motors Corporation (GM), the Ford Motor Company, and the Chrysler Corporation, then as later among the world's largest business enterprises. Those in control of these giant corporations had sworn in public and private, so far with success, never to recognize and bargain collective contracts covering wages and working conditions with an industrial union of their employees. Although under pressure they would eventually yield on these points, their hostility to the union remained. Few of the delegates attending the South Bend convention came from the industry's southeast Michigan heartland, where the Big Three's plants and influence were concentrated. Nearly all represented small UAW locals in the shops and factories of independent car makers and parts suppliers scattered along the industry's midwestern boundaries in cities large and small in Wisconsin, Illinois, Indiana, and Ohio. Although the union at first lacked a presence in the factories of the major manufacturers, the convention delegates knew that its permanence and success hinged on the outcome of confrontations with the Big Three. They were confident that among workers in the unorganized shops and factories there were both hopes and resentments on which to build.[4]

DRAWING UPON AND THEN surpassing the automobile's European inventors, turn-of-the-century American mechanics and manufacturers took command of automotive development. Assembling cars and trucks quickly became the nation's leading manufacturing industry, one that provided, as Henry Ford had proclaimed it would, cars for "the great multitude." By the end of the 1920s, with a car on the road for every five persons, the automobile and its manufacturers had transformed American economic, social, and cultural life, securing for the family car an honored place in upper-, middle-, and even some working-class households. Originally scattered across the nation's northeastern quadrant in many—mostly small—shops, the industry moved gradually toward consolidation in both location and structure. Well-situated to connect the capital, raw materials, and labor necessary for manufacturing cars with the markets in which to sell them, Detroit, Michigan, became the headquarters of the major manufacturers and the location of many of their assembly and parts plants. Sinclair Lewis captured the booster spirit of this boom city of the nation's Second Industrial Revolution in a fictional letter from the head of a Detroit automobile company to the protagonist of his novel, *Dodsworth*, in distant Zenith, Minnesota: "Come up to Detroit and see how we make things hum! . . . Talk about Napoleon! Talk about Shakespeare! Why we're pulling off the greatest miracle since the Lord created the world!" By the end of the 1920s, an oligopoly of three giant firms, each of sufficient size to achieve the economies of scale essential for lowering production costs, manufactured 80 percent of all American-made cars in their Midwestern, mainly Michigan, factories. With an average employment in 1929 of 450,000 wage earners, the industry had one of the largest workforces in the world.[5]

The production methods used in the earliest auto shops were simple and conventional for the times. Most manufacturers were assemblers who bought parts and subassemblies—axles, transmissions, brakes, frames, bodies, and so on—from the machine shops, forges, foundries, and carriage and wagon makers equipped to produce them. A car was put together by a small gang of workmen assembling a single machine. A typical layout consisted of several such gangs scattered with their piles of parts around the factory floor. When they had a car up and running, they collected the parts for another from storerooms and went to work on it. For assembling cars, workers had to possess metalworking tool and bench skills in order to shape and fit the rough castings and forgings with hand files and grinders. Finishing the car by fabricating, painting, and upholstering its partly wooden and partly steel body also required cadres of skilled workers. Consequently, as many as three out of four workers in these early auto plants were classified as skilled. With their indispensable skills, the workmen shared control over the content and pace of the work process, and in body making and foundry work (but not assembly) many were organized in craft unions. Because of these craft methods of manufacture, it took days to fabricate and assemble a single car. As the automobile caught on with the public and demand escalated, pressures to standardize the product and expand output became irresistible. The manufacturer who could supply reliable vehicles by the thousands while reducing unit costs would be repaid with fame and fortune. Several saw the opportunity; Henry Ford seized it. In flooding the nation with his Model T's, marketed at lower and lower prices, produced at less and less cost, and generating more and more profit, he offered the most popular car of the times to eager buyers and in the process invented modern factory work. Ford's organization of work, "Fordism" as it is sometimes called, became the model for manufacturing hundreds of items as the assembly line, interchangeable parts, division of labor, a progressive layout of machines, and other elements of the mass production system spread throughout the industrial economy.[6]

Mass production soon transformed work in the auto plants as the design of the automobile stabilized with standardized components. The skilled workmen of the early years gave way to machines designed by engineers and operated by semiskilled or even unskilled factory hands. The production process was continuously analyzed and reorganized, with the work force redeployed to increase speed, enhance efficiency, lower costs, and centralize control in the hands of management. Although dramatic moments of advance, such as Ford's introduction in 1914 of a moving assembly line to mate the car's chassis and body, were publicized and heralded, in fact the reinvention of production took place gradually, requiring at least ten years to experiment, identify bottlenecks, and devise improvements in design, materials, manufacturing procedures, and factory layout. Even the factory buildings underwent redesign based on "rational" rather than traditional principles. The Ford plant in Highland Park, Michigan, and the massive River Rouge complex of facilities in Dearborn, Michigan, were conceived and constructed as integral parts of the production process. Although Ford made the major advances and received the lion's share of the acclaim, other manufacturers, particularly Buick's production chief Walter P. Chrysler in Flint, were exploring and implementing similar strategies.[7]

When the mass production system was fully in operation, materials in Ford factories flowed through a vast mechanical river fabricated of steel, with each tributary contributing to the main channel in a logical order. A pattern of sequential operations was devised for making parts, with the machines located so that the work flowed from one operation to the next with a minimum of movement, labor, and lost time. Special purpose metal-shaping machines that could perform only a single operation, but could do that one job quickly and well, were designed and installed. Equally important, the division and subdivision of each step in the manufacturing process into the maximum number of separate operations, with each task as fully mechanized as possible, allowed the work to be performed by factory hands who lacked a machinist's training and skill. The Ford Motor Company demonstrated the savings in time, labor, and money that could be achieved by mass production methods with the magneto, the heart of the Model T's ignition system. By the traditional method, a single workman doing the entire job could assemble a magneto in fifteen to twenty minutes. In a nine-hour workday he produced thirty to forty magnetos. When the job was divided into twenty-nine separate operations, each assigned to an unskilled worker, with gravity slides and later conveyors moving the pieces from one workman to the next, the time needed to assemble a magneto shrank to five minutes of worker time. Averaged over the entire crew, each worker produced ninety-five magnetos in an eight-hour day. The new arrangement had more than doubled productivity.[8]

Ford production engineers subdivided operations and extended the conveyor lines into the factory's farthest reaches. By the old methods about ten hours of labor were required to assemble an engine; following a few months of experimentation in stationing workers along a moving line, the time was reduced to less than six hours. The crowning achievement came in 1913–14 on the chassis line, where the subassembly lines and conveyors flowed together into a mighty stream. Chassis assembly at Ford had once required nearly twelve-and-one-half hours to produce a single car; with the moving assembly line in operation the time was reduced to about one-and-one-half hours, nearly tripling production. An endless chain, winched along at six feet a minute, drew a row of cars past its parallel lines of servicing attendants. The modern factory had been born. The new methods brought forth cars and, when applied elsewhere, many other products in unprecedented abundance, adding immeasurably to human comfort and convenience, and eventually producing a higher material standard of living for nearly everyone. The achievement, however, was bought only with the payment of a heavy human price.[9]

A part of the cost was paid by skilled workers, since much of their assembly work could now be performed by semiskilled and even unskilled laborers. Some skilled trades, such as hand painting, coach building and traditional upholstering, disappeared from the factories. Owing to the great and rapid expansion of the industry, few skilled metal workers were actually displaced, although the contraction of their role in production compressed wage

The magneto assembly line at Ford Motor Company's Highland Park, Michigan, plant, c. 1913. Walter P. Reuther Library, Wayne State University

differentials between them and the unskilled and challenged their status as blue-collar aristocrats. Their work changed, with perhaps some loss of prestige, but they were still needed, and jobs were usually available. No longer required to hand file and fit parts, they were absorbed into making the dies that stamped out interchangeable parts, the tools that aligned parts for assembly, or in maintenance trades such as electrician and pipe fitter. Some became inspectors and others were promoted to supervisory positions. As a result, skilled workers constituted 10 to 15 percent of a greatly expanded 1920s work force.[10]

The larger share of the human price of mass production was paid by the production workers. The popular image of *the* auto worker as an assembler engaged in brief, endlessly repeated motions was soon established and has long endured. In fact, assembly work has always been only one element in auto labor. When counted in 1924, the largest number of workers in the car plants, about 40 percent, consisted of the pressmen, grinders, metal finishers, painters, welders, seamstresses, trimmers, and others who operated the machines that made, shaped, and installed the car's thousands of different parts. The measure of skill required varied enormously, but for most of them their work was as repetitious, strenuous, and stressful as that of assemblers. Another 45 percent were equally divided into three occupational classes: assemblers, helpers, and laborers. They worked the assembly lines, moved stock and parts from one location to another, sweated in the foundries and paint shops (among the most disagreeable and unsafe jobs), and performed routine, unskilled, often heavy maintenance chores. Thus, about 85 percent of the workers were assigned to semiskilled and unskilled job classifications, with only about 15 percent of the total engaged in assembly work. The work of all required strength, stamina, speed, and dexterity.[11]

Little training was needed to become proficient in most branches of production work. According to Henry Ford, who may have understated the amount of time required to learn jobs in his factory as a way of touting his industrial innovations, by the 1920s 43 percent of the jobs required only one day or less of training; another 36 percent required from one day to one week; and 6 percent required from one to two weeks. Fourteen percent required a month to one year of training, and only one percent, tool and die making, the most demanding of the metal trades, from one to six years.[12]

Whether the worker sweated on an assembly line or tended a machine, the rapid repetition of a single operation became the defining feature and symbol of auto production work. A particular operation might require minutes or be completed in seconds, but it was each worker's endless, quick round of identical movements that captured the attention of observers and workers alike. Repetition did not mean relaxation. Although the conscious mind might partially disengage as movements were learned and became routine, the body and nervous system remained tightly attached. Not all manufacturers drove the assembly lines at equally high speeds or set impossibly high production rates on presses and other machines, but production meant profit, and the lines and machines tended to move as fast as the workers' physical and nervous constitutions permitted. The Ford lines moved fast; some other manufacturers, such as Dodge Brothers, had a reputation for a less hectic pace. With all elements, human and mechanical, tightly linked in an interdependent whole, the failure of a worker to perform his job in the allotted time would be felt throughout the factory. The pressure was, therefore, relentless. The cardinal industrial sin was delaying or stopping the line, throwing dozens, possibly hundreds, into idleness and thereby escalating costs. The line had to move and the worker had to move at its command. "Hurry up!" in whatever variation and in whatever language, resounded on the factory floor.[13]

The long days of hard work wore men down. With their shifts completed, streetcar passengers slumped in their seats if they were lucky enough to get one, sleeping as they rode home—which for many was a rented room. For some, alcohol was a source of quick energy and a reprieve from the grinding fatigue of the job. Out of the factory and into a neighbor-hood bar during a brief lunch break for a drink and a sandwich was a common practice at some plants. Anywhere in Detroit one was never far from a tavern. During Prohibition the city had thousands of speakeasies and blind pigs serving bootleg liquor, with many of them located near the plants and in working-class neighborhoods. Liquor by the glass was sometimes sold during lunchtime or at shift changes out of automobiles parked next to plant gates.[14]

SINCE AUTO WORKERS WERE seldom asked what they thought and felt about their jobs, one looks for clues in their actions as well as in their few recorded words. The findings are mixed. Many actions and words reveal hostility, even hatred of the work. For whatever reason, or combination of reasons, many workers simply did not report for work regularly. High rates of absenteeism and turnover as the industry embraced mass production methods reflected dissatisfaction with the harsh physical nature of the toil and the boredom induced by many of the jobs. The contemporary labor economist John R. Commons observed that prior to the introduction of the $5 day in 1914, Ford workers were "conducting a continuous, unorganized strike" by their chronic absenteeism. In 1913 Ford had an astounding turnover rate of 370 percent; it had to hire more than 52,000 production workers in that year in order to maintain a workforce numbering 13,600 on average. The daily absentee rate at Ford in 1913 averaged an unprecedented 10.5 percent of the workforce. Other Detroit auto makers faced similar, if less extreme, situations. The annual turnover rate at the Packard Motor Car Company's East Side plant was nearly 200 percent. By interrupting production and adding to training time for new employees, absenteeism and turnover sharply raised costs. Although management efforts to reduce turnover had some effect by the 1920s, the industry's rate remained high. In 1928 over 5 percent of Michigan auto workers quit every month, the highest rate for any of the state's industries. Some workers incorporated absenteeism into their weekly routine. A Ford official observed that "we have a large number of men in our employ who work only enough days per week to enable them to earn enough to live on—in lots of cases working every other day, making the total number of days worked, three per week." The laconic reply of a welder when asked why he worked only four days a week—"Because I can't get along on three"—has become industry legend and been repeated many times. Turnover was heaviest during the first month of employment, as some quickly found the stresses and fatigue of the modern factory intolerable; another peak of departures occurred after four or five months.[15]

The evidence of absenteeism and turnover, however, is ambiguous since the staggering rates reflect, in part, the high demand for labor, which made changing jobs alluring, easy, and free of risk. In good times labor was scarce in the auto manufacturing centers, so one could take off for a few days of holiday or job-hunting and be certain of hiring in elsewhere. A change of jobs might bring more congenial work and better pay, offer an escape from an oppressive foreman, or provide a work location more convenient to home and transportation. Since companies offered few or no incentives keyed to length of employment (such as pension plans, opportunities for advancement, job security, or seniority wage increases), there was little reason for a workman to remain with a firm when an immediate advantage elsewhere beckoned. In addition, a significant portion of turnover was due to discharges by foremen, who might fire a worker for reasons of inefficiency, personal dislike, or because of poor planning of labor requirements. Workers left of their own volition or were turned out for many different reasons.[16]

THE STRONGEST EVIDENCE of a positive attitude toward the job lies in the industry's ability to recruit its workers from all corners of the world. From near and far, those seeking work looked to Detroit and other auto cities for good-paying jobs. Over the years hundreds of thousands of migrants uprooted themselves to forge new lives in the industry. Between 1900 and 1930, largely in response to the growth of auto making and the service industries needed to support it, Detroit's population increased six times over, from 285,284 to 1,720,000. Priming the pump, the Employers' Association of Detroit placed ads for workers in nearly two hundred newspapers. An extraordinary variety of foreign-born workers and their descendants— English, Canadian, Scots, Irish, Polish, German, Russian, Ukrainian, Italian, Hungarian, Bulgarian, Roumanian, Greek, Croatian, Slovenian, Serb, Lithuanian, Finn, Swede, Mexican, Syrian, Belgian, and so on—were to be found throughout the industry, particularly in Detroit. The city's foreign-born population tripled between 1900 and 1920, to some 290,000 persons in a population of nearly a million. A 1917 survey of Ford Motor Company employees showed that 60 percent were immigrants, of whom three-quarters came from eastern and southern Europe. Of 93,159 Detroit auto workers listed in the 1930 census, nearly half (43 percent) were foreign-born whites, and an undetermined but substantial portion of the 41 percent who were listed as native-born whites were in fact first-generation descendants of immigrants. Large areas of the city were inhabited by immigrants of one or several ethnic groups. When Douglas Fraser, UAW president from 1977 to 1983, was growing up in a teeming West Side Detroit neighborhood, predominantly Polish but including Scots like himself and a few Italians, he did not have a playmate or acquaintance whose parents, including his own, were born in the United States. Lacking for the most part factory or urban experience, the foreign-born in the auto plants were concentrated in the less skilled classifications, although immigrants from the British Isles and western Europe were well represented in the skilled trades.[17]

RURAL AND SMALL-TOWN FOLK from midwestern and southern states also streamed into the auto cities. Outstate Michigan, Ohio, Indiana, Illinois, and Wisconsin sent in their thousands. Some migrants sought to escape declining regional economies. Hard times and unemployment in the copper mines of Michigan's Upper Peninsula, for example, stimulated a flow of ex-miners to the auto factories in the state's southern cities. Equally significant was a massive influx of migrants from the upper- and border-state South. In some auto factories more than half of new hires in the 1920s were southerners. By the end of the decade as many as 100,000 southern whites, mostly from farms and small towns in Missouri, Arkansas, Tennessee, and Kentucky, lived in Detroit and Flint, where the auto plants provided work for the breadwinners. Flint had its "Little Missouri," many of its residents lured to the plants by ads proclaiming "Come to Flint and earn $10 a day." Detroit, Pontiac, and other auto cities also had their "hillbilly" neighborhoods. Protestant fundamentalism flourished in some plants and auto cities. The evangelical preacher who worked in a plant during the week and held forth in a storefront church on Sunday became a not uncommon figure in the workforce. Lloyd Jones, a future UAW activist who began preaching in Kentucky at twelve years of age, abandoned that calling for a Detroit auto plant when he failed as a faith healer. A Ku Klux Klan presence rose and fell in plants and neighborhoods in Detroit, Flint, and Lansing in the mid-twenties, drawing much of its support from the ranks of southern white migrants, both auto workers and others, with a "true Americanism" message targeted against immigrants, Catholics, African Americans, and wets.[18]

Many of these rural and small-town recruits, especially young unattached males, adjusted to the seasonal ebb and flow of auto production by joining the "suitcase brigade," becoming transient workers who arrived by bus or train in late winter and early spring when the plants were hiring, moved into the boarding houses or rental rooms for the duration of their auto employment, then moved on to jobs elsewhere or returned home when layoffs came in the fall. Through such labor mobility, the growth and contraction of the workforce correlated with seasonal shifts in the level of demand.[19]

Although most rural migrants had no experience with or predilection for unions (and some employers saw them as a hedge against unionization), a significant number of newcomers from the coalfields of West Virginia, Kentucky, and Pennsylvania brought with them a prounion outlook, including, in some cases, earlier membership in the United Mine Workers.

A number of the early activists and officers in Local 600 at the Ford Motor Company's River Rouge plant, eventually the UAW's largest and one of its most influential locals, harked back to such origins.[20]

AFRICAN AMERICANS FROM THE SOUTH, although fewer in number, were also part of the migrating throng. In the early years few blacks were employed in the industry, but with the interruption of European immigration during World War I recruitment of blacks mounted rapidly. Though they comprised only .5 percent of the 1910 auto workforce, by 1920 their participation had risen to more than 4 percent, and the number continued to climb slowly through the rest of the decade. Michigan's black population tripled between 1910 and 1920 and tripled again by 1930 to 169,452. Most settled in and around Detroit. By 1926 the Ford Motor Company, with 100,000 employees in the Detroit area, had a black workforce of about 10,000 and a national reputation as an employer of blacks. It was the only auto company to hire blacks as a matter of policy, employing at its River Rouge plant alone about half of those with jobs in the industry. A blues lyric of the 1920s captured some of the ambivalence felt when contemplating a job at "Ford's," as the Ford Motor Company was popularly known.:

> Say, I'm goin' to Detroit, I'm gonna get myself a job, I'm tired of layin' around here workin' on this starvation farm. Say, I'm goin' to get me a job now, workin' in Mr. Ford's place, Say, that woman tol' me last night, "Say, you cannot even stand Mr. Ford's ways."[21]

While conditions in the plants and crowded ghettos of the auto cities left much to be desired for blacks, they were better than those many knew in the shanties and on the depleted lands of the rural South. Joe Louis, the future Brown Bomber, recalled that his stepfather, Pat Brooks, a sharecropper in Alabama,

> made the decision that we couldn't do any worse, so why not try to do better?—and plans went ahead for moving to Detroit. They said the Ford factory didn't mind hiring Negroes, and for once we'd have solid money we wouldn't have to share with the landlord. . . . We moved in with some kinfolks. . . . The house was crowded there, but I was used to being crowded and didn't know that there were more private ways to live, and it seemed fine. How could I notice, anyway, when I had electric lights to pull off and on and a toilet indoors that flushed and flushed when I pulled that chain string? . . . . Ford paid more on the job than you'd ever get on the farm. I thought we were doing pretty well, and I looked forward to working in the plant when I got older.

Louis was by no means the only black athlete to find work in the plants. Norman "Turkey" Stearns from Tennessee, an outstanding baseball player for the Detroit Stars of the Negro National League—judged by Satchell Paige to be "as good as anybody who ever played baseball"—worked at the Briggs Manufacturing Company during the off-season along with his team-mates. "We worked in the paint shop in the winter and played ball in the summer," he recalled. "All that gang, about nineteen of us, with the secretary and manager and all, about twenty-two or twenty-three of us." The black players' auto industry wages tided them over until the next baseball season rolled around.[22]

Ford stood out as a partial exception in the hiring and treatment of African American employees, although the racism that pervaded the community, nationally and locally, was evident in the Ford plants. Using the good offices of ministers of several Detroit black churches to screen candidates, the company recruited black workers, confident that they would be grateful and loyal employees. One especially favored church, which had expanded its horizon from the sacred to the secular, was known within Detroit's black community as "the gates to the kingdom of Ford." Ford jobs, offering better wages to blacks than any other available industrial employment, were highly prized. Only at Ford's did a few blacks attain jobs in the skilled trades, and a handful even rose to low level supervisory posts. In the Ford plants a small number of blacks were also employed on assembly lines and as machine operators, a very rare occurrence elsewhere. But most black Ford employees, about 60 to 70 percent, were assigned to the foundry, working at some of the factory's least desirable, most dangerous and unhealthy jobs. Some parts firms, particularly those with foundries, hired blacks, but most auto companies had few or none. Altogether, blacks comprised 14 percent of Detroit auto workers in 1930. Manufacturers assigned them to the most disagreeable, lowest paid jobs, in foundries and paint shops or in materials handling or janitorial work. When Shelton Tappes, later a UAW and civil rights activist, hired in at the Briggs Mack Avenue plant on Detroit's East Side in 1928, the only job he was offered was the dirty, unpleasant one of wet-sanding car bodies. Other blacks were hired at Briggs for the hazardous job of cleaning paint spray booths and as low paid janitors. One white worker told an investigator that there were "some jobs white folks will not do; so they have to take niggers in, particularly in duco work, spraying paint on car bodies. This soon kills a white man." The investigator asked if the work didn't kill Negroes. "Oh yes," he replied, "it shortens their lives; it cuts them down but they're just niggers." Race-based pay differentials were common. When Hodges Mason, later a UAW activist, worked as a chipper, knocking out the cores of foundry castings for parts maker Bohn Aluminum and Brass Corporation, he received 45 cents an hour for the same work for which some whites were paid 75 cents. A rarely breached Jim Crow color line marked off black from white occupations.[23]

UNSKILLED AND SEMISKILLED auto work, which struck observers from privileged backgrounds as monotonous, unsatisfying, and even degrading, represented for many rural migrants a liberating improvement in status, prospects, and job satisfaction as well as in pay and material standard of living. For many, the factory offered a welcome escape from dead-end farming. As one Buick assembler in Flint recalled, his work on a farm in the harsh climate and thin soil of Michigan's Upper Peninsula had led nowhere. "I was working on shares. I had no farm, and I just rented it, and I could not make a living." Now possessed of a car and home, his employment at Buick had brought economic security, comforts, and conveniences previously out of reach. For many former rural laborers the improvement of factory work over their previous occupations was striking. Workers of Mexican birth who entered Detroit auto plants to escape from backbreaking, low-paid labor in Michigan sugar beet fields or came directly from Mexican agricultural areas took pride in auto work and valued the improvement in status it bestowed. The Ford employees' badge was highly prized, emblematic of achievement and a better life, although most Mexican workers at Ford's were in the lowest paid, unskilled classifications. Instances were known of deceased Ford employees, Mexican and otherwise, who chose to be buried with their Ford employees' badge pinned to the lapel of their burial suit. With about 4,000 workers of Mexican birth in 1928, the Ford Motor Company was one of the largest industrial employers of Mexican labor in the Midwest.[24]

AS IN MANY OTHER AMERICAN workplaces, industrial and otherwise, during the first half of the twentieth century, the auto workforce from top to bottom was notable for an ethnic, cultural, racial, and gender stratification tightly correlated with occupation. Management was entirely white and male, usually Protestant, sometimes Masonic, largely native-born with a thin admixture of western European first- and second-generation immigrants; they were often highly skilled workers who had moved up the occupational ladder. The skilled tradesmen, the factory aristocrats, likewise male and white, either hailed from western Europe, including the British Isles, or were native-born Americans. The semiskilled production workers, mostly male with concentrations of females in a few, selected occupations, were of mostly rural or small-town origin, either native or foreign-born. The unskilled laborers were male and either immigrants or blacks. Many of the men were young and, for the time being, unattached to families. In 1920, the percentage of young men twenty-five to twenty-nine years of age employed in the industry was about double the percentage of that age cohort in the population at large. Detroit's population then contained 119 males for every 100 females (among blacks the ratio was 137 men to every 100 women), a sexual ratio whose imbalance was surpassed in the nation's seventy largest cities only by Akron, Ohio, another city whose growth stemmed from the auto industry.[25]

Shop floor culture and language reflected and reinforced the ethnic, racial, gender, and class segmentation of the workforce. Culture and language were heavily infused with a dominant macho element and commonly employed crude ethnic and racial designations and stereotypes. As a UAW committeeman noted in a 1950s grievance case, expressing a sentiment that had been present for years, "the language of the shop is not the language of the parlor." The ordinary semiskilled and unskilled auto worker was either a "hillbilly," a term most apt for those from the hill country of the border South but which might be stretched to include any white rural migrant of native birth; a "polack," which could be stretched to include any immigrant of Slavic background; a "dago," for an Italian; or a "nigger," the lowly black mired at the bottom of "Detroit's scale of ethnic snobbery." Ethnic and racial slurs and insults were common and sometimes led to quarrels and fights. A Jewish youth who got a job at the E. M. F. factory operating a drill press, for example, became the target of antisemitic remarks from a gang of somewhat older and stronger Polish youths similarly employed. A fight ensued in which the Jewish boy came off second best, prompting him to embrace a regimen of physical culture that included weight lifting in order to be able to better defend himself. The ethnocentric prejudice the terminology disclosed divided the workforce before and into the union era, creating internal schisms and conflicts that hampered the development of a common workers' consciousness and threatened worker solidarity, thereby reducing prospects for unionization. Judgments of worth based on ethnic and racial assumptions were commonplace, often used informally by management to classify employees. As a Detroit executive remarked in 1920, "one German is worth a dozen Polacks or Dagoes." Such judgments always favored males of white, western European origin, whether that origin was immediate or removed by one or more generations.[26]

A SMALL BUT SIGNIFICANT number of workers, both foreign- and native-born, brought to the workplace the prized skills of those craftsmen essential to a metalworking industry: tool and die makers, electricians, millwrights, pipe fitters, and so on. Although much of the work process had been de-skilled, a cadre of skilled workers was needed to keep the machines and assembly lines up and running. Foreign-born and -trained skilled workers were prominent, particularly in Detroit. William Stevenson, born in Glasgow, Scotland, and later president of UAW Local 157, an amalgamated unit of Detroit tool and die shops, estimated that 70 percent of the tool and die men in Detroit plants in the 1920s were of European birth. Ethnic identities in skilled trades shops, where workers' skills and status often gave them effective power over hiring in cooperation with a foreman, were strong and exclusive, drawing upon the ancient craft tradition of passing down the mastery of the trade from one family or tribal generation to the next. As Leonard Woodcock recalled, when his British diemaker father came to Detroit in the 1920s, "there were Swedish tool rooms, there were German tool rooms, there were Scotch tool rooms, there were New England tool rooms, there were English tool rooms. But unless you belonged to that particular group . . . you couldn't get a job, no matter what your skills were." Ties of common origin, skill, language, and, for some, of ideology and political outlook prepared skilled workmen for a major role in the industry's unionization.[27]

One of these skilled workmen, of native birth but immigrant parentage, who entered Detroit's auto industry toward the end of the "prosperity decade" of the 1920s was Walter P. Reuther, a young diemaker born in 1907 in Wheeling, West Virginia. Of medium height and solid build, energetic and ambitious, Reuther arrived in the Motor City in 1927 at the age of nineteen, eager for work that would employ the skills he had acquired in an uncompleted diemaker's apprenticeship at the Wheeling Steel Company. His parents had migrated from Germany, met and married in America, and established a family that included three sons—Walter, Roy, and Victor—all destined for prominent places in the UAW's organizing campaigns and its later history, with Walter, the oldest of the three, the union's president from 1946 until his death in 1970. Val Reuther, the boys' father, was both a committed unionist and a socialist adherent of Eugene V. Debs, the leading American working-class politician and spokesman of the times. The sons were brought up with a fervent faith in worker solidarity, in labor unions, and in the need for sweeping economic and social reforms of the capitalist system. Once in Detroit Reuther worked briefly in a production job at Briggs Manufacturing Company, a builder of car bodies notorious for harsh working conditions and low pay, but within a few weeks, after demonstrating his skills to a skeptical foreman, the young man talked his way into a diemaker's job at Ford's, first in Highland Park then later in the River Rouge plant, where he remained for five years.[28]

EMPLOYERS, WHEN THEY EXPRESSED an opinion, often showed contempt for their semiskilled and unskilled workers and the tasks they performed. Henry Ford, the world's most famous automaker and one of its wealthiest men, whose views on many subjects were well-publicized, proudly noted that the skills once possessed by manual workers had been transferred to the new machines and production processes that were created and installed by engineers, machine designers, and management. Commenting on the unskilled workmen who manned the foundry, Ford wrote they "must be skilled in exactly one operation which the most stupid man can learn within two days." "We have made it unnecessary," he continued, "for the highest types of mental ability to be engaged in every operation in the factory. The better brains are in the mental power-plant." In his view the industry's new workers were well-suited to the mindless character of their tasks. "I could not possibly," he boasted, "do the same thing day in and day out, but to other minds, perhaps I might say to the majority of minds, repetitive operations hold no terrors. In fact, to some types of mind thought is absolutely appalling. . . . The average worker, I am sorry to say, . . . above all . . . wants a job in which he does not have to think." The Ford company, its founder pointed out, offered to transfer workers to different jobs but found few takers. "If [a worker] stays in production," Ford complacently added, "it is because he likes it." Workers might have replied that since the choice offered was seldom if ever between dull and interesting work, it made little sense to transfer from one monotonous job to another. In many observations, Ford workers of that era confirmed the mindless and oppressive character of the work. As one said, "A man checks 'is brains and 'is freedom at the door when he goes to work at Ford's." Management's contempt for so much of its workforce, and its failure to enlist the intelligence and cultivate the cooperation and creativity of so many of its workers in improving the company's products and processes made a major contribution to the adversarial hostility that surfaced with the advent of the unionization movement and would continue to limit the industry's well-being and prosperity throughout the century.[29]

Many observers, both friendly and hostile to the industry's management, employed a machine metaphor to portray "Fordism's" impact on its workers. A consulting engineer admiringly described the workers in Ford's factories as "animate machines . . . [trained] to do their work with all the precision of the most marvelous engine." Or, as a ten-year veteran of Ford factories remarked, "workers cease to be human beings as soon as they enter the gates of the shop. They become automatons and cease to think. They move their arms spontaneously to and fro, stopping long enough to eat in order to keep the human machinery in working order for the next four hours of exploitation. . . . Many healthy workers have gone to work for Ford and have come out human wrecks." A friendly automotive industry journalist conceded that "labor turnover, discontent, industrial unrest and kindred problems confront industry as a result—partially at least—of the intensive development of the machine-man"; the author Matthew Josephson, in a 1929 essay published following a tour of Detroit and its auto plants, wrote "nowhere in the world did men seem so *automatised*, submissive, and monotonous." When Diego Rivera, the radical Mexican artist, was commissioned to create monumental frescoes of "Detroit Industry" for the Detroit Institute of Arts in 1932, he portrayed Ford workers at their jobs as strong and dignified but robot-like figures, invisibly but tightly chained to the machines and assembly lines, responsive to the exacting, relentless, mechanical rhythms of production. In a compelling visual metaphor, Rivera rendered a giant press in the Ford shop in the image of the Aztec goddess Coatlicue, a creator of humanity to whom, according to Aztec religious beliefs, human sacrifice was owed in return.[30]

FOR MANY AUTO WORKERS the relatively high wages they received were the most attractive—perhaps the only attractive—feature of their jobs, reconciling them to its stresses and hardships. From the industry's earliest days hourly rates of pay were high compared to other manufacturing jobs, reflecting labor shortages in the rapidly growing manufacturing centers and the physical grind of the work. As mass production methods brought booming sales and fabulous profits to the successful firms, wages continued to climb. As a general rule, hourly wage rates in the auto industry were about one-third higher than the average wage for all manufacturing workers. In wages, as in the development of mass production methods, the Ford Motor Company led the way. In January 1914 Ford announced, to worldwide publicity and acclaim, that he would pay $5 a day to each worker, more than $2 above prevailing rates in Detroit and a sudden jump in wages of more than 75 percent. The new wage structure consisted of two parts. Every worker continued to draw his base pay. If he qualified for profit sharing, as Ford called the added sum, his pay would rise to $5 per day. This wage policy, according to Ford, was simple equity, giving workers a fair share of the fabulous returns from the Model T's success just as stockholders, consumers, supervisors, and management had all benefited. In addition to raising pay, Ford announced that the company would go to three shifts of eight hours each instead of two shifts of nine hours, a move that would add several thousand jobs as well as reduce the hours worked by individual employees. Sceptics pointed out that Ford may have had more in mind than a simple desire to be generous and fair, noting that by paying high wages Ford would get the pick of the labor force, reduce the number of costly turnovers and absentees, and quiet stirrings of worker unrest that threatened to lead to union organizing. The day following the announcement, Ford was swamped with applicants: 10,000 massed outside its employment office, and police resorted to clubs and high pressure water hoses to beat back the mob of job seekers. Word of Ford's wages spread rapidly throughout the United States and even around the globe. Thanks to dramatically lower turnover and absentee rates, and accelerated production, Ford workers ground out more cars per dollar paid in wages after the $5 wage was introduced than they had before, prompting Henry Ford later to boast that raising wages was one of the best cost cutting measures in the firm's history. Although the new rate was understandably popular, some workers thought the restrictive qualifications for its payment and the rapid production pace that was demanded made it a bad bargain.[31]

The new pay rate was not granted across the board. Ford required a minimum age of twenty-one years, as well as a six-month residence in Detroit followed by a six-month probationary period in the plant. Young men were warned that they would not be allowed to waste their new riches in "riotous living," whatever that vague phrase might mean. Female employees and office workers were excluded at first, but within two years the rate was extended to them. By 1916 three-quarters of Ford's employees were on the new wage scale. By the end of the decade other auto manufacturers in Detroit, responding to the competitive pressure, had brought their wage rates close to the Ford standard or instituted other kinds of compensation plans. Although the new Ford policies reduced wage discrepancies, some remained. It was still possible for employees working side by side at the same tasks to receive different wages owing to a foreman's favoritism or a similar cause.[32]

High wages drew workers to Detroit by the thousands and produced a rich and lasting harvest of favorable publicity for the manufacturers, but to focus exclusively on timed rates is misleading. For one thing the use of piece rates in parts manufacturing remained the standard practice at all firms with the important exception of Ford. Sometimes payment by the number of parts produced worked to the advantage of the machine operator by giving him a degree of control over work pace. By working faster he could increase earnings or, once a quota had been met, work in a more relaxed way. But these opportunities were present only as long as the employer did not cut the rate. Generally speaking, workers disliked piece rates. They pitted one worker against another and could easily be manipulated to set a standard rate that only the very fastest could meet; all those who fell short were penalized. At Hudson the piece rate was cut whenever the fastest worker's rate exceeded pay of $1 an hour. Although mass production methods rendered individual piece rates obsolete on assembly lines, many companies used group piece rates, sometimes called "bonus plans," as production incentives. These schemes, which employed peer pressure to stimulate laggards, created divisions within the workforce and were often so complicated that it was impossible for an ordinary worker to know his actual rate of pay. Pay day could bring an unpleasant surprise.[33]

Other practices scaled down the high daily and hourly rates. Workers were sometimes required, as a condition of keeping their jobs, to put in some work for no pay at all. George Addes, for example, when working for Willys-Overland in Toledo, sometimes had to punch out at the end of the shift but then work an additional two hours for no pay. When wet-sanding bodies at Briggs, Shelton Tappes was paid only for the time he actually worked, a common practice in plants where production was frequently interrupted by mechanical breakdowns or parts shortages somewhere up the line. "When a string of bodies were coming down the line" he recalled, "then our time began. The wages were 27 cents an hour, but we were only paid for the time worked. It wasn't unusual to spend ten to twelve hours in the plant and only get paid for three hours. Usually, we averaged from five to six hours per day." In preunion days employees on piece rate at auto upholstery supplier McInerny Spring and Wire in Grand Rapids, Michigan, might be in the plant for as long as 100 hours a week but be working and earning pay for only one-third of that time. Even skilled workers might report to work to find they had to wait, unpaid, until a job came along.[34]

The greatest reduction in pay stemmed from irregular employment. Layoffs for longer or shorter periods were common. Demand was seasonal, peaking in the spring and early summer, flat for much of the rest of the year. Model changes and retooling could mean layoffs of weeks or even months. Consequently, average annual wages are more significant figures than hourly and daily wage rates in determining the workers' return, although the press and the public paid more attention to the latter. By this comparison, auto industry wages still make a strong showing but they were not as far out of line with wages in other industries as hourly and daily rates suggest. In 1914, the auto industry ranked seventh among American industries in average annual wages; in 1919 it was fifth; in 1925, a good production year with few layoffs, it was first, and in most subsequent years in that decade it ranked either first or second. In dollar terms, in the good years of the late 1920s, the minority of auto workers who were skilled earned from $2500 to $3000 annually, while semiskilled metal finishers and upholsterers took in about $2000 a year, and the less-skilled machine operators and laborers brought home between $1200 and $2000.[35]

HIGH WAGES ALONE, Ford feared, would fail to guarantee the degree of worker loyalty the company sought. To create an environment conducive to a stable, productive workforce, Ford launched an ambitious experiment in social control in 1914 to accompany the $5 daily wage. The company designed a body of personal and social behavioral rules intended to shape workers' values, habits, and characters. Its Sociological Department, staffed by 150 investigators, screened and monitored Ford employees to determine whether their personal lives qualified them for the new wage. Calling on workers and spouses in their homes, carefully observing and sometimes

photographing the houses and their contents, the investigators obtained
answers to a daunting list of questions about marital status, nationality,
religion, citizenship, home ownership, health, recreation, debt, and savings.
As a Ford worker dryly remarked about the company's intrusive, paternalistic investigation, "it was kind of a funny idea, in a free state."[36]

Reprehensible, in Ford's eyes, was the common practice of taking single, male boarders into a married man's household, a practice that sometimes led to severe overcrowding. In one case Detroit public health officials
found fifty-two boarders sharing a twelve-room tenement, and boarding-
houses frequently rented the same bed to workmen on different shifts: one
slept while the other worked. In the rapidly expanding city, with its housing shortage and thousands of unattached male workers, boarding was
essential for many of them. It was also an important source of income for
many families, but Ford saw it as a threat to a settled domestic life, and to
marital fidelity. Employees also failed to qualify for the wage on grounds of
harmful personal habits such as excessive use of liquor, gambling, or "any
malicious practise derogatory to good physical manhood or moral character." Booklets, sporting titles such as "Helpful Hints and Advice to Employees," were issued that urged cleanliness, the cultivation of vegetable
gardens, proper care and rearing of children, thrift, prudent spending, and
the purchase of life and fire insurance. A worker who failed to meet Ford's
standards was given six months to comply; if he failed to improve during
that probationary period, he was fired.[37]

Within a few years, as Ford management became disillusioned with
the results of the program, it was abandoned, and the company turned to
coercive methods of control. By the late 1920s, Ford's Service Department,
a private army thinly disguised as a plant protection force, strictly enforced
an oppressive set of plant rules. The department was under the command
of Harry Bennett, an ex-sailor and boxer who hired paroled convicts for his
staff because they were tough and had useful connections with the gangster
underworld. Employees were kept under surveillance, rest rooms were
checked to prevent malingering, and no smoking was permitted. Employees were forbidden to sit while in the plant, nor could they talk on the job
about matters unrelated to work. According to reports, many Ford workers
mastered the ventriloquist's art of speaking without moving their lips or
spoke out of the sides of their mouths in order to communicate with others undetected by the "servicemen." A cloud of oppression descended upon
the Ford factories that did not lift until the UAW was established there.[38]

The Ford company also, like many other employers of immigrant labor,
required non-English speaking employees to make progress in learning the
English language and in adopting "American" customs as conditions of maintaining employment. Ford provided instruction in English in its Ford English

School, or "Melting Pot School," as it was less formally known, in a thirty-six week, after working-hours course using materials that emphasized the industrially valuable traits of punctuality, reliability, efficiency, concern for health, and other domestic habits of settled middle-class life. The course also taught a racism lesson. Students were told that "Black people came from Africa where they lived like other animals in the jungle," and that "white men brought them to America and made them civilized." The graduation ceremony ushered students through an elaborate "melting pot" pageant where, dressed in old world costumes, they descended by ladders from a mock immigrant ship into a mammoth, fake pot. There, with the students hidden from view, the pot's contents were vigorously "stirred" by their teachers, and the students emerged attired in American-style clothing, waving small American flags. The ceremony underlined the irrelevance, even harmfulness, of the immigrants' preindustrial cultures in their new setting. On occasion more severe measures were taken at Ford's to teach American ways. In January 1914 the company fired between eight and nine hundred Greek and Russian Orthodox Christians, about 6 percent of Ford's workforce, who had been absent from work on the day their faith celebrated as Christmas. A Ford official explained: "if these men are to make their home in America they should observe American holidays."[39]

Less intrusive attempts to win the loyalty of workers and stabilize the work force were tried by some other companies. Most simply hired the workman, paid the agreed wage, and let the relationship between employer and employee rest on the dual foundation of the cash nexus and the foreman's shop floor authority. But during World War I and the 1920s, several companies adopted elements of a welfare capitalist program that sought to forge bonds between employer and employee as well as enhance economic security and render unnecessary a resort to worker-controlled, independent unions. Different programs, tried at one or another auto company, included bonus plans based on length of employment, company stock purchase plans, home ownership plans, savings plans (promoted as a substitute for pensions), death and disability insurance, training programs for job upgrades, unpaid vacation plans, recreational opportunities, plant lunchrooms, sponsored social events, and company orchestras, glee clubs, and sports teams.[40]

The most comprehensive program, and the one that affected the most workers, was conducted by the General Motors Corporation in Flint, Michigan, the center of its production system. Skilled workers, with their higher earnings and greater value to the corporation, were the usual participants in GM's savings and stock investment plan, its training programs, and company housing. GM required its Flint employees to belong to the Industrial Mutual Association (IMA), whose offerings of insurance plans, recreational facilities, a dance hall, and auditorium programs attracted thousands of workers and their families. In 1926, when GM offered noncontributory group life and health insurance plans to its employees, the IMA administered the program. Far more than larger, more diversified Detroit, Flint— with its huge Buick, Chevrolet, and parts factories and a total General Motors blue-collar employment of as many as 60,000 men and women in the 1920s—took on the lineaments of the classic "company town," with its civic and political culture reflecting the interests and tastes of the automaker elite. With some exceptions, these measures collapsed or at best barely survived during the depression. It seems likely that they had little lasting effect on workers' attitudes toward their jobs or their employers. As ever, high wages were the best card in the employers' hand in recruiting and retaining an efficient work force.[41]

FEMALE WORKERS IN THE AUTO PLANTS, while they shared many work experiences with their male counterparts, stood apart in important respects. For one thing there were far fewer of them. At all occupational levels, the early auto industry was largely a male preserve, with a heavily macho shop floor and office culture. Women constituted about 5 percent of the work force in motor vehicle plants, about 10 percent in auto body plants, and about 20 percent in auto parts plants. Particular employers such as Hudson, Chrysler, Continental Motors, and the parts-producing AC Spark Plug and Ternstedt Manufacturing divisions of General Motors employed thousands of women, a majority of the workforce in some of their plants. In Flint, the AC Spark Plug plant was the city's largest employer of women. Ford as a matter of policy employed very few. Women could be found in nearly one-fourth of the industry's many occupational classifications, but in fact they were concentrated in relatively few jobs. These included tasks requiring close and light hand work, such as manufacturing and assembling small parts and accessories like spark plugs and other electrical equipment items, body hardware, the "cut and sew" departments that prepared upholstery in body plants, metal finishing and polishing, small press operation, and inspection. Many were young, unmarried, and living either at home or in rooming houses, although a growing minority were married women who worked in order to supplement a husband's income.[42]

Employing women helped reduce costs, and employers sometimes directly substituted female for male labor, although this seems to have happened rarely. In 1925 women's average earnings in the industry were 47 cents an hour compared with 73 cents for men, or about 65 percent of the male wage. The women employees at AC Spark Plug were Flint's lowest paid auto workers. A Ford worker laid off in 1927 reported that his wife landed a job running a drill press for 30 cents an hour, half of what he had received for the same work. "She could do the work as well as I could," he said, "so the firm hired her because she was cheaper. If she had refused some other woman would have taken it." A loosely worded Michigan statute prohibiting discrimination "in any way in the payment of wages as between sex" was unenforceable, and another law restricting women to ten hours of work a day and fifty-four hours a week suffered the same fate. A prosperous industry's financial ability to pay high wages in order to stabilize its workforce reduced the incentive to employ women at a lower rate.[43]

Although gender segregation by occupation within factories may have shielded some women from unwelcome attentions and pressures, sexual harassment was a frequent, though not systematically documented, occurrence, engaged in by both supervisors and male fellow employees. The scope and severity of harassment is unknown, but the macho culture and the unequal distribution of power on the shop floor created an environment in which it could flourish. Reports and recollections of demands by foremen and other supervisors for sexual services in exchange for favorable job assignments or other work privileges, or to ward off punishments for alleged infractions of the rules, including threats of being fired, are too common to ignore. Fellow workers also might engage in harassment, rationalized by its male practitioners as innocent teasing. A young male Briggs employee, working on a seat cushion line, recalled relationships with a "crew of girls" on a neighboring line. "[W]e fellows always found time to fuss around with these gals, asking them for dates or reaching down the line to give one of them a pinch or a pat. Most of the gals were buxom Polish lasses . . . who endured our sportiveness with tolerant good nature. They cracked back at us with ready wit, belittling our boasted amatory powers and advising us to take our passions to the Hamtramck brothels." For women the auto plant environment and milieu all too often meant hurts and indignities.[44]

FOR BOTH WOMEN AND MEN, the factory environment—always noisy, even deafening, from the bang and clatter of machinery, and often dirty— was unpleasant and dangerous. Although not as hazardous as mining and several other occupations, early auto work entailed serious risks to health and safety. Foundry casting, metal finishing with lead solder, the use of lead-based paints on car bodies, and the use of toxic chemicals in chrome-plating and other processes threatened health, even life itself. One metal finisher reported that in his plant "there was no attempt to guard against lead poisoning." Silicosis and other respiratory and lung diseases, in addition to lead poisoning, were the most serious problems. Of the Ford Highland Park foundry, an observer, one generally friendly to the company, reported that "the air during working hours cannot be endured by any workman save those possessing respiratory organs of the most robust description and many visitors are unable to walk through the Ford greyiron foundry . . . because they cannot breathe the air."[45]

The unforgiving machinery, the fast pace of production, and the mind-numbing repetition of the same movements led to industrial accidents in the stamping and parts plants and on the assembly lines. In jobs for which piece rates were set, workers had an incentive to take shortcuts that might prove injurious or even fatal. It was no coincidence that the Ford Motor Company, with the industry's best record in health and safety, did not employ piece rates. The huge presses that stamped body parts out of sheet steel, and which could amputate a hand or an arm in a fraction of a second, often were operated by foot pedals, a dangerous device, rather than by safer but slower hand controls. Despite Ford's better record on safety, under its harsh disciplinary regime of the late 1920s workers risked and even lost their lives as a result of management's insistence on getting out products. Years later, Walter Reuther recalled one such episode from his stint as a diemaker at Ford. Service Department "plug-uglies" forced a reluctant diemaker to undertake a dangerous die repair in a massive press by threatening to fire him. The repair went awry, the press slammed down, and the man was killed. Speaking for those who witnessed or experienced similar instances of indifference to a life, Reuther concluded his telling of the story to his UAW audience with the words, "I don't forget these things."[46]

Companies maintained clinics or first aid stations in their factories to render assistance to the injured, to secure evidence to defend against a worker's compensation claim, and to guard against fraudulent allegations of injury and illness. Companies promoted safety on the job through publicity campaigns but insisted that workers themselves were primarily responsible for whatever happened to them. On the whole, the industry's record, despite its many inherently dangerous operations, was better than in many comparable lines of work.[47]

A COMPREHENSIVE PORTRAIT of auto workers' material standard of living is unavailable, but data suggest that by the end of the 1920s the wages of a steadily employed auto worker provided a decent, working-class standard of living for himself and his family. Many auto workers among the skilled and even semiskilled purchased or built modest homes in working-class neighborhoods. For most, little remained after the basic necessities of food, shelter, and clothing were provided. Expenditures for these three items, including fuel, light, and household furnishings, absorbed more than 75 percent of the auto worker's pay. Ford workers averaged $1,712 in earnings in 1929 and expended a virtually identical amount for necessities. Only 7 percent of the Ford workers surveyed had funds available for an annual vacation, on which they spent an average of $37.[48]

The claim that auto workers had risen to middle-class levels of comfort, convenience, and consumption by the end of the "prosperity decade" is more myth than reality. Although some drove their cars to work, others rode streetcars or took a bus. Since small and medium-sized parts plants were often located in or adjacent to residential neighborhoods, many of their employees walked to their jobs. Of 100 Ford families surveyed in 1929, 47 owned cars, 45 had phonographs, 36 radios, 19 electric vacuum cleaners, and 49 washing machines. Auto workers undoubtedly enjoyed a higher standard of living than most working-class Americans, one that gave access to some of the consumer products and the popular culture entertainments that flooded American society in the twenties, but abundance and economic security were still distant, elusive goals. However limited their material possessions might appear to later generations, for many auto workers their car, the house, access to baseball games, the movies, and other popular entertainments reconciled them to the tedium of the assembly line.[49]

First-generation immigrant and black auto workers, with their work and community lives confined by bigotry and unequal opportunity, gained a less exalted standard of living and had to contend with greater economic insecurity. Segregated housing, as in Detroit's East Side ghetto, "Paradise Valley," forced black auto workers to devote a larger share of their income to housing expenses, leaving less for other needs.[50]

FOR MANY AUTO WORKERS the worst part of the job was the abuse, humiliation, and insecurity inflicted by arbitrary supervisors. According to Walter Reuther, in the old days before the union won a place on the shop floor, "injustice was as commonplace" in the factories "as streetcars" were on city streets. Although most large companies established employment offices to accept applications and screen prospective hires—and in some of these companies turnover was reduced when hiring and firing decisions were partially centralized—the department foremen always had an important say in employment decisions. Abuses by foremen of their authority may not have been the norm, but they were far from uncommon. Family, religious, ethnic, and other kinds of favoritism entered into decisions respecting hiring, promoting, and firing employees. At the Fisher Body plant in Cleveland, as in many others, workers were laid off every summer to make room for high school and college students, usually relatives or friends of foremen and other supervisors, in need of temporary employment. Work assignments, transfers, layoffs, and rehires might be determined by bribery, perhaps only a bottle of whiskey or "a few drinks" at a nearby "beer garden." A Ford worker in the 1930s paid $20 to the foreman for his job but did not feel cheated, since some others were paying as much as $100. At Ford's some workers were hired only after they promised to buy a car—and then were laid off once the car was paid for. In General Motors Flint factories prior to the 1930s, there were "no unions, no rules: you were at the mercy of your foreman. I could go to work at seven o'clock in the morning, and at seven fifteen the boss'd come around and say: you could come back at three o'clock. If he preferred somebody else over you, that person would be called back earlier, though you were there longer." Although such instances may have occurred only rarely, a foreman might "suggest" that a worker paint his house, wash his car, cut his grass, or do other chores on the worker's "day off" or after work in order to keep his job. Even in plants where seniority was nominally recognized for layoff, rehire, and transfer to a better job, the foreman was still the key figure in determining employment and equity in the workplace.[51]

Upper management recognized that favoritism, exploitation, and bribery marred the workplace and poisoned attitudes but hesitated to restrict too severely the authority of those immediately responsible for production and discipline. The foreman's rule was implemented through a phalanx of subordinates, variously known as crew chiefs, lead men, set-up men, gang bosses, straw bosses, pushers, and other more derogatory terms. Hired by the foreman, these subordinates, production workers themselves, received a little extra pay to set and maintain a rapid production pace, and served as the foreman's eyes and ears on the shop floor. When Frank Marquart, later a union activist, recalled an encounter at the Chevrolet Gear and Axle plant in Detroit, his passion was evident. "One night I had machine trouble and fell behind in production. The straw boss, a sub-human pusher who had the authority to hire and fire, bellowed like a bull. When I tried to explain that I had machine trouble, he roared: 'I don't give a damn what you had, you get out production or you get fired—that's the rule around here and no goddamn excuses!' " Marquart walked out of the plant. Beneath the surface calm of labor relations flowed massive, if largely unarticulated, currents of unrest and dissatisfaction. The turbulent worker militancy that was to come drew on years of resentment.[52]

Like Marquart, many workers did not meekly submit to the foreman's autocratic regime. Restricting output to foil the pushers and the time-study men who set the job rates was one way to exert a degree of workers' control, although available only to some and often not to those who worked on assembly lines. By this stratagem workers would not be worked out of a job nor have their pay jeopardized. In one transmission plant, the night shift, a time when supervision generally was more lax, met its quota one or two hours before quitting time, "and then the men read newspapers, played checkers or slept." Sometimes straw bosses and foremen, who stood to benefit from realistic rather than inflated production standards, collaborated with the workers. The "hungry bastards" who exceeded the rate set informally by the workers were pressured by their fellows through ostracism and sabotage of their work. As one temporary worker observed, it was difficult, even impossible, to resist the pressure in his plant to only "get by" or do as little as possible. "This developing of a 'get-by' attitude is almost inevitable," he wrote, "because a man does not need to be a hard worker to win the approval of his fellow workers. In fact I found the opposite to be true. The old workers disapprove and curse the new man who comes in and works 'as if he were on a farm'—unless he has to, as is the case on many line jobs." Workers in parts plants could sometimes build up a reserve supply of completed parts, dubbed "putting it in the bank," that they drew upon to meet their quota in case they wanted a few moment's rest or ran into delays. These devices created solidarity on the shop floor and gave workers a degree of control over their environment when technology, manufacturing processes, and the structure of authority in the plant made that difficult to attain.[53]

No prolonged strikes occurred in the industry before the onset of the Great Depression but spasms of protest further call into question any sweeping claim of worker satisfaction. No comprehensive account of walkouts in early auto plants is available. The extant records show that they were brief—usually lasting less than a day—involved only a portion of a plant's workforce, and often went unrecorded in the press. Rarely was there union involvement or an organized effort of any kind. The most common cause was a wage cut, usually a reduction in piece rates, that threatened the workers' standard of living. Workers almost never used these informal strikes to seek a higher wage or improved conditions. Walkouts were defensive in nature: protests, often desperate, against a worsening of one's situation.[54]

Employers' reactions to strikes were swift and severe. Collective bargaining in any guise rarely took place. Rather the companies either replaced strikers, if other workers were available, or took back the strikers on the company's terms. Typical was John W. Anderson's "take it or leave it" experience when in 1926 the Seaman Body Company in Milwaukee cut the piecework rate for door hangers.

> When the men were notified of this most of them refused to work. They didn't walk out but just sat around talking about what ought to be done. There was no union or talk about a union. There was some hostility toward those men who turned in too many pieces and thus brought about the cut in piece rates. Some of us got tired of standing around. We went home at noon and returned the next morning. Most of the men had returned to work at the reduced piecework rate.

Later, when Anderson worked in several Detroit plants, he encountered and participated in similar disruptions: work stoppages called on the spur of the moment by a small work group, without formal organization or union involvement, usually as a result of wage cuts imposed without warning. Occasionally workers won their point, sometimes by threatening violence. A strike by seat back and cushion makers at Briggs Manufacturing Company in 1929, where "some of the workers threatened to take the bosses outside and beat hell out of them," resulted in rehiring the workers at the previous rate. Such outcomes were rare. At best rehiring at the reduced rate, at worst loss of the job and perhaps a place on a blacklist, were the more common results.[55]

These protests showed workers' determination to defend their interests but they seldom led to a permanent improvement in their working conditions. For that, an effective union that could demand a hearing on grievances, protect its members against being penalized for protesting, and build incrementally from one gain to another was necessary. Only a powerful and permanent workers' organization could counter a powerful corporation. Auto manufacturers were opposed to engaging in collective bargaining with an independent workers' organization and most disliked mere union membership. The Employers' Association of Detroit, which was supported by many manufacturers, was dedicated to maintaining an open shop industry free of union interference. The association, founded early in the century to rid Detroit of craft unions—an endeavor in which it largely succeeded—furnished strikebreakers, circulated lists of radicals and known union members and sympathizers, and encouraged its members to refuse to have any dealings with union men. Some companies paid spies and stool pigeons (ordinarily other workers within the factories) to report on union or radical activity, although the great expansion of spying and infiltration materialized only when the depression posed a realistic threat of unionization. Showing sympathy or mere interest in a union message could be grounds for dismissal. Many workers would not accept leaflets at factory gates from union organizers for fear they would be observed and lose their jobs.[56]

The antiunion position of the manufacturers was generally supported in public discourse within the auto communities, including expressions of opinion in the newspapers. In 1926 a few Detroit ministers invited a handful of American Federation of Labor organizers to address their congregations on the problems of the laborer, provoking what Reinhold Niebuhr, then the pastor of a local congregation and later an eminent theologian and social reformer, called an "uproar" of protest against the churches and demands from the business community that the invitations be withdrawn. "The idea," Niebuhr commented, "that the A. F. of L. leaders are dangerous heretics is itself a rather illuminating clue to the mind of Detroit." Detroit deserved its reputation as "the graveyard of organizers," yet other auto cities were not far behind.[57]

In addition to the active opposition of auto management and other community elites, the character of the workforce was an obstacle to union organizing. It was and remains true that worker organizing cannot occur unless a critical mass within a workplace is determined to bring it about. Before the depression, this critical mass was missing. The proportion of skilled workers in the industry, normally the readiest to organize, was small and shrinking. They were also the best paid and most likely to be promoted during the boom years of the 1920s. The semiskilled and unskilled workers who did more and more of the work, whether they came from midwestern farms or small towns, from the South, or from Europe, had, with few exceptions, insufficient experience with unions to grasp their potential. Moreover, such workers were often entirely dependent on the paychecks that from week to week kept them and their families alive. They could not afford to jeopardize them. For many immigrants and other rural migrants, the ethnic ties, the culture, and the consciousness that were engaged and sustained through religious, social, professional, business, and other civic and community institutions were more binding than the shop floor's ties of class and occupation. Some workers declined to think of themselves as permanently bound to auto factory production employment. They expected to find better work, be promoted to supervision, or return to their former homes, perhaps to set up a business of their own. Realistically, prospects of upward economic and social mobility inside or outside the factory were remote, although a few workers were recruited as supervisors and occasionally an auto worker acquired a small business. Ownership of a tavern, cafe, or similar service operation in a working-class neighborhood became for a few a route out of the factory. During Prohibition a recently laid-off Port Huron, Michigan, auto worker borrowed a small sum from neighbors and friends, secured a supply of bootleg whisky, beer, and wine from nearby Sarnia, Ontario, and converted his basement into a speakeasy, complete with a bar, tables and chairs, and a slot machine. The business flourished until a police raid closed it down. The prospects for other small businesses were about as precarious.[58]

DESPITE THE HOSTILITY AND INDIFFERENCE arrayed against them, unions were never entirely absent from the industry. Prior to the founding of the United Automobile Workers, a tiny contingent of skilled workers were organized in craft unions affiliated with the American Federation of Labor, at times even engaging in collective bargaining with auto manufacturers. Although antiunion in outlook, a management might be prepared to deal collectively on an informal basis with a small group of indispensable

skilled workers as long as it was clear that the masses of production workers would remain union free. Nick DiGaetano, who went to work as a
skilled metal polisher at Chrysler in 1928 was, like most of Chrysler's metal
polishers, a member of the Metal Polishers International Union (AFL).
Although the corporation did not formally recognize the union and would
not sign a contract or put an agreement in writing, a polishers' committee
bargained with foremen to set the rates the polishers would receive.[59]

While no industrial union was successfully established before the
UAW, three attempted to gain a foothold in the industry's early days. All
three did so outside of, and in opposition to, the craft-oriented and conservative AFL. Never more than token organizations in the auto plants, they
received no more than a passing glance from the mass of workers, yet each
served as something of a school for activists who later took part in the
industrial union movement. All stood for industrial organization, seeing
that the industry's reliance on the mass production instruments of
machines, assembly lines, and semiskilled laborers made organization by
crafts irrelevant.

The Industrial Workers of the World (IWW), founded in 1905 as an anticapitalist, revolutionary movement, claimed to have 200 auto worker
members in Detroit by 1913. In that year the IWW sent organizers to the
city to launch a campaign for an eight-hour day aimed at the Ford Motor
Company. When Ford effectively countered the IWW's effort, the union
redirected its campaign to Studebaker, then with production facilities in
Detroit, where a recent change in pay policy had upset many workers and
a cadre of IWW members was employed. In June 1913, 6,000 Studebaker
workers, few of them IWW members, went on strike under IWW leadership,
the first mass walkout in the industry's history. The strike lasted less than
a week, temporarily disrupting Studebaker's production, but failed to
achieve its objectives. IWW membership in Detroit shrank to a minute
number, though the union maintained educational programs, ran relief
agencies—including an "IWW Flop" for the homeless—and resurfaced for a
time in an active role in the first depression era strikes in 1933.[60]

The Carriage, Wagon and Auto Workers Union (CWAWU), founded in
1891 as an AFL affiliate, claimed the right to organize all auto workers
regardless of their particular jobs. Its anomalous position as an industrial
union within the craft-oriented AFL was resolved in 1918 when it was
expelled from the federation for refusing to honor the claims of the AFL's
craft unions to the industry's skilled workers. Ironically, the CWAWU's
greatest success came in organizing skilled auto workers (painters, wood-
workers, upholsterers, sheet metal workers, and the like) rather than the
masses of machine tenders, assemblers, and laborers. Its membership, consisting largely of workmen in the shops of custom, low-volume body manu-

facturers mainly in the New York City area, peaked at 40,000 in 1920. Strikes at the Wadsworth Manufacturing Company, a body maker for Ford in Detroit, and at the Willys-Overland plant in Toledo failed. In Toledo three persons were killed in the course of a battle between strikers throwing bricks and police firing guns. The union's greatest victory came as a result of a seventeen-week strike in New York City body shops, where skilled workers won a contract and created a local with 2,500 members. In 1921, amid a short-lived but sharp depression, CWAWU members launched a strike at Fisher Body plants protesting pay cuts and other setbacks that was broken by the company. With that defeat membership quickly collapsed to its earlier level of a few thousand.[61]

The third organization, the Auto Workers Union (AWU), grew out of the failed CWAWU, with the difference that the AWU's leadership and a portion of its membership consisted of Communists. By the end of the 1920s the AWU and the Communist Party had established shop nuclei in at least a half dozen Detroit auto plants, including such major manufacturers as Ford, Dodge, Fisher Body, Chrysler, and Packard. The number of AWU members was small, ranging from as few as 100 to perhaps as many as 3,000 between 1926 and 1934, with a larger circle of sympathizers. Although incapable of instigating strikes on its own, the AWU was quick to volunteer support and offer leadership when strikes occurred. Most of the strikes failed and few new recruits for the AWU resulted from them, but the union did make its presence known to auto workers and their communities through shop papers and leafleting. At Packard, where the AWU put out a shop paper that condemned speedups and abusive foremen and publicized other worker grievances, a union member on the motor assembly line surreptitiously inserted copies in the engine block's cylinders as they passed his station for those further down the line to find and read. "The foreman tried very hard to find out who the culprit was who was responsible for this, but he never succeeded." By such methods grievances were communicated and awareness of a union's presence was shared by at least a few.[62]

On two occasions during the 1920s the AFL made feeble efforts to unionize auto workers. Its adherence to the principle of craft organization guaranteed its failure. In 1920 its executive council instructed each of the eight craft unions with a claim to a portion of the auto workers to assign an organizer, but nothing happened. The 1926 AFL convention, meeting in Detroit, approved a resolution calling for the assignment of craft workers to the appropriate affiliated trade union and the recruitment of the remainder into federal labor unions, linked directly to the AFL. If all went according to plan, the members of the federal labor unions would eventually be parceled out among the affiliated trade unions. A few organizers went to Detroit, where they encountered hostility from the manufacturers and

indifference from most workers. The campaign director sought to persuade
Henry Ford "to try collective bargaining," but he was not interested.[63]

Although workers' class and job consciousness were insufficient to
create and sustain mass unions, an industrial working-class subculture was
in existence in preunion Detroit and in other auto cities. Although rent by
internal divisions, the preunion working class nevertheless developed some
instruments of cohesion. Ethnicity and class overlapped in defining the
neighborhoods where workers lived and in many instances had their jobs.
Paths of upward mobility later taken for granted were not, for significant
numbers, available to working-class youth. That higher education might
offer an escape for the talented and ambitious from the working class was
not a realistic prospect when American college and university youth came
almost entirely from the ranks of the affluent. Douglas Fraser recalled that
in his Detroit immigrant neighborhood the thought of attending college did
not cross the minds of his school friends and acquaintances. As a matter of
course, a factory job succeeded schooling, with sons, and sometimes daughters, following parents into the plants. Thus workers' consciousness and
identity were forged across the generations.[64]

Critical perspectives on society's institutions and reigning ideologies
were articulated, if in muffled tones. Radical political parties, including the
Communist Party, the Socialist Party, and the Proletarian Party, while they
could claim few active members and had little electoral impact, spread a
message among a larger audience that condemned capitalism and sympathized with workers. Informal discussion of labor issues was common.
"Soap boxing," as one auto worker remarked, "was quite an institution in
Detroit in the early 30's and in the 20's. Sometimes the whole area of Cadillac Square would be packed with people; there would be hundreds of people coming to hear soap box orators." Grand Circus Park, a few blocks north
of Cadillac Square, was another gathering place for soap boxers and their
audiences. Although these street corner orators might talk on any and every
subject, conditions in the factories and topics concerning economic, social,
and political conditions, reform, and revolution were among the staples.
Workers also gathered in restaurants and taverns near the factories and in
working-class neighborhoods both to relax and to discuss their jobs and
working conditions. Such informal discussions, leading to networks of
association and the articulation of shared experiences and convictions,
were another strand in the cord that would ultimately build and sustain an
auto workers' union.[65]

A HISTORIAN OF EARLY AUTO WORK has observed that a tacit bargain was
struck between auto employers and their employees in which workers
yielded pride in and control over the work process in return for the jobs and

wages that supported their material standard of living outside the workplace. For most of those who flocked into and remained at work in the auto factories, this bargain, although it came at the price of a heavy work load and subjection to autocratic control, was deemed acceptable. Class consciousness failed to take deep root when wages were good, jobs abundant, and the work steady. Left undisturbed by external forces, the arrangement might have lasted indefinitely.[66]

An observer in 1929 would readily have concluded that the auto manufacturers had mastered the art and technique of operating in a union-free environment. Outwardly, the workforce appeared loyal or cowed. The feeble efforts to establish unions had so far failed. A change was in store, however, as the layoffs, short time, wage reductions, deteriorating working conditions, speedups, and harsher discipline that came with the Great Depression eroded acceptance of things as they were. The "prosperity decade's" bargain between auto manufacturers and their employees would soon be undermined by the economy's profound and prolonged collapse.

CHAPTER 2

"The genie is out of the bottle"

Toward an Auto Workers' Union, 1933–37

THE AUTO WORKERS' REBELLION AROSE OUT OF THE UPHEAVALS of the Great Depression. At first, the prospects for founding a union were not promising. The manufacturers, on record for many years as opposed to unions and collective bargaining, would resist with all their strength. Little support could be expected from national or state governments whose earlier interventions in conflicts between labor and capital had nearly always favored the latter. Few auto workers had experience with unions or seemed convinced that an independent workers' organization would contribute to their welfare. With little agreement on what, if anything, should be done, the early years of building an auto union were bound to be marked by uncertainty and experimentation. False starts were pursued, then remedied or abandoned before workers settled on an industrial union, a single encompassing organization recognized as the bargainer for all, regardless of the particular job of each worker or the particular employer. The task was challenging and fraught with difficulties, so much so that years of struggle passed before it was completed.

The onset of the depression, triggered by a stock market free-fall that exposed weaknesses in the economy stemming from both a lopsided distribution of income and wealth and structural defects, shook the nation out of its Coolidge-era ideological slumbers but gave no immediate direction for the future. Radical movements, invigorated by the spreading disillusionment with a collapsing economy, glimpsed new possibilities for redistributing income, wealth, and political power. They now sought vantage points within a newly angry and self-conscious working-class and labor movement from which to guide events toward their goal of economic and social reconstruction or even revolution. Although many Americans were stunned and dispirited by the depression's destructive force, to others it offered a rare, perhaps unique, opportunity to shape a future in accord with their ideas of social justice and industrial democracy.[1]

THE FORTUNES OF AUTO WORKERS were, as always, tied to those of the industry. Within a generation the automobile's utility, convenience, and appeal as a status emblem had created the nation's leading industrial enterprise, but the depression dealt the industry staggering blows. Even strong companies barely survived while the weak and the small went down by the score. Sales, profits, and employment plummeted. The sale of 5.3 million motor vehicles (including 4.5 million automobiles) in 1929, the last prosperous year—when the industry employed an average of 450,000 wage earners, marked a peak of car, truck, and bus production not surpassed for another twenty years. In 1932, when the economy hit bottom, the industry produced only 1.3 million vehicles, using a mere 20 percent of its massive capacity, and employment averaged only 250,000, a decline of 45 percent from the pre-depression high. Owing to wage cuts and part time work schedules (few now worked more than four days a week), the earnings of those still blessed with jobs shrank by more than one-third. The minimum wage at Ford Motor Company dropped from $7 a day in 1929 to $4 in 1931. Except for General Motors, which made a small profit and paid dividends even in the depression's worst years, all other companies lost money, and many shut down forever. Insolvency and mergers erased dozens of nameplates from the rolls of auto manufacturers, with the result that at least some, even all, of their employees were cast into the abyss of a bottomless job market. By the end of a decade of depression, the Big Three had captured 90 percent of the market for new passenger cars, with General Motors, the market colossus, accounting for 40 percent of sales. Chrysler had passed a faltering Ford to become the number two concern, and five surviving independent firms—Hudson, Nash, Packard, Studebaker, and Willys-Overland—scrambled for what was left. The midwestern motor cities of Detroit, Flint, Pontiac, Lansing, Toledo, Cleveland, South Bend, St. Louis, and Milwaukee reeled under the weight of the industry's collapse.[2]

In time, and as a result of several circumstances, the auto workforce became more internally unified, with fewer of the ethnocultural differences that divided workers in earlier decades. With the coming of World War I and the restrictive legislation of the 1920s, waves of fresh immigrants had ceased to sweep through the ranks of the blue-collar workforce. For a decade or more, immigrants and second and third generations of their children had begun to acquire the language and take on the customs of the American mainstream. In a further contribution to a more homogeneous and stable workforce, the proportion of auto workers consisting of the rootless "suitcase brigade" of young, single males shrank as hiring fell off and the seasonal cycle of production contracted, leaving an older, more settled and family-centered workforce in place. While the "hard times" pressured

A Detroiter seeks work during the Great Depression. Walter P. Reuther Library, Wayne State University

everyone to look out for themselves, it became clear that remedies for economic ills were beyond the reach of many if acting alone. Collective action, based upon recognition of a common plight and the need to devise a common solution, assumed a larger place in the nation's consciousness. Traditional ethnic, racial and occupational divisions by no means disappeared, but they did contract and lose some of their sharp edges. With fewer internal conflicts and tensions to divide them, the workers became more aware of their common destiny and of the potential of their collective strength.[3]

At first the depression's economic pressures enhanced the shop floor power of employers and racheted up the rigors of the job. Working conditions deteriorated as companies, desperate to cut costs, resorted to fierce speedups. On a Chevrolet assembly line, where no relief was provided, a worker who needed to go to the rest room would work faster to "try to get ahead of the line so [you] could get a few minutes and rush right back and try to catch up." In a letter to President Franklin D. Roosevelt another auto worker likened the pace of the assembly line to the dark days of slave drivers. "If Simon Legree," he wrote, "were to come back to life and see a modern conveyor line in operation, when it is really strutting it's stuff, he would dig Uncle Tom up and kick Hell out of him because of not doing anywhere near his possibilities." At the Briggs body plant in Detroit "there was always a constant harassment . . . by management to get more." At Chrysler, metal polisher Nick DiGaetano recalled, "I never worked so hard in my life." No one could accuse the young Joe Louis of lacking strength or stamina. Following the loss of his first amateur fight in 1932 he took a job at Ford's loading truck bodies on a conveyor, one of the most demanding jobs in the plant. By the end of the day his back was so sore he couldn't straighten up. After two months on the job, he recalled, "I couldn't stand it anymore. I figured, if I'm going to hurt that much for twenty-five dollars a week, I might as well go back and try fighting again."[4]

Threats to health and fears of injury became more pressing. Conditions at the Briggs Manufacturing Company were among the worst. In the paint shop, where drying ovens added to midsummer heat, "they would carry them out just as fast as they would come in. Briggs had two or three people going around the lower East Side in the colored neighborhood hiring colored guys as replacements. Just as fast as they would bring some in, some would drop off because of the extreme heat. . . . Fans or any ventilating systems were unheard of . . . in those days." At times the intense heat activated the Briggs plant's automatic sprinkler system.[5]

As layoffs and plant shutdowns multiplied, employment became sporadic and insecure. Since most manufacturers were not bound to honor seniority, age discrimination in layoffs and rehiring was common. Since experience was of minor significance in unskilled and even some semiskilled jobs, older, presumably less energetic workers often lost out to the young. Even those with jobs might not get enough work to support themselves and their families. Many companies still did not pay for "dead time," when lines were temporarily shut down. A couple of hours of work, with the rest of the day spent in unpaid idleness, was common at the Studebaker plant in South Bend, but one had to remain in the plant in case jobs came along.[6]

Hanging over every worker was the threat of replacement by a soldier from the reserve army of the unemployed, a threat used by some employers to beat down wages and intensify the speedup. At General Motors' Fisher Body plant in St. Louis production standards were raised, with an increase in the group bonus rate, but a short time later the pay was cut to the previous level while the speedup remained in effect. When there were protests, a time-study man told the workers: "I understand a lot of you men think you got [obscenity deleted] on your last pay. Maybe you did and maybe you didn't. Whenever you don't like the pay you are getting, go out to the gate and get your check. There are four hundred men out there every morning willing to work for less than what you men are working for." Leonard Woodcock, a new hire at the Detroit Gear and Machine Division of Borg-Warner Corporation, saw "the unemployed men . . . come and look into the [factory] windows. . . . There were dozens out there who wanted that job you have." At many factories there was a line of men standing at the door of the employment office day after day, hoping that something would turn up.[7]

HISTORICALLY, HARD TIMES were tough times for unions. If jobs were scarce and the supply of workers abundant the economic odds favored employers, and a threat to withhold labor by going on strike exerted little or no economic pressure. With inventory on hand and few sales in prospect, employers might even prefer to close their plants, sell off what they had, and await the return of better times to resume production. A union had strong appeal only if it could hold out the prospect of improving working conditions and defending or raising living standards. Earlier depressions had sometimes provoked strikes in other industries, usually as desperate protests to resist wage cuts, and frequently hard times brought lockouts in which employers cut wages and broke unions.

In the Great Depression's early years there was little organized protest among auto workers. Many hoped and expected that the economy and the industry would bounce back from this downturn as had happened before. This expectation was harder to sustain as bad times persisted, but waiting out the depression seemed to many the safest and perhaps the only tactic. Equally important in deterring protest was the fear that striking or merely showing an interest in a union would lead to the loss of one's job when another might be impossible to find.

Despite the risks, desperate men began to grope toward collective action and to go out on strike. The first major depression era strike came in 1930 at Fisher Body 1, the supplier of bodies to Buick, in Flint, a city as hard hit by the depression as Detroit. As car sales and profits fell, the General Motors Corporation cut the piece rate for trimmers and metal finishers, forcing a speedup if workers were to maintain their wages. Several hundred walked off their jobs. After Auto Workers Union organizers hurried up from Detroit, the struggle escalated into the depression's first plant-wide strike. Metal finishers and trimmers marched through the plant urging fellow workers, also disaffected by the speedup, to join them. At least 3,600 struck and 7,500 more were idled. After two days the corporation reopened the plant under police and state trooper protection, despite the 1,500 pickets on the scene. The strike collapsed when the company hired replacements among the unemployed and thousands of workers chose to return to their jobs. General Motors had made no concessions and twenty-three of the most active strikers were fired. Not an encouraging beginning.[8]

In Detroit the first demonstrations of class protest and collective action appeared among the unemployed and their sympathizers. Those without jobs to lose could more safely express their discontent than could the employed. Unemployed Councils appeared in many industrial cities during and after 1930, about a dozen in and around Detroit alone. Set up and usually headed by radicals—often Communists, sometimes Socialists or members of other left-wing groups—the councils attracted thousands of unemployed workers and supporters to marches, picketing, eviction protests, and other demonstrations aimed at pressuring local officials and employers to respond to the need for relief and for jobs.[9]

In Detroit, a journalist reported, "mass idleness" at the Ford Motor Company's plants hung "like a dead weight on the city—on the world." Although most of Ford's laid-off workers were residents of Detroit, the company, with its properties located in Dearborn and Highland Park, paid no taxes in support of the city's welfare funds. In March 1932 the Unemployed Councils obtained permission from Detroit authorities for a "Hunger March" targeted on Ford's River Rouge plant to petition the company for jobs. The march's organizers sought to broaden its appeal to include current Ford workers by calling for an end to speedups, equal treatment for Ford's black employees, free medical care for auto workers at Ford Hospital, the abolition of the Ford Service Department, rest periods for production workers, a seven-hour day without loss of pay (sought in the hope that the number of employed would increase), and the right to organize with union

The Ford Hunger March, 1932. Walter P. Reuther Library, Wayne State University

recognition— formulating an agenda whose main objectives Ford workers would pursue for more than a decade.[10]

Among the three thousand persons who gathered on March 7 were many former Ford employees. Communists were the chief march organizers and leaders, but the participants were drawn from no particular ideological or political faction. The *Detroit News*, no friend of radicalism or protest demonstrations, reported that "nobody could look at the marchers themselves and accuse them of any destructive purpose." The marchers proceeded without incident through Detroit, but to reach the gates of the plant they had to cross into Dearborn, a Ford company town. At the boundary dividing the two cities they encountered a line of the local police, with tear gas at the ready and drawn weapons, backed by an armed force from the Ford Service Department. In the ensuing battle four marchers were killed by police gunfire (a fifth died later) and at least fifty were wounded. On the other side of the barricades, police and Ford servicemen (including Harry Bennett, the Service Department's chief) were struck by the rocks, bottles, and other missiles thrown by the marchers, but they suffered no fatalities.

A few days later a funeral procession estimated at eight to ten thousand, with many thousands more looking on, bore the martyrs to their graves in a Detroit cemetery, where they were interred beneath the shadow of the Rouge power house's towering smokestacks. "Ford Gave Bullets for Bread," read one of many banners carried by the mourners. After three years of depression, a deadly struggle had erupted in the Motor City, inaugurating a protest movement that would last for a decade and leave, as its most important legacies, the establishment of the United Automobile Workers and the transformation of Detroit into a union town. For a considerable number of present and future Ford employees, the march and its bloody suppression was a consciousness-transforming event that made them unionists in the factory and radicals in politics. The tragedy set the life course of Dave Moore, a black youth and a future Rouge plant employee, radical, and union activist, who recalled, "On that day, that's when I grew up to be a man."[11]

Only a few months after the Ford Hunger March, the presidential campaign and election of 1932 signaled a new departure in national politics. As the Hunger March and acts of protest elsewhere showed, the conventional wisdom which held that the nation's economic policy decisions and affairs were best left to businessmen and like-minded politicians was under assault. In November voters elected Franklin Delano Roosevelt, Democratic governor of New York, as their president on his promise of a New Deal. His campaign statements were vague and sometimes contradictory, but more importantly he promised to take whatever actions were needed to bring about economic recovery. In the auto cities voting majorities decisively and permanently shifted to the Democrats, as masses of ordinary citizens seeking change redistributed political power. In Flint the turnout in the 1932 election was double that of the presidential election of 1928, and for the first time in memory a majority of Flint's ballots were cast for the Democratic Party's presidential and congressional candidates. In Detroit, where 63 percent had voted for Herbert Hoover in 1928, Roosevelt received over 59 percent of the votes running against Hoover in 1932. Both cities, Republican for generations, would be solidly Democratic in the future. The contraction of the business community's authority on economic, political, and ideological fronts opened the door for an advance by labor.[12]

With this turn of political fortunes and a rising indignation in the workers' ranks after three years of hard times, a new spirit of militance and daring exploded. In early 1933, "strikes just burst like lightning" in Detroit's auto industry. Although a handful of Auto Workers Union members took part, these early depression era strikes could not be credited to union planning and agitation. An accumulation of hardships, brought to a boil by recent company cost-cutting measures and the new political environment that was taking shape, sparked the walkouts. For the first time in

Funeral procession for the Hunger March martyrs, 1932. Walter P. Reuther Library, Wayne State University

the industry's history a substantial number of auto workers at different Detroit factories—though none at plants of the Big Three—were ready to risk their jobs through strike action.[13]

In January and February 1933, workers in the Detroit plants of Briggs, Motor Products, Murray Body, and Hudson struck in response to wage cuts. At Motor Products, a cut of 10 percent reduced the hourly pay of Leonard Woodcock's father, a skilled machinist, from 71 to 64 cents, while women workers on the plant's assembly lines took a cut from 15 cents to 13–1/2 cents an hour. Completely shut down by the strike, the company quickly rescinded the cuts. Most of the other walkouts were similarly successful in gaining partial or full restoration of the pay rates.[14]

At Briggs a tough management refused to back down and the strike continued. Briggs was the largest independent body maker in the industry, a supplier to both Ford and Chrysler. Conditions in its plants gave it the "worst reputation in Detroit." "Bodies by Briggs" was the bitter, ironic title of a poem published anonymously in the *Auto Workers News* a few years earlier that condemned the company for an explosion and fire in one of its plants that took the lives of twenty-one workers. Auto workers branded the Briggs factories, with their huge and dangerous presses for stamping body parts, as "the butcher shop" and "the slaughterhouse." A Briggs press operator pulled on a glove that "had the remnants of somebody's finger there," an incident by no means unique. After offering limited concessions on base pay and promising to pay for dead time—an offer which was rejected—Briggs management refused to meet with a strikers' committee and charged that the walkout resulted from an Auto Workers Union conspiracy orchestrated by its Communist leadership. Imperfectly organized and with few resources, workers began to drift back to the shop as the company, drawing upon the labor reserve army of Detroit's estimated 175,000 unemployed, filled the places of 3,000 of those on strike. Fights between strikers and scabs broke out along the picket lines, but by the beginning of March production had resumed and the strike was effectively over. It was not entirely without positive results since Briggs had raised some wage rates and eliminated some of the worst abuses, but a stiff price was paid as about half the strikers lost their jobs and many of them were blacklisted. The Briggs strike, with the other disturbances involving 15,000 to 20,000 participants, revealed the breadth and depth of discontent and left a legacy of resolve and bitterness. "The smouldering" recalled one Briggs employee, "could be felt by people who worked in the plant. You could see that underneath the surface there was rebellion in the hearts of the workers."[15]

SHORTLY AFTER THE STRIKES ENDED, the Roosevelt administration and Congress wrote a new chapter in the history of the federal government's dealings with labor. Historically more often an adversary than a friend of unions, the government would now tolerate and even offer some encouragement to union organizing. In June 1933, Congress passed the National Industrial Recovery Act (NIRA). Buried among a host of complex provisions was Section 7(a), a federal guarantee of the right to collective bargaining for those employed in industries engaged in interstate commerce. Employees, it stated, had "the right to organize and bargain collectively through representatives of their own choosing," and they were to be free from "interference, restraint, or coercion" by employers in making their choice.[16]

As auto workers were soon to discover, serious flaws in NIRA belied these brave words. Key terms were so ambiguous that employers and the courts could define them much as they pleased. Employers could launch, support, and control a company union, "bargaining" with it on trivial matters and using it to obstruct formation of an independent organization. Intimidation, coercion, and discrimination against union members in hiring, firing, job transfers, and promotions were still possible. Nor were effective administrative and enforcement mechanisms put in place. Yet through its minimum wage and maximum hours provisions, the law eventually had an impact in auto parts plants as well as other businesses. Leonard Woodcock's

Strikers at the Briggs Manufacturing Company, 1933. Walter P. Reuther Library, Wayne State University

weekly hours of work at Borg-Warner's Detroit factory were reduced to forty and his pay rose from 45 to 60 cents an hour. But as a guarantor of unions and collective bargaining, the law was a failure.[17]

Despite its weaknesses, the law's passage sparked the depression era's first nationwide outburst of union organizing, foreshadowing the role that government's direct and indirect support would play in the union drives of the 1930s and 1940s. Broadcasting slogans such as "The president wants you to join a union!" organizers fanned out across the land to drive home the message that Congress and the president now saw union membership as a worker's right. Immediate gains were made in industries such as coal mining and the garment trades, where once strong unions had suffered setbacks in the 1920s.[18]

With organization now urgent and imminent, auto workers faced crucial questions. Should unions be established on a craft or industrial basis? Should there be a single union for all auto workers or separate organizations in each company, perhaps even in each plant? Would a new union pursue political goals and embrace political activism or keep politics at arm's length in the spirit of the "pure and simple" unionism that had guided the

American Federation of Labor since the days of Samuel Gompers? The answers to these questions were not obvious and the outcomes not predetermined. In the next few years they were asked again and again, and as answers were found, a foundation was laid for the establishment of the United Automobile Workers.

Soon after the passage of the National Industrial Recovery Act, the leaders of the American Federation of Labor announced a drive to organize auto workers. William Green, the federation's president, appointed William Collins to lead the campaign. Collins, whose appearance struck one observer as resembling that of "a middle-aged Sunday School teacher," had been briefly and superficially exposed to the auto industry in the 1920s, but for all intents and purposes he was an outsider. Since the AFL was committed in principle to craft organization and consisted largely of craft unions, some with claims to portions of the auto workforce, it could not make a strong, unequivocal appeal to the many semiskilled and unskilled auto workers. Organization of the workforce at the Studebaker plant in South Bend, Indiana, on a craft basis, as the AFL contemplated, would have required, according to one calculation, thirty-two different unions within a single factory—not a recipe for successful bargaining. The AFL's craft exclusiveness, reinforced by ethnic and racial prejudice, limited its appeal and hindered effective organizing. Sometimes called the "aristocracy of labor," the skilled tradesmen's attitude toward those with less skill or with none at all reflected the characterization. A machinist at Chrysler conceded that "we took a very snobbish attitude toward the poor production workers," and a Cleveland AFL official told a delegation of workers from White Motors, who came to him seeking assistance, that "no one can organize that bunch of hunkies out there." Although it was structurally, philosophically, and temperamentally unsuited to the organization of undifferentiated industrial workers, the AFL was a going concern, ambitious to extend its reach into the ranks of the industrial millions. Initially it elicited a positive response from auto workers. Belying the employers' talk about contented employees, many workers were eager for organization and only awaited a credible effort from whatever direction it might come.[19]

The organizing unit used by the AFL in industrial settings was the federal labor union. Chartered by the federation rather than by one of the craft unions, a federal union was set up for each major plant or location. All told, the AFL chartered 183 federal unions in the auto manufacturing and auto parts industries. By the summer of 1933 some officials were claiming an AFL membership of 100,000 among auto workers (undoubtedly an exaggeration), with perhaps half of the total in Flint's GM plants. In fact, membership fluctuated wildly. On the rare occasions when a federal local scored a victory or had one in prospect, membership soared. In defeat, particularly if AFL leadership got the blame, disillusioned members tore up their cards. Nevertheless, for the first time substantial numbers of auto workers joined independent unions and gained experience in their methods and operations.[20]

The federal unions undertook to conduct organizing campaigns through leafleting and other publicity devices, sign up members, collect initiation fees and dues, eventually divide the members among the craft unions, secure recognition, engage in collective bargaining, and sign contracts. Once in place, the unions would administer the contract and the grievance procedure. Although it was hard to grasp how the masses of auto workers could be classified and parceled out on the basis of skills they did not possess, that was the declared objective. An additional handicap of the federal unions was that they lacked the autonomy enjoyed by most local unions. Their officers were usually elected by the membership but occasionally they were appointed, and the federation tried, not always successfully, to exercise close control over their actions. Most of the sums raised in fees and dues went to the AFL. Federal union members were not eligible for support from the federation's strike fund until they had been in good standing for a year, a long probation in the circumstances. Instead of using the strong to support the weak, the AFL seemed to use the weak to support those who were stronger. Activities of the federal unions within the auto industry were uncoordinated, a serious defect in the face of centralized corporate power. Each federal local was tied to the federation, but they had no ties to each other. In June 1934, in response to demands from union members, a national council of auto federal locals was set up to provide a forum for consultation, but not until August 1935 was an international union, the United Automobile Workers of America (UAWA) chartered by the AFL.[21]

Disagreements and tension developed almost immediately between the AFL's national leadership and some of the federal locals. Some locals were eager for action, including strikes for recognition, but the AFL held back. Collins, a timid organizer, assured employers that "I never voted for a strike in my life. I have always opposed them." Nevertheless, several federal locals confronted their employers. Strikes or lockouts stemming from diverse circumstances occurred at Bower Roller Bearing in Detroit; Ford assembly plants in Chester, Pennsylvania, and Edgewater, New Jersey; the Nash plant in Kenosha, Wisconsin; the Budd Company in Philadelphia; several Cleveland auto plants; and elsewhere. The results were mixed. In some instances the federal locals failed and then disintegrated. In others workers won partial victories and their local union survived, with some later transformed into strong UAW-CIO locals. In Flint, where thousands of General Motors workers were ready to strike the auto giant, AFL caution and the Roosevelt administration's moves to negotiate a settlement provoked the complaint that "everybody said we got sold down the river."[22]

THE AFL WAS NOT ALONE in seeking to organize auto workers. The workers' willingness to challenge management, as shown by the strikes of early 1933, prompted several new entries in the field. One of the first to appear, the Mechanics Educational Society of America (MESA), set out to organize skilled tool and die makers, the elite of the auto workforce, thereby challenging the AFL on its home ground of craft jurisdiction.

Skilled auto workers divided into two groups. A cautious, conservative outlook, befitting labor's well-paid aristocrats, characterized some, but those whose experience included the trade unionism and radical working-class politics of contemporary Great Britain formed a militant workers' vanguard. A significant number of skilled workers had emigrated from the British Isles to the auto factories in the 1910s and 1920s. In their native land a working-class consciousness, labor solidarity, trade unionism, and a left-wing political outlook—sometimes expressed through membership in one of the anticapitalist political parties—were shared values and commitments. One immigrant recalled a shop floor education in Scotland centered on the shop steward, who held lunchtime classes "on the industrial history of England, and Political Science. This was where we gradually began to pick up the drift of the whole system of capitalism and its economic impact on society." Some skilled workers from other immigrant backgrounds, as illustrated by Walter Reuther's German-American parentage, inherited a critical perspective on capitalist society that reinforced commitment to the union cause. Protected from employer retaliation by virtue of the skills that made them difficult if not impossible to replace, skilled workmen had much to gain from a union but incurred less risk than others in fighting for one. From the founding of MESA in 1933 until the strike of the General Motors tool and die makers in 1939, skilled workers of immigrant origin often took the lead in strikes and other organizing struggles.[23]

The driving force behind MESA was Matt Smith, a British-born socialist and firebrand speaker with a cutting wit. From September to November 1933, MESA conducted the industry's first prolonged strike. It started with skilled workers in the General Motors plants in Flint and spread quickly to other GM plants and to many of the independent tool and die shops in Detroit and Pontiac. With the strikers unable to shut down all the tool and die shops, the struggle dragged on and became violent. The extraordinary "riotcade," the "wild ride of the die-makers," occurred in Detroit on October 30, when an automobile caravan carrying two to three thousand MESA strikers roared through the city from one tool and die shop to another, breaking windows, overturning cars, throwing industrial blueprints on bonfires—in short, shutting down the shops by any and all means. Pursuing police chased the strikers from shop to shop and finally caught up with them but managed to arrest only eight.[24]

Although the strike pried no concessions out of mighty GM, it did bring de facto recognition and informal settlements in many of the tool and die job shops. Most importantly, MESA itself survived the conflict, demonstrating that skilled workers could pursue a militant course without the strikers' losing their jobs or destroying their union. Growth followed upon this partial success. By the end of 1934, MESA had thirty-one locals and claimed a membership of 38,000. In 1936 the newly chartered UAW reaped the benefit of MESA's pioneering when MESA Local 7 became the UAW's East Side Tool and Die Local 155, and MESA Local 9 merged with Local 8 to form the UAW West Side Tool and Die Local 157. Both locals were influential in the UAW for years: Local 155 as a Communist stronghold led by Scotsman John Anderson and business agent Nat Ganley; Local 157, with a socialist and independent left orientation, as part of the Reuther camp. The independent MESA organization that remained after these defections to the UAW was only a shadow of its former self.[25]

As INDEPENDENT UNIONS moved forward, employer resistance stiffened but also became more subtle. Exploiting an administration interpretation of NIRA that permitted "proportional representation" in the plants—that is, as many unions as might gain support rather than a single organization selected by majority vote—General Motors and Chrysler struck back by setting up employee-representation plans or "workers' councils." Employers hoped that these toothless organizations, in which worker representatives could not introduce a motion without their foreman's consent, which merely talked rather than bargained, signed no contracts, and conducted no strikes, would satisfy their employees' aspirations for a voice in their working lives. They did not. Some Buick workers showed their contempt for the councils by writing in the names of Mickey Mouse and Popeye on ballots as their representatives. In fact, official tolerance for these company unions disillusioned many workers with the AFL leadership and to a degree with the Roosevelt administration itself. Some of the employee-representation organizations were, however, later reconstituted as UAW locals and, like some of the AFL's federal locals, they served an educational function by bringing isolated workers together and teaching some of the elements of union structure, solidarity, and procedure. In some plants, for example, the councils provided a forum for the discussion of the kinds of matters—seniority, job classifications, pay equity, and the like—that would later figure prominently in the formal grievance procedures established in the early contracts, creating what a historian has called a "proto-workplace contractualism."[26]

If company unions were the carrot, repression was the stick. The Ford Motor Company, which refused to participate in any NIRA schemes, relied on fear and intimidation to keep workers' organizations out of its plants.

General Motors and Chrysler were not far behind. While the precise extent of dismissals for union membership or activity cannot be determined, the fear of dismissal was the chief deterrent to organization, mocking the law's guarantee of the rights to organize and bargain. Companies went to great lengths and expended large sums to identify and then fire union members and sympathizers. In GM's Flint plants, a reign of "terror" saw sixty-four federal union shop floor leaders fired at Fisher Body and 126 at Chevrolet, where the general manager told his superintendents and foremen, "We expect you to discharge anyone who is found circulating a petition or soliciting names for a petition inside our plants."[27]

Local unions were penetrated by company spies and agents, both to identify leaders and members and sometimes, as agent provocateurs, to influence their decisions. A favorite ploy, exploiting the inexperience with unions of so many of the workers, was to secure the election of a stool pigeon as a local's recording secretary, giving him access to records including membership lists and allowing him to take notes at meetings without arousing suspicion. An early decision rendered by the National Labor Relations Board (NLRB) after it was set up in 1935 involved an effort by the UAW to organize the Detroit employees of Fruehauf Trailer Company, then the largest American manufacturer of commercial trailers. The company had hired a detective "to ferret out the union activities of the men" and to keep the front office "informed of what was going on." The detective was brought into the plant as a production worker, joined the local, and was elected its treasurer, allowing him to turn over a membership list to management. The company fired the union militants and threatened others with the same fate. On appeal the case was heard by the Supreme Court as one of the five cases the Court decided in 1937 upholding the constitutionality of the National Labor Relations (Wagner) Act.[28]

Evidences of spying and other antiunion practices were brought to public notice in dramatic, even sensational, testimony before a United States Senate subcommittee chaired by Senator Robert La Follette, Jr., of Wisconsin. The hearings revealed that General Motors and Chrysler bought spy services from the Pinkerton National Detective Agency, the Corporations Auxiliary Company, and other agencies that supplied operatives. General Motors sought to conceal that it was spying on its employees and to undermine the La Follette committee's investigation by wholesale destruction of pertinent records as the committee prepared for its hearings. GM was both the world's largest industrial corporation and its leading employer of detective agencies, paying Pinkerton's approximately $1 million for its services between January 1, 1934, and July 31, 1936, and large sums at other times. These antiunion countermeasures had their intended effect. Membership in a once large Flint amalgamated GM federal local hit bottom at 120 in 1936, in large part because of espionage and the threat of layoffs for union membership; five of the thirteen-member executive board of the local were in fact spies employed by detective agencies on contract to General Motors. A Lansing GM local shrank to the point where it consisted of five officers, all of them Pinkerton agents, with no genuine worker members whatsoever. "Perhaps nowhere," the La Follette committee concluded, was the failure of union organizing due to spying "more marked than in the automobile industry." Although the repression of the auto workers served the immediate purpose of blunting the drive for unions, the resentments it aroused strengthened the sense of class and class conflict, prerequisites for the future outbursts of labor militance that would carry the UAW to victory.[29]

THE AUTOMOTIVE INDUSTRIAL WORKERS' ASSOCIATION (AIWA), with roots in the Chrysler Corporation's massive Dodge Main plant in Hamtramck, Michigan (an independent municipal enclave within Detroit), explored another path of union development. In this case NIRA procedures led to the formation of an independent organization that, like some of the MESA locals, was later incorporated into the UAW. Unlike MESA, however, from its beginning the AIWA was an industrial union that welcomed semiskilled and unskilled production workers into its ranks along with the skilled.

AIWA grew out of a works council at Dodge Main, a Chrysler company union, which had tackled such housekeeping questions as the size of the milk bottles sold to workers in the plant canteen for their lunches and the maintenance schedule for washing the factory's windows. The works council did, however, center on elections of the workers' representatives and thus laid a foundation for the emergence of an independent leadership cadre. The principal figure in AIWA was Richard T. Frankensteen, a recent graduate of the University of Dayton who returned to a job at Dodge Main in 1933. A husky, likeable, and courageous man with organizing and platform skills, he became the council's secretary. In April 1935 a group within the council, frustrated by the trivial nature of so many of the issues being discussed with Chrysler management in council sessions, formed the AIWA. Rejecting the AFL as autocratic in its dealings with federal locals and biased in favor of craft unionism, the organizers distributed cards at Dodge Main's gates asking workers if they would support an independent, industrial organization. The response was overwhelmingly positive, with fourteen thousand of the plant's huge workforce replying in the affirmative. In the following months AIWA spread to several other, mainly Chrysler, plants. Frankensteen became its president and R. J. Thomas, head of the AIWA local at Chrysler's Kercheval Road plant on Detroit's East Side, became its first vice president. By the end of the year AIWA had approximately 10,000 members in Chrysler plants in Detroit and Ham-tramck, far exceeding the achievement of the AFL in the auto kingdom's capital. In 1936 the AIWA and its locals were absorbed by the newly inde-pendent UAW following its South Bend convention, with Frankensteen taking a place on the UAW's International executive board and becoming director of organizing in Detroit.[30]

In the early years of AIWA, Father Charles E. Coughlin, the famous "Radio Priest" of Royal Oak, Michigan, whose Sunday afternoon broadcasts were heard by millions nationwide, was an influential figure, so much so that AIWA was sometimes called "Coughlin's Union." Drawing on Catholic social doctrine, Coughlin, not yet the voice of strident anti-semitism that he later became, favored industrial unions and urged Dodge workers to transform their works council into an independent organization. Coughlin's message was popular among Detroit's many Catholic workers. Leonard Woodcock recalled that as he walked through working-class neigh-borhoods on Sunday afternoons distributing Socialist Party leaflets in the 1936 presidential campaign, "you could hear the radios" through the open front doors, "Father Coughlin in every house." Dodge Main's work force, heavily first- and second-generation Polish Catholic, formed a large ele-ment in this avid audience. When AIWA held a rally on Belle Isle Park in the Detroit River with Coughlin as featured speaker, a crowd estimated at 30,000 "filled the island."[31]

THE AFL LOCAL THAT MADE the greatest contribution to knitting together the several strands that formed the UAW was Federal Local No. 18384 in Toledo, Ohio. In this major center of parts production and assem-bly the AFL had set up a single local with membership drawn from many plants. The failure of the national AFL to obtain favorable government deci-sions on questions of seniority, employer discrimination against union members, and collective bargaining rights incited the local in the spring of 1934 to break free from the national leadership to conduct its own direct action campaign. The Toledo plants of the Electric Auto-Lite Company, an important parts manufacturer, were the first target. In the most violent and costly strike of AFL auto organizing, thousands of strikers and supporters, many from the ranks of the unemployed and some from radical organiza-tions, manned picket lines and fought pitched battles with scabs, police, and Ohio National Guardsmen, at times witnessed by thousands of specta-tors. Despite mass arrests, the deaths of two strike sympathizers, and scores of wounded, the Auto-Lite plants were shut down and the company yielded, agreeing to sign a contract and rehire the strikers. Through these actions the local, which eventually became UAW Local 12, carved out its place as one of the strongest early autoworker organizations.[32]

Toledo Auto-Lite strikers battle state troops, 1934. Walter P. Reuther Library, Wayne State University

The next year the local struck again, this time against a more formidable target, the Chevrolet Division's Toledo transmission plant. Again defying the national AFL leadership, with a strike that lasted nearly a month in April and May 1935, the local brought Chevrolet production to a halt, forced GM to break its pledge never to negotiate while a strike was in progress, and produced an agreement that, while it fell short of what the local sought, brought de facto union recognition from the leading auto manufacturer. Since GM made no effort to operate the plant during the strike, there was no violence along the picket line. The shutdown of the plant, the sole supplier of transmissions to Chevrolet and Pontiac, idled 32,000 GM employees elsewhere. Since many of the strike's leaders—such as Bob Travis, soon to be a principal in the great Flint sit-down—believed that a push from the AFL to extend the strike to other GM facilities would have produced total victory, the outcome further weakened AFL credibility. A few months later GM, to protect its integrated production system from disruptions by a single, militant local, transferred half of the Toledo plant's machinery to other locations, resulting in the loss of about one thousand jobs. The lesson was not lost on auto workers who saw that no GM jobs would be safe until all GM workers were organized in strong locals, with their actions coordinated by a national union.[33]

AS THE NEW DEAL'S FIRST PHASE came to an end in 1935, auto workers, with only a few victories and many setbacks to show for their efforts, were still largely unorganized, unprotected, and disillusioned. In part the disappointment was due to workers' unrealistic hopes. Without an immediate payoff many did not see the point in a union. As one organizer of that period observed, "a great many people . . . believed that a union was a slot machine that you threw a quarter in. If you did not hit the jackpot, you walked away." The substantial, lasting gains that would make a difference in workers' lives in and out of the plants could be attained only through sustained effort in a more supportive context.[34]

The companies' counterattacks against organizing had been by and large successful. By June 1935, the total paid-up membership of the AFL federal labor unions was a mere 22,687, only 5 percent of the 421,000 employed in automobile and auto parts manufacturing, and a massive decline in membership from the 100,000 claimed at the peak of NIRA-inspired organizing in 1933. In the Michigan heartland of the industry, where corporate resources were concentrated and resistance was unyielding, the AFL's membership of only 3,610 was especially unimpressive. When the AFL faltered in meeting a challenge, members dropped out of the federal locals in droves. In July 1934 a local officer wrote, "since March our membership has fallen away in appalling numbers. . . . Our treasuries have been drained. . . . The few remaining loyal members are discouraged." In Pontiac, where three GM divisions employed 12,000 workers, the Pontiac Motors federal local had only twenty active members, the Fisher Body local had even fewer, and the GM truck local had none at all. At the Rouge plant of the Ford Motor Company, which had ignored NIRA, only nineteen workers were paid-up members of the AFL local.[35]

The AFL federal locals' presence and strength, such as they were, lay outside Michigan in the Studebaker and Bendix locals in South Bend, Indiana; the White Motor local in Cleveland; the Toledo local; the Nash locals in Racine and Kenosha, Wisconsin; the Seaman Body local in Milwaukee; the Norwood, Ohio, Chevrolet and Fisher Body local; the Janesville, Wisconsin, Fisher Body local; and the Atlanta and Kansas City GM assembly plant locals. Organizing in these early locals was carried out by a cadre of activists, without central direction or participation. As one pioneer organizer observed, "our union was built out on the spokes of the wheel, not on the hub." Over two-thirds of the AFL's paid-up membership belonged to these locals, which had, on the whole, been more militant in their actions than the timid AFL national leadership had endorsed, and thereby had gained the respect and support of a portion of the workforce. The composition of the membership in these locals was relatively homogenous, ethnically and culturally, which may have contributed to their ability to create lasting organizations. The workers tended to be white; of American birth; either from the factory city itself or migrants from rural areas, nearby small towns, or Appalachia; and often evangelical Protestants in religious persuasion. By contrast Detroit's workforce, more unified than once had been the case, was yet far more diverse and divided: it was ethnically and racially mixed, with many first- and second- generation, central European immigrants as well as rural native-born migrants; religiously divided among Catholics, secularists, and Protestants; and politically diverse, with radical elements well represented. Except in a few isolated instances these locals had won neither formal recognition nor written contracts from an employer, although informal arrangements at some plants provided a pale facsimile of recognition and negotiation.[36]

The first phase of auto industry organizing produced few concrete results. With only a few exceptions in scattered plants, none of the major manufacturers openly recognized and bargained with an independent union of its employees. Only one manufacturer, Studebaker, granted a federal local "virtual recognition." Its management was unique in not opposing unionization and refraining from antiunion activities. With a tradition of employee-friendly policies, the company paid high wages, ran its assembly lines at relatively slow speeds, and granted the workers almost unlimited job transfer rights within its operations. But the AFL had not been able to mount and sustain a broad organizing campaign. Unaffiliated, rival organizations, such as MESA, AIWA, and the Associated Automobile Workers of America (AAWA)—a union similar to AIWA, with its membership concentrated in the Hudson plant—had established themselves in Detroit with larger total memberships there than the AFL federal locals. One estimate holds that as of June 1935, only 10 to 15 percent of the industry's factory workers belonged to independent, non-company dominated labor organizations; only a tiny, much smaller number were covered by collective bargaining agreements. An attempt by the AFL and the independent unions to cooperate in conducting a strike at the Motor Products Corporation, a Detroit frame maker, collapsed in ignominious failure amid accusations of betrayal and the loss of jobs by many of the strikers. The lesson was clear. Faced with the opposition of some of the nation's most powerful corporations, the small, fragile, rival unions into which the workforce was divided had no realistic prospect of success.[37]

DURING 1935 TWO ISSUES that had plagued auto worker organizing moved toward resolution. First the federal government's commitment in support of unionization was clarified and strengthened. In June the Supreme

Court declared the National Industrial Recovery Act unconstitutional. The act had proved an unsuccessful experiment, inspiring organizing efforts for a time but finally contributing little either to unions or to recovery. To replace section 7(a) of NIRA, Congress passed the Wagner Act, also known as the National Labor Relations Act (NLRA). Besides guaranteeing the right of collective bargaining, the new law adopted the democratic principle of majority rule, familiar and long accepted as the basis of political decision-making, for determining the bargaining agent. If a majority of the employees in a particular plant voted to authorize a union to bargain for them, it became the agent for all. The law reauthorized and strengthened the National Labor Relations Board (NLRB) to conduct elections of bargaining agents and to investigate charges against employers of unfair labor practices; the act named and defined these as including discrimination against union members in hiring and firing, refusal to bargain, and interference with employees' rights and liberties. The NLRB, as a part administrative and part judicial body, could investigate allegations of violations, and, if warranted, issue cease-and-desist orders to offending employers, who could appeal its decisions to federal courts. The act and its instrumentalities rested upon the leading, although not the only, concept of industrial democracy current in those times.[38]

Although the Wagner Act had the potential to greatly strengthen labor's hand in organizing mass production workers, its passage did not ensure any particular outcome. Until a Supreme Court decision in 1937 upheld the law, the act's constitutionality was uncertain. For the present, many employers, including the auto manufacturers, chose to ignore it. Workers now had the promise of better legal weapons, legal protections, and more effective procedures in their arsenal, but in organizing they would still have to rely on their own efforts.[39]

The second issue was the legitimacy and place of industrial unions in the labor movement. At the AFL's 1934 convention the advocates of industrial organization, led by John L. Lewis of the United Mine Workers, urged that new industrial unions be chartered to replace the federal labor unions in mass production industries. Agreement was reached on chartering an auto workers' union, but the jurisdictional rights of craft unions to organize skilled workers in the industry were protected. A vague resolution defining the UAW's jurisdiction contained the seeds of future wrangles. These decisions were unacceptable to auto workers, whose desire for an autonomous industrial union was by this time clear. As a Flint auto worker wrote, "workers believe that the present [AFL] setup is beyond repair and that an entirely new plan as advocated by Lewis must be used."[40]

In October 1935 the issue came to a head at the AFL's Atlantic City convention. Lewis again spoke out for labor organization on the industrial principle. When the delegates spurned his plea, he and other industrial unionists defied the AFL by setting up the Committee for (later Congress of) Industrial Organizations (CIO) to spearhead a union drive in the heavy, mass production, core industries of the national economy. Although it would be two years before the split between the AFL and CIO was set in cement, they treated each other as rivals from the start. For the auto workers the way was now clear to organize on an industrial basis with the support of other unions and of a vigorous, experienced, and resolute national leadership.[41]

TWO MONTHS EARLIER, in August of the same year, with the federal auto unions still under AFL control, the first constitutional convention of the International Union, United Automobile Workers of America (UAWA-AFL), met in Detroit, with delegates representing sixty-five federal unions in attendance. Two issues dominated the proceedings. William Green, president of the AFL, argued that the jurisdiction of the new union did not include craftsmen in tool and die and skilled trades maintenance classifications. Expressing the sentiments of the majority of the delegates, Wyndham Mortimer of the White Motor local in Cleveland warned that "the craft form of organization fits into the automobile industry like a square peg in a round hole." Although acceptance of the charter, with its craft jurisdictional limitation, was railroaded through the convention, unhappy delegates made clear their determination to overthrow the arrangement at the earliest opportunity.[42]

Equally controversial was Green's decision, on the pretext that the new union had to pass through a probationary period, to appoint the International's officers rather than allow their election. Over great protest, he appointed as president the AFL's chief auto organizer, Frank Dillon, never himself an auto worker and a champion of caution and conservatism. The other two leading appointed officers, vice president Homer Martin of the Kansas City Chevrolet local and secretary-treasurer Ed Hall of the Seaman Body local in Milwaukee, had some autoworker experience and standing, but the appointed General Executive Board consisted of AFL loyalists, mostly regional officers with few autoworker followers. Unrepresentative of the membership and unresponsive to the rising militancy within the ranks, this first incarnation of the UAW had little prospect of permanence.[43]

During the next few months what little support Dillon enjoyed among auto workers evaporated. Homer Martin, Ed Hall, and leaders in some of the larger locals, such as Wyndham Mortimer in Cleveland and George Addes in Toledo, were determined to escape the constraints of the AFL's stifling hand. Responding to their insistent demands, the federation scheduled a UAW convention to meet in South Bend, Indiana, on April 27, 1936. Two-hundred and sixteen delegates, representing sixty-nine locals with approximately 20,000 members—only a small fraction of the industry's blue-collar employees—attended this convention, where the UAW was refounded, this time as a self-governing organization. The largest delegations came from Local 5 (Studebaker) in South Bend, Local 12 (Amalgamated) in Toledo, Local 32 (White Motor) in Cleveland, Local 72 (Nash) in Kenosha, Wisconsin, and Local 75 (Seaman Body) in Milwaukee. Delegates from the two major manufacturing centers, Detroit and Flint, were conspicuous by their absence. At the convention's opening, Dillon made a token appearance and immediately withdrew, clearing the way for Homer Martin to become the UAW's first elected president, chosen unanimously by those present.[44]

Although his presidency ended in disgrace only three years later, Martin, previously vice president of the UAWA-AFL, was the obvious choice for president in 1936. The union's most pressing need, so many believed, was for a presidential word magician who could inspire the rank and file and motivate the hundreds of thousands of unorganized auto workers to join the union. Martin was just such a spectacular speaker. Although he had worked briefly in the Kansas City, Missouri, Chevrolet assembly plant, thereby acquiring an autoworker credential, he was by training, experience, and inclination a Baptist preacher. Born into a poor, southern Illinois farm family in 1901, Martin in 1936 was young in years and appearance, like so many of the UAW's first generation of activists. After struggling to complete his education, including graduation from a small, church-related college, he ministered to a Baptist congregation in Kansas City that included current and laid-off workers from the nearby Chevrolet assembly plant. Moved to compassion by their plight, he criticized the plant's management and urged the workers to form a union. That advice, perhaps in combination with other infractions, cost him his pastor's position, adding a martyr's halo to his image. Finding employment at the Chevrolet factory as a trimmer on the truck cab line, he put precept into practice by helping to organize Federal Labor Union No. 19320, becoming its president. In 1934 he was fired from Chevrolet for union activity and thereafter devoted himself to the union, which led to his appointment as UAWA-AFL vice president the following year. From there it was only a short step to the UAW's presidency at the South Bend convention.[45]

Oratory was Martin's great and only strength. "Boy, can that baby speak!" exclaimed one convention delegate. His revivalistic style and diction were readily adapted to a message of this-worldly compassion, redemption, and salvation in a crusade for industrial and social justice. With the union substituted for the church, the Biblical phrases and rhythms marched on. "Homer," another auto worker testified, "could lead you down the sawdust trail." His autoworker sermons had their greatest appeal to those thousands of Appalachian, southern, and rural-born workers, many of Baptist or

Homer Martin in full oratorical flight, 1937. Walter P. Reuther Library, Wayne State University

evangelical Protestant persuasion, who had poured into the factories in the 1920s. First in Kansas City and later in automobile plants and cities scattered throughout the Midwest, Martin's message touched their hearts and bolstered their faith as he urged them to make their decision, not this time for Jesus but for a new cause, a union in solidarity with their fellow workers. As the conflict with the auto makers erupted in sit-down strikes and other protests in the years ahead, some of these Appalachian and rural southerners were among the most class-conscious and militant, if nonideological, unionists.[46]

Martin's oratory helped the UAW to achieve its immediate aim of rallying and enlisting new members, but it fell short of universal appeal. The surface glittered but the inner light of substance was dim. One auto worker, who was exposed to the oratorical fireworks of many labor luminaries during years of active organizing, remarked that Martin's immediate impact on audiences was greater than that of anyone else but it lasted only "while they were listening to him." To auto workers of either a Catholic or secular outlook, large and important elements within the rank and file—especially in Detroit and among the emerging leadership cadres in many of the locals and the International Union—the pulpit oratory fell flat.[47]

Other failings more seriously weakened and eventually undermined his leadership. His knowledge and understanding of the industry were superficial, and his political, organizing, administrative, and negotiating skills infirm. At a time and place when well-articulated and -defended ideological positions counted, his grasp of abstract ideas and debate tactics was weak. In stressful situations, which occurred often, he could crack, becoming erratic and unpredictable in judgment, speech, and action, behavior that betrayed to some observers deep feelings of inadequacy. On occasion he abruptly walked out of important meetings, disappearing for hours at a time, sometimes merely to take in a movie or retire to a coffee shop, where he would hold forth to any listener. More than once the union's executive board had to pass resolutions ordering his attendance at its meetings so that business could be transacted. In a widely publicized incident, when confronted at the door of his Detroit hotel room by UAW members upset over one of his recent decisions, he struck one and threatened another with a pistol. As reports of his bizarre behavior multiplied and spread through the ranks, his standing and credibility irreversibly declined. Soon many hoped and expected that his tenure as president would be brief.[48]

THE MOST INFLUENTIAL AMONG the other officers elected at the South Bend convention, already Martin's critics and rivals, were Wyndham Mortimer, elected first vice president, and George Addes, chosen secretary-treasurer. Mortimer, fifty-two years of age in 1936, was older than most of the new UAW's young leaders. A second-generation immigrant whose English coal miner father and Welsh mother came to Pennsylvania only a few years before his birth in 1884, he followed his father into the mines at the age of twelve as the trapper-boy who opened and closed the underground doors that regulated the flow of air in a mine's ventilation system. Like several early UAW activists, "Mort," as he was known, acquired his working-class and union loyalties within the family circle and from the United Mine Workers. Stints in Ohio steel mills and jobs on railroads and streetcars, interrupted by periods of unemployment, brought him to White Motor Company in Cleveland as a lathe operator, where, deep in the depression's depths, he took the lead in establishing a federal local union. Slight, intense, courageous, committed, and contemptuous of Martin, he was an effective organizer and tactician who recognized that it would take sustained, bold action to build an industrial union of auto workers.[49]

Mortimer was the UAW's leading Communist. His membership in the Communist Party (CP), including its Central Committee, was concealed by a pseudonym in party records and never publicly acknowledged by him, a common practice among party members whose activities and duties took them beyond party circles into the public arena. Regardless of concealment, his party membership was widely recognized within the union. With few exceptions he supported the party's positions on issues, its tactical decisions, and advanced its cause within the UAW as opportunities arose. From the beginning he was the target of anticommunist attacks both from within and without the union. With impressive credentials as an organizer and as an effective local leader and negotiator, Mortimer might well have been the UAW's president if not for fear that his reputation as a Communist would alienate a significant portion of the membership and subject the organization to costly attacks by the press and politicians.[50]

While Communist Party members among auto workers were few in number—only 630 in 1934 according to one estimate—for a dozen years from the union's inception until their defeat by the Reuther forces in 1947 they were an important element in the UAW, and their role and interests had to be taken into account by both friend and foe. In 1934, as part of a tactical shift in support of a Popular Front alliance of all antifascist forces, the Communist Party had dissolved its separatist Auto Workers' Union and, adopting a strategy of "boring from within," encouraged party members and sympathizers to work to establish and then build within and upon an independent auto workers' union. Often well-organized and disciplined, experienced in union and other organizational work, and dedicated to the cause, the party cadre wielded an influence in the fledgling UAW that reached well beyond its limited numbers. The failure of the AFL to mount an effective campaign for an auto workers' union gave the Communists a golden opportunity to come forward as a knowledgeable, reliable organizing force.[51]

The party's union presence was arrayed in two concentric rings around a nucleus. At the core stood a handful of open party members, including John Anderson, president of Local 155, the large tool and die unit on Detroit's East Side; that local's business agent, Nat Ganley; and Bill McKie, a Communist activist, union organizer, and sometime Ford employee. Ganley was sent by the party from New York to Detroit to organize within the autoworker ranks on the party's behalf and to function as its whip at union gatherings. Ultimately, all saw their influence in the union contract as they continued to defend the actions and support the interests of the Soviet Union. The innermost of the concentric rings consisted of those like Mortimer and Bob Travis who were recognized within the union as party advocates and likely members but whose membership, more or less an open secret, was nominally concealed. They were sometimes taunted by critics with the gibe that they were "cheating the party on dues." Concealing membership avoided giving a weapon to anticommunist rivals like Martin, a hostile media, and corporate critics. With a rank and file that was mostly either indifferent or hostile to communism as an ideology, and confronting a negative public and political perception, the concealment of party connection was necessary if these cadres hoped to win a larger following.[52]

The outermost and largest ring consisted of a fluctuating number of allies, neither open nor concealed party members, who supported party positions on particular union and political issues and who could be counted upon to align with the party in the union's internal political battles. Given the nuances in the degrees of affiliation and the frequent changes in the cast of characters, it was not easy for outsiders to identify precisely the depth of commitment and the location on the ideological/political spectrum of any particular individual. This vagueness meant that some of these "fellow travelers" (to use a later terminology) were tied more closely to the party by opponents and critics than was warranted. "Red-baiting" that stated or implied someone had Communist connections became a used and abused tactic within the UAW, employed sometimes as legitimate criticism of someone whose loyalty to the union was conditional, at others to discredit a personal or political rival. At union conventions and local meetings, when suspected Communist sympathizers of any stripe rose to speak, it became a common practice for their critics to heckle them with choruses of "quacks," an allusion to the adage: "if it looks like a duck and quacks like a duck and waddles like a duck, it must be a duck."[53]

Although many auto workers responded enthusiastically to militant rhetoric and tactics, there was little evidence to suggest mass support for the revolutionary goals of economic, social, and political reconstruction that committed Communists pursued as their ultimate objective. Nevertheless, in the UAW's early days, in situations that were always fluid and sometimes chaotic, the Communists were a relatively cohesive, influential force. Many auto workers were prepared to respond to determined leadership regardless of the ideological or political position that inspired it. The Communists themselves tended to exaggerate their impact, overlooking the objective conditions of economic failure and the workers' desire for change that underlay every effort. Saul Wellman, who came to Detroit after World War II to coordinate CP activity in the auto industry, acknowledged, "in the 1930s, a major upheaval was taking place . . . and without that upheaval we would not have been able to play the particular role that we played."[54]

George Addes, the union's new secretary-treasurer, only twenty-five years of age at the time of the 1936 convention, is representative of those who were not themselves Communists (Addes, in fact, was a practicing Catholic) but were prepared to cooperate with the Communists, incorporating them into a broader political coalition. Addes entered the plants as a metal finisher at Willys Overland in Toledo, strongly supported the key Auto-Lite and Chevrolet strikes in that city, was elected financial secretary of Local 12—one of the largest locals represented at the convention—and had already confronted Homer Martin over several political and organizational issues. Neither a stirring speaker nor an energetic organizer, he competently managed the union's finances and other internal business. A loyal unionist and pragmatic politician who welcomed the Communists' support and endorsed their positions on the political issues that mattered so much to them and probably much less to him, he emerged as the leading public figure in the UAW's "center-left" coalition until defeated for reelection to office by the Reuther forces in 1947.[55]

As THE TIME SET for the South Bend convention approached, the different ideological and political tendencies within the union, realizing that the UAW was soon to achieve self-governance, devised the agendas they hoped would bring them to power and shape the union's future. Meeting prior to the convention, a left-wing Progressive caucus, led by Wyndham Mortimer, adopted resolutions calling for an industrial union, a massive organizing drive focused on General Motors, enhancement of the authority of the locals and of the executive board at the expense of the president (a move that reflected distrust of Martin, who was slated for the union's highest office), support for a Farmer-Labor party in national politics (the current Communist Party political position), and incorporation of independent labor organizations such as AIWA, AAWA, and MESA into the UAW. Martin, as vice president of the UAWA, was well-positioned to rally his supporters in locals that would send delegates to the convention. Already the lines were being drawn between Martin and a body of critics and challengers on the left. The Progressive caucus was the first in a series of organized political factions that contended for UAW leadership during the next dozen years. Like many political groupings, each of these factions was a coalition of diverse elements. Shifts and realignments, with old alliances dissolving as new ones formed, sometimes occurred. Changes in nomenclature contributed to confusion. For example, the Progressive caucus of 1936, situated on the far left, became a part of the Unity caucus of 1937 and after, which was then opposed by a second (and very different) Progressive caucus situated on the right, led by Richard Frankensteen and president Martin. Although dismissed by some observers as only political machines narrowly devoted to winning office and aggrandizing power for an ambitious leader and his followers, the caucuses were divided by political, ideological, programmatic, and, to a lesser degree, strictly trade union issues. All of the UAW's factions were situated on the left of the American political spectrum, but the differences among them—which might seem minor to outsiders not caught up in the events—took on major dimensions in the pressured atmosphere of a movement on the verge of growth and power. Most critically, the questions of who would provide leadership and what directions that leadership would take had to be answered correctly if the union was to survive and have an impact on its members' working lives.[56]

A high point of the 1936 convention was Frankensteen's announcement that he would urge AIWA, the largest of the independents, to merge with the UAW. Representatives of MESA and AAWA similarly expressed their support for the new International. Although some of the MESA locals, with their fiery leader Matt Smith, remained outside, their most important Detroit locals and the AAWA and AIWA organizations soon joined the UAW, thus creating a single, undivided union for all auto workers. By and large the rest of the left's program was also adopted.[57]

The election of officers reflected the strength of the left coalition, with first vice president Mortimer, secretary-treasurer Addes, and second vice president, Ed Hall, all associated with it in greater or lesser degree. Among the officers only the third vice president, Walter Wells, in addition to president Martin, was not a part of the left wing. The International executive board of eleven elected members representing the different geographical regions into which the country was divided was about evenly split between left and right, with a few members of flexible orientation in the middle. Among the new board members was former AIWA officer R. J. Thomas, president of Local 7, the large Chrysler local on Detroit's East Side, who would succeed Martin as UAW president in 1939. Reflecting the fact that the UAW had made little progress in organizing workers in Detroit and

UNITED AUTOMOBILE WORKER

Special Convention Number | MAY, 1936. | Detroit, Mich.

UNION WINS SELF-RULE

Dillon Out; New Officers Elected

FIRST DEMOCRATICALLY ELECTED OFFICERS of United Automobile Workers. Left to Right: Wyndham Mortimer, First Vice Pres.; Ed Hall, Second Vice Pres.; Homer Martin, President; Walter N. Wells, Third Vice Pres.; George Addes, Secretary-Treasurer.

Martin President; Mortimer, Hall, Wells, Addes Also Chosen

MAKE PLANS FOR MAMMOTH DRIVE

One of the key points in the program adopted at the South Bend Convention for building the International Union was the decision to inaugurate a great organization drive in the industry, particularly in its heart, the State of Michigan.

Details were left in the hands of Executive Board, though the following plans were specified:

1. Prominent speakers, like John L. Lewis, Charles P. Howard, and other outstanding proponents of industrial unionism, be brought into the auto centers.

2. Organization Committees be set up by the General Officers wherever they are needed.

3. Credentials issued to voluntary organizers upon recommendation of the District Councils.

Widest Publicity

4. Widest possible publicity, through press, radio, sound cars, etc.

5. Enlistment of all liberal and civic-minded groups for assistance.

OFFICERS' SALARIES DRASTICALLY REDUCED

The salaries of all five General Officers were set at $3,000 per annum. This represents a big cut compared with the sums paid last year, the President having formerly received $6,500 and the Vice-President and Secretary-Treasurer, $4,500 each.

The present salaries thus total up to $15,000 or a saving of $500 over those in the past; whereas two extra General Officers will be available for our International despite this reduction.

With the termination of the "probationary period," the question of the election of officers came immediately upon the agenda of the Convention at South Bend. After the constitution of the International had been changed increasing the number of officers to five, this important matter was taken up.

Those elected to office need no introduction to the auto workers of this country. They have all been in the forefront of the battle for the International from the time the original federal locals were set up, and later took up the cudgels for complete democracy.

6. Raising of a "war chest" of $250,000, of which at least $75,000 must come from the affiliated locals of the International Union.

7. Request aid of all local, central and state bodies of organized labor.

8. When necessary, councils of correlated plants shall be established by the General Executive Board for the purpose of discussing negotiations and compiling data on hours, wages and working conditions.

9. Setting up of Research Department in cooperation with the Educational Committee to help compile such data. Locals shall do this on individual scale as well.

This is the plan. By adopting it, the convention showed that the International Union means business. The next few weeks and months ought to witness the unleashing of undreamt of stores of energy, under the guidance of the General Officers and Executive Board, which will mean that our union has finally gone to bat with the tremendous problem of organizing the tens of thousands of unorganized auto workers. But only the completest cooperation and self-sacrificing efforts will bring this aim to a successful termination.

Homer Martin, former vice-president, was elected president by acclamation. Wyndham Mortimer, president of the powerful White Motor local and the Cleveland Auto Council, was designated first Vice-President. Ed. Hall, of Milwaukee, outgoing Secretary-Treasurer, was chosen second Vice-President; while the third Vice-Presidency went to Walter N. Wells, of Detroit, who has been very active in the movement of that city. George Addes, of the famous Toledo local, will fill ex-Secretary Hall's shoes hereafter, keeping the books and finances of the International in order.

It is hard to imagine a better set of honest, upright and aggressive leaders to direct the affairs of the International Union during the coming year.

HUDSON LOCAL VOTES ON MERGER QUESTION

Detroit—A special meeting of the Hudson Local of the Associated Automobile Workers of America (A.A.W.A), headed by Arthur Greer, is being called for May 22 for the purpose of exploring and discussing the question of amalgamating with the International Union.

INDEPENDENTS IN UNITY BANQUET

Working at lightning speed, the General Officers of our International, elected at South Bend, arranged a banquet on Wednesday evening, May 6, (only four days after the closing of the Convention) in honor of the three independent unions which have expressed themselves through their representatives as favoring amalgamation.

Present were Richard Frankensteen, head of the A.I.W.A. with a number of members of the Executive Board of his union; Arthur Greer and two others from the Hudson local of the A.A.W. A., and three representatives of the M.E.S.A.

Speakers Call for Unity

Speaker after speaker rose to his feet, telling with deep feeling how he had been waiting for this day with great longing and expectation. After listening to these men from all the most important auto unions in the industry, it was almost impossible to understand why such a meeting of friendship and solidarity could not have taken place long before this.

President Martin, in a most stirring address which closed the banquet, said that, the time and the reason for disunity were past, and he invited the representatives of the independents to come into the fold so that working together, the common obligation of all to the auto workers and their families could finally be met.

Day of Uniting Closer

This banquet brought the great day of ultimate unity closer than ever, though it was pointed out that a number of matters, some of them technicalities, had to be settled beforehand.

The greatest interest is being manifested in this burning issue by the workers at Hudson's. The place and exact time of the meeting are to be announced late.

AFL HEAD ENDS TRIAL PERIOD

"I am here to perform my duty as President of the the American Federation of Labor, to carry out the decision of the convention of the A. F. of L. and the Executive Council, to end now the administration of your affairs by men appointed by the A. F. of L., to terminate the probationary period and to place the destinies of this great organization in your hands."

These words, of President William Green, which 40,000 auto unionists have awaited—yes, impatiently—for over two years, were finally heard, on the first day of the South Bend Convention, April 26. A great ovation of the assembled delegates greeted this statement, which formally established the complete autonomy of the auto union.

Immediately upon the utterance of these words, President Dillon, Green's appointee of last August, was automatically relieved of his office, and by the suggestion of the President of the A. F. of L., the Convention proceeded to elect a temporary chairman. Vice President Homer Martin was unanimously picked for this honor.

Without delay, the delegates then got down to the business of the Convention, the first of its kind ever held by the auto workers under completely democratic rule.

COUGHLIN MAKES UNITY APPEAL

In a spectacular manner Father Coughlin walked into a party for delegates at the United Automobile Workers' Convention Thursday night in South Bend.

The radio priest had not planned to attend the convention. He was en route from Chicago to Detroit, stopping here for dinner.

Invited to Speak

Richard Frankensteen, head of the Detroit Automobile Industrial Workers organization, and friend of Father Coughlin, who attended the convention, persuaded the radio priest to speak.

He approved industrial unionism along the lines that the organization here is being directed. He said men are not paid on a basis of what they produce but 'on a basis of existence.

"Away with independent unions!" Father Coughlin exclaimed at one point of his short talk in a dramatic appeal for unity.

The UAW's newspaper reports on the South Bend convention, 1936. Walter P. Reuther Library, Wayne State University

other Michigan auto cities, only four board members, chosen from the state at large, represented Michigan workers. With the addition of Dick Frankensteen to the board, all of those officers and board members destined for major roles in the UAW's contentious internal history over the next ten years were now in place.[58]

ONE OF THE MICHIGAN board members elected at the 1936 convention was Walter P. Reuther. Reuther had arrived in Detroit in 1927 at the age of nineteen and had worked for five years as a die maker at the Ford Motor Company. While working he completed high school and took courses at Detroit City College (now Wayne State University). In 1930 a younger brother, Victor, joined him in Detroit, where they lived in a cooperative house with three friends. Drawing upon the working-class sensibilities formed under their father's instruction, the Reuther brothers responded to the depression's demonstration of capitalism's ills with political commitment. They joined the Socialist Party, organized a Social Problems Club at the college, and engaged in local social reform and political activity. In 1932 Reuther campaigned for Norman Thomas, the Socialist Party presidential candidate, organizing "Thomas for President" clubs and giving speeches on college campuses throughout the Midwest. During the campaign he was laid off at Ford's, perhaps because of this political activity, perhaps because of his membership in the Auto Workers' Union, or perhaps simply because the hard times had finally caught up with him as with so many others. Whatever the cause of his dismissal, for the time being he was unemployed.[59]

A frugal man, Reuther had saved in order to finance a sojourn in Europe with Victor. Leaving the United States in February 1933, the brothers first traveled to Germany to visit relatives and observe conditions there under the recently installed Nazi regime, whose brutal treatment of its Socialist and trade union opponents, which they experienced at first hand, deeply impressed the young men. Following travels by bicycle through several European countries, they departed for their ultimate destination, the auto plant at Gorki in the Soviet Union, where Walter's die maker skills were in demand. They returned to the United States in 1935, coming home by way of China and Japan to complete a circuit of the globe.[60]

Reuther's work with the UAW began on Detroit's West Side, where he became an unpaid organizer for Local 86, a fledgling organization seeking to establish itself among the workers in a plant operated by the Ternstedt Division of General Motors. Chosen as the local's delegate to the 1936 convention, his credentials were challenged on the ground that he was not a worker in the Ternstedt plant nor an employee of any of the auto companies. Reuther argued that his one-time Ford employment legitimated his election while left-wing caucus allies testified to Ternstedt employment under a

Victor Reuther and Walter Reuther in Gorki, U.S.S.R., 1934. Walter P. Reuther Library, Wayne State University

pseudonym. (Such irregularities were not unknown in the union's early days.) In any event, Reuther's credentials were approved, although he continued to draw fire from conservative delegates. He shrewdly turned to account the opportunity this controversy offered to speak before the convention on several issues and to secure his election to the executive board as one of the Michigan representatives.[61]

Reuther was still a member of the Socialist Party, associated with its "militant" wing which stood for a Popular Front strategy of cooperation among all antifascists, including the Communists. Reuther's willing cooperation at this time with Communists in the Progressive caucus and in Popular Front activities aroused suspicions of his ideological position among some observers. Combined with the enthusiasm he had shown for the industrial and cultural achievements of the Soviet Union during his stay there and for a time after his return to the United States, some thought it likely that he had in fact become a Communist, maintaining his Socialist Party membership in order to infiltrate that organization on behalf of the CP. Although his cooperation with the union's Communists at this time is well-established, the lack of conclusive evidence for membership in the CP and his denials of it, as well as the testimony of his closest associates, cast serious doubt on the claim. Nevertheless, the charge, leveled from both the left and the right, would dog him for the rest of his life. Although the UAW's Socialist contingent was numerically smaller and less cohesive than its Communist element, it included persons who would play major roles in the UAW's history and would indelibly stamp it as a union with a reform mission that went beyond winning bigger paychecks. In addition to Walter, Victor, and Roy Reuther (the "royal family" as some critics delighted to call them), the early Socialist cadre included Emil Mazey, later the UAW's secretary- treasurer; George Edwards, who would become a Detroit city councilman, police commissioner, and justice of the Michigan Supreme Court and the United States Court of Appeals; and Leonard Woodcock, Reuther's successor as president of the union. A significant number of future influential staff members and activists in local unions also were aligned with the Socialist Party.[62]

THE UNION'S FORMAL STRUCTURE was established in the conventions of 1935 and 1936, with some important alterations at the 1939 convention. The constitutional convention, at first held annually and later fixed at three-year intervals, was the organization's highest formal authority. Convention delegates were elected in the locals and apportioned on the basis of dues- paying members. Any member in good standing was eligible to vote and eligible for election as a delegate; it comes as no surprise that the first convention delegates were those activists who had organized the local and held office in it. In most locals a particular element, adept in prosecuting grievances and conducting local bargaining with management, and often exploiting some combination of ethnic, political, ideological, and personal factors, gained and maintained its position in elections. Nevertheless, rivalries and fiercely contested elections were common. Beginning in 1936 the convention delegates elected the International Union's officers, consisting of a president, a secretary-treasurer, and a varying number of vice presidents. On several occasions the argument was made that a direct election of officers by the entire membership was a more appropriate and democratic method of officer selection, but that argument, whatever its merits, was consistently rejected in favor of election by convention delegates. Regional directors, elected separately at the convention by the delegates from each region, joined with the officers to form the International executive board (IEB), the union's governing body between conventions. The regional directors were responsible for transmitting the international's policy decisions to its locals and for providing locals with assistance in organizing and contract administration. (The number of regions has varied, reflecting fluctuations in the number and distribution of members, but ordinarily there have been between twelve and eighteen.) Local unions were chartered by the IEB when a petition was presented by a work group in a shop or factory. In most locals authority was divided between two elected sets of officers. The president, financial secretary, and recording secretary conducted the local's daily business and managed its relationship with the regional director and the international union. The shop or bargaining committee, supported by a shop floor apparatus of elected stewards or committeemen, prosecuted grievances and dealt with plant management on collective bargaining issues. Amalgamated locals combined units from several, usually small, shops. In the union's early days, the division of power within this federated structure tilted in favor of the large locals where organizing activity was carried out. As time passed and emphasis shifted to conducting negotiations with the major corporations and mobilizing the membership for political action, the balance shifted away from the locals to favor the international union. Establishing a UAW principle of modest remuneration for officers, the 1936 convention set the president's salary at $3,000 annually, less than half the $6,500 that had been paid to Martin's AFL-appointed predecessor, Frank Dillon. The salaries of other officers were lowered accordingly.[63]

IN THE CONVENTION'S DELIBERATIONS on issues that broached the question of Communist influence within the union, the left sought to limit its exposure. Some response was necessary, it was felt, to attacks in the press, led by the Hearst newspapers, that charged the UAW was under Communist control. Walter Reuther created a sensation with a blistering attack on Hearst that threw the convention into an "uproar." A resolution ordering locals to "immediately expel from membership all known Communists" provoked a long and vehement debate, one that "almost," as a delegate later remarked, "dynamited this Convention." This resolution, setting a political test for membership that was obviously at odds with the basic industrial union principle that membership should be open to all workers in a relevant plant, and a companion measure that barred Communists from holding union office, were defeated, being referred back to the Constitution Committee. But the convention proceedings reveal substantial support for these exclusions, helping to explain why Communists in the union might hesitate to declare openly their political affiliation. Later the convention approved unanimously and without debate a watered-down resolution that expressed "unalterable opposition to Fascism, Nazism and Communism and all other movements intended to distract the attention of the membership of the Labor Movement from the primary objectives of unionism," the first in a series of UAW expressions of antitotalitarian sentiment in resolutions and constitutional provisions that have continued to the present day.[64]

Much of the debate at the convention centered on political issues. From the union's earliest days its leadership, alert to the lessons of history, was acutely aware of the impact that political and governmental decisions made in Washington and in state capitals could have on a union's fortunes. As a matter of self-preservation, if for no other reason, the UAW would have to be politically active. On national and state political questions the convention veered back to the left, adopting a resolution endorsing farmer-labor parties in the 1936 elections, a position put forward by advocates of a Popular Front and one that threatened the electoral prospects of Democratic Party candidates. Angry with harmful decisions made by the Roosevelt-appointed Auto Labor Board, and led by Socialists with encouragement from the Communists, the convention initially refused, by a close vote, to endorse President Roosevelt himself for reelection. National CIO representatives, horrified by this rebuff to a president the CIO had endorsed and was preparing to support with a substantial financial contribution, threatened to withhold funding to the UAW of $100,000 for organizing expenses if the decision was allowed to stand. Within an hour, President Martin reminded the delegates of the CIO's position and pointed out that the CIO's financial aid was crucial to the UAW's success. The delegates, seeing the light, jumped on the Roosevelt bandwagon.[65]

As expected, the UAW followed up its convention decisions by affiliating with the CIO in August 1936, a move which promptly led to its suspension followed by expulsion from the AFL. Thus it accepted CIO president John L. Lewis as labor's national spokesman and leader and cast its lot with the other industrial unions that, like Lewis's United Mine Workers, had either defied the AFL or were in formation under CIO auspices. For the next ten years the national CIO, at first under Lewis and after 1940 under Philip Murray, with the support of Sidney Hillman, exerted a powerful influence in UAW affairs.[66]

The South Bend convention rejuvenated the UAW. The timidity and half-way measures of the AFL had been thrust aside in favor of militant action. Organizing was reinvigorated with membership bounding upward in the late summer and autumn of 1936. In some of the supplier companies, whose resistance to the union was weak in contrast to the determined opposition of the major manufacturers, bargaining without formal recognition produced wage increases, seniority systems, negotiated production rates, and other advances. As each improvement proved the local union's effectiveness in bringing about tangible gains, membership grew. Some employers were unable to mount an effective counter strategy. When they responded to the union surge with concessions that they hoped would blunt the union drive, they found they had only whetted the appetite for more and strengthened a union's appeal to their workers.[67]

THE EARLY UAW, like so many of its activists, was a youthful organization. Walter Reuther was only twenty-eight when elected to the executive board, and the two fated to be the principal figures in the Flint sit-down, Bob Travis and Roy Reuther, were in their early twenties when that strike occurred. Many of the local union activists were young as well. Doug Fraser was barely out of his teens and only recently employed at Chrysler's DeSoto factory when he was elected a department steward, and he became president of Local 227 a few years later at the age of twenty-six. The spirit of the organization reflected the youth of so many of its leading figures. It was ambitious, boisterous, hopeful, untested, idealistic, unpredictable, and marked by ideological and personal rivalries—an exciting milieu. With little exaggeration, an observer later remarked that "the UAW at the beginning was a wild scramble of largely inexperienced unionists trying to organize themselves into a functioning union with a number of groups struggling for control."[68]

Although the future and the final outcome were very uncertain, the UAW already had several accomplishments to its credit. It had broken free of the AFL, affiliated with like-minded industrial unions, established the autonomy of its locals, absorbed potential rivals, invigorated its leadership, gained the attention of the workers themselves, and begun their education in the union's potential to give them a voice in shaping their destiny. It now stood poised to face the substantive challenges it had been formed to confront: the enormous and likely dangerous tasks of organizing the auto workers, winning recognition from the auto manufacturers, and negotiating the contracts that would govern the work place and repay the auto workers for their labor.

CHAPTER 3

"Storming the stronghold of the open shop"

The Year of the Sit-Down Strikes, 1937

THE DECISIVE EVENT IN AUTO ORGANIZING WAS THE SIT-DOWN strike at the General Motors Corporation that began on December 30, 1936, and continued for forty-four days until February 11, 1937. The sit-down era in the auto and other industries lasted only a few months, from the fall of 1936 through the spring of the following year, but few and brief as they were, the strikes were one of those transforming events that recast a nation's history and change the lives of all they touch.

A direct action tactic that defied the corporations, the law, and much of public opinion, sit-downs blasted a way through the obstacles that had blocked union organizing at the plants of the major manufacturers. Many workers who were favorably disposed toward a union were hesitant to commit themselves, but they were moved to join as the UAW demonstrated its strength and staying power. Though the early gains in union recognition were partial and the early contracts afforded only modest material improvements, the sit-downs proved to be the UAW's best recruiting device. As victory followed victory, a great surge of energy, resting on confidence in the union's survival and anticipation of the better tomorrow it could achieve, swept through the auto cities.

AUTO WORKERS SOUGHT EMPOWERMENT in the workplace. Visions of gaining control of the shop floor animated few, but all could agree on the need for a greater collective voice in determining the conditions, rewards, and burdens of their working lives. To be recognized in the workplace as human beings, entitled to dignity, security, and respect, was the principal motivation and goal. "People saw the opportunity to become human beings and not machines," recalled Harvey Kitzman, an employee of the J. I. Case Company, an agricultural equipment manufacturer in Janesville, Wisconsin. Bob Stinson, who participated in the Flint Fisher Body sit-down, told an interviewer that when General Motors executive vice president William Knudsen "put his name to a piece of paper and says that General Motors recognizes the UAW-CIO—until that moment, we were non-people, we didn't even exist. . . . That was the big one." Once dismissed as only items in the company's list of assets, auto workers sought acknowledgment of their humanity and an empowerment that would enable them to share in shaping their future.[1]

Union representation was the key to the changes they demanded, which included, more than anything else, protection against the exercise of arbitrary power by supervisors, together with the security provided by a seniority system governing layoffs, rehires, and job assignments. Production standards, especially the speed of assembly lines and health and safety conditions in the plants, were also pressing concerns. Despite the downward drift of wages in the depression, auto workers were still well-paid compared to other manufacturing employees, a fact they recognized; by 1936 the economy, and with it auto production, had begun to rebound from depression lows, bringing slight improvements in wages and renewed company hiring. Martin Gerber, later director of UAW Region Nine, when hired in on a backbreaking job placing frames on the assembly line at GM's Linden, New Jersey, plant, threw himself into the union movement. "It was not so much the wages," he recalled, "as it was the brutal working conditions, the inhuman speedup, the tediousness of the job, the inability to leave the work and go to the bathroom, our being completely chained to the line. . . . I really didn't understand how brutal the speedup could be until I was a victim of it." Or as Red Mundale of Fisher No. 2, a key plant in the Flint sit-down, tersely registered his complaint, "I ain't got no kick on wages, but I just don't like to be drove."[2]

Although a powerful weapon, the sit-down could be used only in the right circumstances. The workers must be emboldened by an expectation of success; the public and government must tolerate, if only temporarily, an assault on the legal rights of private capital; and the employer must suffer economic pain from curtailed production. By the end of 1936, as economic and political conditions took a turn for the better, the prospects for strike action were more promising than at any time in the depression. Car production, sales, and employment were rising along with a general improvement in the economy. The balance of political power dramatically shifted in labor's favor with President Roosevelt's landslide 1936 reelection in a workingman's campaign that mobilized the country's ethnic millions, highlighted and sharpened class divisions, and pitted the president against the "economic royalists" who counted among their number prominent executives of the General Motors Corporation. Roosevelt's triumphal October campaign tour of Grand Rapids, Lansing, Flint, Pontiac, and Detroit—Michi-

SPEED UP!
THREATENS YOUR JOB
The Management Demands of You
FASTER PACE
MORE PRODUCTION
LONGER HOURS

WHY?
TO USE LESS MEN
INCREASE UNEMPLOYMENT
MAKE A SHORTER SEASON
TO ELIMINATE YOUR JOB

THE AUTOMOBILE WORKERS' UNION IS
ACTING TO PROTECT YOU
AND YOUR JOB

Hear

LEO KRZYCKI
CIO Organizer

FRIDAY, OCTOBER 16 - 8 P. M.
8944 JOS. CAMPAU

ACT NOW! TIME IS SHORT!

Dodge Local, United Automobile Workers of America
8944 Jos. Campau   **TR 2-7470**

A UAW organizing handbill, 1936. Walter P. Reuther Library, Wayne State University

gan's auto cities—brought hundreds of thousands of enthusiastic supporters into the streets to welcome and hear him speak. In Flint, the largest crowd in the city's history swarmed to see and cheer him. In Detroit, where a "surging multitude roar[ed] its welcome," more than 150,000, rivaling in numbers those who had turned out for the champion Detroit Tigers "World Series Jamboree of 1935," jammed Cadillac Square and the surrounding streets for

his speech. Roosevelt carried Detroit and other auto cities with record
turnouts and majorities despite a plea from GM president Alfred P. Sloan, Jr.
In a letter sent to all GM employees, Sloan urged them to deliberate carefully before casting their ballots lest "class strife or economic shackles . . .
break the company up or retard its progress." A sentiment attributed to Roosevelt, "if I were a factory worker, I would join a union," was imprinted on
the political leaflets the UAW distributed to its members and other auto
workers. Roosevelt's victory did not stand alone. The election of New Deal
governors in several auto manufacturing states—notably in Michigan,
where Democrat and former Detroit mayor Frank Murphy took office in January 1937—was equally important. Murphy's election had an immediate
bearing, since control of the state's instruments of power and authority,
including command of the state police and National Guard, could be decisive in determining the character and outcome of a sit-down strike or other
labor/capital conflict. The 1936 election at both national and state levels was
a referendum on the New Deal and the union movement, and the decision
was emphatically favorable. The time for action had arrived.[3]

FOLLOWING THE SOUTH BEND convention, the UAW faced its greatest
challenge as it set out to build its membership in the plants of General
Motors, Ford, and Chrysler. By the fall nearly twenty full- and part-time
organizers had been added to the UAW staff. As valuable as it was to have
a paid staff of international representatives, most of the organizing continued to be conducted by the locals and by the members themselves on the
shop floor and in other gathering places. Thousands gave their time in what
quickly became a mass social movement. Owing to their commitment (and
in contrast to the top-down organizing that occurred in steel and some other
industries), the UAW grew from the bottom up in outbursts of grassroots
energy and militance.[4]

The union's officers compiled a list of ambitious objectives to guide
organizers and inspire the rank and file. It included an annual wage (meant
to encourage manufacturers to schedule production throughout the year
without the customary seasonal layoffs); elimination of production line
speedups; the establishment of seniority preference for layoffs, rehires, job
transfers and promotions; a forty-hour week with an eight-hour day, and
time-and-a-half pay for overtime; a reduction in hours for the employed
until all laid-off workers were rehired; better safety protection in the plants;
and, of course, collective bargaining with union recognition. Years would
pass before all were achieved, yet some goals turned out to be within reach.[5]

Conventional strikes, which relied on mass picketing to halt production, placed workers at risk. Scabs could be brought in past unguarded gates
or rammed through the picket line under police protection to resume pro-

A UAW local shows its support for President Franklin Roosevelt's reelection. Walter P. Reuther Library, Wayne State University

duction and break the strike. Such picket line confrontations readily provoked violence, led to arrests, the loss of public support for strikers, deteriorating morale, injuries—even fatal ones—and for many the loss of their jobs. Flint workers remembered the 1930 strike of Fisher Body metal finishers and painters whose picket lines were broken by mounted Flint police and their strike brought to a disastrous conclusion. A sit-down, on the other hand, tilted the balance of forces in the strikers' favor, nullifying some of the weapons and tactics resorted to by some employers in labor struggles. A contingent of determined workers, usually an activist minority, seized a plant and refused to leave. Barriers were erected at doors and gates to guard against attempts to dislodge them by force. A supply of missiles—automobile body hardware, engine parts, and the like—was at hand to repel police and plant security forces. If an attempt was made to retake the plant by force, expensive machinery and inventory would likely be wrecked and lives lost. Restraining the deployment of deadly force against strikers was one of the sit-down's most attractive features and its use contributed to the minimal loss of life in auto organizing. Further, the sit-down strengthened morale and enhanced solidarity. Jobs were protected because scabs could

not be brought in as long as plants were held, and suspicions about the loyalty and steadfastness of one's fellows that might arise in a conventional
strike were averted when the participants banded together within a plant.[6]

On the other hand, a sit-down, as trespass, violated a common-law
property right. Union lawyers won several stays of injunctions from sympathetic judges on the grounds that sit-downers, having been "invited" into
the plants when they were hired, were not trespassers; others argued that a
right to a job took precedence over a property right. These claims were
rejected by the Supreme Court in 1939 in its decision in the case of *Fansteel
Metallurgical Company v. NLRB.* Until that decision, a cloud of legal
uncertainty hung over sit-downs, but there can be no doubt that most people, and certainly most lawyers, judges, employers, and editorial writers in
the mainstream media, considered them illegal. Public opinion, as registered in polls, was ambivalent. Polls conducted by the Gallup organization
during and immediately following the General Motors sit-down strike
showed a majority favoring passage of laws to outlaw sit-downs, but they
also showed a majority in opposition to the use of force to end a sit-down if
that would result, as seemed likely, in bloodshed.[7]

In the exceptional circumstances that existed in 1937, common-law
legality was not the ruling consideration in many minds. To many workers
and to their public sympathizers the fact that the auto manufacturers came
into the contest with dirty hands offset the legally dubious actions of the
sit-downers. It was well-established that the major employers had spied on
workers and fired many of those suspected of union membership and activity, abridging their right of free association in legal organizations. Furthermore, the Wagner Act guaranteed workers a free choice of a union,
collective bargaining rights, and protections against unfair labor practices.
Auto workers knew that employers, hopeful that the Supreme Court would
strike down the law, were defying its clear intent. They maintained they
were acting to implement a national policy established and affirmed by the
president and Congress that was being flouted by their employers. President
Roosevelt conceded that the sit-down "is illegal, but," he asked, "what law
are they breaking? The law of trespass . . . ? [S]hooting it out and killing a
lot of people because they have violated the law of trespass somehow
offends me. . . . The punishment doesn't fit the crime. . . . Why can't these
fellows at General Motors meet with the committee of workers?. . . . It
wouldn't be so terrible."[8]

ALTHOUGH NOT INVENTED by American auto workers, having been earlier employed in Europe and in the United States by the Industrial Workers of the World, sit-downs had their most significant historical impact and
greatest success when taken up by auto workers in the United States.

Following scattered, brief incidents beginning with a 1933 strike at the Nash plant in Kenosha, Wisconsin, the first sustained auto sit-down occurred in the fall of 1936 at the Bendix Corporation, an auto parts manufacturer in South Bend, Indiana, where UAW Local 9 had been trying for months to persuade management to recognize the local as bargainer for its workers. On November 17, Bendix employees, with many women in their ranks, sat down in the plant and halted production for nine days until the company agreed to recognize the union.[9]

Sit-downs then spread like wildfire throughout the auto industry. The day the Bendix strike ended, seven hundred workers, including women and African Americans, sat down at Midland Steel, a frame maker for Chrysler and Ford on Detroit's East Side, and occupied the plant under the leadership of UAW organizer John Anderson, a local union president and public Communist. Shortages of frames soon forced the car manufacturers to shut down assembly lines. Within a week the company settled for union recognition, a 10-cent-an-hour wage increase, seniority in layoff and rehire, and time-and-a-half for overtime—a precedent-shattering settlement. For the first time a major Detroit parts firm had experienced a sit-down and recognized the union, "undoubtedly," as the UAW proudly proclaimed, "the most significant union victory in the history of the automobile industry in Detroit."[10]

A few days later union supporters at Kelsey-Hayes, a manufacturer of wheels and brakes employing 5,000 workers on Detroit's West Side, sat down. An AFL federal local with a fitful existence there had given some workers familiarity with union goals and procedures. Under the leadership of Walter P. Reuther, president of West Side Local 174, a cadre of Socialist activists—including Reuther's younger brother Victor and George Edwards, a recent recruit to the union's cause—infiltrated the plant and plotted the sit-down. A few hundred workers, including fifty women, remained inside. When a rumor spread that the company was planning to retake the plant by force, more than 5,000 pickets, most from other UAW locals and the ranks of the unemployed, were mobilized within an hour's time—one of many instances of a successful appeal to worker solidarity and mutual support in those formative days. Food for the strikers was collected from hundreds of community merchants and local residents by supporters going door to door in the surrounding neighborhoods where many of the strikers lived. Among the gifts, the local A & P gave a pound of coffee; a more generous Peoples' Bakery supplied sixty loaves of bread; and Olga Petrovich baked and donated seventy-seven cookies. A few weeks later a community resident donated her cow to sit-downers at Bohn Aluminum in Detroit. Lacking dues payments or other financial resources, and therefore without a strike fund, all of the union's early strikes relied entirely on the sacrifices of the strikers themselves, their families, non-striking unionists, sympathizers, and other community supporters. Ties of family, ethnicity, neighborhood, and class bound together auto workers' communities within Detroit and in other auto cities.[11]

The Kelsey-Hayes strikers quickly organized an effective social order within the plant. They established a court with policing responsibilities, brought in musical instruments, and sang and played cards for entertainment. The women sit-downers were segregated at night, under the watchful eye of a matron, to protect their reputations and counter rumors of sexual misconduct. When it was charged that the women were being held against their will, they came to the gate and told police and reporters that, free to go or stay, they preferred to stay.[12]

On December 23 the company, under pressure to settle from its major customer, the Ford Motor Company, whose assembly lines were shutting down from a lack of parts, granted a general wage increase, established a minimum rate of 75 cents an hour, and agreed to equal pay for its women employees for their equal work. The strikers saw these results as only first steps and pressed ahead, obtaining within a few months union recognition, a shop steward system for prosecuting grievances, seniority for layoffs, recalls, and job transfers, and a reduction in production line speed.[13]

As the Midland and Kelsey-Hayes strikes demonstrated, even Detroit, that mighty citadel of the open shop, was vulnerable to a sit-down. It was also evident that a victory in one plant could quickly snowball, overpowering the fear of workers that they would lose their jobs by engaging in a strike. In what proved to be a common consequence of a successful sit-down, union membership in the Kelsey-Hayes plants soared. Within days Local 174, an amalgamated local with units at the major West Side factories of Ternstedt, Cadillac, Fleetwood, Universal Cooler, and Ford, in addition to Kelsey-Hayes and some smaller firms, grew from seventy-eight members to more than 3,000; after a year of energetic organizing it had grown to over 35,000, becoming one of the UAW's largest and most influential locals. Growth was hectic. Organizer George Edwards remembered "weeks where we had all the waste baskets in the West Side Local office filled with nothing except membership cards and dollar bills attached to them. . . . Nobody had time to enter membership names on the rolls, issue receipts or get the dollar bills to the bank."[14]

The Kelsey-Hayes sit-down was Walter Reuther's first major credit as a strike leader and negotiator, and as Local 174 grew it gave him the large, solid base he needed for union influence. The Reuther brothers burst on the UAW scene as a unique family threesome, quickly becoming known for energy, intelligence, and commitment. Toward the end of the strike, as Walter and a Kelsey-Hayes official were concluding negotiations in a company office, with Vic just outside in the union's sound car airing a message to the

Kelsey-Hayes sit-downers have a hoedown, 1936. Walter P. Reuther Library, Wayne State University

strikers in the plant, a Flint newspaper was tossed on the desk with a front-page photograph of the third brother, Roy, a key organizer in Flint. "My God!" the astonished Kelsey-Hayes executive exclaimed, "how many of you are there?"[15]

AS VICTORIES AT PARTS FIRMS MOUNTED, attention turned to General Motors, Chrysler, and Ford. With minor exceptions at GM and Chrysler, no union had established a beachhead in their plants and in no instance was a union formally recognized with a written contract. The decisive struggle was joined with General Motors. If the UAW could enlist a critical mass of GM's workers, successfully strike the corporation and gain recognition, then the organization of the entire industry would be within reach; without GM, no foothold was secure. The UAW began to plan an assault on the Chevrolet Division's plants in Flint, Michigan, the manufacturing heart of GM's industrial empire.[16]

Flint was a company town. Two-thirds of its workforce, more than 40,000 persons, were GM factory employees, and 80 percent of its families depended on General Motors for their livelihoods. Four GM divisions—

Chevrolet, Buick, Fisher Body, and AC Spark Plug—manufactured parts or assembled cars there. Chevrolet and Fisher Body had by reputation the hardest-driving managements and the most disaffected employees, while Buick, the original GM division in Flint, had cultivated a "family" atmosphere by hiring successive generations of family members, making it the least likely site of industrial combat. The city government and community institutions reflected the corporation's dominant position and championed its interests. The daily paper refused to print union ads or report union events, and the city's only radio station refused to sell air time to the union. Prior to the sit-down, the UAW had organized only a small and fluctuating fraction of GM workers in the face of the corporation's countertactics. Union leaders were fired and meetings infiltrated by spies. A GM official candidly remarked to the La Follette subcommittee that "there was a very natural growth" of espionage and similar activities in Flint as the union gathered strength.[17]

In June 1936, UAW vice president Wyndham Mortimer arrived in Flint to take charge of the organizing campaign. Dogged by spies, eavesdroppers, and threats, he faced a formidable challenge. An anonymous telephone caller warned him to "get the hell back where you came from if you don't want to be carried out in a wooden box!" Five anemic Flint locals, whose origins dated back to the AFL organizing drive of 1933–34, had a combined membership of only 122 persons, many of them unreliable. Some were spies, others were members of the Black Legion, a violent offshoot of the Ku Klux Klan whose antiunion terrorism, including assassinations of union activists, was exposed in the summer of 1936. With the existing organizations discredited and distrusted by GM's workers, Mortimer secured the revocation of their charters and, in their place, the executive board chartered the amalgamated Local 156 to mobilize the Flint workforce. Despite precautions, several spies and Pinkerton agents engineered their election as officers of the new local.[18]

To find trustworthy colleagues, Mortimer drew on his left-wing connections, recruiting Henry Kraus, a Cleveland journalist, to put out the *Flint Auto Worker*. Radicals were prominent in Flint organizing. Communist Party members were key organizers in several factories, particularly Bud Simons in Fisher Body No. 1, a large facility and one of the first to shut down. Socialists were also active there and elsewhere. According to one estimate, Flint's Communist Party membership in 1936 was between sixty and one hundred persons, with most of the members employed in the auto plants, and small Communist Party units had been established in Buick, Fisher Body No. 1, and several Chevrolet plants. When president Homer Martin, fearful of Mortimer's growing influence and citing allegations that the organizer was building a "Red empire" in Flint, removed him as head of the campaign, Mortimer acceded—provided that Bob Travis, a Commu-

nist activist from the Auto-Lite and Chevrolet strikes in Toledo, should be
his replacement. A brilliant tactician, Travis became one of the key players
in the strike drama.[19]

As winter approached, a skeleton organization was in place in Flint,
with cadres of activists in several plants and membership beginning to
grow. By December, 3,000 workers had joined the UAW, and perhaps as
many as 10 percent of Flint's 45,000 auto workers had joined by the time
the sit-down strike broke out at the end of the month. "Quickie" strikes—
brief, miniature sit-downs in protest against speedups and other company
actions—had occurred in Fisher Body No. 1 and elsewhere. In the Fisher
plants, Henry Kraus observed, "union buttons began to sprout like dande-
lions." The arrival of Roy Reuther bolstered a Socialist Party contingent
that included Kermit and Genora Johnson, destined for prominent roles in
the strike. Roy joined Travis as the leading co-organizer and Vic came to
Flint to take charge of the union's sound car. Travis and Roy Reuther
worked well together, the former excelling as a tactician and one-on-one
persuader, the latter as a "rabble rouser" whose oratory could move the
masses. The violently antiunion Chevrolet manager in Flint, Arnold Lenz,
told the pair—both youthful, vigorous men in their early twenties—that
they were full "of piss and vinegar" and bound to cause a lot of trouble.[20]

A wave of "quickie" strikes hit GM plants elsewhere. Workers at the
Fisher Body plant in Atlanta sat down for a day on November 18 to protest
the firing of several employees for wearing union buttons. On December 15
workers at the Fisher plant in Kansas City sat down in protest of management penalties imposed for union activity and forced the nearby Chevrolet
assembly plant to close for lack of auto bodies. On December 28 the large
Fisher Body plant in Cleveland was shut down by workers who objected to
management's delay in resolving complaints over wage-slashing disguised
as piecework "adjustments." Still the UAW leadership in Flint set no strike
deadline, preferring to complete its preparations and await the inauguration
of Michigan Governor-elect Frank Murphy, due to occur early in January.
Explosions on the shop floor, however, disrupted the leadership's timetable
and forced the issue.[21]

THE STRIKE BEGAN ON December 30, 1936, when the union's ability to
protect its members' jobs and their right to belong to the union was put to
the test. At Fisher Body No. 2 the corporation disciplined three inspectors
who had refused to withdraw from the union when management, which
considered them supervisors, ordered them to do so. Fifty workers sat
down in protest. The plant, small by Flint standards, employed 1,000 workers who built 450 Chevrolet bodies a day. Throughout the early organizing
era, unofficial strike actions tended to begin with occupational groups such

A "hillbilly orchestra" entertains Flint sit-downers, 1937. Walter P. Reuther Library, Wayne State University

as trimmers, metal finishers, and subassembly men in the body shops who collectively possessed a degree of skill, enjoyed personal interaction with workmates, and thereby achieved a greater degree of group identity and cohesion than the atomized and fragmented work force on the main assembly lines. That evening attention shifted to the much larger Fisher Body No. 1, which employed 7,300 workers and produced 1,400 bodies a day for Buick, when it was closed by sit-downers to prevent the corporation from shipping body dies to plants outside Flint—a move the workers feared would undermine their ability to conduct a successful strike. The corporation maintained that while it was ready to discuss grievances with its employees, there could be no talks as long as the plants were occupied.[22]

Strikers inside the plants quickly organized themselves into communities providing for defense of the plants against attack, as well as for internal policing and discipline through a set of rules and duties enforced by informal courts. A rule forbidding destruction of company property was honored. Food was provided by supporters on the outside, and in the large plants like Fisher No. 1 hundreds of hot meals were brought into the plant every day. Sleeping accommodations were no problem in body plants, where cushioned car seats served as beds. Contact with families and union officials on the outside was maintained through correspondence, conversation through open plant windows, and, in the case of union leaders, visits to the plant. On most matters the sit-downers were self-governing, making their own decisions and internal arrangements. To occupy the idle time and maintain morale, strikers employed a variety of games and other diversions, playing cards, dominoes, checkers, and ping-pong, reading, listening to the radio, conducting story-telling sessions, singing, and playing musical instruments. "Hillbilly orchestras" with guitars, mandolins, banjos, accordion, mouth organs, and even violins were very popular. In one plant the orchestra broadcast a program of popular and country music selections nightly over the plant's public address system. Union officers and volunteers conducted classes on parliamentary procedure, labor law and history, and like subjects, aware perhaps that the sit-downers themselves were writing a significant chapter in labor's history.[23]

Workers and their supporters often expressed their thoughts and feelings in song. They sang the old workingmen's standards, many dating from the days of the Wobblies, such as "Solidarity Forever," and the very apt "We Shall Not Be Moved" and "Hold the Fort." New songs were written to commemorate the occasion. The best of these, "Sit Down!"—composed not by a sit-downer but by a UAW attorney, Maurice Sugar—highlighted the strikers' key tactic and urged them to be steadfast in a set of lively verses.

> "When they tie the can
> To a union man
> Sit down! Sit down!
> When they give him the sack,
> They'll take him back.
> Sit down! Sit down!"
> *Chorus:*
> "Sit down, just take a seat.
> Sit down, and rest your feet.
> Sit down, you've got 'em beat.
> Sit down! Sit down!"

Most of the other songs contained lyrics by the sit-downers themselves, put to familiar popular or traditional melodies. The songs expressed and celebrated the themes of winning collective bargaining rights, holding out at all costs, ridiculing company officials, and sharing the bonds of union brotherhood and solidarity. Other lyrics recounted the crucial events of the strike

A Flint sit-downer naps on auto seat cushions, 1937. Walter P. Reuther Library, Wayne State University

and reminded everyone of the anticipated benefits to self, family, and home. To the tune of "The Martins and the Coy's," a hillbilly classic, a set of lyrics commemorated the beginning of the Fisher No. 1 strike:

> "These 4000 Union boys,
> Oh, they sure made lots of noise,
> They decided then and there to shut down tight,
> In the office they got snooty,
> So we started picket duty,
> Now the Fisher Body Shop is on a strike."

The words and music were lively and upbeat, expressing optimism about a successful outcome and resolve in bringing it about. Although many of the songs revealed a sharp sense of class differences and conflicting class interests, they lacked expressions of a revolutionary or destructive intent, such as permanent worker occupation or operation of the factories, or resort to sabotage.[24]

At first GM made no effort to dislodge the sit-downers, but on January 11, in a confrontation that the workers, commemorating the retreat of the

Flint police, called "The Battle of the Running Bulls," the corporation tried to force the strikers from the plants. That evening about thirty Flint policemen attacked the few sit-downers in Fisher Body No. 2 with tear gas. The police were met by blasts of water from the plant's fire hoses and by a barrage of car door hinges, body hardware, rocks, and bottles thrown from the plant's roof and through its open windows. When the wind blew the tear gas back toward the police, they began to retreat, but some drew their pistols and fired into the strikers' ranks. By this time thousands of spectators, mostly cheering for the strikers, lined the streets, and the police fired gas bombs into the crowd, provoking another shower of rocks. Reinforced and reforming their ranks, the police launched a second tear gas attack on the plant and the pickets that continued long into the night, but again they retreated on the run, leaving the strikers in control of the battlefield. There were casualties on both sides but no fatalities. Fourteen strikers and sympathizers were wounded, nearly all by police gunfire. Nine policemen and the sheriff and deputy sheriff of Genesee County were hit by the strikers' missiles. Informed that order had collapsed in Flint and lives were in danger, Governor Frank Murphy, in office only a few days, ordered in units of the Michigan National Guard to keep the two sides apart and prevent bloodshed, not to suppress the strike. He then assumed the role of mediator. By refusing to use force to expel the strikers, Murphy became the key figure both in preventing loss of life and in pressuring the corporation to move toward a settlement.[25]

By this time strikes had broken out at GM plants in Detroit, Ohio, Indiana, Wisconsin, Missouri, and Canada. On January 8 Walter Reuther called a sit-down at Cadillac's West Side Detroit plant, which a few days later was extended to the nearby Fleetwood plant that supplied Cadillac's bodies. In Detroit and in several GM plants elsewhere, the sit-downers agreed to leave the plants, but picket lines, bolstered by the Dodge Main "flying squadron" and supporters from other local unions, maintained the strikes despite attempts by police to break them up. By the end of January, fifty GM plants with more than 125,000 employees were closed, some directly by strikes and others by parts shortages, as the strikes' effects spread. Although the corporation maintained production of some of its car lines, inventory shortages caused its market share to drop. Still focused on Flint, the strike, now nationwide, had become painful. Yet GM still refused to talk with the union.[26]

Hoping to break the stalemate with a crippling blow, the UAW seized the initiative on February 1 when it extended the sit-down to Chevrolet No. 4, a key plant that manufactured the engines for GM's largest division. According to some sources, the idea originated with a cadre of Socialist auto workers and then spread to a few men gathered around Bob Travis and Roy

Cadillac workers, led by Walter Reuther and Homer Martin, march in support of the Flint sit-down, 1937. Walter P. Reuther Library, Wayne State University

Reuther. They devised a clever ruse that exploited the presence of company spies in the union's ranks to mislead the corporation, thereby thwarting GM's countermeasures. At the conclusion of an elaborate charade, word was leaked that the union planned to seize a different plant, Chevrolet No. 9, one less vital to Chevrolet's operations. As expected, spies warned GM's management of an imminent union assault on Plant No. 9. Both sides prepared for battle. The corporation massed plant guards there along with contingents of Flint police and sheriff's deputies. The UAW dispatched pickets and sympathizers to the plant supposedly to bolster the struggle of those on the inside who would seize it, but in fact to sustain the illusion that No. 9 was the target. Only a handful in the leadership and a few loyalists in Chevy 4 knew that Plant 9 was a decoy, with Plant 4 the intended objective.[27]

As the day shift ended in mid-afternoon, UAW members in No. 9 ran through the plant calling for a strike and shutting down the machines. Fights broke out within and outside the plant, with the unionists and their supporters getting the worst of it. Most of them, unaware of their role in the scenario, believed the attack had failed. Meanwhile, a union contingent of a few hundred seized Chevy No. 4 from a depleted force of company

UAW pickets confront Flint police outside Chevrolet Plant No. 9, 1937. Walter P. Reuther Library, Wayne State University

guards and supervisory personnel, overcoming the resistance of employees loyal to the company, who were escorted from the plant. When guards tried to enter, they came under a barrage of pistons, connecting rods, and other engine parts. Once the strikers had secured control of the plant, they barricaded the entrances with heavy crates and other parts containers. No one was killed, but there were many injuries on both sides. The shutdown of Chevy 4, abruptly halting Chevrolet production, exerted an irresistible pressure on the corporation to negotiate.[28]

The talks that led to a settlement began in Detroit two days later, with CIO chief John L. Lewis and Governor Frank Murphy in the leading roles, and a supporting cast of GM and UAW representatives. Lewis was indispensable to the UAW's success. To this point, the union had not developed a leadership with the bargaining and public relations skills required to conduct high- stakes, high-pressure talks in the spotlight of massive national media attention. CIO intervention and support in moments of crisis were crucial to the UAW's survival in its early years, but the relationship was reciprocal. About to become one of the largest CIO affiliates, and already its liveliest, the UAW had the potential to make or break the CIO itself by its

Strike leaders arraigned in a Flint court, 1937. *Left to right:* Victor Reuther, Bob Travis, Roy Reuther, attorney Maurice Sugar, and journalist Henry Kraus. Walter P. Reuther Library, Wayne State University

success or failure. It could hardly be ignored or left to founder by the CIO's leadership. Homer Martin, the UAW's vain, inexperienced, and unpredictable president, was such a threat to a successful outcome of the negotiations that Lewis sent him on a speaking tour of distant UAW locals to keep him away from the discussions. A chagrined Martin learned of the agreement with General Motors while changing trains in Chicago; his signature was not on the UAW's first contract with a major manufacturer.[29]

The corporation's top official, President Alfred P. Sloan, Jr., remained in the background along with members of the DuPont family, then GM's controlling stockholders, who were well-represented on its board of directors. Executive vice president William S. Knudsen, the corporation's production chief, conducted talks for GM. The corporation had refused to negotiate until its plants were evacuated but found a pretext for abandoning that position when President Roosevelt asked it to begin discussions. The basic issue was union recognition. At first the UAW sought the exclusive right to bargain for all employees. GM pointed out that only a minority of its workers were union members, a claim the union could not deny, and the corporation further maintained that the great majority opposed union representation, a very unlikely proposition. When negotiations began the union offered a concession, asking that it be granted bargaining rights only in the twenty plants that were on strike. Once this was agreed to, it said, production could be resumed and the remaining issues settled in collective bargaining. It also insisted that the strikers be allowed to return to their jobs without penalty.[30]

For several days the corporation refused to give ground, while Governor Murphy, under mounting political and judicial pressure to end the strike, considered ways of forcing the strikers from the plants. With further concessions on both sides, agreement was announced on February 11. There were two especially significant provisions. GM recognized the UAW as a bargaining agent only for its own members in the plants that were on strike, and the corporation promised that for six months it would not "bargain with or enter into agreements with any other union or representative of employees of plants on strike," a guarantee that GM would not undercut the UAW by bargaining with a company union. In addition, the corporation pledged not to discriminate against or penalize union members. Although falling well short of what the union had sought, the agreement was GM's first significant instance of formal union recognition. Confident that they could use the six-month period as a window of opportunity to expand the membership, entrench the union in the plants, and bargain a satisfactory supplementary agreement, the UAW negotiators agreed to the compromise.[31]

SEVERAL CONSIDERATIONS ACCOUNT for the corporation's decision to end the strike on terms it had previously rejected. Governor Murphy's refusal to place the state's authority and forces at the company's disposal tied GM's hands. His restraint in using force—he said he would not go down in history as "Bloody Murphy"—limited GM's options and reduced the risk of loss of life. Economic pressures for a settlement were also strong. For the first time in years auto labor was in short supply. Average wage earner employment in the industry had rebounded by 1937 to over 500,000, exceeding even the previous high set in 1929. Probably most important, with an improving economy and strong demand for cars, the nearly total shutdown of GM's production was costing it sales it might never regain. In the first ten days of February both Ford and Chrysler, whose desire for profits outweighed their abhorrence of unions, continued to produce and sell all the cars they could make, while GM built only 151 vehicles in the United States. As a result of the strikes, the corporation lost the production of 280,000 cars, 20 percent of its expected sales for the year.

Nevertheless, the sit-down and the wildcat strikes that followed in its wake fell far short of crippling the auto industry giant since GM, despite the curtailed production, enjoyed in 1937 its best year in profits and sales in a decade.[32]

Even more important for the union's victory than a sympathetic governor and the corporation's economic vulnerability was the determination of the strikers themselves. The workers' willingness to risk their jobs, livelihoods, and even their lives in a disciplined but dangerous seizure of power for a cause they deemed just made the crucial difference. Most of the sit-downers had no formally expressed ideological position, only a conviction that conditions in the plants were intolerable and could be bettered through the actions of an independent union. A segment of the strike's activists and leaders had ties, close or casual, to radical political movements, tendencies, or parties, whether Communist, Socialist, or independent. Whatever their differences, the radicals shared a conviction that American industrial capitalism had failed and that they were actors in a historic drama that would restructure and perhaps replace it.

Most GM employees in Flint and elsewhere did not participate actively in the sit-downs by remaining in the plants. As one Flint worker observed, a lot of his fellows were "just sort of watching" during the strike. Certainly some regarded their employer as a benefactor they should not provoke, and many, fearful perhaps of the corporation's retaliation, cautiously awaited the struggle's outcome before committing themselves. Family ties and responsibilities—the need to put food on the table and make the monthly mortgage payment—held some back. Whatever their position while the outcome was in doubt, clearly once the union was installed and its presence felt on the shop floor and in the pay envelope, it quickly gained majority support. Within a month of the strike's end, membership in Local 156, an umbrella organization that covered all plants, soared to twenty-five thousand, a majority of Flint's auto workers.[33]

The support the strikers received from their families and union brothers and sisters on the outside, both those in other UAW locals and members of other unions, contributed to the strike's success. To guard against demoralization of the strikers by family complications and pressures, members of a women's auxiliary called on strikers' wives, many of them initially suspicious of the strike, to explain the issues involved and enlist their support. A Women's Emergency Brigade, consisting mainly of strikers' wives and other relatives, was formed by Genora Johnson, wife of one of the strike leaders. The brigade courageously confronted the police on several occasions and engaged in hazardous picket duty at critical moments. Its statements and songs stressed the improvement in the quality of family life that the sacrifices required by the strike would eventually

Strikers' children join the Flint picket line, 1937. Walter P. Reuther Library, Wayne State University

bring. The brigade's battle song, set to the tune of "Marching Through Georgia," included these lines:

> "The men are in the factories sitting in a strike we know,
> Holding down production so that we can get more dough,
> The Union's organizing and we'll see that it is so,
> Shouting the Union forever!"

The women's contribution to the strike's success was acknowledged and praised by the union's officers. Even the unemployed supported the strike by picketing and collecting food. Although General Motors launched a "back to work" movement, scab labor was never a problem. Occupation of the plants precluded a resumption of production, and many of the unemployed sympathized with the strikers and believed their interests, in the long run, rested with the strike's success.[34]

The ability of the UAW to mobilize a "strategic reserve" of "flying squadrons," in some cases with numbers reaching into the hundreds, from locals throughout Michigan and northern Ohio to bolster picket lines in

Women sympathizers support the Flint sit-downers, 1937. Walter P. Reuther Library, Wayne State University

Flint and elsewhere demonstrated the broad support for the strike among auto workers and their willingness to share the risks. Workers converged on Flint from all directions during strike emergencies. "In those days," recalled Emil Mazey of Briggs Local 212, "whenever we heard of a strike or heard of picket-line activity, those of us who were dedicated organizers, every strike was our strike." Mazey's eagerness to go into action with Local 212's flying squadron in support of other's efforts laid the foundation for his enduring reputation as a militant unionist. The Dodge Main Flying Squadron from Local 3 operated a "running picket line," available for service wherever and whenever needed. Certain precautions in its use had to be observed. When an emergency arose the squadron met behind locked doors. In order to prevent a spy from revealing the target to police or company officials, no one who came into the meeting was permitted to leave until the squadron marched out as a body. The forging of a common auto workers' consciousness reached beyond the sit-downers themselves to embrace workers in many plants who saw their own future being shaped in the event. To one degree or another, many thousands were involved.[35]

In these early triumphs the UAW operated on several coexisting levels of activity that by and large worked together in harmony. As the story of the sit-down strikes illustrates, the initial commitment to union action took shape on the shop floor, where the immediate conflicts with management occurred. Although organizers from union headquarters were present to offer guidance and encouragement, nothing happened unless workers themselves stepped forward, asserted their rights, and drew up an agenda. Once the struggle was joined, a larger cast of actors came on stage. Assistance came from other unionists and from supportive elements in the community. Seasoned negotiators, experienced in dealing with the media, politicians, government officials, and the corporate elite, took charge of the negotiations and made some of the strategic decisions. As the union moved beyond its formative stage, its continued progress and security could be achieved only through a structure that mated dynamic locals with the national leadership. When challenging adversaries as large and powerful as the automobile corporations, an organization equally large and skillful, drawing authority from an active rank and file was crucial.

The UAW's victory in Flint was decisive for the establishment of industrial unions in America. If the young, untried UAW could bring the country's "most powerful industrial aggregation" to terms, then industrial unionism would survive, perhaps even flourish. A newspaper headline during the strike hit the mark: "Future of C.I.O. Hangs on Auto Strike Result."[36]

THE VICTORY OVER GENERAL MOTORS set off the most furious whirlwind of union organizing in the nation's history. Inspired by the UAW's victory, massive currents of unrest and daring coursed through the auto cities, affecting workers in many occupations and industries. In Detroit, sit-down strikes broke out everywhere. Cigar makers, meat packers, the waiters and maids at the Statler Hotel, clerks in department stores and at Woolworth's, to name only a few, all sat down. Almost overnight, it seemed, Detroit became the country's preeminent "union town," its labor relations environment transformed by the UAW's victories. An unsympathetic newspaper reporter observed that "sitting down has replaced baseball as the national pastime, and sitter-downers clutter up the landscape in every direction." By the end of March, more than 100 sit-down strikes had occurred in Detroit alone. On a slightly lesser scale, sit-downs and other strikes broke out in Flint and some other cities. In the country at large, nearly 500 sit-down strikes of one day's duration or longer occurred, one of the most extensive nonviolent civil disobedience outbursts in the nation's history.[37]

The UAW's next major target was the industry's then second-ranking firm, the Chrysler Corporation, whose assembly plants and parts facilities were concentrated on Detroit's East Side and in the enclaves of Hamtramck

Victorious sit-downers march out of Flint's Fisher Plant No. 1, 1937. Walter P. Reuther Library, Wayne State University

and Highland Park. With several years of organization through the AIWA and then the UAW to draw upon, the workers' pre-strike mobilization in the Chrysler plants had proceeded much further than at GM's plants, and the sit-down which began on March 8, 1937, went off like clockwork. Second in line, the Chrysler strike lacked the fireworks of Flint. Planning for it was so open that even corporation officials knew when and where the strike would begin, but they also knew they could do nothing to prevent it. When Dick Frankensteen phoned John Zaremba inside the Dodge Main plant with the order to launch the strike, Zaremba raised his hand in an arranged signal and the shop stewards shut down the plant. Within five minutes not a machine or assembly line stirred. Again a substantial minority, acting with the sympathy and passive support of the majority, halted the operations of one of the industry's giants. Perhaps as many as 15,000 of Chrysler's workforce of 67,000 were UAW members when the strike began, and about 6,000 were active strike participants.[38]

Although Chrysler sought and obtained an injunction ordering the strikers to clear the plants, no forcible effort to that end was attempted. The sit-downers were supported by thousands of pickets, a mass demonstration

"They Shall Not Pass," Dodge Main strikers, 1937. Walter P. Reuther Library, Wayne State University

of more than 50,000 in Cadillac Square, and a Women's Auxiliary that conducted various activities to boost morale on and off the picket line—including its rendition of "Dollars from Chrysler," with its new lyrics set to the tune of the current popular song, "Pennies from Heaven." The burden of conducting the strike, including feeding the strikers, fell on the Chrysler locals. Although Detroit officials and police were hostile to the strikers, officialdom in Hamtramck, where Dodge Main was located, was supportive, as was its largely Polish-American population.[39]

Governor Frank Murphy and John L. Lewis again played key roles in settling the strike, while the company's president, Walter P. Chrysler, proved to be a less obstinate adversary than GM's executives. Murphy, whose tender treatment of the GM sit-downers sparked much criticism from the nation's editorial writers and spokesmen for its chambers of commerce, refused to call in troops but steadily pressured the union to settle. On March 25, after Chrysler promised and the governor guaranteed that the plants would not operate, the strikers reluctantly evacuated them. An agreement was reached on April 6 in which Chrysler, following GM's lead,

Mass meeting of union supporters in Detroit's Cadillac Square, March 23, 1937.
Walter P. Reuther Library, Wayne State University

recognized the UAW as bargaining agent for its members and promised that
it would not "aid, promote or finance any labor group . . . for the purpose of
undermining the Union." Not until 1939, as the result of another strike, did
the UAW become bargaining agent for all Chrysler blue-collar employees.[40]

In many other respects the fourteen-page Chrysler agreement tracked
the GM pact. Despite the contract's brevity, Doug Fraser, newly hired in
Chrysler's DeSoto plant, remembered it as "a magnificent victory." So
many things that were impossible before the strike were now workers'
rights. "You could dissent, you could argue, you could grieve," and when
layoffs threatened, "you didn't have to look around and say now the boss's
relative is going to stay." Favoritism yielded to rules of fair play. Although
the first Chrysler seniority system made an allowance for "exceptional
employees," seniority in layoff, recall, and job transfers became the general
rule. With its nascent shop steward system within the Chrysler factories
intact and recognized, the UAW was in a strong position in the Chrysler
plants, with the potential to make continuing improvements in working
conditions.[41]

Pickets support the Dodge sit-downers, 1937. Walter P. Reuther Library, Wayne State University

THE RECOGNITION WON from two major manufacturers quickly broke down the resistance of the less powerful. Auto workers who had hung back out of fear of losing their jobs because of union membership now came forward by the thousands. Dozens of new UAW locals were chartered in both the plants of the major manufacturers and in those of the independent parts producers. At Chevrolet Gear and Axle, workers typically joined the union "pretty fast." "In the lunch room everyday," one organizer-worker recalled, "I'd get up on the table and make a speech and then we'd go around signing up everyone to join the union." At the L. A. Young plant in Trenton, New Jersey, where workers resented the arbitrary discharges and other fear tactics that had been used against them, organizing was a snap "just because they were so brutal. They literally drove people into the union. We didn't organize. We just told them where the union office was located." Members and officers of local unions worked extra hours and without pay to sign up recruits. "You would work in the shop all day and work in the office half the night. But we did it because we thought we were right." Nat Ganley, organizer and business agent for Local 155 on Detroit's East Side, observed

Sit-downers march out of Dodge Main, 1937. Walter P. Reuther Library, Wayne State University

that in small and medium-sized tool and die shops "the key organizers are always the people in the shop themselves. You would be surprised how a good deal of the shops I organized . . . I did by just sitting in my local office and have shops walk in."[42]

Packard, a leading independent, recognized the UAW as a result of an NLRB election and then signed the best contract yet obtained by the union; its "exceptional provisions" included rest periods for women, double-time for work on Sundays and legal holidays, and a week's vacation with pay. Studebaker, where the management took pride in a tradition of cooperation and mutual respect between employer and employee, put up little resistance when a brief recognition strike occurred in May 1937. The result for the workers was a favorable contract that gave the union a major voice in setting production standards and a strong internal structure of shop stewards. With the company's acquiescence, a marked shift in shop floor authority from foremen to stewards took place. At Hudson, an East Side Detroit firm, a thirty-five-day sit-down by 600 men had the support of picket lines that at times numbered as many as 9,000. Most of the major parts and components manufacturers, including Briggs, Murray Body, Motor Products, Timken-Detroit Axle, L. A. Young Spring & Wire, and Bohn Aluminum, agreed to UAW representation as a result of sit-downs, conventional strikes, or representation elections—or, seeing the writing on the wall, without contesting the issue. At Murray Body, when UAW membership reached about one-third of the 7,000 employees, members staged a coming out party, flaunting their union affiliation for the first time in a "Button Day." Previously, wearing a union button, which management charged intimidated nonunion workers, would get one fired, but this time, with so many involved, no jobs were lost. Membership soared, and a three-day sit-down led to recognition and negotiation of a contract.[43]

In a last minute attempt to stave off organization, Briggs, the major independent body manufacturer, frantically handed out pay raises. Jess Ferrazza recalled that "in a four-hour period in one day I got a 20-cent raise in 5-cent increments. About every hour the boss would come around and give me another nickel raise." The Briggs workers were not deflected from their purpose by this sudden display of corporate generosity. Threatened with a strike, the company agreed to recognize the union for its members and match the settlement reached at Chrysler. UAW Local 212 at the Briggs plants rapidly gained a reputation for militant action, its "flying squadron" mobilized to lend its presence and strength to picket lines throughout the East Side and elsewhere. With most workers supporting the union, a "Button Day" was used there and elsewhere to bring the reluctant and disinterested into the fold. Stationing fifty to a hundred members at each plant gate, the union allowed inside only those whose buttons showed they were current in dues payments, in effect creating a union shop.[44]

Hundreds of smaller independent parts and component plants were now organized. Although organizing could be carried on more openly, some precautions were still taken. UAW speakers went into Detroit's parks, particularly the large ones on the East Side, almost every night, erected a temporary stand or put together two park benches for a platform, and delivered a prounion message to whomever chose to listen, "whether they were in an auto plant or from a dry cleaning establishment." If necessary, employees could claim they were there for a family or church picnic or casually passing by, not to attend a union organizing rally. Organizers haunted "every saloon and restaurant and bar and every place that workers went to." Sometimes there was little response and sometimes hostility led to fist fights, but the overwhelming reaction was interest and often a commitment.[45]

Although no single small or mid-size auto parts plant or union local is fully representative, many aspects of organizing a plant and founding a UAW local are illustrated at a firm in Hamtramck, Michigan, with about 500 employees. Unionization of this plant's workforce proceeded through distinct stages. Prior to the organizing outburst of 1936–37, there was little cohesion among the workers and no union activity. Workers in different factory departments were divided on ethnic and generational lines between first-generation Polish immigrants, second-generation Polish Americans, Ukrainians, and Anglo-Americans of native birth; these ethnic and generational groups had relatively little contact with each other. As unions were launched in nearby factories in 1936–37 (the example of Midland Steel only a mile away, was influential), two small, separate groups of union activists emerged in different factory departments. Contacting the international UAW's district office in Hamtramck, which was too busy and understaffed in those hectic days to give a small plant much assistance, the two groups became aware of each other's existence and together formed the core of a union cadre.[46]

More than six months of propaganda and effort, concealed at first but in time brought into the open, were required to spread the union message throughout the factory in the face of management opposition and workers' caution. Workers reacted to the union appeal in part along generational and ethnic lines, with the young, second-generation Polish workers initially most responsive, followed by first-generation immigrants, with native-born Appalachians and Yankees coming on board last. Contrasting experiences, present fears, and future expectations shaped the different reactions. An alarmed management's tactical errors calmed workers fears of losing their jobs. An offer of a raise, intended to evoke gratitude and blunt the drive for a union, was taken as a sign of weakness. The open declaration of commitment came when members defiantly wore their union buttons in the factory. When no one was fired, momentum grew and new waves of workers joined. Recruitment became more aggressive. As factory discipline crumbled, organizers moved through the plant during working hours and confronted the reluctant in the "can" and at the bar across the street, where a back room was always available for meetings.

Finally, with about half of the plant's workers signed up, the leaders decided to seek a contract. By producing immediate improvements, a contract would expand the membership and put down the union's roots in the factory. The initial contract gains in seniority and a grievance system, won from a disheartened management without a strike, were modest and flawed, but they demonstrated that the union was in the plant to stay and that it could give workers more control over their jobs. A "dues strike" in 1938, which threatened the few remaining holdouts with loss of their jobs, established a union shop, completing the process. In some other plants a few people who refused to join the union or fell behind in dues were simply thrown out of the plant. The workers themselves often took the initiative in creating an ad hoc union shop, where membership would be a condition of keeping one's job. The leadership cadre of the local in question, which had left-ist leanings, remained stable for years, reflecting the standing and prestige that followed upon success and, perhaps, the predilections of workers whose individual and family origins in precapitalist cultures were not so distant as to be without effect. In dozens of small and medium-sized plants, a similar scenario, with many local variations, was played out.[47]

As this instance suggests, organizing was often carried on more by workers themselves than by representatives of the International Union. A pioneer organizer observed: "Our own members were the best organizers. We staff men could leaflet a plant but when we were able to 'get' to these workers by word of mouth from our own rank and file members we had a far better chance of success." The personal relationships of workmates, relying upon friendship, trust, the appeal to solidarity, and peer pressure were the keys to successful organizing. For many the union movement in its early days represented a relatively rare instance of vital human contact in the depersonalized, atomized setting of a modern industrial factory. The UAW grew from the bottom up and it grew through contact of one worker with another.[48]

IN THE 1930S APPROXIMATELY 7–9 PERCENT of the auto workforce con-sisted of women. As part of the rank and file and as organizers and sup-porters, women played important roles in the union campaigns. Women workers were still concentrated in the upholstery departments of body plants and in the manufacture and assembly of small parts and accessories. At that time few were employed in the assembly plants where the most highly publicized union organizing and strike activity occurred.[49]

Women's impact was felt in many ways, both traditional and innova-tive. At Flint, as elsewhere, it was common practice for members of a women's auxiliary, formed when the strike began, to call on the wives of striking husbands to convince them of the union's potential benefits and enlist their support. The morale and determination of strikers could be, of course, strengthened or undermined by reactions at home. The auxiliaries also provided support through picketing, collecting food and money for the strikers, helping in the preparation and delivery of food, and performing other tasks. In the Flint sit-down, the Womens' Emergency Brigade took a very active part in the strike.[50]

The question of whether women workers should participate in a sit-down was a sensitive matter since, if women remained in the plant, hostile publicists were certain to charge that the strikers, with time on their hands and lacking supervision, would go on an immoral rampage. By undermin-ing public support and disrupting domestic harmony in striker's families, such charges, whatever their merit, were bound to be damaging. Women workers usually were asked to leave the plant when a sit-down began, but in a few instances they remained, with the internal policing arrangements which were part of every sit-down assuring gender separation. At Bohn Aluminum in Detroit, where a sit-down lasted twenty-eight days, about half of the employees and many of the sit-downers were women. At a General Motors Delco-Remy plant in Anderson, Indiana, which employed many women, women workers conducted a brief sit-down without male participation in successful opposition to a speedup.[51]

The idea that women workers were difficult to organize was rooted in labor lore and widely accepted by men. The emotions and aspirations of women, so the argument went, were not centered on the workplace but on home and family. Presumably, demands for workplace equity meant less to them than to their male counterparts. The assumptions, often at odds with the facts, that women workers did not require a household head's income and that they were only temporarily in the workforce were also thought to make them poor prospects for union membership. Although women were a relatively small minority in the total auto workforce, their concentration in certain occupations and plants meant that in some of the parts plants they were a substantial element, even in some cases a majority. If such plants were to be organized, women workers would have to take part.

The Ternstedt Division of General Motors, which produced small body and trim parts, operated the largest plant on Detroit's West Side. Nearly half of its 12,000 employees were women. At first, Local 174 officials had no plans to organize the Ternstedt workers, but they allowed one of their organizers who had successfully organized women in Detroit cigar factories to give it a try. A few weeks after the conclusion of the Flint sit-down had demonstrated GM's vulnerability, the organizer, Stanley Nowak, working with an enthusiastic group of union women, brought the Ternstedt management to the bargaining table by means of a slow-down—a deliberate, severe, and disciplined reduction of production, less risky than a sit-down but, when widely supported by the workers as this one was, almost as effective. Victor Reuther, a Local 174 organizer, found the Ternstedt women the "easiest to organize and . . . the strongest supporters of the solidarity concept" because, he thought, "they knew what justice and the denial of it meant." Such instances of successful organizing by, with, and for women auto workers gradually eroded the idea that they were indifferent and could not be organized.[52]

WITH GENERAL MOTORS AND CHRYSLER workers in the UAW fold, along with thousands of others from independent plants, attention turned to Ford, the remaining major holdout. When the sit-downers marched out of the Cadillac and Fleetwood factories in Detroit only two miles from Ford's

River Rouge plant, they carried a banner optimistically proclaiming "Today GM—Tomorrow Ford." But everyone knew that Ford would be tough, even after the Supreme Court in May 1937 upheld the constitutionality of the Wagner Act, with its collective bargaining and worker protection guarantees. Henry Ford deserved his reputation for stubbornly going his own way in defiance of the law and employees' wishes. At the beginning of the UAW's drive, following the Court's decision in the Wagner Act cases, the automaker announced flatly that "unions are the worst things that ever struck this earth," adding "we'll never recognize the United Automobile Workers Association or any other union." Carrying banners in demonstrations and rallies that read "Fordism is Fascism! Unionism is Americanism!" and "Make Dearborn a Part of the United States!" union activists drove home the point that Ford's refusal to permit the union to organize workers without interference was contrary to the spirit of American values and to the letter of American law. Ford was unmoved.[53]

Ford would fight by any and all means. Harry Bennett's Service Department, with its ranks bolstered by recruits from organized crime brought into the organization through Bennett's membership on the Michigan Parole Board, was adept at spying on and terrorizing Ford employees. From 1937 to 1941 over four thousand Ford workers suspected of union membership were fired in violation of their legal rights. A union sound truck was hijacked, doused with gasoline, and burned by two armed Ford thugs. A bomb blew up its replacement. Violence against union supporters occurred frequently. Servicemen locked Paddy Saroli, an employee and union organizer, in a tool cage one Friday night and left him there until Monday morning. Another employee-organizer was beaten up in one of the toilets by servicemen. The family owned firm, whose internal affairs were closely guarded, was less subject to public scrutiny and pressure than its publicly owned competitors.[54]

Ford's methods may have intimidated some workers, but others became committed union members in reaction against them. Pat Greathouse, who left an Illinois farm family with no union associations to work in Ford's Chicago assembly plant, saw older workers laid off and replaced by the young, people fired for getting a drink of water or going to the rest room, even for taking a bite out of an apple, and later declared "Ford Motor Company made a union man out of me."[55]

A nucleus of courageous union members worked in Ford factories, and the UAW, recognizing that the union's position in the industry would never be secure until all the major manufacturers were organized, was eager for battle. With Homer Martin floundering as the UAW's president, leadership of the union was up for grabs. Whoever gained credit for organizing Ford would have the best shot at becoming Martin's successor.

The UAW's campaign began in April 1937 when a few Ford workers met secretly with union officials to devise tactics. For the sake of security, inconspicuous offices were opened in areas remote from the Ford plant. Bulletins and leaflets were issued in English, Polish, Serbo-Croatian, and other languages to reach the polyglot workforce. Later, over 200,000 copies of Upton Sinclair's muckraking novel about Ford, *The Flivver King*, were distributed. Homer Martin appointed the veteran organizer and executive board member, Dick Frankensteen, to head up the Ford drive in Detroit and Dearborn. In outlying Ford plants, organizing work was done from the inside with little help or guidance from the International.[56]

Handbill distribution at a plant's gates was a standard way to reach employees with a union appeal. Frankensteen, Walter Reuther, and Bill McKie, a Ford worker fired because of union activity, organized a massive handbill distribution by hundreds of union sympathizers at the River Rouge plant for May 26, 1937. The low-key, single-sheet leaflet, with a headline reading "Unionism not Fordism," consisted of quotations from the Wagner Act and an appeal to the reader to join the union. The volunteers, including many women, began to assemble at the appointed gate. Frankensteen, Reuther, and a few others arrived early at the Rouge plant's Gate 4 on Miller Road, where an elevated footbridge across the road gave access to the plant from a parking lot.[57]

In the "Battle of the Overpass" that followed, Ford brutality was amply demonstrated. Once on the bridge, the unionists—Frankensteen, Reuther, Robert Kantor, and J. J. Kennedy—were surrounded and severely beaten by a gang of about forty Ford thugs. As Reuther stated immediately after the beatings:

> The men . . . picked me up about eight different times and threw me down on my back on the concrete. While I was on the ground they kicked me in the face, head and other parts of my body. . . . Finally they got me next to Dick who was lying on the bridge . . . and with both of us together they kicked us again and again. . . . They picked me up and threw me down the first flight of stairs. I lay there, and they picked me up and began to kick me down the total flight of steps. There are three flights.

Frankensteen, a large man and a former college football player, fought back. For resisting he was even more severely beaten. Many others, including some of the women, were assaulted, and one man suffered a broken back. Police posted nearby did nothing to stop the attack, although the UAW, complying with legal requirements, had obtained a permit for leaflet distribution. The Ford servicemen even attacked newsmen, grabbing their notes

Union organizers await the attack by Ford servicemen in the "Battle of the Overpass," May 26, 1937. *Left to right:* Robert Kantor, Walter Reuther, Richard Frankensteen, and J. J. Kennedy. Walter P. Reuther Library, Wayne State University

from their hands and ripping photographic plates and film from the cameras of those photographers they could catch. The outraged newsmen repaid their attackers with eyewitness, widely publicized testimony to the day's events. The attack was fully documented in the local press, and a set of photographs with commentary was reproduced in *Time* and other national periodicals. Testimony by the victims at a National Labor Relations Board hearing a few weeks later produced more negative publicity for Ford, drawing attention not only to the beatings but also to other harsh actions, the "Ford terror" of the Service Department and the company in its treatment of employees. Despite the barrage of bad news, Henry Ford's personal reputation as "labor's best friend," as measured by public opinion polls, remained largely intact. Such was the extraordinary hold of the lingering memory of the $5 day and the impact of Ford's public relations campaigns.[58]

UAW organizers at other plants were also victims of Ford violence. When a UAW organizer arrived at a Ford assembly plant in Memphis in September 1937, he was publicly condemned by the mayor, the head of the chamber of commerce, and the police chief; beaten twice, he was nearly

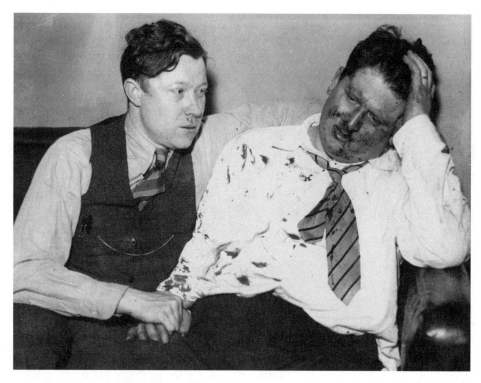

Walter Reuther and Richard Frankensteen following the beatings, May 26, 1937.
Walter P. Reuther Library, Wayne State University

killed in the second attack. Out of concern for his life, the UAW ordered
him to withdraw. At the Ford plant in Dallas terrorism was equally horri-
ble and even more sustained, while in Kansas City Ford enlisted the assistance of police to help with the dirty work.[59]

Although the union continued to publicize its cause, the campaign to
organize Ford bogged down, the result of internal union disputes and rivalries among the leaders as well as of Ford's resistance. Although the company took some care after the Battle of the Overpass to avoid outright
assault and battery, and the unfavorable publicity such tactics generated, in
other respects Ford's opposition to the union was unabated. For the time
being, the organization of Ford workers would have to wait.

DESPITE ITS FAILURE to crack Ford on the first try, the UAW grew rapidly
and achieved substantial results. In the six months following the GM sit-
down, dues-paying membership averaged 220,000, and from the South Bend
convention in April, 1936, to the Milwaukee convention in August, 1937,
membership increased from 30,000 to 375,000, with nearly 500 agreements
negotiated and signed with different employers. The UAW seemed destined

Distributing a union paper to Ford workers, August 11, 1937. Walter P. Reuther Library, Wayne State University

to became a leading union—perhaps, as CIO president John L. Lewis surmised, American labor's preeminent organization. Still, even with the impressive growth and the dramatic victories, much remained to be done before the union would be securely rooted in the industry's workplaces. Few plants were organized completely in the initial, emotional surge of a strike. There were many "hitchhikers" who readily accepted the benefits the union had won or promised to pursue but refused to join and pay dues. In some plants as few as half or even less of those who originally signed up maintained membership in good standing. Only the barest beginnings had been made in curbing arbitrary power on the shop floor and in laying a foundation for a rule of law in the industrial workplace.[60]

The brief sit-down era, compressed into a few months in 1936–37, decisively changed the industry and, equally, the lives of those who bore the struggle's burdens and dangers and gloried in its triumphs. Engagement brought new meaning to many lives. "[T]he feelings" the GM strike engendered "of hope, of optimism, the courage and sometimes the desperation," Frank Winn, a Reuther associate observed, would never be forgotten. When

George Edwards marched out of Chevy 4 with the Flint sit-downers as they celebrated their victory, "It seemed," he recalled, "as if every human being in the world was moving in one stream . . . and they were moving with a unity and a spirit of deliverance and joy that was indescribable. It was the most powerful thing that I [had] ever experienced. . . . It was some night." For Ford employee Paul Boatin, as for many, engagement in the struggle for the union was a path to self-discovery and growth. Like learning to swim, he said, "you've got to get in the water and feel your body sinking, and you develop a lot of abilities and understanding that you didn't know you had." Sit-downers looked back to the stirring events of 1937, like soldiers after a battle, as a defining experience: "'37," one recalled, "everything happened in '37. In '37 I lived my whole life." The loyalties formed then to the union and its mission were enduring; for many they shaped the rest of their lives.[61]

CHAPTER 4

"An insecure person
who happened on historic times"

President Homer Martin, 1937–38

UNCERTAINTY AND STRIFE CLOUDED THE UAW'S FUTURE FOR the rest of the decade. Soon after its victories over General Motors and Chrysler, the union nearly disintegrated. Its position in GM was especially precarious. The corporation launched a strong counterattack that convinced many observers the union would not be around long, perhaps only for a few months. Shop floor relations in GM's plants were unsettled and contentious. Still looming on the horizon was an immense and possibly dangerous organizing drive at the Ford Motor Company. Homer Martin's weak leadership inadequately addressed the many problems the union faced and contributed to the internal factional rivalries that threatened to exhaust the union's energies in factional power struggles. As the union's membership bounded upward in the spring and summer of 1937, the warfare within intensified. Power was all the more worth pursuing if the UAW was to become the leading American union. Assailed from without and divided within, the UAW still had to secure its place in the auto industry.[1]

The battles over direction and leadership and the struggles with the corporations were played out against worsening economic and political conditions. After a few years of recovery from the depths of the depression, the economy fell into the "Roosevelt Recession" of 1937–38, which sharply reduced auto production, put thousands out of work, cut deeply into the UAW's membership and its financial resources, and aggravated shop floor tensions. The auto economy's contraction was sharper and more severe, if less prolonged, than that experienced in the early 1930s. By the end of 1937, 60 percent of auto workers were unemployed and the rest were working part-time. In response to the sudden increase in unemployment, the UAW started a Welfare Department to assist unemployed auto workers in qualifying for benefits and to cultivate and maintain support among the auto unemployed—an early undertaking in community relations as distinct from representation of the employed auto worker. In pursuit of the same objective, the union also established Works Progress Administration (WPA) auxiliaries in areas where UAW members constituted a majority of those enrolled in the federal government's work relief program, with union officials pledged to protect the workers from "speed-up on WPA work."[2]

In national politics a reaction against the New Deal's leftward movement set in that tilted the political balance back toward the center and even to the right. President Roosevelt's defeat on a plan to revamp the Supreme Court's membership and the outcome of congressional and state elections in 1938 indicated that the New Deal had passed its peak as a reform movement. The nation's political thrust to the left had moved as far in that direction as it would go. A counterattack against leftist movements and ideologies was launched. The issue of an alleged Communist presence and influence in national institutions, largely dormant since the Red Scare following World War I, returned to life, with the CIO and its unions, including the UAW, among the principal targets.[3]

HOMER MARTIN'S MISCASTING as UAW president became ever more apparent and divisive. His poor judgment, erratic behavior, political clumsiness, and administrative bungling alienated the most engaged and perceptive union members. The need for new leadership was widely recognized, but Martin, fighting hard to keep his post, refused to step aside. Soon after the Flint sit-down, he launched an attack on his critics, firing or exiling them from union positions. Roy Reuther and Henry Kraus were dismissed. Victor Reuther and Bob Travis were demoted and transferred. As criticism of Martin's performance mounted, he accused his persecutors of plotting against him. General Motors, he feared, had targeted him for assassination. Union opponents, he believed, employed dirty tricks in attempts to get him out of the way, a suspicion that may have had some justification. When Wyndham Mortimer, his chief rival, referred him to a doctor who diagnosed a heart condition and recommended his immediate resignation as president, a skeptical Martin obtained a second opinion from another physician who assured him that his heart was perfectly sound.[4]

Unable to sustain his presidency unaided and convinced that the UAW's openly contemptuous Communist contingent was his principal opposition, Martin turned for support to Jay Lovestone, onetime secretary of the American Communist Party, but now, after a falling out with Stalin, the head of a militantly anti-Stalinist sect, the Communist Party (Opposition)—or, as less formally known, the Lovestoneites. Headquartered in New York City, Lovestone was eager to engage the American Communists on any battlefield. The UAW became only one of many. "The filthy Stalinist lice," he reportedly said, "are crawling all over the UAW. They must be stamped out!" In Homer Martin he hoped he had found the man for the job.[5]

Operating as a power behind the throne, Lovestone urged Martin to mount an anticommunist crusade within the union, something the president already favored, and to appoint Lovestoneites to key union positions where they could advise the president and implement their leader's plan. Martin obliged, appointing Lovestoneites—despite their lack of autoworker experience or a large following in the plants—to UAW positions as organizers, research director, administrative assistant to the president, head of the Women's Auxiliary, and editor of the union's newspaper. In all, Lovestone despatched about thirty agents from New York to Detroit to take positions with the UAW. According to Lovestone's patron, David Dubinsky of the International Ladies' Garment Workers Union, "we gave [Lovestone] one hundred thousand dollars to help the autoworkers build their union." The Lovestone faction conspired to run the UAW autocratically from the top down, an arrangement that agreed well with Martin's inclinations. Given a union whose origins lay in the shop floor and picket line actions of its rank and file and their locals, this put Martin on a collision course with his membership and with the organized opposition. For many, Martin's reliance on Lovestone to oppose the Communists meant he was merely substituting one nonunion, outside influence with its own agenda for another. A movement to curtail the Communists' role certainly had some support within the union's ranks, but Martin's crusade exaggerated their impact, used "guilt by association" tactics, and in any event was insufficient to overcome his inadequacies as president.[6]

The outbreak of unauthorized wildcat or "quickie" strikes immediately following the sit-downs at General Motors and Chrysler, a shop floor rebellion of unprecedented proportions, soon became entangled in the struggle between Martin and his critics. According to the corporation, by June 1937 GM's workers had engaged in 170 unauthorized strikes in the four months since the sit-down ended, and within two years there were 270 more work stoppages in the company's plants. Whatever the actual number, there was no question that wildcats were rampant. As one Flint worker remarked, "every time a dispute came up the fellows would have a tendency to sit down and just stop working. . . . We had short work days for quite a while as a result." In many instances these wildcat strikes, brief and explosive as they usually were, led to settlements of shop floor issues over production pace, job assignments, the role of union representatives, reinstatement of fired union members, and so on. Although GM was more troubled by wildcats than the other manufacturers, similar strikes and stoppages occurred in other organized plants. In the two years after June 1937,

Chrysler reported 109 stoppages, Hudson (where conditions were "a sort of anarchy," according to one employee) more than fifty, and Packard thirty-one. Following adoption by the executive board of a resolution categorically denouncing all unauthorized strikes, their number sharply declined, but they by no means disappeared. Local officers were loathe to surrender the weapon since it was useful in getting action on stalled grievances. Although there seemed to be little if any correlation between the occurrence of wild-cats and the presence of Communists in a local's leadership, Martin hoped to use the wildcat strike wave, which provoked a massive outpouring of hostile editorial comment and strong condemnations from auto manage-ment, to rid himself of his left-wing antagonists. The Lovestoneite editor of the UAW's paper, alleging that wildcats were a Communist stratagem to embarrass the president by exposing his inability to control the member-ship, accused "a small 'left wing' group" of employing the "helter-skelter use of strike action" to "prevent the growth of the whole organization rather than risk loss of [their] control."[7]

Responding to Martin's charge that radical opponents fomented wild-cats in order to discredit him, Communist spokesmen and others coun-tered that the strikes stemmed from causes that had little or nothing to do with union politics or ideologies. The exuberant workers, freed from fear, wanted to test the limits of their newly-won shop floor power by exercising it. Long denied any say in working conditions, many workers now believed that through collective action they could gain a share of the power that governed the industrial process. On the other side of an indis-tinct line, foremen and other supervisors, nervous and insecure in the new regime but reluctant to make further concessions without a struggle, pro-voked disturbances by sometimes acting as though no realignment in the distribution of power had taken place. General Motors' top leadership was still unprepared to acknowledge the union's permanent presence, and lower level supervisors reflected that attitude. In seeking to expand, con-solidate, and defend their portion of the shop floor's "contested terrain," both sides contributed to the production interruptions. As a union activist recalled, many of the elected stewards and committeemen who took the lead in representing workers' grievances and in organizing wildcats "just tried to settle . . . problems by a loud voice and a thumping of the bar-gaining table, and threatening to strike." Martin's self-pitying complaint that the intent of the wildcatters was to embarrass him by demonstrating his lack of control lacked credibility.[8]

NEGOTIATIONS TO PRODUCE A "supplementary contract" to the UAW's original, brief agreement with General Motors, conducted on the union's side by Wyndham Mortimer, were concluded in March, 1937. The corporation fought hard to limit the union's gains, although it unilaterally granted a 5-cents-an-hour wage increase. It turned down the UAW's proposals for a company-wide minimum wage and a thirty-hour workweek without reduced pay, and turned over to individual plants authority over piecework rates and line speed. The UAW made limited progress on seniority, providing transfer, layoff, and rehiring entitlements and some protection for workers from discriminatory discharges. The provision of seniority protection for women employees reduced but fell far short of eliminating opportunities for sexual harassment and demands for sexual favors. Instead of the shop steward system favored by the UAW, which would have provided a steward to represent every twenty-five workers, the union obtained a shop committee arrangement, with the committee to consist of five to nine committeemen in any one plant, each representing hundreds of workers. The committeemen at GM were spread thin. Although workers informally elected stewards in many GM plants and looked to them to take the lead in discussing problems with foremen and other supervisors, stewards had no contractual role in the grievance resolution process. A grievance was raised by a committeeman with a departmental foreman, then, if unresolved, it moved upward to a meeting of the entire shop committee with the plant management, and then to a review by the UAW president and the GM vice president in charge of the division. If still unresolved, the two parties, but only by mutual consent, could refer the dispute to an impartial umpire. In the event, effective third-party resolution of grievances at GM was not established until 1940. Some form of outside decision-making was included in many UAW contracts.[9]

Shop floor authority and the grievance procedure remained matters of fierce controversy. Two supplementary agreements that became effective on April 12, 1937, and March 7, 1938, provided additional committeemen in large plants, and paid them their current wage for up to four hours a day of grievance work. In return the union agreed to a clause expressly prohibiting shop stewards, although in some plants stewards continued to function on an informal basis—even, in some cases, for years. But in some of the large, recently organized plants, the union would have little more than a skeletal structure on the shop floor. At a GM workers' conference called to approve the agreement, a proposal to require that committeemen would have to be elected from the stewards's ranks was narrowly defeated. Many of the shop militants condemned the union negotiator's concessions on representation as a "sell-out," maintaining that only a dense stewards' organization grounded in cohesive rank-and-file cohorts with the threat of wildcat strikes could bring democracy and justice to the shop floor. But the opposing forces in corporate headquarters and in the union were too strong for them to prevail.[10]

General Motors was adamant, fearing formal recognition of stewards would dilute and undermine management's authority. The corporation was determined to restore order, discipline, and control in its factories. "The whole trouble in the UAW," complained Stephen DuBrul, GM's chief economist and a scourge of the union, "is that it is too democratic. Thus, it can't be controlled by its leaders. They are out in front and the mob, led by the belligerent minority of radicals, are always at their heels." GM, in contrast, did not suffer from excess democracy within its corporate ranks. When the union sought to reopen negotiations on general, corporation-wide objectives, like across-the-board wage increases, General Motors made it clear that it would grant nothing until the wildcat strikes were curbed. With internal divisions and deteriorating economic conditions undermining the union's clout, GM cracked down. For the next two years, bargaining with GM at the national level was stalemated. Although the wildcat strikes were the corporation's principal complaint, it also strenuously objected to other union practices, such as solicitation (intimidation in the corporation's view) in collecting dues and recruiting members during working hours on company property.[11]

The International Union officials were caught in the middle between GM's stubborn refusal to yield and the restiveness and insistent demands for local power from below. All of the union's top officers, regardless of their ideological, political, or factional alignments, deplored wildcats. They were responsible for conducting negotiations on a national contract and for holding the union together, and they feared that a balance of power that tipped too far in favor of the locals would weaken, fragment, and possibly destroy the union. With stewards free to call wildcats on any provocation, the local's bargaining position would be undercut, the workers turned against each other, and the grievance procedure rendered irrelevant. When wildcats in one department or factory of an integrated firm produced layoffs in other departments or factories that had little or no stake in the grievance, worker solidarity could be stretched beyond the breaking point. If wildcats proliferated, management had little cause to recognize the union, and the strikes created an opportunity to identify and pick off the shop floor militants for actions that violated agreements. Although the number of wildcats soon declined, they by no means entirely disappeared, and the issue of the precise division of authority between the International Union and the locals with their shop floor contingents remained unsettled and controversial. The fact that the International's leadership had in common with management an interest in averting wildcats and other unauthorized actions put it at odds with shop floor militants and opened it to the charge of acquiescing in "accommodationist" relationship with the employers, in which the union cooperated to maintain plant order and production.[12]

The new agreements initiated discussion on a broad range of issues at GM on a plant-by-plant basis. On many disputed items, such as wage minimums, line speed, job timing, elimination of piecework, redefinition of job classifications, seniority in transfers and upgrades, and provision of relief time, discussions often proceeded to settlements that laid the foundation for a "workplace rule of law" that defined and protected workers' rights in unprecedented ways. Eventually, agreements restricting production work to union members forced management to abolish the foremen's subordinates, the hated pushers, straw bosses, and the like, who then had either to be promoted to the foremen's ranks or consigned to production jobs. Once even limited union representation was achieved, a positive impact began to be felt by workers on the shop floor.[13]

MARTIN'S ATTACK ON THE UAW's left wing launched a decade of civil war within the union. From 1937 until Walter Reuther's reelection as president in 1947, a central struggle in the union's history was the rivalry of factions for influence, office, direction of contract negotiations, and control of policy. Carried on both in the open and behind closed doors, the struggle was a whirlpool that sucked extraneous issues and events into its vortex, making it impossible to debate many issues on their merits. The potential impact of events and decisions on factional rivalry within the union always intruded, even becoming the decisive consideration. Sometimes dismissed as merely a rivalry among union politicians hungry for office with little relevance to the vital interests of the members, in fact the factional battles posed significant questions concerning the union's identity and direction, and its present and future place in the nation's political-economic system. In the worst case, and by no means an impossibility, unchecked factionalism could lead to a permanent division into dual unions, with energy expended in fighting each other and little left for advancing members' interests. Only somewhat less damaging, unrestrained internal battles could cripple the union, leaving no group sufficiently strong to represent effectively the interests of a disillusioned and strife-ridden membership confronting hostile corporations.[14]

Since no single element was sufficiently large and powerful to dominate alone, coalitions quickly formed. On the "right" in the UAW's political/ideological spectrum (well to the left of center on the much broader national political spectrum) emerged the Progressive caucus, the conservative grouping. It included Martin's following in GM factories in Flint, Pontiac, and Lansing, and in GM assembly plants in other midwestern cities. Southern and border state migrants, constituting the majority of the workforce in many of these plants, were the most likely auto workers to stand by the embattled president. "So-called hillbillies or people from the

South," as Briggs activist Ken Morris observed, formed the core of Martin's support in that company's factories on Detroit's East Side. Many still thrilled to the memory of his stirring oratory in the organizing campaigns, and as evangelical Protestants and patriotic Americans they were often hostile to the secular, radical influences at work in the union. A large bloc in the Progressive caucus comprised followers of board member Dick Frankensteen, whose strength lay in the big Chrysler locals in Detroit and Hamtramck, especially Local 3 at Dodge Main. Many, though not all, of his supporters, among whom first- and second-generation Polish and other eastern European Catholics predominated, also looked with distaste on the union's communist element. The anticommunist fulminations of Father Charles E. Coughlin, to which they had been exposed for years, helped shape their views. Although an internal Protestant-versus-Catholic division could be discerned within the Progressive caucus, their shared dislike of the secularist, even antireligious radicals and "Reds" who were conspicuous on the opposing side, was sufficient, for the time being, to create an ecumenical entente. Frankensteen remained personally popular and retained his place as one of the UAW's top officers until the end of World War II, but he broke and reformed his alliances so often that the charge of opportunism eventually damaged his credibility and reduced his following. A small band of Trotskyists—consistently and fervently opposed to the "Stalinist" Communist Party (CPUSA), and, in their view of themselves, constituting the only genuine left—added another zestful ideological component to the Progressive caucus mixture. At first formidable in numbers, claiming the allegiance of a majority of involved unionists, the Progressive caucus was vulnerable because of Martin's failings.[15]

On the "left," the Unity caucus, a broad coalition of militant, secular, and urban-oriented unionists, provided the opposition to Martin and the Progressives; its leadership comprised, as Victor Reuther later remarked, "quite a collection of political activists of the so-called left." Unity included Walter, Roy, and Victor Reuther, and their following, consisting of the rapidly growing West Side Local 174 and other Detroit locals in which fellow Socialists and independent radicals were influential. Reuther's support tended to be located in body and parts plants, with their cadres of skilled workers and large contingents of semiskilled metal finishers and welders. The strong Briggs Local 212 under fellow Socialist Emil Mazey, for example, was a main source of strength, and Reuther competed with the Martinites for support in many of the GM assembly plants. Although the Reuthers drifted away from the Socialist Party as they became fully absorbed in the UAW's activities and prospects, they retained many elements of its outlook in the form of a social-democratic perspective that

championed a strong union, a role for workers in making the economic decisions that affected them, government regulation and stimulation of the
economy, and creation of comprehensive minimum standards of wages and
welfare entitlements for all citizens.[16]

The cluster of locals with Communist leadership, such as the East Side
Tool and Die Local 155 in Detroit, Fisher Local 45 in Cleveland, and Plymouth Local 51 in Detroit, was another major element in the Unity caucus.
Vice president Wyndham Mortimer, the top UAW official to sign the first
contract with General Motors, was its spokesman. For the UAW's Communists, whose position in the union, despite Martin's aroused hostility, was
strengthened by the victory in the Flint sit-down, American capitalism's
depression crisis afforded the rare opportunity to establish and build positions
of strength within the newly empowered institutions of the working class.[17]

Although relatively few auto workers were avowed Communists or
Socialists or were drawn to Communism's revolutionary goals, a strong
sense of class differences and of conflicting class interests with the management of the auto companies provided a fertile field for the militant
rhetoric and tactics offered by the Communists and other radical elements.
Communist Party membership among auto workers ranged from 550 in
1935 to a prewar peak of 1,100 in August 1939, before disillusionment stemming from the signing of the Nazi-Soviet pact reduced the numbers. A high
turnover rate, the result of several factors, meant that many more passed
through the party's ranks than the membership figures at any one time
reveal; one estimate holds that one-time party members in the auto industry numbered between 14,000 and 20,000. Whatever the case as to numbers,
backing for the party's positions and support for its leadership cadres were
considerably greater than membership figures indicate. Usually well-organized, informed, dedicated, energetic—and sometimes unscrupulous—the
Communist leadership exercised an influence greater than the membership
numbers warranted. Communist strength, for both members and their
wider circle of supporters and sympathizers, was centered in Detroit and
the large auto cities of Cleveland, Flint, and Milwaukee.[18]

Most of those active in the Unity caucus and the rank-and- file members they represented had no specific ideological affiliation. In terms of the
American political spectrum they leaned to the left, but they lacked political connections beyond favoring President Roosevelt and other representatives of the liberal wing of the Democratic Party. Above all, they wanted
a strong, effective union, with substantial autonomy for the locals, shop
floor protections, and, when necessary, a vigorous strike policy. Many
looked for leadership to the union's secretary-treasurer, George Addes,
whose hold on office was secure and who was trusted and admired by most

of the union's squabbling elements. For the time being, Addes kept caucus
battles at a distance and forebore to build a disciplined personal following.[19]

Emotions boiled over as warriors of the two caucuses wrangled on
through the summer of 1937, exchanging verbal assaults in print and
speeches and even occasionally coming to blows in confrontations at local
and executive board meetings. At a board meeting preceding the fractious
Milwaukee convention, Martin became so angry with Reuther that he
jumped up from his seat, ran around the conference table, and started
pounding on his head. Reuther, who had recently survived a professional
beating by Ford thugs, remained calm, telling the president "to go back and
sit down and behave himself." At another board meeting Frankensteen, a
burly former football player, threw a punch at fellow board member Lloyd
Jones, breaking a front tooth.[20]

THE STRUGGLE BETWEEN the Progressive and the Unity caucuses burst
into the open at the union's convention in Milwaukee, Wisconsin, in August
1937, "the most boisterous and disruptive convention," Emil Mazey
recalled, "I had ever seen." Many delegates on both sides came prepared for
battle, carrying 2" x 2" clubs onto the convention floor. In his opening
remarks president Martin predicted, with understatement, that "this convention will be very difficult to handle." Although the Martin-Frankensteen
Progressive forces were thought to be in the majority, their margin was
unknown. A series of votes eventually showed that they comprised about 60
percent of the delegates. Bitter battles within the rules, constitutional, credentials, and resolutions committees repeatedly spilled onto the convention
floor. Although the immediate issues were different, at bottom the two sides
confronted the same question again and again: which caucus, by prevailing
in that particular contest, would emerge from the convention fortified and
encouraged, better positioned to shape the union's future as it wished?
Always hovering in the background was the threat of a split that would
result in two rival, drastically weakened organizations.[21]

The Progressive forces had to make some concessions, but won more
often than they lost. Martin made clear his desire, for example, to reorga-
nize the UAW along the lines of the United Mine Workers, with authority
centralized in the hands of a strong president. The delegates authorized the
president to suspend an officer in an emergency, to bring suspended officers
to trial before the executive board with a possible penalty of expulsion, and
to appoint replacements when vacancies in the officer ranks occurred. Martin suffered a reverse on a patently undemocratic, politically motivated proposal to reduce the convention representation of large locals, where Unity's
strength lay, in favor of increasing representation of the smaller locals,
where his support was concentrated. A proposal to give the president more

authority to rein in wildcat strikes met a similar fate. Martin also sought to muzzle his critics on the executive board and to censor the newspapers of locals that were in the hands of the opposition. In the event, Martin was unable to enforce these restrictions on free expression.[22]

Martin's Progressive forces came into the convention intent on removing from office two Unity caucus leaders, vice presidents Wyndham Mortimer and Ed Hall, both closely tied to the Communist Party, and they hoped also to find the votes to remove George Addes from his post as secretary-treasurer. Over the objections of many Progressives and to Martin's disgust, CIO President John L. Lewis, fearing a split and distrustful of Martin, forced through a compromise that increased the number of vice presidents from three to five, retained the three vice presidents currently in office, added two vice presidents from the Progressive ranks, and as part of the deal elected all officers, including Addes and Martin himself, by unanimous votes. In addition, the executive board would be enlarged from twelve to twenty members through the creation of additional regions. Although calming the strife by making places available for factional warriors was a consideration, this expansion of the officer and regional director corps reflected the union's growth and would better equip the leadership, it was argued, to conduct the organizing campaigns and collective bargaining confrontations that lay ahead. Lewis once again, as in the sit-down strike, played a key role in resolving a UAW crisis.[23]

The outcome essentially followed the CIO's recommendation. The existing officers were reelected. Dick Frankensteen and R. J. Thomas, the latter an amiable figure from Chrysler Local 7 and a Martin supporter, were chosen as the two additional vice presidents. As to the division between Unity and Progressive caucuses, the left's position among the officers had been weakened, since now it could count on the support of only three of seven (Addes, Mortimer, and Hall) instead of three of five, but it still had a position, which might not have been the case without the CIO's intervention. Elections of the regional directors to the executive board at the convention's close resulted in a two-to-one working majority for the Progressives. For the time being, Martin remained in control.[24]

The struggle over the credentials of eight delegates from the Fisher No. 1 unit of Flint's large and growing amalgamated Local 156 sparked the greatest controversy and outrage. When Martin rammed through a ruling that eight Unity delegates from the local would not be seated, Unity followers, demanding a roll call vote, created an uproar. In the restrained words of the proceedings, "The President was not permitted to finish his statement by reason of the confusion among the delegates," and "a number of delegates were standing on tables, and tables and floor were pounded with sticks, and there was a general condition of disorder," and finally "the

UAW officers elected at the Milwaukee convention, 1937. *Left to right:* Vice Presidents Ed Hall, Wyndham Mortimer, and Richard Frankensteen, Secretary-Treasurer George Addes, President Homer Martin, Vice Presidents R. J. Thomas and Walter Wells. Board member Walter Reuther views the scene from the background. Walter P. Reuther Library, Wayne State University

noise assumed such proportions the President was unable to make himself heard."[25]

Martin discharged a chairman's duties with heavy-handed partiality. Time and again he ignored opposition speakers who asked for the floor. The credentials committee majority, under instruction, delayed its report until the convention's last day in the hope that Unity delegates would exhaust either themselves or their funds and be forced to return home. Martin kept a small metal box on the podium, an "applausograph," that he claimed could record the volume of voice votes with scientific accuracy. Not surprisingly, with the president announcing the results, the close voice votes went in favor of the Progressives, while the Unity delegates vainly shouted for a roll call or howled in rage. Adding to the noise and confusion and further skewing the results, guests seated in the balconies loudly joined in the "yeas" and "nays" of voice voting.[26]

The Reuther brothers (Roy, Victor, and Walter) at the Milwaukee convention, 1937. Walter P. Reuther Library, Wayne State University

With blows exchanged on the floor and a full-scale riot imminent, George Addes stepped forward to quell the disturbance, saying that in the interests of harmony the credentials committee's decision to deny seats to the eight Unity Local 156 delegates should be accepted. Walter Reuther, who had carried most of the debate's burden on behalf of the Unity caucus, registered a protest against the decision but agreed that it was time to move on. For many, Martin's handling of the convention was the clinching evidence of his dictatorial designs. He seemed willing to bend and break rules whenever it was to his advantage.[27]

DIVISIVE AS IT WAS, the Milwaukee convention was only the prelude to a more serious and enduring split. At issue was responsibility for disciplining workers who engaged in wildcat strikes. The UAW had argued that only the union could take action against its members, a position that General Motors resisted by refusing meaningful negotiations. In September Martin yielded, sending the corporation a "letter of responsibility" that acknowledged GM's right to fire or otherwise discipline members it charged with instigating unauthorized strikes. In return GM gave nothing. Emboldened by a faltering economy that threatened new layoffs, and aware that the national CIO was pressuring the UAW to restrain its members, the corporation's negotiators refused to concede anything on wages, hours, or working conditions. At the same time, Martin launched a new round of firings of his critics from their UAW positions and sought to clamp down on the independence of locals' newspapers.[28]

When a conference of nearly three hundred delegates from GM locals met in Detroit in November 1937, Martin's proposed GM contract called on the union to endorse the president's letter on discipline and to make further concessions on the union's shop floor activity and authority. Disorderly interruptions, points of order, and cries of "sell-out!" showed the delegates' displeasure and held up the proceedings. When the vote was taken, Martin's proposals were unanimously rejected with instructions from the delegates to reopen negotiations. Belatedly trying to jump on the bandwagon, Martin announced that he would gladly authorize strikes, shouting "General Motors has got it coming and they are going to get it!" With the conference concluded he led the delegates in a snake dance through downtown Detroit's Grand Circus Park, singing "Solidarity Forever!" Despite the grandstanding, the episode was another blow to Martin's status, straining the Progressive's ranks and alienating additional important local officers and the rank-and-file members they represented.[29]

A test case with General Motors, and the last important GM sit-down, soon arose when workers at the Fisher Body plant in Pontiac, Michigan, sat down over a speedup and a loss of jobs to a nonunion GM plant. The plant management agreed to negotiate the grievances but was overruled by GM's top brass, which, citing Martin's "letter of responsibility," fired four of the strike's leaders. In protest, workers again seized the plant and prepared for a siege. General Motors refused any concessions and threatened the union with all-out war if the strike continued. John L. Lewis condemned the strike action and Governor Frank Murphy warned that if troops were sent in, their mission would be to remove the sit-downers, not protect them as in Flint earlier in the year. Finally, when the Communist Party threw its weight against the strike's continuation, it collapsed. The strike leaders remained fired; General Motors had prevailed. For the auto workers, the sit-down era was over.[30]

GENERAL MOTORS DREW FURTHER encouragement in its uncompromising course from the UAW's political failure in the Detroit municipal elections of November 1937, the first foray of UAW leaders into Detroit electoral politics as candidates and, for most of them, the last. A "Labor Slate" filed for the nonpartisan ballot: Patrick H. O'Brien, a former judge and state attorney-general with a record of labor support and sympathy, for mayor; and five candidates for the Common Council. Four were prominent UAW figures—Tracy Doll, Dick Frankensteen, Walter Reuther, and R. J. Thomas—while one, Maurice Sugar, was a leading leftist Detroit attorney and politico who had provided legal services and other advice to the union and would become its counsel. The campaign, intended to test the waters for an independent labor party, provoked great interest and controversy. The Detroit newspapers condemned the candidates as labor bosses out to seize control of the city and castigated their proposals as profligate taxing and spending that would bankrupt Detroit and drive away business, turning the city into an "experimental laboratory to test out communist doctrine." The "Labor Slate" platform, a collection of union grievances against hostile city officials with some mildly socialistic and social-democratic schemes, proposed firing the "dictatorial" police commissioner with whom the union had had many run-ins, public ownership of gas and electric utilities, a public housing program, rent control, unemployment relief, free medical and dental care for those unable to pay, more parks and playgrounds, and investigation of high food prices. Reuther, the most visionary thinker on the slate, drew up and published a more expansive program for the city's future entitled "Detroit Can Be Workers' City." All the labor candidates survived the October primary to win places on the final ballot but, in a record turnout for a municipal election, all lost in the November runoff. The unanimous and strident opposition of Detroit's business and media establishment resulted in the election of Richard Reading as mayor and a conservative lineup for the Common Council. Business interests were reassured by this check to labor's political ambitions, coinciding as it did with the UAW's more defensive economic posture under Martin. Just as the New Deal had crested nationally by the end of 1937, so the electorates of the nation's working-class cities had reached the outermost bounds of their leftward political movement.[31]

SENSING THAT IT HAD a divided, fragile union on the run, GM pressed its advantage. As recession set in, car production rapidly declined and auto unemployment rose. By January 1938 all GM workers were either laid off or working no more than twenty-four hours a week. Conditions failed to improve until the end of the year. Passenger car production in 1938 barely exceeded two million, in contrast to the nearly four million cars built and sold the previous year. Union membership and dues collections declined as sharply. As the recession worsened, the inability of the UAW to protect its members' jobs and provide economic security produced disillusionment. Losing on grievances and suffering from discriminatory layoffs and other seniority violations, some members were led to question the value of union membership.[32]

With the union weak and on the defensive, Martin bent over backwards to accede to GM's wishes and prevent protests among the workers. In January 1938, at his insistence, the executive board, on a Progressive versus Unity division, ratified the "letter of responsibility" affirming GM's right to punish wildcat strikers. Taking charge of negotiations, Martin agreed to a further weakening of an already impaired grievance procedure, which saw the surrender of the remnants of a shop steward system, a reduction in the number of committeemen, and restrictions on committeemen's activities and movements within the plant as well as the time they could devote to union duties. As a result, said a later union account, "the grievance procedure bogged down, the workers became irritable, situations were provoked by irresponsible supervision which brought about unauthorized strikes; whereupon workers were penalized by the Corporation." Even Martin's henchmen had to concede that his new agreement was a poor one, but it was, they claimed, "the best that we can get out of the Corporation at the present time." Within a month the Martinites confessed that the agreement was undermining the union in plants where the grievance process was now so heavily weighted in management's favor that workers were too intimidated or dispirited to seek redress of contract violations.[33]

Respect for Martin declined further when he refused to submit the renegotiated agreement to any form of ratification by the membership. The Unity leaders strongly condemned this violation "of the simple fundamentals of democratic procedure," but since Martin had already signed the agreement, they felt they could only go along. As if this were not enough, the president quarreled with CIO head John L. Lewis and exploded in rhetorical outrage over alleged Communist Party domination of the Unity caucus. Finally, he publicly mused that workers should prepare themselves to accept lower wages from employers who were feeling the pinch of the recession.[34]

Not surprisingly, companies large and small responded to Martin's loose talk of wage concessions, prompting struggles that showed the UAW was still fighting for its very existence. An infamous battle, the union's most violent strike ever in Detroit, broke out at the Federal Screw Works, a parts firm on the West Side that had been organized by Local 174 in 1937. The struggle at Federal Screw represented a threat to the UAW's entire position on the industrial West Side. Although the company was profitable, when the recession hit it laid off more than half of its workforce of 300, both men and women, and ordered a wage cut of 10-cents-an-hour to new minimum rates of 50 cents for women and 60 cents for men. Two successive union concession offers, one to take a 5-cent-an-hour cut as a loan that the company would repay and a second to take a 10-cent cut to be repaid out of future profits, were summarily rejected. Reuther and other West Side Local officers suspected the company had received assurances from Detroit's mayor and police commissioner that the police would keep the plant open in case of a strike.

The strike to restore wage levels began on March 28, 1938, with the employees on the picket line joined by many union members from nearby factories and by neighborhood residents. No one tried to break through the first day, although some scabs went in by unguarded side doors and the plant operated at reduced levels. The next day fights broke out, with injuries on both sides.[35]

On the third day the battle escalated. The plant was surrounded by thousands of workers, local residents, and UAW activists from other locals who lined the streets for blocks around. The police appeared in great force, more than five hundred, including a large contingent of mounted officers, with orders to break the picket line and end the strike. Most of the plant's predominantly Polish workforce lived in the immediate neighborhood, a working-class community now being summoned to support its wage earners. As the scabs marched down the street toward the plant protected by a police cordon on either side, the spouses, children, relatives, friends, and neighbors of employees fired sticks, stones, bottles, tin cans, eggs, and tomatoes at them from porches, windows, and rooftops. Some housewives dumped pails of boiling water on scabs and police. Anything that would serve as a missile was used. When strikers grabbed beer bottles from a brewery delivery truck to throw at the scabs, the driver rushed out of a nearby tavern shouting, "Throw the empties, Goddamn it, throw the empties!" A neighborhood was in revolt against a threat to its livelihood. "It was more of a community cause than it was union," one activist recalled, "because all of the people from children on up helped us."[36]

When the police charged to break the picket lines there was a general melee. As the crowd scattered to escape police clubs, housewives opened their doors to rescue strikers from their pursuers and supplied bricks and other objects as weapons. Youngsters used blow pipes to shoot BB's at the police horses, fired marbles from slingshots, and rolled ball bearings down the street to make the horses lose their footing. Many strikers and supporters were arrested, including Jimmy Hoffa, already a rising figure in a Teamsters' local, who worked at a nearby warehouse and came over with others to lend a hand.

Forty pickets and twenty-five scabs were hospitalized, and dozens more injured, including thirteen policemen. Percy Keyes, a black foundry worker at Cadillac Motor Company, tried to surrender to police but was clubbed and kicked anyway, suffering a broken back, arm and skull fractures, and numerous other injuries. Taken to nearby Women's Hospital, he was refused treatment. Although the hospital, established for white women, had previously ignored its rules to treat separate emergency cases involving white men and black women, it refused to accommodate a black

Detroit mounted police and strikers clash at the Federal Screw Works, March 1938. Walter P. Reuther Library, Wayne State University

male. After a two-hour delay, Keyes was taken to Harper Hospital. Not expected to live, he survived with permanent disabilities.

Reuther and Martin appeared before the Detroit Common Council to protest the police action, dividing the blame between Police Commissioner Heinrich Pickert, for whom the event was only one more item on an antiunion record, and Mayor Richard W. Reading, the winner over the UAW's mayoral candidate in the recent municipal election. The community response and the violence jolted the company into negotiations, resulting in a rollback of the wage cuts and a union contract. The incident starkly revealed the serious challenge still facing the UAW and the hostility it could expect from Detroit city officials, but it also testified to the strength of a close tie between workers and their neighborhood community.[37]

BY THE SPRING OF 1938 the balance of forces within the union was shifting decisively against Homer Martin. Whichever way it turned, the union was stymied. Most damaging to Martin's reputation was his failure to achieve a satisfactory collective bargaining relationship with General Motors. The grievance procedure had virtually broken down. The corpo-

ration refused to make significant concessions and the union seemed pow-
erless to mount an effective offensive. The corporation's hard-nosed opposition had resulted, as R. J. Thomas, Martin's successor as president later
put it, in "the almost complete destruction of our organization in GM."
The Ford Motor Company was still unorganized. Limited undercover
organizing activity continued at Ford but the company maintained a vigorous and sometimes brutal opposition. Although the recession had
severely weakened the union, the companies' continued hostility, Martin's inept, dispiriting leadership, and the diversion of energies into factional maneuvering and struggle were equally responsible for the UAW's
deteriorating situation. Summing up the indictment against the president,
the capable and energetic organizer George Edwards wrote to his family,
"here is a young and militant union—the best beyond question in the
U.S.—able and ready to organize its own industry completely . . . and what
does our gallant president do? He fires about a dozen men who organized
and will be essential to maintenance of union success at Ford; caves in to
General Motors; dismisses organizers in the midst of a campaign. Either
they are the most criminally irresponsible acts which any leader has ever
been guilty of, or they amount to what the rank-and-file are openly charging—a sellout." Unfortunately, the worst was yet to come. Before the
UAW could regain the momentum achieved in its sit-down victories of
1937 and fulfill its mission of uniting all auto workers in an industrial
union, working under the terms of good contracts with their employers,
it would have to put its own house in order.[38]

CHAPTER 5

"A fight for the survival of the union"

Resolving the Leadership Crisis, 1938–41

Homer Martin's days as UAW president were numbered. Walter Reuther, with many others, accused him of incompetence. Martin "believed all along," Reuther said in a radio address, "that his emotional oratory was an adequate substitute for a sound union program. For two years this attitude has tossed the UAW from crisis to crisis. Our Union was like a ship in a heavy sea with a drunken pilot. We had no chart to follow, no consistent organization program, no administrative policy to guide us."[1]

The campaign to save the UAW began at the grassroots among rank-and-file auto workers and the officers of local unions. In the spring of 1938 annual elections of officers in numerous locals revealed a rising tide of opposition to Martin and the Progressive caucus. When large Detroit locals like Chevrolet Gear and Axle (Local 235) and the Chrysler Jefferson plant (Local 7)—home local of R. J. Thomas, a vice president and Martin supporter—switched sides to the Unity caucus the shock waves were felt throughout the union. The most significant realignment occurred at Dodge Main, Local 3; this was one of the UAW's largest units, representing thirty thousand workers, and the political base of Dick Frankensteen, the pillar of the Progressive caucus. Within a few weeks of the election of a Unity majority to Local 3's executive board, Frankensteen, already unhappy with Martin's reliance on Lovestone and his coterie, abandoned the president. In Packard, Budd Wheel, Chrysler Highland Park, and Hudson, other large Detroit locals, Unity made substantial gains. Where Unity was already in control it consolidated its position. The West Side Local 174, Briggs, Plymouth, L. A. Young Spring and Wire, Murray Body, and the two amalgamated tool and die locals, 155 and 157, remained solidly pro-Unity. Detroit's auto workers, never firmly in Martin's camp, had shifted decisively away from him. Outside of Detroit, large locals at Seaman Body in Milwaukee, at Studebaker and Bendix in South Bend, at General Motors plants in Atlanta, Cleveland, Saginaw, Bay City, and Tarrytown, New York, and amalgamated Local 12 in Toledo abandoned Martin, as did a large number of smaller locals.[2]

A reshuffling of alliances in the spring and summer of 1938 split both caucuses, leaving Martin isolated and vulnerable. The prime movers in the realignment were Dick Frankensteen and the Communist Party. The Communists in the Unity caucus, perceiving Frankensteen's disintegrating ties to Martin, began to woo him with hints of support for higher office in the future. In a series of contacts spread over several months, Frankensteen edged away from Martin and embraced the left, the first of several similar maneuvers that led to critics tagging him as "Flip Flop Frankensteen." Terms were negotiated with party emissaries and a plan to end factionalism and depose Martin worked out. With Frankensteen available, the Communists were prepared to dump Walter Reuther as a caucus partner who, they now saw, was "unreliable"—that is, would not consent to be led by them. Already established as the leading intellectual force in the UAW's upper ranks, Reuther was too independent, too ambitious, and too shrewd politically to remain closely tied to the CP crowd. Frankensteen, on the other hand, seeking to rescue his political future from the debacle of Martin's self-destruction, was casting about for new allies. In any event, no caucus was large enough to contain both Reuther and Frankensteen, two young, striving men with substantial followings who were obvious candidates for the UAW's highest office.[3]

Reuther had already distanced himself from the Communists. Seeds of distrust had been sewn on both sides well before the open break occurred. Reuther too had been courted by the Communists with promises of future support in exchange for agreeing to closer ties, perhaps including party membership, but he had turned them down. Like many on the left as the decade wound down, he gradually drew back from radical positions and connections as the depression's severity and the popular despair that accompanied it moderated and the New Deal's support for unions and a modified, more closely regulated capitalism improved the prospects for economic and social reforms obtained within the system. The Wagner Act, the Fair Labor Standards Act, the Social Security Act—with its pension, disability, and unemployment compensation provisions—and a host of regulatory measures indicated that reforms of practical benefit to workers and other lower- and middle-class Americans could be won within a revamped capitalistic democracy. The Communists' ultimate goal of a transformed, collectivized political-economic system was becoming ever more irrelevant as the American economy recovered, and their loyalty to a totalitarian foreign state created an unbridgeable gap between them and the American mainstream. Further, by 1938 specific differences between Reuther and the Communists over the union's foreign policy positions, always important to the party because of the Soviet connection, added to the strain. With the Soviet Union under threat from a rearming, aggressive Germany, its leaders advocated collective security, a position echoed by the American Communists and pressed on their Popular Front allies. Reuther, still affected by the pacifistic strain in the American socialist tradition, would not then support a collective security stance that might draw the United States toward war.[4]

The growth of anticommunist sentiment within the United States and among union members contributed to the breakup of the Unity caucus. In Congress's first major inquiry into Communism's impact, the Dies Committee, precursor to the House Un-American Activities Committee, conducted hearings at which testimony was aired alleging that more than three hundred CIO figures, including Reuther and several other UAW leaders, were Communists. Although Martin's leadership was being rejected, his anticommunist message and campaign resonated with elements of the union's rank and file. Reuther, who had spent nearly two years (1934–35) in the Soviet Union as a die maker in the Gorki auto plant, and whose cooperation with the party cadre in the Unity caucus since his return to the United States was well-known, was vulnerable to an outburst of anticommunist feeling from the general public and within the union. He had already been targeted during the General Motors sit-down strike when the charge that he favored a "Soviet America," based in part on forged statements in a letter written from the Soviet Union by Victor and Walter, was reprinted, circulated, and publicized by antiunion propagandists. The accusation was regularly resurrected against Reuther for the rest of his life, from opposite ends of the political spectrum. Left-wing union rivals and critics painted him as a renegade who had abandoned Communist principles and affiliation for reasons of political expediency. Right-wing ideologues, politicians, and bureaucrats, including Federal Bureau of Investigation (FBI) Director J. Edgar Hoover, portrayed him as a closet Communist disloyal to his country. The FBI collected a massive file of rumor, hearsay, and fantasy on Reuther, circulating portions of it among government officials whenever he was under consideration for a government position. In May 1940, for example, two years after his open break with the UAW's Communists, when he was in line for appointment to a government advisory board, Hoover warned treasury secretary Henry Morganthau, Jr., that Reuther was an "avowed Communist," trained at the "propaganda college in Moscow" and sent to this country to promote Soviet interests. The rising tide of anticommunist emotion and exposure, off the target in many cases but widely publicized, gave Reuther reason to welcome a public divorce from the union's Communist faction.[5]

With all parties save Martin signaling readiness for a switch, the open break within Unity came over a political patronage matter. In April 1938, the Michigan State CIO, the political lobbying arm of the state's CIO unions, was founded in Lansing, with election of officers one of its first tasks. The consensus Unity caucus candidate for secretary-treasurer was Victor Reuther, a veteran of the Flint sit-down and of other strikes and organizing campaigns, and a victim of Martin's purge of the UAW's staff. With the pledge of Unity caucus votes, including those of the Communists and their allies, his election seemed assured. At the last moment, the Communists backed out of the deal, throwing their support to Frankensteen's candidate, Richard Leonard, president of DeSoto Local 227. Clayton Fountain, a delegate to the convention from Local 235 and a member of the Communist Party at the time, related that the delegates who were Communists were "hastily rounded up" for a party meeting where, "out of nowhere," party leaders "came up with instructions to desert Vic Reuther and turn on the heat for Dick Leonard." Shortly before the vote the Reuthers discovered what was afoot. "What are you bastards doing?" Walter Reuther recalled demanding. "Do you realize you're going to destroy the Unity Caucus and the Unity Caucus is the only force that can save this union from a disastrous split?" The Communist Party's liaison with the UAW, again in Reuther's perhaps embellished recollection, coldly replied, "We know what we are doing and when you deny us the ability to use the Unity Caucus to advance the party's foreign policy position, we are going to destroy the Unity Caucus. . . . And if the day comes when the party's interests require us to destroy the UAW, we will destroy the UAW." Reuther's response was a declaration of war. "Brother, count me on the other side in every fight and I'm not going to stop until we drive you bastards out of this union." After the switch Leonard, who like Frankensteen had previously been a Martin ally, won easily. The open enmity and struggle between the Communists and Reuther, in the making for some time, emerged as a major theme in the UAW's history, persisting for ten years until Reuther's decisive triumph in 1947.[6]

In another move toward the center of the political spectrum, Reuther and some other UAW Socialists began to dissolve their ties with a Socialist Party weakened by internal divisions and the achievements of the New Deal. They faced a key political test in 1938 when Michigan's Democratic Governor Frank Murphy, whose support for the union during the GM sit-down strike and at other times had been crucial to its success and survival, ran for reelection. The union's debt to Murphy was clear and compelling, and the rank and file—"except for a handful of radicals," as a participant noted—was "firmly committed to the Democratic Party." Any votes diverted to a Socialist candidate were bound to come at Murphy's expense, possibly contributing to his defeat. Although a Socialist Party candidate filed for the office, Reuther broke with the party to endorse Murphy; moreover, the UAW executive board, adopting a motion offered by Reuther, made a substantial financial contribution to his campaign. Reuther later quietly resigned from the Socialist Party. Although he with many others from the UAW later took active parts in national and state Democratic Party politics, he thereafter had no formal political party affiliation. In the event, the union's support was insufficient to secure Murphy's reelection. Weakened by the public's negative reaction to the "Roosevelt Recession," under attack for his tender treatment of the sit-down strikers, accused of being under Communist Party influence, and harassed by a Dies Committee foray into the state that charged him with treason just prior to the election, Murphy went down to defeat. It would be another ten years, when G. Mennen Williams was elected governor in 1948, before the UAW would emerge as the powerful force in Michigan state politics that critics routinely accused it of being.[7]

Following the split in the Unity caucus, Reuther launched a counteroffensive and sought new allies, with the objective of creating a caucus of his own. He fired Communists from the West Side Local's staff and reduced party members and their sympathizers to a "futile minority" on the local's governing council. Socialists and other non-Communist, independent leftists became key members of the Reuther following. He also began to construct an informal alliance with the recently formed Association of Catholic Trade Unionists (ACTU), an organization set up by Roman Catholic laymen and clerics to encourage Catholic workers to participate in union affairs, in part to implement modern Catholic social doctrine's endorsement of unions and in part to limit Communist Party influence in them. The Detroit ACTU chapter would become large, active, and politically astute.[8]

THE CONSEQUENCES OF THE CAUCUS realignment soon began to play out. Frankensteen's alliance with the Communist left created a new executive board majority that, challenging Martin, followed Frankensteen's lead on most issues. On June 8, 1938, Martin lost control of the board when, for the first time, it cast a vote that he opposed. Quickly launching a reckless counterattack, he suspended five officers (the entire officer corps with the exception of vice president R. J. Thomas) on charges of antiunion activity, including subservience to the Communist Party. The officers were handed suspension notices without warning while attending a board meeting. They were to be tried by the executive board where, with the five suspended officers barred from voting, Martin calculated his lost majority would be restored. The trial of secretary-treasurer George Addes, first of the accused, ended when he walked out in protest and six board members followed him, an open rupture within the union's leadership. The rump board of thirteen members stripped Addes of his office and revoked his union membership, actions clearly in violation of the union's constitution.[9]

Undeterred by a mounting wave of protests, Martin moved on to trials of the other officers. When accused by Martin of conspiring to subvert the union, the suspended officers responded that the only conspiracy was one between Martin and an "irresponsible, disruptive political adventurer and intermeddler of New York," Martin's mentor Jay Lovestone, whom they blamed for inspiring the president's assault on his fellow officers. The officers and their lawyer, Detroit attorney Maurice Sugar, now had the evidence to prove their charge that Lovestone was pulling the strings, having acquired, apparently by cloak and dagger methods, a correspondence between Martin and Lovestone that documented the latter's influence. By Martin's and Lovestone's accounts, the letters, whose authenticity was undeniable, were stolen from Lovestone's New York apartment by Soviet agents who turned them over to Martin's Communist enemies, while Sugar claimed that the letters were deposited in his office by a courier who vanished before he could be identified. The fact that photostatic copies of the letters were published in the *Daily Worker* only a couple of weeks after they disappeared from the apartment convinced many that the CP and Soviet agents were at the bottom of the case of the purloined letters. By whatever route the letters came into Sugar's hands, knowledge of their contents soon spread throughout the union, further damaging Martin's credibility and undermining his claim to independence. Nevertheless, as a result of the trials, three more officers—vice presidents Hall, Frankensteen, and Mortimer—were removed from office and expelled from the union, and a fourth vice president, Walter Wells, was suspended for three months. For the time being Martin had purged his enemies, but at the price of alienating virtually the entire union leadership, the CIO's officers, and, most importantly, much of the UAW's rank and file. The hapless ex-preacher was now, so Henry Kraus wrote, "a shepherd who has lost his flock."[10]

Many in the union, at all levels, believed that only John L. Lewis and his CIO colleagues could clean up the mess. Appeals from the expelled officers and from local leaders poured into Lewis's CIO headquarters in Washington pleading for intervention. Some favored calling a UAW special convention to attack the problems, an option initially opposed by Lewis because he feared a riotous convention would irrevocably split the UAW in two, destroying the CIO's most dynamic union.[11]

Lewis proposed a "peace plan" that, in effect, sealed Martin's fate. He despatched his CIO lieutenants, Philip Murray of the steelworker's union and Sidney Hillman, president of the Amalgamated Clothing Workers, to Detroit to investigate and take charge, a move that infuriated Martin but which he was helpless to block. For appearance's sake, Murray and Hillman formed a committee that included Martin and R. J. Thomas to direct the union's affairs until order could be restored. In fact, Murray and Hillman made the decisions. With the "peace plan" approved by an acquiescent executive board, they overturned the trial verdicts and reinstated the expelled officers. They then demanded that Martin remove from the union's staff those associated with Lovestone; eight members of his cadre were ousted.[12]

The CIO's decisive intervention ended the attempt of an outside political organization, largely lacking autoworker representation, to control the union's policies and politics. Its opportunity arose out of Martin's inadequacies and dependency, and from the turmoil of the UAW's founding years. Exploiting the concern felt by many UAW members toward the revolutionary, Soviet-affiliated left, Martin and his backers had sought to blame his failures and problems (most in fact of his own making), on the Communist faction. As a result, he played into their hands. The Lovestoneite-Martin episode was a searing experience that many members and secondary leaders in the locals would not forget. Allowing the union's headquarters to fall under the control of a nonunion, unrepresentative force promoted factional strife and undermined the united front the auto workers' needed in confronting the powerful corporations.

Though mortally wounded, Martin was not yet done. Since he knew only one tactic, frontal assault, it was not entirely surprising, yet shocking to many, that soon after the CIO's intervention rumors began to circulate that he had approached the American Federation of Labor, despised by most auto workers for its earlier failure to organize the industry. The threat of dual unions, a split creating two rival, equally weak auto workers' organizations, each backed by one of the rival labor federations, feared by many as factionalism's final outcome, seemed imminent. Only the manufacturers would gain from such a turn of events, only the auto workers would lose. Supporting suspicions of Martin's disloyalty to the CIO, evidence suggested that he had secretly made contact with Harry Bennett, the head of the Ford Service Department, to negotiate a deal to take his UAW following out of the CIO. In return, Bennett would facilitate the unionization of Ford employees in an AFL-affiliated organization to be headed by Martin but, surely, with Bennett in control.[13]

With the beginning of a new year in 1939, the "long series of incidents which have practically been an earthquake in the auto union field," as characterized by one observer, moved fitfully toward resolution. With the board now back in the hands of Martin's opponents, his maneuvers could be turned aside. On January 7, for example, he suspended the officers of Plymouth Local 51, a Unity caucus stronghold, and ordered new elections; five days later the executive board revoked the suspensions and reinstated the local's officers. Later in the month the board voted to hold a special convention in Cleveland, Ohio, to elect new officers and revise the union's constitution. Martin replied to this provocation by suspending fifteen board members and announcing that he would hold a separate convention in Detroit, decisions that prompted one observer to remark that he "has indeed gone blotto." The ousted board members then threatened to impeach him and named R. J. Thomas, the last of the officers to desert Martin, as acting president until the Cleveland convention could be held. From CIO headquarters in Washington, Murray and Hillman recognized the suspended board members and Thomas as the legitimate officeholders. Homer Martin thereupon resigned from the CIO executive board, with a parting shot at John L. Lewis as a coddler of Communists.[14]

IN SCHEDULING SEPARATE conventions both sides appealed to local leaders and the rank and file for their allegiance. Each local would determine which convention its delegates would attend and whom they would support. At once the locals became forums of intense debate, especially those that were large and not firmly committed to one camp or the other. Spokesmen for both sides debated before large meetings in what was, until Reuther's presidential reelection campaign in 1947, the UAW's most hard-fought and, with its high stakes, historically most significant political contest. Charges of treason against the union flew back and forth in newspapers, speeches, and courtrooms. When debate broke down, both sides resorted to displays of force. "Flying squadrons" roamed from meeting to meeting to protect their adherents and intimidate the opposition; raucous meetings and fist fights were reported in the press; at the Buick plant gate in Flint "there were at least one or two fist fights every lunch hour." In Cleveland, "we had fights all over . . . in local union meetings where we were voting whether to go with the CIO or AFL. Almost all of them wound up in a brawl." Some especially divided locals formed "shotgun brigades" to guard their records and funds against seizure by the opposition.[15]

Demonstrating to the workers the hazards of rival dual unions, the companies moved quickly to exploit the UAW's predicament. With each of the opposing sides claiming to be the legitimate UAW, party to its contracts and legal representative of union members in the plants, Chrysler, General Motors, and lesser companies refused to recognize either Martin or the UAW-CIO as the workers' bargaining agent. Contract negotiations were suspended and the grievance procedures collapsed in plants where rival dual committees were present. The union's newspaper, controlled by CIO adherents, complained: "Under GM's distorted interpretation . . . it can take three stooges in a plant of 10,000 workers and use the phony claims of those stooges to defeat bargaining for the entire 10,000. This is being done in some plants." At Pontiac Motors, a UAW-CIO committeeman related, "if I went to them as a CIO member . . . they said, 'Well, we do not recognize you guys. You do not even represent these people.' So . . . if an AFL guy came to one of them they would say, 'Well, we do not recognize you people. You have got no bargaining rights here.' " In one plant after another General Motors management maintained its refusal to recognize any union. The battle over grievances with Briggs's management was likened to "guerrilla warfare." When President Walter O. Briggs refused to bargain with Local 212, the union threw an informational picket line around Briggs Stadium, the home of the Briggs-owned Detroit Tigers, which was broken up by mounted police. A police inspector testified that the picket line had been peaceful until the police intervened, and the cases against the pickets were thrown out of court. Without a resolution of the conflict, the auto workers stood to lose nearly all the ground they had gained in contracts and on the shop floor since the founding of the union.[16]

Martin's convention met in Detroit in early March to a disappointing turnout. His estimate that delegates represented more than 60,000 workers was deemed three times too high by the opposition. Most of the 360 delegates were from small locals on the industry's periphery; the two major exceptions were the Flint Fisher Body and Chevrolet locals. As expected, the delegates declared their independence of the CIO, initiated an application for affiliation with the AFL, barred Communists from union membership, and reelected Martin president. In June the AFL chartered Martin's UAW-AFL. The specter of dual unions had become flesh and blood.[17]

A MONTH LATER when the UAW-CIO met in Cleveland, it was evident that it retained the loyalty of most auto workers. The officers claimed that the delegates represented more than 370,000 blue-collar employees, although they had to admit that owing to layoffs, factional strife, and incomplete organizing in some of the plants only about 90,000 were paying dues and therefore members in good standing. From the outset the proceedings were guided by President Lewis's two emissaries, CIO vice presidents Sidney Hillman and Philip Murray, "doctors and amateur psychiatrists," as a reporter referred to them, sent to cure the UAW's "feudo-phrenia." In closed convention sessions and during caucus meetings and hotel room conferences—one lasted nine hours—the two CIO leaders urged a program to contain the damage of Martin's defection and restore the union to a solid footing. Murray, fearful that the Communists would try to install Addes or even Mortimer as president, delivered a blistering, angry denunciation of Communist Party union activity to a closed convention session, and Earl Browder, CPUSA chief, eager to deflect the charge that the Communists were exploiting the union's turmoil, turned up to counsel restraint to the comrades in the name of labor unity.[18]

The CIO rescue plan contained several parts. First, George Addes, preferred by most delegates for president, would have to stand aside, contenting himself with reelection as secretary-treasurer. Although Addes, a Catholic, was certainly not a Communist, he had welcomed Communist Party support and relied on Maurice Sugar, the Detroit attorney with a lifelong attachment to left-wing causes and campaigns, for advice. Addes's election as president, the CIO chieftains feared, would be seized upon and exploited by the Martinites and the press to argue that Communists controlled the UAW-CIO, risking new defections to Martin's dual union. Although disappointed, Addes agreed with and supported the CIO plan.[19]

In addition, the delegate count for Addes was tainted, because a portion of his supporters represented locals in which many members were not current in dues payments. Since these delegates had been selected at an earlier date, they were technically eligible to be present at and participate in the convention, but Addes's election on the strength of such "paper votes" would outrage those opposed to him. A push by Addes for president could ignite a revolt and a secession from the union among Reuther supporters unwilling to accept Addes's election by such means, sparking a second dual union threat. Emil Mazey, president of Local 212, which had nearly 12,000 members—95 percent of whom were paying dues—informed Hillman and Murray that he would take the local independent if Addes became president through "paper votes". Mazey pointed out that Plymouth Local 51, a Communist controlled local pledged to Addes, had fewer than 100 members currently paying dues but 75 convention votes, far more than it was entitled to for the number of members currently in good standing. With the union precariously balanced between survival and oblivion and threatened on all sides, the risk of an Addes presidential election was great. Even riskier would have been the election of someone more closely identified with the Communist left such as Wyndham Mortimer.[20]

The CIO's candidate for the office was acting president R. J. Thomas, a nonpolitical middle-of-the-road unionist with neither left-wing connections nor a large following of any character. In his favor it was argued that he would not alienate any important element and, of the presidential possibilities, he was the least vulnerable to Martin's charge of Communist domination. The CIO representatives, especially Hillman, bore down hard on Thomas's behalf, meeting with caucuses and summoning delegates for conferences. One delegate recalled that "it became a joke around the lobby of the hotel that the boys would be singing 'Addes is our leader' [we will not be moved], as they went in Sidney Hillman's hotel room, and they would be coming out saying 'Thomas is our leader.' " Frankensteen, who expected to become secretary-treasurer if Addes moved up as president, recalled his anger at the CIO's intervention in favor of Thomas but conceded in retrospect that Murray and Hillman made the correct choice. Thomas himself acknowledged that without CIO support he would not have been elected.[21]

Many saw Thomas as a caretaker president who would be replaced in due course by Addes, Frankensteen, Reuther, or another more forceful contender. Hillman bluntly but prophetically told Thomas that he should not think his presidency would last long, "because Walter Reuther will be the next president. I don't know how long he will sit still but he's bound to go after it." The offer to Reuther to head the union's General Motors Department, potentially one of its most powerful posts and an obvious stepping-stone to higher office, secured significant support for Thomas's election.[22]

While Thomas was neither ideologically sophisticated nor politically astute, he had popular appeal. An auto worker who entered the union in its earliest days at Chrysler, he shared the tastes and habits of many of the rank and file. He was affable, habitually spoke the rough language of the shop, chewed tobacco, was addicted to poker, and liked to join others for a few beers and some manly talk in the bars down the street from the Chrysler plant. As a historian wrote, Thomas "had no intellectual or leadership qualifications for the presidency of the UAW. But he was loyal, honest, big-hearted, stable, and colorless, all wildly attractive characteristics after Homer Martin." Two other delegates announced their candidacies, but Thomas, with strong CIO backing and accepted by all corners of the union, easily prevailed in the convention vote.[23]

More contentious were the decisions on the vice presidents and the board members. The left wished to retain five vice presidents in order to assure the reelection of its three incumbents, Frankensteen, Hall, and Mortimer. The Reuther caucus, a minority in delegate strength, proposed a single vice president, arguing that a union with too many vice presidents invited factional divisions. The CIO, however, ultimately said the union would be better off with none at all, and its view prevailed. Although this move was publicly defended on the ground that it would reduce expenses and enable the union to deploy an enlarged organizing and servicing corps to greater effect, the motive was to reduce the visibility of the left in order to undercut the hostile charge of Martin and others that the UAW was under Communist control. Wyndham Mortimer saw the Hillman-Murray plan as aimed at removing himself and Ed Hall, another vice president supported by the CP, from the leadership.[24]

In the election of regional directors, where the CIO emissaries had little weight to throw around, the left fared better. By most estimates the Communist Party, with about fifty party members serving as delegates and a larger pool of supporters of varying degrees of reliability, reached the peak of its UAW influence at the Cleveland convention. Although the left took a hit in the election of officers, particularly in Mortimer's loss of his vice presidency, it gained positions on the executive board. Its greater strength there was due primarily to the discrediting of a band of Homer Martin's followers and their failure to be reelected. As might have been expected, the Martinites' departure from the UAW-CIO shifted the political/ideological center of gravity in the upper reaches of union leadership to the left. By no means were all board members tightly aligned one way or the other, but, according to journalists' reports and other assessments, the left could generally count on the votes of twelve of the sixteen regional directors/board members, with the rest aligned with Reuther. A move to create a board seat for Mortimer by fashioning an additional region in Ohio failed. R. J. Thomas, although president, commanded no personal board following.[25]

Electioneering supplied the convention's excitement, but some of its most constructive work consisted of consideration and adoption of constitutional amendments. Aiming to discourage aspiring autocrats, the delegates took steps to decentralize and democratize the union's structure. The president's prerogatives were trimmed by reinforcing restrictions on his power to suspend other officers, by limiting his right to assign officers their duties and by transferring the right to interpret the constitution to the board. Annual conventions were to replace biennial meetings in order to enhance accountability. Executive board/regional director positions became full-time posts, with the stipulation that board members had to relinquish presidencies of local unions, and various mechanisms were put in place to protect locals from interference by the International. Perhaps most important, and a direct response to Martin's abuses, departments and councils for each of the major companies and groups of lesser parts manufacturers were written into the constitution to ensure the membership's role in setting collective bargaining goals and in contract ratification. By virtue of these amendments, the UAW created a more democratic structure and guarded against a future presidency of a Martinite character. In essential respects, the constitution as amended in 1939 remains as the UAW's instrument of self-government.[26]

APART FROM THOMAS, Walter Reuther emerged from the Cleveland convention with the most important new duties and opportunities. In need of Reuther's support and confident of his ability to organize workers, conduct negotiations, and lead strikes, Thomas offered and Reuther accepted appointment as director of the General Motors Department. After the chaos and reverses suffered under the Martin regime, with the locals in many GM plants still divided between pro- and anti-Martin factions, Reuther inherited a rebuilding effort that might have daunted anyone with less self-confidence and energy. By the UAW's estimate, in the spring of 1939 only 12,000 GM workers, constituting 6 percent of the corporation's 200,000 strong blue-collar workforce, were dues-paying UAW-CIO members, with an additional 4 percent in Martin's rival UAW-AFL. In Flint, with 32,000

GM employees, only 500, one in sixty-four, were UAW-CIO members in good standing. Dual committees from the two unions vied for representation rights in eleven, mostly large, GM factories with the corporation ignoring both. UAW-AFL shop committees functioned in twelve plants to the exclusion of CIO committees. In only three GM plants, covering fewer than 2,000 workers, did the UAW-CIO have corporation-recognized sole bargaining rights. From the union's perspective, it was no exaggeration to say that a "deplorable situation prevailed" in all GM plants with a "demoralized and disillusioned" membership.[27]

Rebuilding the union would be a monumental task. Following the convention's mandate, Reuther's first responsibility was to devise and put in place a new structure for the General Motors Department to ensure orderly and responsive consideration of collective bargaining objectives, conduct of negotiations, and coordination of tactics on grievances. Under Martin, arrangements had been haphazard, even chaotic, with at times little or no input from the locals and the rank and file. The plan called for an elected General Motors National Council of twenty-five members, and nine elected regional sub-councils in which all GM plants within the region would be represented. Information and guidance would flow up and down the channels as bargaining goals were formulated and, with negotiations completed, as ratification of a contract was sought. The national council elected an executive committee of five to participate directly in negotiating a GM agreement. At the council's first meeting, Reuther brought forward an ambitious bargaining agenda consisting of a rudimentary version of a guaranteed annual wage, a proposal particularly attractive to the skilled tool and die makers because they were subject to seasonal layoffs alternating with periods of hectic activity. He also proposed to expand employment in the industry by a reduction of the workweek to thirty hours with no loss of pay, to reinstate and formally recognize a shop steward system, and to seek a voice in determining production standards. Tactically, Reuther contended that GM had to be the union's first target because a victory at the industry's dominant firm would set the pattern for the rest.[28]

To reestablish the UAW-CIO in GM, several options were available. The first was a conventional strike of production workers, a tactic that held out little prospect of success. Although the car market was improving from its recession low, it had not fully recovered. GM dealers were still well stocked with cars, therefore the company had little need for uninterrupted production. A production workers' strike would likely be long and costly to the strikers. With the layoffs of 1938 having exhausted many workers' savings and the union without a strike fund, the UAW's ability to sustain a long strike was doubtful. A sit-down was out of the question, since public opinion would no longer tolerate one and Michigan's public authorities, including the state's Republican governor, would be hostile. Reuther was fully prepared to use direct action in order to gain results, but it had to be *"power under control,"* as he often said, mobilized and directed to a common purpose, not the random, uncoordinated protests of wildcat strikes.[29]

Another option was to follow the electoral procedures of the Wagner Act, a course that presented its own problems. The National Labor Relations Board was bogged down in disputes and lengthy delays. A year or more might pass before an election could be held. In the meantime, without a contract that GM acknowledged, the union would most likely weaken and be unable to protect its activist cadres in the plants. An election posed the further risk of Martinite victories in some GM plants, setting in cement a division of the auto workers into two rival unions. To restore its credibility and regain the workers' support, the UAW needed an immediate victory over both Martin's union and the car maker.[30]

Drawing on earlier experiences and observations, Reuther, in cooperation with other tool and die unionists, devised an alternative strike plan that revealed his gifts for shrewd analysis and bold execution. He proposed to maximize pressure on the corporation while minimizing the risk and cost to the workers by calling a strike limited to the loyal and reliable GM tool and die makers, the stoutest union adherents among the corporation's employees, leaving production workers at their jobs. Tools and dies were being completed for GM's 1940 models, counted on by the corporation to lift it fully out of the recession. If only the tool and die makers struck, the far more numerous production workers, still turning out the 1939 models, would continue to draw their pay while the corporation's competitive prospects deteriorated. In addition, since unemployment compensation had recently gone into effect in Michigan, if the strike continued beyond the conclusion of the 1939 model run, laid-off production workers would then be eligible for payments. With the militance and solidarity of the tool and die makers well-established, Reuther expected an enthusiastic response to the call for a strike. The ability to adjust strike strategy to the circumstances of the moment by mobilizing only a small but crucial minority of the union's membership testified to the power and utility of the industrial union concept. Bringing all the industry's workers into a single, cohesive organization added flexibility and force to the union's impact. Production workers had carried the burden in the sit-downs; tool room and skilled maintenance workers came to the fore in 1939. Craft unions with narrow bases, such as MESA and the AFL, would have had difficulty surviving let alone making significant gains in the industry.[31]

Homer Martin tried to beat the UAW-CIO to the punch by calling strikes at GM plants in Flint and Saginaw. At the appointed hour for Martin's strike, four workers started to walk out of the huge Flint Chevrolet plant but, finding that no one followed them, they returned sheepishly to their places. UAW-CIO workers ignored the AFL picket lines, and the plants continued to operate. In calling for a strike, Martin had succeeded only in demonstrating his lack of support.[32]

Still, the "strategy strike," as the tool and die makers' strike was called, was a gamble. The union was internally divided. The Communists, although they dared not oppose the strike openly, did not look with favor on a victory engineered by Reuther. According to his recollection, they agreed to a strike under his leadership "because they thought I would break my neck." Some among the rank and file were hostile, others indifferent or pessimistic. Many workers hung back, since the union still had to prove to them it could produce worthwhile results, and few workers in the plants organized by the UAW were paying dues when the strike began. If the strike flopped, the union would perhaps suffer irreparable damage.[33]

Reuther planned the preliminary rounds carefully. The corporation was asked to enter negotiations but refused, claiming as it had before that it was uncertain whom, if anyone, the UAW-CIO represented. Strike votes conducted by the union at eight GM tool and die shops showed more than 90 percent ready to go out. Another decision was to begin the strike with the most militant shops and then, as GM held out, to extend it to others that might not lead but were prepared to follow. *Time* magazine called this a "new and shrewdly conceived" technique, "not unlike amputating one finger at a time to cripple a hand."[34]

The strike began on July 5, 1939. Fisher 21 in Detroit, which produced welding tools and fixtures, was the first shop to shut down. "Soon as the 10 o'clock bell rang, the power went off and every machine in the plant stopped running. The men quietly put away their tools, washed up, changed clothes, punched the clock, thumbed their noses at the manager, and walked out. By 10:25, not a man was left inside." By the next day, five shops were closed, including Fisher 23, the largest tool and die facility in the world, with 1,600 employees, and the Detroit die shop, also large, of Chevrolet Gear and Axle. The latter's 800 tool and die strikers were joined on the picket lines by 2,500 production workers, a demonstration of solidarity by those who stood to realize no immediate gain. Ultimately the strike spread to eleven shops, stalling GM's preparations for production of its 1940 models.[35]

Reuther orchestrated a range of actions to mobilize union and public support. A demonstration at GM's Detroit headquarters brought out 10,000 production workers marching in columns of ten around the massive building. A Reuther address over a Detroit radio station produced a bonus of favorable publicity when it was disclosed that the station had censored passages critical of DuPont control of GM and of Alfred P. Sloan, Jr., GM's president, as well as lists of the corporation's profits and its executives' salaries.[36]

Corporation moves were countered and its missteps publicized. General Motors executive vice president William S. Knudsen sought a connection with his employees by assuring Reuther during their talks that "I live like any other GM worker. On Sunday, I relax with my family and love to watch my grandchildren swim in the pool in my backyard." Reuther was not moved, nor presumably were GM union members, few if any of whom had backyard swimming pools. GM tried to transfer work from its "captive" tool and die facilities to non-striking, independent tool and die shops, but UAW members there refused to touch the "hot dies." The company encouraged back-to-work movements, but there was little scabbing. Since the workers involved were highly skilled, it was impossible to replace them on short notice. When state police arrived at Pontiac Fisher Body to escort returning workers through the picket lines, few of whom materialized, strikers taunted the state's forces, shouting, "let the state police make [GM's] tools and dies!"[37]

Homer Martin tried to break the CIO strike. According to a Flint worker, the Martinites imported "paid thugs" to intimidate strikers, necessitating the mobilization and despatch to trouble spots of the union's "flying squadrons," at times numbering in the hundreds. In an attempt to minimize confrontations, Reuther cautioned against provocations and admonished his pickets to "stay sober to avoid unnecessary trouble."[38]

Four weeks after it began the strike was settled. Although GM "bitterly fought every inch of the way," it accepted the UAW-CIO as exclusive bargaining agent in the forty-one plants where the Martin union had no shop committees. The price for recognition was a union promise to oppose wildcat strikes. In eleven remaining plants where the CIO and the AFL had rival committees, the corporation insisted that recognition must await the outcome of NLRB-conducted elections. In addition, the corporation agreed to a partial standardization of wage rates for tool and die men in different plants and some other improvements in pay and working conditions. The material gains were not particularly significant. Most important was the UAW-CIO's ability to win recognition by carrying the strike through to a successful conclusion, in sharp contrast to the recent failure of the Martin forces. Emil Mazey expressed a consensus judgment when he later called the strike the "most important single event following the winning of the sit-down strike. . . . At this point, we reestablished the supremacy of the UAW-CIO in the auto industry."[39]

The UAW's success in the tool and die strike marked an important transition in its relationship with General Motors and therefore in the union's position in the entire industry. The corporation lowered the sights of its labor relations policy, substituting an "armed truce" for its previous attempts to eliminate the union. Grudgingly, GM acknowledged the union's existence. In the future General Motors would resist UAW demands, being "tough but fair" (in its own estimation), but it no longer set out to destroy the union.[40]

By demonstrating, for the first time since the sit-downs, that the UAW could successfully confront the world's largest corporation, the strike led to a "rebirth of enthusiasm" in the ranks of auto workers and restored momentum to the union movement. Heartened by the union's success, thousands paid up their dues and thousands more joined for the first time. Buick Local 599 in Flint, which had fewer than 700 paid-up members at the first of the year, had nearly 4,000 by late summer. CIO membership in many of the plants that had been in the Martin camp grew rapidly. As a regional director reported from Flint, "the good old 1937 spirit is here again."[41]

WITH THE UNION REINSTATED in most General Motors plants, and membership and morale skyrocketing throughout the auto workforce, the next step was to invoke the procedures of the National Labor Relations Act in order to secure recognition and exclusive bargaining rights throughout the industry. Soon after the strike ended, the National Labor Relations Board conducted elections at Packard, Motor Products, Kelsey-Hayes, Briggs, and plants of other corporations, resulting in CIO victories, often by huge margins. Eleven of thirteen Chrysler plants voted for UAW-CIO locals with exclusive representation.[42]

The UAW-CIO's landslide electoral victory at Dodge Main set the stage for a confrontation with the Chrysler Corporation over the issue of production standards. Chrysler's determination to set line speed, quotas, and other production standards unilaterally led the corporation to fire a dozen men who refused to work at the new rate. In October a vote conducted by the union showed massive support for a strike to seek a general wage increase and for "joint fixing" of production standards by the corporation and the union. Chrysler would not yield, so the strike began on October 18, 1939, and lasted forty-five days. In desperation, Chrysler mobilized a contingent of the unemployed (mainly blacks with very few whites) to break the union's picket lines with police assistance, but the number of scabs was too small to have an impact. Criticized for its resort to a racial tactic, Chrysler conceded defeat and the strike ended.[43]

The settlement recognized the union's steward system, resting on shop floor units of twenty or even fewer workers, and the legitimacy of bargaining between stewards and foremen to settle grievances. Production rates were to be based on "fairness and equity" for "the reasonable working capacities of normal operators." Foremen could adjust the rate if workers complained it was too fast. In case of continued disagreement, negotiations could move up to the chief steward and the general foreman or superintendent of the department. Beyond that level, the plant committee would take over in meetings with the plant management. Disputes would be settled within each plant with supervisors authorized to make concessions and workers guaranteed a right of appeal. In addition to recognition of a shop floor system, Chrysler workers won a general wage increase, the first since 1937. For nearly twenty years Chrysler workers maintained a steward apparatus that gave them a more powerful voice on working conditions than their counterparts at General Motors and Ford possessed.[44]

Again the make-or-break effort on recognition came at General Motors. Aggressive election campaigns were waged both by the UAW-CIO and by Martin's UAW-AFL, with much of the struggle fought out over Martin's accusation of "Red" domination of the CIO. Despite Reuther's public divorce from the Communist faction, reprints of the Reuther brothers' now infamous letter from the Soviet Union, with its forged closing of "Yours for a Soviet America," were widely circulated to indict Reuther as a Communist. Ignoring no opportunity to score a point, no matter how farfetched, AFL unionists insinuated that UAW-CIO campaign buttons disclosed the Communist leanings of CIO leaders by displaying a tiny American flag with only twenty stars, precisely the number of republics then in the U.S.S.R. "F-L-A-S-H!" a mimeographed handout read, "20 states in Bolshevick Russia. . . . 20 Stars in the flag on the John L. Lewis CIO booster buttons. . . . WHY?" An International representative from Flint told Reuther that some members were removing the buttons and urged him to have the "right amount of stars put on the flag in any future orders."[45]

Reuther launched a vigorous counterattack, with speeches at mass meetings in all the major auto centers. He emphasized the new commitment of the UAW and its General Motors Department to a democratic structure and procedures, with worker representation in all phases of bargaining and the positive benefits that would flow from a single, united organization of all auto workers. Stoutly denying Martin's charge that he was or had been a Communist, he "unreservedly" condemned the European Nazi and Communist dictatorships "as alike as peas in a pod." Throughout the campaign he kept "hammering away that the CIO is American," no foreign import but a legitimate, homegrown expression of workers' legal and moral right to act collectively.[46]

As election day, April 17, 1940, approached, the UAW-CIO was confident of a successful outcome. The president of Local 659 in Flint reported that odds of three-to-one were being offered that Fisher Number 1, once a Martin stronghold, would go CIO by a big margin and "there are no takers. . . . A.F.L. money in this town is very scarce." He asked a correspondent in Baltimore, where Martin had supporters in a GM plant, to put him in touch with anyone willing to bet on an AFL victory in the Flint Fisher plant.

"We don't want chicken feed," he warned, "but if they can produce a reasonable sum we will gladly take care of them with a smile."[47]

The results fully vindicated this optimism. Initially the UAW had petitioned the National Labor Relations Board to hold a single election covering all General Motors plants, but the board decided that each plant should vote as a separate unit. Workers in fifty-five GM plants participated in the vote, the largest exercise in formal industrial democracy ever conducted by the National Labor Relations Board. In all, 128,957 General Motors workers, 94 percent of those eligible in the affected plants, cast ballots. The UAW-CIO received 84,024; the UAW-AFL 25,911; 13,919 were cast for neither; and the small remainder went to other organizations or were invalid. The majorities for the UAW-CIO in "all of the large and key plants" were, the union claimed, "staggering and decisive," with forty-four of the fifty-five plants voting overwhelmingly for the UAW-CIO. In Flint, however, where southerners and other rural migrants formed a major component of the work force, Martin's UAW-AFL garnered a significant if minority share. Since the UAW had previously been charged by the press and the corporations with obtaining representation rights only through coercive strikes—with the implication that most workers would not favor a union if given an unfettered choice—it was important to demonstrate that in a democratic election whose integrity was never challenged two-thirds of General Motors workers chose representation by the UAW-CIO. The democratic decision gave the union a legitimacy and standing it had not previously enjoyed. In the next few weeks run-off elections and votes in additional plants added to the UAW-CIO's total representation. By June the UAW-CIO had sole collective bargaining agreements in sixty GM plants, with more than 130,000 workers. In those plants the UAW became the exclusive bargaining agent for all employees, although there was then no union shop agreement requiring that all employees be members. A few GM plants, small and on the industry's periphery, remained outside for a time, with the last UAW-AFL represented GM plant, a small facility in Meriden, Connecticut, voting to join the UAW-CIO in 1945. As GM through the years brought new plants into production, representation elections were held in each to determine the bargaining agent. Until the 1970s—when GM adopted, in the union's phrase, a "southern strategy" of new plant location—a vote in favor of UAW representation was routine.[48]

The immediate gain for GM workers was a new contract, negotiated in a few weeks, in contrast to the drawn out, stalemated negotiations that were the previous rule, and the first general contract with GM obtained without a strike. It included wage increases and a fund to equalize wages for similar work in different plants, a provision protecting seniority for twenty-four months in event of layoff, and a week's vacation with pay for most GM workers. Although the sum of new money in the contract was not large, the wage equalization feature represented a significant breach of GM's position that wages in its plants should reflect local labor market conditions. The contract provisions also contributed to "wage compression," that is, the wages of the lowest paid increased at a higher rate than the rate received by the best paid. The monetary benefit of industrial unionism would disproportionately go to the lowest paid workers, creating greater wage uniformity across the range of industrial occupations, in different company plants, and across regions. "Equal pay for equal work!" was an auto workers' slogan that would require many years to achieve, and gender discrimination in wages was exceedingly difficult to root out, but wage differentials among production workers at GM and elsewhere in the unionized workforce shrank over time.[49]

The new contract's shop floor provisions brought a measure of stability to plant labor relations after three years of turmoil. General Motors was determined to allow no further encroachment on its managerial prerogatives, its right to run the business. At the corporation's insistence, the contract included a management's rights section maintaining the corporation's right to hire, fire, promote, discipline, and discharge workers, as well as to determine the product, decide the location of plants, and set production schedules for the company's different models, all as the "sole responsibility of the corporation." The company agreed to an increase in the number of plant committeemen and to some other provisions that improved and expedited the presentation of grievances, but it cut shop stewards, where they were present, further out of the grievance process. The only formal function allowed GM stewards henceforth was dues collection, although stewards informally continued to be present and to exercise a limited role in some GM plants. The new contract effectively precluded the possibility of substantial workers' shop floor control. In contrast, at Chrysler, a less determined adversary than GM, workers maintained a shop steward system for many years. As the last step in grievance resolution, the GM contract, drawing on procedures pioneered in the garment industry, established an outside, third-person, mutually acceptable, impartial umpire, whose decision would be final, the first instance of binding, permanent arbitration in heavy industry. Decisions would finally be rendered on grievances. Eventually enforcement of contract provisions through the grievance procedure produced a body of "case law" in arbitration rulings that brought some of the protections of civil society to workers on the shop floor and enlisted union officials among the enforcers of this law. Binding arbitration was extended to Ford and Chrysler in 1943 at the prompting of the War Labor Board. Although Reuther and other defenders of the revamped grievance procedure at GM hoped it would lead to joint determination on a wide range of issues concerning working conditions, GM management successfully resisted expansion of the contract into areas of managerial control.[50]

Some GM workers, particularly in Flint, were loath to forego the wildcat strike as the direct and quick route to settling grievances. The formal grievance procedure often moved slowly, frustrating workers victimized by shop floor injustices for which they wanted immediate redress. But wildcats posed serious risks. They eliminated one of the few incentives that management had for accepting the union's presence, making its long-term survival and effectiveness more doubtful. As contract violations, wildcats posed the threat of adverse legal judgments against the union, with possibly crippling financial results. Even more serious were the potentially harmful effects on worker solidarity and union commitment. Given the integrated production operations within a company, a wildcat strike in one plant or department could idle thousands of workers elsewhere who lacked a vital interest in the particular grievance that provoked the strike. Wildcats put the majority of the workers at the mercy of a minority and, if used frequently, threatened to divide the membership against itself. UAW leaders recognized that the union must aggressively present and pursue grievances, particularly over production standards—especially the "speedup"—or lose the support of the rank and file who would, as Reuther warned, be drawn to "measures of resistance such [as] . . . slowdowns and kindred weapons [which] would result in the wrecking of the union." Strike authorizations could legally be issued by the International Union in cases of unilaterally imposed changes in production standards. The disciplined, strategic application of the union's power in coordinated strikes offered the most hopeful strategy for achieving shop floor fairness and economic security. By 1939 wildcats occurred only infrequently, although in the very different circumstances of World War II they reemerged with a vengeance.[51]

THE UAW's GAINS AT General Motors were matched by its recovery at other firms. The progress the union made in the year between the conclusion of the Cleveland convention and the negotiation of the new contract with GM compared favorably with any similar period in its history and vindicated the course set at that convention as well as the struggle to displace Homer Martin. The UAW-CIO had won all major NLRB elections by landslide votes and thereby confirmed the auto workers' commitment to a single independent, industrial union. It had reestablished enforcement of its existing 321 contracts and signed new contracts covering 327 additional companies or plants. With the economy finally and fully emerging from a depression that had lasted a decade, virtually all contracts, new and renegotiated, were significantly better than the arrangements they replaced. UAW contracts now covered 412,352 workers. Only 13 percent of the contracts provided the local union the security of a union shop, in which union membership was required to maintain employment, and nearly all the union shop agreements were with small, specialized parts firms with relatively few, often highly skilled, employees. The first union shop contract with a car manufacturing firm was negotiated in December 1940 with the Hudson Motor Company. Paid-up memberships, based on per capita payments from locals to the International Union, were at their highest point ever, 294,428 (May 1940), an increase of 93 percent over the May 1939 total of 152,385. If those exonerated of dues payments for unemployment or other reasons are included, the membership in May 1940 was approximately 382,000. The UAW emerged from its time of troubles with a revitalized spirit and renewed confidence, the largest union in the CIO and the second largest in the entire labor movement.[52]

By the end of the depression decade, growing union membership figures alone were insufficient to express the progress auto workers had made. Across a range of rewards and burdens, the conditions of auto labor were improved for those who supplied it. Hours of work on average had been substantially reduced, a reflection of changing economic conditions and government regulation as well as union pressure. Prior to the depression, the New Deal, and unionization, about fifty-four hours constituted the average workweek while sixty or more were not uncommon during rush periods. By the end of the decade, the five-day, forty-hour week was standard. Auto workers now typically enjoyed a two-day weekend with leisure hours at the end of each working day. Although a thirty-hour workweek had been advanced as one of the union's major objectives, it had not been seriously pursued. Premium pay for excess daily or weekly hours of work was now an established principle in federal law and in many union contracts. Hours reductions in contracts were gained only over considerable management opposition.[53]

Average hourly earnings in the industry rose from a depression low of 55 cents in 1933 to over 90 cents by 1939. The result of several factors, including the improved profitability of the companies as the depression eased and the impact of government minimum wage-setting in the National Industrial Recovery Act and the Fair Labor Standards Act, the increase was also in part the result of union pressure both as companies sought to forestall unionization by granting increases and as increases were negotiated once recognition was achieved. Average annual earnings, in most respects a more revealing figure than hourly rates since they reflect the fluctuations in earnings due to seasonal layoffs, show the progress that occurred as unionization went forward, but they also demonstrate that income insecurity was still an acute problem. For car model years from September to August, average annual earnings were as follows:

1933–34	$749
1934–35	$1014
1935–36	$1294
1936–37	$1399
1937–38	$906
1938–39	$1328[54]

Several wage differentials affected the earnings of particular classes of employees. The job differential saw companies paying about 75 percent more than the lowest rate to the most highly skilled employees. An experience differential gave long-term employees a higher rate than the recently hired. A gender differential between male and female employees amounted on average to about a 10-cents-an-hour lower minimum rate for women. Although this was less of a difference than had existed prior to unionization, a contemporary study noted that "sex differentials are firmly established in the industry." Shift differentials, sought by the union and included in many contracts, rewarded employees working on nighttime second and third shifts, considered more disruptive than day shifts of normal life patterns. Geographical differentials caused wage rates to vary greatly from one region to another, with southeastern Michigan sporting the highest rates, followed by other midwestern locations, then the East and West coasts, and finally the South. Regional variations existed in plants owned by the same company, as well as in plants owned by different companies. A demographic differential reflected the population size of the urban area in which a plant was located, with rates generally higher in densely populated areas. With the exception of the job, experience, and shift differentials, all differentials were officially opposed by the union, but it failed to eliminate them, and progress in reducing the spread was slow. More was accomplished in reducing the use of piece rates, with many jobs formerly paid by the number of pieces produced shifted to hourly rates. Piece rates remained, however, a common practice in parts plants. An important argument against piece rates was the charge that the speed of operations could be set unreasonably high with threats to the well-being and health of employees.[55]

In addition to better pay and fewer hours, the quality of work life had improved. Despite company resistance, union workers had begun to shape a body of shop rules affecting, and in some respects governing, shop floor relations. Job classifications, rights of transfer and promotion, reliance on seniority in layoff and recall, production standards, protection against arbitrary discharge and other disciplinary penalties, and safety and health protections were transformed into subjects of bargaining between worker representatives and management. Committeemen and stewards were paid, on company time, to collect and present the grievances of those they represented. At Chrysler the 1939 strike settlement conferred super-seniority on stewards (as long as there was a job in the department, the steward would have it) and guaranteed their right to move about the plant in performance of their duties without loss of pay. To Nick DiGaetano, a Local 7 officer and chief steward at Chrysler, whose industry employment went back to the 1920s, the union's contractual grievance procedure had a profound impact on shop floor relationships. Now a worker could "talk to the foreman on an equal basis." The factory hand of his generation had changed from a "plain, humble submissive creature into a man. The union made a man out of him. . . . I am not talking about the benefits . . . or the rights gained by the union. I am talking about the working conditions and how they affected the men in the plant. . . . Before they were submissive. Now they are men." This reorganization under the union's auspices significantly humanized a hostile industrial environment and, as one historian has written, restored to workers "a self-respect that had been stripped from them in . . . the Great Depression."[56]

While no one would claim that the factory floor had become a paradise of fair ethnic, racial, and gender treatment, the power balance had shifted sufficiently in the workers' favor to afford some protection to those previously subjected to the worst abuses. When a workers' education instructor asked a young woman striker at Midland Steel why she had joined the union, expecting her to cite better wages as the reason, she responded: "When you belong to a union, the foreman can't screw you. Last month my foreman asked me to go out with him. I told him 'to hell with you, Charlie, I know what you want.' He got mad, but he didn't try to spite me. He knew damn well the union would be on his neck if he did.' "[57]

THE UAW'S REMAINING MAJOR TASK was the organization of workers at the Ford Motor Company, where earlier campaigns had accomplished little, despite the efforts of an underground movement in which radicals and other activists had risked and sometimes lost their jobs. At each UAW convention, delegates mulled over the reasons for their failure to organize Ford and vowed to do better, only to fall short again. The Ford company, still under the elderly Henry Ford's control, and still relying on Harry Bennett and his Service Department to keep the union at bay, had maintained intact its apparatus of internal surveillance and discipline, firing union activists without restraint. Dave Moore, a black unionist, "was caught with UAW literature inside [his] shirt. . . . I got the hell beat out of me. . . . They said, 'Nigger, if you ever be caught around the Ford Motor Company again, we'll

Billboard advertisement for the Ford organizing drive, 1941. Walter P. Reuther
Library, Wayne State University

kill you.' And they got me to the gate." Despite the persecutions and
threats, organizing activities went forward. Stacks of union leaflets and
handbills placed on the conveyor lines wound their way through the plant.
Union advocates, touring the showplace River Rouge factory, flashed signs
and buttons at Ford workers with the message "Get Wise— Organize!" So
far Ford had gotten away with violations of labor laws despite attempts by
workers to recover their jobs and back pay through lawsuits and complaints
brought to the National Labor Relations Board. While Ford operated assembly plants in outlying locations, its production facilities were still centered
in the giant River Rouge complex in suburban Dearborn, Michigan, which
employed on average 85,000 workers in 1941.[58]

The UAW's final assault on Ford began in the fall of 1940. According
to Ford employee Ken Bannon, a Reuther adherent and no friend of the CP,
"the best organizers were members of the Communist Party," such as Bill
McKie, Ed Lock, Johnny Gallo, and Paul Boatin, although non-Communists
like Norman Smith, Percy Llewellyn, and Shelton Tappes made essential
contributions. At least half of the Rouge workers were either African American or first- and second-generation immigrants. Second-generation immigrants (Italian, Polish, Ukrainian, and so on) were among the most active
organizers while the least active elements were found among African Americans and those whites with an American ancestry of several generations.

By this time workers had won some favorable decisions before the NLRB and the courts. With its recent victories over GM, Chrysler, and Homer Martin, the union was battle-tested, stronger and more united than ever. Still, rivalries among the claimants to leadership, fueled by the allure of being the successful organizer of Ford, were potentially so disruptive that the CIO sent in a veteran United Mine Workers organizer, Michael F. Widman, to head the drive. Widman was supplied with $100,000 (jointly furnished by the UAW and the CIO) and a staff of fifty-four organizers. A Dearborn judge held that a local ordinance prohibiting distribution of leaflets in congested areas—that is, the gates of the Ford Motor Company during shift changes—was unconstitutional. Leafleting resumed, and 50,000 copies of *Ford Facts*, a UAW publication, were handed out biweekly. Organizers went from door to door in Detroit to locate and talk with Ford employees. The thrust of the union's attack was directed against the Ford system of autocratic discipline and its supervisory favoritism. With a UAW contract, the leaflets read, "the foreman can't set up a patronage system so that the boys who buy him drinks get to work and the boys that won't lick his boots get laid off." By the end of 1940, 14,000 emboldened Ford workers had joined the UAW, which petitioned the NLRB for representation elections at the Rouge and Lincoln plants. The company, through Harry Bennett, discussed grievances over minor issues with union representatives while still refusing to acknowledge formally the union's presence, and Bennett boasted that should the UAW triumph in a "farcical" NLRB election, Ford would "bargain until Hell freezes over, but they won't get anything."[59]

Ford's 10,000 African American workers, constituting about 12 percent of the Rouge workforce, posed critical questions should a strike occur. The Ford plants, where foremen commonly used racial epithets and swore at the workers they supervised, were far from being racially harmonious, but the company was the only major automaker to provide large numbers of jobs for blacks. Most worked in dirty, dead-end jobs in the foundry or as janitors or materials handlers, but there were limited opportunities for employment in production work, parts manufacturing, and even skilled work. Ford provided financial support for Detroit's black churches and used them to recruit its black labor force. Critics said these moves were cynical and exploitative, designed to assemble an amenable workforce and undercut a union's appeal. Nevertheless, the black community, facing discrimination and rejection elsewhere, could see that Ford was doing more for its people than any other employer. The UAW constitution forbade racial discrimination, and UAW leaders often proclaimed the union's commitment to racial equality, but many black workers, aware of a history of antiblack actions and racist policies in some labor organizations, were unconvinced. A cadre of dedicated black unionists, including men such as foundry

Headquarters of the Lincoln Division organizing committee, 1941. Walter P. Reuther Library, Wayne State University

employee Shelton Tappes, worked tirelessly through meetings and other contacts to convince their fellows that the UAW would not countenance racial discrimination, but the distrust of unions generally, reinforced by incidents of racial discrimination at some UAW local unions' social events, was so deep that only a few responded. In fact, Tappes was sometimes physically threatened by other black workers, loyal to Ford, when he approached them about joining the union.[60]

Blacks had taken little part in the sit-downs, with only a handful involved in Flint. In most cases, when a sit-down occurred, black workers left the plants and awaited the outcome, with some fearful that a union victory would confirm or even worsen discrimination. In Detroit, most black community leaders, skeptical of the union's claims, were prepared to stand by their traditional friendliness toward the Ford Motor Company. When the UAW's first campaign at Ford began in the spring of 1937 both sides bolstered their ranks. The International Union hired blacks as representatives, the first being Paul Kirk, a crane operator at the Michigan Steel Casting Company. By summer there were six on the International staff, three full-time and three part-time, including Walter Hardin, William Nowell, and

UAW black organizers at Ford. *Left to right*: Joseph Billups, Walter Hardin, Chris Alston, Veal Clough, Clarence Bowman, Leon Bates, John Conyers, Sr. Walter P. Reuther Library, Wayne State University

Strikebreakers protected by Detroit police march through Chrysler workers' picket line, 1939. Walter P. Reuther Library, Wayne State University

Frank Evans. Several had affiliations with the Communist Party and the old Auto Workers Union. Ford, for its part, added (for the first time) black employees to its Service Department. Some were ordered into action in the infamous "Battle of the Overpass" to beat up unionists, although nearly all of the Service Department personnel in that fray were white.[61]

Racial relations in the Motor City, always tense, had been strained by the attempt of the Chrysler Corporation to use blacks as strikebreakers in 1939. As employer of the second largest number of blacks in Detroit, Chrysler had a relatively favorable standing with the black community, although it had not provided anything like the numbers or the diversity of jobs available at Ford. With the Chrysler plants shut down and surrounded by thousands of white pickets, the company played the race card by recruiting a few hundred black workers to join in a back-to-work movement. Since they alone were clearly insufficient to resume production, Chrysler's apparent objective was to provoke a riot that would lead to police and National Guard intervention and a reopening of the plants. Over a thousand Detroit police were on hand to make the anticipated arrests and break the strike.

Black Ford strikers battle servicemen at the River Rouge Plant, 1941. Walter P. Reuther Library, Wayne State University

On two occasions two hundred workers, nearly all blacks, passed through picket lines, harassed by over six thousand jeering whites, but the pickets refused to accommodate the company's strategy by using force to block their access. Although a handful were hurt in a riot at the plant gates, massive violence was averted due to the restraint shown by the UAW pickets, who were fully aware of the possibility of intervention by police and state armed forces. With the failure of the "back to work movement," the strike was settled within a few days.[62]

Encouraged perhaps by opinion polls that suggested public approval of Ford's labor policies by a two-to-one margin, Bennett precipitated a strike on April 1, 1941, by firing the members of one of the Rouge grievance committees. Without authorization from union headquarters, workers quickly shut down several departments. In short order, over 50,000 stopped work. UAW leaders ordered the rest of the workforce out of the plants and set up picket lines, the first time a Ford plant in metropolitan Detroit was closed by a strike. Barricades of unionists' cars blocked access. Although some of Ford's black workers joined the strike, at least several hundred remained inside the plant and, along with a larger number of whites (including some

Union pickets attack a Ford serviceman, 1941. This photograph, originally printed in the *Detroit News,* won the first Pulitzer Prize awarded for photography, 1942. Walter P. Reuther Library, Wayne State University

skilled workers), occasionally sallied out to attack the pickets. Beatings occurred on both sides. The UAW responded quickly, mobilizing local and national black leaders, including Walter F. White, secretary of the National Association for the Advancement of Colored People, in support of the strike. Bennett's back-to-work movement collapsed and many of the blacks still inside the plant left. The strike became totally effective and the union's relationship with Detroit's black community took a favorable turn.[63]

The recently elected governor of Michigan, Democrat Murray D. Van Wagoner, entered as mediator and brought about an end to the strike on April 10, with an agreement to restore the discharged workers to their jobs and reinstate the grievance procedure. The two sides promised to hasten an NLRB representation election. Encouraged by Bennett, the AFL offered last minute competition by chartering a federal union and applying for a place on the ballot. The UAW-CIO's massive campaign culminated in a rally of more than 60,000 in Detroit's Cadillac Square, featuring an appearance by the black actor, singer, and All American athlete Paul Robeson, who sang "Ballad for Americans" and appealed to his fellows to vote CIO. The election produced stunning results. At the Rouge, 51,886 workers (70 percent)

Wives and other women support the Ford strikers, 1941. Walter P. Reuther Library, Wayne State University

voted for the UAW-CIO; 20,364 (27 percent) for the UAW-AFL; and only 1,958 (3 percent) for no union. At Ford's Lincoln plant, 2,008 voted for the UAW-CIO, 587 for the AFL, and 146 for no union. The minuscule "no union" vote was, according to Ford's production chief, Charles E. Sorensen, "perhaps the greatest disappointment [Henry Ford] had in all his business experience. . . . He never was the same after that." Local 600, destined to be for years the largest and one of the most influential in the UAW, emerged from underground at the Rouge. With the results at other Ford plants equally decisive, the NLRB certified the UAW-CIO as bargaining agent for Ford employees.[64]

In negotiating its first contract, Ford was on the defensive. Scheduled NLRB hearings on charges of unfair labor practices threatened to reveal a sordid story of company brutality and racketeering. Hoping to head off the investigation, Ford moved quickly toward a settlement that gave the UAW far more than it had obtained from any other major manufacturer. Ford granted a union shop, requiring all new employees to join the union, and a dues checkoff, important security measures that the union had hardly dared to hope for from one of the Big Three. The Ford Service Department was disbanded and plant protection employees required to wear uniforms and badges. Ford agreed to pay wages equal to those of any competitor the union might choose (the UAW chose GM for production workers) and granted favorable overtime, holiday, seniority, and grievance provisions. Over 4,000 fired Ford workers were rehired with back pay, and the UAW agreed to drop or settle out of court all cases pending against the company for its unfair labor practices and for personal assaults. At the Highland Park and Lincoln plants the union won smoking privileges in designated areas, breaking down a Ford taboo of many years standing.[65]

Immediately a new spirit of worker empowerment spread through the Rouge. To Dave Moore, unionization produced a "100 percent turnaround. [Workers] were more defiant to their supervisors. They had their say so. [If someone] involved in an argument [with] the foreman disagreed with the supervisor, everybody in that department would stop work and come to [his] defense." Wildcat strikes and other labor disturbances disrupted production almost daily in Ford plants for the remainder of the year, and several hundred work stoppages at Ford's, many provoked by Harry Bennett's abusive tactics, occurred during the war years.[66]

An important strike result for the UAW's, the industry's, and even the nation's future was the entry of 10,000 black Ford workers into the union, by far the largest contingent of blacks to join to that time. Before the Ford strike there were a few black auto unionists, concentrated in locals at Midland Steel, Bohn Aluminum in Detroit, and elsewhere. After the strike the numerous and active black membership in Local 600 transformed the

Signing the agreement ending the Ford strike, 1941. *Seated from left to right:* CIO President Philip Murray, Ford Service Department chief Harry Bennett, UAW President R. J. Thomas, and UAW Secretary-Treasurer George Addes. Walter P. Reuther Library, Wayne State University

scene. Its black officers over the years—Shelton Tappes, Horace Sheffield, Robert Battle III, Marcellius Ivory, and others—played important roles in the local, the International Union, and in public and political affairs. Employment opportunities for blacks within the plants and civil rights questions within the union and society at large were brought forward on the union's agenda as a consequence of their presence. Coming at the outset of the great wartime expansion of production and employment, the creation of an interracial union membership helped to hold in check some portion of the destructive forces of racial animosity that wartime conditions unleashed.

The union's victory in the strike and in the NLRB election was almost more than the elderly Henry Ford, long an international idol and accustomed to having his way, could bear. Charles E. Sorensen later reported that Ford reacted to the terms of the contract with a temper tantrum. Refusing to sign, he shouted: "I don't want any more of this business. Close the plant down if necessary. Let the union take over if it wishes." Something produced a change of heart and Ford eventually signed. By Ford's account, his wife, fearing riots and bloodshed, threatened to leave him unless he accepted the agreement. UAW observers suspected that Ford had been persuaded by Bennett that the union could be infiltrated, subverted, and brought under control. Perhaps the possible threat of a government takeover to maintain military production if Ford closed his plants had some bearing. In any case, the last and most resolute opponent of an auto workers' union among the major manufacturers had been brought into line, ending a long, harrowing campaign and forever changing the working lives of millions.[67]

WITH THE SUCCESSFUL CONCLUSION of the Ford strike and the negotiation of an outstanding contract the UAW had resolved the crises that accompanied its birth: there would be one industrial union for all auto workers. The threat to its existence presented by the Martin split soon faded and disappeared. Although bitter disputes over ideological and political questions remained, the presidency was now in the hands of a down-to-earth, practical, prudent, and loyal unionist, R. J. Thomas. Of equal importance, an experienced and battle-hardened cadre of regional directors and local leaders was in place, and the union was firmly established on the shop floors and in the hearts and minds of its ethnically and racially diverse membership.

CHAPTER 6

"UAW-CIO, makes the army roll and go"

The UAW in World War II, 1941–45

A s World War II advanced toward American shores, a cluster of new pressures and issues insistently washed over the UAW and the auto workers. The nation began to rearm, introduced military conscription in peacetime, and launched the lend-lease program of military aid to Great Britain, pledging, in President Franklin D. Roosevelt's words, that the United States would become the great "arsenal of democracy." The assembly lines and stamping plants in Detroit, Flint, and elsewhere would soon grind out death's instruments in as great abundance as they had once produced cars and trucks. In a "people's war," Walter P. Reuther told delegates to the 1941 CIO convention, workers' actions would carry more force than their leaders' words. "Hitler is not fearful of resolutions," he proclaimed. "The world was resoluting for years while he built up his military machine. . . . We have got to speak, not through microphones but through assembly lines."[1]

War's demands transformed the industry as military production monopolized its vast manufacturing capacity. Except for limited amounts of replacement parts, no cars or auto parts for civilian use were manufactured from 1942 until 1945. After a slow conversion to military production, the industry boomed as it had not in years. It manufactured $29 billion in war materials, including, in addition to all the tanks, trucks, and jeeps, 87 percent of the aircraft bombs, 85 percent of the steel helmets, 75 percent of the aircraft engines, over 12 billion rounds of small arms ammunition, and a host of other products. Comprising the greatest concentration of large-scale, metal-fabricating productive capital, technology, and labor in the world, the industry with its workforce contributed as much as anyone or anything to the Allied victory.[2]

Like the industry, the workforce was transformed. In numbers alone, the change was staggering. More than a quarter of a million UAW members left the factories for the armed forces, their places filled by new hires who were more diverse in gender, race, and age than those they replaced. Women, African Americans, the old and the young filled the vacated places on the assembly lines and at the presses. UAW membership by 1945 had grown to over a million, almost double the prewar peak (with another 250,000–300,000 in the armed forces, still, under wartime rules, members in good standing), making the UAW the largest free union in the world. During the course of the war an estimated 350,000 women passed through its ranks, a number exceeded in only one other union, the United Electrical Workers. During the peak years for women's' employment in the industry, the UAW estimated that women constituted between one-fifth and one-fourth of its membership. The UAW's African American membership of more than 100,000 was the largest number in any union in the nation. The labor force in the Detroit metropolitan area more than doubled during the war, and other auto cities almost equaled that rate of growth. Old and new factories, bursting at the seams, ran day and night. The River Rouge complex employed over 90,000, and Ford's massive, new Willow Run bomber plant in suburban Ypsilanti, Michigan, built with government funds on Detroit's outskirts to produce B-24's, employed as many as 47,000. The turnover in union membership was unprecedented. By the war's end fewer than half of the union's members were veterans of the formative prewar struggles and strikes.[3]

In a reprise of the union's earlier experience, the majority of new employees, whether recruited from midwestern, Appalachian, or southern farms or towns, came from nonunion backgrounds. They had little knowledge of working conditions and wages in the preunion era or of the changes the union had wrought. Investigators at Willow Run, where nearly the entire workforce consisted of new hires, found apathy and negative sentiments toward the union among many workers, some of whom referred to the UAW as an "industrial fifth wheel" or a "gyp organization," with few attending Local 50's meetings or voting in its elections. Union leadership faced the task, not for the first or last time, of convincing a significant portion of the membership of the union's value.[4]

Labor shortages, population migrations, urban and suburban growth, inadequate housing and community services, and social and personal disruptions and tensions—in short, the many stresses that accompanied wartime conditions—contributed to massive currents of unrest among workers as well as the rest of the population. Although a "no-strike pledge" at the war's outset, volunteered by the UAW and other unions, ensured there would be no authorized strikes for the duration, a rash of wildcat strikes in auto and elsewhere interrupted production, expressed workers' dissatisfactions, and perplexed and infuriated government officials, union officers, and much of the public.[5]

The war entangled the union and the workers with an expanding federal government. With only minor exceptions, the government was the industry's only wartime customer. Government-imposed wage controls, rather than collective bargaining, set workers' pay. Officially contracts remained in effect, with grievance procedures intact, but with overburdened government agencies the final arbiter of disputes and the authorized strike weapon in abeyance, long, frustrating delays in resolving grievances became commonplace.[6]

FOREIGN POLICY ISSUES emanating from the war erupted in the summer of 1939, more than two years before the United States became a belligerent. In unions as politically sensitive as the UAW, these issues were quickly reflected in their internal debates and controversies. Only a few days before the German invasion of Poland on September 1, Nazi Germany and the Soviet Union agreed to a nonaggression pact. News of the pact caused a crisis within the American left. To all but the most committed Communists and Soviet sympathizers the pact seemed a cynical betrayal of the Popular Front against Nazism, a sin compounded when the U.S.S.R., soon after Germany invaded Poland from the west, expanded its empire by seizing the eastern half of Poland, annexing the Baltic republics, and invading Finland. Whatever justifications might be offered in behalf of a Soviet security strategy, the proletarian fatherland had joined with its bitter ideological enemy in a course of aggression: an aggression aimed in large part at the ancestral homeland of the many Polish-American auto workers. Anticommunism, as a cause, received powerful reinforcement within their ranks. Although these developments had little immediate impact on the union's economic objectives, they raised pressing questions for elements of the rank and file and for the upper echelons of union leadership.[7]

Within the UAW and in other unions and Popular Front organizations, the overseas crisis eroded the ideological and political standing of the Communists and their close allies. For nearly two years, from August 1939 until the German invasion of the U.S.S.R. on June 22, 1941, the Soviet Union's cooperation with Germany and acquiescence in its conquests was in conflict with President Roosevelt's program of American rearmament and resistance to Nazi aggression. As the CPUSA lined up in support of Soviet policy, the toleration of the American public (including many auto workers) for the party contracted. An important step in the isolation of the American Communists and their exclusion from political life was taken in 1939, years before the onset of the cold war.[8]

A conflict with the national interest as it was proclaimed and championed by President Roosevelt was only part of the explanation for the erosion of the Communists' position in the UAW. By the beginning of the wartime era the union had entered a new phase: it was now a going concern, its position in the industry more secure and the leadership crisis surrounding Homer Martin behind it. Consequently, there was less need for the pioneering services in organizing and mobilizing autoworker strength that the shock-troop Communists had once supplied. An educational process had been launched and largely completed. Whereas initially few auto workers were knowledgeable about unions or skillful or experienced in organizational matters (a vacuum once filled by Communists and other radicals), now many were trained and eager to take part in the union's operations. Building a lasting organization had become the union's major task. Realistically, in a society and culture that counted patriotism, political democracy, capitalism, consumer choice, material abundance, and individual opportunity among its core values, the presence of a visible, Soviet-supportive Communist contingent in the UAW was far more a liability than an asset for the organization.

Walter Reuther, now the Communists' principal UAW antagonist, exploited their vulnerability in a series of attacks. At the union's St. Louis convention in August 1940, its first since the signing of the Nazi-Soviet pact, Reuther isolated the Communists, exposed their lack of support, and embarrassed their allies. Among the delegates (as among millions of Americans) fears had been aroused and feelings inflamed by a string of spectacular and terrifying German victories that brought continental western Europe under Hitler's control, leaving an embattled Great Britain as his lone opponent. The convention debate opened with a resolution introduced and championed by the Reuther forces that condemned "the brutal dictatorships, and wars of aggression of the totalitarian governments of Germany, Italy, Russia and Japan." Such "Commu-Nazi" resolutions, equating and equally condemning Communist and Nazi dictatorships, were adopted by dozens of liberal organizations and unions in the aftermath of the Nazi-Soviet pact as the left's Popular Front strategy of the 1930s went down in flames. Some organizations, the American Civil Liberties Union among them, went beyond denunciation to exclude Communists from their offices and governing committees. John Anderson and Nat Ganley, officers of Local 155 and Communist Party spokesmen on the convention floor, charged that the resolution was motivated by union politics, sneered at Reuther as a renegade who had sung Russia's praises only a few years before, and denied that the Soviet Union was a dictatorship of the same ugly character as the others. Ganley assured the delegates that "first hand observation in Russia showed that it was not a totalitarian nation," an assertion greeted, like much of Ganley's Soviet apologia, with choruses of "boos."[9]

Testifying to the strength of anticommunist sentiment among the delegates, all of the union's top officers, including President R. J. Thomas,

secretary-treasurer George Addes, and board member Richard Frankensteen, supported the antitotalitarian resolution, with Thomas conceding
that his reelection as president hinged on his stand on the issue. Addes and
Frankensteen, allied with the Communist element, gave the resolution a
qualified endorsement, deplored "Red-baiting," and urged the delegates to
direct their attention to the union's many domestic challenges without
worrying excessively about complicated international matters. The resolution on a voice vote "carried by a very large majority"; only about twenty
delegates, far fewer than the number of party members present, voted
against it. Several executive board members with ties to the Communists
"were conveniently in the washroom" when the vote was taken. A second
resolution sought to bar from union office members of organizations
"declared illegal by the government of the United States through constitutional procedures," a test that the Communist Party did not meet. Both resolutions were more symbol than substance, but they nevertheless isolated
the Communists from their usual allies, revealed how fragile their standing within the union had become, and were the most serious public rebukes
they had thus far suffered.[10]

A proposed endorsement of President Roosevelt for reelection divided
the convention along identical lines. Defense of the Nazi-Soviet pact put
the Communists in the worse than awkward position of opposing a president for whom nearly all auto workers felt gratitude and affection. Reuther,
who had already secured adoption by the executive board of a resolution
proclaiming that "President Roosevelt has been the greatest friend of labor
ever to hold the office of president," now sought to put the convention on
record in favor of his reelection. CIO president John L. Lewis's refusal to
endorse Roosevelt, for reasons of his own, gave the Communists a convenient cover for opposing the endorsement. Wyndham Mortimer attacked
the resolution as a "kick in the face" to "the greatest labor leader this or
any other nation has produced"; he announced that he "would not give one
hair of John L. Lewis' bushy eyebrows for all the politicians in both the
Democratic and Republican parties." Reuther ridiculed the Communist
speakers for hiding behind Lewis's skirts and castigated them for their
steadfast defense of shifting Soviet positions. Brandishing a copy of the 1939
convention proceedings, he shouted: "Brother chairman, I wish I had time
to . . . review the beautiful resolutions that Brother Nat Ganley introduced,
praising Roosevelt, because those were the days of collective security and
the People's Front. That is no more; there has been a deal between Stalin
and Hitler, and therefore People's Front and collective security have been
put in the ash can once and for all." Lewis, Reuther added, should continue
to head the CIO while Roosevelt led the nation. The Roosevelt endorsement was approved by a vote of about 550 to 40, a recognition of the fact,

as Victor Reuther noted in a letter to the Socialist Party leader Norman Thomas, that "the auto workers themselves had already endorsed him long before the convention opened." Victor added that the "CP machine," the "greatest stumbling block to the growth of progressive influence in our union," had received "a smashing blow" as a result.[11]

The attack on the Communists produced action as well as rhetoric. In the election of executive board members, the Reuthers and their allies gained enough seats to establish a rough parity with their opponents, allowing them to push through a purge of known Communists from the UAW staff. At the executive board meeting immediately following the convention, about a half dozen were fired, including Bob Travis, a hero of Flint. The communist faction was brought to its lowest point since the union's founding.[12]

A few days before the presidential election, Lewis stunned and dismayed labor by endorsing the Republican Party's presidential candidate, Wendell Wilkie, and threatening to resign as CIO president if Roosevelt were reelected. The UAW promptly rallied to FDR's support in its first open break with CIO leadership, demonstrating its growing strength, independence, and maturity. Officers took to the airwaves to repudiate Lewis and urge the rank and file to stand firmly behind FDR. In a radio broadcast, Reuther predicted that "the personal spite or the hatred of one man" would not switch labor's vote from Roosevelt. "The issue is wholly and simply: Roosevelt or reaction! American labor," he predicted, "will take Roosevelt!" And it did. Sustained by a tidal wave of votes in labor strongholds, FDR swept to victory and a third term.[13]

In December 1940, believing that auto industry management was failing to meet its responsibility to contribute to military preparedness, Reuther conceived a bold plan for the industry's conversion to military production. Following a survey of auto plants, he devised and advanced a proposal to build "500 Planes a Day," using the industry's idle capacity—which amounted, he estimated, to 50 percent of its total. Eager to lay the plan before the highest authorities, he persuaded the new CIO president Philip Murray, who supported the plan's general approach, to present it to Roosevelt. The president turned it over to his new economic mobilization agency, the Office of Production Management (OPM), headed by General Motors' former production chief William S. Knudsen, with Sidney Hillman, the CIO's troubleshooter, second in command. A talented publicist, Reuther launched a campaign to build public interest and support. The union circulated thousands of copies of the plan, with its eye-catching title, "500 Planes a Day"—an astonishing goal when contrasted with the average of twelve military aircraft produced daily in 1940. Prominent columnists commented favorably. A meeting of cabinet officers and other administration officials was arranged. Henry Morganthau, secretary of the treasury, was impressed and urged the president to order a full study of the plan, but he warned, "There is only one thing wrong with the proposal. It comes from the 'wrong' source."[14]

Aircraft manufacturers, auto management, and Knudsen, who referred to Reuther during their confrontation in the 1939 tool and die strike as a would-be "commissar," were all opposed. Automobile mass production methods could not be adapted, they argued, to the precision requirements of aircraft manufacture. The Reuther plan, they said, would require production of a single model, with no allowance for modifications as suggested by experience. One of the key questions was whether auto industry machine tools could be employed in making aircraft parts. Knudsen doubted that they could, although after Pearl Harbor brought a new urgency to American rearmament, most automotive machine tools found their way into war production of one kind or another. Bedrock ideological opposition was generated by Reuther's suggestion that an aviation production board, "with representatives of labor as well as government and business," be created with "full authority to organize and supervise the mass production of airplanes." This takeover of private managerial functions by a tripartite, publicly constituted body was Reuther's first widely publicized, concrete proposal for an industrial decision-making and planning apparatus incorporating union representatives at the highest levels. If implemented, the proposal would have brought a labor voice to bear in such key decisions as employment levels, allocation of materials, investments in machines, new plants and other facilities, and so on, across the whole range of economic planning and coordination for a major and expanding segment of the economy. The proposal also would have positioned the UAW firmly in the aircraft industry. The plan constituted, as a historian later wrote, "a genuine proposal for basic change." As on later occasions when Reuther put forward similar proposals, the opposition prevailed and the plan was laid aside, but the UAW's willingness to cooperate in meeting national security needs had been demonstrated. Reuther's reputation as the labor movement's bright, though controversial, young man dated from this episode. It brought him into contact with a circle of Washington New Deal liberals, including Mrs. Eleanor Roosevelt, with whom he remained friends for the rest of her life.[15]

THE PREWAR PROGRAM of military rearmament that the president and Congress launched raised the ticklish question of the legitimacy of strikes against companies with contracts for arms production. Could a union, in effect, strike against the government in a time of national emergency? The issue was critical for the UAW because many of its members were or soon would be engaged in war-related work. With the Communist Party opposed to American military preparedness from 1939 to 1941, the ground was prepared both for internal strife and a clash with the federal government itself. A dispute at the Allis-Chalmers Company in suburban Milwaukee—where UAW Local 248, a vigorous, militant local with a leftist leadership, squared off against the management—first posed the issue. To the local, the issue in the strike was union security. Fearing that the company intended to wreck the local by recognizing AFL craft unions among its skilled workers, the local struck for a union shop. The Allis-Chalmers management, pointing to government contracts for Navy turbines that formed a small part of its business, blamed the strike on the local leadership's support for Soviet foreign policy, assailed the union's lack of patriotism, and started a back-to-work movement. The company's position received much newspaper and congressional support. The strike went on for seventy-six days before government pressure to reopen the plant led to a bloody confrontation at the factory's gates. Local and state police tried to protect a few hundred workers, out of a labor force of thousands, who wanted to return to their jobs. The strike was ended by a government-imposed compromise that gave the local a watered-down union shop in return for a promise from the union's officers that there would be no authorized strikes, a settlement that foreshadowed the federal government's wartime labor policy.[16]

The strike issue came to a crisis in the aircraft industry, where the UAW faced a massive organizing challenge and the government was eager to expand production of military planes. The UAW's CIO charter authorized it to organize aircraft workers, the jurisdiction granted on the proposition that a single union should organize all those who produced anything powered by an internal combustion engine whether on the ground or in the air. Preoccupied with its central task of organizing auto workers, the union had made little effort in aircraft in its early years. At the 1939 convention, plans for an organizing campaign were approved. Wyndham Mortimer, dismissed as a vice president, was dispatched to California with Henry Kraus to take charge of aircraft organizing, in cooperation with Lew Michener, the West Coast regional director, who was also closely tied to the Communist Party. The party was well-represented in the leadership of several West Coast locals throughout the World War II era. With 150,000 poorly paid aircraft workers (receiving about 50 cents per hour for jobs that in unionized auto plants paid 75 cents), and with the prospect of many thousands more as military aircraft production expanded, the UAW anticipated an enthusiastic response. Its AFL rival for the allegiance of West Coast aircraft workers, the International Association of Machinists (IAM), was favored by the manufacturers and already had agreements with Consolidated, Lockheed, and Boeing. In the East, the UAW moved quickly to organize and gain contracts at Bell Aircraft in Buffalo, New York, Lycoming in Williamsport, Pennsylvania, and Brewster Aeronautical in Long Island City, New York—all plants that would undergo great wartime expansion. As UAW aircraft organizing continued during the war, aircraft workers became the union's second largest cohort after auto workers, themselves soon engaged in military production. UAW organized plants came to include Ryan, several Douglas plants (including Long Beach), Martin, Wright Aeronautical, and the Buick and Dodge aircraft engine plants (the latter, the largest aircraft engine plant in the world, made engines for the B-29).[17]

Mortimer launched the UAW's western campaign with a weekly paper, the *Aircraft Organizer*, distributed to workers in the major southern California plants: Vultee, North American, Douglas, Lockheed, Ryan, and Consolidated. The first target was Vultee, which had many women employees. Although they lacked union experience, many embraced the union cause and served as committeewomen, stewards, and officers of the local, performing most of the organizational work at Vultee in the early stages. In July 1940 the UAW won at Vultee the first representation election conducted by the National Labor Relations Board in the West Coast aircraft industry. At first the company refused to bargain, but an effective strike in November resulted in a contract with a 20 percent increase in the starting wage (from 50 cents to 62–1/2 cents an hour) and paid vacations. A barrage of press, industry, and government attacks charged that the strike was politically inspired, fomented by Communists to delay American military aircraft production in accord with current Soviet foreign policy aims. Although Communists were active in the local's leadership, there was no evidence that rank-and-file aircraft workers were motivated by politics or ideology. The strike was amply justified on the straightforward economic ground of inferior pay.[18]

Similar charges were brought in June 1941 during the most serious prewar defense industry strike, that at North American Aviation in Inglewood, California, where more than one-fifth of United States military planes were then produced. By this time, Richard Frankensteen had been placed in charge of aircraft organizing, although Mortimer and Michener continued to run the daily operation in California. With the North American workforce at 11,000 and rapidly growing, and the IAM competing for workers' support, much was at stake for the UAW. By a narrow margin the UAW defeated the IAM in an NLRB election and began negotiations with the company, another low-wage aircraft manufacturer, demanding a minimum starting rate of 75 cents an hour for new employees and a 10-cents across-the-board raise for the rest. When talks deadlocked and workers voted overwhelmingly to authorize a strike, the dispute was referred to the National Defense Mediation Board (NDMB), a newly created federal agency with responsibility for averting strikes in defense industries. Frankensteen and

government officials agreed that as long as no strike occurred, a wage settlement would be retroactive—in effect granting a no-strike pledge to be in
place while the NDMB deliberated and attempted to mediate.[19]

The agreement failed to take into account the discontent of the North
American workers and the willingness of the Communist faction to defy
the government and the International Union. Impatient with the slow
grinding of the government bureaucracy's wheels, they launched a wildcat
strike on June 4, 1941, with the unofficial backing of the local's leadership,
in which Communists were well-represented. As had been the case at Vultee, low wages were the strike's justification for the rank and file. Picket
lines of thousands, the largest in California's history, surrounded the huge
plant and turned back police attempts to break them up. Frankensteen
rushed to California hoping to end the strike but was shouted down when,
speaking at an outdoor rally in a bean field, he urged the strikers to return
to work. The strikers had enlisted the services of sympathizers from nearby
Hollywood. Disney studio animation artists with radical leanings, themselves on strike, supplied the North American wildcatters with signs featuring painted cartoons of Frankensteen's head perched atop the bodies of
rats, skunks, and snakes. As he spoke at meetings, hecklers raised the signs
and waved them in his face. Under pressure from the federal government,
the CIO, and the International UAW's leadership, Frankensteen lifted the
local's charter, suspended its negotiating committee, and appointed a new
leadership to run the local. Asking Wyndham Mortimer, "Mort, what is
your position?" and receiving the reply, "Well, I am with the rank and file,"
Frankensteen responded, "You sure are because you just got canned; you are
no longer on the staff of the UAW," thus terminating Mortimer's UAW connection. With the strike continuing despite these forceful steps to end it,
Washington took the matter out of the union's hands, determined to show
that strikes in key defense plants would not be tolerated. President Roosevelt, outraged that the strike broke an agreement reached by the NDMB
and the union, cited national security concerns and ordered in 2,500 soldiers, who broke up the picket lines and prevented public gatherings within
a mile of the plant—the first use in the twentieth century of federal troops
to break a strike. California draft boards were told to cancel the deferments
of strikers who refused to return to work. The strike ended soon thereafter,
and production resumed. Within a month the NDMB approved a settlement
that gave the workers nearly everything they had sought, including a satisfactory retroactive pay raise.[20]

For the UAW's Communists, the strike was another defeat. Editorial
writers across the country charged the strikers with a lack of patriotism.
"What kind of Americans are these?" the Detroit News wanted to know.
Public opinion, including most union opinion, was unsparing in its attacks

The United States Army ends the strike at North American Aviation, 1941. Walter P. Reuther Library, Wayne State University

on the local's Communist leadership and the political considerations that were assumed to be behind their support for the strike. The firing of Wyndham Mortimer removed the Communists' most prominent and capable figure from the UAW staff. Deserved or not, they got the lion's share of the blame for the strike and for the government's decision to intervene. President R. J. Thomas condemned the strike as the work of a "subversive group" who threatened "the very existence of the CIO and the UAW," and Frankensteen, whose alliance with the left fell apart as a result of the episode, told reporters that "the vicious underhand maneuvering of the Communist party was apparent in the strike" from the beginning. He later charged in a blistering attack at the UAW's 1941 convention that the wildcat strike was engineered by Communists, inside and outside the union, in order to demonstrate their ability to obstruct national defense preparations.[21]

A reverse of a different kind occurred when the Nazi-Soviet alliance collapsed with the German invasion of the Soviet Union on June 22, 1941. Immediately, the Communist left executed a 180 degree u-turn in its foreign policy posture. Having bitterly assailed the Roosevelt administration for its "war-mongering imperialist policy" of rearmament and aid to Great

Britain, the Communist left now urged rapid American military preparation and the immediate extension of lend-lease assistance to a beleaguered
U.S.S.R. Although the Communists were now back on track with the Roosevelt administration and with the sentiments of most auto workers, it
seemed an obvious inference that Soviet needs, not American national
interests, had dictated the sudden shift. Nevertheless, the realignment
served eventually to enhance CP wartime organizing among sympathetic
auto workers since, in addition to its other claims, the party now stood for
an alliance aimed at Allied victory. In the Rouge, already a plant with a
strong Communist presence, CP membership expanded significantly.[22]

The sudden and startling reversal produced embarrassing episodes,
some becoming UAW legends. The leadership of Local 51 at Plymouth's
Lynch Road Detroit plant, which had faithfully supported the Communist
Party's positions through the years, supplied the leading instance. A few
days before the German invasion of Russia, a meeting of the local adopted
a leadership-sponsored resolution condemning the Roosevelt administration for its aid to Great Britain and its rearmament program. The resolution
was forwarded to the Wayne County CIO Council, the local labor body that
took positions on political issues, to be considered and voted upon as a policy statement. Before the Council could meet, the German invasion of the
U.S.S.R. intervened. The local met again and adopted a second resolution
proposed by the leadership. This one, in direct contradiction to the first,
urged the Roosevelt administration to speed up its military preparations
and rush lend-lease assistance to the Soviet Union. The two resolutions
came up together at the next Council meeting. Amid laughter, the presiding officer, Tracy Doll of UAW Local 154, turned to C. G. "Pop" Edelen, the
president of Local 51, and inquired, "OK Pop, which one do you want?" Taking his stand on the current party line, "Pop" indicated his preference for
the local's second resolution. In Victor Reuther's judgment, the incident
was a key event in exposing the "Communist element in the union . . . as
not a force within the union but rather an external force that was trying to
impose its political views."[23]

THE DRAMATIC WARTIME-RELATED EVENTS and issues of 1939–41 were
hotly debated at the UAW's convention in Buffalo, New York, in August
1941. A fragile Reuther-Frankensteen alliance, hastily assembled following
the latter's falling out with the CP over his handling of the North American strike, was expected to control proceedings. In the event, this new combination fell apart before the convention ended. Since the convention
followed the German invasion of the U.S.S.R. by several weeks, the major
UAW political tendencies were now in agreement on international issues,
strongly supporting American rearmament and lend-lease aid. But despite

the new-found harmony on substance, scores remained to be settled and opportunities exploited. The Reuther forces hoped to gain a decisive grip on the instruments of power, daring even to challenge George Addes as the union's secretary-treasurer. Their achievement fell well short of their goal, but they did win a position approaching parity with the opposition. There was no question that punishment would be meted out to the disobedient North American local and to Region 6, headed by Lew Michener, for the unauthorized North American strike. By a close margin the delegates voted to bar Michener from the executive board for one year, a punishment criticized by many as a mere slap on the wrist. More attention was paid to the credentials of delegates from Allis-Chalmers Local 248, the dispute turning into a complicated merry-go-round of conflicting testimony, investigatory delegations sent to Milwaukee to interview participants, and dramatic appearances and oratory on the convention floor.[24]

Debates on the North American strike and the Allis-Chalmers delegation were a warm-up for the convention's main event, the so-called "Red Resolution," a direct attack on the UAW's Communists through a proposed amendment to the UAW's constitution. Several months prior to the convention, Reuther and Frankensteen, joined in their fragile alliance, announced their intention to introduce an anticommunist constitutional amendment and appealed to "workers in the shops" to support the election of convention delegates favoring it. As brought in by Victor Reuther from the resolutions committee, the resolution stated: "No member or supporter of any organization whose loyalty [is] to a foreign government or who supports organizations which approve of totalitarian forms of government, shall be eligible to hold elective or appointive office in the international Union or any subdivision thereof." A minority report did not challenge the main thrust of the resolution but offered an amendment broadening the ban to include members of Communist, Nazi, Fascist, and Socialist organizations, a poison pill designed to defeat the resolution by bringing Socialist members and friends of the "Royal Family," as their opponents sometimes dubbed the Reuther brothers, within its scope. The attempt by the minority report debaters to link American Socialists (members of a democratic, anemic, fading political faction that lacked any connection with foreign powers) with Communists, Nazis, and Fascists fell flat. The Reutherites responded with the charge that the Communist Party was not a political organization in the normal sense of the term but an agent of a foreign power. The civil liberties implications of the proscription were barely mentioned. After a rancorous debate, a super-minority report was adopted by a margin of nearly two to one (1,969 to 1,026). It stated that "no member of any Local Union shall be eligible to hold an elective or appointive position in this International Union or any Local Union . . . if he is a member of/or subservient to any political organization, such as the Communist, Fascist, or Nazi Organization which owes its allegiance to any government, other than the United States or Canada, directly or indirectly." This represented the first and so far the only political restriction on office-holding in the union's history. Prior to the 1950s, the provision was not enforced by local unions or the International Union; known Communists and sympathizers continued to hold offices in local unions as long as they won election. But its adoption was a clear warning, indicating the extent of anticommunist sentiment and the fragility of the Communists' position. In the more heated anticommunist climate of the cold war the proscription was resurrected and, for a brief period, put to use.[25]

As Article 10, Section 7, the provision remained in the UAW constitution. In 1980 the union's leadership, recognizing that court decisions had made the disbarment from office of members of legal organizations unenforceable, recommended that it be deleted from the constitution. On a voice vote at the UAW's convention that year, the motion to remove the provision was rejected overwhelmingly. As one delegate tersely expressed her sentiment in the debate, "I am opposed. I lost a brother in Korea. That's all I have to say." Reduced to a symbol drained of substance by court rulings, the exclusion still carried emotional and ideological weight.[26]

The strong feelings generated by the political and factional confrontations at the 1941 convention were evident in the disorder on the floor. Whenever Frankensteen rose to defend his actions in the North American strike, delegates from California locals and their supporters vigorously waved tiny American flags in mockery, a heckling device used on several wartime occasions to deflate patriotic pretensions. During the balloting for membership on the executive board, when the official proceedings reported "considerable confusion in the hall," President Thomas plaintively asked, "What is this, a convention or a riot?" In these elections the Reuther group strengthened its position on the board. The Reuther caucus, consisting of a large element of centrist unionists whose basic loyalties were to the UAW itself and the New Deal liberalism of President Roosevelt, as well as anticommunist Catholics, socialists. and social democrats, emerged as one of the union's most powerful forces. In officers' elections, the caucus ran a candidate, Dick Leonard, for secretary-treasurer against George Addes, the first serious challenge to Addes's position. Addes's winning margin was much reduced from previous elections, with Leonard receiving 43 percent of the vote. Association with the Communists, Addes now discovered, could become a liability.[27]

BY THE TIME WORLD WAR II broke upon the United States in December 1941, a strong linkage between patriotism and workers' rights had taken shape in the rhetoric of auto workers and their leaders. This theme sprang from their conception of their right, as free American workers and citizens, to associate in a union to secure and enhance their livelihood and improve their working lives through collective bargaining and action. Americans were guaranteed free association in pursuit of lawful purposes, a freedom specifically and expressly established for workers in the Wagner Act and other measures. The struggle for victory in a war against totalitarian regimes in Germany, Japan, and Italy, where workers' rights had been routed and destroyed, gave deeper meaning and greater urgency to the auto workers' assertion of their rights as free citizens of a democracy. As Reuther pointed out in an address supporting military preparedness, workers and their labor movement had a vital concern in overcoming the threat of Nazism because "wherever Nazism is victorious the precious liberties that differentiate free men and free workers from slaves are destroyed."[28]

With American entry into the war the union's internal political and ideological contentions faded into the background, where they festered, less evident and divisive than before, but still very much alive. Patriotic sentiments and the need for a united national front carried the day. The UAW executive board, meeting on the day after the attack on Pearl Harbor, adopted a no-strike pledge—"an uninterrupted and ever increasing flow of tanks, trucks, airplanes, guns and munitions." Consequently, not a single wartime strike was authorized by the union's officers and executive board. Without the threat of strikes the union's ability to affect wages and working conditions was virtually nullified. In the spring of 1942 an elaborate apparatus of government measures took effect, including price controls, rationing of selected consumer items, and the "Little Steel" formula for pay, which limited wage increases to no more than 15 percent over the pay rate of January 1, 1941. These controls were supposed to assure workers a fair return for their labor and protect all against the threat of inflation posed by shortages of civilian goods. Despite the wage controls, a variety of devices, such as job reclassifications, promotions, and abundant overtime made possible an increase of about 20 percent in auto industry workers' real wages during the war. The war brought about the most rapid and significant redistribution of income in favor of manual workers in the history of the twentieth century. Although there was always serious opposition to the no-strike pledge within the union, and a willingness to defy it through wildcat strikes, most rank-and-file auto workers joined the International's leadership in supporting it. A survey conducted by the UAW Research Department in 1943 showed that 71 percent of the members polled believed the pledge was the union's correct position. Expressing a common sentiment, a Ford worker responding to the survey commented, "I think we can't do enough for our boys in service."[29]

Building B-24s at Ford's Willow Run, Michigan, plant. Walter P. Reuther Library, Wayne State University

UAW officials also offered to forego double time for Sunday and holiday work, a pledge that provoked great opposition from the rank and file. The government and the CIO took the position that there should be no wartime premium pay except for time-and-a-half for hours worked in excess of forty per week as required by law. The UAW position faced its greatest challenge in the aircraft industry because the AFL refused to make concessions on premium pay. More than 20,000 workers at Curtiss-Wright's huge Buffalo, New York, plant voted to affiliate with the AFL Machinists union (IAM), the UAW's rival, over the Sunday pay issue. At its 1942 convention, which lacked the usual fireworks over the election of officers and other politically charged issues, the UAW demanded premium pay unless all unions would forego it, an action aimed at IAM; this resulted in a presidential executive order prohibiting premium rates except for overtime.[30]

Angry over delays in conversion to war production that led to layoffs for more than 100,000 auto workers, the UAW pressured management and government with a barrage of complaints and public demonstrations by as many as twenty thousand persons in Detroit's Cadillac Square. In the opinion of many critics of the industry, the auto manufacturers held back from conversion in order to produce cars as long as possible, since, for the first

The Chrysler Tank Arsenal, Warren, Michigan, 1943. Walter P. Reuther Library, Wayne State University

time in several years, the civilian car market was buoyant and profits good. The auto industry did not complete its conversion to military production until the fall of 1942. When conversion was embraced it proceeded hectically. As a reporter described the scene in Michigan auto plants, "where the assembly lines used to be, one sees swarms of construction workers ripping out overhead conveyor systems, uprooting old machines, rushing discarded equipment to snow-covered parking lots. . . . New machines start whirring even before they have been fully bolted to the floor."[31]

With sacrifices expected of all, the UAW called upon management to do its part in the war effort in a program entitled "Victory through Equality of Sacrifice." The union urged the federal government to set firm price ceilings, extend and strengthen rationing, limit corporate profits to a 3 percent return on investment, fix a maximum salary for businessmen and others of $25,000 a year, and begin planning for the postwar economy. The proposals drew praise from some auto workers, one UAW newspaper proclaiming that "all sections of the population must . . . unite in this effort. . . . [B]ut to us, the men and women who work in our factories and fields, American democracy is more important than [to] any [other] single group. This war is *our* war to protect *our* democracy." Despite President

Soldiers from Camp Atterbury, Indiana, inspect a UAW-built tank, 1943. Walter P. Reuther Library, Wayne State University

Roosevelt's support, most items on the "equality of sacrifice" agenda were not implemented. Eager to stimulate maximum production regardless of cost, the administration and Congress guaranteed manufacturers a profit through "cost-plus" defense contracts, granted tax breaks for expanding existing plants and building new ones, and left defense purchasing in the hands of the military, always more comfortable with business than with labor. "Congress," UAW president R. J. Thomas bluntly remarked, "paid no more attention to the [equality of sacrifice] program than to an individual who would go to church and burp." As it became evident that wartime sacrifices would be one-sided, and unclear how far workers would be pressed to go in making concessions, auto workers began to think in terms of defending rights they feared were endangered.[32]

ALTHOUGH THE UNION'S INTERNAL factional struggle was subordinated to the war effort, beneath the surface "it was still very strong and the undercurrents were very powerful." On occasion it broke into the open. The first issue to disrupt wartime harmony was that of payment of incentive wages.

Before the coming of the union, piece rates were common in auto parts man-ufacturing but generally disliked by workers, who felt they made them vul-nerable to speedups; the union had undertaken, with considerable success, to abolish them. The War Production Board endorsed group piecework plans, promising an increase in wages for all as production rose. With straight-time wage rates limited for the duration of the war by the Little Steel formula, incentive rates offered a possible wage increase. This brought the proposal some rank-and-file support. Most important in turning the issue into an internal union battleground, in 1943 the Communist Party, intent on increasing military production, proposed that incentive wages be adopted throughout American industry. The proposal was bound to be gen-erally unpopular, but the UAW Communists, with the backing of many of their allies, took up the cry. George Addes proposed an incentive pay plan at an executive board meeting, and Dick Frankensteen, now again cooper-ating with the left, argued that the total wages of workers in the aircraft industry, where straight-time rates were still low, would increase if the plan were adopted. Reuther, who objected to incentive wages on principle and had long fought to banish them entirely from the industry, perceived an opportunity to seize an issue costly to his opponents and sure to improve his standing. He attacked the proposal as contrary to the union's policy and the workers' interests, and his supporters decried the subservience its sup-port revealed to the Communist Party's agenda. A narrow majority of the board sided with Reuther, a position confirmed at the 1943 convention.[33]

The lively fight over incentive pay at that convention was bound to affect the election of officers. The Reuther caucus once again ran Richard Leonard for secretary-treasurer against George Addes. Leonard's campaign stressed the support Addes and Frankensteen gave to the Communist posi-tion on incentive pay. Singing to the tune of "Reuben and Rachel," the Reuther forces ridiculed Addes and Frankensteen in biting verses:

> Who are the boys who take their orders
> Straight from the office of Joe Sta-leen?
> No one else but the gruesome twosome,
> George F. Addes and Frankensteen
> Who are the boys that fight for piecework,
> To make the worker a machine?
> No one else but the gruesome twosome,
> George F. Addes and Frankensteen. . . .
> The Auto Workers have their sideshow,
> One is fat and one is lean,
> Who are they but the gruesome twosome,
> George F. Addes and Frankensteen.

The many verses of the song were chanted down the hotel hallways and in the meeting rooms. The likelihood of a close contest between Addes and Leonard stimulated much gambling on the outcome. A reporter claimed that the hotel lobby "has virtually been turned into a betting ring." Addes won reelection by the slim margin of 72 votes, out of a total of 7,424 cast, while Reuther was chosen first vice president over Frankensteen in another close contest, the only time he bested Frankensteen in a direct electoral challenge. Frankensteen then beat Leonard in the race for second vice president, again by a very narrow margin. On the executive board the Reuther following approached parity with Addes's supporters, while President Thomas controlled a few votes in the middle. The incentive pay proposal, forced on Addes and Frankensteen by the CP, dealt a devastating blow to those two leaders and sealed the fate of the Communists within the UAW. Several years before cold war pressures guaranteed their elimination as a force in the union, the Communists started down a road from which there was neither exit nor return.[34]

BY AND LARGE, despite wartime's problems and stresses, the UAW made important gains during this period. The Roosevelt administration, friendly to labor and politically dependent on it, had no intention of undermining unions and creating discord in the midst of a war requiring national unity and sacrifice. It needed union leaders to make its labor mobilization policies work and it relied on labor votes at election time. To provide union security in the setting of a controlled economy, the government included a "maintenance of membership" clause in its procurement contracts with unionized employers. As usually formulated and applied, this established a modified union shop in which workers in an organized plant, unless they withdrew from the union within fifteen days after beginning work, had to remain in the union for the duration of the contract. Despite the fact that many of the wartime labor recruits lacked union experience or deeply rooted loyalties, less than 1 percent withdrew from their unions under the maintenance of membership clauses. With this backing from the national administration and a burgeoning economy, total union membership expanded from 10.5 million in December 1941 to 14.75 million by June 1945, reaching a proportion of the civilian workforce—approximately 36 percent—never since exceeded and rarely equaled. The UAW, with almost all of its members working under government contracts, benefited handsomely from maintenance of membership. In July 1943 the UAW's dues-paying membership passed the one million mark, making it the nation's largest union. Wartime's imperatives and a friendly government's policies completed the organization of the nation's core industries and extended unionization into areas that had previously been exempt.[35]

Although the UAW as an organization grew and prospered during the war, many workers' lives were disrupted by wartime's demands. Maintaining a stable workforce was a problem. Employee turnover was high, with some firms annually hiring several times the number of workers needed to maintain production. Many workers were drafted into military service, and draft boards issued industrial deferments reluctantly. As manpower shortages began to be anticipated, some companies hoarded labor, stockpiling workers for whom they had no immediate use. One UAW official, working with the War Manpower Commission, saw plants "where you could go into any toilet or washroom at any hour of the day and find 25 or 30 men standing around shooting crap[s] or reading or just killing time because the plant was overstaffed." At one plant, workers idled by a shortage of aircraft parts set up a picket line to publicize and protest their lack of work. Sometimes supervision resorted to make-work. A worker was given a bucket of rivets to sort by size; after the rivets were sorted, they were mixed again and given to another worker to sort. Wasteful and demoralizing, hoarding cost the companies nothing since "cost-plus" contracts paid the bills.[36]

Absenteeism adversely affected productivity. Excoriated by newspapers, employers, and patriots (World War I flying ace Lieutenant-Colonel Eddie Rickenbacker observed to an audience of Detroit auto executives that "there are no absentees in foxholes"), wartime absenteeism, which was high compared to peacetime rates, stemmed from several causes. Despite critics' charges, by no means was it always the result of laziness, malingering, or indifference to the national interest. Job shopping, illnesses, fatigue, disruptions of family life due to unsuitable housing, transportation problems, inadequate child care, and difficulties associated with other household duties all had their effects. Much of the absenteeism occurred on and around weekends. Thousands of wartime employees, men and women, were new to factory work. The long working hours in many factories amid the tensions of industrial production contributed to fatigue and inefficiency. At the peak of war production in the fall of 1943, Detroit industrial employees averaged 47.5 hours of work a week, and as many as seventy working hours were not unknown. Work weariness was often intensified by long commutes from home to factory.[37]

Many workers became suspicious of management's conduct of labor relations in the wartime setting. A secret government survey in 1942 showed that a majority of Detroit workers thought that employers were bent on exploiting wartime conditions in order to deny workers their recent collective gains. Grievance processing broke down in many plants. Disputes over line speed, wages, job assignments, transfer rights, and seniority multiplied. In January 1943, a War Production Board representative in Detroit reported to his Washington superiors that "the evidence . . . seems to indicate rather clearly that a well-organized and determined effort is being made on the part of many manufacturers and industrialists to do everything in their power to create incidents which will 'needle' and provoke labor into unauthorized stoppages of work." A UAW survey in February 1943 showed that two-thirds of those who responded believed that employers were taking advantage of the union's no-strike commitment to ignore and refuse to correct harmful conditions in the plants and violations of contractual protections. An inspector at the Chevrolet Gear and Axle plant in Detroit spoke for many when he said that, "Due to [the] no-strike pledge it is harder for our men to get justice in many cases." The manufacturers, another wrote, were "taking advantage of the workers' cooperative attitude." At Dodge Truck, where there was a "good number" of unauthorized wartime strikes, the local's president insisted they could more accurately be called "management-provoked work protests" than wildcat strikes. The management "had developed a habit and a practice . . . of not becoming serious about problems . . . until workers in a particular group began taking things into their own hands." In practice, much wartime grievance bargaining was carried on through confrontations. Since the union leadership could do little to expedite settlements, workers increasingly sought redress through disruptive wildcat strikes. On the other hand, at Studebaker, a company whose management was committed to amicable labor relations, union control over production standards and other working conditions was enhanced by the wartime situation, since the company, working under cost-plus contracts, was content to pass on increased costs to the government. For several reasons factory discipline deteriorated in wartime, with workers becoming more assertive.[38]

"Here we have the feeling of sitting on top of a smoldering volcano, which may explode at any time," wrote the Detroit chairman of the Regional War Labor Board in July 1943. Given the ephemeral nature of auto workers' wartime wildcats and the fact that many went unreported, no entirely accurate and comprehensive count of them can be given, but from 1943 to the war's end in 1945 thousands of stoppages occurred. By one count there were 773 wartime wildcats at the Ford River Rouge plant alone. One estimate holds that 65 percent of Michigan UAW members participated at one time or another in such strikes, many presumably in more than one. Most wartime wildcat strikes involved only a few workers and lasted only a short time, a few minutes or hours, at most a few days. In what seems a typical action, Dodge Truck workers walked out one day at noon and were back the next day. Although there were many strikes at that plant, rarely was it down for as long as two or three days. Some locals were hotbeds of wildcatting. The president of Local 212, whose members were spread throughout several Briggs plants, thought he "had accomplished something if one of the plants had not gone on a strike during the week."[39]

Chevrolet workers in Detroit launch a wildcat strike, 1945. Walter P. Reuther Library, Wayne State University

Some wildcats were provoked by disputes over wages. Although wages rose generally, the government's wage controls restrained the increase. In many cases the companies, with cost-plus contracts, were willing to grant wage increases, but they were disallowed by the government. Related wildcats occurred over job reclassifications since they were one way to get around wage controls. In those parts plants where piece rates were still in use, wildcats occurred in response to increases in production norms. Since piece rates could be changed without violating the wage freeze, workers had an opportunity to raise their pay through unauthorized strike action. Disputes over production standards, seniority, job transfer rights, promotions, and safety concerns also provoked wildcats. Many wildcats occurred in response to company disciplinary actions, such as firing or suspending workers who refused to meet a higher production rate. Measured by hours of work lost, disputes over discipline were the primary source of wildcat strikes.[40]

The equation of wartime supply and demand for labor, reconfigured to the worker's advantage, created an environment in which wildcats could flourish. With labor shortages persisting throughout much of the war, a worker disciplined for wildcatting or other infractions at one shop could usually find a job elsewhere without difficulty or delay. The long hours of exhausting work and the tensions inseparable from wartime conditions contributed to wildcat restlessness. Many workers simply felt the need for some time off, even if only for a few hours. At the DeSoto plant on Detroit's West Side the wartime wildcats were "larks, really larks," in steward Douglas Fraser's view, stemming from the need for relief from the long hours of work. When workers were making good money and shortages of consumer goods gave them little to spend it on, "the result was that some days they were not too anxious to work." Strikes occurred for reasons that outsiders might consider trivial, yet they expressed the workers' desire to gain a greater measure of personal freedom. Cadillac workers, for example, struck to protest company no-smoking rules; at another Detroit plant workers struck to protest a company order banning checker games during lunch. With union resources stretched thin, those responsible for processing grievances often had more to deal with than they could handle. The result: "we threw away valid grievances," one representative confessed, with workers then tempted to wildcat to get relief.[41]

Wildcats rarely seem to have been undertaken to advance a radical political or ideological agenda. The Communists, the most active radical element prior to the war, were (to their political cost) dead set against any work stoppage. Consequently, they were among the union's stoutest defenders of the no-strike pledge. Ken Bannon, a union activist at the Rouge plant's Local 600 and future UAW vice president, maintained that fewer wildcats occurred in Communist-led than in noncommunist-led locals, testifying both to the Communists' desire to maximize production and to the role that local leadership could play in "unofficial" strike actions. Contingents of Trotskyists with syndicalist leanings espoused worker shop floor control on principle, but it seems to be the case that most workers, insofar as they were moved by an ideological rationale for their actions, saw their job actions as a defense of their rights as workers and citizens—in sum as patriotically American.[42]

Despite the many strikes and the swelling chorus of criticism they inspired, their short duration amid scattered locations meant that relatively little working time was actually lost. By and large, military production was maintained without serious interruption. Released from pressure to maximize production by cost-plus contracts and labor hoarding, management, it was frequently observed, tolerated a slower pace in wartime compared to what it had demanded in a time of peace. One effect was to reduce the amount of production lost when strikes occurred. A historian of the auto industry has maintained that "labor disputes caused no obstruction of the war effort in any segment of the automobile industry," and a union calculation showed that all of the stoppages in GM's plants in 1943 and 1944 totaled far less lost production time than that resulting from the plants' shutting down for the July 4th holiday.[43]

UNION LEADERSHIP AT ALL LEVELS was squeezed between the pressures from the shop floor and the loud and sweeping condemnations of labor disputes that issued from the press and politicians. Editorial writers launched blistering attacks on wildcats. Commenting on strikes in several Chrysler plants, the *Detroit News* told its readers that "somebody somewhere will die" because of them, and the *Detroit Times* charged that "so-called American workers" were "little better than traitors to their country and to their sons and brothers who are fighting for that country." Perhaps more telling to auto workers than criticism from normally hostile sources was the criticism that came from within the union. At the 1943 convention, President Thomas, a firm supporter of the no-strike pledge and critic of wildcats, publicly read a letter he had received from Charlie Varos, a UAW member serving in the army in Europe. "What's the matter with those boys [wildcatters at Chrysler and Dodge]?" he asked. "Are they crazy? Don't they know there is a war on and that a lot of boys are giving up their lives just to make a better world for the folks at home to live in?" Heightening the letter's impact, Thomas disclosed that the young soldier had been killed in Sicily by the time the letter was received. A resolution endorsing the no-strike pledge passed by an overwhelming vote at the 1943 convention.[44]

The UAW's top leadership, fearful of government reprisals and the threat of oppressive labor mobilization legislation, deplored wildcats, sought their rapid settlement, and urged the union's members to act responsibly. The passage of repressive labor legislation by Congress, notably the Smith-Connolly Act in 1943, showed that fears of a hostile antilabor government offensive were by no means groundless. Reuther, while arguing that the companies bore a large part of the blame because "collective bargaining in too many plants has become collective begging," pointed out that "no labor movement can strike against the government . . . without literally crucifying itself." President Thomas declared that "public opinion has become inflamed against our union. There can be no such thing today as a legitimate picket line." In a few very serious instances, such as the strike of seven thousand workers at five Chevrolet Gear and Axle plants in Detroit in July and August 1944, union leaders organized back-to-work movements, suspended local officers, and issued statements condemning the action. Within the locals, where officers faced a disgruntled membership in annual elections, the situation was difficult and often tense. Local officers sometimes straddled the issue, taking a public position in opposition to strikes but supporting or acquiescing in them surreptitiously. Both the merits of the disputes and the pertinent political considerations entered into their response to the situation.[45]

The condemnations of wildcats by editorialists, government officials, and UAW leaders appear to have had only a limited effect on workers' willingness to engage in them. When the UAW's 1944 convention met in Grand Rapids, Michigan, a newly formed Rank-and-File caucus, which drew heavily on locals that had usually supported Reuther, forced a spirited debate on the no-strike pledge, merging its attack on the pledge with support for independent political action by labor and the election of a new slate of officers. Political divisions enlivened the proceedings. In some plants Trotskyist, Socialist, and independent radical opponents of the pledge had prevailed, endangering Reuther's political base. The Addes-Frankensteen caucus supported the pledge without reservation, as their Communist allies, who would brook no interruptions of production damaging to the Allied war effort, insisted. "The party line," one observer wrote, "is taking a suicidal turn in favor of the Chamber of Commerce—and such positions do not sit well with the rank-and-file." The patriotic rhetoric issuing from the left excited the ridicule of opponents. When Addes and others defended the pledge, invoking the necessity of wartime sacrifice and other imperatives of patriotism, the delegates from the militant but independent and non-communist Briggs Local 212, who opposed the pledge's continuation, turned the tables on the left-leaning delegates as they waved tiny American flags in mockery.[46]

The convention failed to reach a consensus. President Thomas, recently returned from Europe where he had spoken with many former UAW members, reported that every UAW soldier he met urged the union to reaffirm the pledge. Warned by Addes and others that the pledge's repeal would provoke congressional retaliation against labor, the convention rejected the Rank-and-File caucus's proposal to abandon the pledge by a resounding two-to-one margin. Reuther, in political hot water, advanced a compromise, proposing to maintain the pledge in plants producing war material but to abandon it in those manufacturing civilian goods once the Allies had defeated Germany, since defeat of Japan, the remaining enemy, could be accomplished with reduced production. Critics complained that companies would subvert the compromise by retaining a little war work to avoid authorized strikes while shifting most of their production to civilian goods. The proposal went down overwhelmingly on an unrecorded vote, as left-wing and Rank-and-File delegates combined to defeat it. Finally, the delegates narrowly voted down an unequivocal endorsement of the pledge. All three proposals had failed. An alert Rank-and-File delegate asked if this meant the UAW had no position on wartime strikes, a policy vacuum that would leave each local free to act as it wished. The embarrassed leadership quickly proposed to submit the pledge to a membership mail referendum, as had been earlier suggested by the Rank-and-File caucus. More than one and a quarter million ballots were mailed out, including those sent to soldiers who were still members. Approximately 30 percent were returned, over a quarter million votes, with 65 percent favoring retention of the pledge, probably as accurate an indication of the auto workers' view of the pledge while the war was winding down as can be obtained. Despite the discontent with management's refusal to settle grievances in a timely way, UAW members would not countenance an open repeal of the pledge. Nevertheless, wildcat protests continued, if on a reduced scale, until the end of the war.[47]

THE MOST MOMENTOUS WARTIME CHANGE in the auto workforce and in UAW membership was the recruitment of tens of thousands of African Americans. In response to the labor shortage, management recruited black workers more actively than ever before, and it offered better employment opportunities. Plentiful jobs at good pay, with more opportunities for advancement into machine-tending and assembly work assignments previously closed to them, exerted a strong pull, drawing in blacks already resident in Detroit as well as migrants from the southern and border states. Marc Stepp, later a UAW vice president, left "Jim Crow" Evansville, in southern Indiana, in 1941 for Detroit and a job at Chrysler following his graduation from high school because he "knew that life could be better someplace else." The incorporation of a multitude of African Americans into a workforce densely populated with people of middle European descent and white migrants from the American South transformed a volatile racial mix into an explosive one. With 100,000 African Americans among its million members the wartime UAW became what it has since remained, one of the nation's largest private organizations with an interracial membership.[48]

The wartime expansion of the workforce in Detroit and other auto cities sparked racial tension and conflict. Detroit, the "arsenal of democracy" in its proud boast, was rocked by the nation's worst wartime race riot in June 1943, the culmination of numerous incidents, especially over black residents' access to housing. Two days of savage street warfare resulted in the deaths of twenty-five blacks and nine whites and property damage of more than $2 million. As many as 100,000 white rioters took part, and federal troops were brought to the city to restore order. The auto plants were free of violence during the riot, and UAW officers proudly pointed out that blacks and whites continued to work side by side. But fights occurred at the gates of several plants. High rates of absenteeism among workers of both races, with black absenteeism at 90 percent in some factories, suggest that some workers were involved in the riot as victims or rioters or were afraid to venture out to their jobs. Whatever the case, the UAW leadership presented a constructive, though stillborn, assessment and program for the prevention of future riots, a rare exception in white Detroit in refusing to blame the riot entirely on blacks.[49]

The union's leadership was acutely aware of the contradiction between the defense of democratic values used to justify the war and the racial bigotry and hatred at home. Not long after the riot, Reuther told a labor audience, "we realize we cannot fight against the master race theory in Berlin and permit it to be practiced in the city of Detroit." As a union open to all workers in the auto industry, the UAW's constitution prohibited racial discrimination in membership. All of its principal officers, including R. J. Thomas, George Addes, Richard Frankensteen, and Reuther, championed equal treatment of all members. The union had warmly applauded President Roosevelt's issuance of Executive Order 8802, which banned employment discrimination in companies with defense contracts, and it had taken the initiative, in cooperation with other interested parties, in launching the Metropolitan Detroit Council on Fair Employment Practice. Nevertheless, the distance separating the leadership's commitments from the views of some rank-and-file elements, including some local leaders and some executive board members, was greater on racial questions than on any other wartime issue. Racial discrimination in aspects of employment such as access to jobs, transfers to better jobs, seniority protections, and participation in local union affairs, characterized some UAW-organized plants. Some southern locals, where the worst situations existed, openly segregated black members within their union halls. One Georgia General Motors local, in violation of the union's constitution, excluded black employees from membership. Reuther, as head of the General Motors Department, "read the riot act to them." His threat to suspend the local's officers and appoint an administrator to run the local forced them to accept the black workers as members.[50]

The worst explosions of racial hatred were ignited by challenges to racial occupational segregation, threatening to breach the age-old tradition that drew a line between a "white man's job" and a "black man's job." Although many wartime plants employed black workers in menial or otherwise inferior positions without protests by whites, working side by side at the same or similar jobs struck at the racist principle, deeply embedded in the nation's history during slavery and after, that the desirable jobs were reserved for whites and the undesirable ones for blacks. As one observer reported, "the matter of promotion for Negro workers is the toughest problem the union is facing. There is a very strong feeling among the white workers whenever this issue comes up. . . . White workers have told me, 'I'll be g—damned if I'll work with a g—damned nigger.' Even union officials who would like to see Negroes get the promotions they deserve are afraid to handle the issue." Shelton Tappes, an officer of Local 600 during the war, was called in by Ford officials as a union witness to a voluntary quit by, as Tappes noted they were called in the plant, one of the "hill-billies." The man told Tappes, who was black, that he had to quit because he could not work with "the Ni—colored people. . . . I just can't help it, that's the way I was raised." And so he quit. In the DeSoto plant, which had been "lily white" before the war, blacks were hired as janitors once the war began. When one of the janitors was upgraded to machine operator the steward, Doug Fraser, had to deal with a complaint. "A little Polish guy, spoke with broken English, came up to me, and I knew what was coming. . . . He said, 'You going to do something about this?' I said, 'About what?' He says, 'This nigger working next to me. . . . I want to know what I can do about it.' I said, 'You can go to the employment office and quit; you won't have any problems.'"[51]

With the accession of the giant Ford Rouge Local 600 in 1941, a strong and articulate contingent of black activists pressed the attack on racial discrimination. The union's Communists were vocal champions of black rights, and their position within the Addes caucus ensured that there would be a hearing of their case at the union's highest levels. By the end of the war Local 600 had about 450 Communist Party members, one-third of whom were blacks, the largest contingent by far in any UAW local. (There were an estimated 3,000 Communist Party members in wartime auto plants.) The Communists' appeal to blacks had little to do with revolutionary Marxist doctrine. Saul Wellman, who came to Detroit in 1946 as Communist Party coordinator for the auto workers, later said, "the overwhelming majority of blacks who joined the Party, joined because they met a unique group of white people who were fighting alongside them and also socializing with them. That had nothing to do with the principles of Marxism, Leninism or Socialism or state power or anything else."[52]

Black workers hired during the war had to struggle to gain equal treatment. Some company officials clung to racially discriminatory practices either because of their own prejudice or because they feared the hostile reaction of white workers if the workplace became thoroughly integrated. Some local union officials, fearful of electoral retaliation by white majorities in their plants, hesitated to support black workers' claims to transfers and upgrades to better jobs, and sometimes conspired to block them. Some black workers refused to acquiesce in such treatment. They instigated dozens of wildcat strikes and protests seeking access to better work. In the summer of 1941, following President Roosevelt's issuance of Executive Order 8802, black workers in Chrysler and Dodge plants wildcatted repeatedly in protest of company refusals to transfer and upgrade them when it was taking on whites as new hires for the jobs. Delegations of black workers appeared before the UAW's executive board to urge it to protest violations of seniority rights in upgrades and transfers and to pressure UAW local officers and regional directors to respond to complaints of discrimination. In April 1943, following a long series of discriminatory incidents at the Ford Motor Company, whose reputation as the black workers' friend was in serious jeopardy, three thousand blacks walked off the job in a three-day wildcat strike. Other stoppages by blacks in Detroit plants occurred at Chevrolet Gear and Axle, Timken Axle, Chrysler Highland Park, Chrysler Jefferson, and Packard.[53]

The most serious incidents of racial strife were the widely publicized "hate strikes," when whites wildcatted to protest black occupational advances. The course of events varied, often according to the attitude and response of management. Where supervisors reacted quickly to a wildcat with threats of dismissal or other penalties, the strike was almost always brief. In plants where management refused to act promptly and decisively, wildcats were more frequent and caused longer interruptions of production. Racial wildcats by whites occurred at Dodge Main, Dodge Truck, Chrysler, Curtiss-Wright, Briggs, Timken Axle, and other plants. At Hudson Naval Ordnance, where much of the workforce had transferred from the Hudson Motor Company—including southern-born employees with Ku Klux Klan and Black Legion affiliations—a wildcat strike occurred when two veteran black employees were upgraded from sweeper to machine operator. As vice president Dick Frankensteen walked through the tense plant trying to end the strike, white workers chanted "Nigger lover, Nigger lover, Nigger lover." Frankensteen threatened that if they did not resume work within fifteen minutes he would recommend to the company that they be fired. They went back, but with a lot of grumbling. (In 1945 Frankensteen, hoping to launch a political career, was defeated in a race for mayor of Detroit in a campaign marred by vicious attacks on his record of support for equal rights.)[54]

The worst hate strikes occurred at Packard, where there was an influx of southern white wartime workers. The first was in 1941 and the most serious in June 1943, only a few weeks before the Detroit riot. Since the war's beginning racial conflict had been virtually chronic at Packard, where persistent allegations charged Ku Klux Klan infiltration of both the rank and file and the leadership of Local 190. The UAW's executive board claimed to have conclusive evidence that the Packard strike was "fomented and deliberately organized" by the KKK. The management encouraged white resistance to black promotions and stimulated the hate strikes, apparently in the hope that racial conflicts would divide the workers and at least weaken, perhaps destroy, the union. The company's personnel director openly expressed his racial prejudice, maintaining that a job to which a black was to be promoted was a "white man's job" and telling white workers that they "need not work with Negroes" unless they chose to.[55]

The Packard crisis came to a climax when the company, under pressure from the government, announced the upgrading of three black workers to the aircraft assembly line. For some Packard workers, maintaining racial segregation was more important, at least rhetorically, than victory in the war over the nation's enemies. One was quoted as saying, "I'd rather see Hitler and Hirohito win than work next to a nigger." By the next day, according to reports, 90 percent of Packard's 25,000 white workers were out on a wildcat strike and production had ceased. Thousands crowded the factory gates, cheering the harangues of antiblack, antisemitic, anticommunist, antigovernment, and antiunion speakers, and booing the UAW officials who urged them to return to their jobs.[56]

Although Local 190's leadership was divided and paralyzed, the International's leadership did not hesitate to condemn the hate strikes and take strong action against them. In fact, the leadership reacted more decisively when racial hatred inspired a wildcat than it did when issues of a different nature led to walkouts. President R. J. Thomas importuned the War Labor Board (WLB) in Washington to make a forceful representation to the Packard strikers to return to work, and Colonel George E. Strong, the War Department's Detroit representative, threatened that strikers would be fired from their jobs. Thomas then warned that the UAW, far from defending the striking workers' jobs, would expel them from the union. Other top UAW officials, including George Addes, Dick Frankensteen, and Walter Reuther, consistently took the position that the union would not defend the jobs of hate strikers. Faced with this government and union leadership resolve, Packard workers after three days on strike began to return to the shop, a process hastened when thirty "ringleaders" were suspended, some of whom lost their jobs permanently. Although this conflict was settled on terms that guaranteed the upgraded blacks their new jobs, with seniority to determine future upgrades, racial conflict at Packard did not end. The following year, a large if briefer and less tense white walkout occurred when four blacks were upgraded to metal polishing jobs from which they had traditionally been excluded.[57]

By no means did all plants suffer from such racial conflicts. Black workers were employed and upgraded without incident in many plants, and as the war wound down in 1944 and 1945, hate strikes, for the time being, all but disappeared. Much depended on the attitude of local union leaders and the preparations they made. At the Buick aircraft engine plant in Melrose Park, Illinois, UAW Local 6, Jack Conway, chair of the bargaining committee, was determined to have a black worker put on machine work. He instructed company officials to stay out of the picture, letting the union handle the situation. When the move was made after thorough preparation, there was no hostility. Blacks then were routinely upgraded in that plant. As terrible as the expressions of racial hatred were in some plants, equally remarkable was the progress toward racial equity and acceptance of an interracial work place in others.[58]

AS BLACK MEMBERSHIP EXPANDED, African Americans gained a greater voice within the union. There was a steady increase in the number and proportion of black delegates to the UAW's wartime conventions. Seventy-five black delegates attended the 1942 convention in Chicago, the largest representation to that time. At the 1944 convention in Grand Rapids the number rose to 250, 11 percent of the total, a proportion approximating that of black employees in the wartime workforce. A commitment to protecting black delegates against discrimination was shown by the last-minute decision to move the 1943 convention from St. Louis to Buffalo when the former city's hotels and restaurants refused to guarantee equal treatment of all delegates.[59]

Blacks gained elective leadership positions in several local unions. As early as 1937 a close observer noted that "in almost all locals having one hundred or more Negro members," at least one black, often a steward in a department with a substantial contingent of black workers, had won an elective office. But the sum total of officeholders, which included a handful of local presidents, remained tiny in proportion to their membership numbers, a situation that was substantially unchanged during the war.[60]

Since there was insufficient support within any region to elect a black regional director by the normal process of a majority vote by regional delegates, black unionists proposed to establish an executive board seat for a black. This was first suggested in 1939 at the Cleveland convention following the creation of a black executive board seat by Homer Martin's UAW-AFL, but the idea was summarily rejected. At the 1942 convention the possibility of electing an African American as one of the UAW's vice presidents was briefly aired then quickly dismissed. By 1943 an additional board member, elected at large by convention delegates rather than as a regional director, seemed a possibility. The plan called for the creation of a minorities department to promote racial fairness and resolve racial disputes, headed by an elected board member who, it was understood, would be black, and for the hiring of more black International representatives.[61]

The proposal, like many others, was soon entangled in internal politics. The delegates to the 1943 convention were evenly divided between the Addes-Frankensteen "left-wing" caucus, which included the Communists and nearly all blacks, and the "right-wing" Reuther caucus. The Addes-Frankensteen caucus endorsed the proposal for a black executive board seat before the convention opened, cementing black support for the plan and black support for Addes's reelection as secretary-treasurer against the rival candidate of the Reuther caucus, Richard T. Leonard. Their opponents' endorsement of the plan was viewed by the Reuther caucus as a political maneuver to bolster Addes's reelection prospects and to enlarge their following on the closely-divided executive board by an additional vote. Seeking a compromise that would prevent damage to their political position and possibly merit some black support, the Reutherites announced that while they liked the idea of an African American member of the board, they opposed what they called a "jim-crow" solution ("affirmative action" in modern parlance). As Victor Reuther declared in the convention debate, "if there is a special post for Negroes, then in all justice there should be a post at large for the Catholics, the women, the Jews, the Poles, and all the rest." As a weak concession, they proposed to create a minorities department with a black director to be appointed by the UAW president. The director would not be a board member.[62]

The Addes-Leonard contest for secretary-treasurer resulted in a narrow victory for Addes. The black delegates, urged and expected by the Addes-CP caucus to support the secretary-treasurer, voted for Addes almost unanimously, 150 out of 160 delegates by one count, providing his margin of victory. Especially costly to Leonard was his failure to hold the votes of black delegates from Local 600, the Ford River Rouge plant, whose support he had counted on since he was director of the Ford Department. The proposal for an African American board member was then brought to the floor, where it sparked a "stormy debate" in which its two leading black sponsors, Shelton Tappes and Hodges Mason, and the union's top officers, Thomas, Frankensteen, Addes, and Victor and Walter Reuther, participated. President Thomas backed the Reuther compromise. In the end the convention voted down both the original proposal and the compromise. Nearly all the black delegates supported the proposal, but Horace Sheffield and Walter Hardin, among the few African Americans with ties to the Reuther caucus, refused to go along. The refusal of the Reuther caucus to support the proposal fed black members' conviction that his caucus harbored a racist element.[63]

The issue came up again at the 1944 convention with a different outcome. Again the black delegates failed to secure a seat on the board, but a version of the Reuther compromise was adopted. The UAW set up a Fair Practices Committee to confront racial discrimination in the plants and in the union's locals. Although the person appointed to head the committee, the African American attorney George W. Crockett, a former U.S. Labor Department lawyer and a federal Fair Employment Practices Committee staff member, lacked previous UAW ties, his knowledgeable and vigorous leadership made the committee an active force in investigating

and resolving discrimination issues. In 1946 the committee was elevated
to department status as the Fair Practices and Anti-Discrimination
Department and put under the nominal co-leadership of Reuther, elected
president at the 1946 convention, and William Oliver, a black unionist
from the Ford Highland Park plant. Despite the improvement in status,
the department was less vigorous in combating racial inequities within
local unions than the committee had been. Although the department has
drawn criticism from some historians and others for its failure to attack
energetically and rout out instances of discrimination in UAW locals, it
should be noted that its educational campaigns, designed to forge a consensus among the membership in opposition to racist practices, were pursued more vigorously than in many other unions.[64]

The war brought significant gains for the male African American
minority, but the achievement fell well short of equality. The number of
black workers in the industry, especially in Detroit, increased markedly
and, despite all the troubles there, the wartime auto plants in Detroit were
more fully desegregated than many industrial facilities elsewhere. By the
end of the war, African Americans constituted 15 percent of the Detroit area
auto workforce. Although most were still performing unskilled labor, a significant number had won access to semiskilled production jobs. Their claim
to such jobs would not be seriously challenged in the postwar era, and the
representation of black males in the Detroit area plants rose slowly but
steadily after the war ended. The skilled trades, on the other hand, were
still—and long remained—a white preserve.[65]

A DIFFERENT FATE AWAITED BLACK WOMEN. Although they constituted
a large reservoir of underemployed labor, they found fewer job opportunities than black males and received less support from the government and
the union in obtaining suitable work. Ford, although it continued to have
more black employees than any other major employer, resisted hiring black
females for war production. Black civic leaders in Detroit and many union
officials fought to win job access for black females, with much of their effort
aimed at Ford's suburban Willow Run bomber plant, but the results were
negligible. Before the plant opened, UAW officials, aware that the government expected the bomber plant to recruit female workers, pressed Ford to
agree that blacks would constitute at least 7 percent of all women hired.
The company responded with a vague assurance of nondiscrimination but
dragged its feet in its implementation, claiming that the presence of black
women in the factory would lead to "disturbances" among the plant's large
"hillbilly" southern and rural white workforce. By the summer of 1942,
over 3,000 white women had been hired at Willow Run but not a single
black woman. Mass meetings and picketing by Local 600 unionists, com-

bined with threats of a wildcat strike by black Rouge foundry workers and of FEPC public hearings on Ford's racialist hiring practices, brought the company to a bare token accommodation. In March 1943, the Willow Run plant employed 25,000 women, with fewer than 200 of them African Americans. By the end of the war only 735 Willow Run employees of both sexes were black, 3.5 percent of the total. Although black women eventually constituted substantial portions of employees in several small Detroit plants, tokenism, as at Willow Run, was the common response of large auto firms to pressures from government agencies, the union, and black civic organizations to hire them.[66]

Occupational segregation was more rigidly maintained for African American women than for men. Although thousands of black women were trained for production jobs, such as welding and riveting, they were seldom allowed to fill openings in those occupations. Most of those hired were employed as janitors, washroom matrons, or laborers. Some companies trained black women for production work but fired them during the probationary period before they became entitled to the union contract's protection. Once inside the plant, a black female was not shielded from racial prejudice. At the Willow Run plant a black woman was denied a transfer to a better job for which she had received training because, as she was told by a management representative, "the whole trouble is that Niggers are trying to move ahead too fast."[67]

Some white women resisted working with blacks. At a 1942 UAW women's conference, a female Local 3 shop steward complained, "Once we accept Negro women into the shops even during this crisis we will always have them. When they come into the shops to work you know what that means. They'll be working along side of us, they'll be using the same restrooms." This view was strongly condemned by other speakers at the conference but it represented an important current of opinion in many shops. Resistance, including work stoppages by white women, occurred but, if resolutely opposed by local union officials, usually evaporated. At Bohn Aluminum, which had white and black male and white female employees but no black women, local union officials took the position that no more women could be hired unless black women were included. Opposition to their position, which included a brief wildcat, came mainly from white women. Threatened with the loss of their jobs, they "very reluctantly" went back to work, but continued to lock the black women out of the ladies' rest room. When two black women (one of them the mother of Berry Gordy, Jr., much later the founder of Motown Records) were put to work sewing fabric panels on wings for fighter planes at the Briggs Mack Avenue plant, some white women refused to work with them and walked out. Emil Mazey, president of Local 212, promptly had the strikers informed that the union would support management in firing them. Within ten minutes all were back at work, although the white women were "bitter" and "mad." A similar incident at the Rouge foundry saw white women return to work when the union committeeman, a black male, told them their only alternative to working with the African American women was to collect their pay and leave. Subsequently, they worked cooperatively with the black women. On the other hand, if local union officers caved in, as they did at Packard when management removed a few black women drill press operators from their jobs and returned them to training school in order to pacify wildcatting white women, prejudice prevailed.[68]

Black women did not acquiesce in unfair treatment and as a group acquired a reputation for assertiveness. A few emerged from the ranks to take part in union activities. Lillian Hatcher, a riveter at the Briggs aircraft plant, led a successful protest by a group of white and black women, all with children, in opposition to their transfer to the night shift. She was elected to the executive board of Local 742, organized that local's first women's conference in 1944, and became assistant director of the newly founded UAW Women's Department in the same year.[69]

BLACK WOMEN WERE ONLY a small element in the large contingent of more than 300,000 working women who entered the industry and the union during the war. The demand for wartime labor significantly altered the distribution of age and marital status among women workers. Before the war most of the industry's women were young and single; once war hiring began, older, married women entered in large numbers. Many had not worked previously and very few had any experience with unions. The women's reception, both by the companies and by the union, was mixed. Given the industry's history of gender employment practices, when women entered the factories disputes over fair treatment respecting wages, job classifications, and seniority entitlements were bound to occur, but over time women had opportunities to challenge discrimination.[70]

Meeting family responsibilities while working full-time and often overtime was a continuing source of tension and frustration for women workers. Sometimes a group of women devised a creative response to a particular problem. In one Detroit plant the women pitched in to do the rest room matron's job while she went out to do their shopping. The complex pressures generated by factory occupations and work routines combined with the difficulties in managing household responsibilities contributed to an absentee rate among women that was about 50 percent in excess of that of men and a rate of labor turnover that was more than twice as great.[71]

During the transition from civilian to war production, from late 1941 to the spring of 1942, when many men were laid off because of conversion problems, few women were hired for defense jobs. But the labor shortage that developed by the summer of 1942 brought thousands of women into the defense plants. From a low of less than 6 percent of the industry's work-force, the percentage of women employees peaked at 26 percent in November 1943. There were no women factory wage earners at Ford's River Rouge plant in the spring of 1942, but by the following year there were 5,000.[72]

The war eventually brought access to a wider range of jobs. At first women were employed in jobs traditionally considered "women's work": light assembly, inspection, drill press, punch press, and sewing machine operation. Gradually they were hired for jobs that had previously been available only to men: riveting, welding, heavy machinery operation, and foundry work— sometimes only after a wildcat by protesting male employees had failed. Although women secured jobs previously held only by men, job segregation persisted. Women were unevenly distributed throughout all factory occupations, heavily clustered in some, lightly represented in others. Despite their original hesitancy in hiring women for work traditionally performed by men, many wartime employers conceded that women's productivity matched and not infrequently exceeded that of their male employees.[73]

As the number of women in the plants and in the union increased, the UAW pressed for equal pay for equal work. After innumerable wrangles with employers over job classifications and the pay rates attached to each, the War Labor Board affirmed in September 1942, in a landmark case brought by the UAW and United Electrical Workers (UE) against General Motors, the principle of equal pay, "a milestone in the history of women's rights." The equal pay principle was defined broadly to include comparability, thereby making possible equalization of wage rates by job evaluations. Future GM contracts included an equal pay clause—"wage rates for women shall be the same as for men where they do work of comparable quantity and quality in comparable operations"—but many disputes remained over its application. In setting rates on new jobs, the union argued that the new jobs were comparable to the men's (higher) rate on previous jobs, while management argued that new jobs were comparable to the women's (lower) rate on previous jobs. A WLB arbitrator substituted "light" and "heavy" for "female" and "male" with a 10-cent wage differential, a decision that reduced one traditional differential but left another intact. The UAW objected to this violation of the equal pay principle, but without result. Overall, the gap between men's and women's pay narrowed but by no means disappeared. In 1940 women's share of men's straight-time wages was 67 percent; by 1943 it had risen to 79 percent, and by 1944 it had risen to 90 percent in Michigan plants.[74]

The International UAW had long opposed separate seniority lists for men and women, which left women more vulnerable to layoffs. During the

Riveters at work on an aircraft wing at Willow Run, c. 1944. Walter P. Reuther Library, Wayne State University

war some progress was made in eliminating them but, despite the union's policy and women's protests, separate lists were not abolished across the board. The General Motors contract stipulated that women hired into jobs that had been classified as "male" had seniority only for wartime. Some locals successfully defended their separate seniority lists. When female employees at Studebaker brought a proposal to abolish separate seniority lists to a local union meeting, it was voted down by the union's huge male majority.[75]

Wartime women workers succeeded in adding some of their objectives to the union's agenda. Gaining a voice in union deliberations was of key importance. In February 1942, the first UAW Women's Conference was held, with seventy women from locals in southeastern Michigan in attendance. A year later a conference on UAW policy toward women drew 326 female and male delegates from fifty-two Detroit area locals, and endorsed positions supportive of women on several important issues. The UAW executive board advocated maternity policies, defending the job rights of pregnant women, and pressed these on employers. The International Union also advocated more federal funding for day care centers, an issue of vital importance to many women workers. Wartime day care facilities were never close to adequate, and child care concerns accounted for much of the absenteeism among women workers.[76]

Although some union leaders made remarks critical of women as union members, and some locals discouraged female participation, by and large union leadership recognized the need to draw women employees into active roles. Publications designed to convince women of the union's value, such as the pamphlet *Sister, You Need the Union!*, were prepared and issued. Although home and family responsibilities limited the time and energy that many women could give to union participation, in most plants women workers were generally supportive of the union, and some became active members. Women began to appear in greater number in elective offices. By 1944 there were women shop stewards in nearly three-fourths of the UAW locals surveyed, and in 60 percent of these locals one or more women had been elected to the executive board. A smaller but still significant percentage of these locals, 37 percent, had elected women to plant bargaining and negotiating committees. The percentage of delegates to UAW conventions who were women nearly doubled, from 2.6 percent in 1942 to 5 percent in 1944, though this was still far short of matching their presence in the workforce. Whereas only thirteen locals sent women delegates to the 1941 convention, sixty-nine sent one or more women delegates to the 1944 convention. In one instance a woman unionist, Caroline Davis, became president of a local with a predominantly male (80 percent) membership. Despite the tokenism and half-way measures, women's emergence within the union during the war marked a step toward acceptance and equality.[77]

At the 1943 convention the debate over the establishment of a minorities department prompted a similar query concerning a women's department. The following spring the International executive board responded by authorizing a Women's Bureau as part of the War Policy Division. Although

lacking the status and budget of a department, the bureau could investigate
and publicize women's workplace problems and serve as an advocate within
the shops and to the outside world on issues such as child care. Mildred Jeffrey, a social worker with experience as a union organizer and with the War
Labor Board, was appointed the bureau's first director.[78]

As the war wound down, reconversion to peacetime production occupied national attention. For working women, reconversion wrecked most
of the occupational gains of World War II. In peacetime, women were
directly competing for jobs with men, including the returning war veterans
to whom the nation felt indebted, a competition intensified by widespread
fears of a postwar depression. A large majority of the women working in
auto industry factories hoped to be retained in similar postwar jobs: 86 percent according to a UAW survey conducted in the summer of 1944. As the
end of the war approached, with military contracts abruptly canceled, the
layoffs came with devastating swiftness. On May 5, 1945, the Navy and War
(Army) Departments awarded the Willow Run bomber plant the Army-
Navy E for Excellence in production at a meeting attended by thousands of
the plant's workers, many of them women. Henry Ford II, the company's
chief executive officer, used the occasion to inform the workers that they
were no longer needed and tens of thousands would soon be laid off. Half of
the workers, men and women alike, in plants under UAW contract lost their
jobs in the first week after the war's end. Most of the women laid off were
never recalled to the auto plants. At the Ford Motor Company, where over
20 percent of the workforce had consisted of women, the number dropped
by January 1946 to 4,900, only 4 percent of Ford employees. At General
Motors the decline, while not as steep, was still sharp. From 32 percent of
all GM workers at the wartime peak, the proportion of women working in
GM plants declined to 16 percent by November 1945. In total, the percentage of women working in auto fell from its wartime high of 26 percent in
the fall of 1943 to a low of less than 9 percent by the summer of 1946, only
a couple of percentage points above the average prewar figure.[79]

The seniority system's basic principle of "last in, first out" was bound
to put wartime women workers at a disadvantage. Veterans with prewar
auto jobs received seniority credit for their years of military service. Departmental or occupational group seniority in some plants, instead of plant-
wide seniority, kept women from "bumping" men in other departments or
occupations who had less seniority than they. Some UAW locals were vig-
ilant in protecting women's job rights; others were not. In some cases locals
conspired with companies to remove women from the plants. Grievances
filed by women mysteriously got lost with no action taken. The International Union consistently took the position that women should be treated
fairly and without discrimination, but it made little concerted effort to

implement this commitment and in the circumstances exercised little influence. President R. J. Thomas informed all UAW locals that women workers' legitimate claims to seniority must be honored and that the local's officers should monitor management's actions to insure their compliance, statements that reflected the fact that seniority provisions were being widely ignored in layoffs. The decisions were largely left in the hands of plant management officials and local union leadership.[80]

Seniority, although a serious hindrance to maintaining women's employment, was not as confining as the hiring practices of management. There was no shortage of industry jobs once the postwar transition to peacetime production was completed. As soon after the war's end as 1947, with the auto market booming and fears of a depression evaporating, the number of production workers in the industry exceeded the wartime employment peak. The companies, with control of hiring, simply preferred to fill their jobs with men. Jobs were reclassified from "light" to "heavy" or from "female" to "male" in order to exclude women. In some cases companies simply ignored women's seniority rights by not recalling them as jobs opened up. One company delayed its resumption of production in order not to have to recall women. Others began to enforce previously ignored regulations in order to lay women off. A "common practice" saw women put on peacetime production jobs they could not physically perform and then laid off for inability to do the work, while new male employees were being hired to do jobs within the range of women's physical capability. Women were downgraded to jobs of less skill and less pay such as janitorial work, put on the night shift, or transferred through a series of jobs each more demanding and perhaps demeaning than its predecessor. There were many ways of discouraging and eliminating them. As late as the early 1960s, women's employment in the auto plants, less than 10 percent of the total, had still not rebounded to wartime levels. Women's concerns did gain a more secure place in the union's institutional structure when the International in 1946 gave the Women's Bureau, originally placed in the now defunct War Policies Division, a permanent home in the new Fair Practices and Anti-Discrimination Department.[81]

DEEPLY CONCERNED ABOUT POSTWAR employment for its hundreds of thousands of members and with avoiding a postwar depression, UAW officers brought forward proposals for reconversion of the economy to peacetime production. As usual, the most visionary plans came from Walter Reuther, who formulated a social-democratic program for postwar prosperity. Reuther's thinking emphasized cooperation, public coordination of the economy, full employment, and a broad distribution of income and goods. The postwar political-economic system he foresaw was a mixed one: free enterprise combined with national regulation and planning. In one of many speeches on the subject he said "we say that free enterprise has a right to live only if free enterprise . . . accepts its full social responsibility and that is that the welfare of the workers and the community and the nation come first before the relative position on the New York Stock Exchange." National planning, in which labor as well as government and business would be involved, was, he believed, the key to a prosperous and equitable future. In 1944 he proposed a sixteen-point conversion program that included pooling manpower and machine tools for allocation among corporations, a thirty-hour workweek to create jobs for all, government operation of monopolistic industries as yardsticks for determining costs, the establishment of production quotas based on social need, and a public works program to provide jobs and the infrastructure required for a prosperous economy. Later he urged creation of a Peace Production Board with representatives of labor, management, consumers, agriculture, and government to plan and allocate manpower, materials, and machinery.[82]

The government's huge wartime investment in plants and machinery, Reuther argued, should be put to peacetime uses as quickly as possible once the war ended. The most pressing social need, he believed, was for mass-produced, prefabricated, low-cost housing. Government-owned aircraft factories could be converted to its manufacture. Venturing into more hazardous depths for an auto workers' union official, he proposed that huge government-owned plants in the Detroit area, such as the Willow Run bomber plant and the Chrysler Tank Arsenal, be converted to the manufacture of "modern streamlined light-metal railroad cars." The *Detroit News*, appalled that an upstart union official should have views on such weighty matters and publicly discuss them, urged the UAW to buy Willow Run to "manufacture . . . whatever it thinks may strike the fancy of the market. . . . The experiment would be edifying . . . as a yardstick both on the performance of managements and, even more so, on the union leaders' confident ideas of how management ought to perform." Like Reuther's earlier proposals for codirected national, industrial planning mechanisms, his reconversion ideas encountered more opposition than support. President Thomas flirted with the idea of a UAW purchase of the Willow Run plant but settled for the more modest proposal of urging industrialist Henry J. Kaiser to take over Willow Run and build automobiles there, an undertaking Kaiser already contemplated and eventually acted upon.[83]

BY THE WAR'S END THE UAW had achieved many of its original objectives. It had organized nearly the entire auto industry (only workers in some of the independent parts plants remained on the outside) and established a strong position in aircraft, and a competitive one in agricultural implement manufacturing. Wages and working conditions had by and large been removed from the arena in which the auto companies competed. Most of the companies the union dealt with had, however grudgingly and unhappily, come to accept its existence. It had successfully fought off splinter movements and attempts to control it in the interests of outside groups, and it had won an independent and influential position within the CIO. All auto workers, of whatever occupational, racial, ethnic, or gender group, had been incorporated within the union; by no means was this accomplished without tensions or on terms of equality, but all benefited from the improved wages and better working conditions the union had won. The auto workforce had recreated itself in the image of the union's name. What was once an aspiration was now a reality: they were truly united. All who had contributed—rank-and-file workers, union activists, and local and International leaders—could take pride in what had been achieved.

The greatly enlarged and more diversified auto workforce was one of the keys to Allied victory in World War II. It produced a flood of war materials for the armed forces of the United States and its allies. To a significant degree, the war muffled, but did not end, the union's factional battles, which burst out with renewed vigor once the war was over. Throughout wartime, the balance of power shifted gradually away from the Addes-Frankensteen-CP combination in favor of Walter Reuther and his following. Although there was no challenge during the war to R. J. Thomas's presidency, he was perched insecurely above and apart from the rival caucuses, without a loyal, cohesive force of his own. The war set the stage for Reuther's bid for the union's highest office.

It also left the UAW, like other unions, facing an uncertain future. The federal government had inserted itself into labor-management relations in a massive way; its role in postwar labor and industrial relations was as yet unclear but included the possibility of restrictive legislation. While the war stimulated the union's growth and consolidated its position in the plants of the leading manufacturers, it raised unanswered questions about the organization's and the workers' futures.[84]

CHAPTER 7

"Teamwork in the leadership and solidarity in the ranks"

The Reuther Era Begins, 1945–60

Throughout its early history the UAW rose and fell with the shifting tides of Roosevelt's New Deal. The New Deal's program of economic revival and reform produced important results, but its creative phase was soon over. By 1938 a reaction had set in that halted its forward momentum. Many of the New Deal's achievements, including the reborn labor movement, came under hostile public and congressional scrutiny. The overriding priorities of World War II restrained the backlash for a time, but the public's harsh response to wartime acts of defiance by Lewis's miners' reinvigorated the antiunion movement as the war drew to its close.[1]

For the labor movement the precedents from a previous postwar period were ominous. After the First World War, an aggressive open shop campaign reduced a growing union movement to impotence for a decade, while the "Red scare" indiscriminately targeted leftists and their organizations for suppression. Walter Reuther, with other labor figures, warned that if the movement relaxed its vigilance, "it would be 1919 and the twenties all over again." In many minds, furthermore, was the fear that as the war had brought full employment and a feverish prosperity, so peace would bring the return of labor redundancies, soup lines, and other miseries of the depression decade.[2]

Political prospects were another source of anxiety for postwar labor. With Franklin D. Roosevelt's death on April 12, 1945, the labor movement lost the best Oval Office champion it had ever known. Although his successor, Vice President Harry S. Truman, backed most New Deal measures during his tenure in the United States Senate, to nearly everyone, both friend and foe, he seemed a lesser man than "the champ." Organized labor's influence in Congress, in decline since the elections of 1938, continued to erode. A hostile coalition of congressional Republicans and conservative southern Democrats steadily gained strength and stepped up its opposition to labor's legislative agenda. The first national postwar elections, the congressional contests of 1946, dealt the labor movement a heavy blow. The Democrats lost fifty-four seats in the House and eleven in the Senate, and many labor-friendly congressmen were gone. The election of Republican majorities in both houses of Congress, which the party would control for the first time since the session of 1930–32, together with a bloc of southern Democrats assured a veto-proof vote for legislation curtailing organized labor. Even before the election decimated the prolabor congressional contingent, Congress passed the Case bill, which imposed severe restraints on unions. That bill fell victim to a presidential veto, but political forces were now in place for the passage of the Taft-Hartley Act in 1947 despite President Truman's disapproval. As the political balance of power shifted against labor, antiunion managements became more confident of their ability to resist union demands.[3]

Prospects, however, were by no means entirely bleak. In scanning the present and divining the future, there were grounds for hope that a progressive drive toward the "vital center" of social democracy with a mixed-enterprise economy would produce significant results. Postwar European developments were encouraging. There, with millions determined not to return to prewar economic stagnation, social decay, and pessimism, both the noncommunist and the communist left were vigorous and resolute. For progressive American unionists, the victory of the British Labour Party in the July 1945 parliamentary elections, which produced a Labour government pledged to create a partially socialized economy with health, housing, unemployment, and other entitlements, was an inspiring breakthrough. UAW President R. J. Thomas greeted Labour's triumph as "the most important thing for the cause of organized labor in the United States that has happened for a long time." On balance, however, auto workers had reason to regard an uncertain future with concern.[4]

As that future unfolded, it belied the fears of a floundering economy but confirmed those of a political attack. Following a turbulent transition from war to peace, the economy entered an era of growth and substantial, if uneven, prosperity. For the auto industry, a gap of more than three years (1942–45) in civilian car production had created a reservoir brimming over with demand, ready to burst out of confinement as soon as the manufacturers could supply the dealers with vehicles. Car production and auto employment rose, reestablishing the industry as the heart and muscle of the manufacturing economy. For auto workers, postwar economic conditions by and large proved favorable. On the political front, antiliberal and antiunion sentiments, invigorated and driven to extremes as a new Red scare inflamed American opinion, seized control with a vengeance, throwing organized labor and all those seeking a fulfillment of "freedom from want"—that glowing promise of the late New Deal—on the defensive. Political action was stalemated by the contending forces, unable to go forward but unwilling to go back.[5]

BY WAR'S END, Walter Reuther, a UAW vice president since 1942 and head of the union's General Motors Department, had emerged as the leading auto unionist. Schooled by experience in all of a union officer's duties, he added to his credentials during the war by frequently representing the UAW in national arenas, devising plans to attack production bottlenecks and wage and price control problems, and testifying before government agencies and Congress. A forceful speaker, well-prepared with strong staff support, and keenly aware of public opinion's impact on the union's fortunes, he conducted debates and discussions with representatives of the corporations, government, and the media on at least equal and often superior terms. Although the frustrations of the war years strained the relationships of all UAW leaders with the rank and file, Reuther's standing suffered less than that of others. The CP left was particularly hurt by its wartime support for incentive pay and strict adherence to the no-strike pledge. In the grudging tribute of CP spokesman Nat Ganley, their blunders gave Reuther the opportunity to "ride in as the great hero on the white horse leading the downtrodden masses, which he did and did very successfully."[6]

Reuther had assembled a corps of advisors, administrative assistants, union staff, and other associates, an informal brain trust, whose collective efforts and talents he would direct and rely upon throughout his union service. No one doubted his leadership, but the operation was never a one-man show. Reuther brought into his circle like-minded yet creative and independent colleagues with whom he could test ideas and from whom he could learn. He freely borrowed promising ideas from them or any other source, sometimes giving credit, sometimes not. All, like Reuther himself, came out of the noncommunist, social-democratic left, with or without a previous or current affiliation with the Socialist Party. Although the composition of the group naturally changed from time to time, there was considerable continuity. Most made the UAW their life's work, while occasionally someone departed for related positions in government or with other union agencies.[7]

His earliest associates were his two younger brothers, Roy (1909–1968) and Victor (b. 1912). Roy was the first of the brothers to enter actively into autoworker organizing. Apprenticed as an electrician and then trained as an instructor in workers' education at the socialist-oriented and union-supported Brookwood Labor College in Katonah, New York, he was a pioneer UAW organizer in Flint and a key figure in the great sit-down strike. Outgoing and warm, he was for many years Walter's closest associate, giving his brother frank advice on many subjects. As a UAW International representative, his responsibilities centered on political activity and advising, including organizing registration and voter participation campaigns. Victor, also a student at Brookwood, whose service in the Flint strike included operation of the union's sound car, was, as the UAW's educational director, a key supporter of Reuther's drive for reelection as president in 1947. Later, building on associations with foreign labor leaders and a reputation as the family intellectual, he headed the UAW's International Affairs Office in Washington, D.C. The Reuther inner circle had expanded in March 1936, to include May Wolfman, when she and Walter married. Reared in a family of leftist sympathies and setting comparable to Reuther's, May was a strong and supportive mate and confidant, as well as for several years his secretary, both volunteer and paid, whose advice he sought and respected. Having met at a Socialist Party gathering, they married in a union hall, and on the night of their wedding drove to suburban Algonac, Michigan, in order that Walter could speak at an organizing meeting.[8]

Outside the family circle, an early recruit to the brain trust was Eddie Levinson, socialist, manager of Norman Thomas's 1932 presidential campaign, publicist, journalist, author, and all-around labor intellectual. Brought on the UAW staff in 1939 with Reuther's backing as publicity director and editor of the *United Automobile Worker*, Levinson, with his acute political sensibility, polemical thrusts, cheerful demeanor and wit made valuable contributions and always enlivened proceedings. His premature death in 1945 deprived Reuther of a shrewd, engaging companion, whose judgment he trusted and on whose abilities he relied.[9]

During the war others entered the circle. Reuther brought in Donald E. Montgomery as consumer counsel and representative in the UAW's Washington office. Montgomery was a liberal economist with vast experience in New Deal agencies and knowledge of their policies and operations, including a seven-year stint in the Department of Agriculture as an advocate for consumers' interests. He soon became an influential researcher and advisor on questions of national economic policy and the economic impact of union objectives. Always on the lookout for talent, Reuther added Frank Winn, Leonard Woodcock, Jack Conway, Nat Weinberg, Douglas Fraser, and Irving Bluestone, among others, to his cadre.[10]

By the war's end a reshuffling of political forces within the UAW had shifted power in Reuther's direction. Most of the union's other leading figures had drawn together in a fragile "center-left coalition," as much the product of fear of Reuther's ascendency as of shared ideological position and outlook. President R. J. Thomas, who had long maintained a precarious caucus neutrality, had perforce thrown in his lot with the coalition, but secretary-treasurer George Addes remained its leading figure. Vice president Dick Frankensteen, still with a substantial following, was winding down his union activity in favor of launching a political career. Richard Leonard, Ford Department director, felt his claims to preferment had been slighted by the Reuther caucus and abandoned it for the coalition. Although in ordinary service activities for the members the differences between the "center-left" and the "right," or Reuther faction, were not great, their political agendas and alignments sharply contrasted. The Reuther following maintained that the Communists in the coalition had shown they would sacrifice the union's and the membership's interests as political considerations dictated, dragging their coalition partners with them. Activists on both sides had long anticipated that a showdown would occur somewhere down the road. As Bill McKie, a Communist and pioneer Ford organizer had reportedly predicted, "sooner or later either the Reuther gang or the Addes side will be in full control of the UAW. . . . We're in this fight to see that our side wins and we can set policy." [11]

AUTO COMPANY EXECUTIVES, who chafed under the gains labor made during the New Deal and the war, now feared new encroachments on management's rights and privileges. Many business leaders expected a postwar struggle. As *New York Times* writer James Reston noted of the antagonists, "both sides seem to take the view that they have taken a lot of guff from the other side during the war and are now free to fight it out." Hostilities were not limited to the auto industry. Peace saw a resurgence of strife throughout the industrial economy. From the summer of 1945 through the close of 1946 there were as many strikes with as many participants as in any comparable period before or since, with major disputes in the auto, steel, electrical equipment, meatpacking, longshoring, and trucking industries.[12]

Soon after the war's end, the UAW negotiated new contracts with all the auto manufacturers, but it reached agreement with General Motors only after a bitterly contested strike, which began on November 21, 1945, and lasted 113 days until March 13, 1946—the longest strike against a major manufacturer in which the union had been engaged until that time and the longest national GM strike in its history. As head of the General Motors Department, Reuther persuaded the UAW's officers and its executive board to endorse a "one-at-a-time" strategy in confronting the manufacturers, intended to maximize pressure on the target company. Arguing from a Keynesian economic perspective developed by Donald Montgomery, Reuther called for a 30 percent wage increase and a pledge from the corporation to hold the line on car prices. The 30 percent increase, he claimed, would maintain but not exceed auto workers' overtime-enhanced wartime earnings. Without the increase, an auto worker's standard of living would drop by nearly one-third. From the Keynesian standpoint of bolstering a productive economy, the proposal would enable auto workers to maintain their spending, thus contributing to strong demand, while the elimination of overtime would force the companies to expand employment, reabsorbing into the workforce many who had been laid off. The novel and controversial proposal for a pledge to hold the line on prices was necessary to protect consumers and workers from a price surge that would pay wages in "the wooden nickels of inflation," posssibly resulting in rising unemployment and a depression. All of these objectives could be accomplished, Reuther predicted, while allowing the corporation adequate funds for reinvestment and providing a fair return to stockholders. The ambitious proposal sought, through a contract between the nation's largest industrial corporation and its largest industrial union, a limited version of co-determination, a voice for auto workers in establishing the industry's policies. As later appraised by one historian, the Reuther proposal sought to exploit "the flux of the reconversion period . . . to rewrite the rules governing the management of the American economy and the political and social order it undergirded."[13]

In arguing for mass purchasing power and price restraint, Reuther claimed to speak for the interests of both workers and consumers. The entire community would benefit from a demand-driven, full-employment economy with the profits of industry assured by high-volume, technically advanced, low unit-cost production. "The war," he said in a speech, "has proven that production is not our problem; our problem is consumption." A broad distribution of income quickly converted into massive aggregate demand held the key to future prosperity. Mindful that largely as a result of wartime controversies much of the public believed that organized labor was a greedy special interest concerned only with its own gains, Reuther took pains to frame and articulate a union agenda that both benefited labor and contributed to the common good. "All that we have done in this wage case," he proclaimed, "is to say that we are not going to operate as a narrow economic pressure group which says 'we are going to get ours and the public be damned' or 'the consumer be damned,' " adding, in a phrase he would often repeat, "we . . . want to make progress with the community and not at the expense of the community." Liberal journals responded favorably, with the *Nation* praising Reuther for "fighting the government's battle and the consumer's battle," while the *New Republic* saw the "most advanced unions" following Reuther's lead, acting "not only in the interest of their members, but in the interest of sound national policy as well." Organs of opinion on the center and right of the spectrum were skeptical or hostile.[14]

Angry and dismayed, General Motors' management condemned Reuther's demands as an attack on essential features of free enterprise. A transcript of prestrike talks reveals the ideological chasm separating the

two sides. Following Reuther's assertion that without "a more realistic distribution of America's wealth, we don't get enough to keep this machine
going," a GM spokesman retorted "there it is again. You can't talk about
this thing without exposing your socialistic desires." Reuther replied: "If
fighting for a more equal and equitable distibution of wealth of this country is socialistic, I stand guilty of being a socialist." "I think you are convicted," he was told. Setting the price of its cars, GM maintained, was
management's exclusive prerogative, not a matter to be bargained over with
a union of its workers. To counter the UAW's proposal, the corporation
offered to increase the work week to forty-four hours without payment of
premium rates, which, it pointed out, would increase the incomes of those
with jobs. Reuther was quick to note that the offer fell well short of maintaining workers' wartime income and would do nothing to restore employment for those who were laid off.[15]

Both sides maneuvered for advantage in this prestrike sparring. Introducing another novelty into the bargaining scenario, Reuther offered to
accept less than a 30 percent increase if GM proved it could not pay that
amount and still make a "fair" profit, thus linking even more closely the
union's wage demands with the corporation's ability to pay. But there was
a catch. To make its case, the corporation would have to let the union have
"a look at the books," opening its cost and earnings records to public inspection. By law the corporation was required to issue only a consolidated financial statement, which concealed the cost and profit-and-loss figures of its
many different operations. The union proposal would make public, and
known to competitors, closely guarded corporate secrets. GM officials were
shocked. One candidly confessed, "We don't even open our books to our
stockholders." Again GM charged the union with encroaching on management prerogatives and, escalating the rhetoric, claimed that a union victory
on this point would lead to "a Socialistic nation with all activities controlled and regimented, and with the people the servants of government."
Although by any sober analysis Reuther's proposals fell far short of a socialist restructuring of the economy, they did call for a sharing of powers that
had belonged exclusively to management. If the Reuther approach were to
prevail throughout industry, "the result may not be the end of capitalism,"
the supportive Association of Catholic Trade Unionists (ACTU) publication the *Wage Earner* stated, "but it will certainly be the beginning of a new
kind of capitalism."[16]

Whatever the merits of the ideological debate and the readiness of GM
workers for a strike, in tactical economic terms the UAW was at a disadvantage. Thanks to a provision in the tax laws GM had an important edge.
The wartime "excess profits" tax, which was still in effect, allowed GM to
deduct any losses of revenues it incurred from a strike from its federal tax

bill. For 1945 the corporation had already earned nearly as much as it was allowed before losing all additional "excess" profit to the tax. Since the taxes had been paid in advance on the assumption of uninterrupted production, the corporation would receive rebates if a strike closed it down. In a bizarre turn of events, the government would make strike payments to the company while the union, without a substantial strike fund, could offer little to its members. According to a calculation in *Business Week*, the strike cost GM only 15 cents for each dollar reduction in its earnings. "Never before," the magazine wrote, "has a major employer had so little direct economic incentive to end a stoppage by making concessions to a union." Although GM could be hurt by losing sales to competitors, the direct cost of the strike would be low. From the standpoint of the economic pressure that could be brought to bear on the corporation, a worse time for a strike could hardly be imagined.[17]

From the standpoint of internal politics, however, the time was right. General Motors workers were eager to go out. Strong feelings that had been bottled up during wartime or only partially discharged in wildcat strikes could now be channeled into coordinated strike action. Victor Reuther later went so far as to remark to an interviewer that "the GM strike was designed to take the ball out of the hands of the stewards and committeemen and put it back in the hands of the national leadership." Although the union had only a $4 million strike fund, insufficient to sustain the huge GM workforce for long, wartime savings gave many workers a financial cushion. General Motors workers were estimated to own $300,000,000 in war bonds. A strike vote, required by the wartime Smith-Connally Act that was still in effect, posed the leading question: "Do you wish to permit an interruption of war production in wartime as a result of this dispute?" Since the war had been over for three months when the vote was taken, no one was fooled. Approval of a strike carried by nearly a six-to-one margin. At the last moment the corporation offered a 10 percent raise, which Reuther countered with an offer to go to arbitration framed in such a way that GM would have to concede public examination of its books. On November 21 the strike of 320,000 GM workers (of whom about 140,000 were on temporary layoff owing to reconversion delays) began.[18]

Although the strike's objectives challenged the status quo in industrial relations, provoked heated exchanges in the press and at the bargaining table, and lasted much longer than any previous major auto strike, the strike itself was peaceful. The corporation made no effort to operate its plants. Skimpy picket lines were set up to publicize the strike and sustain morale, but there was no need to block access to the plants.[19]

Reuther, aware of public opinion's potentially critical impact on the strike's outcome, deployed an array of public relations initiatives. A citizens'

Workers and their families on the picket line in support of the UAW strike at General Motors, 1946. Walter P. Reuther Library, Wayne State University

committee of prominent sympathizers was recruited to investigate his claim that GM could afford higher wages without a price increase. Its report, to no one's surprise, supported his position and warmly praised his effort to lift "collective bargaining to a new high level by insisting that the advancement of labor's interest shall not be made at the expense of the public." Local unions were instructed to contact area merchants to solicit their sympathy and support with an appeal to their self-interest. After pointing out to merchants how much new money would be pumped into local economies if GM workers gained the raises they sought, local unionists were told to ask "How many of the DuPonts [GM's major shareholders] do you have among your customers?"[20]

Within the labor movement and among other UAW leaders, Reuther encountered skepticism. Although no prominent UAW official openly condemned the strike or Reuther's conduct of it, there was behind-the-scenes criticism and little enthusiasm for the strike's novel objectives. President R. J. Thomas issued supportive press releases but privately ridiculed Reuther's proposals as offering food for thought for intellectuals but little bread for workers. CIO president Philip Murray endorsed the strike but privately tried to talk Reuther out of the link he proposed between wages and prices. United Mine Workers president John L. Lewis harshly condemned both sides: "The dishonesty on the side of the company," he charged, "is only equaled by the stupidity on the side of the labor organization." No important labor leader supported Reuther's contention that unions bore a responsibility for the general welfare as well as for that of their members.[21]

President Truman, eager to end the strike so that conversion to peacetime production could proceed, appointed a fact-finding board in December. The corporation, fearing that the board would link a wage increase to price stability and demand access to the company's records, improved its wage offer to 13–1/2 cents per hour. On December 20 the fact-finding board met with GM representatives. When a statement from President Truman was read that said the board "should have the authority . . . to examine the books of the employer," GM walked out of the hearings and denounced what it called an attempt to force it to open its books to "the hungry eyes of . . . competitors." The company, a spokesman said, must defend itself against the "revolutionary" and "radical" position of the union and the government. "To yield," it predicted, not for the first or the last time, "would mean the end of . . . free enterprise."[22]

On January 10, 1946, the Truman board recommended a raise of 17–1/2 percent (19–1/2 cents an hour), which it claimed the corporation could afford without a price increase. Although disappointed in a recommendation that amounted to only a little more than half the union's original demand, Reuther announced that he would accept the recommendation if the corporation agreed. GM quickly turned the proposal down.[23]

The General Motors workers' position was weakened by agreements reached with other auto employers. Ford and Chrysler settled with the UAW on hourly wage increases of 18 cents and 18–1/2 cents an hour respectively, with a stipulation that the contracts could be reopened if GM, whose current offer was considerably less, agreed to pay more. Nothing was said about prices, but the Ford contract, while continuing union shop and check-off provisions, contained a "company security" clause that provided for dismissal of any employee guilty of fomenting or participating in wildcat strikes without resort to the grievance procedure, and a tough management rights clause that threatened discipline and discharge of workers who failed to meet production standards. Another damaging settlement, at 18–1/2 cents an hour without a pledge on prices, was signed by the United Electrical Workers (UE), representing 30,000 GM employees in electrical equipment divisions. UAW officials charged that UE had reneged on a promise not to negotiate a separate settlement without prior consultation, a charge UE leaders denied. Reuther and his followers saw a clear explanation for the alleged "betrayal." The UE's leaders were close to the Communist Party, and Reuther believed the agreement was a deliberate, Communist-inspired attempt to sabotage the GM strike and discredit him with GM workers. The UAW's position was further weakened when the United Steel Workers settled for the now customary 18–1/2 cents, with the steel companies promised a $5 a ton price increase by government price controllers. Truman, with the concurrence of steel worker's union president Philip Murray, undercut his own position on price stability in order to end the steel workers' strike. A few days later the rubber workers agreed to the same terms, and a pattern for the first postwar round of wage increases, followed by price increases to offset higher costs, had been set. The outcome that Reuther had feared and tried to avoid, an inflationary spiral for which labor would be blamed, now seemed a certainty.[24]

The GM workers were isolated in both their monetary demands and their philosophical position. As the strike wore on and workers elsewhere reached agreements, pressure for a settlement grew within the ranks. The UAW's strike fund was soon exhausted; the $600,000 in contributions the union raised from nonstriking workers and friends hardly made a dent in the need. With limited concessions forthcoming from both sides, an agreement to end the strike was reached on March 13, 1946. The company offered a raise of 18–1/2 cents an hour; with additional adjustments for plant pay differentials, paid vacations, and overtime that the union claimed (with little evidence), raised the total to slightly more than 19–1/2 cents. In addition, the union gained a stronger seniority clause and a monthly dues checkoff for workers who gave written consent; but, as GM had insisted all along, the agreement was silent on prices. A double-edged sword, but one popular with many workers, assured reasonable smoking privileges in the plants.[25]

Like many a general at the end of an arduous campaign, Reuther proclaimed victory, but most observers were not convinced. The monetary settlement was not materially better than that gained by workers elsewhere who had incurred shorter strikes or none at all. In pursuit of a penny more per hour, the strike had been prolonged for weeks. It would be more than two years before GM workers recovered their pay losses, and not until 1953 would their earnings equal what they would have been if GM's offer of a 13–1/2 cent raise had been accepted. In most nonmonetary respects the GM contract was comparable to the contracts with the other manufacturers. None of Reuther's hopes for a breakthrough that would give the union a say in setting prices had been realized. Again he had brought forward a proposal to restructure the industrial decision-making process through an expansion of the union's role as representative of its members as both producers and consumers. The logical end of this approach, a version of industrial co-determination combined with a broad-based community union, would not be realized and in fact was dropped from the union's (including Reuther's) agenda. The limited objective of protecting auto workers' pay from inflationary erosion, however, was reached in 1948 when General Motors president Charles E. Wilson negotiated a UAW wage provision that included a cost of living adjustment (COLA) that tied wages to changing price levels and over the years would produce the bulk of auto workers' wage increases. Unlike Reuther's proposal, the Wilson plan gave auto workers some protection against inflation but left consumers adrift. In the future the union's collective bargaining agenda would be confined to the workers alone, with broader general interest objectives, which the UAW did not abandon, pursued through the resistant thickets of political and social action. GM's stout opposition to union demands and the high cost of supporting a strike by the corporation's hundreds of thousands of blue-collar employees made the UAW leadership wary of again choosing GM as a target. Although the corporation had to deal with numerous local plant strikes concerning working conditions and other matters, not until 1970 would the UAW again call out all GM workers to "set the pattern" in a full-blown strike.[26]

Prices spiraled upward following the settlements. Over the next six months the car companies were granted three price increases, then Congress abolished all price controls, allowing the manufacturers to charge whatever the market would bear. The government had as little success as the union in restraining price increases. The cost-of-living index rose at a faster pace in 1947 than in any subsequent year until the inflation induced by the oil embargo of 1979. The postwar settlements, prolonged though the strike was in the case of General Motors, had no damaging effects on company returns. By 1949, when the car companies had completed their transition to peacetime production, they had an annual rate of return (net profits after taxes divided by net worth) of over 25 percent, compared with a rate of less than 9 percent for all corporations. GM led the profit parade.[27]

ALTHOUGH THE ECONOMIC and ideological results were disappointing, from a political perspective the strike was a victory for Walter Reuther and his union following. As its leader, he had enhanced his reputation as an energetic, imaginative captain of the union's forces. United Electrical's settlement with GM allowed the Reutherites to blame the Communists for the strike's disappointments. Workers' pay and prospects, they could argue, had been sacrificed in a factional maneuver. The aggressive challenge to the most powerful of the auto corporations, even though the outcome was at best a draw and at worst a defeat, propelled Reuther into the UAW's presidency, a climactic development long anticipated by supporters and feared by opponents and rivals.[28]

As UAW president since 1939, R. J. Thomas had tried to walk a tightwire suspended high above the contending forces. Placed in office as a peacemaker and caretaker at the insistence of CIO officials, he never built the kind of loyal, disciplined following among secondary leaders and rank-and-file activists that was necessary for success in the UAW's highly charged political milieu. He charted a middle-of-the-road course, positioned at equal distances between the shifting boundaries of left and right. With the Reuther forces gathering strength and preparing for a challenge as the war ended, Thomas's strategy became untenable and he threw in his lot with the ramshackle coalition that was taking shape on the UAW's left. A former Chrysler welder, Thomas's personal qualities appealed to many auto workers. His habits and tastes were down-to-earth. He enjoyed a drink, seemed always to be chewing a plug of tobacco (according to one story, on a wartime trip to the U.S.S.R., where his favorite brand was unavailable, he took along a small suitcase filled with Mail Pouch!), and liked playing poker, sometimes to the neglect of union duties. It was said that there was a twenty-four hour poker game at union headquarters during Thomas's tenure, with the president often taking a hand. Where ideas and initiatives were concerned, he reacted to those of others, possessing little creativity or independent intellectual force. From the beginning of his term, he had recognized Reuther as his most serious rival. Although he referred to Reuther dismissively as "the comet" and scorned his "fancy economics," he envied Reuther an upbringing that seemed ideally suited for a union activist and feared his ambition and array of leadership skills.[29]

The contrast between the two contenders was striking. Although Reuther was warm and unreserved among a circle of advisors, relatives, and friends, and easily established a bond with audiences when speaking at large gatherings, he seemed distant and wary to those he did not know or trust. The union brotherhood's rituals of comraderie meant little to him. After meetings he returned home or went to his hotel room instead of joining in the "barroom postmortems" where "the boys hash it all over." Small talk, practical joking, and horseplay had no place in this serious man's social repertoire. Profanity was sparingly used, reserved for those occasions, as in bargaining, that warranted a special emphasis. He neither played poker, drank whiskey, nor used tobacco; he seemed, in fact, to have few if any of those humanizing vices that dissolve barriers and create bonds among those who share them. Admirers and detractors constructed very different images. "The real key to his personality," wrote an admirer (Paul Weber, editor of the ACTU paper, the *Wage Earner*) "is a kind of Boy Scout simplicity and enthusiasm which shines through everything he does. He is never disturbed by any opponent['s] doubts of the justice of his cause or the wisdom of his course." At the opposite extreme, Communist and like-minded critics were relentlessly hostile, viewing Reuther as a cold, ambitious, unprincipled opportunist and renegade, whose decisions and tactics were dictated by political expediency, with his self-promoting maneuvers shrouded in clouds of long-winded,

high-flown hypocritical rhetoric. Repeatedly thrown at Reuther was his condemnation of Red-baiting dating from 1937 and the struggle with Homer
Martin, in which he urged fellow workers not to "play the bosses' game by
falling for their red scare. . . . [T]hose who peddle the red scare . . . are dangerous enemies of the union"—remarks now directly applicable, critics said,
to himself. Such charges were dismissed by Reuther supporters and many
observers as outdated and irrelevant to the current situation or as polemical
distortions resorted to by those who feared they were destined to end up on
the losing side. While he lacked Thomas's common touch, in the view of
many unionists his energy and devotion to his work, combined with demonstrated practical skills as a union leader, a creative intellectual flair where
both union and broader social objectives were concerned, and a finely-tuned
balance between visionary idealism and political realism more than com-
pensated for any deficiencies of the "hail fellow, well met" variety or the
inconsistencies that cropped up in an active life that stretched through
tumultuous times. In 1946 he was a youthful thirty-eight years of age.[30]

THE "REUTHER BOOM" BEGAN EARLY in March 1946 before the GM
strike ended, kicked off when presidents of seventeen large locals, representing a bloc of 250,000 members, urged Reuther to run and pledged their
support. The most direct, least divisive route to the presidency would be to
win over secretary-treasurer George Addes, a coup that would fragment the
opposition, dispense with Thomas, and isolate the Communists. Addes was
told that the Reuther caucus would not oppose his reelection, thus assuring his continuation in office, if he would agree to serve under Reuther.
Since some of Addes's followers had made clear their unhappiness with R.
J. Thomas's "bumbling mismanagement," and the secretary-treasurer himself harbored doubts about R. J.'s adequacy for the job, Addes was tempted
by the offer and at first agreed. Later he changed his mind. His decision to
reject the overture to play second fiddle in a Reuther administration, which
probably came as no surprise to Reuther, insured that there would be a sharp
contest and a continuing division within the union.[31]

When the nearly 1,900 delegates representing more than 800,000
members met in Atlantic City, New Jersey, electioneering was energetic
and intense in the UAW's only closely contested convention presidential
election. Emotions spilled over into heckling and rowdiness on the convention floor and in the hotel. At one point Addes, not known for humorous remarks, unwittingly brought down the house with a plea to the
conventioneers to stop dropping paper-bag water bombs from hotel windows because they might injure "a delegate or a human being." CIO president Philip Murray, who could not afford to antagonize the UAW's next
president whoever he might be, concluded a speech with an indirect but

unmistakable endorsement of Thomas, "this great big guy for whom I have a distinct fondness, the President of your Union"—the last attempt by a CIO head to influence an important internal UAW matter. The statement, indirect though it was, cost Reuther many votes. The Reuther camp counterattacked with a proposal for a wide-open, off-the-record debate between the two candidates at a closed session, confident that the articulate, mentally nimble Reuther would demolish his opponent. Addes, temporarily chairing the convention, blocked the debate with a ruling that a two-thirds vote was required for such an extraordinary session. When a vote was taken on Addes's ruling, the Reuther forces barely fell short of the required margin, easily gaining a simple majority. In what was, in a way, a straw ballot on the presidency, Reuther had prevailed.[32]

The outcome of the election was not determined prior to the convention. Large numbers of delegates were uncommitted or only loosely aligned, free to float from side to side as they were swayed by one or another consideration. Most of the electioneering action was fought out in delegates' meetings, caucuses, and informal gatherings in hotel rooms rather than on the convention floor. Reuther actively solicited votes in caucus speeches and in numerous meetings with small groups of delegates and influential individuals, and his political organization, under the direction of Leonard Woodcock, ran a professional campaign. The stakes were high and the tone serious but humorous touches were not absent. As the rival caucuses gathered in separate rooms off a hotel hallway, a Reuther supporter held up two signs: one read, "This way to Reuther," with an arrow pointing to the Reuther caucus meeting, and the other, "That way to ruin," with an arrow pointing down the hall to the Thomas meeting.[33]

The issue of the Communists' role in the union seldom intruded in convention debates or appeared in resolutions. The "Red-baiting" for which the Reuther caucus was criticized made less of a public appearance than it had at UAW conventions in 1940 and 1941. Of course, since Reuther's anticommunist position was well-known to the delegates and the rest of the membership, little was required in the way of a public reminder. One of Reuther's campaign slogans, "Against Outside Interference," was a sufficient statement. In their remarks in closed caucus meetings Reuther and spokesmen for his candidacy denounced Thomas and the rest of the center-left coalition leadership as "stooges" for the CP who had toed a Soviet-dictated party line even when it conflicted with the interests of the union and its members. They cited the CP's wartime support for incentive pay, for a categorical no-strike pledge, and for mandatory labor mobilization proposals, and assailed UE's alleged abandonment of the UAW in the GM strike. Thomas's contribution was to charge that Reuther was part of a conspiracy to take the UAW out of the CIO and into the AFL. Each contestant distorted his rival's record and position in a scramble for votes.[34]

Three major elements, along with scattered support elsewhere, united behind the Reuther candidacy. The largest and most important was a body of unionists who were convinced that Reuther's leadership was necessary to carry the union forward through the transition to peacetime production and put it on the road to substantial gains in members' living standards through effective bargaining. Among the many local officers and members who saw the union as primarily a service organization for the improvement of workers' standard of living and the efficient processing of shop floor grievances, Reuther had proved his mettle. Many of these same delegates wanted an end to the distracting, divisive, and destabilizing factional bickering and maneuvering. Although these were engaged in by all, the Communists got the major share of the blame. A Reuther victory, these delegates hoped, would inaugurate an era of unity and solidarity within the UAW, lowering the temperature in its over-heated atmosphere. Reuther also had support from the Association of Catholic Trade Unionists, an organization dedicated to eliminating Communist influence from the union, with a substantial Detroit membership. The alliance of the secularist Reuther with ACTU, which went back to 1939, did not rest alone on a shared dislike for the Communists' presence in the union. A kinship (not an identity) existed between their idea of an industrial democracy, expressed in advocacy of a role for labor in governing the workplace, in joint labor-management industrial planning, and in support for specific proposals like a guaranteed annual wage. Drawing upon a concept of "corporatism" formulated in papal encyclicals and the writings of Catholic social theorists, ACTU championed a workers' voice in determining production standards and line speeds, a position with which Reuther, according to an ACTU statement, was "in complete agreement." The statement added that "the solution of industrial problems lies . . . in an increasing share for the union in the functions now exclusively exercised by Management." To the left, contingents of socialists and Trotskyists formed a third element in the Reuther coalition. Although few in number compared to the coalition's other members, the socialists and ex-socialists were close to Reuther in social philosophy, recognizing that a portion at least of their vision of a just social order might be won through his leadership. The Trotskyists, committed to militant, shop floor action as required by their ideal of grassroots, rank-and-file democracy, were not as close to Reuther in outlook, but their ideological differences with the Communists and the years of abuse and opposition they had suffered at the hands of a Stalinist Communist Party prompted their cooperation with the union's anticommunist forces. Both socialists and Trotskyists were sophisticated union activists, capable debaters, and experienced in organizational matters.[35]

Tension mounted on the convention floor as the clerk took four hours to call the roll of the hundreds of UAW locals scattered across the United States and Canada. Reuther defeated Thomas by a mere 114.187 votes (each vote represented approximately 100 members) out of a total of 8,821.093 that were cast. Much of his support came from the General Motors locals that he had served as director since 1939 and recently led in the strike. Both contenders demonstrated strength in Ford and Chrysler locals, with Thomas holding an edge. With the support of Dick Frankensteen, director of the union's aircraft division, Thomas received votes from some aircraft locals, although one of the largest, Willow Run Local 50, went for Reuther. Many of the members of the aircraft locals had disappeared because of postwar layoffs, but under the rules these "ghosts" were still eligible to be represented. Black delegates almost unanimously supported the Thomas-Addes slate. Leonard Woodcock, Reuther's political organizer and vote counter, believed that Reuther's total was reduced by the defection of a number of local leaders who cherished a close division among rivals at the top. Some local officers believed that the independence and influence of their locals were enhanced when factions contended for union offices, and that competition among rival factions contributed to better service. To some, Reuther's capture of the presidency seemed a threat. After the election Woodcock was told by one local president, "Look, Leonard, Walter's just too goddamn smart." Woodcock replied, "Well, that's why we want him for president." "No, no," the unionist said, "That's not what I want." The prospect of strong leadership that many welcomed in a Reuther presidency was feared by others.[36]

Although the correlation was not perfect, the political connection of the regional director was a major factor in influencing the votes of the locals in that region. Undoubtedly this reflected political organizing by the directors and the International representatives attached to the regional staffs, as well as the political leanings of local officers and rank-and-file members. Each side mobilized its base. Reuther had strong support in Region 1D (Western Michigan), 2B (Toledo), 5 (St. Louis and the Southwest), 8 (Southeast), and 9 (Northeast), all headed by regional directors allied with him. But he also received many votes in 1B (Pontiac) and 1C (Flint), regions where directors with Addes-Thomas-Leonard connections held sway. Regions 1 and 1A (both Detroit) and 9A (Northeast) were evenly divided between the two candidates, while 2 and 2A (Cleveland and eastern Ohio), 3 (Indiana), 4 (Illinois, Wisconsin), 6 (California), and 7 (Canada), all headed by regional directors allied with the Thomas-Addes coalition, voted for Thomas.[37]

Walter Reuther and supporters celebrate his election as UAW president, 1946. Walter P. Reuther Library, Wayne State University

In his acceptance speech, Reuther appealed for harmony and affirmed his commitment to a union movement that reached beyond the workplace to the reform of society at large. The offer of unity in fact extended only to George Addes, whose reelection as secretary-treasurer was uncontested by the Reuther caucus. The Reuther forces nominated candidates for the two vice presidencies and for all the regional directors' seats. In these elections they suffered a stinging defeat. Thomas was elected first vice president and his center-left ally, Richard Leonard, was chosen second vice president. On the executive board, consisting of the officers and regional directors, the Thomas-Addes forces gained a working majority. The formula used to determine the distribution of votes among the members of the executive board, which was based on the number of members in each region, gave the Addes-Thomas-Leonard forces a decisive 510 votes to 324 for the Reuther following. The opposition, far from routed, had isolated and surrounded Reuther in the presidency. This turn of events, which destined the UAW to almost two years of the most bitter factional battle, was rooted in a fear that a leader of Reuther's caliber would, unless checked, overmatch the locals and other lesser power centers.[38]

REUTHER SOON LEARNED that he was not in control. Within days, the Addes-Thomas-Leonard group broke with the president, submitting for board approval a union program developed without consultation with Reuther that repudiated many of his ideas. At first he was told by the board, which had to approve his appointments, that he could name only his two administrative assistants, Leonard Woodcock and Jack Conway, but negotiations produced important additions. Thomas, belatedly setting out to build a following, wanted to head the Competitive Shops Department because its large number of appointed International representatives made it a patronage power-house. Dick Leonard was given the union's Washington office, including political and legislative affairs. In return for agreeing to these arrangements, Reuther obtained appointment of his brother Victor as education director and of Frank Winn as publicity director and editor of the *United Automobile Worker*, positions that were immensely useful in the coming struggle. Winn, another ex-socialist and former student at Brookwood Labor College, was a veteran associate of the Reuthers, having come to Detroit in 1937 as public-ity director for Local 174 when Walter was its president. Another important appointment obtained by Reuther was that of Nat Weinberg to the staff of the Research Department. Weinberg, a working-class intellectual and Socialist, had earned an economics degree at New York University by attending night classes and gained experience in the Research Department of the Interna-tional Ladies' Garment Workers Union. The director of UAW Research, James Wishart, an Addes supporter, gave Weinberg a cold shoulder when he arrived in Detroit, indicative of the mood inside a divided headquarters. "The only time I talked to Wishart," Weinberg recalled, "was when I said 'Good Morning' when I met him in the hall. I worked in an airless room that should have been a storage closet. I couldn't use Wishart's secretary, so if I wanted something typed I would walk around the building looking for a secretary who was (a) friendly to Walter, and (b) had some time to type for me." After Reuther gained control of the union in 1947, he appointed Weinberg head of research. A fertile source of economic ideas, who was sometimes referred to by Reuther as his "conscience," Weinberg escaped from the tedium of rou-tine administration to become an advisor without portfolio, the "cloud nine job" as it was sometimes called.[39]

Reuther's two administrative assistants, Leonard Woodcock and Jack Conway, were the political workhorses of the new regime. Woodcock (1911–2001) had been associated with the Reuther brothers since the 1930s. The son of British-born immigrants whose father found employment in Detroit at his machinists trade, Woodcock worked for an auto parts firm, became an active union member, and joined the Socialist Party of America. He conducted successful organizing campaigns in auto plants in western and central Michigan, in the process building a political base. By 1945 he was a major figure in the Reuther caucus and a key organizer of Reuther's election to the presidency, serving as "scorekeeper," keeping track of how delegates were likely to vote and pitching in to persuade the uncommitted. Although he was Reuther's assistant for only a brief period, returning to western Michigan's Region 1D to launch a successful campaign for election as its regional director, he was a loyal supporter and advisor, and eventually, after Reuther's death in 1970, his successor as president.[40]

Jack W. Conway (1917–1998), was a more recent Reuther recruit. Born and reared in Detroit, he obtained bachelor's and master's degrees from the University of Chicago. During the war he worked at the Buick aircraft engine plant in Melrose Park, Illinois, and joined UAW Local 6. He soon became chairman of the shop committee and a delegate to UAW conventions, tied to the Rank-and-File caucus which opposed the no-strike pledge. A socialist, he was a superb administrator and a tough political operative. As Reuther's assistant, he became the chief organizer of the president's 1946–47 successful reelection campaign and, through the 1950s, was the ace troubleshooter who would be handed the most challenging administrative and political problems to solve. On many internal union matters he spoke for Reuther and had his complete confidence. Failing in a bid to establish an independent political base in a campaign for a regional director's seat, he left the UAW for posts in the Kennedy and Johnson administrations and later served in the Industrial Union Department (IUD) of the AFL-CIO in Washington, but he maintained close, cooperative ties with his UAW comrades.[41]

Upset with its election failures, the Reuther caucus began to prepare for the next round as soon as the 1946 convention ended. The organization was constantly active, with the leading roles in its operations taken by Reuther, Conway, and Woodcock. "We organized," Conway recalled, "to the teeth . . . [and] put together a real juggernaut."[42]

The year and a half until the next convention in November 1947 saw a sustained political battle, a do-or-die effort on the part of the anti-Reuther forces. The opposition fired the first shot when Addes, at a board meeting, introduced policy resolutions agreed to by his caucus but of which Reuther had not even received advance notice. Subsequently, the opposition board majority adopted policies with which the president disagreed, condemned him in resolutions, and excluded him from some meetings. Vice president Thomas launched a public attack on Reuther's role in an attempted settlement of Local 248's long, bitter, and finally unsuccessful strike against Allis-Chalmers, to which Reuther responded with denials of Thomas's charges and a blistering criticism of him for airing internal union differences in a hostile press. The Allis-Chalmers management was exploiting the left-wing affiliations of Local 248's leadership to destroy the local, a situation Reuther feared would be the fate of other locals that remained under left-wing control. Well aware that the rising tide of anticommunist and anti-Soviet sentiment in the United States would be used by some employers and their political allies to attack and, if successful, destroy the union movement, he told the UAW board that "what is happening in Local 248 is just a small, a little dress rehearsal compared to what is going to happen in this country. I am not saying we should run. I am prepared and will take my place to fight against the witch-hunt, but I say it is nothing short of criminal negligence for a union not to recognize these basic facts and attempt to get its house in order and get in a position to resist the full impact of that attack." Such incidents as the circulation of Communist Party electoral petitions on the Allis-Chalmers picket lines gave the company's management and the Milwaukee media more than enough ammunition to brand the local as an arm of the party. While Reuther's campaign to reduce Communist influence within the union had several strands, by the "Red scare" days of the late 1940s the principal one was the practical fear that the growing, extremist anticommunism lodged in the minds of a large portion of the American public would, unless headed off, destroy the movement on which he and his comrades had pinned their hopes for a better world.[43]

Reuther became the target of a barrage of "dirty tricks" and false charges, some so extreme that they damaged the reputations and undermined the credibility of those who brought them. Reuther's eventual success in his reelection campaign sprang in part from these self-destructive maneuvers of his adversaries. One instance was the publication of a twenty-four-page cartoon pamphlet entitled *The Bosses' Boy*, produced by left-wing UAW staff members and widely circulated among the membership, in which the union's president was portrayed as a company stooge who repeatedly betrayed the workers. One of *The Bosses' Boy*'s smears was contained in a fabricated letter, attributed to the Reverend Gerald L. K. Smith—a noisy, antisemitic, quasi-fascist—which praised Reuther for doing an "excellent job" in opposing the union's left-wing but cautioned that any public statement of support by Smith would limit Reuther's "sensational usefulness." The letter confided in closing that Reuther was "thoroughly alert to the Jewish issue." In a similar vein, a fugitive publication, *FDR*, was issued to carry the attack on Reuther, its cryptic title subject to several interpretations: the innocuous *Franklin Delano Roosevelt*, a hostile *Fire Damned Reuther*, and a more hostile, obscene version. Perhaps the most ludicrous libel was a rumor, given national currency by the syndicated columnist Drew Pearson, that Reuther would run for the vice presidency of the United States on a ticket headed by Republican Senator Robert A. Taft of Ohio, coauthor of the hated Taft-Hartley Act. Thomas-Addes henchmen supplied UAW local newspapers with a sample editorial that concluded, "We can't dismiss the Taft-Reuther story as too fantastic. It's all so logical."

The executive board proclaimed that Reuther had "exposed himself as the working ally of Labor's enemies" and proposed that the law should be renamed the Taft-Hartley-Reuther Act. Only somewhat less outrageous was the charge, aired in the *Daily Worker* and other Communist Party publications, that because Reuther had argued that greater productivity attained through new technology could support higher wages, he must favor speedups.[44]

Reuther counterattacked with a no-holds-barred campaign, branding his executive board opponents a "mechanical majority" that dutifully voted through any proposal of which he disapproved. From the beginning he declared war on the union's Communist left, asserting that internal unity would be attained regardless of "opinions, programs and plots of those political elements whose loyalties are commanded by groups outside the union or nations outside America." Fearful for the UAW's future, he warned that in the agitated cold war environment of the times, the presence of Communists and close sympathizers in prominent UAW positions exposed the union to possibly fatal attacks from a potent combination of hostile employers, media, and politicians. The union should fire communist sympathizers in its employ whose jobs put them and their views on public display. For example, he told the executive board that the union's chief Washington lobbyist, Irving Richter, should be dismissed because of his record of support for Communist Party positions. Richter and others like him, he said, "make this union vulnerable, at a high time when we should be putting on armored plates." For the time being Richter, protected by other officers, remained in his position. Reuther also threatened that the time had arrived to enforce Article X, Section 8 of the UAW constitution, adopted in 1940, which banned Communists from union offices.[45]

Accusations, denials, and libel suits flew back and forth. Friends and political associates came to Reuther's support. Eleanor Roosevelt wrote in her nationally syndicated newspaper column that the executive board's public attacks on Reuther, launched without informing him of the charges, showed "human nature at its worst." As the contest drew to a close, Reuther issued a long statement to the membership without seeking the board approval he knew would not be forthcoming. He presented concrete reform proposals, such as providing verbatim records of board meetings and establishing a board of trustees to ensure fiscal integrity, and attacked his opponents as the source of disunity and of "outside interference" in the UAW from the Communist Party. Acknowledging that every union member had a right to his personal political philosophy and a right of membership in any political organization of his choice, he added "we must oppose with uncompromising determination the efforts of the Communist party or any other outside group . . . to interfere in the affairs of our union."

Appealing for "Teamwork in the leadership and solidarity in the ranks," the Reuther forces promised an end to factional battles if they won control in the coming elections—perhaps the most attractive plank in their platform to a membership increasingly weary of the struggle and wary of its consequences. Outraged by Reuther's attack, the executive board majority fired its own broadside in the union's paper, in which it denounced Reuther's issuance of his statement without obtaining board approval as a high-handed tactic and further demonized him "as a whole hearted advocate of the restrictive features" of the Taft-Hartley Act, a reference to his belief that union officials must, under protest, sign the noncommunist affidavits required of them by that law.[46]

In addition to the efforts of Reuther and his assistant, Jack Conway, a major part of the Reuther campaign was conducted through the union's Education Department under Victor Reuther's direction. The department became a spearhead of the Reuther offensive, holding large education conferences that were utilized as recruiting grounds for the Reuther caucus, publicizing Reuther's positions on the issues and putting supporters through crash courses in parliamentary procedure, public speaking, and effective argumentation in preparation for the showdown when locals elected their delegates to the 1947 convention. As publicity director, Frank Winn also played a key role. He had the distinction of having been fired for political reasons from previous positions by both the union's right and its Communist left: from a staff position by Homer Martin in 1937 and as editor of Local 600's newspaper in 1944.[47]

IN THE SPRING OF 1947 the Thomas-Addes forces came up with a scheme they hoped would snatch victory from the jaws of defeat. They proposed to incorporate the United Farm Equipment and Metal Workers Union (FE), with which the UAW disputed an overlapping jurisdiction among workers in agricultural implement firms, into the UAW. Several CIO unions, including the Steel Workers Organizing Committee and United Electrical Workers, had members in farm equipment plants, and the UAW, which claimed jurisdiction over all those who worked on vehicles powered by internal combustion engines, had organized workers in some of the truck and tractor plants of International Harvester, J. I. Case, and Allis-Chalmers. In 1938, over UAW objections, the CIO set up a farm equipment workers organizing committee, and in 1942 it chartered the Farm Equipment Workers Union, again over UAW objections, as a permanent organization. Both the committee and the union had a Communist leadership. The FE had organized about 40,000 farm implement workers in some of the large plants of International Harvester, Caterpillar Tractor, and John Deere. The other unions, including the UAW, had organized about half that number. It seemed advantageous and logical, as favored by the CIO, to unite the two organizations through a merger, with the much larger UAW absorbing the FE. But FE had turned down previous merger attempts, and the new merger proposal as presented was clearly intended to trap Reuther and block his reelection. The FE's left-wing leadership was certain to support the Thomas-Addes group with its convention votes. Under the terms of the merger the FE locals would receive approximately 450 convention votes, more than they were entitled to by their numbers, and perhaps enough to defeat Reuther for reelection. In short, the FE merger threatened to pack the UAW convention with an anti-Reuther majority.[48]

The proposal was sprung without warning at a board meeting, with the Reuther supporters given only fifteen minutes to discuss it. A resolution approving it passed, but its backers tactically erred by including a call for a membership referendum, assuming that a favorable popular vote would lock in the merger beyond challenge. Instead, the referendum gave the Reuther forces the opening they needed, and, as Jack Conway later boasted, the merger issue "gave us a forum and we beat their ears off." Reuther threw himself into the struggle, rushing to locals across the country and debating both Thomas and Addes at jammed meetings. More than 1,600 "noisy, cat calling" local union officers, for example, turned out for a Reuther-Addes debate at Detroit's Cass Technical High School. The public exchanges were confined to trade union issues, avoiding any mention of the Communist Party's position in FE, although the subject doubtless came up in shop floor and local union discussions. Far from representing a genuine merger leading to labor unity, Reuther charged, the plan would create a privileged elite within the UAW. FE would become a semiautonomous unit with more power than its numbers warranted. The precedent, he pointed out, was ominous. Other particular interest groups within the union, such as skilled workers, might demand a similar status. Before long the UAW as an industrial union would be irreparably divided and perhaps ultimately undermined. Despite the appeal of a merger, logical in itself, the proposal went down to defeat both on political grounds and on its union demerits, losing in the referendum by a margin of nearly three to one. Particularly disturbing to the Thomas-Addes forces was its defeat in many locals that had previously been counted among their faithful supporters. Since votes were cast only by those who attended a local union meeting, the outcome represented the views of activists rather than those of a cross section of the entire membership. There is no reason to think the result would have been more favorable to the proposal if a more representative group had participated and the turnout had been greater. It was widely interpreted as a forecast of the convention delegate elections, and the Reuther forces' victory now seemed assured.[49]

Elections of local officers and convention delegates were closely watched for their bearing on the contest. When Thomas's home local, the 10,000-member Chrysler Local 7 on Detroit's East Side, chose a slate of officers aligned with Reuther with an unusually high membership turnout of over 70 percent, the tremors were felt throughout the union. Reuther supporters seized the opportunity to organize opposition slates in left-wing locals. The 8,000 member East Side Tool and Die Local 155 had long been headed by the union's two leading open Communists, president John Anderson and business agent Nat Ganley. Early in 1947 Russell Leach and other Reuther backers organized a caucus in Local 155 and challenged the Anderson-Ganley leadership. They brought an array of charges to support their claim that the local's officers subordinated the union's interests to those of the Communist Party. Ganley, they said, spent most of his time on party, not union, business, and they alleged that the *Michigan Worker*, a party newspaper, was published out of 155's office with its financial support, that Anderson gave some employers "soft settlements" in return for their willingness to employ Communists, and that the local's political endorsements and activities promoted factional interests and adhered to the party's preferences. (As one example, when Dick Frankensteen, at the time still a union vice president, ran for Detroit mayor in 1945 with the CIO's endorsement, Local 155, to settle a political score, endorsed his opponent despite the man's antilabor, racist record.) With more than 7,000 votes cast in Local 155's election of officers, a heavy turnout, Leach lost to Anderson for the presidency by 59 votes, but the Reuther forces defeated Ganley, took over the local's executive board, and elected a majority of Reuther supporters as convention delegates. The following year Leach defeated Anderson for the local's presidency, ending Communist dominance in what had been a vocal and influential local. Many anti-Reuther locals underwent a similar reorientation.[50]

IN THE MIDST OF the union's internal struggle, Congress took up the Taft-Hartley bill. Following the election of a conservative Congress in 1946, it was a foregone conclusion that antilabor legislation would be forthcoming. In congressional hearings in Washington and Milwaukee preceding the bill's passage, UAW Local 248 (Allis-Chalmers) was showcased as the leading example of the political and industrial strife, disruption, and even sabotage that could occur in an industry vital to national security when a key local fell under left-wing control. In his account of the bill's passage, Representative Fred A. Hartley, Jr., (Republican, New Jersey) its principal author and sponsor, charged (without supporting documentation) that the Allis-Chalmers strikes before and after World War II "were ordered by Moscow." Ignoring the Allis-Chalmers management's obstinancy and

UAW Local 7's float in the Detroit Labor Day parade urges defeat of congressmen who supported the Taft-Hartley Act, 1947. Walter P. Reuther Library, Wayne State University

many provocations, the congressman heaped blame on the local leadership's political commitments for all the troubles. The bill's requirement that union officials sign a noncommunist affidavit stemmed primarily from committee hearings on Local 248, a demonstration of the political cost to the entire labor movement of a visible left-wing leadership in a local union. The UAW mounted a spirited campaign in opposition to the law's passage, but its effort, like that of other unions, failed. Massive rallies in Detroit, attended by as many as 200,000, and in other cities utilized work stoppages in auto factories to swell the crowds, although a threat by GM to discipline workers who walked out held down participation.[51]

Supported by nearly all Republicans and most southern Democrats, the bill passed Congress easily, becoming law over President Truman's veto. For the long term, the act represented a serious setback for organized labor, tilting the balance in industrial relations in management's favor, enhancing the states' powers to impede union organizing, and reviving the federal government's authority to obtain injunctions to block or delay strikes in certain

circumstances. In the near term, the law's impact was felt through its requirement that union officers sign affidavits affirming that they were not members of the Communist Party. Refusal to sign carried no criminal
penalty—the Communist Party was not, after all, an illegal organization—
but a perjured statement could result in stiff fines and jail sentences for individuals. The penalty for a union was practical rather than legal, but life
threatening nonetheless. Unions whose officers failed to comply would be
deprived of certification under the Wagner Act and denied the right to appear
before the National Labor Relations Board, crippling them in their dealings
with other unions and employers. Since they could not appear on NLRB ballots, they would be vulnerable to raiding by rival unions, and the NLRB would
not hear charges of unfair labor practices they brought against employers.
Several thousand pending charges initiated by UAW members would die if its
officers refused to sign. In the first court test of the law in 1950 the Supreme
Court upheld the affidavit's constitutionality, but in 1965 the Court reversed
that ruling when it held that a later statute incorporating the requirement of
an affidavit was an unconstitutional bill of attainder.[52]

The noncommunist affidavit sparked an agonized debate within the
labor movement. Should officers sign or refuse to do so? Labor officials
objected to being singled out as of dubious loyalty, to the affidavit's breach
of civil liberties, and to the threat it posed to their organizations. At first
there was much sentiment in favor of refusing to sign, but it soon became
evident that such a course put a union at risk and threatened its ability to
serve its membership. Most unions came to the position that, distasteful as
it was, union officers should sign under protest, complying with the law in
the hope that a future Congress would repeal it or the courts overturn it. A
divided UAW executive board supported this position, which was ratified
by the convention delegates a few weeks later by a three-to-one margin. All
of the UAW's officers then signed.[53]

The government's anticommunist campaign, of which the Taft-Hartley affidavits were only one part, had a profound impact on the struggle
between the UAW's two factions. The United States Congress, in cooperation with many state and local governments, was determined to eliminate
any Communist presence in union officialdom, as in other major institutions such as the government bureaucracy itself, the mass entertainment
industry (especially Hollywood), and schools and universities. Those who
refused to cooperate in this campaign would pay a heavy price in public
scorn, economic and legal penalties, and a loss of political influence. Labor
officials were mindful of the political toll levied on the labor movement as
a result of right-wing charges of Communist associations brought against
the CIO and its Political Action Committee (CIO-PAC) in the congressional
elections of 1946. With candidates for Congress supported by CIO-PAC win-

ning in only 75 of the 318 races they entered, the stage had been set for the passage of hostile legislation. The Taft-Hartley affidavits might easily turn out to be only the first step in a mounting government crackdown on all union political activity. This new "Red scare" gave a cutting edge to the message that Reuther and other union noncommunists had been sending: given the mounting hostility of the government and public opinion, the UAW could not afford a prominent Communist element within its leadership.[54]

THE CONVENTION DELEGATE ELECTIONS in the locals showed Reuther the clear winner. The only remaining question was whether any of his opponents would survive in other offices. In his keynote address Reuther repeated the slogan of his campaign for unity—"teamwork in the leadership and . . . solidarity in the ranks"—and laid out a program of union objectives, including pensions, an annual wage, opposition to speedups, a daily newspaper under labor auspices, community consumers' cooperatives, and organizing those still unorganized. He pledged a vigorous effort to mobilize the union's potential political power: "we have the job," he said, "of making our people realize the relationship between the bread box and the ballot box. . . . The surest way to guarantee to have your ice box filled with good food is to see the ballot box is filled with good votes." Atop the list of political objectives was repeal of Taft-Hartley.[55]

Rejecting a plea from Philip Murray to spare Addes, the Reuther caucus ran candidates for every office. The opposition, soundly whipped, conceded Reuther's reelection by putting up no prominent candidate for president. John De Vito, from the radical Fisher Body Local 45 in Cleveland, ran against Reuther, along with an unknown; together they received 339 votes to Reuther's 5,593. The 1,219 delegates who abstained provided a fuller measure of the remaining opposition to the Reuther presidency. (Combining abstentions and votes for the other candidates gives Reuther a margin of about four and a half to one.)[56]

The results of the other races were equally decisive, bringing a Reuther team into all the International Union's offices. The caucus candidates for office reflected a politician's effort to construct a majority coalition from diverse elements. Most importantly, Emil Mazey, former president of Local 212 (Briggs) and an Eastside Detroit regional director, defeated George Addes for secretary-treasurer, the union's second-ranking post. A scrappy, militant, Socialist, and anticommunist unionist, Mazey was the key figure in organizing Briggs workers in the face of that tough company's opposition. A "perennial picket captain," in the words of journalist Murray Kempton, Mazey had built a firebrand's reputation in leading the Briggs "flying squadron" into numerous demonstrations and picket lines in support of strikes in Detroit and elsewhere. Mazey had an independent power base within the UAW and was not a member of the inner circle of Reuther's close associates. While in general agreement with Reuther's objectives as president and his leadership of the union, Mazey had no fear of disagreeing with him and sometimes did, most notably in the 1960s over the union's position on the Vietnam War.[57]

The Reuther caucus candidates for the two vice presidencies, John W. Livingston of St. Louis and Richard T. Gosser of Toledo, also had independent political bases. Both handily defeated their opponents, Richard Leonard and R. J. Thomas, rolling up better than two-to-one margins. Livingston was a pioneer organizer in General Motors' St. Louis plant, president of Local 25, and director of Region 5. An experienced negotiator, he had worked with Reuther on GM matters during the war and inherited the General Motors Department when Reuther became president. Gosser, a skilled tradesman, similarly rose through the ranks as president of Local 12 in Toledo and director of Region 2B, which he ran with a heavy hand. Both Livingston and Gosser were conventional trade unionists, lacking the social-democratic political and reform interests and commitments of Reuther and others in his inner circle, and neither ended his career in the UAW. Livingston left for an AFL-CIO position when he found his hope of replacing Reuther thwarted, and Gosser, of whom Reuther long felt uneasy, left under a cloud, and was later convicted on a tax fraud charge unconnected with his UAW duties. Following electoral victories in several regions, the Reuther forces now enjoyed a solid eighteen-to-four majority on the executive board. There would be no serious internal challenge to their position until Reuther's presidency neared its close. The collapse of the center-left coalition at the office-holding level of the International was complete.[58]

The triumph of Reuther's following in the UAW had important consequences for the labor movement and liberal politics. It was the critical defeat of the center-left coalition that led in a few years to its virtual disappearance both in the UAW and elsewhere. The UAW's left-wingers, with all their credits as union pioneers and organizers, had always had to contend with the suspicions and mistrust of a significant number of auto workers; now, in the cold war era, they were fatally handicapped by a connection, close in some instances but remote in others, with a hostile foreign power. Reuther and his allies had little difficulty in persuading a majority of the UAW's members that the present and future costs of "outside interference" outweighed any possible benefit. Mrs. Eleanor Roosevelt, a leading spokesperson for the New Deal's legacy, greeted the electoral sweep as a heartening development and acclaimed Reuther as a labor leader "who gives hope for a sane and wise leadership both in labor and in the liberal movement." Liberal thinker and historian, Arthur M. Schlesinger, Jr., of Harvard University, likewise hailed "the extraordinarily able and intelligent leader of the United Auto Workers" as "labor's man of vision and will." Dissenting from these plaudits and positive predictions, critics on the left deplored the center-left's loss of its position in the UAW, fearing that the organization would lose its fighting spirit and dull its idealistic edge.[59]

In his acceptance speech Reuther envisioned a future of social justice with the auto workers leading the way as "the vanguard in America, in that great crusade to build a better world." He staked out a grand mission for the union: "We are the architects of the future, and we are going to fashion the tools and weapons with which we will work and fight and build." He pledged the UAW to social and economic pioneering and offered to work with anyone "who believes in the basic Trade Union fundamentals that this Union stands on, and the idealism and principles for which America stands." In a climactic ceremony that symbolized the continuity of working-class loyalties across the generations and paid tribute to the faith in which he was reared, he introduced his father, Valentine Reuther, "an old soap boxer, an old rabble-rouser . . . an old fighter in the ranks of labor." Val Reuther, following a brief, stirring address, was accorded honorary UAW membership by the delegates.[60]

AFTER HIS REELECTION Reuther moved quickly to unite the union and consolidate his control. None of the defeated officers remained active in the union. As an observer later wrote, "both sides [had] worked under the grim realization that the defeated faction would not occupy the opposition benches . . . but would be cast out of the assemblage." Havens were found for some of the displaced. R. J. Thomas moved to a CIO staff position; Richard Leonard announced that he would return to his welder's job in the DeSoto factory and reforge his ties with the rank and file, but in fact soon followed Thomas to the CIO staff; George Addes, to whom Reuther offered a UAW staff appointment, chose instead to go into business; Dick Frankensteen had left the union earlier to pursue interests in politics and business. Attorney Maurice Sugar, the union's counsel for ten years, was dismissed. Close to the Communists and a policy advisor and strategist in the factional battle, Sugar was often considered the behind-the-scenes mastermind of the Addes faction. Reuther gave no quarter to most of the opposition leaders, who neither expected nor asked for any since they knew that in his position they would have acted in the same way.[61]

"To the victor belong the spoils," is an ancient rule of politics, and in the UAW the art of patronage was practiced by all. With the defeat of the center-left coalition, there occurred the largest turnover in office-holding ("purge" in the terminology of critics) in the union's history. As implemented, it was not as sweeping as some had hoped and others had feared. In accord with UAW custom, at both the International and regional levels most staff members and representatives had been active in the political battle on behalf of one side or the other. In determining the fate of staff members, of whom about one hundred were dismissed (approximately 30 percent of the total), Reuther and the other officers drew a distinction. Some were dismissed for their political affiliations and activity, others because those now in charge were not favorably impressed with their job performance. It was not always easy to determine if someone was dismissed for political reasons or for incompetence. The Reuthers drew another line, as Victor later remarked to an interviewer, between "opponents" and "enemies": "one [the first] you win over, the other you destroy." With those who had been enemies, the "true believers" whose primary loyalty lay outside the union, there could be no reconciliation. There were others, however, as a Reuther supporter said, who were "basically trade-unionists, who happened also to be Communists. But if you strip away the myth of the Party hold on them and bring them further and further into the union and train them, they became just like everybody else." These the Reutherites were prepared to retain, or co-opt, without vindictiveness or revenge, letting bygones be bygones.[62]

As always with the politically astute Reuther, calculations of the likely effects were at work. Beyond recognizing the positive contributions former opponents could make in the future, he understood that a forced exile back to the shop would sow seeds of resentment and opposition. After years as union "porkchoppers," many were in no condition to return to the rigors of the assembly or press lines. As one former local union president explained, "we got bought off. . . . [W]hat kind of a fool would I be if I didn't accept Walter's offer? At my age and with my broken health, how long would I last if I went back to the Dodge paint shop? I've been out of the factory for years; if I had to go back now and buck production, I'd probably drop dead in a week's time!" So many former oppositionists were retained that UAW insiders joked that the surest ticket to a staff appointment was to have been against Reuther at one time or another, and some loyalists complained that their just claims of preference were being overlooked.[63]

Reuther promoted loyal staffers to vacated senior positions and for new appointments drew heavily on local officers— presidents, shop committee chairmen, and the like—who had proved their mettle in the crucial struggle over admission of FE to the UAW. Among the important appointments were those that reorganized the UAW's Washington, D.C. office. Donald Montgomery, upon whom Reuther had come to rely for economic analysis of government policies and proposed legislation, became its director, and Paul Sifton, another ex-socialist, experienced journalist, former employee in the Department of Labor, and lobbyist for the National Farmers' Union, was named national legislative representative, the union's chief lobbyist. Joseph L. Rauh, Jr., a bright, energetic lawyer, soon to become one of the nation's leading civil rights attorneys, was retained as Washington counsel. The Washington office was given considerable latitude in drawing up and issuing statements on current governmental and legal issues and quickly came to be recognized as one of the ablest operations in the capital.[64]

Next to those dismissed from their positions, the most adversely affected group was the UAW's contingent of African American activists. In view of their just and rightful claim to fair treatment, the increasing number of blacks employed in the plants, and the imminent emergence of a national civil rights movement, a seriously negative consequence of Reuther's victory was the diminished presence of African Americans in the UAW's upper ranks. The great majority of activist blacks were tied to the Addes-Thomas coalition, and the Communists had been vocal champions of black participation in the union. When the center- left coalition collapsed, it took most of the union's black activists down with it. Perhaps the greatest loss was the dismissal of George Crockett, closely tied to the left-wing caucus, as head of the Fair Practices Department. With Crockett's departure most of the department's vigor was lost. Although Reuther was personally and ideologically committed, like nearly all of the UAW's top leadership, to equal treatment of all and support for civil rights, by the rules of political conduct he owed blacks little and others much. He was not prepared to make an active campaign for black advance within the union a major priority. Among some of his supporters in the two southern regions (Region 5 in the southwest and Region 8 in the southeast), and in some of the northern plants where white, southern-born workers were employed in large numbers, there was no enthusiasm and some hostility for concessions, symbolic or substantive, to black employees in terms of either expanded employment opportunities or union participation. These elements, by and large Reuther supporters in the factional battles, had been and remained a constraint on progress toward internal racial equity. Some of the black International representatives were among the dismissed, although others were later added to the International staff. Through the 1950s there were only about a dozen black International representatives in the Detroit area, with a few more elsewhere. For ten years, until the question of adding a black board member resurfaced in the late 1950s, there was no black caucus activity, and not until the 1960s did black representation in the UAW's upper echelons approach and begin to exceed what it had once been.[65]

The UAW's Fair Practices Department, placed under Reuther as nominal director with William Oliver, a black unionist, as codirector and operating head, had only a modest impact on internal racial issues. Oliver was not vigorous in pursuing charges of discrimination within the locals and the plants, concentrating instead on liaison with interracial organizations such as the National Association for the Advancement of Colored People and the Urban League, an emphasis that must have reflected Reuther's wishes in the matter. During the 1950s the UAW, whose constitution mandated 5 cents of each member's monthly dues to fund fair practices activities, contributed thousands of dollars to the NAACP, and many locals, particularly those in the Detroit area with large numbers of African Americans, actively recruited within their ranks for NAACP members with considerable success. Internally, the department's effort centered on educational initiatives: holding conferences on civil rights questions, preparing statements for use in education programs, and so on. Reflecting the reliance on education as a long-term solution to the problems of racial injustice, few locals, perhaps no more than 10 percent, had Fair Practices committees that actively investigated and sought remedies for racial problems.[66]

Repercussions from Reuther's reelection were felt throughout the broader labor movement. Though always harboring strongly felt anticommunist sentiments, CIO president Philip Murray had tried to muffle ideological conflicts within the federation. He now edged toward a showdown with those unions that had regularly endorsed Soviet policies. The Communist Party, a fervent supporter of the American government's military effort in World War II, lurched to the left after the war's end as the cold war set in and intensified, expressing its opposition to the Truman Doctrine and the Marshall Plan and its support for Henry Wallace's Progressive Party 1948 challenge to President Truman's reelection. When the outbreak of the Korean War in 1950 brought American casualties in the fight against a Communist state and Soviet ally, and as many Americans were swept up in a popular fear of Communist subversion and espionage within the United States, all organizations and persons with any kind of connection with communism, real or imagined, total or partial, came under fierce attack. The CIO unions that were suspected of being under "communist domination" or "influence," whatever the substance and nuances that lurked behind those vague terms, represented about 20 percent of the CIO's six million members, no negligible force. With the UAW, the CIO's largest union, now unequivocally committed to an anticommunist position, Murray prepared to move against them. Eventually, eleven unions were expelled from the CIO, including the United Electrical Workers (UE), the third largest in the federation. Reuther, who declared at the 1948 CIO convention that "they are not trade unionists, they are agents of a foreign government using the trade unions as an operating base," played a leading role in the trials of the accused, and UAW convention delegates strongly supported the expulsions.[67]

THE REFUSAL OF SOME UNION'S OFFICERS to sign the Taft-Hartley non-communist affidavits in combination with the CIO expulsions opened the door to raids on their membership by other unions. Since jurisdictional lines were vague and in several cases overlapping, pretexts for raids were not lacking. Reuther proclaimed that the UAW would accept members from such unions who wanted to affiliate with a democratic organization, and the UAW executive board declared that where the rank and file were in revolt against a leadership that refused to follow national CIO policies, the UAW would issue charters to new locals. Splitting semantic hairs, UAW organizers denied they were poaching on another's territory, declaring, "it's not a raid, it's a rescue." A few locals of UE and Mine, Mill came over to the UAW on their own volition.[68]

The UAW had long been at odds with one of the unions later expelled from the CIO, the Farm Equipment Workers (FE). In 1946 it laid plans for a major organizing drive, and in 1947 the convention authorized the establishment of an Agricultural Implements Department. At that time the UAW represented agricultural implement workers in truck plants of International Harvester in Ft. Wayne, Indiana, and Springfield, Ohio, some of the John Deere and Company plants, and most of Allis-Chalmers, J. I. Case, Oliver, and Massey-Harris. The aborted plan of the Addes-Thomas forces to bring FE into the UAW as an autonomous division in order to defeat Reuther reinforced the new leadership's desire to bring the farm equipment workers into the UAW on its terms. The refusal of FE officers to sign the Taft-Hartley affidavits put their locals at risk in NLRB certification elections, since their union was denied a place on the ballot. A worker favoring FE had to vote for "no union," an obvious impediment to winning an election, and then hope that his employer could be brought to negotiate a contract with an uncertified union. One of the first FE locals to switch was at the Deere plant in Dubuque, Iowa, where, in the UAW's version of events, "some of the leaders of FE Local 241 contacted our staff and indicated that their membership wanted to get into the UAW-CIO." The UAW was chosen bargaining representative in the subsequent election. In the spring of 1948 the UAW won out in an NLRB election over its rivals—UAW-AFL; International Association of Machinists (IAM), also an AFL affiliate; and FE, i.e., "no union"—in the huge Peoria, Illinois, Caterpillar local, FE's largest with about 20,000 members. With FE pickets blocking the plant's entrances, UAW organizers walked from house to house in Peoria and East Peoria to locate and win over Caterpillar workers. The first round of the election resulted in the elimination of IAM and "no union" from a second-round ballot, where the UAW-CIO defeated the UAW-AFL by more than 2,000 votes. The UAW also won an election at the International Harvester local in Memphis, Tennessee, when FE was barred from the ballot.[69]

Following FE's endorsement of Henry Wallace in the 1948 presidential campaign—in violation of a CIO political ruling elevated by president Murray to the status of a test of CIO loyalty—the CIO executive board ordered

FE to affiliate with the UAW, approved the UAW's raids on FE locals, and at the next CIO convention revoked FE's charter. The UAW declared war on FE at its 1949 convention, opening the way for a full-scale assault under the direction of vice president and Agricultural Implements Department director, John W. Livingston. Some FE locals, where there was disgust with the Communist leadership, were readily absorbed. Reuther and other UAW officials denied that these were raids at all, referring to them as "liberating operations" for workers "who don't want to tolerate Communist domination of their unions." But in a number of FE locals the union was entrenched, thanks to strong organization and decent contracts. This was particularly true at several John Deere and International Harvester plants. In these locals it took years of campaigning, marred in some cases by fights between UAW organizers and FE loyalists, to bring them into the UAW. In February 1949, for example, 300 members of FE fought pitched battles with 100 UAW organizers who were distributing handbills at the gates of the International Harvester plant in East Moline, Illinois. The lubricating oil of political deals and patronage played a role in resolving some of the conflicts as a number of key FE local leaders received staff positions in the Agricultural Implements Department in return for shepherding their locals into the UAW. In addition, FE suffered a devastating defeat in a 1952 strike at International Harvester (IH), opening the way for UAW absorption of its membership. By 1957, with UAW election victories at the Harvester plant in East Moline and at IH's three plants in the Chicago area and at the John Deere Planter Works and Plow Works in Moline, the great majority of agricultural implement workers had united with the UAW.[70]

As the formerly FE plants were brought one by one into the UAW, the union's primary objectives were to clean up a huge backlog of unresolved grievances at International Harvester and to establish uniform wage, benefit, and working conditions among agricultural implement workers out of the diversity that had previously prevailed. Contracts at different plants of a single company had varied widely, with even greater discrepancies between contracts at plants of different companies. As in its negotiations with the auto companies, the UAW sought through pattern bargaining to eliminate differences in compensation and working conditions from plant to plant and company to company by bringing everyone up to the highest standards. Achieving uniformity, obviously beneficial to the workers, was facilitated when all the plants were united in a single organization. By 1957 agricultural implement contracts, with modified union shops, supplemental unemployment benefits, and improvements in insurances, pensions, and wage levels approximated those in the auto industry. Such gains were not won easily; they required long strikes at International Harvester and John

Farm Equipment (FE) members at John Deere's East Moline, Illinois, Plant oppose Reuther and the UAW, 1952. Walter P. Reuther Library, Wayne State University

Deere, and a continuing battle with J. I. Case, one of the most resolutely and viciously antiunion employers with which the UAW had to contend.[71]

REUTHER'S REELECTION, though decisive for setting the UAW's future course, did not end internal dissent. Organized factions centered on International officers of the stature of Addes, Thomas, and Leonard had disappeared, but some lesser figures and their locals, including Local 45 (Fisher Body) in Cleveland and Local 51 (Plymouth) in Detroit, remained opposed to the Reuther administration and to one or another of its policies and practices. The most prominent of the opposition locals was Ford Rouge Local 600, still the UAW's largest, although its membership was contracting as Ford embarked on a program of decentralizing its assembly facilities. The confrontation between the administration and Local 600 began soon after the election of Carl Stellato as its president, who ran initially as a Reuther supporter. Stellato, a savvy politician, broke with Reuther when the latter proposed a dues increase at the union's 1951 constitutional convention. At the administration's insistence, five officeholders in Local 600 who refused to sign the Taft-Hartley affidavits were put on trial for violating the clause in the union's constitution (Article X, Section 8) that barred Communists and those who adhered closely to Communist Party positions from union offices. When opposition to the trials mobilized in the local, Stellato executed an about-face that brought him into alignment with the local's still powerful left-wing. The atmosphere was tense inside the Rouge. The members were under speedup pressure from Ford and threatened by a loss of jobs as the company, pursuing a production and jobs dispersal strategy, was building new plants in distant parts of the country.[72]

At this point, in March 1952, the House Un-American Activities Committee (HUAC) descended on Detroit for an inquiry into Communist control of labor unions, with Local 600 its principal target. Although Communists were the committee's stated concern, many labor leaders and independent observers believed its purpose was to undermine unions by linking them in the public's mind with the Communist Party and the Soviet Union. Currents of anticommunist and anti-black feeling, which often merged, had already surfaced in several auto plants. Shortly after the Korean War began, and for a few years thereafter, there were incidents of "violent ejection" of Communists and suspected Communists from auto plants in Detroit, Flint, Milwaukee, Linden, New Jersey, and Los Angeles. Some of the victims were so-called "colonizers," dispatched by the party to find employment in the plants in order to win the workers' trust, spread the party's message, and rebuild its cadres. Few of the colonizers remained for long in the plants. As auto workers, many of them blacks, were named in testimony before the committee as Communists, some were thrown out of the plants and in some instances never allowed to return to their jobs. According to newspaper reports, a wave of sit-down strikes in defiance of UAW policy occurred in Detroit plants instigated by rank-and-file workers who refused to work alongside an accused Communist or suspected sympathizer.[73]

After some hesitation, the UAW executive board undertook to protect the job rights of members against mob action, stating that the union would support grievances of those who were forced from the plants, lost pay, or were discharged by the companies. Reuther and Emil Mazey condemned the vigilantism in letters or telegrams sent to locals where incidents had occurred, pointing out that it was wrong to use violence against those accused, whether correctly or mistakenly, of CP/U.S.S.R. support. In some plants where mobs formed, a conflict was evident between a local leadership that wanted to protect members' rights to their jobs and an element in the rank and file that wished to cleanse the plant of political/ideological nonconformists.[74]

In Local 600 the trials of the five Communist officeholders were stalemated. The trial committee established to its satisfaction that they were Communist Party members and adhered to Communist Party positions, but the local's governing body, the General Council, dismissed the charges. Following well-publicized testimony before HUAC concerning CP activity in Local 600, Reuther decided to break the stalemate with charges of "division and disruption caused by political manipulation engineered by a small but well-disciplined Communist minority." The International executive board set up an administrative board under Reuther's assistant, Jack Conway, which took over the local and suspended its officers. The board clamped down in various ways, including removing the five alleged Communists—Paul Boatin, John Gallo, Dave Moore, Nelson Davis, and Ed Lock—from their union offices. But even Reuther, powerful as he was, could not keep a local under an administrator indefinitely. By the UAW's constitution, a new election of officers was to be held within sixty days of the takeover, although an extension to six months could be, and was, authorized by a two-thirds vote of the International executive board. Ultimately, control of the local had to be returned to the members. The International's heavy-handed, much resented intervention made martyrs of Reuther's foes, and when home rule was restored and elections were held an anti-Reuther slate was returned to office. Throughout the 1950s, Local 600 continued to be a thorn in the flesh to the Reuther leadership. The removal of Communists from union office, a political maneuver to rout the few remaining opponents and an accommodation to the anticommunist hysteria of the times, violated the civil liberties of its victims, regardless of the fact that it was legal under the UAW's constitution and probably had the support of most of the membership outside of Local 600. Since the CP element in the UAW had by then been thoroughly defeated, the imposition of administrative control over the local was as unnecessary as it was unfair. The episode smacked of revenge targeted against a remnant of a once potent force; few if any would defend it today. The five members, demoted to second-class union citizenship when ruled ineligible for office, regained full standing after a long struggle and many appeals, when they filed affidavits denying CP membership for the previous five years. Years later, in a calmer time, Ken Bannon, a Reuther loyalist and director of the union's Ford Department, offered Dave Moore a place on the department's staff.[75]

In 1954, when HUAC returned to Michigan for a second probe of labor unions, the UAW took a position on the use by a UAW member or employee of the Fifth Amendment's protection against self-incrimination. At a time when some employers, including movie moguls and even some university presidents, were dismissing and blacklisting employees who refused on constitutional grounds to respond to the committee's questions, the UAW leadership vowed that "no member, employee or officer of the UAW [would] be prejudiced in any degree in his relationship to the union merely and solely because he claims the privilege" of the Fifth Amendment. The union pledged to resist the discharge or discipline by an employer of any member on the sole ground that he claimed the privilege. An exception to the rule was allowed in 1957 in the case of union employees who sought Fifth Amendment protection when questioned in connection with racketeering charges under investigation by the Senate's McClellan committee.[76]

Disturbed by the reckless forays of congressional committees into citizens' political beliefs, the UAW fought an important legal battle to limit the scope of congressional investigations. When UAW staff representative John T. Watkins, a left-winger and former FE organizer in the Quad Cities agricultural implement plants, was hailed before HUAC, he followed the UAW's recommended response for its employees by speaking openly of his own political affiliations but refused to give the committee the names of others he had known as one-time party members. The committee, following its standard practice, cited him for contempt. With the backing of Reuther and the executive board, UAW attorney Joseph Rauh appealed Watkins's case to the Supreme Court. In a decision that imposed a major restriction on the investigating power of Congress, the Court, reversing Watkins's contempt conviction, ruled that his First Amendment rights had been violated and that HUAC had no power to investigate political beliefs for the sake of exposure alone. The commitment of the UAW leadership, Rauh recalled, "made these kinds of [civil liberties] victories possible."[77]

The victory of the Reuther forces ended factionalism and reduced the Communist and CP-allied presence in the UAW to that of a small minority with little influence. Reuther's attack provoked charges of "Red-baiting," the accusation that the anticommunist campaign was merely a device for political opportunists, exploiting the "Red scare" hysteria of the times to use against their rivals in the factional battle. There is no question that anticommunism, linked as it was to an appeal to the strong sentiments of patriotism in the auto workers' ranks, was a politically powerful weapon. The argument that CP loyalists put Party and Soviet interests ahead of workers' interests persuaded many. For Reuther, the crackdown on Local 600 struck a blow at a potential rival, Carl Stellato, by associating him with a Communist cadre. Equally true, Reuther's fear of a destructive antiunion crusade aimed against the UAW, shielded behind anticommunist rhetoric, was genuine and, given the circumstances of the times, well-founded. But political advantage and fear of damage to the union were not the whole story. A principled objection to Communism was also important. Believing that a democratic left, of which they were a part, and a totalitarian left were locked in a struggle to shape humanity's future, Reuther and his followers saw the UAW's committed Communists as apologists for a dictatorial regime that denied principles of human freedom, including the rights of free labor, and threatened the freedom of other nations. The fundamental solution was to champion and create an effective democratic alternative, as Reuther declared on many occasions. "There is only the never-ending task," he wrote, "of making democracy work, keeping it alive and fighting against injustice; expanding and enriching it by tangible achievement. Stopping Communism is only a negative aspect of that positive, infinitely more important work."[78]

A corollary to this position, as Reuther further explained, held that "honest liberals must guard against the temptation to join forces with or accept help from those whose only badge of fraternity is their anti-Communism." Both an anticommunist and an opponent of extremist anticommunism, Reuther warned in a report to the 1947 UAW convention: "We must fight against . . . home-grown varieties of fascists . . . and we must guard against the technique of smearing every decent liberal and progressive with the brush of communism. On the other hand we must fight against the Communist Party and their efforts to employ the same smear technique in reverse by branding as a Fascist and Red-baiter everyone who has the courage to oppose or to criticize the Communist Party line." The UAW condemned those politicians, like Wisconsin Republican Senator Joseph McCarthy, who exploited and magnified the anticommunist hysteria for political advantage. The union contributed large sums of money to McCarthy's electoral opponents, distributed leaflets and other materials critical of the senator and his methods to its members and the public, and provided a forum at its conventions for McCarthy's critics. The irony that its strictures were applicable to some of its own actions probably escaped the union's officers.[79]

THE 1947 VICTORY OF THE REUTHER forces was one of several turning points that saw the internal balance of power between the International Union and the locals tilt in favor of the former. In the early days the locals often set the pace in organizing, strike activity, and grievance handling, with the International's officers and staff scrambling to keep up. The union's founding strike at GM began when local activists took the initiative. The weak and divisive leadership of Homer Martin and, to a much lesser degree, that of R. J. Thomas contributed to the locals' ability to maintain their strong position. The chronic factional struggle, which lasted ten years and at times created chaos in the union's upper reaches, preoccupied the rivals, leaving the locals in a state of benign neglect and with considerable discretion in managing their affairs. Despite the wildcat strikes, World War II marked the start of a trend toward a more centralized, bureaucratic organization. Several strands were woven together to enhance the International's authority. The companies (and the government) pressed the union to centralize authority and responsibility, to honor contracts, to maintain production, to respect the prerogatives of management, and to define (and thereby confine) divisions of authority with precision. Many of the new locals founded during the war with inexperienced members and leaders relied upon regional and International officers for guidance in bargaining and contract administration. When wartime regulations transferred final authority in disputes over wages and grievances to Washington, the burden of dealing with these legalistic, technical matters increasingly fell on the International. With the Big Three and the union tied to binding arbitration, many of the most serious contract infractions were no longer argued out between steward or committeeman and foreman, but sent up the ladder and ultimately, if unresolved, out of the plant to an arbitrator. As rulings accumulated, they built up a body of case law that International staff members kept track of. With precedents in place, the outcomes of many disputes arising on the shop floor were already settled. In another step toward central control, in 1946 the union signed "company security" agreements with Ford and Chrysler (something similar had been agreed upon with GM in 1940) that acknowledged the right of the corporations to discipline local union officers who participated in wildcat strikes.[80]

Once the war was over the International leadership dominated in formulating and implementing bargaining and strike strategy. When Reuther took the initiative in instigating and conducting the General Motors strike, he established the precedent that major conflicts were the responsibility of Solidarity House. The adoption of pattern bargaining—negotiating with a target company what was, in effect, a set of common contract provisions that all the major manufacturers would be required to conform to—further strengthened the International's position. Local strikes over job classifications, seniority provisions, production standards, safety questions, and other plant issues were bound to and frequently did occur, but the company-wide settlements of wage and benefit packages negotiated by the International commanded the public's attention and comment. As the wage and benefit provisions moved into new areas, such as cost-of-living escalators, pensions, health insurance, and a host of others, the contracts became more complex and technical, the province of the bargainers and their specialist consultants and advisors. Thus the distance between the International and the locals grew and the role of the International continued to expand.[81]

Services once provided by locals, if at all, were incorporated into International departments that handled matters such as legal counseling, veterans' affairs, education, unemployment insurance, civil rights, health and community services, and women's concerns. Concurrently, the social, recreational, and educational activities of the locals, while still vigorous in those large enough to sustain them, occupied a lesser place in many workers' lives. In the postwar world of television, spectator and participatory sports, hobbies, travel, and inexpensive popular entertainment, workers found many new opportunities for leisure activity and family activities apart from their local union.[82]

Corporation and government bureaucracies spawned union bureaucracy. As the union grew and contracts expanded to cover new subjects and contingencies, the necessity of constructing and operating a more elaborate apparatus with professional personnel was apparent. The International representatives who maintained contact with and provided services to locals were union members who came out of the autoworker ranks, but specialized training and competence were prerequisites for a growing number of staff positions. The corporate and government agencies the union now regularly dealt with were themselves mammoth organizations with intricate divisions of labor among their white-collar employees. The corporations employed thousands to prepare and fine-tune their bargaining positions and proposals. The UAW could never fully match their resources, but an effective presentation of the union's case on a multitude of issues required recourse to a skilled cadre that combined commitment to the union's cause with a command of the techniques of economic and social analysis.[83]

A blunt instrument for asserting the International executive board's control was the appointment of an administrator, usually a regional director, to take over and run a local that was allegedly breaking the rules. If the board received information that a local union's officers were derelict in performance of their duties, it could, following a "show cause" hearing and a two-thirds vote, appoint an administrator to take over the local for sixty days. At the end of that period, new elections would be held and the local would regain its autonomy. Under certain circumstances, the administrator's reign could be extended to six months. Administratorships, often controversial and resented, were resorted to reluctantly and only in particular circumstances. The leading instances included managing a local union's financial assets as it was winding up its affairs when a plant closed, investigating charges of fraud or other misbehavior in local elections, dealing with racial discrimination within a local, cracking down on in-plant gambling where gangsters and local officers were allegedly involved, and, in the case of Local 600, enforcing the union's ban on office-holding by Communists.[84]

Although the International gained in power and status the locals retained much of their vigor on matters of vital interest. On issues of day-to-day importance to the membership—such as production standards, health and safety concerns, and a host of other locally determined matters—they enjoyed substantial autonomy through both formal and informal means. For maximum effectiveness in promoting the interests of the members, both strong locals and a strong central organization were necessary, with a distribution of functions and authority between the two linked together in a dynamic balance.

FOLLOWING REUTHER'S REELECTION the UAW's only permanent, internal political organization was the Reuther caucus or, as it came to be called, the Administration caucus. The basic caucus rule allowed for the expression and debate of all views and for any nominations for office in caucus sessions, but once decisions by majority vote were reached all were bound to support them in conventions, executive board meetings, and other official gatherings. Caucus decisions were rarely defied by caucus participants. To do so was to place yourself in opposition to the leadership and the majority will. The caucus and the union's structure of councils, educational programs, and internal communications had a two-fold purpose. They were instruments for maintaining the leadership in power and winning support for its proposals, and they were a means of expressing the reactions and concerns of the union's secondary leaders and, through them, of rank-and-file members. The existence of a binding caucus made conventions and board sessions sometimes cut-and-dried affairs. The outcome was known in advance since key decisions on many issues were made in the caucus, ordinarily acting on the leadership's recommendations. On some issues the caucus took no position, allowing participants a free vote, and modifications of caucus positions were possible as a result of convention or board debates. The caucus was organized on three levels. The board caucus consisted of supportive board members, which included nearly everyone after Reuther's reelection. Meeting as needed prior to a board meeting, it considered, debated, and ordinarily endorsed recommendations that came from the officers. The caucus steering committee, which excluded board members, consisted of elected leaders from each region, normally officers of some of the larger locals. It met two or three months before a convention and formulated a set of consensus recommendations for convention action. The entire caucus, consisting of all those elected convention delegates who chose to attend, met a day or so before the convention and adopted the program, ordinarily following the recommendations of the steering committee. Caucus expenses—meeting hall rentals, dinners, travel expenses and the like—were met out of a "flower fund," made up of contributions from officers, staff members, and others. A small amount of "flower fund" money was actually spent on flowers for occasions such as weddings and funerals of staff members and their families.[85]

Although most policy proposals and officer nominations came down from above for ratification, the caucus provided a forum for convention delegates to express their views. The importance they attached to this channel of communication was demonstrated early in Reuther's presidency when the caucus was temporarily disbanded. The leadership mistakenly assumed that without an electoral campaign to conduct there was no need for it. At the 1949 convention several unpopular proposals, including a dues increase, were brought forward without first being given a caucus airing and vote. This provoked an uproar that forced the leadership to call an immediate caucus meeting. The delegates made plain their dissatisfaction with the abandonment of the caucus. Reuther, belatedly recognizing that the caucus was a necessary device for discovering and monitoring the views of his constituency and convincing the delegates of the merits of his program, conceded "you're absolutely right." Lacking the formality and procedural constraints of a convention session, the caucus setting allowed for a more complete exchange of views between the leadership and the convention delegates.[86]

Although the caucus was an important leadership tool, it would not have worked effectively without Reuther's personal qualities. He rarely lost touch with the membership. His greater participation in public affairs as his presidency progressed reduced opportunities for personal contact, but an understanding of the auto workers' world and the cultures of work and family that shaped his life helped to bridge any gap. As one associate recalled, he had a "remarkable sense of an average auto worker and what was bothering him. . . . It wasn't from reading books. It was an ability to catch it in a meeting, in a conversation, in a dialogue back and forth between contending forces." In his dealings with local leaders and rank-and-file workers he never underestimated their intelligence nor the importance of their concerns, and in his speeches and other messages he communicated economic, political, and social concepts in terms that could be readily understood but were not patronizing. As Nat Weinberg, a close associate for more than twenty years, observed, "I've never seen anybody in a leadership position dealing with enormous numbers of people who could persuade them to follow him as effectively as he could."[87]

Committed to rising with his class rather than out of it, Reuther believed that union officers should not receive salaries so high they would distance them from the members. His salary, set like those of other officers by the convention, was always at the low end, often the very lowest, among heads of major unions, despite the UAW's size, wealth, and prominence. In 1960 his annual salary of $22,000 was the lowest of the salaries of presidents of the eight largest American unions and was less than half of the amount paid to AFL-CIO president George Meany. When a move was made on the floor at the 1953 convention to increase officers salaries beyond a committee's modest recommendations, Reuther opposed it, saying, "I am not in the union for what you put in my pay check. I am in this for what is in my heart." His position, which was endorsed by the delegates, did not endear him to some of the other officers and staff members whose own pay could not be increased unless the president's salary was raised.[88]

SOME CRITICS HAVE CHARGED that the disappearance of factional alignments, the installation of a single ruling party, and the expansion of the
International's role at the expense of the locals signaled the decline, even
the demise, of democracy in the UAW. At one time the union's internal
political structure had somewhat resembled that of a two-party system,
with an ongoing competition for power between evenly balanced rivals.
Rarely, however, has any union reached decisions through give-and-take
between more or less permanent, internal political organizations. In fact,
the UAW was unique among major industrial unions in maintaining a rough
balance among its competing elements for as long as it did. The question of
UAW democracy is complicated by the contradictory pressures and expectations that were brought to bear on the organization. On the one hand it
had to be a participatory democracy in which each member had a free and
equal voice; on the other it had to function periodically as a cohesive force,
unified and mobilized for action and economic struggle with powerful
adversaries. Inescapably, conflicts between diversity and unity, more
broadly between freedom and order, would occur. The task of leadership
was to find a balance that acknowledged the legitimacy of both principles
and permitted it to evaluate where circumstances at any particular juncture
required the emphasis to be placed.[89]

The Reuther administration was organized to secure the degree of
unity and order it judged necessary to assure the union's survival and effi-
cacy. This was reflected in the rules that governed the operation of the constitutional convention, the union's supreme authority. Convention
committees contained only administration supporters, and committee resolutions could only be amended once the original resolution was voted
down and resubmitted. Such restrictive procedures precluded unfettered
debate. In an earlier time committee memberships reflected the factional
division, and committees submitted majority, minority, and even "super-
minority" reports, sparking vigorous convention debates on the merits of
conflicting proposals. By contrast, in the Reuther era administration proposals were challenged infrequently and debate was often routine. Requirements for convention roll-call votes were difficult to meet, and there were
few of them. In the name of punishing and preventing actions that harmed
the union's cause, the administration accused two opponents, with some
justification, of actions that damaged the union's organizing activities and
obtained their expulsion, in the process violating the union's expulsion procedure. Invoking the need to protect the union against harm, the International leadership insured that the newspapers put out by local unions
publicized leadership views and refrained from criticisms the leadership
considered irresponsibile and damaging. Charging that the *Searchlight*, the
paper of Local 659 (Flint Chevrolet), which had an editorial policy of print-

ing articles submitted by any union member as long as they were not libelous, had published false and malicious pieces accusing International officers of dishonesty, the executive board appointed an administrator to take over the local and suppress the offending paper, leaving an embittered local convinced that its right to free expression had been trampled on. Educational and publicity activites emanating from union headquarters supported the leadership's agenda. On occasion the International sought to influence the election of a regional director, but ordinarily incumbents were reelected without serious challenge. International intervention in a local election was rare, although International representatives assigned to a region were often active electioneering agents.[90]

On the other hand, one-party control by no means meant that all avenues for the expression of oppositional views were closed. Elections of officers and convention delegates in the locals were substantially free of outside interference and often vigorously contested. Heated discussions of controversial issues at conventions occurred, and committee recommendations were sometimes modified, defeated, or withdrawn. Convention debates were conducted to give those opposed to leadership positions an opportunity to express their views by alternating speakers for and against a proposition. On important and potentially divisive issues—such as a dues increase (always a controversial matter), extending the interval between conventions from one to two years, adopting the practice of a direct vote by the entire membership for the election of officers, or extending terms of local officers from one to two years—Reuther insisted on more than a bare majority in favor; sometimes he ruled that a motion had failed when it had narrowly carried in order to obtain additional discussion, possible revision, and broader support. As a rule of thumb, he wanted a consensus of at least two-thirds and preferably three-fourths of delegate support for important decisions. Controversial proposals were not rammed through conventions over opposition protest. To gauge support for such proposals he liked to take straw votes in convention sessions, withdrawing the proposal before a final, binding vote was taken if it lacked strong support.[91]

An important test of union democracy requires due process rights for individuals. Are they protected against abuse by union officials, including protections against the use of strong-arm or otherwise unscrupulous methods, and are they guaranteed fair and equal treatment? Perhaps more than any other American union of similar scope and size, the UAW met this test. The most careful academic student of the UAW's governance concluded, "few unions rank higher on the democratic spectrum than the UAW with respect to . . . the guarantee of fundamental individual rights." In a more sweeping statement, secretary-treasurer Emil Mazey claimed that "labor unions are the most democratic institutions we have in our country in which the rank and file members play a much greater part than the stock-holders in a corporation, or citizens in our government"—a boast to be sure, but not off the mark.[92]

In order to place the members' right to due process on a firm institu-tional foundation, the convention in 1957 (at Reuther's insistence, there being little rank-and-file sentiment on the matter and some opposition on the executive board) authorized the establishment of a public review board. As Michael Harrington later wrote, "paradoxically, the anti-bureaucratic reform was carried out by the bureaucracy." The appeals procedure previ-ously in effect required a member who had a grievance against the union or who had been found guilty by trial of a violation of the union's constitution to appeal to the executive board for review, with a final appeal to the con-vention. Recognizing that the decisions of the executive board and of the convention could be unduly influenced by the officers, Reuther insisted that a panel completely independent of the UAW be established as an alternative final review body for internal grievances. Its membership consisted of seven prominent "impartial persons of good repute" from outside the union. Over the years, judges, clergymen, and university professors with a professional interest in the internal activities of unions have been favored as final review-ers. The board's hearings are public, its expenses paid without question, and appellants entitled to counsel. In its first three years the review board heard twenty-nine cases on appeal following an executive board decision; it affirmed the executive board's decisions in twenty-three and reversed it in six. In comparison, the conventions of 1953, 1955, and 1957 heard thirty cases on appeal from executive board decisions and reversed on three. In its first official decision the public review board upheld the right of five former Communists to retain UAW positions. Most of the cases involved alleged misdeeds by a local union against one of its own members over issues aris-ing out of disputed elections, failure to prosecute grievances, the duty of fair representation, and the like, with the board's decisions based on due process rights guaranteed in the union's constitution. The board has no jurisdiction over collective bargaining issues and scrupulously avoids involvement in them. A major instrument for protecting individual rights and therefore union democracy, its establishment, according to an early independent assessment, represented the "broadest grant of authority over its internal affairs ever voluntarily given by a labor organization—or any other organi-zation for that matter—to an outside body."[93]

Reuther's continuing success as president was a more important part of the explanation for the failure of strong oppositional groups to emerge than the use of internal manipulations and constraints. He was a shrewd politician, opportunistic and flexible, "very agile politically," in Nat Wein-berg's words. He showed no reluctance to drop proposals that were proving unpopular or met only a lukewarm response, and he reversed his position on occasion—for example, on a cost-of-living escalator, a concept he had once opposed. He readily adopted popular proposals brought forward by others and made them his own, most notably a demand for an early retirement program that forcefully emerged in the 1960s and that could, if ignored, have led to the growth of a significant opposition. Obtaining superior contracts, the union's primary purpose in the view of most members, sealed the Reuther group's hold on power. In the face of a steady flow of popular wage and benefit improvements producing more stable employment and income, achieved through union bargaining, it was exceedingly difficult for opposition factions to form. External factors were also important in contributing to one-party rule. The redistribution of the membership out of Detroit and throughout the country in new plants, a development initiated by the corporations for their own purposes, may well have made organization of a permanent opposition more difficult. The cold war decline, suppression, and disappearance of radical movements in the United States, a process the UAW leadership contributed to but which occurred independently of it, removed an important base of factional formations.[94]

A SERIOUS PHYSICAL THREAT to the union stemmed from the interconnected worlds of gambling, crime, and union-busting by hostile employers. Gambling on horse races and sports events, and playing the numbers, which then faced no competition from state-operated lotteries, were popular diversions in many plants. The thousands of workers employed represented an enormous potential for gambling operations and profits. Probably all of the big Detroit plants, and many elsewhere, had an active numbers operation. Even small wagers of a quarter or less a day added up to large sums when collected from many players. One union officer estimated that the numbers handle at the Rouge plant alone was $7 million a year, mostly in nickels, dimes, and quarters. An estimate, probably conservative, as of 1948 held that the yearly gambling take in Detroit auto plants was at least $20 million. While union rules forbade officers from becoming involved in gambling operations, local union officials were sometimes recruited as runners or bookies. Union committeemen, free to move about the plant in order to investigate and discuss grievances, and in some cases authorized to leave the plant during working hours, had a perfect cover as numbers runners. Not surprisingly, the profit potential in gambling attracted the underworld's attention. Gangster control of gambling ordinarily required at least the acquiescence, and sometimes the active cooperation, of both union and management elements. The numbers payoff brought hope and excitement to the factory floor, and from the point of view of management, such gambling, unlike shooting craps in an out-of-the-way corner of the factory or a rest room, had the virtue of causing little interference with work.[95]

Reuther and other UAW officials condemned gambling, fearful that some workers were losing more than they could afford and that gambling operations could corrupt a local's leadership. Reuther and secretary-treasurer Emil Mazey believed gambling could be eliminated if law enforcement wished to do so and pointed out that it "cannot exist in any plant without the knowledge and consent of some level of management." They warned that the union would not protect the jobs of any members running gambling operations, opening the way for dismissals or other disciplinary penalties if management chose to take action. The UAW's constitution was amended in 1951 to provide removal from office of any local or International official found guilty of participating in organized gambling rackets. As part of its "war on gambling in the plants," the union prepared and issued a booklet, that reviewed common forms of gambling and warned that the odds of winning were always against the bettor. The victory of the Reuther forces in 1947 threatened to curtail plant gambling, although one of his key supporters, vice president Richard Gosser, was rumored to have a hand in gambling operations in the Toledo plants.[96]

The union's antigambling stance clashed with the interests of the gangsters who wanted to run the lucrative operations. A critical situation developed in plants of the Briggs Manufacturing Company on Detroit's East Side, whose workers were represented by UAW Local 212. There a deal was struck between elements within the Briggs management and Santo Perrone, a Detroit gangster also known as "the Shark" and "the Enforcer," who, among other criminal activities, used beatings and threats of violence to keep unions out of plants. Perrone would establish control of plant gambling and obtain a generous contract to haul away the company's scrap metal, a job which could be subcontracted on advantageous terms to a legitimate disposal firm. In return the thugs would intimidate the local's leadership and perhaps succeed in driving the union out of the plants, using any means to do the job.[97]

Within a year's time, four officials of Local 212, including Ken Morris, its president, were attacked and seriously injured. Morris, beaten unconscious with lead pipes, suffered fractures to his skull, jaw, arm, and legs. Moving on, gangsters targeted president Reuther. On the night of April 20, 1948, as he was finishing a late dinner at his Detroit home, he was shot through a window by an assailant using a twelve-gauge shotgun loaded with heavy double-O buckshot at a distance of nine feet. Only a quick turn at the moment the shot was fired saved his life. As it was, one of his arms was shattered and nearly severed; the nerves were in shreds and doctors feared he would never recover its use. Intricate surgery and years of physical rehabilitation eventually led to partial restoration, although the arm never regained full strength. After the shooting Reuther said that in the union's early days he had received many threats, but that in recent years he had received few. Two threatening letters, one objecting to his defense of civil liberties for Communists and another attacking his campaign to win admission for blacks to bowling tournaments, had arrived the week before the shooting. Thirteen months later Victor Reuther was similarly shot through the living-room window of his home in Detroit. The blast took out his right eye.[98]

Although large rewards were offered, mainly by the UAW, neither attempted murder was solved. Investigations were carried on as late as 1968, and the State of Michigan extended the statute of limitations when it appeared there might be a break in the case. The Detroit police department, never friendly to the union, mishandled its investigation. Material evidence and even witnesses mysteriously disappeared from police custody, and investigators hired by the UAW found the police uncooperative. Federal authorities were no more helpful. When pressed to enter the cases, FBI Director J. Edgar Hoover privately replied that his agency could not become involved in a criminal investigation "every time some nigger gets [obscenity deleted]." A General Motors executive who had always been rough on the union stated at the bargaining table that "it's too bad they didn't kill the son of a bitch." The union broke off negotiations until a GM official, though not the one who uttered the offensive remark, offered an apology. Among official bodies, only a United States Senate committee under Senator Estes Kefauver made a serious attempt to get to the bottom of the crimes, but its resources and jurisdiction were limited. The underlying attitude of some of the law enforcement agencies and the newspapers seemed to be that the beatings and shootings were the work of rival labor gangs trying to bump each other off; the sooner they succeeded, the better.[99]

Many rumors and hypotheses were aired. Some anticommunists and media pundits surmised that Communists were involved, a suspicion that may have inspired the Michigan Communist Party to contribute $500 to the reward fund. The police inspector assigned to the case mysteriously intoned to a reporter that "only Moscow knows" who the assailants were. Although never proved, some evidence suggested a link to oppositional elements within the union, but if in fact that was the case, the motivation was financial rather than ideological or political. The most plausible suspicions centered on the Perrone gang.[100]

Following the assassination attempt, the UAW adopted strict security measures to protect Reuther, including purchasing an armored Packard sedan for his transportation, hiring body guards, and relocating his residence to a more easily protected semi-rural site. Reuther was a potential target for the rest of his life. The union occasionally received threats to blow up Solidarity

Solidarity House, the UAW's headquarters, 1958. Walter P. Reuther Library, Wayne State University

House, its Detroit headquarters, and there were anonymous threats to plant bombs on airplanes on which Reuther was scheduled to fly, but no further incidents occurred. Victor Reuther left Detroit soon after recovering from his wounds, first for Paris and later Washington D.C., where he took charge of union foreign policy and International operations.[101]

WITH REUTHER'S REELECTION in 1947 the UAW entered an era of internal stability and outward progress, aptly represented in the new headquarters building it occupied in 1951. After years in offices in a structure overshadowed by the mammoth General Motors headquarters, the union's new status found expression in a striking building of its own. Erected on acreage fronting the Detroit River that had once been the site of Edsel Ford's mansion, "Solidarity House" was a stone and glass symbol of the victories won in the contests with the auto companies that had brought into existence a powerful and permanent workers' organization. Beyond celebrating the union's history, the modern Scandinavian-inspired design of the building and its furnishings was a physical representation of the union's aspiration to serve as a vanguard pointing America toward a social-democratic future. In the event, there would be as much frustration as fulfillment in the pursuit of that dream.[102]

CHAPTER 8

"The glory days of growth and rich settlements"

Better Lives for Auto Workers and Their Families, 1948–60

W ITH THE VICTORY OF THE REUTHER FORCES, THE UAW's attention turned from internal struggles to the challenges of raising the members' standard of living and enhancing their economic security. In its early years the union was most intent on winning recognition and a shop floor voice. In postwar America, the emphasis shifted to material gains, to more dollars in the pay envelope and an expanding array of fringe benefits that would, taken together, enormously contribute to family and personal security. Winning higher pay, pensions, medical, surgical, and life insurance, dental coverage, paid vacations and holidays, sick leave, shift differentials, and other kinds of premium pay and benefits assured the UAW a place in the front rank of workers' organizations. Most industrial workers and some service employees, both union and nonunion, shared these gains, but the auto workers often set the pace and always exceeded the averages.[1]

Although UAW membership fluctuated, sometimes dramatically, from year to year depending on industry employment, it remained between 1.1 and 1.5 million from the late 1940s until the end of the 1960s, making the UAW either the largest or second largest (after the Teamsters) of American unions. The great majority of members were employed in auto assembly and parts manufacturing for the Big Three and independent companies, but significant numbers were also present in aerospace and agricultural implements. Bargaining power was securely based on the near total membership in the auto manufacturers' plants. Of the five firms producing cars in 1961, General Motors employed 310,000 UAW members, Ford 122,000, Chrysler 90,000 (of whom about 10 percent were salaried office, clerical, and technical workers), American Motors 23,000, and Studebaker—close to shutting down as a car maker—6,000. Throughout the entire auto industry approximately 90 percent of the hourly-rated workers were UAW members. Only in some of the parts firms were nonunion workers to be found, and no foreign-owned "transplant" factories had yet been established in the United States to create a major nonunion element within the auto workforce.[2]

The real wages and living standards of auto workers rose dramatically. Measured in constant dollars, the 1947 average weekly wage in the industry of $56.51 had doubled by 1960 to $115.21, and tripled by 1970 to $170.07. In contrast, the average wage in miscellaneous manufacturing occupations was approximately two-thirds of the auto workers' wage; the average in ordinary service occupations, such as retail trade, was less than half as much. The spread between autowork pay and pay in other manual occupations steadily increased throughout the postwar years. In 1966, Flint, Michigan, riding on the crest of General Motors revenues, was the top hourly wage area in the United States as reported by the U.S. Department of Labor, with factory workers there, nearly all UAW members, earning a weekly average of $166.26. Average weekly earnings of factory workers in Michigan at $143.79 were higher than those in any of the adjacent forty-eight states; Ohio, the state with the second largest number of UAW members, was second in earnings at $127.02. Many auto workers could now afford some of the perquisites of middle-class life. Home ownership soared. Detroit and Flint had the highest proportion of owner-occupied houses of any American cities of their size, and modern household appliances had become standard possessions. Car ownership appropriately symbolized the auto workers' rising status. Prior to World War II, streetcars and buses carried many to their factory jobs, but now most drove their own cars or light trucks. One reason, among several, that the car manufacturers located new plants on the outskirts of industrial cities and in small towns was that land for employee parking lots was relatively inexpensive.[3]

Creative innovations secured wages and living standards against the hazards of a historically volatile industry. Wage increases were tied to gains in productivity and to increases in the cost of consumer goods. Linking raises to productivity improvements guaranteed that workers would share in the fruits of new technologies and thus have less incentive to oppose their introduction, a point of prime importance to the manufacturers. Tying wages to the cost of consumer goods guaranteed that the buying power of their wages would not be undermined by inflation. The UAW also secured a substantial payment to supplement unemployment compensation, the first step toward guaranteeing an auto worker a year's wages in case of layoff. Other forms of compensation, such as pensions and paid holidays, added to personal and family security and well-being. Hospitalization insurance and medical and surgical benefits promoted the health of workers and their families and shielded them against the devastating financial blows inflicted by the costs of modern medical treatment. Some insurances, such as group life insurance, had been available previously under company programs, but only as contributory plans with the costs borne by the insured. The companies had to be persuaded to take the first step in assuming the costs and expanding the coverage, and then another step and then another, through successive rounds of bargaining. By securing these fringe benefits, the UAW created for its members through collective bargaining a private "welfare state" whose scope rivaled that of the social-democratic entitlement systems then emerging in the nations of western and northern Europe. Owing to the possibility of capital flight to lower cost labor areas, the UAW's "welfare state" was not as securely based.[4]

Although these gains were genuine and even dramatic, they were unevenly shared. Periodic and even chronic unemployment represented a problem as companies shut down many older factories, particularly in Detroit, replacing them with new plants in suburbs and in distant towns and cities. Some of the smaller manufacturers abandoned the business entirely. A series of recessions in the 1950s, most severe in 1958, saw several hundred thousand auto workers on temporary layoff, with union membership shrinking by about 300,000, forcing cutbacks in the locals and reductions in pay for staff. Layoffs occurred unevenly across the workforce, thanks to seniority rules. African Americans and women employees, typically over-represented among the most recent hires, were the industry's "shock absorbers" in downturns.[5]

The UAW's bargaining effectiveness was predicated on a prosperous industry, on competition for market share among the manufacturers, and on union dominance of the labor market that produced the cars Americans bought. The achievement of internal unity and focus within the union coincided with the dawning of a golden age for the industry. Demand for cars seemed insatiable. Owing to wartime's lack of production, the existing stock was depleted and worn-out. Despite bursts of inflation and periodic recessions, the postwar economy produced an unprecedented rise in real incomes. Most American income earners chose to spend a substantial portion of their wealth on cars, whose possession was exalted far beyond that of a mere utilitarian provider of transportation into the leading "status symbol" of the times and a prime example of conspicuous consumption. In 1948 only half of American households owned automobiles; twenty years later the figure had risen to over 80 percent. In the twenty-five years from 1946 through 1970 American manufacturers built 156 million passenger cars and 34 million trucks and buses, more than twice as many motor vehicles as had been built in the industry's earlier years.[6]

Auto manufacturing was the most prosperous of major industries. For nearly every year from 1947 to 1967, the annual rate of return (net profits

after taxes divided by net worth) was twice as great in the auto industry as
in all manufacturing corporations. For those twenty-one years the industry's
average annual return was 17 percent, a figure that includes the losses of
firms that failed, such as Kaiser-Frazer and Studebaker-Packard, as well as
the profits of those that succeeded. General Motors, the profit leader in those
years, averaged nearly a 21 percent annual rate of return; the corporation
could recover its capital investment out of profits in less than five years. The
UAW calculated that the profits of the Big Three from 1947 to 1969 were
$3.5 billion, fourteen times their invested capital. No other major American
business matched that record. Since the companies, an oligopoly that followed GM's price leadership, did not compete on price and faced little sustained foreign competition in the market's major segments until the 1960s,
they simply passed higher costs, including the cost of labor, through to buyers. General Motors labor relations officials took pride in the claim that
despite the substantial monetary gains won by the UAW, the corporation's
labor costs, as a percentage of all costs, remained remarkably stable.[7]

Although the companies were dedicated to tough bargaining and were
prepared on occasion to take a strike, the prosperous years drained some of
the acrimony from the exchanges between the union and the manufacturers. The corporations became resigned to the union's presence as, in present
circumstances and for the time being, unavoidable. They had learned that
the workers would stand by the union in a struggle and that prolonged or
continuous conflict was harmful to the business. In part, a more acquiescent attitude on management's side came with new personnel. Many of the
top executives of the hard-nosed, prewar generation had passed from the
scene. At General Motors William S. Knudsen, formerly the company's
president, did not return to GM's management following his wartime service in Washington. Alfred P. Sloan, Jr., remained board chairman but ceded
executive control to a new president, Charles E. Wilson. The role of the
DuPont-family interests, whose controlling stock holdings in GM came
under attack in a tangled and finally successful antitrust suit, was diminished and their representation in GM's management and on its board of
directors withdrawn. Unlike earlier GM chief executives, who regarded the
union as an affront and avoided personal dealings with it as much as possible, Wilson, who later told Reuther that the union's 1945–46 strike had convinced him that "you were going to be around for a long time," was an
active force in labor relations. He relished the bargaining table's battle of
wits. His contests with Reuther stretched back to the 1939 tool and die
strike when Wilson carried the bargaining burden for the corporation. In a
marathon session near that strike's conclusion, Wilson "offered Reuther"
(in a participant's words) "about eight different positions, all variations of
the thing, and it got to be about midnight, and Walter pushed his chair back

and laughed like hell and he says: 'I'm going to offer a recess until morning. I damned near took that last position of yours and it's not as good as the first one you offered." Following their 1950 bargaining, Wilson told Reuther during a chance encounter that he would enjoy a poker game with him sometime when there was "not a billion dollars in the pot." Compared to his predecessors and successors at GM and to executives at other auto companies, Wilson was imaginative and audacious in labor relations and even respectful of his union adversaries. His relationship with the union dismayed some other GM executives, one of whom told a reporter long after Wilson's death, "we would like to go out and piss on his grave." Reuther acknowledged that he had always found Wilson to be "a very decent genuine human being," but he could not refrain from adding, "the test of that is that if you can still act as a human being after going through the General Motors Corporation's machine, it means you're not only a good human being, you're an unusual human being." After Wilson's departure in 1953 to become secretary of defense in the Eisenhower administration, GM management became less creative, although it did not revert to its former relentless hostility.[8]

At Ford, too, new faces brightened the scene. The elder Henry Ford died in 1947 and Harry Bennett, his sidekick, was fired by the company's new chief executive, the founder's grandson, Henry Ford II. He brought in a management team consisting of General Motors veterans and "whiz kids" from the United States Air Force office of statistical analysis to lift the ailing company out of the doldrums. These newcomers were prepared to work with the UAW and responded favorably to some of the union's demands. It became a bargaining rule of thumb within the UAW in the 1950s and 1960s that if the union wanted mainly money in a new contract, it went first to GM because that's where most of the money was and GM would spend in order to avoid a work stoppage; but if the union had a new idea that it wanted to put across, it went first to Ford.[9]

Although Walter P. Chrysler had long since left the scene, the Chrysler Corporation management had changed the least among the Big Three. Its policies and decisions were still shaped by executives whose views on labor relations dated from an earlier era. It was not surprising that the longest and most bitterly contested strike of the Reuther presidency, that of 1950 over pensions, occurred at Chrysler.

MANY OBSERVERS SAW A CONTRAST between the engagement and idealism of the founding generation of the UAW, when an almost continuous sense of crisis and the challenges of overcoming the depression and reforming society mobilized the ranks, and an alleged indifference of the workforce in the postwar years. Reuther acknowledged to the executive board in 1951 that "reaching our membership" is the "most serious problem we have. Half of the membership . . . are people who came into our Union after its original struggles were over, and they do not appreciate what it used to be like in these plants before we had a union"—a refrain repeated many times down through the years. Labor leadership's main task, he told a CIO convention, was to "unionize the organized." Reuther often expressed alarm over the state of the labor movement. As he told the 1962 UAW convention: "A labor movement can get soft and flabby spiritually. It can make progress materially and the soul of the union can die in the process." A share in prosperity and an increase in leisure (both due in considerable part to the union's efforts) could draw workers away from the union and its activities. One veteran claimed that in the 1930s "they were willing to spend some time at the union hall in educational classes and so forth . . . because they did not have much money and they did not have anything else to do." Board member Martin Gerber remarked that the current members "do not need a . . . [union] to occupy the idle hours. . . . I used to go to membership meetings because I had nothing else to do." Gerber suggested that to accommodate the interests of a new generation of auto workers, meetings should be scheduled when they did not conflict with televised football games or other entertainment attractions. Ten UAW officials testified to the shrinkage of members' loyalty and expressed other critical views in a Center for the Study of Democratic Institutions publication. They maintained that companies now gave workers the things unions had fought for and said that to remain viable unions must find new objectives which employers were reluctant to concede. Reuther added that "we are not going to change the fact that as we increase the level of affluence we are going to, in effect, be intensifying the competition to get the time and attention of our members."[10]

A generational change clearly had taken place. Many of the UAW's early leaders and rank-and-file activists, shaped by capitalism's 1930s crisis, had a philosophical-political outlook as liberals, social democrats, independent leftists, Socialists, Communists, Trotskyists, or Catholic labor activists that gave motivation, direction, and meaning to their actions. By the 1950s there were fewer radicals. Some had been outvoted and dismissed from office by political opponents; others had retired, died, or simply suffered a loss of energy as they aged. The rightward drift of American politics after the war, driven mainly by cold war pressures, was disillusioning and discouraging. Whatever led them to drop out, most were not replaced. The idealistic fervor and eagerness for change that were evident in the 1930s had diminished in the UAW as in society at large. Frank Marquart, a Socialist with experience in worker education, lamented in a 1968 interview that "there is none of that fraternity, the feeling of solidarity; they don't sing anymore like we used to in the old days."[11]

Although routine participation in union affairs fell off as the experiences and memories of the early years faded, material gains increased, and competing opportunities multiplied (some locals had difficulty holding meetings owing to the lack of a quorum), Reuther and other UAW leaders maintained that "when there is a big crisis coming up—a big layoff or where there is a strike threat, then you are going to get much broader participation because the rank and file under the pressure of that crisis is going to respond." Events vindicated this view. Loyalty was tested and demonstrated during strikes. The major strikes of the Reuther era, from that at General Motors in 1946 until the 1970 GM strike, were warmly, even fervently, supported by most of the membership. The UAW leadership never had a problem with worker loyalty when it was put to the test. In 1958, when contracts lapsed for several weeks without a strike, the companies were under no obligation to collect dues and turn them over to the union. The union reverted to the "old-fashioned way," sending stewards and committeemen through the plants to collect in person from each member. According to union records, 98 percent of the members paid dues without the checkoff, prompting Reuther to remark that the episode "was one of the best things that ever happened to the union."[12]

The differences in degrees of union participation and commitment between the generations, while real enough, should not be overdrawn. Even in the sometimes romanticized days of the union's founding, attendance at meetings had often been sparse. Looking back, Sam Sage noted that the average rank and filer had been "more interested in putting up the storm windows or taking the wife some place . . . than . . . in attending the local union meeting." Only a member "with an ideology," he thought, felt that the "meeting is the important thing in his life"; the attendance of the politically committed had allowed them to exercise a disproportionate influence on union decisions. Some UAW locals had drawn turnout by providing entertainment. The best attended meetings at the big Chrysler Local 7 in Detroit in the late 1930s occurred when the local staged boxing matches. Members' interest in sports was catered to by some local union officials. Al Nash, a popular night shift committeeman in the Melrose Park, Illinois, International Harvester plant, strolled through the factory during baseball season wearing a signboard with postings of the latest scores: "Tigers 2, Yankees 1, sixth inning."[13]

Union leaders were well-aware that they had to compete with the companies for the loyalty and support of both the auto workers and the larger public. The companies, which had been on the defensive during the depression, built upon the praise they garnered from the production achievements of World War II to launch a counteroffensive aimed at containing union influence. The struggle for public support was joined in the General Motors strike of 1945–46 when Reuther asserted that the workers wanted to "make progress with the community," not at its expense, while the corporation mounted a lavish public relations campaign that cast it as the defender of free enterprise and managerial rights against the union's socialistic designs.[14]

The UAW launched a series of ambitious projects to tie ordinary members more closely to the union, efforts that were only partly successful. An extensive education program reached thousands. Throughout the 1950s over 50,000 auto workers enrolled annually in the union's education classes, making the program the largest sponsored by any union. Summer schools and weekend institutes supplemented the ongoing classes that local unions offered under the supervision of the International's active Education Department. These programs dealt with both practical methods of making union members more effective—such as public speaking, contract administration, parliamentary procedure and the like—and with presentations on current issues reflecting the leadership's point of view. The principal means of internal communication was the monthly paper the *United Automobile Worker*, produced by the International Union and mailed to all members. Many of the larger locals with adequate financial resources put out their own paper, which would include local news and additional material on national issues and the International Union supplied by Solidarity House. In 1958 the publication was renamed *UAW Solidarity* in recognition of the fact that a large number of members consisted of nonautomotive agricultural implement and aerospace workers. *Ammunition*, a monthly magazine, was sent to twenty thousand local union officials. It was, a historian judged, a "sophisticated and radical magazine that pushed the left edge of mid-century political orthodoxy."[15]

Hoping to exploit opportunities afforded by modern communications technology, the union obtained licenses from the Federal Communications Commission (FCC) for noncommercial FM radio stations in Detroit and Cleveland with programming that featured union news, public affairs discussions, and music. At the time, relatively few auto workers, the main target, possessed FM radios, so the effectiveness is doubtful. In any case, lacking revenue from advertising, the stations were too costly to operate, and by 1952 the union abandoned its ownership, donating its Detroit station, WDET-FM, to municipally-owned Wayne University. More successful and enduring were sponsored programs on commercial AM stations. By the mid-1950s more than forty stations located in areas of concentrated UAW membership broadcast two half-hour UAW-produced news and public affairs programs: "Eye Opener," a morning program directed at day-shift workers on their way to the factory, and "Shift Break," a similar afternoon program for second shift workers. Under the direction of Guy Nunn, a talented radio journalist and announcer, the programs seem to have been popular with the targeted audience. A check of automobile radio dials in the parking lot of a UAW-organized plant one morning showed that 89 percent were set to the "Eye Opener" station, while a more scientific survey of auto plant workers concluded that about one-third of the autoworker audience regularly listened to the program. One rating service reported that "Shift Break" had more listeners in its 2:30–3:00 p.m. time slot than any other program. The broadcasts did not escape controversy. When a Cincinnati station refused to sell the union air time for "Eye Opener" because its management disapproved of the program's message, the UAW successfully appealed to the FCC to hold up the station's relicensing until it agreed to put the program back on the air.[16]

The most costly and presumably the most effective means of communicating with the general public were beyond the union's financial reach. The union contemplated entry into the rapidly expanding TV medium, but, discouraged by high costs, abandoned a project for setting up its own TV station in Detroit. It established instead in 1951 a weekly TV program, "Meet the UAW-CIO," aimed at the general public more than the membership, and later added a daily "Telescope" program, a variety show with interviews, news, sports items, buying tips for consumers, and so on, all presented from a union standpoint. The UAW also discussed with other unions establishing an editorially-independent, eight-page, general circulation weekly newspaper (with perhaps a daily paper sometime in the future), setting a goal of 30,000 subscription pledges to get the project started. The goal was never reached and that project too was abandoned in recognition of its high costs and the probable lack of advertiser support. A far more modest program, the UAW Labor Book Shelf, provided more than 3,000 sets of books on labor history and related subjects to schools and libraries, with the books paid for and donated by UAW locals.[17]

The union also sought to "unionize the organized" by serving its members' consumer needs, recognizing that a worker's standard of living was determined as much by the prices he paid as by the wages he received. The union's collective bargaining strategy, Reuther commented, needed to be supplemented by a "collective buying strategy," and so several cooperative ventures under UAW auspices were launched. By 1947 Detroit had four large cooperative warehouses, supported by one hundred UAW locals, with smaller operations in Flint and Pontiac, offering groceries, auto supplies, hardware, work clothes, and household goods and appliances. The union also operated a bookstore in Detroit for a few years in an attempt to encourage and enrich a union-oriented, working-class culture. A few locals ventured into cooperative housing projects. All of these undertakings carried risks, were undercapitalized, suffered from a lack of experienced management, and were relatively short-lived. Most either never got started or

UAW Local 12's grocery co-op, 1949. Walter P. Reuther Library, Wayne State University

quickly failed. After one failure Reuther exploded at a board meeting: "God damn it! When we engage in collective bargaining there's nobody better than the UAW because we know the business. We're good at that business. But when it comes to operating a grocery store or a bookstore, we don't know which end is up." Far more popular, successful, and permanent were the credit unions that were formed by more than 250 locals.[18]

A major effort was made to provide recreational and other leisure activities, often in competition with programs under company auspices. More than one-quarter of the larger UAW locals provided basketball, softball, or bowling leagues for their members, and 900 locals fielded teams in industrial or community leagues. Other activities sponsored by locals included golf tournaments, children's summer day camps, family picnics, Christmas parties, choral and other musical groups, sportsmen's shows, retiree drop-in centers, and hobby exhibits and demonstrations. According to a UAW estimate, over 600,000 members participated in one or more such activity in 1960; they were joined by many more thousands of nonmember, usually family, participants. Although by union standards the UAW's program was massive, it was limited and underfunded compared to the car companies' programs. In 1952, Reuther noted, "the entire recreation program of the UAW must operate on a budget so low its total would appall the average person connected with industrial recreation." No union had the recreational grounds and facilities available to corporate programs. Local 600 at the Rouge plant was unusual in being able to afford a full-time recreation director. The Ford Motor Company employed a staff of fourteen to operate a recreation program for workers at the Rouge plant, adding the cost, of course, to the price of its cars. In 1950 Local 600 sponsored one bowling league with twenty teams; by comparison, the company had sixty men's leagues and thirteen women's leagues for its blue- and white-collar employees. Union officers urged members to patronize the union's program but it was hard to compete with the companies' superior resources. A racial factor may have inhibited fuller participation. Some white workers chose not to participate in union-sponsored activities because by the 1950s they were racially integrated. Company programs, on the other hand, remained segregated for a time.[19]

The business community's postwar offensive, aimed at the workers as well as the general public, defined "Americanism" as a belief in the values and virtues of capitalistic free enterprise. Companies sought to convince their employees that their interests were better served by their employers than by unions. A steady drumbeat of activity and propaganda was maintained. General Motors installed information racks in its plants, distributing seven million copies of pamphlets in a single year that lauded the corporation and presented its point of view. In 1947 GM, accentuating the positive, sponsored an elaborate essay contest for employees on the topic "My Job and Why I Like It," offering new cars, refrigerators, electric ranges, washing machines, ironers, and home freezers as prizes. Reuther suggested that the title should have been "What I Like *or What I Don't Like* About My Job." Not surprisingly, in view of the cornucopia of consumer goods offered, many GM employees—over 178,000—submitted entries, and, equally predictable, all found something good to say about their jobs. For most, it was the wages, the fringe benefits (on the verge of a great expansion), and a seniority system that provided some security and fair treatment. GM's claim that the results revealed the innermost thoughts and feelings of its blue-collar workforce was viewed with skepticism owing to the loaded terms of the contest and the participation of thousands of white-collar employees.[20]

The union ridiculed the companies' attempts to engineer human relations, calling their efforts to communicate "baloney" and dismissing supervisors' training in human relations as ineffective. *Ammunition* sarcastically noted that "foremen are attending school throughout the country to receive training in the art of convincing workers that they are deeply beloved by the boss." The UAW's Education Department regularly published exposés of the methods used by employers in their "secret struggle" for workers' loyalty.[21]

While no precise measurement is available, the overall result of the battle for workers' hearts and minds may well have been a draw. In a workplace or bargaining crisis, including assuming the risks and sacrifices involved in a strike, the union could count on workers' support—the critical test. But it could not shape their way of life, which more and more conformed to the middle-class standards, values, and culture that pervaded the society—and which the union's success in bargaining was bringing within auto workers' reach. It was not uncommon for workers to acknowledge bonds to both the corporation, to which they owed their jobs and in whose products many took pride, and to the union, which strove to improve and protect their working conditions, represent their interests in public matters, and secure for them a fair share in pay and benefits of the wealth they helped to produce.

THE COLLECTIVE BARGAINING ENTERPRISE, like the union's operations in other respects, was brought more directly under central control, a continuation and elaboration of trends that extended back to the activities of the War Labor Board in World War II and beyond. Both management and the union moved toward a more centralized structure. For the union, centralization was imperative since the corporations could play off workers at one plant against another if they were fragmented, lacking a common, coherent strategy and agenda. Contract bargaining, grievance processing, and servicing activities to locals and members all became more centrally directed. In part, too, the greater degree of central control was attributable to Reuther. Collective bargaining, he believed, occurred in a complex pattern of economic forces involving consumer demand, profits, prices, employment levels, and the health of the economy. Effective action in that context required a systematic analysis and disciplined pursuit of strategic objectives. The UAW continued to bargain separately with each firm, eschewing industry-wide negotiations, but the Reuther group devised a coordinated approach, "pattern bargaining," that exploited the competition for market share among the manufacturers, maximized the union's bargaining clout, and reduced the likelihood of long, costly strikes. The union chose as its target the company it thought most able and likely to grant what it most wanted. Then, threatening it with a strike that would halt its production but leave its competitors free to continue, induced it to "set the pattern" by meeting the union's demands. The settlement, achieved with or without a strike, then would be taken in turn to the other firms with the requirement that they match it. Auto managements, realizing their vulnerability, professed to despise the approach but found its removal of labor costs from competition to have some merit; at any rate, they were unable effectively to counter it.[22]

With the parties still locked into annual contracts, the 1947 round of bargaining reflected the union's divided condition. Following the dismantling of the government's price control apparatus, an inflationary surge quickly swallowed up the wage increases of 1945–46. The executive board proposed to seek an increase of 23–1/2 cents an hour as a general wage increase, arguing that this raise would merely restore to workers the 18 percent loss in real wages they had suffered from the rise in prices since the beginning of the year. Although the industry's production was hampered by materials shortages, the potential profits once full production was achieved were so great that again the union argued the raise it wanted would not dictate or justify an increase in prices. In addition to a wage increase, the union put forward a "social security" program of health benefits and a proposal for a pension plan. Still riven by its internal conflicts, the UAW was in no condition to press its case aggressively or to strike. The terms agreed to were closer to the companies' original proposals than to those of the union, and closely tracked a settlement GM had already reached for those of its employees who were members of United Electrical Workers. The general wage settlement was for 11–1/2 cents an hour, plus 3–1/2 cents an hour to fund six paid holidays: New Year's Day, Memorial Day, Independence Day, Labor Day, Thanksgiving, and Christmas. Payment for holidays represented a significant breakthrough since previously some companies had given workers the holiday off but without pay, a no-win situation. If the holiday came during the week, as it often would, the worker could take the day off and lose a day's pay. If the holiday fell on a weekend, it was simply an unpaid, nonworking day. An improved vacation plan, providing GM and Chrysler workers with a two-week paid vacation, was thrown in. The corporations maintained they were not obliged to bargain on the union's "social security" proposals and turned down the union's demand that the 3–1/2 cents' segment of the package be put into a health insurance fund.[23]

By 1948, following Reuther's reelection as president, the union was poised to make greater progress at the bargaining table. That year's contract with General Motors was the first postwar contract to mark a general advance. Reuther, recovering from the gunshot wound suffered in the assassination attempt, played no direct part in the negotiations, but he was kept informed and participated in important decisions. Secretary-treasurer Emil Mazey served as acting president in Reuther's absence, and negotiations for the union were led by vice president John Livingston and GM department assistant director Thomas "Art" Johnstone. In general terms the UAW demanded that some provision be made to protect workers' wages against inflation and that the results of greater productivity gained through technology and more efficient organization of production be shared. A specific proposal came from the company. Conceding that workers deserved a steadily rising, annual increase in their standard of living as the corporation became more efficient and prospered, GM proposed that an annual improvement factor (AIF) be built into the wage structure. The factor represented each worker's share of rising productivity, measured by output per hour worked. The calculation was based not upon General Motor's own production experience but on the rate of productivity improvement for the entire economy, a formula that benefited the corporation: owing to heavy investments in new machinery and plants, its productivity gains consistently outpaced those of the economy at large. For 1948, the proposal called for a 2 percent wage increase, about 3 cents an hour, in each of the two years of the agreement. Despite the formula's imbalance, the proposal assured to workers a share in the gains to be realized from more efficient technology and work organization and—an important concession by the corporation—it established the expectation of an annual wage increase. From the corporation's standpoint, it gave workers and the union a stake in the introduction of new technology.[24]

The second specific wage proposal also came from the company's side of the table. This was a cost-of-living allowance (COLA) that would raise or lower a worker's wage in accordance with price changes as measured by the Bureau of Labor Statistics' consumer price index. Although not the first such plan to be negotiated, it was the first to be implemented in a mass-production industry that historically confronted volatile demand for its products. The formula adopted provided that an increase of 1.14 points in the index during a quarter would trigger a pay raise of 1 cent an hour. A decline of the same amount would correspondingly lower wages, although the company agreed to a maximum reduction of 5 cents an hour per quarter regardless of how low the index fell. With some merit, Reuther claimed that the escalator was a modification of, and inspired by, his 1945 proposal to link wages to prices and protect workers' buying power against the ravages of inflation. The improvement factor and COLA increases immediately added 11 cents per hour to the workers' pay, 3 cents from AIF and 8 cents from COLA, raising the average pay from $1.50 to $1.61 an hour. When the wage increases secured from GM (and the other manufacturers) in 1946, 1947, and 1948 are added up, they approximate the 30 percent increase that Reuther had unsuccessfully sought in the first round of postwar bargaining.[25]

Many labor leaders were suspicious of cost-of-living adjustments, fearing they would impose a ceiling above wage rates but place no floor below them, and Reuther himself, perhaps out of factional considerations, had once been opposed. In view of shrinking wages in the depression, still fresh in everyone's memory, the fear seemed well-founded in experience. There was considerable criticism of COLA within the union, with many favoring the traditional locked-in, straight-time increases. The GM plan, however, met some of the specific objections to escalators, and in any case better anticipated the economy's future course, which brought far more inflation than deflation as the postwar boom gathered steam.[26]

Over the years COLA and the annual improvement factor proved their worth. The first COLA upward adjustment, a 3-cents-an-hour increase, came in August 1948 only three months after the contract was negotiated, and over the years COLA and AIF provided the bulk of the auto workers' wage increases. In 1948, the straight-time wage, without benefits, averaged $1.50 an hour. By 1980 it was $10.77. Of the $9.27 increase, $5.44 came from COLA and $2.71 from the annual improvement factor; together they accounted for 75 percent of the total wage. The remainder of the increase, $1.12 an hour, came from general raises, the correction of inequities, and additions of higher-paying jobs to the workforce. Thus the greater part of auto workers' wage increases can be attributed to keeping pace with inflation and to greater productivity. By 1968, COLA and AIF had added more than $22 billion to the pay of UAW members and 92 percent of them were covered, including many in nonautomotive occupations.[27]

Charles E. Wilson remained the industry's leading champion of COLA, and he publicly took issue with the charge, frequently brought in the media, that the union's wage demands were the primary cause of inflation. "The working people," he wrote in a 1952 *Reader's Digest* article, "did not make . . . inflation. They only want to catch up with it in order to be able to pay their grocery bills. I contend that present high wages are more the result of fundamental inflationary money pressures than of unreasonable wage pressures by the union." Instead of the *"wage*-price spiral," he continued, "we should say the '*price*-wage spiral.' For it is not primarily wages that *push* up prices, it is primarily prices that *pull* up wages." Reuther could not have said it better, and he delighted in quoting Wilson's words when a speech touched on the causes of inflation.[28]

Although GM could well afford an innovative pay settlement, it firmly resisted most of the UAW's demands for enhanced worker power on the shop floor. It consented to a greater role for committeemen in representing workers in disciplinary proceedings but denied union proposals for recognizing stewards and for improvements in union security, the seniority system, and negotiated production standards.[29]

Wilson, not surprisingly, wanted something in return for the annual improvement factor and COLA: a longer-term contract. Most previous contracts had been for only a single year, or even less, a practice that made sense when the future was unpredictable but which was costly, time-consuming, aggravating, and stressful to both sides when conditions were reasonably stable and workers had contractual protection against inflation. For the corporation the most serious disadvantages of annual contracts were that they undermined long-range planning and increased the risk of strikes. Without knowing labor costs in advance, the company had to be cautious and tentative in investing in plants, machinery, and product development. Both General Motors and Ford, anticipating strong future demand, were embarking on extensive investment programs in new parts and assembly plants. They wanted to secure an agreement of at least two year's duration as a beginning, and were prepared to pay to get it. Although there were some benefits for both sides in longer-term contracts, a prolonged period between negotiations carried risks for the union, contributing to an accumulation of unresolved disputes over working conditions, which, in turn, could lead to an increase in local strikes over such issues. There was no ideal contract length, perfectly suited to everyone's needs. In 1948 the UAW took the first step toward longer-term agreements, signing contracts that ran for two years.[30]

FOR MANY AUTO WORKERS, as well as those in other industries, pensions were as important an objective as wage increases. Partly as a result of winning seniority for layoffs and recall in the 1930s and 1940s, the average age of auto workers was gradually rising, a fact that naturally stimulated interest in pensions among the rank and file, pushing the issue to the top of the bargaining agenda. Retirement on a decent pension was about the only practical means available to an auto worker to escape from the rigors of the assembly line; this helps account for the popularity of pensions as a bargaining issue and the sustained campaign in the 1960s and 1970s to lower the age of pension eligibility. The Social Security old-age benefit provided only $32 a month, an amount that had not been increased since the system was introduced and which postwar inflation rendered utterly inadequate. Efforts in Congress to increase the Social Security payout had failed. With retirement threatening workers with a staggering contraction in their standard of living, company-funded pensions became an irresistible bargaining goal. Most companies, even those that had made some provision for pensions, took the position that they were not required to bargain with a union on pensions since the beneficiaries were no longer employees nor were they eligible for full membership in the union. Granting a pension, they maintained, was a management prerogative in which a union had no voice. In 1947 the Ford Motor Company had offered its workers a choice between a wage increase and a pension plan funded mainly by employee contributions with no union participation in its administration. Reuther's caucus opposed Ford's pension plan and Ford workers chose the wage increase, but Ford's offer of a plan, even an unsatisfactory one, convinced the UAW leadership that when the time came for the union to move on pensions, Ford should be the target. In order to gather the data on the health and security needs of its members and to prepare for the negotiation and administration of pensions and other benefits, the UAW established a Social Security Department in 1948. Although strongly supporting publicly-funded social spending in order to provide economic security for all, Reuther and other UAW leaders recognized that the postwar political stalemate, securely in place by the late 1940s, was unlikely to permit bold expansion of government programs in pensions and health coverages. Only a few days after the outcome of the 1946 elections signaled a strong conservative political movement, Reuther realistically assessed the effect of the current political situation: "in the immediate future," he said, "security will be won for our people only to the extent that the union succeeds in obtaining such security through collective bargaining."[31]

Reuther believed that since employer pension contributions were a part of compensation they were a legitimate subject for bargaining, and the UAW's success in bringing the auto companies around to this view would contribute to its acceptance throughout industrial America. Certain safeguards in a pension plan were necessary. It was essential for the union to ensure an impartial administration, including the investment of pension funds. The amounts accumulated for pensions by such industrial giants as General Motors, Ford, and Chrysler would be huge and therefore tempting if left under exclusive company control. Employees had to be protected against a scheme to raise capital disguised as a pension plan.[32]

Although there was already a lively interest in pensions among the workers, Reuther launched a vigorous campaign to build support and throw the companies on the defensive. Contrasting the treatment given high company officials with the indifference accorded ordinary workers, he pointed out that GM President Charles E. Wilson would have a pension of $25,000 a year, although his annual salary and bonus payments came to $516,000. "If you make $258 an hour, they give it to you. If you make $1.65 an hour, they say: 'You don't need it, you're not entitled to it, and we are not going to give it to you.' " Reuther claimed to have invented and he certainly popularized the emotionally powerful slogan, "too old to work and too young to die," to dramatize the plight of many aging workers. As he recalled, he first used it in 1949 at a mass meeting of 7,000 older Ford employees at Detroit's Cass Technical High School, where he pledged there would be no new Ford contract without a pension plan. The phrase inspired the Joe Glazer song of the same title:

> You work in the factory all of your life,
> Try to provide for your kids and your wife.
> When you get too old to produce any more,
> They hand you your hat and show you the door.

Chorus:
Too old to work, too old to work,
When you're too old to work and you're too young to die,
Who will take care of you, how'll you get by
When you're too old to work, and too young to die?

Threatened with a strike in the midst of a highly profitable year, Ford agreed
to pay the entire pension cost of $20 million a year, contributing 8–1/2 cents
an hour per employee—the first negotiated pension program of its type in a
heavy, mass-production industry, and a vast improvement over the plan
Ford had offered in 1947. Ford employees with thirty years' service at age
sixty-five were eligible for a pension of $100 a month, triple the amount
then available from Social Security alone. The union insisted that the company actually reserve the funds from which the pensions would be paid; that
is, the pensions must be fully funded. Furthermore, in order to guarantee a
lifetime pension, the funding of the plan must be actuarially sound: the
amount set aside had to be keyed to the life expectancies of the retirees.
Well-aware of the uncertainties of the car business, UAW negotiators took
care to guard against a company that made promises but might not be
around to keep them.[33]

Following agreement with Ford, the UAW moved on to Chrysler with
its pension demand. Chrysler agreed to match the $100–a-month figure but
refused to fund the pensions, offering instead a "pay as you go" plan that
would not set aside the funds. Reuther, emboldened perhaps by the union
convention's decision to establish a substantial strike fund, insisted on a
strike despite evidence that some workers did not appreciate the importance of the funding issue. The strike, which began on January 25, 1950,
lasted 104 days, the longest in Chrysler's history, and it dealt a fatal blow
to the company's hopes of regaining its standing as the industry's number
two firm. After nearly three months, the company offered to deposit $90
million in the bank as a sign of good faith. Reuther pointed out to a meeting of auto workers that while this did not amount to full funding, it was a
step in that direction. "Yeah, Walter," a voice called out from the rear of the
hall, "but is it actuarially sound?" With both sides making concessions to
end the strike, Chrysler agreed to a fully funded, jointly administered, noncontributory, actuarially sound pension program. The full pension became
available to workers sixty-five years of age with twenty-five years of service
to the company. Defying tradition, Reuther refused to shake hands with the
shocked Chrysler negotiators at the conclusion of the settlement because
he had all along maintained that a strike to establish an employees' right to
a pension should never have occurred. A few weeks later General Motors
came aboard with a pension of $125 a month, including Social Security. The

Chrysler workers on strike for pensions, 1950. Walter P. Reuther Library, Wayne State University

UAW had remedied the inadequacy of Social Security's old-age benefit for its members and taken long strides toward assuring them a retirement of dignity and economic security.[34]

The pension payouts had an immediate impact. By the end of 1952 nearly 30,000 auto workers had retired with company-funded pensions, and the number mounted rapidly. In 1949 the typical monthly retirement income for an auto worker and his wife under Social Security was a mere $54. By the end of the following decade the sum available from Social Security had doubled to $108, and the addition of the negotiated pension brought the total to $245 a month. Pension checks were going out to retired UAW auto workers in forty-four states and twenty-seven countries, displaying American affluence even in distant parts of the world. A retiree who had returned to his native Sicily wrote the UAW president, "Brother Reuther, when I get my check every month I'm the richest man in this village." In the decade following establishment of the Chrysler pension fund, it paid out more than $22 million to nearly 11,000 retirees. By 1970 Ford and Chrysler had paid more than $660 million in pension benefits to their former UAW employees.[35]

As the UAW leadership had maintained from the beginning of the pension fight, the success of the UAW and other unions in securing company-funded pensions would stimulate increases in Social Security payments to the benefit of all workers, unorganized as well as organized, white-collar as well as blue-collar. While Social Security was funded by a payroll tax levied equally on employer and employee, negotiated pensions, as in the auto industry, were usually funded solely by the employer. Thus the greater the share of pension costs the employer could shift to Social Security, the less pressure to increase his liability. Employers had successfully opposed any general increase in the Social Security tax since its inception in 1935, but with the adoption of employer-funded pensions their opposition faded. In 1950, following speeches by Charles E. Wilson of GM and Ernest Breech of Ford endorsing increases in Social Security taxes, Congress for the first time raised payroll taxes, making possible improved benefits for all covered workers. As Nat Weinberg remarked, "whenever we can, we hope to pursue essentially the . . . strategy of using collective bargaining leverage to win gains not only for our people but for all other people who have similar problems." Ford Department head Ken Bannon recalled, "I'm proud, so proud, that we not only helped the people who were part of UAW and part of the Ford contract, but everyone else."[36]

IN ADDITION TO ITS PENSION PROVISIONS, the 1950 General Motors agreement contained several other new departures. The corporation was pleased with the results of the 1948 contract. Since postwar inflation had leveled off between 1948 and the beginning of the Korean War in June 1950, the cost of COLA was not excessive. Company planning had proceeded smoothly without the disruptions and uncertainty inseparable from annual negotiations. The contract agreed to on May 23, 1950, raised the annual improvement factor to 4 cents an hour, continued COLA, and marked an important and expensive breakthrough in hospitalization and medical care insurance, with the company agreeing to pay half the premium cost for each worker and his family. The UAW estimated the settlement was worth 19 cents an hour immediately and would ultimately reach at least 35 cents an hour, promising an astounding 20 percent increase in auto workers' standard of living over the contract's term—one of the greatest single economic gains in the history of the union movement. A banner headline in the *Detroit News* proclaimed "Billion Won in GM Pact," the largest sum negotiated in a settlement to that time.[37]

In another breakthrough, a "tremendous change for corporate America," as Leonard Woodcock later remarked, the contract established a modified union shop, the first time GM had made such a union-security concession to the UAW. Along with other wartime employers GM had been forced to recognize maintenance of membership. That arrangement ended as war contracts expired, but the UAW gained partial restoration as a result of the 1945–46 strike. By the terms of the 1950 settlement all new employees had to join the UAW and all present members had to remain in the union, but those currently employed who were not members were not required to join. In 1955 GM became a full union shop with all hourly-rated employees in UAW-represented plants required to belong to the union. An exception was made for members of religious sects who opposed union membership and dues payments on grounds of conscience. For these few employees the company deducted an amount equivalent to dues and contributed it to charitable organizations and causes mutually acceptable to the union and the worker. Ford workers had previously confirmed their allegiance to the union shop. A 1948 referendum on mandatory membership, called for by the Taft-Hartley Act, saw more than 98 percent of Ford workers backing union membership for all, a result that Ford management characterized as "astonishing." The GM contract received a "heavy and enthusiastic vote of approval" from the membership.[38]

In return for its concessions, GM wanted a contract of five years' duration, an unprecedentedly long term. Despite opposition and reservations within the union, the UAW bargainers eventually agreed, and similar terms were extended to Ford and Chrysler. In the business press the agreement received high praise. Characterizing it as "astounding," "imaginative," and (in case anyone missed the point), "amazing," *Fortune* dubbed it "the treaty of Detroit" and concluded: "G.M. may have paid a billion for peace [but] it got a bargain." With five strike-free years in prospect, management had tightened its control over long-range planning of production, model changes, and tool and plant investment. Reuther's reputation as a labor statesman rose in business circles and elsewhere. A year later *Fortune*, pointing out that the auto workers had gained 24 cents an hour in their basic rate under the contract without a single strike of consequence, wrote: "most labor leaders are accustomed to puffing and heaving, and sometimes striking, for the pennies per hour they get for their men, but Walter Reuther makes it look easy." In addition to Ford and Chrysler, most major supplier firms, independent car producers, and agricultural implement manufacturers under UAW contract—including Briggs, Hudson, Allis-Chalmers, Packard, Mack Truck, Studebaker, and many others—followed suit by agreeing to comparable wage hikes, pension plans, medical insurance benefits, and union shop provisions in their 1950 contracts.[39]

The extravagant praise bestowed by the press on the contract and management and union leadership was premature, for it soon came under fire from auto workers and union officers. Only a month after the agreement was signed, the outbreak of the Korean War ignited an inflationary firestorm, inadequately restrained by government price controls, that pushed prices to record highs. The COLA adjustment of wages failed to keep pace. Rank-and-file workers and local leaders complained that the contract's constraints were exacting a heavy toll in real wages. In 1952 Reuther, feeling the heat from below, declared that contracts are "living documents," and demanded that GM and the other companies reopen negotiations on the wage provisions. If unanticipated events such as wars and inflation undermined real wages, he argued, there was sufficient justification for a new agreement restoring the equity originally established. When GM and Ford refused to reopen the contracts, strikes over production standards, coordinated from union headquarters, broke out. Grievances that in ordinary circumstances would have been settled led to local strikes. Production at GM and Ford nearly came to a standstill. One strike in particular, dubbed the "Canton Can Opener," at a Ford foundry in Canton, Ohio, by cutting off the supply of 75 percent of the forgings needed for parts, led to the layoff of 58,000 Ford employees and received credit for producing the contract reopening the union sought. In May 1953 the union prevailed over the car companies by securing an upward revision of the contracts, in effect a major contract negotiation. GM gave production workers a 10-cent-an-hour raise with an additional 10 cents for skilled workers, revised the cost-of-living formula upward, raised the annual improvement factor to 5 cents an hour, improved pensions to $137.50 a month, and arranged group health coverage for retirees. Ford and Chrysler made similar concessions. The union leadership learned the lesson that long-term contracts carried too much risk. When the contracts expired in 1955, the union and the corporations settled on three years as the standard contract term.[40]

Although the "treaty of Detroit" tag overstated the case, the agreements of 1950 and 1953 were milestones in labor relations. The corporations confirmed their acceptance of the union as a permanent presence, the legitimate representative of their workforces, and committed themselves to funding a rising standard of living through regular wage increases and an expanding array of fringe benefits. On the other hand, they stoutly resisted union attempts to gain a share of management functions. As a later GM executive reportedly said, "give the union the money, the least possible, but give them what it takes. But don't let them take the business away from us." Both sides now acknowledged a boundary line that protected the vital interests of each.[41]

The reopening of the contracts, which the companies bitterly resented and made the occasion for considerable moralizing about the sanctity of obligations, would later prove a useful precedent for the auto manufacturers. In 1979 the Chrysler Corporation, compelled to take action by the federal government as the condition of receiving loan guarantees, availed itself of the "living documents" theory to reopen its contract with the UAW in order to erase promised wage increases and secure other concessions. Although not under pressure from the government, General Motors and Ford soon demanded and obtained similar relief.

THE MOST DARING AND CONTROVERSIAL innovation in compensation sought by the UAW was the guaranteed annual wage (GAW). The idea that manual workers should be paid on an annual rather than an hourly basis was by no means new. Unemployment compensation, initiated by the federal government in the Social Security Act of 1935, established an entitlement to a continuation of income during a layoff, but, limited in duration and amount, the payment fell far short of being an annual wage. A few companies in industries where demand and employment were stable and predictable, such as food processing, had installed GAW's, but no company in an industry with the irregular employment pattern of auto had attempted it. Auto manufacturing was a challenging place to seek an annual wage since it was both a seasonal and a cyclical business, subject to sudden and drastic changes in the level of demand; with its hundreds of thousands of employees, a GAW fund would require setting aside millions of dollars. By the same token, with layoffs always a threat, auto workers were among those most in need of the protection a guaranteed wage would provide. Even in the generally prosperous 1950s, prolonged layoffs during model changes and periodic declines in demand were not uncommon. In 1955, at the very time the UAW was preparing to negotiate a guaranteed annual wage, the wife of an auto worker, complaining that her husband had been laid off for seven months, plaintively asked in a letter to a Detroit newspaper, "Isn't there any place one can find some small security?"[42]

The guaranteed annual wage would serve a double purpose, maintaining income for laid-off auto workers and their families and giving manufacturers a powerful economic incentive to plan production to avoid shutdowns, thus stabilizing employment. Back in 1936, President Franklin D. Roosevelt, campaigning for reelection in Detroit, had noted the problem of seasonal and cyclical layoffs in the industry. While not endorsing any particular remedy, he stated his "belief that the manufacturers of automobiles . . . must, by planning, do far more than they have done to date to increase the yearly earnings of those who work for them." In 1951, when Reuther proposed the plan to the UAW's convention, he pointed out that "the surest way to guarantee that you will have full employment in your plant is to make the company pay you if there is no work to do, and when they have got to pay you for not working they'll find a way to keep you working." Furthermore, again expanding their horizon to encompass the social and economic needs of a broad segment of the population, UAW officials argued that a guaranteed wage plan would win support among employers for a federal government full employment policy, since a robust economy with a growing aggregate demand would reduce an employer's liability to fund a guaranteed wage and, by maintaining purchasing power during down times, the plan would further contribute to a stable economy. In the most sweeping sense, the UAW argued that a GAW would put "people above property, men above machines," by ending "the immoral double standard under which the worker, of all those who draw their incomes from industry, has the least protection against economic adversity."[43]

Discussions in general terms of an annual wage went back to the days of the UAW's founding. Reuther was seriously interested by 1945, and in 1951 he launched a complex process of formulation and negotiation that was later characterized by Sumner Slichter, a leading economist, as the "classic" example of postwar collective bargaining. Linking the union's objective with a reading of history and the nation's needs and interests, Reuther declared: "The guaranteed annual wage is more than a matter of economic justice to the wage earner; it is a matter of economic necessity to our nation, for freedom and unemployment cannot live together in democracy's house."[44]

Many problems had to be addressed in preparing a feasible plan. A major question was whether payments made to temporarily laid-off workers could be combined without penalty with unemployment compensation benefits. If a state could reduce unemployment compensation as privately paid benefits increased, a company-funded plan would be of no advantage. In 1951, when Reuther was convinced the idea would work, the union's convention endorsed the annual wage by a unanimous vote as "the next major goal of our Union," ahead of four weeks' vacation with pay, a $200-a-month pension, and fully paid hospital and medical insurance for the worker and his family. Two years later, following further study, a detailed plan was approved, again with no dissent. No major demand advanced by the UAW received more thorough preparation before being brought to the bargaining table. The union also undertook the most elaborate and intensive educational campaign in its history to convince the membership of the GAW's value.[45]

At the conclusion of the process in 1955, Reuther announced that "we are not irrevocably committed to our specific proposal. We are irrevocably committed to the principle that the workers in our industry are morally and economically entitled to a year-round wage." If adopted the fully developed plan would provide income sufficient to maintain living standards for laid-off workers, give employers a strong incentive to plan year-round employment, protect against the imposition of short workweeks, integrate the companies' payments with unemployment compensation, and establish a joint administration of the fund. The delegates to the 1955 convention affirmed their support for the plan and, in preparation for any contingency, authorized assessments to build a war chest of $25 million, the largest strike fund in the union's history to that time. The companies were unanimously and stoutly opposed to an annual wage, and there was much backing for their position throughout corporate America: the Michigan Manufacturers' Association denounced the annual wage as a "fanatic, dishonest, un-American, foreign, socialistic nightmare," adding, for good measure, that it was "plain crazy." But with demand soaring and the industry headed toward a record annual production of nearly eight million cars, the Big Three desperately wished to avoid a strike.[46]

Reuther's "brilliant generalship," as Leonard Woodcock later characterized it, in what was perhaps his most hard-fought and remarkable bargaining triumph, ultimately produced a union victory. General Motors, as was often the case after C. E. Wilson's departure for Washington D.C. in 1953, adopted a rigid position, viewing the annual wage demand as a challenge to management's control of policies. In a long reply to the union's statement, GM said it was being asked to pay wages for work that had not been performed, which it had never done and would not do, and it grimly predicted the corporation's doom and the death of free enterprise if it were forced to yield. The corporation put forward a generous financial offer, among other things extending to factory hands a voluntary, subsidized stock purchase plan already available to white-collar employees. To provide income during layoffs, GM offered to make interest-free loans on the security of employees' stock to be paid back out of future earnings. Reuther denounced GM's offer. "Hell," he exclaimed, "that's for the provident," and GM workers quipped in a reference to Alfred P. Sloan, Jr., GM's board chairman, "If you want a loan, see Sloan!" GM's refusal to consider a GAW forced the union to move the negotiations to Ford.[47]

Expecting Ford to put forward an independent proposal, the UAW team was shocked when the Ford negotiator, John Bugas, began to read from a near copy of the GM stock ownership plan. Reuther replied: "This is the General Motors Corporation proposal and what you've done by presenting it is that you've just bought yourself a strike." When Bugas denied that it was GM's proposal, Reuther shouted, "Don't give us that bullshit. We've got it [the GM plan] right here." Continuing, he added, "We do not question your right to stooge for the General Motors company. But I'd like to suggest that it's very bad policy and it will get you nowhere. You guys have got rocks in your head." He went on to recite how a long strike against Willys-Overland had started that company's decline and pointed out that the 1950 strike against Chrysler had prevented it from overtaking Ford in sales. Reminding Bugas that the union had extended its contract with General Motors while it bargained with Ford, he taunted, "How will you produce Fords on the Chevrolet assembly line?" Jack Conway, Reuther's assistant, thought it "the roughest exchange I've ever seen in an auto set of negotiations. It was just as intense as it could be." Ken Bannon, director of the union's Ford Department, recalled it as "a nasty, nasty session."[48]

Bugas countered with a claim that the workers favored Ford's offer over the union's guaranteed wage plan by a margin of nine to one and added that he had a survey to prove the point. Reuther, confident of rank-and-file backing, quickly put the issue to the test. He invited Henry Ford II to attend an open union meeting to tout Ford's plan—an invitation promptly declined by the company's chairman—and asked Bugas "Will you agree to have a referendum vote of Ford workers . . . on our proposal? . . . If they vote for yours, we'll sign a contract containing your proposal. If they vote for ours, we'll sign a contract with that. Since you say they want yours by nine to one, you're not taking any chances." Reuther later recalled, "Poor John! I thought he'd die."[49]

Ford did not take up the challenge. It withdrew its original offer and proposed instead a "supplemental unemployment benefits" (SUB) plan, which accepted the essentials of the union's position as the basis for settlement. Much hard bargaining lay ahead since Ford's first SUB proposal was a far cry from the union's idea of wage security. Even with further threats of a strike, Ford would yield only so much. Negotiations concluded on June 6, 1955, when the company agreed to put 5 cents an hour for each worker into a SUB trust fund totaling $55 million that would be drawn on to provide payments of $25 a week for up to twenty-six weeks for laid-off workers. When unemployment compensation was added, a worker would receive 65 percent of take-home pay for the first four weeks of layoff and 60 percent for the next twenty-two weeks, with the duration of payments conditioned on seniority, attendance record, and the availability of reserves in the trust fund. With only twenty-six weeks of income maintenance pledged, the original SUB plan was a semiannual commitment to a partial wage rather than a genuine annual wage, but Reuther and other UAW leaders believed it responded effectively if incompletely to the problem of income insecurity and viewed the 1955 settlement as a key step—but only the first step. Although the establishment in principle with limited implementation of an annual wage was the most important gain in that year's negotiations, the new contract provided numerous enhancements, including improved health insurance and pensions, a better productivity increase rate, pay inequity adjustments, added vacation time, additional paid holidays, and an improved COLA rate. All in all, it was one of the best contracts the UAW ever negotiated. It elicited a wide range of evaluations, from a sympathetic editor's praise of it as "a landmark of industrial democracy" to the National Association of Manufacturers' prophecy of its "damaging effects . . . perhaps leading to a socialistic state and controlled economy."[50]

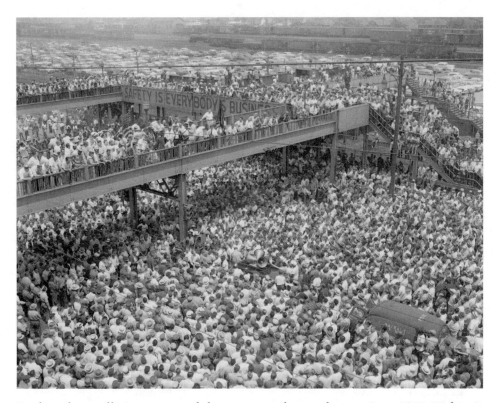

Ford workers rally in support of the guaranteed annual wage, June 1955. Walter P. Reuther Library, Wayne State University

GM executives opposed the SUB plan and bluntly told Reuther that they would never have been the first company to agree to it. But with auto sales booming in the industry's best year to date and Ford's uninterrupted production now guaranteed, they wanted no part of a strike. Forced to endure Reuther's taunt that "There's a Ford in GM's future," the GM negotiators accepted a "Chinese copy" of the Ford contract, that is, an exact replica that included all the defects and "patches" that GM deplored. One of the GM negotiators announced at a press conference following the signing, "This is the first time that the president of the General Motors Corporation has ever signed a contract that he didn't understand." The successful conclusion of the negotiations was a striking vindication of the pattern bargaining approach the UAW pioneered in its 1950 contract negotiations, the principal instrument used to remove wages and other labor costs from employer's competitive cost-cutting.[51]

By stabilizing income the SUB plan arguably had a greater positive impact on the everyday lives of auto workers and their families than any other gain won by the UAW. The plan soon proved its value in maintaining income during layoffs. In its first three years, from 1956 to 1959, more than

Signing the UAW-Ford contract, 1955. Walter P. Reuther Library, Wayne State University

$105 million was paid out, mostly during the recession of 1958 when car sales dried up, the national unemployment rate rose to more than 7 percent, and hundreds of thousands of auto workers were laid off. Reuther made increased SUB funding and extensions of benefits priority bargaining items, winning improvements gradually in a series of negotiations. In 1967, in a settlement reached with Ford following a two-month strike, a laid-off worker received 95 percent of take-home pay for up to fifty-two weeks, less a $7.50 weekly deduction for savings in commuting and lunch costs. SUB was now a genuine annual wage guarantee. The SUB trust funds, together with the more accurate production scheduling the plan stimulated, were adequate for smoothing out most of the normal ups and downs of auto employment, but the widespread and prolonged layoffs that followed the OPEC embargo on oil shipments in 1973–74 showed that the SUB funds could run dry. Neither Ford nor Chrysler replenished their funds sufficiently to maintain the contracted level of benefits, although both funds recovered when full production resumed. Unable to cope fully with a deep and continuing unemployment crisis, SUB yet provided a significantly greater degree of income security in an industry notorious for irregular earnings.[52]

*"I'm not saying it will <u>work.</u> I'm just saying has
anyone ever <u>asked</u> Walter Reuther to come in as v.-p. at a hundred grand?"*

"I'm not saying it will *work*. I'm just saying has anyone ever *asked* Walter Reuther to come in as v.-p. at a hundred grand?" The *New Yorker* Collection 1958 Richard Decker from cartoonbank.com. All Rights Reserved.

With or without strikes, SUB soon spread to the other auto and agricultural implement makers with which the union had contracts and then into other industries. Chrysler, American Motors, Allis-Chalmers, Bendix, International Harvester, Studebaker-Packard, Deere, Caterpillar, Budd, White Motor, Spicer Gear, Eaton, McInerney Spring and Wire, Kelsey-Hayes Wheel, and the many tool and die shops in Detroit all incorporated SUB in their 1955 contracts. In time, over 90 percent of the UAW's membership was covered. In 1956 the United Steel Workers negotiated a similar but more liberal plan with the steel and railroad car industries. By 1962 over 2.5 million workers in the rubber, plastics, garment, and electrical equipment industries, in addition to the millions in auto and steel, were covered by SUB plans. Paralleling the spread of negotiated pension plans, a gain by workers in one industry benefited those elsewhere, including some nonunion workers. In addition, as UAW leaders had anticipated, employers who were obligated to fund annual wage programs now had an incentive to lobby state legislatures to liberalize unemployment compensation payments, since more in compensation would constrain the demand for larger SUB payments. As a result of such pressure, thirty-three states increased their level of unemployment compensation in 1955 alone. Thus once again, nonautomotive workers and nonunion members directly benefited from a bargaining victory won by the UAW.[53]

PROVIDING FOR PAYMENT of medical expenses was almost as important as a guaranteed wage for protecting income and a family's standard of living. Hospitalization and doctor bills could destroy a family's budget. Since the adoption of Social Security in 1935, many of its advocates, including those in the UAW, had considered a national, tax-funded health insurance plan as its logical extension. During World War II, liberals in Congress introduced the Wagner-Murray-Dingell bill to amend the Social Security Act to create a comprehensive national health insurance system, including hospital, medical, dental, and nursing home coverages, financed like Social Security through a payroll tax. The bill was enthusiastically endorsed and supported by the UAW and other labor organizations, but it went down to defeat at the hands of the American Medical Association and private health insurers. In the postwar years the UAW supported President Truman's proposed comprehensive, universal prepaid medical insurance plan and, when that failed, less sweeping medical coverage legislation. During the 1950s Reuther was an active member of President Truman's Commission on Health Needs of the Nation, and he later became chairman of the Committee for National Health Insurance, which revived the movement for a national health-care system in the late 1960s. None of these efforts produced the national health plan the UAW, in combination with others, sought. The only successes were registered in the establishment of Medicare, providing payroll-tax-supported medical care for the elderly, and of Medicaid, providing care for the poor.[54]

Although clearly preferring a national system with universal coverage, the auto workers, like other unionized workers, did not choose to wait patiently for government action that might never come while health care costs soared and their needs and those of their families went unmet. The choice they faced was not between a publicly-financed health plan and a privately-financed health plan, but between a union-negotiated plan and no plan. As it became evident that the opposition of the medical professions, the private health insurers, and antitax organizations would delay or prevent government action, the union turned to seeking protection for its members through collective bargaining. The conservative postwar political climate effectively precluded any other course.[55]

Reuther dramatized the failure to provide adequate health care protection with a story about GM president Charles E. Wilson's prize bull. He told the UAW convention in 1949 of a young man he had met in the hospital the previous year while undergoing treatment for the gunshot wound he had suffered in the assassination attempt. The man had been paralyzed for nine years but had run out of money just as the treatments were taking effect and had to leave the hospital. Reuther contrasted the treatment received by gentleman-farmer Wilson's bull:

> C. E. Wilson had a bull and the bull had a bad back. We are sorry about that. But what happened to C. E. Wilson's bull compared to this boy who was paralyzed for nine years? In the case of C. E. Wilson's bull, the General Electric Company sent a special 140,000-volt X-ray machine into Detroit on a special chartered airplane. It was picked up by a General Motors truck and taken out to C. E. Wilson's farm. The bull didn't even have to leave home to get medical care. Then when they got the 140,000-volt machine there they couldn't operate it because they didn't have enough power, so the Detroit Edison Company ran a special power line out to C. E. Wilson's farm. Then medical specialists flew in from all over the country and they gave this bull the best medical care that modern medicine and science knows how to deliver. Now why? Why? I ask that simple, honest question. Why did C. E. Wilson's bull get the best of medical care while millions of these kids all over America are not getting that kind of care? It is because C. E. Wilson's bull cost $16,000, and you get boys and workers for free.[56]

The major manufacturers maintained they were not required to bargain about company-financed medical benefits, and they refused to do so—the same position they had originally taken in respect to pensions. The only concession they made was to agree to a payroll deduction to finance prepaid hospital and surgical coverage for employees who elected to buy it and pay the full premium. Employees could choose between a private insurer and Blue Cross/Blue Shield coverage. Following the war the UAW tried to persuade the companies to bargain on medical benefits but the only manufacturer who agreed to do so was Kaiser-Frazer, whose presence in the auto industry was destined to be brief. In 1948 that firm established a company-funded hospitalization and medical program for its employees and their dependants, financed by 5 cents for each employee-hour worked. In the meantime, the UAW charged General Motors with an unfair labor practice for its refusal to bargain on health benefits, and the union's position was eventually upheld by the National Labor Relations Board. The board's decision opened the way for company-paid health coverage in the auto industry and elsewhere, a victory of tremendous significance for both union and nonunion workers. Forced to bargain, GM agreed in the 1950 negotiations to pay half the cost of hospital and surgical coverage for the worker and his family. Ford and Chrysler followed suit. By the end of the year more than one million UAW members plus their families were covered by plans for which employers paid at least half the cost. Health benefits quickly spread to other employers with whom the UAW had contracts. By 1954 virtually all UAW members and their families were covered for hospitalization and surgical care, and most were covered for office visits and other kinds of medical treatment, with employers ordinarily obligated to pay one-half of the cost of the insurance.[57]

As with many other bargaining objectives, these were only the first steps, "the foot in the door," as Reuther often said in justifying any compromise settlement that fell short of the union's original demands. Almost every major contract negotiation following the breakthrough in 1950 saw some improvement in the health coverage system the UAW was creating. Periods of coverage were extended. Co-pays and deductibles were reduced and finally eliminated. Coverage was extended to nursing homes, home care, and rehabilitation. In 1964 the UAW negotiated a mental health outpatient benefit, another health care advance.

Many in the UAW leadership were not satisfied with the hospitalization and surgical coverage provided by Blue Cross/Blue Shield and the commercial insurers. The coverage was too limited, omitting some critical and expensive medical procedures, and it failed to give adequate emphasis to preventive care, early diagnosis, and outpatient treatment. Too much of the additional money the UAW won for health benefits in its rounds of negotiations simply went to raise the incomes of doctors (Reuther claimed that Michigan doctors had the nation's highest average medical profession incomes owing to the UAW's successful bargaining) and to increase the revenues of hospitals. The UAW's social security experts and most of its leadership favored comprehensive programs like Health Insurance Plan (HIP) in New York and the Kaiser Health Foundation in California, which utilized group practice with physicians on salary to provide expanded coverages and services at the same or less cost than Blue Cross/Blue Shield and the commercial insurers. UAW members in those states could join these managed-care plans. In 1957, at the UAW's prompting, the Community Health Association (CHA) was established to provide prepaid, comprehensive health services in the Detroit area. Reuther, who had once favored a UAW-owned and -operated health service and hospital for its members, became convinced that a community organization, open to any group, was a sounder approach. CHA, which began operations in 1960 with Reuther as board chairman, provided about 35 to 40 percent more in services than Blue Cross/Blue Shield, at about the same cost. Negotiations in 1961 won for most UAW members in the Detroit area the right to choose which plan they preferred; within two years 30,000 had selected CHA.[58]

THE AUTO TALKS IN WHICH these advances in economic security were won were the major leagues of collective bargaining. Given the industry's massive impact on the economy and the public's fascination with its automobiles, the periodic encounters between the UAW and the car companies captured public and media attention, both favorable and hostile, in the postwar decades. Except for the GM strike of 1945–46, Reuther's conduct of negotiations was rarely criticized within the union. Employing all the arts and ploys of the negotiator, from the humdrum and routine to the dramatic and unexpected, and inventing some new ones, Reuther masterfully played the bargaining game. A flexible strategist and tactician, he could depart from bargaining dogma when circumstances warranted. In 1958, for example, when the union's bargaining position was undermined by collapsing sales and massive layoffs (during the first half of that year 220,000 of the Big Three's 580,000 UAW members were laid off at one time or another, and the companies had a backlog of nearly one million unsold cars), the union had its members continue working for three months after their contracts expired. The companies maintained pay rates and funded fringe benefits despite the contracts' lapse but refused to check off employees' dues, forcing UAW locals to collect dues directly. When conditions improved, the UAW negotiated new contracts incorporating modest gains.[59]

Preparation of the union's case was prolonged and thorough. Ideas were welcome from any source. Reuther could pick them up anywhere, in meetings, casual conversations, periodicals, and so on, but most often he drew on his close staff members and fellow officers. These included, over the years, special advisor Nat Weinberg, public relations director Frank Winn, administrative assistants Jack Conway and Irving Bluestone, Woody Ginsberg, Weinberg's successor as research director, and fellow officers Leonard Woodcock, Doug Fraser and Emil Mazey. Reuther would call together a group and run an idea by them, in effect conducting a policy seminar. Everyone was free to speak and usually did. Often someone would start off with, "Walter, you're crazy as hell. That won't work." Reuther would "question and probe." "He never told you he was president, never. He never exercised his authority, and he let you argue and argue and argue." Following staff formulation, proposals went to either constitutional or special collective bargaining conventions for a presentation to the membership. Refinements were worked out in the council and subcouncil meetings. A rough division of labor gave the councils, which consisted of representatives from each local in a particular manufacturer's plants, a major voice in demands concerning working conditions issues, while union staff employees took the lead in formulating the more technically complex wage and benefit demands. If the issue was likely to be an important one, Reuther would be engaged in these preliminary discussions, defining the issue, gauging the membership's response, and shaping the outcome. If of lesser significance, he was less involved. With the approval of officers, executive board, and convention delegates, the agenda was constructed.[60]

Debate and endorsement in conventions ideally was balanced between two different tactical objectives, both expected to contribute to a successful negotiation. One was to give the delegates an opportunity to express publicly and forcefully their determination to achieve particular bargaining goals. This was designed to demonstrate to the corporations that concessions were necessary to avoid a strike and to secure ratification of a tentative agreement. The other objective was to state the bargaining agenda in sufficiently vague terms that the union's negotiators would have room to maneuver as bargaining proceeded, conducting a juggling act in which, as a strike deadline approached, some balls fell to the ground while others remained in play. The final ordering of priorities often occurred only at the last moment. In 1958 the UAW held its first special convention to construct a bargaining agenda, thereby adding a meeting free from the distractions of constitutional issues and elections, timed just prior to the expiration of contracts in order to get up-to-date input from delegates and generate support for bargaining goals.[61]

Both skilled in publicity and mindful of the need for public and autoworker support, Reuther began negotiations with a presentation designed to rally the troops, woo the public, and put the companies on the defensive. Weeks before the contracts expired, trailed by a small army of aides, he went from company to company for opening sessions, dominating these meetings with a long and impassioned exposition of the workers' needs and the union's demands. The companies had to be convinced that the union would strike but kept in the dark as to the exact concessions that would prevent one. At these affairs, company representatives made little attempt to counter or upstage Reuther, well aware that the rhetoric was aimed at them only in part. They sat back to watch the show, content with restrained and often condescending responses.[62]

Once contract talks began they were largely in the hands of the department director and the national bargaining committee, with Reuther taking little direct part until the deadline approached and a strike loomed. In the meantime, with issues assigned to joint committees, subordinates on both sides moved along on lesser matters, leaving the money settlement and major innovations, if any, for the principals.

In the small group that came together from the two sides as negotiations moved toward a conclusion, Reuther made no lengthy speeches aimed at the public, the company, or the membership, becoming strictly a tough and resourceful bargainer. "This is where," as Jack Conway, his closest associate in the 1950s, observed, "Walter is absolutely magnificent." Although in some instances the combative stances and harsh words seemed to follow a scripted challenge-and-response dialectic, genuine passion and spontaneous departures from conventional norms of intercourse broke through the surface on both sides. Reuther maintained a balance among the union's demands, sacrificing something here in order to gain something else there, and kept in touch with the bargaining committee, an essential for contract ratification. Obtaining ratification—that is, what you could "sell" to the membership—was always a key concern in the multifaceted negotiations, with the threat of a negative ratification vote a useful bargaining tool for pressuring company negotiators. The corporations' representatives recognized that the UAW was a democratic, highly political organization whose leaders, at all levels and like all political figures, had to score victories or risk losing their positions. While their interests on most matters conflicted, company and top union negotiators shared a common interest in fostering the perception that the union had won a victory despite company opposition, when in fact the outcome of negotiations invariably represented a compromise. Reuther was quick to discern chinks in the opponent's armor and to turn unanticipated developments to advantage, sometimes with humor, sometimes with profanity. In September 1955 difficult negotiations with GM coincided with Reuther's birthday. Louis Seaton, GM vice president and chief negotiator, presented him with a birthday cake; the reporters covering the talks provided another, larger one. "Like the GM offer," Reuther quipped at a press briefing, "Mr. Seaton's cake was inadequate." The traditional way to conclude talks was in a marathon session carried down to the strike deadline. Reuther, who rejuvenated himself during long sessions by periodically brushing his teeth, tipped off reporters that he expected such a session and therefore a settlement by brandishing his toothbrush as he entered the room where negotiations were being conducted.[63]

Reuther's mental and physical energy and stamina—the result of a lifetime of exercise, regular habits, abstinence from alcohol and tobacco, and a strong physical and mental constitution—paid off at the bargaining table. His mastery of the techniques of tense, high-stakes bargaining was fully appreciated in the UAW. Coming out of a session a few hours before a strike deadline, he found some bargaining team colleagues calmly playing cards. "How can you characters sit there and play poker and have a damned good time," he asked, "and we're six hours away from a possible strike?" "We just know you'll figure out the answer," one replied, and he did. On other occasions, when negotiations were deadlocked and no one knew what to do, Reuther stretched out on a sofa to think, "and all of a sudden he would sit up and say, 'I've got it,' and it would be some major turning point in negotiations."[64]

During the Reuther presidency the UAW functioned superbly as a bread-and-butter union. Sufficiently in touch with rank-and-file sentiment to know that most workers expected the union in a generally prosperous economy and industry to produce a rising standard of living and that they judged the leadership in large part by its ability to do so, Reuther never ignored or treated with condescension the material needs and wants of those he represented. His efforts were repaid with nearly unanimous worker support for the UAW and its bargaining priorities. While sympathetic to members' demands for the material means to a more fulfilling and secure life for themselves and their families, the UAW leadership did not neglect the goal of social and economic justice for all citizens, a goal that transcended the limits of business unionism.

ALTHOUGH THE UAW's INTENT and policy was to equalize wages among its members for the same work wherever and by whomever performed, implementation of this policy encountered management resistance. Management contended that differentials were necessary to provide incentives, reward merit, and correlate with skill. Although the victory was by no means complete, by and large the union successfully overcame these objections. Equally difficult to root out were pay differentials between plants of the same company, where the companies took the position that pay should reflect local labor market conditions. The union, fearing that differentials would lead to the transfer of work from high to low wage areas, and concerned as well to honor the equity principle that work of comparable character should receive the same pay, regularly sought equalization funds during negotiations. By the 1950s the union had substantially eliminated differentials at Ford and Chrysler, but at GM, whose many parts and assembly facilities were scattered throughout the country, some differentials remained in place.[65]

DESPITE THE INDUSTRY'S GENERAL prosperity and an overall increase in auto employment, which peaked in 1955, periodic unemployment and its consequences were still threats to auto workers. The industry still swung back and forth between peaks and valleys of production, creating an underlying anxiety within the workforce. As the union's president and chief public spokesman, Reuther devoted more time and effort to formulating and publicizing union positions on unemployment and economic stagnation and their consequences than to any other of the many public issues the union addressed. He testified frequently before congressional committees, published essays, and gave speeches on these subjects, urging the federal government to adopt Keynesian fiscal and monetary policies to stimulate employment when the economy failed to perform. Repeating a well-worn theme, he argued that the key to an abundant economy lay in expanding effective consumer demand, thereby bolstering purchasing power. In stagnant times, with annual growth rates in the 1–2 percent range, as was the case toward the end of the 1950s, interest rates should be kept low and a deficit in the federal budget accepted. Public spending on infrastructure and other capital asset improvements—schools, water systems, highways, airports, public facilities of all kinds—should be targeted in areas of high unemployment. Combined with these Keynesian-inspired remedies was a steady criticism of the "administered pricing" policies evident in the auto industry and in other oligopolistic and monopolistic segments of the economy that kept prices high for consumers, condemned industry to operate below capacity, and contributed to unemployment. Such price-fixing could be blocked by antitrust prosecution and government-imposed price ceilings. As Reuther summed up the union's point of view in testimony before the Joint Congressional Economic Committee, "only by adopting programs, at home and abroad, which will expand our power to consume and make new demands on our power to produce can we stimulate the economy to respond . . . and achieve full utilization of our productive capacity."[66]

Belying the popular perception of the postwar auto economy as uniformly prosperous, deindustrialization—the dismantling and abandonment of factories and even of communities—was an ongoing concern. This was especially the case in the city of Detroit, which lost a staggering 134,000 manufacturing jobs between 1947 and 1963. The city's auto economy went through a downsizing in the 1950s from which it never recovered. The State of Michigan also felt the effects. In 1950, 56 percent of all auto employment was in the state; by 1960 that figure had fallen to 40 percent. Deconcentration of auto manufacturing facilities began with General Motors in the late 1930s as that corporation built several new assembly plants in distant locations. The movement accelerated in World War II when the auto companies, with the government supplying most of the funds, constructed huge one-story plants on the outskirts of Detroit, such as the Willow Run bomber plant in Ypsilanti, Michigan, the Chrysler Tank Arsenal in Warren, Michigan, and massive aircraft engine plants operated by Buick and Dodge in suburban Chicago. In the postwar era, General Motors and Ford, with capital-short Chrysler lagging behind, built new factories in Detroit suburbs and in sections of the country remote from the old auto centers. Between 1947 and 1955, the Big Three built twenty new parts and assembly plants in the Detroit metropolitan area employing 70,000 workers, but all were in the suburbs, none within the city itself. A UAW investigation disclosed that between 1950 and 1957, 163 Detroit factories engaged in auto parts manufacturing left the city for the suburbs and twenty-nine more moved to sites in outstate Michigan. In the same period sixty-eight new parts factories came to the suburbs but only one located in Detroit itself. While Ford, GM, and Chrysler made no systematic effort to keep the UAW out of their new plants or to undercut established wage rates, for many of the smaller firms removal of plants from the centers of union strength figured in their relocation decisions. Other considerations factored in as well. The old-fashioned, multistoried auto plants of early twentieth-century vintage, whose basic design dated from the onset of the industrial revolution, were obsolescent. Materials and subassemblies could be moved for less cost horizontally in new, one-story plants with adequate space overhead for conveyors than vertically by lifts in multistory factories. The availability of large tracts of land at relatively low prices, combined with the added incentive of lower taxes, guaranteed that the new plants suitable for more highly automated mass production would be built outside the central cities.[67]

The unemployment situation in the old auto manufacturing centers was drastically worsened by the mergers or shutdowns of undercapitalized, inefficient, unprofitable firms and factories. The slim ranks of the remaining "independents" were decimated. American Motors Corporation, the result of a merger between Willys-Overland and Nash, took over the Hudson Company in 1954 and closed its East Side Detroit plant. The factory was torn down and its site turned into a parking lot. Two years later, Studebaker, whose main facilities were in South Bend, Indiana, absorbed the Packard Motor Car Company, closing down another major East Side Detroit employer. Packard workers were stunned. As one recalled, when the factory closed "I felt like some one had hit me with a sledge hammer"; others said "they just threw us out and didn't say nothing . . . they just threw us out on the street," and "I could have cried. It's like losing your home." With a pension fund at Packard that had been in existence only a few years, the little money available went to those sixty-five and older. Others got nothing. Older workers, blacks, and the less skilled all had difficulty in finding new employment. Ten months after the shutdown, 23 percent of Packard's former workers were without jobs, long after unemployment benefits had expired. Another third of the workforce found jobs but lost them within two years of the shutdown. Since they had little seniority in their new positions, they were vulnerable to layoffs. By 1958 only about half of those with jobs were working at skill and pay levels comparable to their Packard employment.[68]

Studebaker's turn to abandon car manufacturing came in 1963. It left behind 7,200 active members of UAW Local 5, at the time the oldest UAW local, with a history stretching back to its founding as an AFL federal local in 1933. It also left behind a $30 million—80 percent—unfunded pension obligation (portions of the pension fund had been raided for last-minute acquisitions in a desperate attempt to stave off bankruptcy), and an unemployment rate in South Bend that exceeded 9 percent. Eight months after the plant closed, about one-third of Studebaker's workers were still without jobs; the rest had either found work in other auto plants or in service jobs, or, particularly among those too old to secure new employment, retired on "extremely modest" retirement checks or minuscule lump-sum severance payments. The failure of the Studebaker pension fund ignited a UAW campaign to secure a federally administered pension reinsurance fund, similar to the protection provided bank depositors by the Federal Deposit Insurance Corporation, a campaign that finally proved successful in 1972 after years of lobbying. Thanks to relatively prosperous times in the mid-1960s and a federally funded Manpower Development and Training Center set up in an old Studebaker plant, most of the young and middle-aged ex-Studebaker employees were eventually able to find jobs.[69]

Chrysler, the largest East Side Detroit employer, also took jobs out of that area, cutting its workforce at Dodge Main—for years second only to the Ford River Rouge complex as the industry's largest facility—by several thousand jobs. Overall, Chrysler reduced its employment in Detroit by nearly 50 percent during the 1950s. The effects were not limited to these companies since important suppliers, such as Motor Products, also lost business, and many had to close. Many of the small supplier companies, tool and die shops and the like, either closed or followed the move to out-lying areas. The effect when a big assembly plant closed was, an observer noted, "like a bowling alley, like one pin knocking down the others." By one count these closings cost Detroit's once vibrant East Side over 70,000 auto jobs, an economic devastation that turned the working-class communities of that part of the city into an "economic slum." Older plants were shut down in scattered locations outside Detroit with similar consequences. When the Plainfield, New Jersey, plant of Mack Truck closed in 1960, workers had to reduce their food and clothing expenditures substantially and turn to borrowing and installment credit for many necessities. An officer of Local 348, who negotiated distribution of pension and SUB money and transfers when a Toledo, Ohio, machine and tool plant closed in 1958, poignantly observed, "It's incredible how many sad details there are to take care of when your plant closes."[70]

Instances of the abandonment of old plants and the building of new multiplied. Ford's main target for downsizing was that one-time wonder of the industrial world, the massive Rouge complex. The number of hourly-rated employees dropped from 83,000 in 1941, to 65,000 in 1950, to fewer than 30,000 during the 1960s. In the single year 1951, Ford reduced the number of its Rouge employees by more than 20,000. The loss of jobs decimated the workforces in several previously large and militant Rouge departments, such as motor manufacturing and the foundry. Ford completely shut down one of its oldest assembly plants, that in Chester, Pennsylvania, which had an aged workforce with high seniority. A transfer agreement provided an option for some to move to a new assembly plant in

Mahwah, New Jersey, about 150 miles away, but four months after the closing most were without work, and only about 20 percent chose to transfer.
Other hard-hit areas included the once bustling manufacturing district
around East Grand Boulevard in Detroit. Murray Body, a major employer in
the area, lost its contract to build bodies for Ford when that company shifted
production to its factories. Murray was forced to close its huge but outdated
plant, and with its closing UAW Local 2 disappeared.[71]

The ripple effect of plant closings cascaded through surrounding neighborhoods. Restaurants, taverns, pharmacies, grocery stores and other small
businesses went under as they lost their autoworker clientele. Commercial
and residential property values plummeted as businesses closed and those
workers able to do so sold their homes to follow the jobs out of the city. Tax
revenues declined and public services from education to trash collection
deteriorated. Cities like Detroit, Reuther pointed out, were in danger of
becoming "ghost towns" without a tax base or a steadily working population. His prediction that "you can scrap your old model jalopy, but you can't
scrap a whole city," proved to be seriously wrong as vast stretches of industrial cities and towns were abandoned and turned into wastelands.[72]

As companies left the city, some workers followed their jobs, relocating in the developing areas and thereby creating blue-collar suburbs. Ethnic
and socioeconomic class communities within the city fragmented. Labor
solidarity and union participation came under pressure as distances
between home and work lengthened and competing interests came into
play. The impact of relocation did not fall evenly across the workforce.
Owing to lack of seniority and white opposition to integrated housing,
blacks found following the plants a difficult, sometimes impossible, transition. One effect of deconcentration was to reinforce the racial lines dividing the workforce. The impact on age cohorts also was uneven, with older
employees less likely to be able or willing to obtain new employment or
move to new locations.[73]

Some auto parts firms that left Detroit and other auto cities blamed
the UAW for demanding unreasonably high wages, protecting uncompeti-
tive job rules and working conditions, and harboring a destructively hostile
attitude toward employers. Federal-Mogul and Fruehauf Trailer are two of
many examples. One small, family-owned firm engaged in wheel cover
manufacturing threatened to move to Mississippi unless its workers agreed
to take a cut in compensation of nearly 50 percent. When the bargaining
committee countered with an offer of a 15-percent reduction, it was told
"Boys, it is not enough," and the company shut down in Detroit and moved.
The Ex-Cell-O Corporation, a manufacturer of machine tools with a UAW-
organized workforce, built new plants in rural Indiana and Ohio, citing
labor union hostility as its main reason for leaving Detroit. In a parting shot,

its president warned the union that "Industries, like people, will not go where they are insulted and vilified daily. If Michigan labor leadership is seriously interested in job opportunity for their members, they must change their attitude from one of conflict to one of cooperation with industry."[74]

In order to discourage migrations, the UAW sought to organize the new workforces of those concerns that fled, while the companies that relocated out of antiunion sentiment were equally determined to resist. A notorious instance of such a struggle concerned the Monroe Shock Absorber Company, originally located in Monroe, Michigan, where it had a long-term contract with a UAW local. The company built new plants in Georgia and Nebraska, moved its production to them, recruited a new workforce, and fought the union tooth and nail. With official and community support in Hartwell, Georgia, Monroe put up a violent resistance. Episodes eerily reminiscent of the "Battle of the Overpass," occurred in the spring and summer of 1963 when six UAW organizers, including vice president Pat Greathouse, were beaten by a "rock-throwing, knife-wielding, club-brandishing mob" of about 150 "company underlings," who prevented the organizers from passing out leaflets at the plant's gates. When one of the assailants was told his actions violated the American way, he replied, "Well, this is the Monroe way." The county sheriff, whose forces stood by during the attack and who later testified in court that he "didn't see anything," told Greathouse, "We jus' don't want you around." The next year a Reuther effigy was hung from a tree branch, then shot up, burned, and buried beneath a gravestone whose legend read:

> Less [sic] we forget
> Here lies the UAW
> Born in Greed
> Died in Defeat

The local paper, pushing the populace's hot buttons, carried articles "proving" Reuther was a Communist and showing that the union (truthfully in this instance) made donations to the National Association for the Advancement of Colored People, Americans for Democratic Action, the Leadership Conference for Civil Rights, and the Jewish Labor Committee. UAW organizers persisted despite the risks. In 1966 the union won a representation election at the plant by a vote of 342 to 264, but with the company exploiting every opportunity for delay, it had—even eleven years later—still signed no contract. Although the struggle with Monroe received more publicity than other incidents, it was only one of many where independent companies fought the UAW. Even in western Michigan, a generally conservative area but close to the union's center of strength, organizers moved warily in the face of community disapproval. Threats to close plants if the union was voted in were common. One organizer was advised to pose as an insurance agent, carrying blank policy application forms, when calling at the homes of prospective members. Despite the opposition, on the whole autoworker organizing was successful in the 1950s and 1960s. The Big Three did not resist unionization in their new plants. In 1956, a good year for organizing, the UAW won 253 of 312 employee representation elections, bringing in about 40,000 new members and giving it one of the best records of any major union. In an ordinary year, the UAW won about 60 percent of the several hundred representation elections conducted by the National Labor Relations Board in which it participated.[75]

Thompson Products (now part of TRW) was one large auto parts concern that successfully resisted unionization in a struggle carried on over several years. The UAW organized small Thompson plants in Toledo and Detroit, but failed at the company's major facilities in Cleveland. Thompson was a "welfare capitalist" firm that employed a mix of legal and illegal tactics, paternalistic and hardball programs and rhetoric, captive audience pressures, use of anticommunist attacks, wage increases just before votes on union representation, and a company union among other devices to resist unionization. The company's antiunion campaign was shrewdly led and effective. Despite large expenditures of funds and personnel, the UAW repeatedly failed to organize the Cleveland plants.[76]

UNION OFFICIALS WERE UNABLE to mount a fully effective counter to companies' decentralization strategy. Decisions on all capital investment matters including plant locations were a hallowed management right, and there was every reason to expect management to resist union encroachment on this prerogative as fiercely as it had resisted similar threats in the past. There was no basis in current law for holding companies responsible in location decisions either to their workforce or to the communities in which they operated. Although by law workers could not be laid off for union activity, employers otherwise had a free hand in letting them go as long as they complied with contractual seniority and severance provisions. Local 600, whose members bore the burden of Ford's relocation and automation strategies and feared that the Rouge was destined to become a "ghost plant," brought suit against the company in federal court, asking for an injunction to block layoffs that resulted from plant relocations. The International Union refused to support the suit, considering it hopeless, and a United States district court judge contemptuously dismissed it, holding that such decisions were a management right unabridged by any contract provision. In its 1961 negotiations the UAW, taking note of the protections provided for workers in other industrialized nations, particularly France, sought from Ford a right of prior consultation on possible plant closures—a proposal that elicited a negative response from the company and produced "from the nation's editorial writers the biggest single howl of the 1961 negotiating period."[77]

In the end, the union fashioned a two-fold response. First was the negotiation of transfer rights to assure that workers in a closed plant would have first call on jobs that opened elsewhere. Such provisions were initially negotiated on a plant-by-plant basis as shutdowns threatened. Then in the 1955 contracts the union obtained general provisions on preferential hiring rights for members in new plants, the right to transfer with the company when it moved to a new location, and severance pay for those who chose not to relocate. The second response was to mount vigorous, and nearly always successful, organizing campaigns in the new plants of the major car makers as they opened.[78]

THE AUTOMATION OF MANUFACTURING, a key to rising productivity and standard of living, similarly challenged secure employment. Going back to the production innovations of the early days, the industry had been known for its receptivity to any new technology that promised to cut costs and increase output. In the postwar world, automation, embraced by all the companies, loomed ever larger and threatened more workers' jobs. For the union automation was a double-edged sword. By increasing productivity it lowered costs and contributed to the companies' profits, enabling them to fund the wages and benefits the workers wanted; but the same productivity increase threatened unemployment as workers were replaced by automated machines and processes. As one measure of the productivity improvement brought by automation and other innovations, between 1947 and 1962 annual production of motor vehicles increased by 70.4 percent while employment in the industry declined 11 percent. At Chrysler in 1956, 128,399 production and salaried workers turned out 961,000 vehicles; nine years later, in 1965, 126,000 employees produced 1,611,000 vehicles, an increase of 649,000 vehicles requiring 2,000 fewer workers. Some of the new machines would handle routine, physically-taxing jobs that could be lost with little regret. Others, however, such as metal-forming and shaping machines and the transfer devices that integrated a sequence of separate manufacturing operations into a single automated process, threatened to displace some of the industry's most skilled workers. For finishing cylinder heads at one factory in 1949, six machines, representing an investment of $240,000, were required to produce 108 cylinder heads an hour at a labor cost of 20 cents per piece. Five years later a single automated machine, costing $230,000, reduced labor costs to 4 cents a piece with the same production. Five machine operators were no longer needed. A union study maintained that more than 4,000 jobs were lost in Ford plants alone due to automation between 1949 and 1953.[79]

Despite the threat to jobs, the UAW leadership welcomed new technology as the means to a more abundant life. Once when asked if he favored a ban on new technology, Reuther replied, "Nothing could be more wicked or foolish. You can't stop technological progress and it would be silly to try it if you could." In the long run, progress would bring numerous benefits, freeing workers "from the monotonous drudgery of many jobs in which the worker today is no more than a servant of the machine," raising living standards, making possible a shorter workweek, longer vacations, and earlier retirement, and thus creating a dramatic increase in leisure time. "Creative expression in our leisure hours," as Reuther saw it, mandated a vast expansion of educational, community, trade-union and church opportunities and activities, but it must occur within a framework of economic security. Someone who is laid off has leisure, he pointed out, but owing to anxiety about the future and insufficient income could not use it constructively.[80]

In the short run, technological innovation would be a disruptive force for individuals and even entire communities. Its dislocations could undermine purchasing power, throw local economies into recession, even contribute to a national depression. When Reuther toured a new, highly automated Ford engine plant in Brook Park, Ohio, a company engineer taunted him with the remark, "You know, Walter, not one of those machines pays union dues." Reuther shot back, "And not one of them buys new Ford cars, either." Automation, economists pointed out, replaced physically exacting factory jobs with skilled, well-paying jobs in the design, manufacture, and operation of more sophisticated machines. But there was little likelihood that the displaced unskilled or semiskilled factory worker could qualify for such work. "*How,*" Reuther asked, "does the hand trucker become an electronics engineer—or a skilled technician?" Only a massive retraining program could conceivably make the transition to highly skilled work possible, and only a vigorous management of the economy would guarantee the demand necessary to achieve prosperity.[81]

Since all shared in the benefits of greater productivity, it was only fair that all share the burdens. Workers displaced by automation needed protection. Companies must retrain them for new jobs where possible, job classifications would have to be renegotiated, displaced workers given preferential hiring status, lost wages replaced during retraining, and those too old to retrain offered early retirement. Only a nationally planned and funded retraining program could fashion a fair and prosperous future, but the Eisenhower administration, so Reuther charged, was "looking through a rear-view mirror" rather than up the road ahead. The UAW supported bills introduced by Senator Paul Douglas of Illinois to provide capital and planning for high-unemployment communities. Congress was urged to establish a community development authority that would target areas for technical assistance and public works, and revamp the unemployment compensation system to provide job training and help in meeting moving expenses. President Eisenhower vetoed such bills in 1958 and 1959, but with John F. Kennedy in the White House after 1960 a scaled-down version of the program, the Area Redevelopment Act, was enacted.[82]

Union officers believed that unemployment could be alleviated through collective bargaining initiatives and through voluntary actions by employed workers. Proposals to reduce the workweek, which had a long history in the American labor movement, were one response. Regularly brought forward in the postwar era, the reduced workweek was one popular proposal Reuther refused to embrace. At times he said it should give way in negotiations to other objectives, such as a guaranteed annual wage, that he deemed more important. Usually he could be found arguing against it, and his support, when forthcoming, was half-hearted. He was convinced, he said, that few companies engaged in durable goods manufacturing could afford to pay a forty-hour wage for thirty or thirty-five hours of work without going broke. An across-the-board reduction in working hours that left younger, more energetic workers free to work overtime or take second jobs would do less to increase employment than more vacation time, more paid holidays, and restrictions on overtime. Besides, he believed it would be impossible to mobilize the American public in support of a negotiated or legislatively mandated thirty-five-hour week because "they are already influenced by the idea that all labor is trying to get is more for less." The fact that proposals for reduced hours were championed by the union's remaining left opposition doubtless also contributed to Reuther's lack of interest, although he was known to adopt proposals as his own that he had previously opposed once they demonstrated their appeal. He advocated an experiment with a flexible full employment workweek that would vary the hours of work depending on the unemployment rate, an idea that had as little chance of acceptance as a straightforward reduction in hours. In 1962, at the end of a decade in which as many as two hundred thousand production jobs had been lost in the auto industry due to automation and other causes, Reuther proposed to the companies a plan to facilitate the transfer of qualified production workers threatened with layoffs to white-collar jobs, but the companies were not interested.[83]

The companies' growing reliance on overtime rather than new hires to meet production needs, a cost reduction strategy predicated on the increasing cost of fringe benefits as a proportion of total compensation, contributed to unemployment. A premium pay rate of time-and-a-half had once been sufficient to restrain assignment of overtime, but, in a classic instance of an unintended consequence, with fringe benefits now accounting for nearly half of total compensation that was no longer the case. It cost the companies less to require overtime and pay the wage premium to an employee whose costs for medical insurance, pension, and other benefits had already been met than to fund both wage and benefits for a new hire. With the industry reporting "heavy overtime" of almost five hours per week per worker in the last quarter of 1962, the union claimed that overtime alone currently kept 60,000 laid-off and prospective auto workers unemployed. Overtime was understandably popular with many rank-and-file workers for whom it meant a substantial improvement in wages and standard of living. As a General Motors executive (with some exaggeration) quipped, "overtime is an evil of which everyone wants a share." Many workers, especially those younger ones entering the workforce in the late 1960s, objected to the unilateral right of the companies to require overtime, arguing that its excessive use interfered with family obligations and leisure activities. UAW leaders realized that some overtime must be allowed both to satisfy the wishes of the membership and to give the companies flexibility in matching the workforce to production needs, but they wanted to limit its availability. Reuther argued that overtime rates should be increased to double time for all work over forty hours a week or eight hours a day, "because it is morally wrong for workers to work excessive overtime in plants when there are millions of workers who are trying to work one hour a week." Union leaders also disapproved of workers taking a second, moonlighting job when there was unemployment, although they recognized that the union had no practical way to address the problem.[84]

SOME UAW CRITICS ARGUED that the union's leadership, pressured by management's assertion of its rights and prerogatives and beguiled by employers' demand for "responsibility," traded shop floor power that could have been used to resolve workers' problems and even expand the boundaries of their control in exchange for material gains such as wage increases and fringe benefits. According to this interpretation, while the workers gained higher wages and benefits, giving them access to some of the pleasures (and perhaps burdens) of a burgeoning consumerist culture, the manufacturers obtained greater freedom to determine working conditions. Since the major companies were so profitable, it was easy for them (so the argument goes) to concede money, especially since they were free to relocate their plants, automate their production, and squeeze more work from their employees. As their part of the bargain, in return for the material gains that kept the rank and file in line, the union leadership made sure that worker complaints and shop floor rebellions over unsatisfactory working conditions were kept to a minimum, a strategy that had the additional and not incidental benefit, from the leadership's point of view, of blunting the emergence of critics and potential rivals from the ranks. One writer asserts that the Reuther leadership "worked hand-in-hand with management to discipline workers."[85]

In fact, the picture was more complicated. Reuther and the rest of the UAW's top leadership deplored wildcat strikes in nearly all circumstances and believed the union was obligated to honor the no-strike clauses of its contracts. Grievances against the companies, they insisted, should be pursued through the established procedures for dispute resolution, and when settlements were not reached in the lower stages, appealed to an umpire's arbitration. "Workplace contractualism," in a historian's phrase, was fully in place and functional by the 1950s. The grievance procedure was vigorously and frequently employed to protect shop floor rights and working conditions, and there was a marked increase in the number of grievances filed in the postwar era. At General Motors the grievance rate per 100 employees more than doubled from 12.8 in 1947 to 31.7 in 1961, reflecting mounting tensions over working conditions issues. When the slow working of the grievance procedure failed to satisfy, criticisms were voiced in convention debates and other forums.[86]

Although the no-strike clauses in the national contracts prohibited strikes over wage and benefit issues while the contract was in force, it was possible for auto workers to have an authorized, legal strike during the term of a contract over company-imposed speedups and over health and safety issues, elastic terms that were occasionally stretched. The 1946 contract with Ford prohibited unauthorized strikes and maintained the company's authority to discipline wildcatters, but it exempted disputes over health, safety, and production standards from the arbitrator's jurisdiction and the no-strike rule. The ordinary grievance process was followed for these issues up to the point where the matter would be referred to the umpire for a binding decision. If not satisfied, the local could then ask the UAW's executive board for a strike authorization, the "five day letter," notifying the company that a strike was imminent. Strike authorizations were not provided on demand nor without requiring the local to make a strong case for direct action, but they were almost automatic in situations where companies were unilaterally raising production standards, and in hundreds of instances the strike authorizations alone were sufficient to restart negotiations and bring about settlements. In the twelve months preceding April 1949, as the companies pressed for more production, the UAW authorized 386 strikes and approximately 200,000 workers went out in the first four months of that year alone. For a slightly longer period, from the 1947 convention to 1949, the UAW international executive board (for the first time controlled by Reuther loyalists) granted more strike authorizations than in any earlier comparable period in the union's history.[87]

The leading instance was the twenty-four-day strike by Ford employees in May 1949. Instigated in part by left-wing elements in the Dearborn Assembly and Lincoln plants when Ford fired workers for refusing to work at higher line speeds, a strike was authorized by the International, and Ford workers elsewhere were called out in its support. The union contended that the speedup imperiled the health and safety of employees; the company's position would have left the workers and the union with little if any role in influencing the pace of work. All Ford assembly and most production operations were shut down, and additional thousands stopped working in supplier plants. Reuther, in a flamboyant gesture, challenged Henry Ford II to a public debate in Briggs Stadium on the issues before a mass audience of striking Ford employees. The invitation was declined. With Ford production halted in the midst of a record-breaking sales year, the company settled on terms that guaranteed there would be no arbitrary, unilateral increases in line speed in the future, with determination of some disputed facts left to a third-party arbitrator. In the words of historian Robert Asher, the strike "was a significant victory, perhaps the most important gain of a degree of workers' control on the shop floor in the auto industry in the post-World War II era."[88]

In another significant development, GM locals in 1958 were authorized to carry on negotiations on plant working conditions subsequent to a national settlement, continuing or launching a strike if necessary to settle their local problems. Such negotiations became a common occurrence with a particular local plant—often seeking resolution of a stalled backlog of grievances—going on strike after the national settlement of wage and benefit issues had been reached. Local union bargaining gained greater authority and local strikes occurred more frequently. As Don Ephlin, a UAW vice president, recalled, in the 1950s and 1960s "nothing [was] more important to people than production standards and discipline at the lower level. Finally getting a chance to fight on those issues was very, very important to the local people." In one historian's summary assessment, as "executive officers of a highly vulnerable institution and the elected representatives of an aggrieved workforce, UAW leaders could neither endorse a level of militancy that would bring the union down, or refuse to resist the speedup that so angered their membership. UAW leaders thus accepted management's goal of uninterrupted production, but also insisted that management, as well as workers, had to honor contracts that defined production standards and stipulated that they would not be altered capriciously."[89]

Although officially frowned upon by the International leadership, wildcats by no means entirely disappeared. By one author's count, perhaps conservative, there were more than 400 wildcat strikes in the auto industry from 1946 to 1963, occurring mainly in operations such as trim lines

YOU'LL NEVER BRING BACK THOSE DAYS AGAIN

"YOU'LL NEVER BRING BACK THOSE DAYS AGAIN," 1949. © Ben Yoman, originally published in 1949 in *Ford Facts*.

where solidarity and trust could develop among a closely-knit work group, rather than in the more atomized milieu of the assembly line. At Ford alone in 1951 there were fifty-six unauthorized work stoppages and one authorized strike, involving 16,629 workers in all. In the Ford plants and elsewhere, hot summer days with soaring temperatures produced "heat strikes" in the poorly ventilated, unairconditioned factories. In 1953, as the union's top officers looked the other way, wildcats occurred because of discontent with provisions of the five-year contracts negotiated in 1950. According to

Ford Motor Company sources, there were 123 wildcat strikes in Ford plants, with forty-seven of them pertaining to working conditions. Another wildcat outburst occurred in 1958 when, owing to the expiration of contracts, the companies had an opportunity (exploited especially by Chrysler) to raise production standards and otherwise chip away at the shop floor rights and representation of employees. General Motors, quicker to discipline workers who violated contractual no-strike guarantees, was less troubled by wildcats but was by no means immune. The UAW leadership felt committed to contracts which banned strikes in all but particular circumstances, but it did not resist shop floor militancy when an inequitable or threatening situation cried out for correction.[90]

The union's pursuit of material gains through higher wages and improved fringe benefits was not something foisted on a reluctant or indifferent rank and file. While working conditions were always a matter of vital concern, the evidence shows that postwar workers prized and expected the wage and benefit improvements the leadership was able to obtain. The contracts negotiated in the 1950s were ratified by large margins. Samplings of membership attitudes conducted in 1960 by the Lou Harris organization and in 1967 by Oliver Quayle and Company show a high level of approval of the UAW leadership's goals and of the gains it had achieved. By a two-to-one margin the surveyed rank and file approved of the leadership, with the highest endorsements of specific objectives given to the winning of pensions and the guarantee of wages. Improvements in other fringe benefits, in general wage levels, hours of work, working conditions, and production standards, while of importance, were of lesser priority than the security of a guaranteed income during the working years and the opportunity and promise of leaving the factory at retirement with a decent income. Generally speaking, the highest priorities of the membership guided the goals and strategies of the leadership, and the leadership received credit for its accomplishments. Confidential interviews with delegates to the UAW's 1959 convention showed that 87 percent considered Reuther the outstanding labor leader in the United States.[91]

BY LAYING CLAIM TO ALL THOSE who worked with internal combustion engines, the UAW acquired jurisdiction over production employees in the aircraft industry. Unlike the situation it once confronted in the agricultural implements industry, in aircraft the UAW faced no rival organization within the CIO, although the International Association of Machinists (IAM), an AFL affiliate, was an active organizer and competitor in the industry. Preoccupied with auto organizing, the union did not launch a serious effort in aircraft until 1939, just as the military buildup before World War II was getting underway. Representation rights were won at North American Aviation and several smaller California firms before the United States entered the war, the effort punctuated by the 1941 strike at North American that was broken by the federal government. That strike illustrated a key difference in union representation and bargaining between the auto and aircraft industries. For most of its product, the aircraft industry had a single customer and that customer was the United States government. This fact severely limited the use of strikes. In a time of national emergency (and the emergency status inaugurated with World War II stretched into a less intense but permanent state of emergency during the cold war and the Korean and Vietnam conflicts), the government would not tolerate long stoppages of aircraft production. World War II expansion of the aircraft industry brought more than 400,000 aircraft workers into the UAW. In addition to North American, where Local 887 was for years the largest UAW local on the West Coast, the UAW gained representation rights for workers at several Douglas plants in California and at Chance-Vought. Among eastern manufacturers Curtiss-Wright, Brewster, Bell Aircraft, and Glenn L. Martin had UAW representation. The Willow Run facility in Ypsilanti, Michigan, built to manufacture the B-24 under Ford management, harbored for a time one of the largest UAW locals, Local 50, the "Bomber Local," with 50,000 employees. Aircraft employment declined as the war wound down, and when it ended in August 1945 the jobs quickly disappeared. The staff of the UAW's Aircraft Department was reduced almost overnight from its wartime peak of ninety-seven representatives to a mere two.[92]

Although the industry never regained its wartime size, the contraction was soon over; both military and civilian aircraft production emerged as major postwar industrial enterprises. The UAW rebuilt its organizing and servicing apparatus, maintaining or adding representation rights at Douglas plants in Long Beach, Tulsa, Tucson, and Charlotte, at North American and Ryan, at Bell, Chance-Vought, Fairchild, Sikorsky, AVCO, and at many smaller operations. It engaged in a lively competition with IAM, winning some representation elections and losing others. Among the major manufacturers, IAM represented Douglas workers at plants in Santa Monica and San Diego, and at plants of Consolidated-Vultee, Boeing, and Lockheed. Both unions expended a great deal of energy in raids on each other's membership and both eventually recognized the raids had resulted in little net change. By the mid-1950s, with more than 90 percent of the industry's production employees represented by one or the other of the two rivals, with membership about evenly divided between them, and with the CIO and the AFL approaching a merger, the two unions were content to "live and let live," signing a "no-raiding" agreement while continuing to compete in nonunionized plants. As military aircraft production ballooned in the early 1950s, the number of workers covered by UAW contracts tripled. Neither union succeeded in organizing Northrup, the most resolutely antiunion firm in the industry. With more than 1,000 Northrup workers voting in a representation election, the UAW fell short of winning a majority by sixty-two votes; using a time-honored tactic, the company granted a substantial wage increase on the day the National Labor Relations Board announced an election would be held.[93]

Sensitive to charges by aircraft workers that their interests were neglected in the autoworker-dominated UAW, the union leadership fought to bring auto industry standards to aircraft, where, by labor market factors and tradition, pay and benefits were relatively poor. In some respects the struggle replicated the history of auto industry labor relationships. The management ranks of military contractors frequently included retired military officers, a group generally unfriendly to unions. Strikes were difficult and risky, in part because the government was a party to the negotiations and in part because production times of aircraft were so drawn out that a strike, to be effective, had to go on and on, sapping the resources of the union and the resources and morale of the workers. A long strike at North American almost broke the union there when, under government pressure, thousands of workers returned to work, forcing a settlement largely on the company's terms. The union's pattern bargaining approach could not be transferred to aircraft. Because the products of each company were unique and required by their government contracts, one company could not be played off against another. Aircraft employers generally disliked union shops. Through a long effort continued over many negotiations, union shop agreements spread from the eastern plants, where they were more readily accepted, to those in the southwest and west. Largely achieved without strikes, by the 1960s the union shop was standard in the industry. Although the relationship with IAM continued to show some strains, once a no-raiding pact was concluded progress was made toward coordinating bargaining for agreed-upon objectives, with a further agreement that neither side would settle before the other. Where the IAM and the UAW represented different plants of the same manufacturer, as was the case with Douglas, the two unions stayed on the same track, but where that did not apply settlements were sometimes reached by one that were unsatisfactory to the other. With Leonard Woodcock director of the UAW's aircraft division, a joint committee to discuss cooperation in negotiations was set up in 1956. A steady push toward eliminating "merit" wage scales, raising rates, adding COLA escalators, extending fringes in pensions, insurances, supplementary unemployment benefits, and so on, brought the aircraft and auto components of the UAW's constituency substantially together by the 1960s. The carefully cultivated friendly relationship the UAW had with the presidential administrations of John F. Kennedy and Lyndon B. Johnson during the first half of that decade facilitated the progress aircraft workers made.[94]

WHITE-COLLAR WORKERS IN AIRCRAFT, auto, and elsewhere constituted another growing UAW constituency with a distinctive organizing and bargaining history. By the end of the 1960s the UAW had more than 80,000 members in white-collar occupations. Chrysler employees formed the largest group of any single employer with about 8,000, but the aerospace industry supplied 27,000 of the total, many more than the 17,000 in all of auto. The rest were scattered throughout a great variety of service and production enterprises. Nearly all UAW white-collar members were in clerical and technical classifications, with few in professional levels. At Chrysler, technicians such as tool, die, and fixture engineers, clay modelers, designers, and draftsmen were among the represented employees.[95]

The UAW's white-collar organizing originated in several ways. In 1941 the Marysville, Michigan, Chrysler Parts Depot, Local 954, was chartered, the first local of Chrysler office workers. The UAW launched an organizing campaign among other Chrysler white-collar workers that the corporation did little to oppose. The interest of these workers in union representation stemmed from the company's "chaotic" white-collar rate structure and job classification systems, which were riven with favoritism, arbitrary promotions, demotions and discharges, and salary "secrecy." Corporation backwardness and inattention, more than an aggressive union campaign, accounted for the success of the movement. The Society of Designing Engineers (SDE), with a following among technicians and engineers in other auto maker's plants and in some of the supplier firms, petitioned for affiliation with the UAW in 1942. General Motors mounted a more effective resistance to white-collar organizing than Chrysler, but UAW Local 160, with a membership of technicians, emerged at the General Motors Tech Center in Warren, Michigan, out of an SDE local. At Ford, where the UAW's first contract in 1941 included a clause prohibiting an attempt to organize white-collar workers, the union made little progress. The division between white- and blue-collar workers was most pronounced at Ford, where some production workers were actively hostile, on ideological/class grounds, to including white-collar workers in the union. White-collar workers resented this attitude, and their resentment contributed to the UAW's loss of several white-collar representation elections at Ford. Both GM and Ford actively resisted the UAW's appeal to their white-collar employees by devising more rational and fairer personnel policies, introducing seniority protections, and "voluntarily" extending to white- collar employees the gains that were won by the UAW for production workers at the bargaining table and on the picket line.

Middle- and lower-level white-collar employees stood on the sidelines and silently cheered as the union sought wage and benefit improvements for its membership, hopeful and confident that the gains the union wrested from the corporation would soon be extended to them. On occasion, an unrepresented salaried employee wrote to Reuther, usually anonymously, expressing "gratitude and appreciation" for the benefits received as a result of the union's efforts. In aerospace, with the largest number of white-collar UAW members, there was less separation between blue- and white-collar occupations since many of the former required some technical training and skill. Consequently, both blue- and white-collar aerospace workers tended to be organized at the same time and in the same locals.[96]

The small numbers of white-collar workers involved minimized their influence. White-collar workers could be organized in separate locals, in amalgamated locals of white-collar employees at different locations, or submerged within production workers' locals. In the last case they had little influence on the local's bargaining priorities and political dynamics. At the 1959 convention, when 5 percent of the membership consisted of white-collar workers, only 2 percent of the delegates were drawn from their ranks. Dissatisfaction similar to what had appeared among skilled tradesmen emerged. In 1957 contract ratification procedures were changed to permit white-collar workers, as well as skilled tradesmen, a separate vote on contract provisions that exclusively affected them, while the local continued to vote as a unit on matters of common interest. In 1966 the procedure was strengthened to permit separate votes on common matters as well as on those exclusive to the group.[97]

To service white-collar locals the UAW set up an Office Workers Department in 1953, but it was relatively inactive. Dissatisfaction among white-collar workers, and the leadership's desire to mount a more energetic campaign, both within and beyond the workplaces it had traditionally targeted, led to the reorganization and renaming of the department in 1962 as the TOP (Technical, Office, and Professional) Department, with Douglas Fraser, a dynamic and popular UAW board member, as its director. For the rest of the decade the UAW did noticeably better in winning certification elections and gaining new white-collar members, although Ford and, to only a slightly lesser extent, GM white-collar employees, remained outside the union. By a union estimate there were more than 300,000 potential white-collar union members employed in the industries in which the union was active, with many thousands more in other, unorganized industries.[98]

IN AFFLUENT POSTWAR AMERICA a reformulated bargain between auto workers and auto management was put in place. Resting on the dual foundations of the industry's prosperity and their union's bargaining, auto workers received more in higher wages and other forms of compensation than any other factory hands in the world. Although income and employment were not guaranteed in perpetuity, a substantial income during layoffs and retirement was assured. Thanks to the vigilance of workers, their local unions, and the International, the arbitrary exactions of an oppressive factory regime had been, by and large, eliminated. For the auto workers and their families unionization had paid off in many important ways. Management had yielded some ground on the shop floor and at the bargaining table, but it had by no means been routed. Major management prerogatives and rights—such as setting prices, determining products, production schedules, plant locations, levels of investment, and employment—while not unchallenged, were intact. Adjustments and concessions had been made but no revolution had occurred, as management mounted a successful defense of those prerogatives that were not immediately and visibly present in the workplace. The work itself, not on the whole as physically exacting as in preunion days, was still demanding and, for many workers, intrinsically unsatisfying due to its repetitive character and the absence of opportunities to develop new skills. A workplace compact, resting upon a complex blend of separate adversarial and overlapping common interests, had been achieved.[99]

The grander hopes, entertained by Reuther and others, that the UAW's collective bargaining gains would be emulated throughout the economy failed of full realization. Less prosperous industries with weaker unions, or none at all, lagged behind in the compensation their workers received. Similarly, the hope that company-financed entitlements would enlist management in a movement for the expansion of publicly-financed benefit entitlements fell well short of reaching the intended goal. Still, the impact of the UAW's bargaining outside the ranks of its production workers should not be underestimated. The UAW contracts were an inspiration and of direct value to the hundreds of thousands of both blue- and white-collar workers whose employers granted higher wages and improved benefits in response to the presence of the UAW and other strong unions.[100]

CHAPTER 9

"Give 'em hell, Harry!"

The Political Battlefront, 1948–60

S INCE THE UNION'S BEGINNINGS ITS LEADERS AND MOST OF ITS members had been aware of the crucial connection between its fortunes and the tumultuous world of politics. For the union, a political program and political action were necessities, not luxuries. Milestones in the union's history, like Governor Frank Murphy's support during the great sit-down strike, the federal government's control and direction of the economy in World War II, and the passage of the Taft-Hartley Act, amply demonstrated that the actions of government could impart vitality, even life, to a workers' organization—or take them away. Political influence was needed both to defend the union and advance a positive program. Reuther's failure to establish a larger role for the union in industrial decision-making through collective bargaining made him all the more determined to use the political system to advance workers' interests. Effective collective bargaining was always the union's first priority, but its political program was a close second.[1]

Working-class Americans and their unions had three options in politics: a permanent alignment with the Democratic Party, a separate party of and for labor, or a "reward your friends, punish your enemies" approach, without a binding party commitment. Those who believed that the two major parties were so thoroughly dominated by interests hostile to or indifferent to labor were drawn to the second option. In 1936, for example, when President Franklin D. Roosevelt's popularity was at its height, sentiment for a "farmer-labor" party was so strong in the UAW's leadership echelons that delegates to the South Bend convention had to be pressured by the CIO to endorse Roosevelt for reelection. Among the UAW's postwar leaders, a number had been members of the Socialist Party, including Reuther and his two brothers, vice president Leonard Woodcock, regional director Martin Gerber, and several other regional directors, staff members, and local union officers. Most had drifted away from a formal affiliation by the end of World War II, at odds with the party's pacifist position, discouraged by its poor electoral prospects, and aware that more votes for unelectable Socialists meant fewer votes and possible defeat for electable Democrats. Secretary-treasurer Emil Mazey, the union's second-ranking officer, maintained a Socialist connection longer than most. Sentiment for a labor party still occasionally surfaced, inspired in part by the surge of labor parties in Europe and Canada as World War II drew to its end. In 1944 a number of secondary UAW leaders organized the Michigan Commonwealth Federation and entered candidates in several districts heavily populated by union members and their families. When they polled less than 2 percent of the vote, the federation folded.[2]

Given the "winner take all" principle of the American electoral system and the dynamics of the interlinked class and ideological structure, any narrow, strictly labor-based party, unless it relished the role of "a voice crying in the wilderness," was doomed to an ineffectual existence. The UAW leadership recognized that a party that wished to construct a majority in order to participate in government had to be built on a coalition of classes, interest groups, and ethnic and racial minorities. No single element, including labor, had the size, cohesion, and consciousness of separate identity needed to form a majority party's sole support. The absence of a labor party in America was rooted in the nature of its class system. "In Europe," Reuther observed in an interview with a British journalist, "labor parties are a natural political expression because there you have a highly fixed . . . class society. But America is a society in which social groups are in flux, in which you do not have this rigid class structure." Classes there were, to be sure, but they did not conform in many particulars to the European model, especially the lack of a developed class consciousness. To have a political impact, the labor movement had to enter into alliances with middle-class liberals, friendly elements of business, professionals, farmers, organized consumer groups, and racial and ethnic minorities. Successful coalition building required finding common ground within a diverse assemblage and mastering the challenging, sometimes treacherous, art of compromise. Such reasoning pointed the UAW toward the New Deal wing of the Democratic Party, despite the racialist base of its southern element and the presence of conservative business interests within it.[3]

Although a labor party seemed an impossible dream, many UAW leaders were attracted to the less ambitious but still formidable challenge of realigning the two major parties more sharply along ideological/class lines by uniting liberal Democrats, progressive Republicans, and liberal independents in a party facing left, while placing the northern and southern economic and social conservatives of both parties in the other looking to the right. As the 1948 elections approached, with the Democratic Party under siege and threatening to break apart because of internal contradictions, such a realignment did not seem unrealistic. A resurgent Republican Party had won control of Congress in the midterm elections of 1946 and was confident it would capture the presidency in 1948. Southern Democrats, outraged as the party's northern wing embraced a civil rights agenda, openly talked of leaving the party. At the opposite end of the spectrum, a portion of the party's left-wing, upset with President Harry S. Truman's cold war stance·and rhetoric, was threatening to break away. Change was in the air; the party needed rejuvenation, a new direction, and, in the view of many, new leadership in order to defend the achievements of the New Deal and go forward from them.[4]

A new direction required a road map. In January 1947 Reuther and other liberals met in Washington, D.C., at the invitation of Reinhold Niebuhr, the Protestant theologian and liberal activist, to found Americans for Democratic Action (ADA) for the purpose of mobilizing the "enormous forces in American life which are both progressive and non-Communist." The disastrous results for liberalism in the recent Congressional elections, when only thirty-six of seventy-seven incumbent congressmen who had received a *New Republic* rating as consistent liberals won reelection, made the task of reviving liberal forces an urgent one. With its purpose of developing and propagating a liberal position on all public questions, ADA was more issue-oriented than politically activist. To ADA, Communism was, along with Nazism and Fascism, the totalitarian antithesis of liberal democracy, so Communist Party members were excluded from its offices, and its charter condemned their ideology. The UAW became an important ADA financial backer, donating $10,000 in the spring of 1948 and making additional contributions thereafter. As a liberal-labor, noncommunist organization that sought to draw the Democratic Party toward social democracy, ADA was a comfortable affiliation for many in the UAW's leadership.[5]

In general terms, the ADA's agenda was in harmony with the UAW leadership's political goals. Each saw legitimate roles for both private capital and the public in directing and overseeing a mixed-enterprise economy. Important objectives included a national, democratic planning mechanism to direct investment and production, an institutional structure that integrated labor and government into the economy's decision-making process along with private capital, public spending to stimulate the economy and provide jobs when unemployment threatened, and a redistributive, progressive tax system. Entitlement programs would guarantee all citizens a minimum standard of living, including retirement and disability benefits, a national health service or health insurance plan, subsidized housing for workers and the poor, and improved benefits in unemployment compensation. A commitment to advancing and protecting civil rights and equal employment opportunities was held out to racial minorities. In terms of foreign policy, the highest priority was economic reconstruction under American auspices in war-torn western Europe through the Marshall Plan.[6]

The UAW's political direction was set by the leadership within the broad boundaries established by the members' sentiments. Since many rank-and-file auto workers saw political action as less central to the union's purpose than its economic function, the leadership enjoyed considerable freedom of action in formulating specific political goals. Unlike contracts, political agendas required only the stamp of approval of convention resolutions; they did not have to be submitted directly to the members for ratification votes. Resolutions on both general and specific issues were brought before UAW conventions by the leadership and often approved with little debate or strongly expressed opposition. Using these convention resolutions as general guidelines, two groups formulated and implemented specific political positions and strategies. The Detroit cadre included Reuther and key officers and assistants, such as Leonard Woodcock, Roy and Victor Reuther (the latter until 1950 when he left for posts in Paris and later Washington, D.C.), Frank Winn, Jack Conway, Nat Weinberg, and Doug Fraser, joined by Mildred Jeffrey, Brendan Sexton, and others—a group that could be expanded or contracted as changing issues and circumstances required. The Washington office, responsible for drawing up and releasing statements on current issues and lobbying Congress and government agencies, included Donald Montgomery, Paul Sifton, and Joseph L. Rauh, Jr. In both Detroit and Washington all were noncommunist social democrats.[7]

THE 1948 PRESIDENTIAL ELECTION presented a dilemma to the UAW. President Truman, a man "with his heart in the right place but a man not adequate for the job he inherited," as Reuther bluntly remarked to a reporter, was not, in the view of critics from all sides of the political spectrum, of presidential stature. His floundering on reconversion, labor strife, and the removal of price controls seemed to confirm this judgment. He had surrounded himself with cronies and conservative businessmen and had shown neither the liberal vision nor the political skills needed to hold the Democratic Party on a New Deal course, let alone build on its achievements. If Truman ran for reelection, his defeat, the UAW's leaders feared, would drag down the friendly liberal senators and congressmen on whom the UAW and other unions relied. Although conventional political wisdom argued that dumping an incumbent president ensured his party's defeat, ADA leaders began to search for an alternative to Truman. Some, including Reuther for a time, hoped to persuade General Dwight D. Eisenhower, whose political sentiments were then little known but whose popularity was enormous, to accept the Democratic nomination. Convinced by UAW staffers that Eisenhower was more conservative than Truman, Reuther turned for a candidate to Supreme Court Justice William O. Douglas, a New Dealer and a favorite of Roosevelt's, though handicapped by lack of a solid political base. In July 1948, shortly before the Democratic convention met to nominate Truman for reelection, Reuther called for an open convention and personally endorsed Douglas. His advice was ignored.[8]

However grudgingly, the UAW leaders had little choice but to give formal support to the Truman candidacy. Considering the alternative, the Republican candidate Governor Thomas E. Dewey of New York, he was much the lesser of two evils. As Donald Montgomery had earlier pointed out to Reuther, Truman was "the only instrument at hand for keeping the Republicans out" of the presidency, the UAW's primary political objective. Furthermore, Truman had adopted the shrewd and effective strategy of rallying the New Deal coalition, his only hope of reelection. Vetoing the Taft-Hartley Act and pledging to work for its repeal restored his ties to organized labor. He put forward a progressive program that promised to fulfill some of the New Deal's hopes and go beyond it in other respects. A key item was the support he gave, equivocal though it was, to the recommendations of the Civil Rights Commission he had appointed in his first year as president, the first formal presidential backing for a civil rights legislative program since Reconstruction. The proposals included a permanent fair employment practices commission, a law making lynching a federal crime, the abolition of the poll tax, and desegregation of the armed forces. Overcoming opposition from southern Democrats, liberals placed a strong civil rights plank in the Democratic convention's platform, prompting many disaffected delegates from southern states, fearful that their section's veto over civil rights legislation was in danger, to "take a walk." The departure of these "Dixiecrats" threatened Truman's electoral prospects in the "Solid South," but made it easier for liberals to rally to him. Truman had also promised to back legislation expanding the New Deal's rudimentary welfare state, including establishment of a national health insurance plan, a program of public housing and urban renewal, and price supports for farm commodities. Despite Reuther's fear that Truman was doomed to defeat, the UAW had no choice but to endorse his candidacy, which the executive board did in September following Truman's campaign kickoff speech before a Labor Day crowd of more than 100,000 in Detroit's Cadillac Square. Reuther contributed a lukewarm endorsement in a radio address a few days before the election. In line with the pessimistic assessment of Truman's chances, the bulk of the UAW's 1948 electoral activity was directed to supporting liberal congressional and state candidates.[9]

The third party that appeared on the left in 1948 was anathema to the UAW. Henry Wallace, former New Deal secretary of agriculture and vice president, was dismissed by Truman as secretary of commerce for speaking out in favor of a postwar conciliatory relationship between the United States and the Soviet Union. Convinced that world peace depended upon the reestablishment of US-Soviet cooperation, Wallace criticized the hardening positions of the Truman administration, including both the Truman Doctrine, which promised military aid to countries threatened with communist takeover, and the Marshall Plan, which supplied economic aid to the nations of western Europe. Supported by the remnants of Popular Front sentiment, including those within and without the UAW that the Reuther following had long battled, Wallace announced his candidacy for the presidency as a Progressive and received the public endorsement (which was not repudiated) of the American Communist Party. Wallace denied that he was following anyone's "line" but his own, but added that if a Communist or anyone else chose to follow *his* line, "I say God bless 'em"—perhaps not the best choice of words in the circumstances. Communist spokesmen meanwhile put forward the exaggerated boast that they were behind the launching of the Progressive Party and the recruitment of Wallace as its candidate. Progressive candidates filed for Senate and House seats in some of the states where labor and liberal sentiments were strong, a threat to the election of supportive Democrats.[10]

As a prominent New Dealer, Wallace appeared to pose a serious challenge to the election of a Democratic presidential candidate. The Wallace candidacy drove the UAW leadership, along with that of most CIO unions, into the arms of the Democrats. Whatever they might think of the emerging cold war and the foreign policy debate, most union leaders saw the entry of a Progressive ticket that threatened to cause the defeat of liberal Democrats as a hostile challenge to labor's interests. Wallace's election was an unlikely outcome of his campaign; more likely was Truman's defeat by Governor Dewey, already the heavy favorite to win the presidency. With a Dewey victory and a Republican Congress, any hope of repealing the Taft-Hartley Act and obtaining a fulfillment of the New Deal, let alone expanding it, would be dead. In the worst case scenario, a Republican sweep could lead to hostile legislation, including the repeal of the Wagner Act.

The UAW leadership swung into action to defeat the Wallace initiative. Reuther launched a harsh, personal attack on Wallace and his acceptance of Communist Party support. His remarks to reporters were widely circulated:

> Wallace has become a lost soul. He has been a great disappointment, for he might have been a great help and made a major contribution. . . . People are using Henry Wallace. The Communists are doing for him what they do for any other important figure they can bring under their wing. They furnish a complete political valet service.

They will write your speeches. They will do your thinking for you. They will arrange and take you to meetings. They will supply the audience and lead the cheering. And, when necessary to keep you in camp, they will inflate your ego.

The UAW executive board declared that the Progressive Party was "a Communist Party maneuver designed to advance the foreign policy interests of the Soviet Union," and the political literature the union distributed to its members portrayed Wallace as a Communist dupe. Reuther took the lead in urging the CIO to forbid its affiliates to support Progressive candidates. Labor supporters of Wallace countered with the argument that political endorsements were the prerogative of the affiliates themselves, not of the federation and its officers. Following a bitter debate, the CIO executive board voted 33–11, with president Philip Murray in the majority, to denounce the Wallace candidacy. Reuther pushed ahead in condemning the eleven CIO unions, including United Electrical Workers, the third largest in the federation, that defied the CIO executive board by endorsing Wallace's candidacy. The UAW executive board ordered all UAW locals to oppose Wallace and, when some local officers refused to follow orders, took steps to undermine their credibility with their members, even bringing charges of antiunion activity against them. Whatever hope Wallace may have had of obtaining UAW support was quickly quashed.[11]

With the UAW leadership convinced by virtually all the political pundits and opinion polls that Truman was doomed to defeat, a strategy to minimize losses and plan for a post-Truman future was devised. Distancing itself from the president's campaign, the union concentrated its electoral efforts in support of candidates for Congress and for state offices. In the spring of 1948 the executive board had declared its official political objective to be the "formation after the 1948 national election of a genuine progressive political party" that would draw together liberals whatever their previous party affiliations in order to mount an opposition to the anticipated conservative Republican regime. As the first step in implementing this strategy Reuther participated in planning and promoting a national conference scheduled for January 19, 1949, in Washington, D.C., timed to coincide with Dewey's inauguration. The plan was rendered embarrassingly irrelevant by the underdog Truman's victory in his classic come-from-behind campaign. The Wallace movement faded as he failed to carry a single state, while the Dixiecrat States' Rights Party carried only four states in the Deep South. Truman, uniting many elements of the New Deal coalition, swept to a decisive victory. In addition, the Democrats regained majorities in both houses of Congress, although a southern Democrat-Republican coalition there would continue to exercise effective control over the legislative agenda. The Washington gathering of disaffected liberals was canceled and, with Democrats on the rebound, the UAW was more firmly tied to that party than ever. Truman, who told reporters that "Labor did it," acknowledged the crucial support he received from union voters. Regardless of the UAW leadership's lack of enthusiasm, there was no question that UAW voters, 89 percent of whom cast their ballots for the president, favored Truman. Reuther referred to the election's outcome as a "holding operation" that had the merit of warding off worse damage to the union movement.[12]

The UAW's political mobilization in 1948 was unprecedented in the union's history and set the pattern for the future. Despite the fact that many auto workers came out of cultural-social settings that did not emphasize political (or other community) participation, the UAW in 1948 and later elections stimulated a remarkable outpouring of political activity. More than $136,000 in voluntary donations was raised from members and expended by the International, with many thousands more raised by locals through contributions and the sale of campaign buttons. More than 10,000 precinct workers were recruited from the union's ranks, and over eight million pieces of CIO-PAC campaign literature distributed to members and the public—both totals conservative estimates, according to the union. In the ninety-seven congressional districts that contained an appreciable number of UAW members, forty-five antilabor congressmen were defeated and twenty-seven prolabor congressmen reelected, but twenty-five anti-labor incumbents prevailed over the union's opposition. Among the new congressmen was Tom Burke of Toledo, Ohio, a former officer in Local 12 and the first UAW member to be elected to the United States House of Representatives. More would follow. New senators supportive of labor were elected in Illinois (Douglas), Minnesota (Humphrey), Montana (Murray), and Tennessee (Kefauver). Governors friendly to labor were elected in Michigan, Indiana, Illinois, Iowa, Missouri, and Connecticut, all states with substantial UAW membership. The union endorsed candidates and provided support in thousands of contests for state and local offices.[13]

THE MOST SIGNIFICANT TRIUMPH for the UAW in the election of 1948 was revitalizing local and state politics in Michigan, the union's home base. Operating through the CIO-Political Action Committee (CIO-PAC), the UAW poured thousands of dollars and, of greater importance, thousands of workers, both volunteer and paid, into the Michigan campaign. At the state level, this effort was led by August "Gus" Scholle, director of the Michigan CIO-PAC, UAW vice president John Livingston, and Roy Reuther, his administrative assistant and successor as coordinator of the union's political action programs. They urged union officials and rank-and-file members to enter the state Democratic Party, seek election as precinct delegates, participate in district, state, and national conventions, and secure positions in the party's apparatus. The union organized a massive commitment of manpower by freeing hundreds of International and regional staff representatives from their regular duties to work in campaigns, and by mobilizing hundreds of unpaid volunteers to distribute handouts, organize voter registration among both union members and supportive elements of the general population, obtain signatures on nominating petitions, and assure a big turnout of favorably inclined voters on election day. By 1953, political action committees had been set up in over 90 percent of the UAW's local unions to organize and coordinate these activities at the community level. Not every UAW member participated, but many threw themselves into the political campaigns with enthusiasm, and surveys showed a solid majority of the members approved of the union's activism.[14]

In Michigan the UAW gained a position in 1948 as the single most powerful force within the state Democratic Party. A coalition consisting of the UAW and other CIO unions joined with reform Democrats, some representatives of minority groups, and some AFL unionists to elect hundreds of precinct delegates and thereby gain control of the party apparatus and the state convention, defeating old-line Democrats and a conservative AFL group led by Jimmy Hoffa's Teamsters. About 1,000 liberals, mostly UAW members, filed for precinct delegate in 1948 in Wayne County alone, the state's most populous and most unionized jurisdiction, and over 700 were elected. In Wayne County the labor-liberal coalition took control of the Democratic Party organization in four of the six congressional districts, and three years later the CIO-PAC reported that it had met its goal of recruiting four block workers for each Detroit precinct. Enlisting union activists from its locals in the western and northern portions of the state, the UAW built the Democratic Party in outstate Michigan, a region where it had scarcely existed before, recruiting and endorsing Democratic candidates for office where none had run earlier, creating a competitive, statewide, two-party political structure. In some outstate cities and towns a UAW local office or union hall was the only place available for a Democratic Party meeting. With control of the state party came an opportunity to select liberal candidates for local offices, write a liberal party platform, secure appointments of labor-endorsed candidates to positions on government regulatory commissions and administrative bodies, and send liberal delegates to the national convention. UAW members formed the core of all these activities.[15]

The signal Democratic victory within the state in 1948 was the election as governor of G. Mennen "Soapy" Williams, to whose financially strapped campaign the UAW contributed $10,000, the largest donation he received. Williams, an ADA member, held the state's highest office for twelve years through five reelection campaigns, all won with UAW support, locking the labor-liberal coalition into the state's political system. His election in the presidential year of 1948 was not so surprising since a Democratic candidate had won in the previous presidential election years of 1936 and 1940. Far more astonishing was Williams's narrow victory in the non-presidential election of 1950, since Republicans had prevailed for decades in off-year elections. In addition, liberal Democrats George O'Brien and Louis Rabaut were elected in two new congressional districts. In subsequent elections union political forces built upon these victories. In 1954, CIO-PAC workers saturated Detroit, Flint, and other CIO cities in a successful campaign to defeat incumbent Republican Senator Homer Ferguson, replacing him with the victorious Democrat, Patrick V. McNamara. In addition, two PAC-endorsed candidates for the House of Representatives from Flint and Detroit won, and, for the first time in many years the Democrats gained as many as one-half, fifty-five of one hundred and ten, of the seats in the Michigan House of Representatives. In the next senatorial election in 1958, Lieutenant governor Philip A. Hart, a UAW-endorsed candidate, defeated his Republican opponent, giving Michigan—for the first time in its post-Civil War history—two Democratic United States senators, both with close ties to the labor movement. By the end of the 1950s only the state Senate remained in Republican hands, owing largely to districting that favored sparsely populated rural areas and small towns. It is no exaggeration to assert that the UAW and its allies had transformed the state's politics and its representation in the national government. With its influence in state Democratic Party organizations in Michigan and elsewhere, "by the 1950s," as summarized by historian Kevin Boyle, "the UAW sent more delegates to the national Democratic convention, contributed more money and personnel to election campaigns, and maintained a more extensive congressional lobbying apparatus than any other American union." As another observer put it, "The UAW takes politics seriously."[16]

Although the UAW forged a firm and enduring bond with the Democratic Party it never became totally identified with it. Rather the union operated as a force within the party, free to criticize positions and candidates of which it disapproved. Reuther was never formally a party member, and Emil Mazey maintained a connection with the Socialists. The charge repeatedly brought by the newspapers and Republican politicians that the UAW and CIO had "captured" the Michigan Democratic Party overstated the case. The union's leaders recognized that only as part of a coalition could they hope to win general elections, and they chose to cooperate as partners rather than seek to dominate. Political opponents in the heated "Red scare" atmosphere of the time sought to make political capital out of

the UAW's activism; for example, in 1950 a Republican candidate for governor alleged that the "kings and the kingmakers," with Reuther prominent
among the latter, "are getting ready to turn loose 5,000 paid workers to try
to stampede Michigan into Socialism."[17]

Money, of course, was essential for an effective political voice. The
Smith-Connally Act and the Taft-Hartley Act forbade the use of union dues
money for direct contributions to presidential candidates, but the legislation did not prohibit a number of other political expenditures, including
donations to candidates for state and local offices. Following a favorable
court decision, unions were at liberty, as an exercise of freedom of speech,
to make political endorsements of candidates for national, state, and local
offices, and to publicize these endorsements in their newspapers, radio and
tv programs, and press releases. Unions could legally collect voluntary contributions from staff employees and members and donate the funds to
endorsed candidates or use them for other political purposes. Union officers
urged local unions to ask their members for a donation of $1 each to CIO-
PAC, and thousands responded. In 1954 the national CIO-PAC spent over
$1 million on endorsed candidates, and UAW political committees spent
about half that amount on, by and large, the same candidates. In that year,
95 percent of UAW locals participated in the CIO-PAC "Buck" campaign,
collecting over $300,000. Although unavailable for direct contributions to
presidential candidates, dues money could legally be used to prepare "educational" materials, such as compilations of candidates' voting records and
position statements for distribution to union members and the general public. The union's Education Department took the lead in disseminating such
material. By 1964, following convention approval, the UAW constitution
allocated 5 cents of each member's monthly dues to an "Educational Fund"
for election-related materials. The constitution also allocated 10 cents a
month in dues money to a "Citizenship Fund," with the money divided
between the locals and the International to mount voter registration campaigns aimed at UAW members and others, for "get out the vote" drives on
election day, and to provide candidate information. Members who objected
to this use of their dues could direct that their money be used for other purposes, but few chose to do so. Summoned before the Senate Subcommittee
on Privileges and Elections, Reuther defended the UAW's political fund-
raising and expenditures in a hot and amusing exchange with Senator Carl
Curtis (Republican, Nebraska), and followed up by proposing electoral
reforms, including limitations on political contributions. Congress chose
not to act on the proposals.[18]

Although heavily promoted by the top leadership, political activity
across the union's broad expanse was uneven. The International leadership
could not compel regional directors to mount vigorous campaigns if they

were disinclined. In the Detroit area, outstate Michigan, and several other midwestern states strong efforts were made with impressive and lasting results. A survey of UAW voters in Detroit in 1948 showed 89 percent had cast their ballots for President Truman, compared with only 11 percent for Governor Dewey; none reported voting for Henry Wallace. Votes for Democratic presidential candidates among Detroit Polish American and African American voters from the 1940s to the 1960s frequently topped 90 percent. In 1952 the UAW Detroit area vote for the union-endorsed presidential candidate, Democratic Illinois Governor Adlai E. Stevenson, was a solid 75 percent. Dodge Local 3 had over 100 volunteers working in Hamtramck, an enclave within Detroit and a heavily Democratic area, to publicize the union's endorsements and organize voter registration and conduct get-out-the-vote drives. Like many union activists in 1948, Douglas Fraser spent election day checking off UAW members as they came through his precinct polling place, and late in the day he rounded up all the slackers he could reach before the polls closed. Such efforts turned out a large vote. But in some other areas, particularly in the South and in one of the Ohio regions, little was done. No effective effort to collect CIO-PAC contributions materialized, staff members were not released for political duty, and volunteers were not encouraged or coordinated. Despite all the vaunted clout of the "Reuther machine" and the union's bureaucratic structure, the International leadership could not compel indifferent regional directors to make more than a token effort.[19]

IN DETROIT CITY ELECTIONS, where one might expect UAW political influence to be at its most potent, the results were disappointing and, by revealing the profound racial division within the community and the union, deeply disturbing. With a high proportion of owner-occupied homes and with many neighborhoods having a clear ethno-racial identity, civil rights sharply collided with property rights, undermining the prospects of union-endorsed candidates for mayor. Two campaigns produced stunning defeats for the union. In 1945 veteran organizer and vice president Richard T. Frankensteen, his UAW career stalemated, challenged incumbent Detroit mayor Edward Jeffries in the nonpartisan primary. Frankensteen placed first in the primary, beating Jeffries by 83,000 to 69,000 votes and eliminating the rest of the field from the runoff. With UAW endorsements, the CIO-PAC spending over $100,000 on his behalf, and some 550 Detroit precincts organized with union block workers, Frankensteen's victory seemed assured. But a massive outpouring of antiblack, "protect my property" sentiment buried him in a humiliating loss, with 275,000 votes for Jeffries to 217,000 for Frankensteen. Racial fears dominated the campaign. Frankensteen had endorsed the CIO's platform of equal rights for minorities. Memories of his support for black employment and promotion opportunities in war plants still rankled with some white union members, and (doubtless the most important consideration for white property owners and renters) the expansion of the black ghetto into previously all-white neighborhoods was held to be an imminent threat if Frankensteen should win. Thousands of copies of leaflets were distributed charging that with a Frankensteen victory, "you couldn't keep the niggers out of City Hall." Jeffries and his supporters flooded white residential districts with handbills accusing Frankensteen of plotting "racial invasions" of their neighborhoods, and his posters assured homeowners that "Mayor Jeffries is Against Mixed Housing." Behind the plot to open access to housing, it was implied, was the UAW's "Red" leadership, out to communize Detroit and its citizens. In the voting, majority black precincts went heavily for Frankensteen but white areas of the city, inhabited by both Polish and southern-born migrants (white working-class districts with many union member residents), joined with middle-class areas to give Jeffries the victory. Union supporters of Frankensteen were shocked at the size of the Jeffries vote and the evidence of his support in precincts with significant autoworker populations. The UAW leadership had received a painful lesson in the limited reach of its political influence, even among its own membership, when confronting the racial divide.[20]

Four years later, in 1949, another UAW-endorsed candidate for mayor suffered an equally distressing loss. George Edwards was a pioneer member of Local 174, the West Side Local, a friend and early associate of the Reuther brothers, and an articulate and well-educated man who was on excellent terms with the UAW's leadership when he left the union for public service. Even more closely than Frankensteen, he was associated with fair treatment of the city's black minority. As head of the Detroit Housing Commission and an elected member of the city's Common Council, he had consistently championed fair and open housing, with access for blacks to public housing projects located in white neighborhoods. Edwards's principal opponent for mayor was city treasurer Albert Cobo, a conservative, former accountant who promised to keep taxes low and otherwise make the city hospitable to private businesses. Edwards, who broke the election's traditional nonpartisan status to run as a Democrat, advanced a New Deal-Fair Deal program of active municipal government, expanded public services, and equal protection for all across the entire spectrum of civil rights concerns. The UAW and CIO-PAC mounted a vigorous campaign on Edwards's behalf, spending nearly $30,000, distributing over 1.3 million pamphlets, and mobilizing an army of campaign workers. Volunteers went door-to-door spreading the message while UAW sound trucks roamed the streets. Although Cobo and his supporters muffled the racial appeal under a blanket of code words—in contrast to its blatant use in the 1945 election—that message was clearly present, along with countless thrusts at Edwards's "radical" spending plans. The result was a stunning defeat for Edwards and his union leadership backers. Most disheartening was the lack of support in white working-class districts. As one UAW shop steward at the time later wrote, "To the astonishment of secondary UAW leaders, the new homeowners in Detroit among the auto workers spoke openly in the shops against 'labor's man.' " Edwards carried no precincts on Detroit's West Side, with its largely white population, and on the East Side he ran strongly only in those wards that mostly contained black residents. Cobo won easily as a record setting 529,360 voters turned out, nearly 62 percent of those registered; 309,067, 58 percent of voters, chose the city treasurer as their next mayor. Perceived threats to neighborhoods and property values from the feared movement of blacks into white areas accounted for much of the failure of union members, including auto workers, to support the leadership's political endorsements. In part, as a UAW political coordinator observed, their votes for Cobo were the result of the union's success in bringing its members into the property-owning classes. As he reported, "I think in these municipal elections we are dealing with people who have a middle class mentality. Even in our own UAW, the member is either buying a home, owns a home, or is going to buy one. . . . George was beaten by the housing program." Affirming racial bigotry as the American way and thereby testifying to the union's failure to transform the racial perspective of a portion of its membership, one union member chastised Edwards after his defeat in these words: "We don't want you or any part of your stuff. . . . I suggest you go to Washington they take care of lame ducks there. . . . We may belong to the CIO in the shops but when we vote we vote American." Edwards's defeat soured a chastened UAW leadership on heavy involvement in Detroit local elections. The progressive candidates its leadership could in good conscience support appeared to have little chance of winning, given the conservatism, racial and otherwise, of the electorate. To lose consistently, especially when some of the union's own members contributed to the loss, was demoralizing and seemed a waste of energy and resources. Although by no means withdrawing from the local political scene, the UAW kept a lower profile in the future.[21]

On the other hand, in local elections that did not arouse fears of disrupted neighborhoods and declining property values, Detroit voters were prepared to back candidates supportive of civil rights. In 1954 the UAW endorsed Charles Diggs, Jr., a Democrat and African American, for election to Congress. Diggs was the first of his race from Michigan to be elected to the House of Representatives. He received 66 percent of the vote in an East Side district with an estimated black population at that time of about 38 percent, the first instance of the election of a black congressman in a district with a minority of black voters. Although no voting records by union membership or by union families are available, with approximately 43,000 UAW members residents of the district, it is safe to say that a large number of white unionists voted for a black congressional candidate.[22]

Unable to make progress in securing equal rights in access to housing through local elections, the UAW pursued other ways to promote fair housing but enjoyed no greater success. One focus of controversy was a proposal for the construction of the union-supported and privately financed School-craft Gardens Cooperative on Detroit's northwest side, in a "white" neighborhood. The design was presented as model "workers' housing," consisting of modern townhouses in a beautifully landscaped garden setting. The project received financial and administrative support from the UAW, which hoped it would be the first of many cooperative housing projects throughout the city. The union and other private agencies supporting the project resisted pressure to guarantee that housing would be reserved for whites, thereby unleashing a barrage of protests from real estate interests, neighborhood associations, and fundamentalist ministers. A spokesman for the Detroit Real Estate Board condemned the project for "pitting class against class or race against class or race . . . " and promoting "the socialistic theory of a cooperative society." A zoning change passed by Common Council to permit construction to proceed was vetoed by Mayor Cobo, and the project died on the drafting table.[23]

The experience of the UAW in its political actions revealed both common ground and sharp cleavages within the union's ranks. Both the leadership and the membership were committed to a national social-democratic/ working-class program of progressive taxation, economic stimulation through government fiscal and monetary policies, and expanded social security entitlements. On these and other issues that directly affected livelihoods, living standards, and economic security, the union spoke with one voice. A national civil rights agenda that focused on ending southern racial segregation and discrimination, including denial of voting rights, received substantial support across the union's ranks, but with something less than unanimity. In the local political arena, where ethnic and racial homogeneity, as well as property values, were threatened by unrestricted access to housing, schools, and neighborhoods, cleavages emerged and became acute. Leaders and many members parted ways, inevitably reducing the union's ability to contribute to a solution of local racial and ethnic issues.

Racial issues cropped up in other settings. The union's culture, structure, and internal political dynamic raised barriers to reforms imposed from above. Despite the centralizing tendency of recent years, the union's origins and much of its history and continuing activity were rooted in local initiative and control. Local officers and regional directors, who routinely faced

reelection campaigns, felt pressure to accommodate rank-and-file sentiments. The remedies available to the International for correcting an errant
local—expulsion or installing an administrator—were resented and resisted
whatever the issue. Some regional directors in southern and border states,
whose cooperation in ending discrimination in southern locals was necessary if results were to be obtained, paid little more than lip service to equal
rights principles. These circumstances limited the union's response to conditions its International leadership deplored and condemned. The dilemma
posed by popular support for undemocratic objectives was not, of course,
limited to the UAW.[24]

The auto companies were less than helpful in moving toward fair hiring and promotion practices. Repeated UAW attempts to negotiate nondiscriminatory hiring clauses in its contracts were rebuffed by the companies
on the ground that the union could not bargain for persons not yet
employed. Management was determined to resist any loss of control over
hiring, and the issue of fair hiring was not sufficiently vital to the entire
membership for it to occasion a strike. In the southern states where General Motors opened factories in the 1950s, blacks were not offered a fair
share of the jobs or assigned to the better jobs on an equal basis. The corporation's policy was to leave hiring decisions to local plant managers, who,
following the line of least resistance, bowed to regional custom. As the
manager of a GM facility near Atlanta, which employed few blacks and confined those few to janitorial work, explained, "when we moved into the
South, we agreed to abide by local custom and not hire Negroes for production work. This is no time for social reforming in that area and we're
not about to try it." A Fisher Body plant in Atlanta employed twenty-seven
blacks in a workforce of 1,400, and a nearby Buick plant employed eighty
blacks out of a total of 1,700, none in production work. Ford Motor Company plants in Atlanta, Dallas, Memphis, and Norfolk employed less than
1 percent African Americans out of a combined workforce of more than
seven thousand. Although a color line remained in place in these southern
plants until the 1960s, the situation affected a relatively small proportion
of the UAW's members, since in 1955 the fifty-six UAW locals in southern
states represented only 5 percent of the membership. In some border state
plants—as, for example, the GM plant in St. Louis—discriminatory practices persisted into the 1950s, resting on collaboration between the local
union and management. In this instance separate seniority lists for white
and black workers were maintained, making blacks more liable to layoffs
and ineligible for upgrades.[25]

The most explosive racial conflicts pitted some southern locals against
the International UAW. Racial feeling among many southern whites was
inflamed as the civil rights movement gathered momentum and swept

across the South. The Supreme Court's attack on segregation in public schools, launched in its 1954 decision in *Brown v. Board of Education,* incited a monumental backlash in the white South whose effects were seen in the formation of White Citizens' Councils throughout the region and many other instances of both nonviolent and violent opposition to civil rights advances. The extreme case of a local refusing to admit black employees to membership, a blatant violation of the basic principle of industrial unionism and of the UAW's constitution, no longer occurred. In 1946 a General Motors local in Atlanta admitted black employees only under a threat of expulsion, and as late as 1951 the UAW expelled a small local of airplane mechanics and maintenance workers at a Braniff Air Lines facility in Dallas, which had refused to admit African Americans and Chicanos to membership—the last instance of the expulsion of a defiant local for racial transgressions.[26]

White racist organizations actively recruited and agitated in some southern plants and locals. According to an International Union estimate, 80 percent of the white members, including half of the officers of Local 988 in Memphis, joined the White Citizens' Council. A staff member of the Fair Practices Department, sent to the South in 1956 to report on the situation, was told by one of the local's officers during a tumultuous meeting, "the time is soon coming when the workers of the South will decide whether we want your union with desegregation or we want our own union with segregation. When the showdown comes we'll take segregation and leave you guys up in Detroit. We won't stand for it." In Atlanta, perhaps as many as 5,000 members in three large locals joined the Ku Klux Klan, which underwent a revival throughout the South in the mid-1950s, and a member of Local 34 was the Georgia Klan's Imperial Wizard.[27]

In Jacksonville, Florida, at a meeting with UAW Local 20, the representative encountered more outbursts and threats. He defended the union's support for the National Association for the Advancement of Colored People, its opposition to the White Citizens' Councils, and its support for politicians who championed fair practices. The president of the local then rose and "charged that the NAACP is communistic, that Walter Reuther was a communist; that Walter Reuther went to Russia; that all Walter Reuther wanted was the 'nigger' vote so that he could be president some day...." "Shaking his finger in my face," the representative continued, "he said that when the time comes, and 'nigger' loving Reuther lined up his 'niggers,' Reuther would be the one he was going to draw a 'bead on.' "[28]

A sustained conflict involved workers at the International Harvester plant in Memphis, Tennessee, Local 988. The plant, built after the war to manufacture cotton pickers, hired an interracial workforce, with the black employees, about one-third of the total, assigned to foundry and non-production jobs as tradition dictated. A black member, George L. Holloway, challenged the racial employment prohibitions and other instances of segregation, calling on the International Union to live up to its principles. In the spring of 1953 the promotion of a black to a welder's job, to which he was entitled by seniority and skill, provoked a wildcat walkout by white workers that shut down production and soon began to affect other International Harvester operations. The UAW leadership condemned the strike as a violation of the contract and the union's constitution, threatened to expel the local, ordered the strikers to return to work, and informed the company that it could penalize strikers, up to and including their dismissal, without union objection. Rather than be fired, the strikers returned to their jobs.[29]

The same local fought a prolonged battle with the International UAW over the racially segregated toilets and drinking fountains in its union hall. In 1960, after years of chiding by the Fair Practices Department, negotiation, delay, broken promises, threatened law suits, and assaults in the hall's parking lot on International representatives sent to Memphis to settle the matter, the local was put under an administrator when it refused a direct order to remove "white" and "colored" signs over the rest room doors and water fountains. With the International finally in control, four local officials were removed from office and the offending signs taken down, actions that were upheld by the Public Review Board. Despite the dogged opposition of white workers within the local, black workers there made genuine progress in gaining access to better jobs, thanks to pressures generated by the black workers themselves, national civil rights organizations, and, belatedly, the International Union.[30]

Although in the early postwar years scattered "hate strikes" still occasionally occurred in a few northern factories, employment prospects there for blacks improved. Wildcats by whites protesting black promotions at the Cleveland Fisher Body plant in 1947, the Ex-Cell-O facility in Detroit in 1951, the Toledo Champion Spark Plug plant in 1955, and the St. Louis GM plant in 1956 were among the last of their kind. By the mid-1950s the occupational color line for production work had been breached, even broken, in northern and most border state auto plants. Especially in the Detroit plants, the workforce became multiracial. Although present in greater numbers and proportions than had previously been the case and spread farther across the occupational spectrum, black workers still tended to be clustered in particular occupations, ordinarily those that were least desirable. Most egregious was their virtual exclusion from the skilled trades, the factory's best paid and most prestigious jobs. Compounding the harm to African Americans, tradesmen exerted an influence disproportionate to their numbers, occupying positions in the factory and union hierarchies from which blacks continued to be excluded. They remained barred until the racial strife of the late 1960s forced the union and the companies, jointly responsible for entry into the trades, to allow limited access. Opportunities for African Americans to fill production jobs on more than a token basis in the auto makers' southern plants awaited the passage and implementation of the nondiscrimination hiring guarantees in the Civil Rights Act of 1964. The force of law was required to break down the ancient barriers to equal access to employment in that region.[31]

The large Detroit locals with their contingents of black members were in the vanguard of the attack on racial discrimination both within and without the factory. Ford Local 600 had the best record on racial equity and harmony. Reflecting their important place in the plant's workforce, particularly in the foundry and several other large departments, African Americans had been active in the union since the local's beginning, holding elective offices and influencing the local's political positions and alignments. The local's social functions were conducted without racial discrimination. Like Local 600, Local 212, on Detroit's East Side, carried on a vigorous campaign of desegregating bars, restaurants, and other businesses in the plant's neighborhood. "We cannot effectively unite our members," the local's Fair Employment Practices Committee wrote, "and permit bigoted, narrow-minded cockroach businessmen to flagrantly practice discrimination right outside the plant." Integrated committees from the local called on the offending businesses to demand they change their ways, and boycotts of recalcitrant companies were organized. Thousands of auto workers from these and other locals, mostly blacks but also many whites, joined the Detroit branch of the National Association for the Advancement of Colored People making it the largest and one of the best-funded and most active chapters in the nation.[32]

In contrast, some other locals were indifferent or hostile to integrating social affairs and the community and business services patronized by members. Even in plants where workers of both races accepted working side-by-side at the same or similar jobs as the normal arrangement, and where union participation was open to those of all races, social occasions, particularly dances sponsored by a local, remained tense. Some UAW locals refused to sponsor dances because the officers did not want to face the resentment and possible political retaliation of those whites who opposed "mixed dancing." Other activities that challenged traditional social mores, such as the campaigns to desegregate restaurants and taverns near the plants, might also encounter white resistance. A celebratory Christmas holiday kiss between workmates on the Dodge assembly line, a gesture of friendship by a black man and a white woman that was perceived as a violation of the rule of sexual separation between the races, incited an explosion of racial hostility and resulted in a cruel and swift punishment for those involved.[33]

Racial segregation in local union recreation programs came under fire from both important locals and the International. In the 1930s and early 1940s the first UAW-sponsored softball and baseball teams were usually racially segregated in conformity with the rules of community leagues, but by the postwar era integrated sports teams had become the common arrangement. Bowling, a popular recreation among both white and black auto workers (and more fundamentally a social occasion than a baseball game, since eating, drinking and conviviality among the players were part of the activity) had remained racially segregated. Local 600 had begun to desegregate Detroit bowling alleys in 1941, sometimes putting up picket lines of more than a thousand. The American Bowling Congress (ABC), which sponsored the nation's major tournaments and limited team members to "the white male sex," was the greatest obstacle to progress. The UAW executive board condemned the racial restriction in 1944 and urged its repeal, but without result. Mounting an offensive, the union formed the National Committee for Fair Play in Bowling, demanded that the ABC change its policy, and refused to sanction participation by UAW teams in ABC tournaments. When the staff of the union's Recreation Department tried to persuade locals to boycott ABC tournaments, it encountered strong opposition. White bowlers, especially in but not limited to southern and border state locals, attacked the leadership's crusade. In 1948 the UAW, failing to persuade the ABC to remove the Jim Crow restriction from its constitution, started a new bowling league, a very unpopular step with large sections of the rank and file. A protest to Reuther on this issue from the troublesome Memphis International Harvester local contained a reminder, a veiled threat as well as a piece of advice: "Remember you are only President of the U.A.W. (C.I.O.) so please let President Truman handle the racial situation, also remember Mr. Thomas is out. Read your Bible and history." The issue was resolved when the union, in association with other interested parties, obtained a court decision in 1950 holding that racial discrimination by the ABC violated the terms of its charter, thus opening its tournaments to integrated teams and play.[34]

The UAW's response to racial segregation and discrimination reflected the differences over the issues within its ranks. Officially, the organization condemned racial inequities. Its efforts to remedy racial injustice through the mechanisms of national politics were second to none. Within the plants and in the locals, however, racial divides existed. The International Union pressured recalcitrant locals to conform to the union's principles but, concerned to avoid a schism, it did not act as quickly or firmly in some cases as it might have and as critics, then and later, wished it had. Racial wildcats were suppressed in cooperation with management's threat to fire strikers, a response that was adequate to put an end to hate strikes. Pressure was

A UAW bowling team, 1955. Walter P. Reuther Library, Wayne State University

exerted to end unfair practices such as separate seniority lists and "Jim Crow" facilities in union halls, but obstruction and delay were tolerated at times. The strong position and firm resolve of skilled tradesmen allowed them to maintain a near monopoly of these positions for whites, which the union leadership did little to combat. The response to racial injustice, in short, contained elements of both politics and principle. Where the International leadership had the political resources to enforce fairness without provoking a disruptive level of turmoil, it did so. Where the resources were in question, it applied pressure but temporized by withholding the full force of its disapproval.[35]

THE CONSERVATIVE POLITICAL MOOD that crystallized during the cold war era afforded opportunities for the liberal pioneering the UAW favored but little fulfillment. Repeatedly, the union's public objectives were thwarted. The conservative southerners who led the national Democratic Party in Congress were hostile to the UAW's reform agenda, and many Democrats from all regions, their patriotism under attack by the Republican opposition, shrank from embracing exposed liberal positions. Although the union continued to press its views, it was unable to break the hold of a conservative consensus.

Adlai E. Stevenson, the Democrats' presidential candidate in 1952 and 1956, received the support and endorsement of the UAW but was far from being a "labor candidate." Fearful that the Democratic Party would be tagged as a "labor party," he made it clear that as far as he was concerned there was much in the Taft-Hartley Act worthy of support, and he bluntly told ADA members that he did not share their views. Convinced that his only chance of winning was to regain the southern states that had deserted the Democrats in 1948, while maintaining a competitive position in the northeast, midwest and far west, he backed away from Truman's civil rights pledges and in 1952 selected a southern senator, John Sparkman of Alabama, as his running mate. Swallowing its disappointment with the positions Stevenson took on civil rights and labor law, the UAW strongly backed his campaign with money and volunteers. With Roy Reuther hitting his stride as the UAW's political organizer, the CIO-PAC raised substantially more money that it had in 1948, produced and distributed Stevenson campaign literature in abundance, and paid for three national television speeches in which Reuther endorsed the candidate. Stevenson's southern strategy worked in part but fell short of reaching the goal. He carried most of the southern states (including those that defected to the Dixiecrats in 1948), but he lost to the popular former general Dwight D. Eisenhower everywhere else (442 electoral votes to 89). The 75 percent vote for Stevenson of those UAW members who participated far exceeded the Democratic vote percentage generally, but it was well below the 89 percent of their votes that Truman received in 1948. At the next Democratic party convention in 1956, Reuther and Joseph L. Rauh, Jr., the union's Washington attorney, sought without success to strengthen the platform's civil rights plank by endorsing the immediate implementation of the Supreme Court's decisions desegregating schools and other public institutions, a position that was anathema to the party's southern wing and opposed to Stevenson's wishes. With Republicans controlling the presidency from Eisenhower's inauguration in 1953 until the conclusion of his second term in 1961, and with Texas Democratic Senator Lyndon B. Johnson—a consensus politician who was determined to prevent wedge issues from dividing his party—the Senate majority leader for most of the decade, the prospects for passage of the legislation the UAW favored were dim to nonexistent.[36]

The union advanced and defended its agenda in Washington but had few results to show for its efforts. The national planning mechanism its leadership believed essential for an economy of abundance had few champions and many opponents in a business-dominated administration and Congress. Its proposals to stimulate growth and reduce unemployment in an economy plagued by periodic recessions, which hit hard in the auto cities, failed to win congressional or administration support. An attack on "administered prices" in the auto industry, which the union charged effectively priced new cars out of the reach of many potential buyers, produced a congressional investigation but no legislation. A broad program of federal aid to education, including funding for school construction, teachers' salaries, scholarships for college students, and programs for gifted children, met a similar fate. Prospects at first seemed better for the Fair Deal legislation Truman proposed to Congress after his reelection, but the southern Democrat-Republican coalition blocked passage, and rampant McCarthyism terrorized liberal Democrats. Despite the odds against success, the UAW supported Fair Deal proposals, going beyond them in numerous instances, only to suffer defeat. Foremost was the struggle for civil rights legislation including establishment of a permanent Fair Employment Practices commission, abolition of the poll tax in federal elections, and a law to make lynching a federal crime.[37]

The key to passage of civil rights legislation lay in limiting the filibuster, the rule that allowed unlimited "debate" in the Senate thereby permitting a minority to talk a bill to death. With the UAW's chief lobbyist Paul Sifton coordinating the scheme, a proposal was put forward to change the Senate's rules by lowering the required margin for cloture, the rule to set a time limit on debate, from a two-thirds vote of those senators present and voting to a simple majority. The change would have made passage of civil rights bills a realistic possibility, but the plan backfired when the Dixiecrats and Senate Republicans joined to adopt a new cloture rule requiring the approval of two-thirds of the entire Senate. Instead of facilitating enactment of civil rights legislation, the bar to its passage had been significantly raised. With a successful filibuster now a foregone conclusion, most of President Truman's civil rights bills died in committee. The following year, 1950, a fair employment practices bill reached the floor of the Senate, where it was killed by a filibuster.[38]

In 1949 anti-civil rights forces in the Senate moved aggressively to lock in the filibuster by changing the cloture rule, Senate Rule XXII, to read that there could be no cloture vote on a motion to change Rule XXII itself. The rule was now placed beyond reach; there would have to be unanimous consent among senators to bring about any change in it. Working through the Leadership Conference on Civil Rights (LCCR), which it helped organize, and cooperating with the National Association for the Advancement of Colored People (NAACP) and other civil rights organizations, the UAW coordinated the attack on Rule XXII. Paul Sifton took the case to the Senate while UAW attorney Joseph L. Rauh, Jr., devised the argument. Rauh maintained that the Senate was not a continuing body from one session to the next but started afresh at the outset of each session and therefore could adopt new rules, including a different Rule XXII, by a simple majority vote. The maneuver produced near hysteria among some southern Democrats, one senator calling this application of the principle of majority rule the "death blow to our institutions of government." The UAW and the LCCR persuaded liberal senators to introduce a motion at the opening of the 82nd Congress in 1953 to alter Rule XXII, but the southern Democrat-Republican coalition held firm to administer the motion an overwhelming defeat. A second attempt in 1955 ignominiously ended when a number of liberal senators, choosing not to defy Senate majority leader Johnson, who wielded the power of committee appointments and threatened to use it against them, withdrew their support for the motion. Consequently, civil rights legislation had little chance of reaching the floor of the Senate in the first half of the 1950s.[39]

The second half of the decade seemed to hold more promise for a civil rights program. The union had supported the NAACP's attack on school segregation in *Brown* and related desegregation cases with amicus curiae briefs, and it offered moral and financial support to the Montgomery bus boycott, Martin Luther King, and the Southern Christian Leadership Conference. LCCR expanded its civil rights agenda. It endorsed the Eisenhower administration's mild civil rights proposal, which failed of passage in 1956 owing to Johnson's opposition. The union's civil rights initiative suffered a setback in the 1956 Democratic platform's vague, innocuous civil rights plank. In 1957 the LCCR and the UAW supported passage of an emasculated Eisenhower civil rights bill, which contained a fatally weakening provision that authorized jury trials in southern courtrooms for those accused of civil rights violations. Weak as it was, the bill was still the first civil rights legislation passed since Reconstruction. A second civil rights bill in 1960, intended to protect voting rights, was, in Reuther's words to the executive board, "nothing to be proud of. It is a feeble step forward when we ought to be taking giant strides." For all the effort (Reuther claimed the UAW had done more to support strong civil rights legislation than any other organization aside from the NAACP), the record of accomplishment was very thin. It came as no surprise that the failure of a Congress in thrall to racially conservative forces pushed the civil rights movement into the streets.[40]

In Michigan the UAW was a primary force in efforts to enact civil rights legislation. G. Mennen Williams, governor from 1948 to 1960, was deeply and enduringly committed to equal rights for all the state's citizens. He fashioned a coalition of liberal, religious, minority, and labor organizations—with the UAW a key element—that attacked discriminatory racial practices and sought remedies through legislation. The first and most important objective was a fair employment practices law to guarantee equal access to jobs and fair treatment at work. Williams secured the introduction of a bill in 1949; six years of public pressure, parliamentary maneuvering, and weakening compromises were required to move the state legislature, grossly malapportioned and dominated by members from rural and small-town "rotten boroughs," to enact a law. Although craft unions were either opposed or indifferent to enactment, the state's industrial unions, led by the UAW, gave consistent and ardent support. Ed Carey, a former UAW member and Chrysler employee and now leader of the Democrats in the Michigan House of Representatives, was one of the chief craftsmen of the bill, which barred employment discrimination on grounds of race, religion, nationality, and ancestry, and set up a Fair Employment Practices Commission (FEPC) with enforcement powers. On other state issues, the UAW strongly advocated a graduated income tax, although it finally was able to obtain only a flat rate tax, and it planned and helped finance the challenge in the courts to the malapportioned state Senate that eventually led, joined with other cases, to the U.S. Supreme Court's "one man-one vote" decision. The decision mandated legislative redistricting that gave the state's urban and suburban areas a fair share of representation. Outside of Michigan, UAW locals in a number of midwestern cities supported municipal FEPC campaigns.[41]

Among the Fair Deal issues was publicly-supported housing, a subject in which Reuther and other UAW leaders had a long and serious interest. The wartime housing crisis in overcrowded Detroit alerted the union to the need for a rapid expansion of available housing. A devoted family man, Reuther believed that every worker's family deserved a comfortable, secure, and attractive home. On many occasions he sought to use the UAW as a platform to launch large-scale public housing projects. At the end of World War II he proposed to utilize vacant war plants to mass-produce prefabricated houses, providing not only houses but jobs for displaced war workers. A government corporation similar to the Tennessee Valley Authority, he recommended, should be established to determine which factories could be adapted for the purpose. The facilities could then be operated by the corporation or leased to private manufacturers or workers' cooperatives. In 1945 he wrote that "the same mass production miracles which have made us a nation on wheels can place a modern, durable, healthy home within the economic reach of the common man. . . . The entire vicious circle of primitive methods and restrictive practices in the building industry can be broken." Such words did not endear him to building tradesmen and contractors, but he never conceded that anything less than mass production methods would solve the problem of outworn, inadequate housing. In 1949, testifying before the Senate as chairman of the CIO National Housing Committee, he argued that thousands of two-bedroom houses could be erected by establishing a self-replenishing revolving fund that would initially require a government investment of $500 million. Truman's Fair Deal housing proposal was a much more modest program of slum clearance and mixed public-private development. The UAW and CIO backed the Truman plan but wanted to go beyond it with their new version of a prefabricated housing program. The UAW-CIO plan received little support elsewhere and, in the event, only a watered-down version of the Truman plan survived congressional scrutiny.[42]

IN PART BECAUSE OF REUTHER'S personal interest in working and union conditions in other countries, and in part owing to the global nature of automobile manufacturing, the UAW became one of the nation's most active unions in the international arena. To rebuild Europe's war-torn economy, integrate it into an American-led international trading system, and construct a barrier to the U.S.S.R.'s westward penetration beyond the boundaries of its eastern European satellites, the Truman administration in 1947 proposed the Marshall Plan, consisting of nearly $20 billion in economic aid. The Soviet government reacted negatively, and American Communists and their sympathizers, including those in CIO unions, condemned the Marshall Plan as another instance of American imperialism. Crippling strikes, led by Communist-affiliated unions, broke out in Italy and France in opposition to acceptance of Marshall Plan aid. To Reuther, whose close concern with the fate of labor in western Europe could be traced to his personal witness of Hitler's destruction of the German trade unions, these actions betrayed the cause of free labor. He believed the United States had to encourage the development of stable, open economies abroad in which independent unions could take root and flourish. Upset with excessive business influence on aid policies and decisions, and with the AFL's anticommunist obsession, Reuther devised through the CIO a European trade union support activity detached from the AFL and at arm's length from the government. In 1951 the CIO opened an office in Paris under the direction of Victor Reuther to encourage and strengthen a democratic trade union movement in Europe free from Communist control. The CIO's approach, in the words of a leading academic student of the subject, "tended to be more sensitive than other American groups to the traditional values of European labour and cautioned government representatives against the blanket export of American labour relations norms and standards."[43]

In 1949 a new organization, the International Confederation of Free Trade Unions (ICFTU), was formed, with both CIO and AFL participation. Reuther was a CIO delegate to its first convention and served as chairman of a committee that drew up its manifesto on the basic rights to "bread, peace, and freedom." He had to guard against the attempts of the AFL, which ran an active and relatively well-financed operation in Europe largely under the control of Jay Lovestone, the UAW's old nemesis, to turn the ICFTU into a rigid anticommunist bloc with little by way of program beyond opposition to the U.S.S.R.[44]

Reuther's desire to support noncommunist unions in Western Europe led him in one instance to become a disburser of US government funds. With Communist-controlled unions providing strong competition to noncommunist organizations, the Central Intelligence Agency sought covers for its subsidization of noncommunist unions, asking the Reuthers in 1952 to channel $50,000 of the agency's funds through the CIO to them. According to Victor Reuther's recollection, they "reluctantly" agreed. The money went to unions in France and Italy, countries where Communist-controlled rival unions were particularly strong. When this episode became public knowledge in 1967 it caused the Reuthers, who had been critical of the AFL-CIO's government-supported overseas operations, considerable embarrassment.[45]

While opposing and strongly criticizing denials of personal liberties in Communist-controlled nations, including denial of the right to found and join a free union, Reuther rejected the simplistic and self-defeating argument that an anticommunist stance alone entitled another nation to American support. He frequently criticized both the AFL's foreign policy positions and those of the United States government for a blind anticommunism that failed to distinguish between democratic and authoritarian regimes. "The chief weakness of American foreign policy," he wrote in a 1948 article, "is the predilection of our State Department for dealing with anybody who will promise to hate Communism. It is fatal to resist Communism by courting reaction." Both American foreign policy and trade unions in foreign countries, he argued, should aim to encourage the positive results that would flow from a free economy and society, countering the false promises of the Soviet Union by building the free, democratic institutions that would bring genuine, lasting progress. Taking issue with those on both sides of the Iron Curtain who divided the world between two rigid, monolithic blocks, he denied that the choice before humankind and nations was limited to Communism or capitalism. A third way, a social-democratic state created through democratic political means and including strong, free unions, was possible and superior to either. As he put it on several occasions, "we have got to make it clear that the choice in the world is not between Stalin and Standard Oil, that the choice is between freedom and dictatorship." Reuther criticized the dangerous tendency of anticommunist zealots to cast aside all restraint and sink into a destructive monomania. "I've been preaching for years," he told a reporter, "that you can't lick the Communists with hysteria. You've got to have a positive program to do the job."[46]

A MAJOR ISSUE FACING THE UAW in the 1950s was the question of labor unity. The division over industrial versus craft organization that originally split the AFL and the CIO was long since resolved. The CIO industrial unions were now established on the economic scene, and several large AFL affiliates, such as the Teamsters, Machinists, and Ladies' Garment Workers, were primarily industrial in nature. The deaths in 1952 of two of the original combatants, president Philip Murray of the CIO and president William Green of the AFL, removed an obstacle to reconciliation. Murray was replaced by Reuther and Green by the AFL's secretary-treasurer, George Meany, neither of whom had been caught up in the bitterness of the split. The disadvantages in having two competing labor federations were demonstrated daily. Organizing workers into unions was sufficiently challenging without adding inter-union rivalry and raiding into the mixture. Several major organizing drives planned for the postwar years, especially a massive CIO campaign in the South—intended to give the union movement national, not merely regional, scope—bogged down. The passage of the Taft-Hartley Act in 1947 demonstrated the labor movement's political vulnerability. Perhaps similar setbacks in the future could be averted through mobilization of a united front.[47]

Both Meany and Reuther pronounced in favor of unity shortly after their elections respectively as AFL and CIO presidents. There was opposition within the UAW from those who saw the AFL as unimaginative, wedded to conservative business unionism, and lacking a dynamic social reform commitment. UAW support for unity was conditioned on AFL progress in disciplining and, if necessary, expelling corrupt or gangster-ridden unions. Reuther also insisted that a united federation must commit itself to eliminating racial discrimination within the movement, still a problem in some AFL affiliates. These conditions satisfied some of the UAW critics, but an uneasy suspicion that a reuniting of labor would dull the UAW's crusading edge remained. The reform spirit of the CIO would be diluted, these critics feared, when labor policy had to clear an executive council of craft unionists under Meany's control. The AFL unions, with about twice the membership of the CIO, would dominate the new federation no matter how hard Reuther and other progressive unionists pushed liberal causes. Events soon revealed the merit in these reservations.[48]

With a no-raiding pact between AFL and CIO unions negotiated in 1953 as a first step, on February 9, 1955, Meany and Reuther announced that agreement on a merger had been reached. In the new AFL-CIO the affiliated unions' autonomy and integrity were guaranteed, and each retained its existing jurisdiction. Where jurisdictions overlapped, merger would be encouraged but not forced. A no-raiding agreement would be maintained on a voluntary basis. Along with the separate departments of the AFL, a new Industrial Union Department (IUD) was established with Reuther as its president, giving CIO industrial unions a formal place in the organization's structure. Reuther expected that the IUD would become the dynamic force within the federation, driving a united and enlarged labor movement along the path to social democracy.[49]

The program to which Reuther and Meany pledged themselves reflected the UAW's ideas, but the means of reaching the goals were in several instances left unclear and unspecified. The federation itself would become active in organizing the unorganized, a task Meany believed should be left to the affiliates. It would launch a campaign against racketeering, guarantee equal treatment and the benefits of organization to workers regardless of race, and protect the union movement from "the undermining efforts of the Communist agencies and all others who are opposed to the basic principles of our democracy and of free and democratic unionism." Reuther believed that a merged labor movement had to face up to the most difficult and important challenge of all: it had to take on the task of "unionizing the organized, of making the millions of workers in America who have trade union cards in their pockets understand what trade unionism means in their hearts." The decline in the movement's morale and its loss of vigor were controversial subjects, but Reuther and many others realized that much needed to be done to restore its fighting spirit. Memories of the struggles undertaken in the 1930s to establish a strong labor movement were fading. Millions of new members had entered labor organizations with little or no recollection of preunion working conditions and wages or of the sacrifices, courage, and determination that had gone into creating and nurturing the unions. Since they took the achievements of the past for granted, the consciousness of these workers had to be raised to revive the crusading spirit of the CIO's early days. Unfortunately, exactly how this daunting task could be accomplished in an age of spreading contentment and apathy was by no means clear.[50]

There was never any question that Meany would become president of the AFL-CIO. Not only did the AFL unions bring more members into the new federation, but Meany, unlike Reuther, had no independent base outside it. For the time being, the new organization required full-time attention, which Meany could provide, and Reuther realized it would be foolish, even if possible, to exchange the presidency of the UAW for that of the AFL-CIO. In the long run, to guard against the impact of AFL conservatism, Reuther could reasonably expect that at some future time he would become the federation's president. Sixty years old, Meany was more than ten years senior to Reuther. His retirement at a normal age would open the way for the succession of Reuther or a like-minded colleague. The expectation, suspected and much resented by Meany, proved to be wishful thinking.[51]

Even before the merger was consummated, Meany and Reuther differed over issues of foreign policy. Meany relied on Jay Lovestone, the rigid anticommunist and antagonist of the UAW's left in the 1930s, for foreign policy direction. Like Lovestone, Meany divided the world into two camps: there were supporters and there were opponents of Communism; everyone was on one side or the other. Meany particularly scorned neutralists who tried to protect their nations and reduce tensions by allying with neither of the two superpowers. Soon after he became AFL-CIO president, Meany denounced Prime Minister Nehru of India and Marshal Tito of Yugoslavia (the latter had broken decisively with the U.S.S.R. in 1948) as "aides and allies [of Communism] in fact and in effect, if not in diplomatic verbiage." Reuther stood for a more nuanced, less simplistic, analysis of world affairs. Though firm in opposing Communist totalitarianism and the threat of Soviet aggrandizement, he did not believe that fervent anticommunism, militarism, and undeviating support for American foreign policy was the wisest course to follow. His views soon brought him into conflict with George Meany. Shortly after Meany's public criticism of Nehru, Reuther visited India. In public statements there and on his return he described Nehru as "truly one of the great statesmen of the world" and criticized United States policy in Asia for placing "undue emphasis upon military power, military pacts, and military alliances. This . . . has, in my opinion, tended to trade reliable democratic friends for doubtful military allies." He repeated his often-expressed view that "military preparedness is but the negative aspect of a dynamic foreign policy. I believe that the struggle between freedom and tyranny is essentially a struggle for men's minds, and their hearts, and their loyalties, and that such a struggle cannot be won with military power but rather by a positive peacetime program of economic and social construction." "Freedom's struggle in Asia," he added, "will be won primarily in the rice fields and not in the battlefields." By showing the Indian government and people that an influential American labor leader recognized and appreciated their commitment to democracy, independence, and neutrality, Reuther's well-publicized remarks were, as an Indian newspaper wrote, "a most welcome whiff of fresh air," but they did nothing to endear Reuther to George Meany. The neutrality question was only the first of many issues, both foreign and domestic, on which the two would differ.[52]

To give substance to his belief that world peace depended on a vast and continuing sharing of resources, skills, and wealth, Reuther proposed that the United States pledge 2 percent of its gross national product for a period of twenty-five years to a United Nations-administered fund to assist less developed nations in improving their standards of living, health, and education. The U.S.S.R. and other industrialized nations would be challenged to do the same, launching, he hoped, an era of peaceful competitive coexistence. Reuther also proposed the establishment of a United Nations task force of skilled, idealistic young Americans to provide technical and educational assistance to other countries, the germ of the Peace Corps later established by President John F. Kennedy. "The more young Americans we send throughout the world as technical missionaries with slide rules, with medical kits, with textbooks, to fight Communism on a positive basis," he told an educator's conference in 1956, "the fewer young Americans we will need to send with guns and flame-throwers to fight Communism on the battlefields of the world." He elaborated on and championed this proposal through the rest of the decade. Reuther also supported a food-for-peace program utilizing American farm surpluses. American economic aid, he believed, should "be made available to every free and independent nation without any political strings whatsoever," a formula that included nonaligned nations like India but omitted those in the Communist bloc. Once again proposing to channel action through the UN, he suggested formation of a permanent multinational "voluntary police force" that could be dispatched to trouble spots for peacekeeping purposes. The immediate stimulus for the recommendation, which anticipated a direction the UN would ultimately take, was the brutal Soviet suppression of the Hungarian uprising in 1956.[53]

The differences between Meany and Reuther were sharply and publicly drawn in their disagreement over the wisdom of meeting with Nikita Khrushchev and Anastas Mikoyan during the Soviet leaders' visits to the United States in 1959. Meany refused to meet with them in any forum because to do so, he argued, would endorse their captive, state-controlled workers' organizations. Reuther thought the Soviet leaders should be confronted directly by representatives of American workers so they would know the full measure of workers' objections to their principles and policies. At a dinner that Meany refused to attend, Khrushchev and Reuther engaged in acrimonious exchanges on a broad range of topics, from the nature of Soviet society, to American foreign policy, to the vulgarities and corruptions (in Khrushchev's view) of American popular culture, particularly as created and disseminated by Hollywood. Khrushchev was so upset by Reuther's well-publicized, aggressive debate tactics that, following his return to the Soviet Union, the newspaper *Trud*, the Soviet trade union journal, denounced Reuther as a "traitor" to the workers' cause and a "lackey" of monopolistic capitalists, and published an interview that charged him with bigamy for having married, and then abandoned, a Russian woman during his sojourn there. The undocumented charges were denounced by Reuther as lies. At his summit meeting in Vienna in 1961 with President John F. Kennedy, a grim Khrushchev, expressing his contempt for social democrats, told the president, "We hung the likes of Reuther in Russia in 1917."[54]

Meany's and Reuther's disagreements over policy and principle were aggravated by personal conflicts. Meany resented what he saw as Reuther's attempts to usurp his authority, and he disliked Reuther's aloofness and austere code of personal conduct. Nor did Reuther's censorious judgments please colleagues on the AFL-CIO's executive council. At one of the council's first meetings that he attended, Reuther asked the assembled labor chieftains, gathered in an opulent Miami Beach hotel, if they wished to "wallow in luxury like a bunch of capitalists?" One looked up and growled a one-word reply, "Yeah." In 1959 Reuther complained to the UAW's executive board: "We don't have a labor movement. We have a club. It is a very exclusive club; stays in the best hotels, in the finest resorts. . . . But it isn't doing a job."[55]

THE UAW's POLITICAL PROGRAM and well-publicized activities exposed it to almost constant attack in the 1950s from one direction or another. Although the union itself and its effectiveness were the ultimate targets, Reuther, as the union's prominent head, bore the brunt of this campaign. The FBI's J. Edgar Hoover, despite the evidence of Reuther's anticommunist position and convictions, never wavered in his belief that Reuther was a Communist. On several occasions Hoover, operating behind the scenes, blocked Reuther's appointment to important government committees and advisory bodies by planting suspicions of his ideological orthodoxy and loyalty. Early in 1957 antiunion forces in the Senate went on the offensive when that body established a special committee under the chairmanship of Senator John McClellan, Democrat of Arkansas, to investigate "criminal or other improper practices or activities . . . in the field of labor-management relations." Although most labor leaders opposed the investigations as an attempt to smear honest labor organizations, Reuther took the position that corruption should be exposed wherever it existed by whatever means necessary. He urged, however, that equal attention be devoted to corruption within management, advising the committee, "Go after the crooks in the labor movement, but go after the crooks in management's side of the problem. When you find a crooked labor leader who took a bribe from a crooked employer, put them both in jail for about fifteen years and give them plenty of time to talk it over between themselves." The committee, focusing its investigation on labor leaders, declined to follow Reuther's suggestion. In the view of the committee's counsel, Robert F. Kennedy, who first met and gained respect for Reuther during the hearings, several of the committee's Republican members hoped to "get" the UAW because of its actions in a bitter strike against the Kohler Company of Sheboygan, Wisconsin. They hoped to bring down Reuther and cut the UAW down to size (the hearings would bring down Dave Beck as head of the Teamsters' union and ultimately lead to the trial and imprisonment of Beck's successor, Jimmy Hoffa). These hopes were disappointed because Reuther proved to be both a highly effective, even aggressive, witness and an honest man running a union in an honest way. No charges

were ever brought against Reuther although the committee scrutinized his
and the union's financial records, including individual items in his expense
account right down to his modest dry cleaning bill, with a fine-tooth comb.
The committee's expert accountant testified that he had never seen a more
carefully kept set of books than those of the UAW. As the *New York Times*
noted, the committee uncovered no evidence of corruption in the UAW, and
the paper's editorial went on to give Reuther high marks for his convincing,
forthright testimony.[56]

Although Reuther emerged from the hearings with a clean bill of
health, he and the UAW figured in a well-publicized committee side excur-
sion. Senator Barry Goldwater (Republican, Arizona) and two other Republican members of the committee insisted on an investigation of the strike
of UAW Local 833 against the Kohler Company—a Wisconsin manufacturer
of bathroom fixtures—the nation's longest major labor dispute of the postwar decades. The UAW had won a representation election at Kohler, but
contract negotiations had broken down. The strike began in April 1954,
with over 2,500 workers on the picket lines, and lasted until September
1960, although the company, which had obtained an injunction, reopened
after fifty-four days with scab labor. Beatings of nonstriking Kohler workers by two members of a Detroit UAW local were the focus of the committee's investigation. The two men testified that the local paid them to go to
Wisconsin and support the strikers but gave them no instructions. One got
into a fight in a bar with a nonstriking Kohler worker, for which he served
thirteen months on an assault conviction. While he was in jail, the UAW
helped support his family and paid for his lawyer. The other attacked a non-
striker who was working in a service station as well as his father, knocking
both unconscious. A warrant was issued for his arrest, but he returned to
Michigan, and Governor G. Mennen Williams refused extradition without
assurances of a fair trial. In his testimony, Reuther deplored the beatings
and conceded that the Detroit local was at fault in failing to control its
agents. There was no evidence that UAW officers had ordered the attacks.
Reuther argued that the Michigan suspect should be extradited to Wisconsin when the authorities there agreed to a change of venue. Eventually that
was done, the assailant was tried, convicted, and served eighteen months
in prison. After the strike ended, the UAW pressed cases before the National
Labor Relations Board (NLRB) to win reinstatement, back pay, and pension
credits for discharged strikers. In 1962 a new contract was ratified, and two
years later the NLRB found Kohler guilty of causing and prolonging the
strike. A year later, in 1965, a settlement of the twelve-year struggle was
negotiated, which included reinstatement of fired strikers and a $4.5 mil-
lion fund for back pay and pension credits. Through the course of the strike,
the UAW paid out more than $12 million in strike benefits. Following the

"Sweetiepie, Tell Us Little Old Judges In Your Own Words What A Scoundrel That Reuther Is"

"Sweetiepie, Tell Us Little Old Judges in Your Own Words What a Scoundrel that Reuther Is." From Herblock's *Special for Today* (Simon & Schuster, 1958)

conclusion of Reuther's committee testimony, Goldwater privately remarked to Robert F. Kennedy concerning the Kohler hearings, "You were right. We never should have gotten into this matter."[57]

Reuther often seized the initiative during his questioning by the committee, particularly in a series of sharp exchanges with Senator Goldwater. At one point he proposed that he and Goldwater each select three clergymen as members of a panel to judge the merits of the charges they had hurled at each other. Goldwater declined. The UAW leader brought up a television statement of Goldwater's in which the senator said that Kohler had a "right not to have a union if he can win a strike." Reuther made the remark the occasion for a lecture to the senator, pointing out that "only the employees under the law of these United States can make a decision whether they want a union and which union. An employer cannot make that decision without violating the law." "I would like to know," he persisted, "whether you think under the Taft-Hartley law a company can decide not to have a union and destroy that union? I maintain they can't." Goldwater dodged the question and tried to change the subject. "I will tell you what," he said, "someday you and I are going to get together and lock horns." He then reminded Reuther that witnesses were not supposed to ask questions at committee hearings. Not long after this confrontation Goldwater informed a Detroit audience that "Walter Reuther and the UAW-CIO are a more dangerous menace than the Sputnik or anything Soviet Russia might do to America." But, as often happened in these public encounters, Reuther had the last word. In a nationally televised interview with Mike Wallace in 1960, he responded to a question about Goldwater with the acid remark, "Well, you see, I have nothing against Goldwater. I think he has the finest eighteenth-century mind in the U.S. Senate."[58]

Although the UAW and its president emerged relatively unscathed from the hearings, the political attacks continued. In the 1958 midterm elections they became the prime target of a campaign to "fight the labor bosses." Hoping to capitalize on the antiunion sentiment generated by the committee, some Republican candidates and party officials launched a slanderous attack, concentrating on California, Ohio, and other states with antiunion right-to-work referenda on the ballot and large numbers of congressmen. Republican Senator William F. Knowland, running for governor of California, circulated a pamphlet (later withdrawn) on Reuther entitled, "Meet the Man Who Plans to Rule America." The ancient charge that Reuther championed a Soviet America, based on a forgery, supported by no positive evidence, and belied by years of anticommunist rhetoric and actions, was revived and given wide currency in newspaper ads and elsewhere. Vice President Richard M. Nixon complained that money was being diverted from needy Republican candidates to fund inane propaganda. "There is more money wasted by big business on screwball committees and pamphleteers," he told reporters, "than the Republican party gets in a campaign." Significant financial support for the smear effort came from Donaldson Brown and C. S. Mott, both members of the General Motors Corporation board of directors. The antiunion campaign seems to have had little if any effect on the outcome of the 1958 elections. Thanks to both a

"Comrade!" 1959. *St. Louis Post-Dispatch.*

national recession and a vigorous UAW counterattack, the liberal contingent in Congress emerged from the elections much enlarged and strengthened. Republican losses in Congress were their worst since the Roosevelt landslide of 1936, resulting in Democratic majorities in both houses that approached two-thirds. The right-to-work referenda went down to decisive defeat in all states where they were on the ballot—with the exception of Kansas—and the ballot proposals received some of the credit for drawing a large turnout of Democratic and union voters.[59]

BOTH AS A REPRESENTATIVE of a leading American labor organization and by drawing on his own talents as a public figure, Reuther gave the UAW in particular and American labor in general a visible national and international presence and witness. No American union or its leader was better or more favorably known abroad in labor and working-class circles. In 1957 Reuther delivered a speech to the British Trade Union Congress of which the *London Daily Express* wrote, "No overseas visitor in living memory has made such an immense impact by his personality and tempestuous oratory." In 1959 he delivered a similarly rousing address on May Day in Berlin, to a gathering of hundreds of thousands, assuring the residents of the surrounded, embattled city, "You do not stand alone. Your American trade union colleagues stand firmly with you." Only fifteen minutes in length, it was one of the briefest, but most stirring, of his speeches. He spoke in carefully rehearsed German, "which delighted the crowd."[60]

The 1950s, a decade of consensus and conservatism, saw the UAW fighting an action on two fronts, both in the vanguard of social change and in warding off hostile attacks. On most of the public issues that mattered to the UAW, national politics was locked in a stalemate, unable to go forward and unwilling to retreat. The major objective of combining all noncommunist progressives into a national political party, still on the agenda, was unrealized. Southern conservatives, entrenched in power in Congress by virtue of the seniority principle and in the Democratic Party's councils, still exercised a veto over any action taken by the Democrats, while the Republicans, drawn to anticommunist excesses since the beginning of the decade, were more remote than ever from a progressive perspective.

Critics have argued that the UAW's close tie to the Democratic Party was a one-way street in which the union expended its political substance but received little in return, with the implication that a political alternative—a labor party or independent action—would have been more productive. Perhaps so. Such speculations cannot be conclusively disproved. While it is true the UAW failed to achieve most of its political and legislative objectives, it was able to defend itself against the attacks of opponents, and it survived the 1950s with its fighting spirit and determination intact. Politics may have brought more frustration than fulfillment, but the prospect of a new decade and new national leadership kindled hopes for a progressive resurgence.[61]

CHAPTER 10

"Some frosting on the Chrysler birthday cake"

New Frontiers in Bargaining, 1960–68

A S THE 1950S DREW TO A CLOSE THE AMERICAN AUTOMOTIVE industry and the auto workers' union stood on the threshold of a global economic revolution that would transform them in coming decades. From the beginning, the American auto market was dominated by American-owned and -managed companies, and American workers supplied the labor that built the cars. This was about to change. A competitive international auto market was taking shape as foreign manufacturers, rebuilding after the destruction wrought by World War II, challenged the American manufacturers' at home. Exploiting the failure of U.S. companies to offer small, reliable, and relatively inexpensive vehicles, first Volkswagen, followed in a few years by a parade of Japanese and other imports, established a beachhead in the American market, which in time would expand to include a full range of models, from the plain and economical to the most luxurious and expensive. By 1959, 10 percent of the cars sold in the United States were imports, and the popularity of small cars had forced the American manufacturers to respond with compacts of their own. This American counterattack temporarily stemmed the import tide, but by the end of the 1960s foreign manufacturers claimed 15 percent of U.S. passenger car sales. Eventually one-third of American domestic vehicle sales would consist of those produced by foreign-owned companies, either manufactured abroad for export or in "transplant" factories located in the United States. With more price and product competition in the marketplace, higher costs could no longer be so readily passed through to consumers. Manufacturers came under greater pressure to restrain cost increases and strive for greater efficiency. The aggregate American auto market expanded significantly in the 1960s, and in good years manufacturers could sell all the cars they produced. Consequently, the full impact of the new competition was not immediately felt. For the time being, the bargaining environment for the UAW remained favorable, but by the end of the decade auto workers recognized that both restraint and a reordering of priorities were necessary. Henceforth, raising wages and benefits would yield to bargaining objectives that promoted job and income protection. As Reuther warned a UAW skilled-trades conference, American auto workers had reduced bargaining power. Contrasting auto work with the building trades, he said: "They have a monopoly. You can't build a skyscraper that you need in New York in Japan, but you can build automobiles in Japan and you can make tools and dies in Japan, or you can make them in Germany." These could all be made elsewhere and sold in the United States.[1]

WHILE THE UAW CONTINUED to press for higher wages, better benefits, and other compensation enhancements, negotiations in the 1960s, responding to an insistent rank-and-file demand, put greater emphasis on improving working conditions. By the end of the decade the union's number one bargaining priority was a lower retirement age with full pension eligibility, attractive primarily because it permitted an earlier escape for thousands from the stressful, unsatisfying character of many factory jobs. Working conditions also drew attention because the corporations' ceaseless quest for lower costs through the introduction of automated machinery and processes required retiming and rescheduling of jobs and the setting of new pay rates. Devising equitable adjustments in workload in an environment of rapid technical change was a tremendous challenge. The proliferation of models, as firms sought to blanket the market with a product for every taste and pocketbook, required modifications in assembly procedures that raised more questions of job timing, scheduling, and rates. Production innovations generated a torrent of speedup charges, unlike anything seen since the union's early days. The number of grievances filed soared. Despite the gains the union had made on the shop floor, foremen, under pressure to produce, could still abuse employees and put their safety at risk. In a Ford plant in 1964, as only one example, a group of workers, including local union officers, protested and blocked operation of an unguarded welding machine that discharged electric flashes, demanding that a shield be put in place to protect the operator. Their position was supported by the plant's safety engineer. The foreman, however, shouted at the operator, "F___ the UAW, run this stock (drive shaft) and if they get in your way knock them down with it." When the stock rack ran low the foreman ordered a Hi-Lo operator to "come on in . . . and run over them if they don't get out of your way." Although the foreman was reprimanded by management, he continued to display an "arrogant attitude." "We sincerely believe," the local's president reported with remarkable restraint to the UAW's Ford Department director, "this touches on the issue of humanizing the plants."[2]

Lead soldering a car body in a Ford plant, 1964. Walter P. Reuther Library, Wayne State University

Especially at General Motors, tension between workers and management increased, and the number of demands made by local unions dealing with working conditions issues rose sharply. Local bargaining, a General Motors statement conceded, had "become an increasingly difficult problem." At GM the sum of local demands leaped upward with each contract expiration, from 11,600 in 1958, to 19,000 in 1961, 24,000 in 1964, 31,000 in 1967, and 39,000 in 1970. Local shop floor issues delayed settlements and caused strikes to be extended at many plants. According to a General Motors calculation, from 1958 to 1976 more than 100 million hours of labor were lost in its plants due to strikes over local demands. Although many of these strikes were of short duration, there were exceptions. In 1969–70 a strike by 3,500 members of Local 598 at Fisher Body Plant Number 2 in Flint lasted 136 days, the longest walkout over local plant issues in GM's history to that time. At issue were the speed of the assembly line and the number of workers needed to operate it. Local demands ranged over issues of work pace, health and safety, seniority rules, wage and shift preference agreements, cafeterias, parking lots, locker rooms, washing facilities, and a host of other day-to-day matters. Although media reportage of these disputes was often dismissive and patronizing, local issues arising within the broad universe of job conditions and factory culture often meant as much or more to those affected than the highly publicized wage and benefit compensation gains that dominated the national negotiations, a valid assessment as acknowledged by the union's leadership. Asserting that the contracts bargained at the plants by shop committees intimately acquainted with the problems was an essential element of industrial democracy, Reuther called the local contracts the UAW's "greatest contribution" to its members' welfare. They had given the men and women in the plants "some voice with respect to the conditions of their employment" and a "feeling of worth and dignity inside the factories."[3]

A General Motors' reorganization of its assembly operations worsened working conditions and racheted up tensions. In 1965, as part of a defensive strategy against a pending antitrust court decision that threatened to divide GM into its separate manufacturing divisions, the corporation removed assembly operations from the divisions and placed them in the hands of a new General Motors Assembly Division, appropriately dubbed GMAD. For the rest of the decade GMAD absorbed and merged assembly operations from Chevrolet and other GM divisions and folded Fisher Body plants, previously separately organized, into the combined operations. New, hard-driving managers reclassified jobs and reorganized assembly lines to reduce labor and speed up production, provoking a workers' rebellion. Strikes erupted in eight of the first ten plants GMAD took over. In some instances, relatively minor matters that would previously have been resolved in local negotiations with foremen proved impossible to settle without a strike. In 1969, six GM plants undergoing consolidation under GMAD's direction went on strike over production standards, halting more than one-third of the corporation's output. All told, the International Union issued seventy-one intent-to-strike notices against GM plants for speedups from 1963 to 1969.[4]

Locals could conduct an authorized strike, even while national contracts with no-strike clauses were in effect, when contractual production standards were unilaterally changed by management and over conditions threatening to health or safety. The latter justification was flexible, suitable for use beyond its stated purpose. As Ken Bannon noted, "there was always oil or something on the floor." The International supported local strikes for these purposes in principle, and authorized many. An incomplete list for

A Local 155 member tacks up a strike poster, October 1966. Walter P. Reuther Library, Wayne State University

1966 gives these examples of authorized strikes: (1) a Local 862 strike at the Louisville, Kentucky, Ford plant over working conditions, which lasted two weeks; (2) a Local 890 strike at the Ford Metuchen, New Jersey, plant over working conditions, which lasted five weeks; (3) a Local 1250 strike at three Ford plants in Brook Park, Ohio, over unresolved grievances, idled over 30,000 in thirteen plants in five states and Canada, which lasted less than a week; (4) a strike at the Twinsburg, Ohio, Chrysler stamping plant, which lasted four days, idled 14,300 workers in three plants in Detroit and Newark, Delaware; (5) a GM strike at the St. Louis Chevrolet plant that caused layoffs elsewhere of 2,400; (6) a strike at Local 216, the GM plant in South Gate, California, which lasted almost two weeks.[5]

International officers disapproved of unauthorized wildcat strikes, opposed any weakening of the strike authorization procedure, and sought to end wildcats as quickly as possible. Beyond the problem of contract violations and possible legal liability for damages, wildcats often forced layoffs for workers whose jobs were unaffected by the issue and threatened to divide the membership. Three examples illustrate the problems that could arise when wildcats occurred and the International responded. In August

1963, at the Ford Chicago Stamping Plant, five officers of Local 588 blocked operation of a press for safety reasons. The corporation penalized them with layoffs; the workforce responded with a wildcat strike that shut down thirty-one Ford plants in the costliest unauthorized strike in Ford's history. The International's order to end the strike provoked great resentment, and Ford threatened to fire those who failed to return to work. A court injunction forced the end of the strike and Ford fired two local officials, including a former president of the local, who then started a movement for the local's withdrawal from the International. The strike violated the contract, the UAW constitution, and the Taft-Hartley Act. The local was put under an administrator, and the president put on trial and expelled from the union.[6]

A wildcat strike in 1967 at the Fisher Body plant in Mansfield, Ohio, brought pressure from the International on Local 549's leaders to call off the strike when 133,250 General Motors' workers at other plants received layoff notices because of parts shortages. A threat to take over the local temporarily ended the strike, but it resumed when five members were suspended for their actions in the previous wildcat. The executive board appointed an administrator to take over the local and the plant resumed full operations.[7]

In April 1969, 4,000 members of Local 1264 at a Chrysler stamping plant in Sterling Heights, Michigan—a plant with a history of contentious safety issues—wildcatted. Workers had refused to obey a supervisor's orders to handle knife-edged scrap metal from a malfunctioning conveyor while standing on a slippery, oil-covered floor. When the company suspended the local's officers, seventy workers walked out, refusing to work without union representation. When the seventy were fired, hundreds more walked out. The plant was shut down for eight days, and more than 35,000 Chrysler workers elsewhere were idled. The International executive board imposed an administrator, Doug Fraser, who assured the workers that the International Union would authorize a strike if the members formally voted for it. The board insisted that the strike be ended as soon as possible in view of Chrysler's eighty-eight-day inventory of unsold cars and the fear that the unauthorized strike would cause 90,000 Chrysler employees to be laid off without unemployment compensation or supplementary unemployment benefits—a graphic illustration of how a major segment of the union's membership could be damaged by the actions of another.[8]

RANK-AND-FILE BARGAINING priorities changed from time to time in response to current problems, but the general goal of an improved retirement plan, permitting an earlier exit from the plants with full pension rights, was at the top of the list throughout the decade. If layoffs were occurring or threatened, as was the case in the early 1960s, then members not surprisingly tended to value job and income security measures. Convinced that both collective bargaining and constitutional issues could not be fruitfully addressed in a single convention, the UAW established the practice of holding a special convention for exclusive consideration of collective bargaining proposals and building support for upcoming negotiations. International officials traveled widely to tap worker sentiment. In preparation for the 1961 special collective bargaining convention, secretary-treasurer Emil Mazey chaired a series of ten hearings in different cities to get local unions' views on union-wide problems, and vice president Leonard Woodcock, head of the General Motors Department, visited each of General Motors' 131 local unions for the same purpose. That convention saw a slogan of "30–40–60"—thirty hours of work for forty hours of pay with the eligibility for retirement age set at sixty—receive considerable publicity. An early retirement program had an appeal that reached far beyond those who would immediately become eligible for retirement. Those who remained in the plants would gain new opportunities for transfer to better jobs, and the threat of layoffs for lower seniority workers would be reduced. A 1961 survey of 2,681 union members in General Motors' plants in Flint and in Janesville, Wisconsin, and a Ford plant in Cleveland showed that a "better retirement plan" was the "most important" objective, followed by a "guaranteed work week," "improved health and medical insurance" (meaning full payment of premiums by the companies), and a "steadier work week." The objective of a "shorter work week with same pay" received a low mark as "most important" and the next to the highest mark as "least important," while "higher wages" were chosen by only 7 percent as "most important" and received the highest mark, 46 percent, as "least important." Since recent layoffs had resulted in a loss of income for many workers, the emphasis on income maintenance and employment security was understandable. Referring to the "30–40–60" slogan, the survey's authors concluded that the "30 for 40" part is "not at all representative of the UAW rank-and-file's most urgent demands today. On the other hand, the '60' part is both legitimate, popular, and representative."[9]

At the 1961 bargaining convention the leadership formulated its program for the coming negotiations. With layoffs occurring throughout the industry, the focus was on increasing employment. Although much of the press characterized the demands as self-serving exercises in reducing the amount of work, Reuther contended "we aren't fighting for more leisure. We are fighting for more jobs." As good fortune would have it, the measures the union proposed to increase employment would also increase the amount of leisure and provide some relief for employees from the pressures of a demanding work routine. A summary of bargaining objectives included demands for replacement of hourly wages with annual salaries (an income maintenance device as well as a way to blur the social-economic-cultural division between blue- and white-collar employees), shorter hours, early retirement, longer vacations, additional paid holidays, "industrial sabbaticals," and reductions in overtime. Implementation of all but the first of these measures would require additional hiring.[10]

A visionary proposal to combat unemployment was put forward by Nat Weinberg, the union's leading economic thinker. With the nation's unemployment rate at 6.1 percent, its highest point in fourteen months and still higher in the auto cities, Weinberg proposed and the convention endorsed a "flexible work week." Forty hours of work would remain the norm, but hours would rise or fall depending on the unemployment rate. A rising unemployment rate would trigger a reduction in hours; but as the unemployment rate fell, hours of work would rise, returning to the norm and even exceeding it, if warranted, with overtime rates put in effect. The complicated plan would require both company participation and government action. An amendment to the Fair Labor Standards Act would be needed to maintain the forty-hour wage and establish a National Work Week Adjustment Fund, financed by a "small" payroll tax, to keep pay up to the forty-hour rate during periods of reduced work time. Neither the companies nor the federal government was interested, and the union was unprepared to make the plan a high priority.[11]

In the 1961 negotiations, the UAW reached agreement with American Motors (AMC) on a profit-sharing plan, a favorite of AMC chairman George Romney, and then tried to use this agreement as a pattern with the major manufacturers. The union did not push the profit-sharing concept with the other manufacturers, who had clearly indicated their disapproval, but profit sharing remained a long-term goal. Reuther told the Detroit Economic Club, where auto barons were well-represented in the audience, that management should become "emotionally adjusted" to the idea of profit sharing because it was "knocking on your door." In the event, many years would pass before profit sharing made its way into UAW contracts with the major manufacturers.[12]

Failure to reach agreement with Ford led to a ten-day strike in October 1961, the first general strike at Ford since 1941. As would often be the case in the 1960s, monetary issues had been settled before the strike. The walkout turned on production standards, the number of committeemen, the use of outside contractors, Ford's steelmaking operations, and working conditions and job classifications in the skilled trades. In addition, there were many unsettled local issues, ranging from wash-up times at the end of a shift, to protective clothing, to parking lots. After a national agreement was reached, twenty-five locals remained on strike for varying periods of time.[13]

In a letter to General Motors vice president and chief negotiator Louis Seaton, Reuther emphasized the necessity of dealing with the problem of job insecurity. Short workweeks had reduced earnings and placed the burden of coping with fluctuations in demand and production scheduling on the backs of hourly-rated employees. While there were short workweeks in some plants, in others workers were forced, in some cases against their will, to put in many hours of overtime. In 1960, Reuther pointed out, with over five million unemployed throughout the United States, General Motors required about 60 million hours of overtime, a practice for which, he said, "there can be no moral defense." The union leadership continued to oppose mandatory overtime, despite the understandable popularity of added pay with many workers, on the ground that it kept thousands off the job rolls. In addition, the UAW demanded that GM provide adequate relief time during the workday, a more effective shop floor representation system comparable to those in force at other automobile companies, and better pension benefits and hospital and medical care.[14]

General Motors refused to sign a national agreement until local settlements on working conditions were reached. Both authorized local strikes and some wildcats began in early September. Although no general strike was called at GM, the effect was nearly as devastating: 255,000 GM production workers at ninety-two plants halted virtually all operations. Reuther castigated GM as a "glorified, gold-plated sweatshop," a line he often used in the 1960s when discussing working conditions at the corporation. In many of the plants on strike, relief time was the critical issue, with workers "chained to the line" for four hours without a break. Practice and rules on relief time varied widely from one GM plant to another, so one of the union's objectives was to establish a uniform minimum standard for relief. General Motors agreed to provide one relief man for every twenty workers. This would provide twenty-four minutes of relief time to each worker per day, divided between twelve minutes before and twelve minutes after lunch, but GM's plan as originally proposed assumed that someone would be relieved as soon as he started work at the beginning of a shift and others right after finishing lunch, when the respite from labor would be of little value. UAW negotiators finally persuaded the corporation to block out the first hour in the morning and the first hour after lunch, an arrangement that GM had resisted because it necessitated hiring additional relief workers. At first the Fisher Division refused to go along, and by the time its executives had agreed, telegrams had already gone out from union headquarters authorizing local strikes. The strike was dubbed the "toilet strike" by the media and called "the most needless major strike in U.S. history" by an unsympathetic journalist, who apparently thought that a guarantee of a few minutes to go to the washroom during a long, wearisome working day—a privilege taken for granted by white-collar employees—was a frivolous matter. The workers did not think it frivolous, however, and it took four weeks to get everyone back to work.[15]

The 1961 national settlements provided important improvements in fringe benefits and went some distance in meeting the union's goals of enhancing security and stimulating additional employment. The gains included hospital-medical insurance for workers and their families fully paid by the companies, including payments of premiums for laid-off workers for up to twelve months (benefits envied by workers in many less-favored industries); SUB improvements; improved pension benefits, including payment by companies of half the cost of both present and future retirees' hospital-medical insurance (an important retirement incentive); improved life insurance; increased severance pay; and improved paid vacations. Moving-expense allowances were a response to the companies' plant dispersal strategy. After years of refusing to comply with a union demand, GM agreed to contract language forbidding discrimination in employment decisions on the basis of race, color, creed, or national origin. Other provisions of the settlement strengthened the union's factory floor presence by improving the status and privileges of committeemen and shop chairmen.[16]

WHEN CONTRACTS WITH THE companies expired on August 31, 1964, the industry was in the midst of one of its most profitable years, selling at a good price every car it could manufacture, unemployment was at its lowest figure in years, and no serious inflation was yet in sight. Earnings for the companies exceeded a 20 percent return on assets for the previous year. Even Chrysler, close to bankruptcy only a short time earlier, had made a remarkable recovery. Such economic conditions were, of course, conducive to union bargaining success. Reuther announced that "we go to the bargaining table under the most favorable economic circumstances that we have ever enjoyed in a major set of negotiations," and he mapped out an ambitious and costly bargaining agenda that stressed early retirement and improved working conditions, while not neglecting increases in straight-time wages. The potential costs alarmed government economists who feared an inflationary settlement. Walter Heller, the chairman of President Kennedy's Council of Economic Advisors and a friend of Reuther's, issued a call in a speech before the Detroit Economic Club for an auto wage settlement within the federal government's guidelines of 3.2 percent. At a subsequent press conference Reuther told the assembled journalists that he was "not going to let any son of a bitch professor in the White House tell us what we can settle for"; yet he quickly turned aside and whispered to a mutual acquaintance, "Tell Walter [Heller] not to take that personally."[17]

Once again working conditions were the hottest issue. Disputes over production standards had contributed to a significant rank-and-file discontent, with the result that more than the usual number of local union officials had been ousted in recent elections. Officers were voted out, for example, at seven of ten locals serving Ford assembly plants. More than one-third of the top officials in UAW production locals failed to be reelected in 1963. As an officer of the Tarrytown, New York, Fisher Body local explained: "There is a revolt in our plants and we of the secondary leadership . . . are the first casualties." Although the International leadership at first underestimated the seriousness of the uprising, they could not ignore it indefinitely, regardless of the fact that the companies were likely to resist concessions on working conditions more strenuously than on wages. Reuther observed that "when the job controls the man, he loses his dignity. . . . We have to restore a measure of dignity on the job . . . [and] assert the worker's sovereignty over his machine." Increased relief time, five-minute halts of assembly lines each hour, curbs on production speedups, longer vacations, and an increase in the number of committeemen would contribute to this end.[18]

A closely related question was whether the union could devise ways to increase employment. The most important means was early retirement, a popular step with the approximately 40,000 production workers over sixty and with the many thousands more approaching that age. Pressures generated in the big Flint locals left the leadership with no choice but to make an early retirement program a major objective. Reducing the amount of overtime would also increase employment. Claiming that an end to overtime would create 60,000 additional jobs, the union leadership advocated an increase in overtime rates in order to give the companies an economic incentive to reduce its use. Again, the companies were sure to resist, since putting current workers on overtime, despite the premium pay required, resulted in substantial savings over hiring additional workers who would have to be paid costly and numerous fringe benefits. By a bizarre twist that confounded expectations when premium pay for overtime was mandated, extensive use of overtime in place of additional hiring had become one of the chief ways the companies controlled labor costs. Other demands that would both give existing workers a break and encourage additional hiring were longer paid vacations and extended relief time.[19]

The auto companies offered a 3.5 percent increase in wages and benefits, which Reuther rejected, paraphrasing a wartime remark of Winston Churchill's: "never have so few with so much offered so little to so many." Although there was much agitation within the union to tackle General Motors, UAW negotiators, exploiting an inadvertent revelation by Chrysler chairman Lynn Townsend that the corporation, with its strong sales and improving profit margins would make any concession to avoid a strike, chose that firm as their target. Only minutes before a strike was scheduled to begin, with additional relief time (a large cost item for the company since its implementation would necessitate thousands of new hires) the final obstacle to a settlement, the bargainers reached agreement. Chrysler contracted for a 4.3 percent wage and benefit increase (a 60-cents-an-hour increase spread over three years and a cost-of-living adjustment of another 10 cents an hour). In a breakthrough of great significance, early retirement pensions providing $400 a month for workers retiring at age sixty with thirty years of service were won. Other gains included an increase in relief time to thirty-six minutes a day from twenty-four for those whose jobs were paced by machine or assembly line, and an additional week of paid vacation for those with one year's seniority. The week could be taken as a Paid Absence Allowance—that is, one could work during a vacation and earn double pay (a provision that reduced the potential contribution additional vacation time would make to new hiring but one that was very popular with workers who wished to increase their earnings). The agreement also included two additional paid holidays (Good Friday and the employee's birthday, the latter touted as an acknowledgment of each employee's individuality); moreover, the company agreed to pay all premiums for life, sickness, and accident insurance. In another important breakthrough, the contract provided substantial improvements for those already retired as well as future retirees. Most notably, Chrysler agreed to pay the full premium for health coverage for retirees and their spouses (until then it had been paying half of the premium), a boon to retirees themselves but also a retirement incentive for active workers and thus a way of creating opportunities for better jobs and employment for others. Retirees greeted the settlement rapturously. As one said, "You get to where you can hardly say anything, you feel so much gratitude for what the union did for retirees in this new contract." The early retirement provision was a welcome road out of the plant for many. At Chrysler, early retirement rose over 1,000 percent above the pre-1964 average, with 4,417 Chrysler workers choosing early retirement in the first sixteen months. Ford matched the retirement provisions with similar results: whereas in 1953 only 5 percent of retirees left their jobs before reaching sixty-five, by 1968, 73 percent of retirees had not yet attained that age. For the industry as a whole, retirements in the first year of the program soared to 24,159, about three times the number pensioned in the previous year. Of that total, 17,975 retired before reaching age sixty-five. Further innovations were the inclusion of coverage for psychiatric care, pre- and postnatal care, payment of employees' college tuition for a course of study related to their work, and agreement that an employee could volunteer for the Peace Corps without loss of seniority and with reemployment rights after two years of service. The mental health coverage, included largely as the result of a campaign by Melvin T. Glasser, director of the union's Social Security Department, was the first to deal with all kinds of mental problems, including depression, emotional upset, and anger. A major innovation was coverage of out-of-hospital mental health treatment. The 1964 Chrysler contract, unparalleled in sweep and innovation, was one of the best ever negotiated by the UAW, and it forced the corporation to hire additional workers to keep its machines and assembly lines humming.[20]

Reuther claimed the Chrysler agreement was "the most historic in the history of the American labor movement with respect to the broad problem of pension security for workers," and many agreed with him. Through providing early retirement at a decent income level, adding vacation and holiday periods, and increasing relief time, the contract helped humanize the workplace and provide employment for thousands of additional workers. The UAW claimed that 10,000 jobs opened up in the auto and agricultural implement industries in just three months (September–November 1965) as a result of the 1964 pension provisions. Retirement eligibility was determined by a point system, with eighty-five points needed—the points representing the sum of one's age plus years of service (for example, age sixty plus twenty-five years of service provided the requisite eighty-five points). Relief time went up from twenty-four minutes daily to thirty-six minutes (eighteen minutes before and eighteen minutes after lunch, which could be divided into four nine-minute periods), an increase regarded by a Chrysler worker as "one of the greatest rewards of the pact . . . the added time away from the dismal monotony of the job." When Reuther called President Lyndon B. Johnson after concluding the Chrysler agreement, the president asked "What did you do to the guidelines?" "Mr. President, we bent the hell out of them," Reuther replied. After Reuther related some of the contract's provisions, the president responded with congratulations, particularly on early retirement. "He thought it was wonderful," Reuther told the executive board.[21]

A week later Ford accepted essentially the same contract, even adding the "frosting on the Chrysler birthday cake" of a Christmas bonus, but local negotiations and strikes over working conditions delayed ratification and resumption of full production by two months.[22]

General Motors, sporting enormous profits and handsome executive bonuses, was prepared to accept the economic terms of the package but not the noneconomic agreements. The company refused to make concessions on greater union representation in the plants (the union wanted released time for committeemen comparable to what it had at Ford and Chrysler), overtime limitations, health and safety regulations, production standards, disciplining of workers, and subcontracting of work to outside producers.

Claiming, as always when faced with demands of this character, that its authority to run the business was at stake, the company prepared for a strike, the first national strike at GM since 1946. Reuther was eager to avoid a strike in an election year that could embarrass the Democratic presidential candidate—Lyndon B. Johnson, favored by UAW leaders—and was prepared to accept GM's final offer. Yet he was overruled by the union's GM negotiating committee of local representatives, one of the rare occasions he failed to get his way. He then proposed arbitration of the shop floor issues, but GM turned him down.[23]

Officially the national strike (while not a pattern-setting strike) lasted only a week, but again the issues of production standards and accumulated unresolved grievances in dozens of locals (by one count 17,000 grievances awaited action) led to local plant strikes that effectively shut down GM's production for more than a month. The strike was "selective," in that forty-one GM plants producing parts for GM's competitors (GM was a major supplier of parts to the other manufacturers) were not shut down, only the eighty-nine parts and assembly plants manufacturing solely for GM's car divisions. This tactic was intended to increase the pressure on the corporation to settle. Issues were resolved on a plant-by-plant basis, and by early November, just in time for the election, everyone was back at work. Although the results of the decentralized negotiations were decidedly mixed, the union claimed a victory. According to Reuther, this was "a strike for human dignity. They wanted more rational and humane treatment on the job. . . . The fact that in many G.M. locations the workers had to demand that doors be installed on toilet stalls symbolized the resistance to degrading personal treatment by the Corporation and the struggle to achieve dignity at the work place." GM's chief negotiator, Louis Seaton, insisted that the corporation had not "agreed to anything that is going to impair our responsibility to our shareholders to run an efficient business . . . and that's what the strike has been about."[24]

WITH PENSIONS WON FROM the auto companies and the number of retirees rapidly growing, the UAW addressed the question of its retirees' status within the union. The 1951 constitutional convention had adopted a very broad concept that entitled a retiree "to all the privileges of membership except that he shall not have to pay membership dues." Not only could retirees attend membership meetings, they could also vote for local union officers and even participate in strike and ratification votes. Although the International Union did not create a retirees' organization until 1957, many locals had already established their own retirees' clubs and activities. A resolution at that year's constitutional convention earmarked 2 cents of each active member's monthly dues to finance a retired workers' program, set up a Retired Workers Department within the International, and required each local to create a standing committee on retired workers' programs. In 1966 a more elaborate, four-tiered structure was created, with retired workers' chapters in the locals, area councils, regional councils, and the International Retired Worker Advisory Council. Each elected member of the International Council was made a delegate to the constitutional convention, with voice and vote. Voluntary dues of one dollar a month were put in place to fund activities. By 1968, 359 UAW locals had retired workers' chapters, and there were nearly 70,000 dues-paying retired members.[25]

As the number of retirees increased, problems cropped up pertaining to the voting entitlement. Active members began to complain when the rising number of retirees' votes threatened to determine the outcome of local elections, strike authorizations, and contract ratifications. In response, the 1959 convention restricted voting rights. Retirees could no longer vote for stewards or committeemen, the direct representatives of the workers in the shops, vote on a contract ratification, or participate in a strike authorization vote. Reuther pointed out that giving retirees a vote in negotiations bestowed power without responsibility. The retirees' income would not be jeopardized by a strike, but "when a fellow who is punching his time clock votes to strike it means he gives up his pay check." These voting restrictions by no means deprived retirees of all important union participation. They could attend local meetings with voice and vote, run for office and vote in local elections except for steward and committeeman, and vote for and run for constitutional convention delegate. Two members of the Retired Workers Advisory Council were entitled to attend International executive board meetings without a vote but with the right to be consulted on matters affecting retirees. Thus, retirees had opportunities for significant input into the union's activities, including collective bargaining matters through several channels. Allowing retirees to vote for local officers led to unsatisfactory results in some of the large locals with many retirees, such as Local 600, where they constituted as much as one-third of the total membership of approximately 45,000. In at least one election in that local the retiree vote brought in officers who did not have the support of a majority of the active members. Nevertheless, the voting privilege was not taken away.[26]

Some of the retirees' activities were social in nature, an opportunity for old-timers to get together to renew friendships and commemorate their collective struggles. In the 1950s and 1960s an annual picnic on Belle Isle Park in the Detroit River drew thousands. The 1960 picnic, for example, was attended by more than 14,000 retirees. In 1969 the Local 600 retirees' chapter had more than 17,500 members, claimed as "a world's record." Other services included preretirement planning, "drop-in" centers for social and recreational activities, and many opportunities for citizenship and political work, such as working on election day to get out the vote, lobbying on issues of particular concern to retirees like Social Security, voter registration drives, volunteering for service in community organizations, and so on. In direct support of union actions, retirees served on picket lines and in strike kitchens and conducted educational programs for active members.[27]

The closest bond was created by the UAW's success in meeting some of the retirees' needs through collective bargaining. Obtaining paid medical benefits for retirees and their spouses and raising pension pay-outs to keep pace with inflation were material boons of the greatest value for those otherwise on fixed incomes; these and other benefits cemented retirees' loyalty to the union. The affection was reciprocated, with union leaders and activists grateful for the retirees' past and present services. After relating a story to the executive board of an emotional encounter with a retiree veteran of the 1937 Fleetwood sit-down, in which Reuther had participated, the union's president said, "these are the kinds of guys that make up our retired workers. They are pure gold."[28]

As contract expirations approached in 1967, the UAW prepared for the next round of bargaining. With the UAW's skilled tradesmen restive and in some cases in revolt, and with inflationary pressures mounting as demand ballooned due to the Vietnam War and other government spending, the negotiations threatened to be among the most difficult in the union's history. Reuther neutralized the possible opposition of the Johnson administration to a generous auto settlement by averting a threatened strike against the Lycoming Division of AVCO, a company with a tumultuous and contentious labor relations history and the sole supplier of engines for the Army's helicopters in Vietnam. The company was operating under a Taft-Hartley eighty-day "cooling off" injunction that was about to expire. Pressed by President Johnson and a host of high level White House aides, Reuther promised to do his best to prevent resumption of the AVCO strike. According to Reuther's later account, he received the famous presidential "treatment." Johnson wrapped an arm around him as they walked on the White House lawn and said, "You put this one to bed, and as far as I'm concerned you've got a green light to strike these others for the rest of the summer." "I shook his hand. I said: 'We have an understanding.' " With Reuther and other UAW officials taking over the negotiations, the AVCO dispute was resolved on very generous terms without a strike—with the administration, in effect, picking up the bill. The eventual auto settlement exceeded the administration's wage guidelines, but not a word of criticism was heard from the White House.[29]

In preparation for negotiations the union once again surveyed the membership. Those surveyed were asked to rate seventeen bargaining issues as "most important" and "least important." A better retirement plan still headed the list, with 57 percent declaring it the most important objective. Other issues that received high marks were a guaranteed workweek, guaranteed income, and better handling of grievances—but, as the organization conducting the survey remarked, "better retirement is virtually in a class by itself." Not surprisingly, support for a better retirement plan correlated with the advancing age of respondents, with 76 percent of those over fifty-five rating it as most important, but even in the youngest age cohort, those under twenty-five, it received the highest rating (36 percent). Such strong support among the young reflected the expectation that their own retirement prospects would brighten and the likelihood that openings to better jobs and more security for themselves would occur as those with higher seniority retired. Broken down by race, there was little difference in the responses to most items, but a reformed seniority system was of more importance to blacks than whites, no surprise in view of the fact that blacks were much more likely to be recent hires. Raising the wages of skilled tradesmen to equal those paid in the building trades was of less importance to blacks than whites, again no surprise in view of the very small number of black skilled tradesmen. A yawning gap existed on the question of skilled trades wages equal to those paid to building tradesmen, with 59 percent of UAW skilled workers rating it as the most important issue and only 5 percent of those in production agreeing. Questioning by those conducting the survey showed that production workers thought tradesmen's wages should, in fairness, be equal to the wages paid in the building trades, but as a goal they gave it little weight.[30]

A CONTINGENT OF THE SKILLED TRADESMEN, who altogether constituted about 18 percent of the union's auto membership, had long been resentful and restless at being submerged within an industrial union. As a General Motors official pointedly remarked, the UAW was "an industrial union with a skilled trades bellyache." In the union's early days many tradesmen were in the forefront of the union movement, drawing on left-leaning commitments that sprang from their British and western European origins. By the postwar period a new cohort of tradesmen had entered the plants, who largely lacked the social and political orientation of the earlier generation. A minority within a democratic organization, they felt their interests had been ignored and overridden by the majority. They had seen the wages of production workers rise more rapidly than their own, creating a convergence that would, they feared, ultimately undermine their higher status. Their hourly rate was usually less than that received by skilled workers in the building trades, some of whom might be working alongside them in the auto plants as outside contractors, and they were often paid less than tradesmen working in the independent tool and die shops. In both instances, however, their annual pay was usually about the same or even better, since auto industry tradesmen employed by the Big Three had steadier employment than those on the outside. They also feared the dilution of the trade and its loss of integrity by the incorporation of "upgraders," production workers trained not in the full dimensions of a trade but in only one of its operations. Upgraders came into the industry in large numbers during World War II, and since they cost less than the fully skilled to train and employ, employers were tempted to utilize them. Skilled trades discontent was stronger at General Motors and Chrysler than at Ford because the first two companies had diluted their trades through greater use of upgraders and outside contractors, causing a degree of fear and resentment not present at Ford. There was also a racial element in the tradesmen's discontent as African Americans came to constitute a large proportion of the production workers and therefore of the UAW's members. Since very few African Americans had gained admission to the trades, a separate tradesmen's union would be in fact for "whites only." The skilled tradesmen's "episodic fluctuation between class militancy and parochialism," reflected, in the words of one historian, "a precisely calibrated social opportunism." In any event, the tradesmen provided the UAW leadership with its most serious internal challenge since the struggles with the Addes caucus in 1946–47.[31]

The "skilled trades revolt," implicitly threatening the establishment of a rival, dual union, surfaced in General Motors plants in the mid-1950s. The International Society of Skilled Trades (ISST) appeared on the scene and quickly gained thousands of members, stimulated by the tradesmen's unhappiness with the small raises they received in the 1955 negotiations. Perhaps as many as 50,000 joined ISST, and another 20,000 joined the Maintenance, Construction and Powerhouse Council, another potential dual union. The ISST attacked the industrial union concept and argued that skilled tradesmen would never obtain equity within a UAW dominated by production workers. In 1957 a National Labor Relations Board ruling on an ISST petition undercut the rival organization's threat by holding that a trade, such as electrician, could be removed from a bargaining unit only on a company-wide, not a plant by plant, basis. Nevertheless, resentment remained so strong that the UAW leadership expanded and strengthened the bargaining role of skilled trades representatives in an attempt to calm the storm. The leadership, eager to show technical, engineering, and other white-collar workers it hoped to organize (as well as the tradesmen) that the industrial union concept was sufficiently flexible to serve the needs of nonproduction workers, amended the union's constitution to give representation on local and national bargaining committees to skilled tradesmen and

white-collar workers. Union leaders also conceded to them separate ratification votes on agreements that concerned only their interests and the right
to strike, subject to International approval, if they were not satisfied with
the agreement reached. These significant concessions quieted the revolt for
the time being.[32]

Skilled trades dissatisfaction peaked again in the mid-1960s. The leadership was under pressure to obtain wage increases for skilled trades to
match those won by the construction unions, which had done very well in
those buoyant, inflationary times. Reuther sought a 50-cent hourly raise for
skilled workers in 1966, fourteen months before the contracts expired, but
the companies turned him down. An important, if controversial, concession by the union's leadership—"one of the biggest mistakes we ever
made," in Ken Bannon's view—was adopted at the constitutional convention in May 1966. It gave skilled tradesmen a separate ratification vote on
tentative agreements. If the contract in its entirety was rejected by a majority of either production or skilled workers, then there was no agreement.
Although strictly construed this violated the industrial union principle by
creating a privileged minority with a veto over a tentative agreement, the
concession gave skilled tradesmen a lever to make the union address their
concerns, and it could be used to enhance the union's bargaining clout,
since negotiators could now point out that a company proposal would never
win skilled trades approval.[33]

Despite the concessions, an ISST resurgence sparked new interest in
leaving the UAW. The crisis occurred in early 1967, in a series of wildcat
strikes at the Fisher Body plant in Mansfield, Ohio. The strikes, lasting
three weeks, forced the layoff of two hundred thousand workers and infuriated GM executives, who threatened to sue the UAW for violating the contract's no-strike provision and demanded heavy monetary damages.
Reuther read the riot act to the Mansfield strikers, and the executive board
took over the local. The Mansfield shop committee chairman later went to
work as an organizer for ISST. A substantial wage increase for tradesmen
negotiated in 1967 quieted the uproar and ended threats of secession by an
important portion of the union's membership.[34]

While many white skilled tradesmen agitated to leave the UAW,
African Americans, steadily gaining access to production work but still disproportionately confined to the industry's worst jobs, demanded entry into
the skilled trades. Closure of skilled trades apprenticeships to racial minorities had long been one of the sorest points in the industry's racial relations.
Even as the civil rights movement dramatically and courageously confronted racial injustice in the 1960s, the auto industry trades remained
almost exclusively white. In 1960, when 24 percent of Chrysler's Detroit
area production workers were black, only twenty-four out of 7,425 skilled

workers at Chrysler (.03 percent) were from that minority group. (Ten of Chrysler's 3,000 Detroit area salaried employees were African American, and there were none among the 1,890 Chrysler engineers.) At General Motors' Detroit area plants there were sixty-seven skilled black workers out of 11,125. At Ford's River Rouge complex, where 40 percent of 35,650 workers were black, there were 259 black skilled workers out of 7,450. Faced with obstacles, most notably the threat of a skilled trades secession from the union, the UAW leadership shrank from an affirmative action program to correct the situation. The craft tradition bestowed on tradesmen themselves the right to grant admission to the craft, and for years ethnic and family associations and identities had affected decisions on entry. Breaking the color barrier would require a commitment from the companies, a sustained effort by the union's leadership, support by the union's black membership, pressure from civil rights organizations, and a strong push from federal and state governments through legislative, administrative, and judicial rulings. Recognizing that one of the problems was the inadequate educational preparation of both minority and white youth, the UAW contracted through the Manpower Development and Training Act to provide pre-apprenticeship training for "hard-core" blacks and whites to prepare them to pass apprenticeship entry tests. These efforts had little impact because of the resistance of white tradesmen. With the union facing criticism for its failure to attack the problem more aggressively, Reuther expressed his frustration and skepticism of the tradesmen's claims: "All this business," he told the executive board in 1969, "about lowering standards . . . is so much pious hogwash to hide the central question that these people want to maintain these jobs on a monopoly basis and exclude the right of blacks to participate."[35]

REUTHER OPENED A SPECIAL COLLECTIVE bargaining convention in April 1967, with a typically lengthy explication of the union's objectives. He pledged a major effort to improve working conditions, saying, "let us never forget that this union was not organized for just another nickel in the pay envelope, although this is important. This union came out of the struggle of the workers against the inhumanity of the speedup of the production lines." A heightened concern about protecting jobs threatened by outside contracting, a growing practice favored by management, surfaced. "If you can strike during the life of a contract to protect yourself against unfair production standards, we ought to insist upon the right to strike during the contract to protect our jobs from being stolen by outside contracting." Reuther reaffirmed the union's commitment to upgrade the SUB system to a guaranteed annual income, indicating that would be a major goal. He also pledged there would be "no tampering" with the COLA escalator, a promise which in the event he failed to fulfill, and committed the union to achieving wage parity for Canadian auto workers with U.S. wages. Both prior to and at the convention itself there was a militant mood, with the leadership subject to criticism in leaflets, speeches, and the like. For example, leaders of six Cleveland locals criticized Reuther for proclaiming the guaranteed annual wage as the UAW's major goal; in their view, job security and the thirty-five-hour workweek were more important objectives.[36]

Ford was selected as the target. The union proposed a wage and benefit package that amounted to 90 cents an hour, and the company responded with an offer of about two-thirds that amount. In prestrike talks neither side made any important concessions. A strike was so taken for granted that on the final day of talks the negotiators for the two sides spent most of the time in their abbreviated sessions talking about the previous night's Detroit Tigers' baseball game and coho salmon fishing in Lake Michigan. The strike, involving 160,000 Ford employees, began on September 6, just as the 1968 models were being launched, and lasted until October 20, the UAW's longest general strike against a major auto manufacturer since the Chrysler strike of 1950. General Motors and Chrysler workers stayed at their jobs without a contract, with the companies refusing to collect dues or be bound by union shop agreements. With a strike fund of $67 million, the union seemed well prepared, and strike benefits of $20 to $30 a week—the amount scaled to seniority—were paid out. But the fund was rapidly depleted as the strike went on, and strikes at several other nonautomotive companies added to the demand for benefits. In October a special convention imposed a substantial monthly assessment on working members to replenish the strike fund, an indication of the depth of support for the strike among non-strikers which perhaps encouraged Ford to settle. Dues were increased from a flat $5 a month to a sum equal to two-hours' pay per month. From the union leadership's point of view, the trickiest question was to determine where to strike a balance between a wage increase for skilled workers and one for production workers at a point that would result in ratification by both parties.[37]

With an overall money increase of more than 6 percent, the settlement was a substantial, but by no means total, victory for the union. A guaranteed annual wage, a major priority for more than a dozen years, was finally achieved. Laid-off workers with seven years seniority were now guaranteed 95 percent of their pay, including unemployment compensation, for up to a year, less a small amount to compensate for savings in lunch and travel costs. The wage settlement met most of the demands of the skilled workers, who had seen the differential between their pay and that of production workers shrink over the years. They received a mammoth increase of 50 cents an hour, The 20-cents-an-hour raise for production workers seemed puny by comparison. In a further effort to humanize the workplace, Ford workers got twelve minutes a day additional relief time (a significant boost), bringing the total to a minimum of forty-eight minutes per day, with an upper limit of eighty minutes; the existing upper limits were retained where they had been in effect, for example, in foundries and other particularly harrowing workplaces. Two more paid holidays were added to the package. In separate ratification votes, the skilled workers approved the contract by a three-to-one margin, with production workers voting for it by an overwhelming nine to one. Despite the lackluster money settlement for production workers, they were ready for the long strike to end. Disputes over local issues once again delayed resumption of full production.[38]

In order to obtain the settlement and end the strike, Reuther made an important and costly concession. He agreed to an annual 8-cents-an-hour ceiling on cost-of-living increases over the life of the three-year contract. Apparently assuming that President Johnson would soon be able to bring the Vietnam War to a conclusion and avert a new inflationary surge, Reuther and the rest of the leadership believed the COLA cap would prove harmless. As it turned out, military and other government spending overheated the national economy. Measured by the previous COLA formula, the ceiling, which of course was incorporated into the contracts with Ford's competitors, cost each worker between $700 and $1,000 over three years, produced a loss of real wages for that period, and saved the companies hundreds of millions of dollars. Auto workers complained that their wages were falling behind inflation, which contributed to an opposition movement that surfaced at the next UAW convention. Reuther later admitted that he had miscalculated and erred in agreeing to the ceiling, although holding out could have prolonged for weeks an already long and costly strike. As inflation roared ahead and left wages behind, the discrepancy between the 50-cents-an-hour increase for skilled workers and the limited raise for production workers with the constraint of the COLA cap caused a lot of discontent in the ranks.[39]

Moving on to Chrysler the UAW persuaded the company, by threat of a strike, to match the Ford agreement, provide a wage increase for Chrysler's unionized white-collar employees, and raise the wages of Canadian Chrysler workers to the levels paid in the United States. The contract stipulated that Canadian Chrysler workers would achieve wage parity, phased in over two and a half years. Equalizing the wages of Canadian auto workers removed a threat to American jobs, so this was a step supported by U.S. workers as a contribution to job security and an implementation of the union's "equal pay for equal work" principle. The national agreement was ratified by production workers at all but one local; the margin of the skilled workers' vote was narrower, but they also ratified. Nearly half of Chrysler's workforce was on strike for brief periods over local issues.[40]

*"If Walter Reuther had his way,
there'd be a guaranteed annual everything!"*

"If Walter Reuther had his way, there'd be a guaranteed annual *everything!*" 1967. The *New Yorker* Collection 1967 Dana Fradon from cartoonbank.com. All Rights Reserved.

General Motors followed the pattern. As had become customary, local strikes over working conditions issues delayed GM's resumption of production. Even after the two sides reached a tentative agreement, 114 GM locals still had unsettled local issues. These included washing-up time for those with particularly dirty foundry jobs, protective clothing for those with dangerous foundry jobs, shift preferences, job transfers, production standards, relief time, adequate lighting, plant cleanliness, water fountains, and overtime preferences—the nitty-gritty of daily auto factory life. Strikes at GM foundries throughout January and February idled over 100,000 workers. At issue was the company's refusal to grant a six-minute, pre-lunch washup period in the grimy foundries; some workers ended up getting three minutes. An epidemic of GM local strikes broke out from January through April over production standards and unresolved grievances.[41]

THE PATTERN IN THE AGRICULTURAL implements industry was set at Caterpillar following a strike of 25,000 workers, the first at the company in nineteen years. The other firms, John Deere, International Harvester, Allis-Chalmers, J. I. Case, and White Motors, matched the Caterpillar settlement. The major gains were precedent setting income guarantee provisions that protected workers from a loss of income during short-term layoffs and from a reduction in income if they were downgraded in job classifications. Other gains at these firms matched the Ford settlement.[42]

The UAW still shared organization of aerospace workers with the International Association of Machinists (IAM). UAW contracts were in effect at Bell, Hayes Aircraft, Douglas (Long Beach, Charlotte, Tulsa, and Toronto), North American, Curtiss-Wright, Vertol, LTV, Ryan, and DeHaviland, a Canadian firm. IAM had organized workers at Aerojet, Rohr, McDonnell, Douglas (some plants), Lockheed, and Boeing. Relations between the two international unions, which had once been reasonably cooperative, became competitive and fractious as the decade drew to its end. Charging that IAM had reneged on agreements and tried to raid UAW-organized plants, the UAW canceled the mutual assistance pact with IAM, in effect declaring a state of belligerence. The IAM countercharged that the UAW had adopted its own raiding program. The two unions waged a bitter campaign to determine representation for about 21,500 McDonnell Douglas production and maintenance employees, with one election ruled a tie by the NLRB before the IAM narrowly prevailed in a run-off vote. In bargaining the UAW still sought to bring aerospace workers to the levels achieved in auto. One major accomplishment was that all major West Coast aerospace agreements provided either a full union shop or an agency shop.[43]

SINCE THE UNION'S EARLIEST DAYS, its International component had consisted of Canadian auto workers. The establishment of the UAW in Canada was concurrent with its origin in the United States, beginning with Local 195 at Kelsey Wheel in Windsor, Ontario, in December 1936. While clearly inspired by events in the United States, Canadian auto workers essentially created their own union with little outside assistance. As in the U.S., the key event occurred at a General Motors facility, in this case in a strike in 1937 at the corporation's Oshawa, Ontario, plant. By and large the union developed along parallel lines in the two countries, although in most respects developments occurred first and were more securely grounded on the United States side of the border. Organizationally, the Canadian locals were grouped into their own region with their elected regional director, bound by UAW constitutional provisions and administrative rules and procedures but with considerable autonomy. In recognition of separate sovereignties, a division on political matters was maintained. The Canadians did not participate in U.S. political activities or take positions on U.S. political issues, and they were free to make their own political decisions on Canadian affairs without American interference. All three of the major manufacturers produced cars in Ontario, with the original Chrysler and Ford plants located in and around Windsor and the main General Motors plant in Oshawa, east of Toronto. As more facilities were added, plants were built in other Ontario cities. During World War II, Ford's Windsor plant was the largest supplier of military vehicles in the British Commonwealth, and by 1950 the UAW, with 60,000 members, was the largest Canadian union. In the postwar era Canadian auto workers maintained a political position to the left of their U.S. counterparts. A few Communists were active. Other leftist tendencies with representation and some support within the union included the Canadian Commonwealth Federation, with a social democratic orientation, and later a social democratic party, the New Democratic Party (NDP), with which the Canadian region had close ties.[44]

A landmark in trade relations between the two countries occurred with the negotiation of the Canada-U.S. Automotive Products Agreement in 1965. The pact opened trade without tariffs in auto components and cars, allowed the companies to integrate their operations across the border, and guaranteed a larger investment in Canadian manufacturing. Canadian production grew rapidly after the pact went into effect, and the size of the workforce (and UAW membership) increased in the late 1960s at a rate about double that in the U.S. Wages in the industry had always favored American workers, while the Canadians claimed to enjoy more favorable working conditions. The smaller size of the Canadian market, which meant economies of scale could not be as fully exploited, had been an obstacle to wage parity. The international auto pact worked to equalize production costs and efficiency, giving Canadians a stronger claim to wage parity and U. S. workers an incentive to support them out of concern about a lower wage Canadian competitor. Wage parity, now with the support of all sections of the union, was won by the UAW first at Chrysler in 1967, to be implemented gradually; General Motors and Ford followed suit reluctantly. Canadian workers, who received large wage increases as a result, were the prime beneficiaries. Influence was by no means a one-way street. Canadian activists in the union were a relatively militant, ideologically sophisticated, left-leaning element. Their influence tended to pull the UAW in that direction. In 1968 the Canadian regional director, Dennis McDermott, became one of the UAW's five new vice presidents, an acknowledgment of the Canadians' importance within the organization.[45]

RECOGNIZING THE MULTINATIONAL character of automotive manufacturing, the UAW joined with the International Metalworkers Federation

(IMF), an organization supported for years by European metalworkers' unions but with little following in the United States. The purpose of the collaboration was "to work with representatives of the free labor movement throughout the world in developing a program to protect the working conditions, the wage standards, and general interests of the workers in these basic industries." The IMF emphasized improvements that could be won through collective bargaining. When Reuther consented to head a World Automotive Department within IMF, many European trade unionists at first were skeptical of American leadership, but at an IMF convention in Zurich he won them over with his progressive social and economic ideas. With a broad plan for free trade, recovery assistance, and establishment of international standards in working conditions, the IMF enjoyed some success in encouraging the development of free trade unions at the grassroots level.[46]

Although the powers of the World Automotive Department were limited, its establishment provided a forum for exchange of information on problems facing auto workers around the world. Its first project was a pathbreaking study of automotive contracts in many countries in order that unions entering into negotiations might know what their counterparts elsewhere had won. The information was invaluable in formulating demands and conducting negotiations. The department also organized training sessions for union activists and, in general, sought to uncover and publicize the means whereby the experiences of workers in one country could be brought to bear in assisting others. In 1956 Reuther proposed the establishment of auto workers' councils to facilitate exchange of information on wage rates, working conditions, and collective bargaining objectives in plants around the world for employees of General Motors, Ford, Chrysler, Volkswagen, and other multinational companies. No American union of the postwar period was more active than the UAW in promoting international contacts and cooperation among free workers and their organizations.[47]

Unity and understanding among the world's free auto workers assumed greater significance with the internationalization of car manufacturing. The extension of free trade encouraged manufacturers to locate new facilities to take advantage of low labor and material costs, producing parts and cars wherever that could be done most cheaply and shipping them elsewhere for sale. The potential impact of this transformation of manufacturing on the jobs and living standards of American workers was evident. "The day of the purely U.S. auto corporation is gone forever," Reuther noted. "Profits know no patriotism. . . . Technologies are the same and corporate policies are uniform, yet the workers are divided by national differences in social policies and in trade union custom and development. This is a division we must bridge." Following a visit to Germany in 1959, as Volkswagen exports to the United States leaped upward, he maintained that wages there must rise to the level of a "reasonable relationship" with American wages, not necessarily equivalent, if fair competition was to be maintained. For the UAW it was crucial that foreign workers move toward wage parity with their American counterparts.[48]

Reuther realized that differences of language, living standards, and political and cultural values impeded the establishment of effective international autoworker cooperation. Nevertheless, he preferred to aim for common standards and free trade instead of sealing off the United States market through protectionist legislation. Not until 1962 was the first world conference of auto workers held, and the first world auto council, which brought together representatives of General Motors, Ford, and Chrysler workers from fourteen different countries, was established only in 1966. Whether such efforts would ever result in multinational unions bargaining with multinational corporations was uncertain. The obstacles increased as rising fuel prices and inflation shifted demand toward smaller, more fuel-efficient vehicles. With capital needs for model development and plant investments rising, manufacturers were driven to reduce costs. Whatever the outcome, Reuther and the UAW recognized the implications of the creeping globalization of the auto labor market and tried to find ways to move toward solutions of problems that would recognize and protect common interests. In the words of the leading student of Reuther's and the UAW's overseas' union activity: "His overseas interests were the clearest indication of his belief that freedom and democracy were indivisible and that auto workers in Detroit would benefit in the long run from improvements in economic and social conditions of workers in other countries. His international idealism was genuine, and though pressures of commitments at home sometimes constrained his work in this field, the truth was that he was a 'doer' whereas other union leaders were content to pass resolutions."[49]

As early as 1962 the UAW created the Free World Labor Defense Fund; its convention authorized a contribution to the fund of more than $1.5 million to "support international solidarity among workers, to equip the International Metalworkers Federation to carry out organizing tasks and to promote higher wages and improved working conditions for workers in foreign countries." As Reuther pointed out to the delegates, this was an exercise in enlightened self-interest. "By helping our brothers throughout the world, we help ourselves by protecting our own standards." The money would be drawn from the interest earned by the union's strike fund. Grants from the fund supported oppressed workers and endangered unions in France, Italy, Spain, Turkey, Zambia, and Jamaica, among other countries, but most of the expenditures went to the IMF in support of its programs to organize more effectively and extensively those who worked for multinational auto corporations. At the time, fewer than 15 percent of Ford's employees in Germany were unionized and only 30 percent of those at Volkswagen. If successful in raising wages, lowering hours, and winning other improvements in working conditions in factories abroad, the undertaking would help to protect the jobs and the standards of the American workforce. Not only would the prices of imported cars rise, American auto corporations would have less incentive to shift production abroad to take advantage of lower costs. The UAW also took note of the growing threat to American jobs from the Japanese industry. In 1962 Reuther spent ten days in Japan, where auto workers' unions were fragmented and weak, in an attempt to persuade them to unite and adopt a more aggressive bargaining stance and establish mechanisms for identifying and publicizing Japanese wage levels. All of these efforts, which the UAW continued to pursue throughout the 1960s, provoked controversy and had, in fact, only a limited effect. For the rest of the decade Reuther offered plans in international forums for standardizing wages and working conditions, and he used his considerable oratorical powers to call on the unions of the world to "mobilise . . . against the 'super corporations.' "[50]

IN ITS COLLECTIVE BARGAINING ENTERPRISE, the UAW made significant advances during the 1960s. The union proved to be a flexible instrument for advancing and protecting the interests of auto workers. Without diminishing its commitment to a rising standard of living for its members, it adroitly placed new emphasis, in response to rank-and-file demands, on protecting income and increasing time away from the job through more relief time, more paid holidays, and early retirement, with economic security afforded by an adequate retirement income and company-paid medical and hospital benefits. American auto workers were still among the best paid factory employees at home or abroad, thanks to the industry's prosperity and to the efforts of their union. Vigilance on the shop floor was a shared responsibility of the local unions and the International. The locals took the initiative in bringing grievances, and the International provided guidance in their prosecution and resolution. Given the pressures to increase production being brought to bear on a workforce of younger persons less and less tolerant of the authoritarian factory model common in the past, tensions within the plants markedly rose. Mindful of the need to mold a common purpose and resolve out of a welter of conflicting interests, the International Union searched for the course that would advance the vital interests of all while sacrificing those of none.

CHAPTER 11

"Something short of perfect"

New Frontiers in Politics, 1960–65

T HE RECAPTURE OF THE PRESIDENCY IN 1960 BY JOHN F. Kennedy, the Democratic Party's candidate, raised hopes in the UAW that the pursuit of the New Deal's pledge of economic security and plenitude for all would now be resumed. "I am confident," Reuther told members of the UAW executive board a month after the election, "that Senator Jack Kennedy, when he takes the presidency on the twentieth of January, will implement the program upon which he was elected. There is no question whatsoever in my mind about that." With the White House and Congress under Democratic control, creating a unified, national government committed to stimulating the economy through federal spending to end unemployment, to federal aid to education, to civil rights legislation, and to other economic and social policies the UAW favored and the Democratic platform endorsed, progress seemed assured. In the event, Kennedy, in his brief time in office, proved less the ardent reformer than a cautious politician of consensus, with Congress remaining in the hands of the conservative southern Democrat-Republican coalition. Although the presidency of Lyndon B. Johnson began with the greatest outburst of reform energy and action in a generation, the American failure in the Vietnam War and a civil rights backlash shattered Johnson's political base and drove him from office. The assassinations of Robert F. Kennedy and Martin Luther King in 1968, five years after John F. Kennedy's own death by an assassin's bullet, brutally annihilated the reform movement's national leadership. A decade that began with the UAW's hope for a new dawn for American social democracy ended with a strife-ravaged nation embracing conservatism.[1]

With the approach of the 1960 election, the UAW leadership believed the Democratic party was poised to regain power. After eight years of a Republican administration, with the controversial Richard Nixon that party's likely presidential nominee, the political pendulum was due to swing to the Democrats and a progressive government. Senators John F. Kennedy, Hubert H. Humphrey, Stuart Symington, and Lyndon B. Johnson, and former governor of Illinois and two-time presidential nominee Adlai E. Stevenson were candidates for the Democratic nomination; all except Johnson were acceptable to the UAW. Officially the UAW remained neutral during the pre-convention battle, making no endorsement, although officers, regional directors, and staff members were free to support the candidate of their choice, with the understanding that all would rally behind the Democratic candidate once he was selected. Some supported Humphrey, with whom the UAW had close ties over the years, and some supported Kennedy. When Humphrey, with UAW prompting, dropped out after suffering defeat in the West Virginia primary, leadership support for Kennedy became virtually unanimous. Saddled in his early years as congressman and senator with a middle-of-the-road, lackluster record, Kennedy had followed the straightforward advice Reuther offered in 1956 when the senator asked what he must do to merit the UAW's support: "Improve your voting record," the UAW leader replied. Kennedy's votes thereafter closely tracked the UAW's policy positions. As a member of the McClellan committee, the Massachusetts senator provided valuable assistance to the UAW during the hearings. Union attorney Joseph L. Rauh, Jr., later testified, "Every time we were getting into trouble, Jack would enter the hearings room, take his seat on the committee dais and help us out." Kennedy's string of victories in the primaries showed that his Roman Catholic faith would not be an electoral handicap and that he could mount a strong, well-organized, and well-financed campaign. Reuther's friend, Eleanor Roosevelt, begged him not to foreclose the possibility of supporting Stevenson for a third try for the presidency, but the UAW leader believed Stevenson's two previous, unsuccessful campaigns were all that he deserved; moreover, Reuther feared that any weakening of Kennedy's position would work to Johnson's advantage.[2]

At the convention, after a boomlet for Stevenson collapsed, Kennedy won on the first ballot with the support of Reuther and the forty UAW delegates to the convention, the largest contingent from any union. The hottest issue was the vice presidential nomination. Reuther favored Humphrey, but the Minnesota senator had alienated Kennedy with his support for Stevenson, and he may have, in any case, preferred to remain in the Senate. Kennedy stunned Reuther and all liberal delegates by offering the place to Johnson. Although Reuther had many reservations about Johnson's record on issues of importance to labor and the civil rights movement, at Kennedy's request he quashed the opposition to the Johnson nomination within the UAW's ranks, stepped in to head off a revolt in the Michigan delegation—which wanted to challenge the nomination in an open floor fight—and dissuaded George Meany from pushing a critical resolution through the AFL-CIO council. As it turned out, the Texas senator's pres-

ence on the ticket gave it a crucial lift (the electoral votes of seven southern states, including Texas, were essential to Kennedy's narrow victory),
and after Johnson succeeded Kennedy in 1963, his liberal accomplishments
at home surpassed those of any president since FDR.[3]

The UAW threw itself into the campaign with money and the efforts
of thousands of volunteers. Roy Reuther, with much experience in the
union's nuts-and-bolts political operations, became codirector of a Democratic Party voter registration drive aimed at blue-collar workers, and when
Kennedy kicked off his campaign with the traditional Detroit Labor Day
speech, 80,000, by the union's estimate, turned out to hear him praise the
UAW and endorse some of Reuther's ideas on economic stimulation to produce full employment and economic growth. In a later campaign speech
Kennedy, at Reuther's urging, pledged to create a Peace Corps, an idea
Reuther, along with others, had supported for years; this proved to be one
of Kennedy's most popular and enduring accomplishments. Nixon, believing he could turn the visibility of the UAW and the Reuthers in the campaign to account, denounced Walter as a "labor leader turned radical
politician" and warned that with Kennedy in the White House Reuther
would "have a lot to do with calling the tune," remarks that perhaps cor-
ralled votes but certainly exaggerated the influence the UAW president
would exercise in the Kennedy administration. In the extremely close election, Kennedy carried Michigan, Illinois, Missouri, New York, and
Delaware, states with large numbers of UAW members, but lost Ohio, Indiana, and Wisconsin, which also had many auto unionists. According to a
post-election Harris poll, 73 percent of UAW voters cast ballots for
Kennedy, compared to 59 percent of their blue-collar neighbors in similar
economic and social circumstances, and 49.6 percent of the electorate as a
whole. Concerns about unemployment (the number of auto jobs had
declined significantly since reaching a peak in 1955) and other "bread and
butter" issues dominated the members' thinking. Despite this strong UAW
support for the new president, the poll revealed some fragmentation of the
UAW vote, trends that would gain strength in future elections. Skilled,
white, younger workers and those who had only recently become union
members were slightly less likely to vote for JFK than production, black,
older, and high-seniority workers. There was no appreciable difference in
voting patterns by gender. Speaking to a UAW convention after the election,
Kennedy, with characteristic wit, paid tribute to the union's contribution
to his victory. Noting that he had received such cool receptions in recent
appearances before Chamber of Commerce and American Medical Association audiences that, "I began to wonder how I got elected," he acknowledged the union's fervent electoral support and its uproarious convention
welcome by adding, "And now I remember."[4]

John F. Kennedy campaigns for the presidency in Detroit on Labor Day, 1960.
Walter P. Reuther Library, Wayne State University

THE NARROW KENNEDY VICTORY and the slight changes in the distribution of power in Congress, where the Democrats had majorities in both
Houses but the conservative Republican-southern Democrat coalition
remained intact and in control of key committees, did not augur well for the
UAW's progressive program. Although the union's public and Reuther's personal relationship with Kennedy remained strong and cordial, the payoff in
policy and legislation was thin. Kennedy had pledged in the campaign to "get
the country moving again" and had accepted a Democratic Party platform
that established an annual economic growth rate of 5 percent as a national
goal—slogans and commitments that were interpreted by the UAW and
many others as pledging a vigorous assault on a national unemployment rate
which, since the recession of 1958, had climbed to 8.7 percent in early 1961,
its highest point since 1950. With the UAW strongly supporting the legislation, Congress passed the Area Redevelopment Act, twice vetoed by President Eisenhower, which targeted chronically depressed areas with federal
funds and for the first time began job retraining for displaced workers. But
the limited funding for the program guaranteed it would fall short of meet-

ing the need. Ever hopeful of seeing the federal government take on a role in democratic economic planning akin to that being employed in most western European nations, Reuther proposed a National Planning Agency with government, labor, and management representatives to set economic goals. The agency would exert some influence on tax policy, federal spending, business regulation, pricing policies, and plant closings and locations in coordinating public and private economic activity to achieve maximum output and employment. As an immediate stimulus to consumer demand, the union favored a Keynesian program of tax credits primarily benefiting low-paid workers combined with government spending for housing, public works, health and educational facilities, resource conservation, and recreational development. A tax credit for low-income families, Reuther wrote Kennedy, "is both morally right and economically sound . . . ," for such "families will reflect their tax savings in high velocity purchasing power"; he told the president that the "most irresponsible fiscal policy is a government policy that tolerates mass unemployment and the underutilization of our economic resources." A restructuring of economic management and decision-making and a redirection of policy toward massive government spending had little chance of winning congressional approval, and it was not at all what Kennedy, fearful of reactions on Wall Street and in corporate boardrooms, had in mind. When, in 1962, a Kennedy tax cut proposal was forthcoming, its benefits went primarily to the affluent. Acutely disappointed with such a cautious, conservative approach, the UAW criticized the president's proposal but eventually accepted a limited tax cut as the only economic stimulus obtainable.[5]

Reuther keenly felt the frustrations of powerlessness. A political realist as well as a visionary, he knew that the system responded only to pressure. "There is not a chance in the world of the President doing any of these things," he told the UAW's executive board, "excepting as the American labor movement is prepared to carry the ball and mobilize this country so that politically it is feasible for the President of the United States to do these things." Eager to remain on good terms with the president, Reuther directed his strongest public criticisms at a sluggish Congress's refusal to act. He accused the lawmakers of conducting the longest strike in America and added "there's more featherbedding on the Hill in one week than in the labor movement in a year." Although careful to avoid a public break with the Kennedy administration, he did not spare it in private. He had been forced to recognize that the UAW, despite its support for Kennedy's election, had little leverage with the administration because it had, as Kennedy's chief economic advisor Walter Heller noted, "nowhere else to go." To the union's executive board, Reuther acknowledged the frustrating political dilemma the UAW faced when a liberally inclined president was in office: "It is more difficult during the Kennedy administration than it was during the Eisenhower administration because when you get an administration that is reasonably friendly it tends to immobilize the left." Such immobilization would have far more serious consequences in the future. Still, the options of a nonpartisan stance or support for an independent third party promised only worse frustration and greater futility, and a break with the national Democratic Party could come at a price, since the affiliation still seemed to be a defensive necessity. With the erosion of the majority political coalition Roosevelt had assembled, the two major parties could be kept in balance only as long as labor remained firmly within the Democratic camp. If labor withheld support or struck out on an independent path, it risked tipping the balance of power in the Republicans' favor.[6]

ON QUESTIONS OF FOREIGN POLICY the UAW and its leaders were in closer agreement with the actions of the Kennedy administration. Initiatives like the Alliance for Progress program of aid to Latin American nations, the reduction of trade restrictions through agreements on lower tariffs, and negotiated limitations on nuclear testing accorded with UAW policy positions, and the union leadership applauded as appropriate steps were taken toward these goals. Similarly, the president's handling of the Cuban missile crisis in October 1962 evoked public expressions of UAW support. The establishment of the Peace Corps represented the fulfillment of an idea Reuther had championed for years. In 1950, as part of his "Proposal for . . . A Total Peace Offensive," he recommended creation of an organization that would provide young Americans with an opportunity to "use their energies, training, and creative ingenuity to assist and train the people of under-developed countries to restore and increase the productivity of their land and to improve their health and living standards." Elaborating on the concept in speeches and other statements, he proposed in 1953, shortly after the end of the Korean War when the draft was still in effect, offering young men government-funded college scholarships. Those who accepted them would, on graduation, have the option of serving abroad for three years in a civilian service capacity or for two years in the military. With Reuther and others urging him on, Kennedy introduced a Peace Corps proposal during the campaign, although he quickly dropped the option of civilian service as a substitute for military service when Nixon charged that the plan would create a haven for draft dodgers. Once in office, Kennedy established the corps by executive order, adding provisions which made women eligible to serve. On arms control, another important foreign policy issue, Reuther argued in a 1963 essay in a popular magazine that "We *Can* Make the Russians Disarm." He proposed drawing the Soviet Union into an economic competition that the United States, with its powerhouse economy, would win; in order to keep within shouting distance, the Soviets would have to sacrifice parity in arms and military capability—a scenario that events many years later and long after Reuther's death approximated.[7]

Reuther, at the request of an embarrassed and humiliated Kennedy administration, took on the task of organizing a rescue effort for the more than one thousand Cubans captured by Castro's forces in the disastrous Bay of Pigs invasion. At first Castro demanded five hundred bulldozers, a proposal rejected by the administration on the ground that the equipment could be used for military construction projects. Proposals to substitute agricultural implements and a cash payment of $28 million likewise fell through, and the Reuther effort came to an end. Much later, an arrangement in which Reuther played no part secured the release of the prisoners in exchange for pharmaceuticals.[8]

BY THE BEGINNING OF THE 1960s the moral fervor and potential political force being generated by the civil rights revolution promised a resurgent progressive movement. The UAW's record in support of a national civil rights program was solid, more than sufficient to entitle it to a place in the "coalition of conscience," as Reuther and others referred to the assemblage of unions, civil rights groups, and religious organizations that formed the core of 1960s reform. Welded together, these forces could become the new dynamic in American politics, moving government to undertake a legislative reconstruction of American society. A long-time member of the board of directors of the National Association for the Advancement of Colored People, Reuther enjoyed credibility with that organization and the thousands who supported it. The UAW had given moral and financial backing to several of Dr. Martin Luther King, Jr.'s, campaigns. Two historians of civil rights saw Reuther as "the one white labor leader of national stature who was close to both the NAACP and Martin Luther King." The emergence of a militant, uncompromising civil rights movement, Reuther believed, offered an opportunity to restart forward momentum across the entire spectrum of social, economic, and political reform. The movement marked a rebirth of the struggle for justice that the unions had begun on behalf of their members thirty years earlier. To a hesitant George Meany of the AFL-CIO, he pointed out: "[T]he Labor Movement morally was obligated to be in the front ranks of this great effort. After all, the Labor Movement is about the struggle of the people who are denied their measure of justice, and if the Labor Movement is not in the front rank then I think the Labor Movement begins to forfeit the loyalty of the people whom I profess to represent and lead." In addition to supplying funding and the active support of many of its members and leaders, the UAW could make a special contribution as a result of its experience in national politics and its contacts with influential government officials in Congress and elsewhere, a knowledge and expertise in political and legislative methods that few other members of the coalition of conscience could match.[9]

During the Kennedy years Reuther was a forceful advocate of civil rights measures, steadily pressuring the administration and Congress to move farther and faster than they were prepared to go. In an appearance before the 1960 Democratic convention's platform committee, which adopted the strongest and most comprehensive civil rights planks in the party's history, he urged the party to demand personal pledges from its candidates for president and vice president to support the platform's civil rights proposals. Appointed by Kennedy to the President's Committee on Equal Employment Opportunity, he took an active part in its deliberations and acquired an appreciation of committee chairman Vice President Lyndon B. Johnson's recently surfaced commitment to civil rights. Reuther was one of many who urged President Kennedy to fulfill his preelection pledge to forbid racial discrimination in access to federally-funded housing programs by issuing a broadly worded executive order, an action the new president delayed for months.[10]

The UAW provided important funding for the civil rights movement. It raised money to support the Montgomery, Alabama, bus boycott, endorsed the national boycott of Woolworth stores in support of the lunch counter sit-ins, denounced the violent assaults on the freedom riders who were attempting to desegregate southern buses and donated funds for bail money when they were arrested, underwrote voter registration campaigns in areas with large black populations, and in 1963 alone contributed over $100,000 to the Southern Christian Leadership Conference, Martin Luther King's organization. In May of that year, when hundreds of civil rights demonstrators were jailed in Birmingham, Alabama, Attorney General Robert F. Kennedy, anxious to find a peaceful solution to a conflict that threatened to turn more violent, asked the UAW to organize the raising of funds to provide bail money for the release of the 840 jailed demonstrators. With at least $160,000 required, the UAW pledged $40,000, and Reuther, as president of the AFL-CIO's Industrial Union Department, pledged an additional $40,000 from that organization. A reluctant George Meany was persuaded to provide $40,000 from the AFL-CIO after Reuther assured him the UAW's money would be used to provide bail for those posing the greatest risk, thus providing some security for the AFL-CIO's funds. The United Steel Workers put up another $40,000. Governor Nelson Rockefeller of New York and Mike Quill, head of the Transport Workers Union, provided additional sums. The Birmingham authorities required that the bail money be paid in cash, so Irving Bluestone, Reuther's administrative assistant, and William Oliver, the African American who headed the union's Fair Practices Department, strapped on money belts containing $50,000 in cash and flew from Detroit to Birmingham. As Bluestone recalled "I was scared to death; black and white coming down to deliver bail money" during one of the nation's most tense racial crises. In the event, the bail money was deposited and the jailed demonstrators were released, but the entire amount of the UAW's funds was not repaid until 1970.[11]

Although Kennedy originally showed little interest in securing civil rights legislation, being more concerned to maintain the Democratic Party's precarious balance between northern liberals and southern conservatives, as the movement gathered force and momentum with the success of demonstrations in Birmingham and elsewhere, he now supported a civil rights initiative. In the spring of 1963 a Kennedy civil rights bill containing provisions on public accommodations and school desegregation was introduced in Congress. With the focus of civil rights action now on Washington, the UAW's role in the movement took on greater significance. Kennedy's bill was the most sweeping civil rights legislation introduced by any American president to that time, and Reuther praised the president's willingness to embrace the civil rights cause with a legislative proposal. Yet the bill's inadequacies were disturbing. The public accommodations and school desegregation titles would have only limited effect, and the bill entirely lacked voting rights and fair employment practices sections. In congressional testimony Reuther urged the addition of titles providing for the appointment of federal voting registrars in states where African Americans were not registered and a fair employment practices section that would grant limited special hiring treatment for blacks but deny specific quotas.[12]

The UAW launched an energetic lobbying campaign to strengthen the Kennedy bill, go beyond it in important respects, and obtain its passage. The "coalition of conscience" wanted a law that would eliminate segregation in all public accommodations, guarantee fair employment practices, prohibit federal aid to any organization that practiced racial discrimination, provide federal voting registrars, reduce congressional representation in states that denied blacks the vote, and empower the attorney general to sue on behalf of victims of discrimination. The lobbying, coordinated through the Leadership Conference on Civil Rights (LCCR), which the UAW had helped found in the 1950s, focused on moderate Republican congressmen from rural, small-town and suburban districts (not areas of UAW strength) who would have to supply votes to offset the opposition of many southern Democrats—a tactic that depended on lobbying by religious groups for its success. The UAW gave LCCR critical financial and staff support and cooperated closely with the religious groups. Thanks in part to this lobbying effort the bill was significantly strengthened in committee but had not passed Congress prior to Kennedy's assassination. Further strengthened, it became the basis for the landmark Civil Rights Act of 1964.[13]

THE GREAT PUBLIC CIVIL RIGHTS demonstration of the Kennedy years was the massive March on Washington for Jobs and Freedom on August 28, 1963, initially proposed by A. Philip Randolph, the head of the Brotherhood of Sleeping Car Porters and civil rights activist, and the most memorable setting for Dr. King's "I Have a Dream" speech. The UAW, one of ten officially sponsoring organizations, insisted upon the link between jobs and freedom in the march's official title, reflecting the union's view that any substantial improvement in the condition of the nation's black minority had to be grounded in access to good jobs and the higher standard of living and the greater degrees of security and independence such access would bring. A dress rehearsal for the march had occurred in Detroit under the auspices of black ministers and the UAW only months earlier, when Reuther, Dr. King, Mayor Jerome Cavanagh, and other local figures led an estimated 125,000 blacks and whites down Woodward Avenue in, as King noted, "the largest and greatest civil rights demonstration ever held in the United States"—a tumultuous, electrifying event. The UAW supplied much of the manpower, experience, and organizing expertise for the march, with King and Reuther addressing the crowd at Cobo Hall at its conclusion.[14]

As plans for a civil rights demonstration in Washington went forward, Reuther found himself caught in a web of conflicting pressures. The Kennedy administration feared that a massive demonstration might result in violence and that an all-black demonstration employing civil disobedience tactics would infuriate southern Democrats and some Republican congressmen, solidifying their resistance to any civil rights legislation. In some measure, Reuther shared that fear. He persuaded the sponsoring organizations to abandon the plan for a civil disobedience demonstration on Capitol Hill, while also helping to mobilize and incorporate into the march sympathetic white elements, including many UAW members, other labor groups, and representatives of religious organizations. The union provided bus transportation to Washington for 5,000 rank-and-file UAW members, the largest contingent from a single organization, and made other financial contributions to help meet the march's expenses. The result was the most impressive public demonstration of interracial backing for civil rights in the nation's history, a festive occasion that was, despite the forebodings, unmarred by violent episodes and added immeasurably to the momentum that led to the passage of the civil rights acts of 1964 and 1965.[15]

Reuther tried to obtain Meany's cooperation and the official endorsement of the AFL-CIO for the march, but Meany, predicting riots and blood-

Detroit's "Walk to Freedom," 1963. Walter P. Reuther Library, Wayne State University

UAW and other union members march for civil rights in Washington, D.C., August 28, 1963. Walter P. Reuther Library, Wayne State University

shed, feared AFL-CIO sponsorship of a demonstration it could not control; in any event, Meany preferred to access government's power through Washington's back corridors rather than on the streets. The AFL-CIO council turned down Reuther's request for an endorsement and funding when Meany made the issue one of personal support for his leadership, after which the council passed a weak resolution acknowledging the right of affiliated unions and their members to participate in the march and support it financially. An irritated Reuther snapped, "That resolution is so anemic it will need a transfusion to get to the mimeograph machine," but it was all he could get. Meany's refusal to support the march embittered Reuther for the rest of the decade. "It bothered the living devil out of him," recalled Irving Bluestone, his closest associate in civil rights matters.[16]

Reuther served as a behind-the-scenes conciliator in holding together the coalition of conscience when it threatened to fall apart at the last moment. One of the speakers, John Lewis of the Student Non-Violent Coordinating Committee (SNCC), proposed to deliver a fiery address that dismissed President Kennedy's civil rights bill as not worth the paper it was written on, claimed that blacks could not obtain redress within the American constitutional system, and threatened that he and others would march through the South like General Sherman's army in a "scorched earth policy"—in short, a call for revolution. With the other sponsoring organizers appalled and King, the champion of nonviolence, pointing out that "this is completely contrary to everything we are doing," the Roman Catholic archbishop who was scheduled to deliver the invocation as representive of one of the sponsoring organizations threatened to pull out if Lewis's speech was delivered as written. In a flurry of activity that secured the archbishop's agreement to proceed with only minutes to spare (Reuther later remarked to his UAW colleagues, "You talk about bargaining against deadlines!"), Reuther and others persuaded Lewis that a speech whose ideas were so contrary to the nonviolent, legalistic, and legislative approach of the sponsoring organizations could not be included. Lewis, whose right to say whatever he wished in a different setting and under different sponsorship was not in question, chose to allow the speech to be reworked to bring it within the boundaries set by the participants' agreement. Reuther recalled his relief when the archbishop and his retinue of fourteen bishops mounted the steps of the Lincoln Memorial only moments before the invocation was scheduled to begin the program: "I never saw a Bishop look so good in my life."[17]

Reuther was the only white labor leader to address the assembled multitude. In his impassioned style he chided the Kennedy administration for its hesitant support and iterated the longstanding UAW view that substantial and lasting progress in ending racial injustice could only come by making good jobs available to all in a full-employment economy. In formulating the equation for progress "the job question is crucial," he asserted, "because we will not solve discrimination in education or housing, or public accommodations as long as millions of Americans, Negroes, are treated as second class, economic citizens. And so our slogan has to be 'fair employment'— but fair employment within the framework of full employment so that every American can have a job." In a remark that Reuther treasured when later told of it, Irving Bluestone overheard one black woman at the march identify Reuther to another as "the white Martin Luther King."[18]

Although the UAW leaders sometimes chafed at Kennedy's hesitancy to support a vigorous attack on racial and economic problems, they recognized the political constraints that hampered his actions and looked forward, with him, to the 1964 presidential election with its prospect of a stronger mandate. Following Kennedy's death, the delegates to the UAW's convention unanimously authorized a donation of $230,554.60 to the Kennedy presidential library fund. The warm feelings between the Kennedys and the UAW were mutual and reciprocated. In February 1964, Robert Kennedy—making, as he noted, his first public appearance since the assassination of his brother—briefly addressed at his request a UAW council meeting in Washington, D.C. Expressing great appreciation for all the

UAW and its members had done in support of the martyred president, he said, "I wanted to come to this organization because there was no organization in the United States with whom the President was more closely associated and identified than the UAW."[19]

THE CIVIL RIGHTS MOVEMENT had repurcussions in the auto plants and within the UAW's ranks. By the 1960s undercurrents of racial tension and expressions of racial animosity long present in northern plants exploded in outbursts of rage and demands for change. This coincided with and reflected the vitality of the civil rights movement and a recomposition of both the factory workforce and the union's membership. In only five years, between 1962 and 1967, the UAW admitted 842,000 new members, over half of the total. During the 1960s employment of African Americans in the auto industry increased dramatically. Although the UAW did not record its members' race, UAW sources estimated that African Americans constituted approximately 18 percent of the membership by the end of the decade; estimates by others ranged as high as 25 percent. African American employment was concentrated in auto plants (in contrast to aircraft plants and other non-auto UAW-organized workplaces), particularly in urban auto plants; it was highest in Detroit and there were significant variations between manufacturers and between plants. In 1960 General Motors' Detroit area black employment averaged 23 percent of the workforce, ranging from a high of 60 percent at Chevrolet Forge to a low of 1 percent at a Fisher Body plant in the largely white suburb of Livonia. The average at Chrysler plants was 26 percent black, ranging from 48 percent at the Lynch Road assembly plant to 11 percent at Amplex. Incomplete Ford data showed 41 percent (12,500 out of 30,000) at the Rouge plant, still the largest Ford faciltiy and probably the Ford plant containing the highest percentage of African American employees. In blue-collar occupations in 1968 at Big Three plants the proportion of blacks varied from a low of 3 percent among skilled tradesmen, to 21 percent of production operatives (the largest occupational category in the industry with more than half a million employees), to 27 percent and 20 percent for the smaller, yet still substantial numbers of service workers and laborers, respectively. In contrast, only 1.4 percent of managers employed in the Big Three were African Americans.[20]

Black auto workers, whatever their particular jobs, materially benefited from the contract advances negotiated by the union. In Detroit, as one historian wrote, "they became an aristocracy of labor among the city's African American population," with good wages and benefits and some job security. Buoyed by the industry's high wages, black industrial workers in Michigan led the nation in income. In 1960 their earnings were 80 percent of the income of the state's white industrial workers, whereas nationally the comparable figure was 56 percent. The seniority provisions in the UAW's contracts prevented employers from discriminating against blacks when layoffs came, but, as so often the last hired, they would by the same token be among the first to go when downturns occurred. The lack of high seniority similarly restricted opportunities for promotion and transfer.[21]

For years, black unionists had pointed out that, given their numbers in the union, they were underrepresented in the leadership. Locals with substantial numbers of black members, such as Local 600, had always had some elected black officers, and blacks would be present in their delegations to conventions and other union gatherings. In other locals, African Americans began to win election to office as their membership numbers increased, usually in coalitions formed with some whites, sometimes confronting and overcoming openly expressed appeals to racial prejudice. When African American Marc Stepp, later a UAW vice president, ran in 1960 for vice president of his local in the Chrysler Highland Park, Michigan, plant, his campaign manager, a white skilled tradesman, "was called nigger lover and all that . . . but anyway, we won by 54 votes." By the end of the 1960s eleven locals in the Detroit area had African American presidents, and there were hundreds of elected officials of lesser rank, such as committeemen and stewards. As late as 1968, however, only 7.5 percent of the representatives and other staff positions in the International, including those on regional staffs, were held by blacks, while about 30 percent of the clerical staff at union headquarters was black.[22]

Although some steps toward racial integration of office-holding within the locals had been taken, domination of local union offices by those of one race with token representation for the other remained a common pattern. The union's official position of opposing discrimination and favoring integration pressured racially mixed locals to avoid a "lily-white slate" in elections, a "political 'no-no,' " according to Stepp, by the 1960s. Locals with a racially mixed membership in which blacks were in the majority tended to elect black officers with a token white, with the reverse occurring in locals with a white majority and a black minority. Racial tensions and expressions of prejudice remained high in some plants, and verbal clashes and even physical assaults occasionally occurred. Symbolic actions in tense situations could provoke protests. After the assassination of Martin Luther King, Jr., in 1968, white workers at two Flint factories threatened wildcat strikes if flags were lowered to half-mast as many black workers were demanding. At some other plants, the flags were lowered without protest.[23]

In the late 1950s, blacks began to organize to secure recognition and a more influential role within the union. An ad hoc committee of Detroit black unionists that met with Reuther, Leonard Woodcock, and Douglas Fraser evolved in 1957 into the Trade Union Leadership Council (TULC), with the purpose of bringing blacks into leadership positions in unions, politics, and community organizations. Although its interests extended beyond the UAW, most of the membership came from the union, a testimony, in part, to the stimulus to activism and the training in organizational methods and forms the UAW had cultivated among its members. TULC played a crucial role in mobilizing Detroit's large black working class for community and political projects and it helped prepare the way for the expansion of the civil rights movement from its southern base to the cities of the north. Its two leading figures, Horace Sheffield and Robert "Buddy" Battle 3rd, were prominent black unionists from Local 600. Sheffield was on the UAW staff and had been a Reuther supporter since the struggle with the Addes-Thomas faction, while Battle was the head of the largely black division of Ford foundry workers. TULC was integrated. It invited white unionists to join, and several white UAW officers and staff members, including Woodcock and Brendan Sexton, responded, but its membership, which once numbered 7,000, was predominantly black. The relationship between TULC and the UAW was strained at times. In 1961 the union's political apparatus, cooperating with the Detroit AFL- CIO, endorsed Mayor Louis Miriani for reelection; Miriani's labor record was worthy of support, but his lack of response to black citizens' concerns had created dissatisfaction within that community. TULC leaders refused to go along with the Miriani endorsement, preferring Jerome Cavanagh, a young, liberal newcomer to politics, whose advocacy of racial justice and fairness, in a city whose electorate was shifting from white to black, carried him to victory. Ironically, the UAW, which had twice supported racially enlightened Detroit mayoral candidates only to see them go down to defeat, now found itself backing the more conservative candidate with the same result. The UAW leadership quickly came around in support of Detroit's dynamic new mayor, a political New Frontiersman in the Kennedy mold.[24]

TULC set out to secure a UAW executive board position for a black, an objective that had not been seriously pursued since World War II. Although the total African American membership now constituted a substantial minority in the union as a whole, it still lacked the concentrated numbers within a single region necessary to elect a board member. Consequently the strategy was to build momentum for the election of an African American by the entire convention as an International officer, a position that carried with it board membership. The question was raised at an Administration caucus session prior to the 1959 convention. Introduced and backed by several black members of the caucus, the proposal received no support from any of its white members. In fact, some whites were openly hostile, clapping and shouting "sit down" as blacks attempted to speak. Despite the caucus's rejection of the proposal, when the convention met to

elect officers Sheffield nominated Willoughby "Bill" Abner, a black unionist from Chicago and a UAW International representative, for a vice presidency. The nomination's purpose was to draw attention to the inequity
represented by the absence of a black board member and to nudge the leadership toward a solution. Abner, as arranged, declined the nomination.
There had been no expectation that, lacking a caucus endorsement, he
would run or could win. Annoyed with the often repeated excuse that a lack
of qualified candidates excluded blacks from election to the executive
board, Sheffield sarcastically noted during the convention debate, "Negroes
are sick and tired of the matter of qualifications being raised . . . because I
think it is fairly evident to everyone here that it is not necessary to be a
Rhodes Scholar to sit on the International Executive Board." Some members of the Administration caucus demanded that Sheffield be fired from his
staff position for insubordination in defying a caucus decision, a punishment warranted by caucus rules, but Reuther refused to accede to their
wishes.[25]

By 1962, as the next convention approached, the leadership had taken
the matter in hand, fashioning an arrangement that would both respond to
the need of blacks for recognition and muffle charges of racial favoritism.
The solution was to create three new positions of board members-at-large,
the occupants to be elected, as were all International officers, by the convention delegates, with an understanding that an African American would
be included as one of the new board members. The caucus nominees for two
of the positions were stalwarts of the Reuther leadership cadre but not currently board members: Ken Bannon, director of the Ford Department; and
Douglas Fraser, formerly president of Local 227, administrative assistant to
Reuther, and codirector of Region 1A. The nominee for the third position
was African American Nelson Jack Edwards, an International representative and TULC member. Edwards had been active in the campaign to secure
a board position for a black but by no means so prominently as Sheffield and
some others. Although many blacks preferred Sheffield, as perhaps did
Reuther himself, Edwards's selection had the support of the black leadership and of influential members of the Reuther caucus such as Fraser. He
proved to be an effective spokesman for black interests and concerns in
board deliberations. In 1968 a second black unionist, Marcellius Ivory of
Local 600, joined the executive board when he was elected director of
Region 1B, covering West Side Detroit and adjacent suburban areas, and
with a substantial but still minority black membership. Reuther prepared
the way for his election by persuading the two leading contenders for the
vacant position, both white, to step aside, obtaining from each of the two
rivals a promise not to run if the other would likewise abstain. Although
requiring presidential intervention, the election of a black regional director

was an important breakthrough that reflected a growing black membership and the pressures generated by the civil rights movement. At the same time African American unionists, led by Local 600 vice president Robert "Buddy" Battle III, focused on increasing black representation on the union's staff, pointing out that although approximately 25 percent of the membership was African American, only seventy-five blacks held appointments as International representatives.[26]

The UAW's Fair Practices Department under William Oliver, with Reuther himself as nominal codirector, had historically functioned more as an ambassador to the nation's civil rights organizations than as a solver of the UAW's internal race relations problems. Reflecting the rise of the civil rights movement and the passage of effective civil rights laws by Congress, the department became more active in the 1960s. Its case load rose dramatically. In 1964 it handled only twenty-three cases but the number then climbed rapidly, reaching 136 in 1970. Of these 136 cases, 115 originated pursuant to Title VII of the Civil Rights Act of 1964, the section dealing with equal opportunity in employment, or through the federal Equal Employment Opportunity Commission or state equal employment opportunity commissions—through the mechanisms, that is, of recently enacted federal and state laws. The remaining twenty-one cases originated internally, through local unions, letters of complaint to the president's office, or through the Fair Practices Department itself. Much of the final push to make the department an effective advocate of internal racial equity came from the outside, but it should be added that the UAW, in its political activity, had played a major role in securing the legislation from Congress and state legislatures that supplied the thrust.[27]

Fair access to housing was another civil rights cause supported by the UAW leadership. Some UAW staff members were victims of housing discrimination. When African American attorney William B. Gould, later a distinguished law professor and head of the National Labor Relations Board during the Clinton presidency, arrived in Detroit in 1961 to take up a position as UAW assistant general counsel, he was denied an apartment lease because of his race. As one of many such cases, the incident was brought to the attention of Michigan Governor John B. Swainson, a strong supporter of establishing a state civil rights commission with authority over access to housing. Effective state legislation to prevent discrimination in the sale and rental of housing was not forthcoming until, in the aftermath of the Detroit racial uprising of 1967, the Michigan legislature passed a strong open-housing law. The UAW took steps to improve access to housing where it had influence. A leading instance involved construction of an open-housing project, "Sunnyhills," in Milpitas, California. When the Ford Motor Company closed an old plant in Richmond, California, moving production to a new factory in the Santa Clara valley, African American members of Local 560 who transferred to the new plant were unable to find affordable housing there. To remedy the situation the union persuaded Ford to commit $1.2 million from the Ford-UAW pension fund to finance start-up costs for a housing development and secured additional federal funding for construction. The result was a racially integrated community of over 1,000 three-bedroom homes, available for a down payment of $199 plus closing costs. United Nations officials who visited the site called it a "model example of integrated democratic living." This was the breakthrough in the UAW's effort to persuade corporation and pension fund trustees to invest in socially progressive projects.[28]

THE FEMALE ELEMENT in the industry's workforce took heart from the human rights/civil rights movement to advance its claim for equal treatment. Averaged over time, the percentage of women employed remained stable in the 1950s at about 12 percent, but there were fluctuations when layoffs occurred. During the 1960s the number of women employed grew slowly, to around 14 percent. As with race, the union's gender policies were officially nondiscriminatory, but in some locals the male majority benefited from and maintained gender-based discriminations, including separate seniority and job classification lists. The Women's Bureau, which had been set up in 1944 within the Fair Practices Department, was upgraded to a free-standing Women's Department in 1955, placed under the direction of Caroline Davis, and given additional staff. It encouraged women employees to take action in their locals, and some piecemeal moves toward equal status and treatment were recorded. The International's leadership was supportive but unprepared to make gender equity a major cause. With some success, the leadership pressured delinquent locals to relent in their opposition to the employment of married women, although in some locals, even after contract language was changed to end such discrimination, restrictive verbal agreements with management remained in effect. The percentage of married women within the female auto workforce gradually increased, from 61 percent in 1950 to 68 percent in 1960. Not until 1969 did the executive board extend strike benefits to a married woman on the same terms as to a married man.[29]

The most contentious gender issue was that of equal pay for equal work. The spotlight was on General Motors, the only major manufacturer to resist the equal pay principle and, not coincidentally, the employer of the largest number of women. In the 1955 negotiations the union made equal pay a priority and won concessions that narrowed some pay differentials by about 50 percent, but gender inequities remained, due primarily to the continuation of separate "male" and "female" job classifications. Following passage of the federal Equal Pay Act in 1963, the UAW used the law to secure equal pay for women and men on the same jobs in many plants, but many jobs were unaffected because of slight differences in the definitions of the work for men and women.[30]

The adoption of Title VII of the Civil Rights Act of 1964, forbidding discrimination in employment based on sex and on other grounds, introduced a new and potentially powerful instrument for asserting and protecting equal rights to and on the job. The UAW, which had been a strong advocate of state protective legislation for women workers, reversed its stand, holding that the federal law superceded state protective laws, making the UAW the first large labor union to take this position. Studies conducted by the Women's Department concluded that the legislation had been more discriminatory than protective. By the time the Civil Rights Act was passed, women were under new pressures. Companies were finding it cost-effective to require overtime from current employees instead of hiring additional workers. State laws limiting the daily hours of work for women made it impossible to require as much overtime of them as employers might like. Consequently, employers were both refusing to hire women for jobs where overtime would be needed and were not able to offer as much overtime to some women employees as both they and their employer wanted. Women were being laid off and denied transfers and promotions because the jobs might require overtime beyond the legal maximum of hours worked per week. UAW women, however, like women in other occupations, were by no means united on the question of repeal of protective legislation. Many feared that repeal would lead to mandatory overtime (as was the case with men), which would interfere with fulfillment of responsibilities to home and family. The debate ended when the Equal Employment Opportunity Commission, on the UAW's urging, ruled in 1969 that state laws restricting employment opportunities for women conflicted with Title VII. In the following year the Michigan attorney general declared that the state's laws limiting women's hours of work had been superceded. A few months later, at its 1970 constitutional convention, the UAW endorsed the proposed Equal Rights Amendment to the United States Constitution, becoming the first union in the nation to do so. The endorsement, backed by female and male delegates, was an important demonstration of support by working women for an amendment that had historically been associated with middle-class and upper-class women. At the same convention the delegates adopted a set of sweeping proposals for reform of women workers' treatement, characterized by the *Detroit Free Press* as "the most far-reaching stand any international union has ever taken in favor of women workers." Among the measures endorsed was repeal of state laws outlawing abortion (this was prior to the *Roe v. Wade* decision), paid maternity leaves with job seniority protection, application of remaining workplace protective legislation equally to women and men, a system of national child care centers, tax deductions for child care where both wife and husband held jobs, recruitment of more women into the skilled trades, and better opportunities for women in union staff positions.[31]

The campaign to secure an executive board seat for a woman was reinvigorated by the decision to add a black repersentative in 1962. An attempt was made in 1964 to secure an additional at-large board seat for a woman but the campaign was launched without sufficient preparation and failed. Given the relatively small number of women working in the plants and the few women union activists, there was little rank-and-file sentiment for creating another at-large seat. Some board members were opposed because an additional board member would be assigned some administrative units to manage; such redistribution of responsibility would dilute the voting power of affected board members and deprive them of challenging tasks. A push from the top—particularly from Reuther, with support from Woodcock and Fraser—was crucial to the movement's success. Women activists campaigned for a board seat before the next convention and obtained Reuther's public endorsement of their goal, but the opposition was still formidable. In April 1966 the executive board voted 16–8 with one abstention in favor of an additional seat, and the convention delegates followed with their approval. Olga Madar, director of the UAW's Recreation Department and a Reuther loyalist, was chosen as the new board member. In the local unions, as the number of women working in the plants increased, more women were elected to office, although the percentage of elected officers and of appointed staff representatives who were female lagged well behind the 14 percent figure for women members. These steps toward equity did not establish gender equality in the workplace or in union affairs, or end sexual harrassment in the plants. Women could still be treated with disrespect and subjected to exploitative pressures, but the new federal legislation and the commitment to a greater voice for women in the union's councils marked significant progress.[32]

ALTHOUGH OPPOSED TO THE SELECTION of Lyndon B. Johnson as the Democrats' vice presidential candidate in 1960, Reuther had reached a more positive assessment of him during the Kennedy years and quickly rallied to him following Kennedy's assassination. Johnson, a consummate and energetic politician who was doubtless aware that the UAW could give him much valuable political and legislative support, called Reuther the day after the tragedy, as he called other leading liberal and labor figures, pleading with Reuther, as the UAW president recalled, "My friend, I need your friendship and support now more than ever before." Prior to Kennedy's death Congress had been inching toward passage of legislation the UAW had long advocated. Now Johnson's political skills and the desire to fulfill and build upon the martyred president's agenda were added to the momentum for reform already generated by the civil rights movement. In flattering terms, Johnson asked for Reuther's advice, prompting the first in a steady and voluminous flow of memos and other communications from Solidarity House in Detroit to the White House in Washington, D.C. These communications were supplemented by frequent conversations between the two by telephone and in the Oval Office, contacts that continued until the Vietnam War and its domestic repercussions chilled the relationship.[33]

Till then, Reuther fulsomely pledged "my heart and my hand" in the president's support, becoming, as he once put it, "a member of your team and a part of the Great Consensus," a "devoted member of your working crew." In response to the new president's invitation to state a legislative preference, Reuther indicated that passage of a strengthened civil rights bill was the UAW's highest priority. When later asked to submit suggestions for the president's first State of the Union message, he replied with a paraphrase of the UAW's national legislative agenda, emphasizing the need to launch "a massive national effort to provide a better life for America's submerged third" through improved public assistance, special educational opportunities for underprivileged children, expanded public housing, job retraining, and improved social security support and health care for the elderly. When consulted on legislative tactics, Reuther held that the administration's civil rights and social reform bills should have priority over the union movement's chief objective, the repeal of section 14(b) of the Taft-Hartley Act, a provision that had hampered organizing in southern and some western states. From the standpoint of obtaining passage of the legislation needed to attack the nation's racial and economic inequities, it would be a "serious mistake," he explained, to expend precious political capital on a measure primarily of benefit to organized labor. The national interest came first. Most of the UAW's items were endorsed in Johnson's message, in which he declared an "unconditional war on poverty." An exception was the union's plea for a national planning agency, a red flag to the champions of a private market economy that Johnson chose to omit, although he did pledge to establish a national commission on automation which might in time have formed the nucleus of a planning agency. With that exception, the address was everything the UAW leaders could have hoped for. With a politically skillful and passionately committed president in support of its program, the UAW and with it the nation seemed on the verge of a historic breakthrough. The first payoff came when LBJ pushed the civil rights bill through the House and then, concentrating on gaining sufficient Republican votes in the Senate to break a filibuster, obtained its passage by that body in May 1964.[34]

The outcome of the 1964 presidential and congressional elections bolstered the UAW's optimism. Before Kennedy's assassination, when it appeared certain that he would be renominated, Reuther had expressed the hope in an interview that the Republicans would make conservative Senator Barry Goldwater of Arizona their presidential candidate in order to give voters a clear choice and to realign the parties with the clear ideological division he had long favored. He must have rejoiced when the Republicans, possibly for the first and only time, followed his advice. During the campaign, the Republican vice presidential candidate, Representative William Miller, claimed to have discovered a "plot" by his Democratic counterpart, Senator Hubert H. Humphrey, to have Reuther appointed secretary of labor in the new Johnson Administration. With a Republican presidential candidate who drove millions of independents and moderate Republican voters over to the Democratic ticket, Johnson won reelection in a landslide, bringing in with him the largest liberal congressional majorities in a generation, including as a key member of the House of Representatives, Frank Thompson, Democrat of New Jersey, a former member of UAW Local 731 at General Motors' Ternstedt plant in Trenton. Johnson won the votes of 85 percent of voting auto workers, 10 percentage points higher than his support among other blue-collar voters. Reuther welcomed the result, proclaiming that "the American people have given the leadership of the Democratic party a clear mandate. We can by working together fulfill that mandate and successfully complete the task of dealing with the unfinished work on the agenda of American democracy."[35]

Like nearly everyone drawn into Johnson's furious orbit, Reuther was pressed to render political services and thereby learned the cost of playing the political game with a determined, wily practictioner like the president. At the Democratic convention in 1964, the Mississippi Freedom Democratic Party (MFDP), an integrated, predominantly black group formed largely as a result of a SNCC campaign, challenged the credentials of the all-white "regular" Democratic delegates from Mississippi. The Freedom Democrats truthfully contended that the regulars neither agreed with the national party's position on civil rights nor fairly represented the state's many black and moderate white citizens. In pre-convention activity, the UAW registered its support for the MFDP cause. Johnson, fearing that a convention walk-out by southern whites over the issue would cause the loss of their states to Goldwater and detract from his anticipated large majority and mandate, wanted a compromise that would keep divisive disputes off the floor and all the delegates inside the convention. His operatives first proposed to seat the regulars and allow the Freedom Democrats to appear on the floor but not vote; they were offered a pledge that rules changes would ensure representative delegations in the future—that is, delegations that included some blacks. The Freedom Democrats turned down the deal. Furthermore, they threatened to remove the struggle from the seclusion of the credentials committee to the convention floor, where many delegates from northern states would support them, creating the open rift and southern walk-out that Johnson feared. Applying the "treatment" with all the many expletives at his command, Johnson instructed Senator Hubert Humphrey, who hungered for the vice presidential nomination, to take charge of the operation, telling him to "get ahold of Walter Reuther and see if he can help you." Aware of Reuther's standing with black civil rights leaders and of the fact that Joseph L. Rauh, Jr., legal advisor to the Freedom Democrats, was an attorney and lobbyist for the UAW as well as Reuther's friend, Johnson expected Humphrey and Reuther to bring the matter swiftly to the conclusion he favored.[36]

At first Reuther, involved in tense negotiations with General Motors, was reluctant to take on an assignment that would pit him against an African American delegation that he sympathized with, had supported, and whose actions contributed to the party realignment he had long hoped to bring about. But Humphrey, desperate to obtain Johnson's promise of the vice presidency and thus the prospect of his own succession to the presidency in the future, prevailed on him for help. Eager to place a liberal of social democratic convictions like Humphrey in line for the presidency, and after weighing the pros and cons, Reuther flew to Atlantic City. At the convention he met with Johnson's advisors and the Freedom Democrats and fashioned a compromise that largely reflected the president's wishes but added two Freedom Democrats—Aaron Henry, a middle-class African American, and Ed King, a white—as voting delegates. None of the Freedom Democrats liked the proposal. Some held it acceptable if a representative of poor, black Mississippians, Fannie Lou Hamer, was included. Others rejected it altogether, charging Reuther and Humphrey with compromising principles of black representation they had agreed to support. As talks continued an incorrect public announcement that claimed the deal had been accepted infuriated the black leaders. Rauh, who resented Reuther's heavy-handed approach in the negotiations, believed that given a little more time he could have worked out an agreement that would have avoided the bitter resentment felt by many blacks over the white liberal pressure and betrayal. The Reuther-Rauh relationship was never again as close as it once had been. In the end, Henry and King were seated and the white Mississippi delegates walked out of the convention in response to the demand that all delegates pledge to support the platform's civil rights plank and the deal's assurance of fair treatment for blacks in future delegate selections. As Johnson had feared, Goldwater carried Mississippi and four other Deep South states, the first Republican presidential candidate to do so, but the president so overwhelmed his opponent elsewhere that these defections were not immediately missed. Nevertheless, the episode signaled an ominous split between white liberal advocates of civil rights and militant African Americans, leaving wounds that never healed. As serious in its political ramifications, the election tolled the death knell of the Democrats' "Solid South" with the rapid emergence of the Republicans as the party of southern racial conservatism. The voter realignment that Reuther and the UAW favored was launched on these stormy waters without any assurance that the result would be the longed-for national liberal majority. In fact, the election, despite the liberal landslide in the presidential contest, witnessed the formation of one strand in what would emerge before long as a national conservative majority.[37]

FOR A HISTORIC MOMENT from 1964 until 1966, before massive countercurrents flowing from the Vietnam War and backlashes against black nationalism and ideological and countercultural extremism undermined the fragile liberal consensus, the federal government produced the greatest flood of innovative legislation since the height of the New Deal, an achievement to which the UAW contributed as much as any private organization. With little if any exaggeration, Reuther characterized the 1965 session of the 89th Congress as "the most productive . . . in the history of the United States." In a remark to the UAW's executive board, he paid Senator Goldwater a backhanded tribute, saying the new laws were "Goldwater's great contribution to American democracy. In his defeat he made a much greater contribution than some Presidents made when they got elected."[38]

With a strong public accommodations and equal employment opportunity act on the books, civil rights activists moved on to secure guarantees of voting rights. Following the pattern set in Birmingham, King and the Southern Christian Leadership Conference selected Selma, Alabama, a city notorious for its severe restrictions on black voting, as the site of demonstrations. Following a brutal attack by Alabama state troopers on African American marchers, outraged supporters of voting rights from throughout the country poured into Selma. One of their number, James Reeb, a Unitarian minister, was fatally assaulted, others beaten. The UAW established a memorial fund with a donation of $10,000 for the benefit of Reeb's family, particularly to insure educational opportunities for his four children, and Walter and May Reuther led a UAW delegation of more than 2,000 to a memorial service in Selma. In the aftermath, the personal witness of Reuther and other UAW officials elicited many responses from UAW members. By far the greater number of telegrams from UAW locals expressed pride in the union's stand on the great moral issue of the times, but there were also protests. A division on racial issues still existed at the rank-and-

file level. Local 34 in Atlanta, Georgia, sent a petition to the executive
board, with the signatures of more than half of the membership, objecting
to UAW financial contributions to the NAACP, the Congress on Racial
Equality (CORE), and other civil rights organizations, and to Reuther's participation in civil rights demonstrations.[39]

At the height of the Selma crisis President Johnson addressed a joint
session of Congress, proclaiming in the words of the civil rights anthem,
"We shall overcome," and throwing the administration's weight behind the
struggle for a strong voting rights bill. Following a cloture vote in the Senate, the bill passed in July 1965. Reuther had great hopes that the enfran-
chisement of millions of southern African American voters would end the
southern Democrat-Republican coalition's control of Congress, producing
an enduring liberal majority in the country and in Congress. To the union's
executive board he predicted, "instead of Southern Democrats, coming out
of the deep South and joining forces with the most reactionary Northern
Republicans to block social legislation, you are going to have some of the
most progressive Congressmen and Senators coming out of the deep South.
This is going to make one tremendous difference in the whole relationship
of forces in the political arena of American society." To German Chancel-
lor Willy Brandt he wrote that a "historic process of . . . fundamental political realignment of forces" was underway in the United States. Although
the emergence and growth of the southern black electorate ended the
overtly racist rhetoric and politics of the southern past (no small victory!),
it failed to establish the UAW's liberal, social-democratic position as a
national consensus.[40]

As the civil rights movement achieved its triumphs in access to
accommodations, equal employment opportunities, and voting rights, the
horizons of its most influential leader, Martin Luther King, expanded in the
direction of the UAW's social-democratic economic agenda. With Jim Crow
on the run in the South, King recognized that the logical next steps must
be toward greater economic opportunity and a more equitable distribution
of income and wealth. In Sweden to collect the Nobel Prize for Peace, King
praised that nation's social-democratic regime, long admired by Reuther
and others in the UAW leadership as a model for the United States. Referring to the situation back home, King added, "Call it what you may, call it
democracy, or call it democratic socialism, but there must be a better distribution of wealth within this country for all of God's children."[41]

AS THE CIVIL RIGHTS BILLS moved through Congress, the Johnson administration concurrently launched its War on Poverty. Featuring an assort-
ment of programs that were narrowly focused and inadequately funded, the
antipoverty rhetoric far outstripped what the legislation could deliver.

Although the War on Poverty fell short of the comprehensive social-democratic approach the UAW leadership favored—including levels of social spending and vigorous Keynesian economic stimulation contributing to the redistribution of income and wealth—the president's effort was supported in the hope that it could be improved upon and expanded in the future. Although Reuther told the president that he, the UAW's officers, and the union's one and one half million members had enlisted "with you for the duration in the war against poverty," he considered the Johnson program superficial, telling a reporter that it was "a good beginning, but . . . only a beginning." "Poverty," as he testified before a House committee in April 1964, "essentially, is a reflection of our failure to achieve a more rational, more responsible, more equitable distribution of the abundance that is within our grasp. Therefore, we will not deal with the problem of poverty until we deal with the problem of the maldistribution of the national income." Despite his reservations, Reuther assured Johnson, on behalf of the UAW, that "as commander in chief, you can count on us as you lead America into battle against poverty and want."[42]

Beyond mobilizing its lobbying forces in Washington and urging, futilely as it turned out, a quantum leap expansion of the program, the UAW's contribution to the antipoverty campaign was directed at the Community Action Program (CAP), one of the legislation's most controversial features with its principle of "maximum feasible participation" by the poor in planning and implementing antipoverty measures. Sargent Shriver, director of the Office of Economic Opportunity (OEO), appointed Jack Conway, Reuther's former aide and right-hand man, as OEO's deputy director in charge of CAP. Conway adapted the tripartite model of decision-making, long favored by the UAW and Reuther, to the community action programs, creating local poverty boards that included representatives of local governments, of private agencies, and of the poor themselves. To support the government's efforts, Reuther proposed a Citizens' Crusade Against Poverty (CCAP), initiated by the UAW and reflecting union organizing principles, to channel private funds, activity and other input into the antipoverty program. From start to finish, CCAP, which Reuther boasted was "the broadest coalition of citizens that has ever joined together for a common purpose," was a UAW project. More than 125 union, liberal, civil rights, religious, and student organizations affiliated with CCAP. The 1964 UAW convention authorized a $1 million grant of union funds to CCAP, and Reuther became the new organization's chairman. With Johnson's blessing and Conway's eager cooperation, CCAP and the Community Action Program closely integrated their activities. The crusade coordinated the antipoverty efforts of private agencies, conducted important inquiries into poverty-related problems such as the extent of hunger and malnutrition, and planned a program of massive proportions, supported by Ford Foundation funds, which trained more than a thousand antipoverty workers and community organizers. In several urban areas CAP, CCAP, and the Industrial Union Department of the AFL-CIO organized "community unions," often with substantial participation from UAW regional staff and locals, to initiate remedial education classes, youth conservation corps, youth summer camps, and consumer protection services. An important objective was to develop and train indigenous ghetto leadership. In defending the union's involvement, Reuther invoked a parallel between the empowering of the autoworker rank and file in the 1930s and that of the urban ghetto masses in the 1960s. He told the UAW's executive board,

> What we have really got to do is to train people in the poor neighborhoods to do . . . what we did thirty years ago. . . . We developed the guys inside the factories who organized these factories. It is true there were people from the outside who helped us, but John Lewis didn't go into a single General Motors plant and Phil Murray didn't go into a single Chrysler plant. They worked from the outside and the guys in the plant did the job and that is what has got to be done with the poverty neighborhoods.[43]

The antipoverty campaign soon stalled. Although some of its programs, such as Head Start for preschool children, proved their worth and were maintained, others faded away. The programs had many critics. Some local politicians and government officials were hostile to a program which placed blacks in positions of authority and whose funds they could not control. In Mississippi powerful politicians, headed by the state's senior senator pressured Shriver to cancel a successful Head Start program, drawing from Reuther the comment that the Mississippi politicians were "more interested in preserving the status quo . . . than they are in helping disadvantaged children." Some ghetto residents took exception to the CCAP's effort to identify and train leaders in their communities as an instance of white-establishment intrusion into their affairs. Most seriously, appropriations for the campaign dwindled as escalation of the war in Vietnam absorbed available funds. As funding dried up, Reuther became openly critical of President Johnson and Sergeant Shriver, the poverty program's administrator, noting in a speech to a Poor People's Poverty Convention in 1966 that poverty could not be abolished by doling out money "with an eye-dropper" and that the Johnson administration had erred in requesting appropriations that were politically palatable but inadequate for the purpose. "It is a mistake," he chided the president, "to trim your sails before the fight." Sums at least as large as the billions going each year to Vietnam would be required if the campaign was to have a lasting impact.[44]

In a last gasp—and despite Johnson's opposition—the antipoverty campaign organized "Resurrection City" in Washington, D.C. in the summer of 1968. The UAW contributed $55,000 to the campaign and pledged to send 2,000 members to Washington. Reuther reported that 7,000 rank-and-file members would give up a day's pay and participate in a march. Reuther spoke at the march—the only labor leader to do so—in support of a just share of affluence and dignity for African Americans, Hispanic Americans, American Indians, and poor whites. Eight busloads of UAW members attended the march, the largest delegation from any organization. Pointing out that "we shall not be serious about winning the war against poverty at home until the budget for that total war against poverty is equal to the budget for the war in Vietnam," he called for a reordering of national priorities that would put first things first. Specifically, he called for a decent job at a living wage for every American able and willing to work, a guaranteed minimum family annual income, increases in Social Security benefits and expanded medical and drug provisions for the elderly, and a massive community rehabilitation program to wipe out slums and ghettos.[45]

AN URBAN CRISIS, with run-down housing stocks in deteriorating cities, was closely linked to urban poverty and racial friction. Reuther's interest in public housing and planned city development and rebuilding predated World War II. In collaboration with Oskar Stonorov, an architect and urban planner he had previously worked with, he initiated a "Demonstration Cities" plan. This was a sweeping proposal to incorporate all federal aid to cities into an "urban TVA" (Tennessee Valley Authority), in which the national government, through expenditures of billions of dollars, would "create architecturally beautiful and socially meaningful communities" in six selected cities, including Detroit, the UAW's hometown. Reuther saw massive urban redevelopment as one way to attack the nation's racial crisis by inducing voluntary residential integration. What we must do, he explained to the UAW's executive board, is "rebuild the whole inner cores of our great cities and produce in those inner cores an attractive, healthy, wholesome living environment that will be so exciting that everybody will want to live there and the racial thing will get lost in the shuffle." The plan was a pilot project but on a grand scale, intended to show how a coordinated, well-financed initiative could transform American cities as TVA had transformed its region. The heart of the proposal was a program that avoided the massive land clearances and sterile apartment blocks of public housing's past. Instead there would be integrated, low-density units compatible with existing communities. But far more than new housing was envisaged. The Demonstration Cities neighborhoods would include new schools, sites for social service agencies, neighborhood parks and recreation areas, and modernized public facilities to reduce air and water pollution. Local nonprofit corporations, bringing together government officials, local business interests, labor officials, and residents, would prepare the plans for federal government approval and subsidy. Reuther presented the idea directly to President Johnson, who responded with enthusiasm and authorized a task force, with Reuther as the labor representative, to move the proposal from concept to plan. Meeting in closed sessions, the task force, with Reuther, according to one of its members, supplying "the vision, drive and sometimes mere rhetoric that has kept us moving," completed its work in time for Johnson to incorporate its recommendations in his 1966 budget proposals. Reworked within the Johnson administration, the task force's plan was both enlarged and diminished. It now was paired with a proposal to create a federal Department of Housing and Urban Development (HUD) within which Demonstration Cities would become a major agency. Reuther had also proposed that CAP be moved from the Office of Economic Opportunity and placed in HUD. On the other hand, to broaden the plan's political appeal and enhance its prospects for congressional approval, the number of sites was greatly increased, diluting if not undermining its impact as a demonstration project. As the plan's major author and supporter, Reuther was given serious consideration for appointment as secretary of HUD and indicated he would accept the post if offered. If CAP were then incorporated in HUD, he would have become in effect the head of the War on Poverty as well as chief architect of urban reorganization and renewal. As it happpened, the appointment was not offered: Robert Weaver, a seasoned black administrator, was named HUD's first secretary and became the first black member of a presidential cabinet. Even the Johnson administration's pared down program encountered problems. It did not fare well in Congress, where the recommended appropriations were scaled down by more than 60 percent. In a public relations move, the project was renamed "Model Cities" to distance it from current urban disorders. Most seriously, LBJ's and the nation's attention as well as its funds were diverted from domestic reform to the war in Vietnam. The urban rebirth program never assumed anything approaching the scale and structure Reuther had envisaged and thought necessary.[46]

ALTHOUGH CIVIL RIGHTS, antipoverty, and urban policy were the UAW's main public domestic concerns, throughout the 1960s the leadership expressed a union position and brought its political weight to bear, sometimes with positive results and sometimes not, on a wide array of domestic and international issues. A stream of telegrams, letters, reports, convention and board resolutions, and personal testimony bombarded the White House and Congress with UAW position statements on a multitude of public questions. These included support for federal aid to education, enhanced consumer protection, freeing international trade, economic sanctions against South Africa to halt the "dirty profits" coming to U.S. companies operating there, ending nuclear proliferation, solutions to the problems of air and water pollution, and creation of additional national parks and other civic beautification and recreation projects. All this was promoted without neglecting such labor perennials as increases in the statutory minimum wage and expansion of its coverage, improvements in unemployment compensation, and reform of labor law to eliminate some of the restrictions on union activity imposed by the Taft-Hartley and Landrum-Griffin acts. The UAW sponsored a clear water conference, attended by more than 1,000 union officers, which adopted resolutions urging massive federal spending to combat water pollution, one of the earliest instances of union concern about an environmental issue. In 1970 UAW convention delegates called for an environmental bill of rights and held that pollution control laws had to be drastically strengthened and vigorously enforced. The UAW joined six conservation groups in urging Congress to set tougher air pollution standards even if that meant banishing the internal combustion engine within five years.[47]

For years the UAW had supported adoption of a national health plan. Following congressional establishment of Medicare and Medicaid, which provided health care for the elderly and the poor, a new mobilization of public opinion through the Committee of One Hundred for National Health Insurance was constructed, with Reuther as its chairman and with the objective of completely reshaping health care in the United States. The committee, whose members included Senator Edward M. Kennedy, the preeminent congressional supporter of health legislation, Mrs. A. D. Lasker, Dr. Michael D. DeBakey, and Whitney M. Young, Jr., championed a comprehensive, universal system of national health insurance. A private meeting with representatives of the American Medical Association failed to break the stalemate over a national health plan. The union also urged passage of federal legislation for reinsurance of private pension plans, a concern of union members and other employees whose pensions were in jeopardy through the failure of their employers.[48]

Aside from civil rights activity and support, few public issues on which the leadership took a stand provoked a strong adverse reaction among UAW members and locals. Although the leadership felt relatively unencumbered in adopting and promoting its views, it was careful to remain within the parameters set by convention resolutions. As in the case of a proposed resolution opposing prayer in public schools, the leadership was willing to modify and even withdraw proposals that encountered strong opposition from convention delegates. On some controversial issues, such as endorsing a pro-choice position on a woman's right to an abortion, the strongly expressed leadership preference prevailed despite considerable opposition among the rank and file and some local leaders. A board stand on an issue that arose without previous convention discussion and decision might provoke a negative reaction. When the executive board, with a sense of urgency, endorsed gun registration legislation following the assassinations of Dr. Martin Luther King, Jr., and Robert F. Kennedy in 1968, some members objected by telegrams, and resolutions were adopted in several local unions claiming that the leadership's views were unrepresentative. Although in an organization with more than a million members there was bound to be a diversity of opinions, the leadership could ordinarily count on the support of the membership, active or merely acquiescent, for its public stands. The contentious issues of the second half of the decade would subject the relationship of leaders and membership to greater strain.[49]

CHAPTER 12

"A stressful time"

The Issues of War and Racial Justice, 1965–70

CRISIS FOLLOWED CRISIS IN THE LATTER HALF OF THE 1960S AS the progressive coalition that the UAW had helped build, and which had seemed close to winning a strong voice in national policy, fell apart. Americans experienced their angriest, most violent decade of the century. A costly, lost war abroad, assassinations and civil disturbances at home, and a sweeping countercultural challenge to mainstream moral codes and lifestyles polarized opinion across a vast range of issues and behaviors. The Vietnam War struck at the coalition's core by dividing and disheartening liberals. The equal rights movement fragmented in response to the urban crisis, angry black nationalism, and antiwar and countercultural protests, which together provoked a destructive backlash that swept across the political landscape. Progressive leadership was irreparably damaged with the assassinations of John and Robert Kennedy, Dr. Martin Luther King, Jr., and other civil rights martyrs. How quickly the mood and expectations of progressives changed from hope and confidence in the early 1960s to pessimism and despair as the decade came to an end! The UAW felt in full measure the strains of these conflicts and the consequent polarization. In the factories and within the union's leadership, divisive issues of war and race cut through the ranks. Another source of contention for the UAW saw a smouldering dispute between Reuther and George Meany burst into flame, resulting in the UAW's departure from the AFL-CIO. A climax came in the watershed presidential election year of 1968 when the forces bent on destroying liberalism came together to set the nation on a conservative course.[1]

IRONICALLY THE ISSUE THAT UNDERMINED the UAW leadership's hope and expectation of a progressive advance at home arose out of a foreign war. As an organization the UAW, with Reuther as its spokesman, had taken a liberal position in foreign policy, deeply skeptical of reliance on military solutions to international problems. Speaking for himself and for the UAW, Reuther often expressed concern at the domination of American foreign policy by a rigid, militaristic anticommunism that divided the world into two monolithic, hostile blocs. Although acknowledging the need for a military establishment adequate for the nation's defense, Reuther always emphasized the priority of peaceful solutions to international problems. He favored maintaining contact with Communist regimes in the hope that exposure to the world beyond the Iron Curtain would eventually undermine their authoritarian governments (a view vindicated when the Soviet empire finally collapsed), and he defended the neutralist position of nations such as India that refused to align themselves with one or the other of the two great power blocs. He repeatedly and insistently argued that instability, popular disaffection, and injustice in restless Third World countries could be resolved and cured only through the economic and social development that would bring an end to colonial empires and hold out the promise of reducing poverty, providing personal and economic security, and bringing a higher standard of living. An obligation rested on the United States, as the world's wealthiest nation, to fashion the well-funded aid programs, preferably through the United Nations, that would stimulate and carry forward such development. To resist justified demands for social, economic, and political change with military force was dangerous and futile. To align the United States with reactionary, autocratic, self-styled anticommunist regimes in Third World countries was worse. Despite this long, well-articulated record, Reuther bound himself to an American president who placed his faith and the fate of his administration in war.[2]

Reuther's willingness to compromise his commitment to peaceful means of international change was a calculated decision made not on the merits of the issue but in the hope of maintaining and even enhancing the UAW's ability to achieve its domestic political and economic goals. He was prepared to swallow a mistaken, even immoral military adventure in the hope that the war would soon be ended and President Johnson's passion for domestic reform would return to dominate the national agenda. Taking issue with Johnson on Vietnam would alienate the president, whose demand for total loyalty from all who came within his orbit was legendary. As the UAW's Washington counsel and political advisor, Joseph L. Rauh, Jr., observed, "Walter wanted to keep in line with Johnson [and] Johnson wanted 100 percent loyalty." Doug Fraser, as close to the UAW president as anyone on political matters, recalled years later that Reuther's desire to stay on good terms with Johnson "held Walter in place [on Vietnam], I'm sure longer than he would have liked." Having for years worked to gain the political access necessary to carry forward the UAW's reform agenda, Reuther, whose relationship with Johnson was for a time the closest he enjoyed with any president, fell victim to the president's manipulation. It was flattering to have a president who solicited and seemed to respect his views and whom he credited with a sincere desire to fulfill the noble dream of a society with equal rights for all and poverty for none. Reuther was not alone. The president took many hostages in the ranks of liberals won over by his recently compiled, yet impressively strong, record as a domestic reformer. Paul Schrade, the UAW regional director on the West Coast and one of the union's leading doves, later testified that when he pleaded with Reuther and vice president Leonard Woodcock to join the antiwar movement, "They knew the country was wrong. They knew they should be doing something about it. But the politics of the Union and the country dictated siding with Johnson."[3]

For the duration of the president's term, the UAW and Reuther urged a peaceful settlement in Vietnam achieved though negotiations and a deemphasis on waging war, but they urged pursuit of these goals in terms sufficiently narrow and measured to avoid an open break with Johnson. Not until the approach of the presidential election of 1968—when Johnson's days in office were numbered, liberal ranks were broken, and Reuther's closest UAW associates had committed themselves to one or another dovish position—was he prepared to move the UAW toward public criticism of the administration's policy. The failure of the UAW leader openly to condemn and oppose the war contributed to the disintegration of the reform coalition he was dedicated to creating and preserving.

Public attention was drawn to the Vietnam conflict in the spring of 1965 when Johnson made the United States a full participant by launching bombing raids on North Vietnamese targets and committing American combat troops to the ground war in South Vietnam. Until then, although the worsening conflict had produced shocking incidents like the self-immolation protests of Buddhist monks and the assassination of a South Vietnamese president, and the Congress had granted President Johnson in its Tonkin Gulf Resolution broad authority to conduct military operations, neither the American public nor the UAW gave the question of an American role in the war full consideration. *UAW Solidarity*, the UAW's monthly publication for its membership, contained an ample stream of articles on current social, economic, and political problems, foreign and domestic, throughout the early 1960s: poverty, civil rights, hunger, Social Security, education, the economy, unemployment, world peace, military spending and waste, consumer protection, pollution, the grape boycott, health insurance, and more were all analyzed and reviewed. But the publication had almost nothing to say on Vietnam. Suddenly the war became a burning issue, particularly on university campuses, where it sparked an unprecedented outburst of student protest. In March 1965, the UAW executive board, spurred by secretary-treasurer Emil Mazey's memo expressing his "deep concern" over the "Vietnam crisis," conducted its first serious debate

on the war. Reuther presented a "middle ground" resolution that rejected
the two "unacceptable alternatives" of immediate withdrawal of American
forces from Vietnam and further escalation of military activity. The statement itemized escalation's dangers and argued for an unspecified political
solution worked out through negotiations with North Vietnam, and it
called on the United Nations to supply an international peacekeeping force.
The three propositions of no unilateral withdrawal, no escalation, and pursuit of a negotiated peace remained the UAW's official position for the next
three years.[4]

The executive board debate, reflecting the division then splitting the
citizenry into "hawks," "doves," and other unnamed birds that fluttered
uneasily in the middle, found the UAW leadership more deeply at odds on
a public issue than at any time since the Reuther group came to power. Secretary-treasurer Emil Mazey, the union's second highest ranking official,
and regional directors Martin Gerber (East Coast) and Paul Schrade (West
Coast) argued for an unequivocal condemnation of the Johnson administration's escalation in Vietnam and called for the withdrawal of American
troops as hostilities contracted, or, at the least, a suspension of bombing in
North Vietnam. Their views were supported by several key staff persons
with whom Reuther had close ties, particularly Nat Weinberg, his all-pur-
pose policy advisor, attorney Joe Rauh in Washington, Victor Reuther, the
head of the UAW's International Affairs office, and others. None of the
board dissidents, all union and Reuther loyalists, were prepared to vote
against the board resolution they had criticized, thereby publicizing an
internal dispute and risking an open break with the UAW's powerful and
respected president. Their position at first was not unlike that of Reuther
when he weighed the pros and cons of remaining on good terms with President Johnson. Considering the various missions of the union and the need
for unity, the advantages of going along with Reuther's dubious, "middle
ground" position seemed to outweigh the negatives of open opposition. In
transmitting the board's resolution, which was adopted unanimously, to
Congress, Reuther spoke of the "increasing disquiet among our own members over the implications of our government's policy."[5]

The clash of views within the leadership came into the open in the following months, when Emil Mazey repeatedly and publicly stated his opposition to the war in speeches before union, religious, and academic
gatherings, becoming a leading war critic. The United States, he charged, had
compromised its principles by bolstering and maintaining an oppressive military dictatorship in South Vietnam, and President Johnson had made a "serious mistake in escalating the war" by attacking North Vietnam. Mazey
called for an immediate de-escalation and cease fire. In September 1965,
speaking with the passion of a veteran union orator, he addressed an audi-

ence of more than 3,000 University of Michigan students and faculty members in Ann Arbor, exhorting his listeners to "tell the President we don't like to be lied to." Reuther tried, without success, to persuade Mazey to moderate his criticism but took no stronger action against the independent-minded secretary-treasurer, whose standing in the union was second only to his own. When questioned by journalists about Mazey's public statements, Reuther allowed that he had every right as a private citizen to take a contrary position as long as he did not claim to speak for the UAW. Publicly opposing the union's position was difficult for a life-long loyalist like Mazey; according to some testimony, at one point he considered resigning from the union but decided the better course was to stay and fight from within for his views and his right to speak on the issues. Reuther approached other leading union doves, like his brother Victor and Paul Schrade, attempting to moderate their opposition, but again without success.[6]

The UAW's reaction to Johnson's defense of his Vietnam policy in a speech at Johns Hopkins University illustrates the determination to construe the president's words as containing an opening to a peaceful settlement. Although the burden of Johnson's remarks charged North Vietnam with aggression and invoked the shades of Munich to condemn appeasement, Reuther seized on the president's promise of an economic aid program to Vietnam and his willingness to enter into, in Johnson's phrase, "unconditional negotiations." In fact, none of the parties to the conflict were willing to negotiate without conditions at this stage. In a "redefinition" of its position, the UAW board, again unanimously despite the reservations of some of its members, stated its support for the "current administration policy of insuring against Communist military victory while holding forth the hand of unconditional negotiations," a formula that the board hoped would preclude further escalation.[7]

In May 1966 a UAW constitutional convention adopted a weak declaration of support for the administration that discouraged escalation but rejected unilateral withdrawal. Protests against the war on campuses and elsewhere around the country were now in full bloom. When Johnson addressed the convention delegates by way of a telephone connection (by this time the president made few public appearances, fearing hostile demonstrations), his speech was disrupted by noisy, youthful, antiwar protestors, as was the convention itself the following day. Angry convention delegates stormed the demonstrators "and started beating the hell out of [them]." Doug Fraser and other UAW officers put a stop to the assault, and the next day, during the debate on the foreign policy resolution, Emil Mazey condemned the attack as "disgraceful."[8]

A similar incident had occurred at the AFL-CIO convention in December 1965, exposing the gap that was opening between the UAW and the AFL-CIO on the war question. President George Meany, outraged that a band of antiwar demonstrators heckled Secretary of State Dean Rusk as he defended the administration's record, ordered the sergeants-at-arms to "clear the kookies out of the gallery," which those officials were only too glad to do, to the cheers of some of the delegates. Mazey, a UAW representative, in his speech to the convention chastised the delegates: "I was sick with the vulgar display of intolerance that some delegates showed to some college students . . . here the other day. . . . [I]t seems to me that the labor movement has to take the lead and has to demonstrate and fight for the right of people to disagree, whether it is on Viet Nam or on any other subject matter." His remarks, which included a list of American policy errors in Vietnam going back to 1950, drew "scant applause" from the AFL-CIO audience.[9]

Middle level UAW officials began to mobilize a labor protest against the war. Edward F. Gray, assistant director of Region 9—whose director, Martin Gerber, was one of the antiwar board members—helped organize one of the first labor groups to oppose the war. About a dozen union officials met in his office in New York City and expressed their regret that no labor group had spoken out against the war. About two hundred responded to their call for a public meeting. They issued a statement under the auspices of the Trade Union Division of the National Committee for a SANE Nuclear Policy (SANE) that attacked the AFL-CIO's pro-war position and called for immediate de-escalation.[10]

Mazey was one of the organizers of the National Labor Leadership Assembly for Peace, which sponsored, again under the auspices of the Trade Union Division of SANE, the era's largest gathering of antiwar labor officials in November 1967 in Chicago. In a wide-ranging review of American policies that extended far beyond Vietnam, he criticized the war and defended the right to dissent. At the same conference, Victor Reuther launched a "scathing attack" on the AFL-CIO's International Affairs Department's hardline support of the war and called for an end to the bombing of North Vietnam without conditions. Shortly after the conference ended, George Meany publicly charged that it had been "planned in Hanoi" and that he had read "every line" of its antiwar statement in the *Sunday Worker*, a Communist publication, prior to the conference. Mazey denounced Meany's statement, accusing him of the "big lie" technique, "character assassination," and "suppression of dissent." Meany refused to retract his charges, even after it was demonstrated to him that the *Sunday Worker* published the antiwar statement after, not before, the meeting. While steadfast in opposing the war and defending the right to dissent, Mazey was critical of the radical, provocative, and unpatriotic tactics of some New Left protesters. He denounced "flag burners," "VC flag carriers,"

UAW Secretary-Treasurer Emil Mazey addresses an antiwar rally in New York City, October 13, 1971. Walter P. Reuther Library, Wayne State University. Photograph from *The Distributive Worker.*

and other protestors of the "lunatic fringe" for their counterproductive actions, and he warned that the UAW would not condone them.[11]

Although the UAW remained officially, if uncomfortably, supportive of the war, the public activities of Mazey, Paul Schrade, and a significant number of staff members and representatives testified to the existence of strong antiwar sentiment within the ranks of the union's leadership. As casualties mounted and the war's futility became ever more evident, other UAW officers, who earlier had expressed no qualms about supporting the administration, began to entertain doubts. Vice president Leonard Woodcock and board member-at-large Douglas Fraser, two of the most loyal and politically active figures in the leadership, were beginning to question the war. Reuther himself took a step away from Johnson's position in September 1967 in a "Meet the Press" interview where he called for a halt in American bombing of North Vietnam in the hope there would be a reciprocal gesture that would lead to negotiations, something the president was unwilling to order. Reuther, a man usually sure of his course, was beset by doubts. Those he was closest to in the UAW leadership were turning distinctly dovish. He sometimes complained to Schrade, Rauh, Victor Reuther and others about their antiwar stance—that it was at variance with the union's official position and at odds with President Johnson—but at other times he seemed to envy their position on the moral high ground in condemning the war. His two teenage daughters identified with the antiwar movement as did some of the college-age sons and daughters of other UAW leaders, creating arguments, tense moments, and outbursts at home. In a revealing moment at an executive board meeting, Reuther, who rarely called for divine guidance, confessed: "I wish God would give somebody the wisdom to say with absolute certainty: 'This is the right position.' I wish somebody had that kind of Divine wisdom because I think the world could use that right now." Slowly the gap between the union's position and that of President Johnson was widening.[12]

BELIEFS ABOUT RANK-AND-FILE workers' views of the war are heavily colored by the "hard hat" stereotype, which, drawing on an incident involving a brutal attack by New York City construction workers on antiwar demonstrators in 1970, holds that blue-collar workers supported vigorous prosecution of the war and assaulted the dissenters. The stereotype may conceal as much as it reveals. On the one hand, the union's top leadership felt little pressure from below to abandon its support of President Johnson and the war. Looking back, Doug Fraser observed, "I cannot recall any local union leader coming to the leadership of the UAW and saying, 'Let's change our policy on Vietnam.' There may be an isolated case, but there was no pressure that I can recall, none, to change our position on Vietnam." On the other hand, evidence from several polls and other sources suggests that UAW members were more likely, if only marginally, to hold antiwar sentiments than the general public. In June 1966, 51 percent of Michigan union members, a pool that included many from the UAW, favored a negotiated settlement of the war, and 19 percent of union families favored immediate withdrawal. In November of the same year, the city of Dearborn, Michigan, the residence of many UAW members, conducted the nation's first municipal referendum ballot on the war. The results showed that war opposition, including support for immediate withdrawal, was centered in working-class areas of the city. In 1967 Oliver Quayle and Company polled UAW members on Vietnam and other public questions. The survey showed that 54 percent of UAW rank and file preferred a negotiated settlement or immediate withdrawal to the present state of war. At the time, other polls showed that 60 percent of Americans favored escalation. The survey's authors concluded that "UAW members are considerably more dove-like than is the electorate as a whole. . . . So that the moderate position adopted by the UAW leadership accurately reflects the feeling of the rank and file."[13]

Elements in Local 600 spoke out against the war well before the International UAW. A small but outspoken group calling themselves "Concerned Unionists" formed there, issuing antiwar statements and participating in demonstrations. Although opposition to the war was strong in the local, it was constrained by the need to support the "boys in Vietnam," some of whom were the sons, relatives, or neighbors of the workers. The obligation to support the soldiers, on personal and patriotic grounds, set a limit to blue-collar, antiwar protest. Opinion in Local 600, with its large African American membership, moved somewhat in advance of general opinion among the American public toward an antiwar posture, fed as much or more by war weariness and a growing sense of the war's futility as by moral, class, ideological, or other considerations.[14]

Class resentment was a powerful force affecting workers' views of war protest. Both enlistments and conscription drew disproportionately on working-class youth. The sons of working-class families, white and black, were sent to fight and, for many, to die, while the privileged offspring of the comfortable and affluent went to college or found some other means of keeping out of harm's way. Death was unevenly distributed. Many workers were hostile toward student antiwar demonstrators more for reasons of class, patriotism, and culture than for the merits of the war versus peace issue. To them, students got deferments, evaded service, and (not compelled to show up for work every day) had the money and leisure to go to Washington, San Francisco and elsewhere to engage in well-publicized protests. When a journalist interviewed leaders of Local 36 in Wixom, Michigan, following the invasion of Cambodia, he found that while they had doubts about the wisdom of the invasion, their outrage was directed at students, like those at Kent State University, who had engaged in violent protest. As the antiwar movement evolved, some of the behaviors that became associated with it were obnoxious to many workers. They saw and resented the anti-American, nonconformist gestures—the flag and draft card burning, sympathy expressed for the Viet Cong, long hair, drug use, public displays of rowdy behavior and filthy language, and the condescending rejection of the goals of economic security and modest comfort that workers had struggled to attain and that many of the protestors could take for granted. The experience was both mystifying and infuriating. "We can't understand," said one worker, "how all those rich kids—the kids with the beads from the fancy suburbs—how they get off [military service] when my son has to go over there and maybe get his head shot off."[15]

Years later Leonard Woodcock assessed the development of antiwar views within the UAW's leadership echelons and within its rank and file, telling an interviewer "you had one group relatively small that was opposed to the war on philosophical principle and you had a much bigger group that finally came together on the basis, 'We're not going to win it—let's get the hell out' which I think essentially is what happened with the population generally."[16]

UAW LEADERS ORIGINALLY SAW THE New Left, along with the mobilized masses of the civil rights movement, as an integral part of a new progressive reform coalition and welcomed its advent. By the end of the 1950s, UAW leaders, like many observers within and outside the labor movement, were concerned about the ebbing vigor and commitment of labor. The movement, including the UAW, needed an infusion of youthful idealism, something akin to the energy, vision, and determination the Reuther brothers and so many others had brought to autoworker organizing in the 1930s. A Socialist organization that dated back to the early years of the century, the Student League for Industrial Democracy (SLID)—which had counted several UAW staffers among its members in the 1930s—remade itself as Students for a Democratic Society (SDS), destined to be the main instrument of 1960s' youth radicalism, even though it represented only a small minority of the college-age population before opposition to American intervention in Vietnam gave it something of a mass base. The relationship of the UAW to SDS seemed "practically maternal," to a historian. A key connection was provided by a number of youths from UAW families attending the University of Michigan, where the strongest and one of the earliest SDS chapters was formed. They included Sharon Jeffrey, daughter of Mildred Jeffrey, a leading UAW political staff activist; Leslie Woodcock, daughter of vice president Leonard Woodcock; and Barry Bluestone, son of Irving Bluestone, Reuther's key administrative assistant in the 1960s. In 1961 SDS received a UAW grant of $10,000 to fund an SDS organizing drive on college campuses. With the UAW leading the way, the flow of funds from industrial unions was SDS's principal source of income in its early years, and there were expanded personal contacts, with Bluestone and Jeffrey the UAW's liaison persons. The SDS manifesto—the "Port Huron Statement," a key document of the 1960s—was drafted and adopted at a 1962 meeting held at a UAW-owned summer camp and conference center in Port Huron, Michigan. The statement revealed much common ground between SDS and the UAW, with its paraphrase of many standard UAW positions and goals, particularly on needed economic changes.[17]

In line with UAW thinking, SDS linked progress in civil rights with economic change and undertook its own campaign to reduce poverty. In September 1963, SDS launched its Economic Research and Action Project (ERAP), which consisted of assigning SDS members to organizational activities among the black and white poor in lower-class sections of northern cities. The UAW provided financial support, and the relationship between the two organizations remained close, although SDS submitted proposals for several grandiose projects that the UAW declined to fund. Bluestone called SDS one of the most active of "the socially progressive forces in this country."[18]

The alliance broke down once the American phase of the Vietnam War began. Some in SDS had always been suspicious of organized labor, including even a benefactor like the UAW, seeing it as part of a reigning "corporate liberalism" that coopted and marginalized radicals instead of forging partnerships with them or, even better, following their lead. The UAW's failure to condemn the war on moral and ideological grounds and break with the Johnson administration over it was taken as proof of a corrupt alliance with "the establishment." Soon an SDS social and political critique was directed against organized labor with all the considerable vehemence the organization could muster. The hostility of the New Left to labor weakened the position of the doves in the UAW hierarchy, leading Emil Mazey to charge that the New Left "did a great deal of disservice to those of us who feel strongly about Vietnam." The UAW's hope that a new, idealistic youth movement would form part of a progressive coalition with the UAW was another casualty of Vietnam.[19]

When, toward the end of the decade, SDS fragmented into rival splinter groups, the UAW and SDS became totally estranged. Some SDS splinters advocated violence and other illegal actions, some cheered for the Viet Cong, some adhered to a Maoist version of Marxist-Leninist doctrines, and others veered into a drug-based hedonistic counterculture; all were equally repugnant to the UAW leadership and most of its rank and file. In contacts with antiwar youth, Reuther, a civil man with polite manners, whose obscenities were reserved for occasional use at the bargaining table, might be subjected to their rude shock tactics. In 1969 he addressed a group of student newspaper editors on Vietnam. After the speech a young woman came up and launched an attack on his position. As Walter tried to explain, she broke in to say "Mr. Reuther, you're full of shit." According to an observer, Reuther was "stunned" but gamely continued with his explanation. She interrupted again, this time to say "Mr. Reuther, go [obscenity deleted] yourself," ending the exchange.[20]

The destructive acts and rhetoric aroused an impassioned response. In April 1970, less than a month before his death, Reuther criticized New Left elements that had turned toward violence, including extremist blacks in his condemnation. He charged that the New Left in its latest manifestations had embraced destruction without offering a constructive alternative. While its adherents typically announced that their demands were nonnegotiable, the union, never shrinking from a fight, always sought to reach an agreement. Before a UAW audience he invoked a contrast with the struggles attendant on the UAW's birth: "I said [to them] we knew what we were fighting for. And you only know what you're fighting against. And that's not good enough. You have no moral right to destroy something unless you think you've got something better to put in its place."[21]

THE UNION'S AFFILIATION WITH the AFL-CIO, under pressure since the labor federation's inception in 1955, bent and then broke when the UAW withdrew in 1968. A tangled skein of issues eventually drove the UAW out. Reuther and George Meany's association was never close, although on some matters, such as civil rights, their goals if not their methods were similar, and at times they worked together effectively in pursuit of common objectives. In part, their disagreements reflected conflicting ideas of a union's purpose. Meany was a conventional unionist, comfortable with a limited role for the labor federation: it should confine itself to representing the workers' interests in routine political matters, policing ethical standards in labor organizations, and resolving jurisdictional disputes. This contrasted with the UAW leadership's more expansive view, which sought to cast unions as active agents of social change, the core of a national progressive movement. Although some contemporary observers dismissed the differences between Meany and Reuther as having little substance, the view from the perspective of business management saw much at stake. In 1967, when Reuther was attempting to revitalize the AFL-CIO, an industry journalist commented:

> Walter Reuther epitomizes the kind of labor leader many managers abhor. He crusades for ideals. He refuses to stage bargaining tangos that mislead his membership. He won't make "cynical" deals. He exerts every bit of strategic muscle at his command. What's more, he understands—but rarely sympathizes with—managerial economics. All of which makes him a tough, aggressive, thoroughly unpleasant adversary. . . . [Y]ou're not likely to cheer about what may follow if he does get the labor movement going again.[22]

The lifestyles of the two men reflected contrasting values. Meany drew a large salary and lived well. Although he retained his New York working-class accent and delighted in referring to himself as merely a former Bronx plumber, he acquired a gourmet's taste in food and wine, smoked expensive cigars, and belonged to a country club. The AFL-CIO council's annual winter meetings, at which he presided, were held in luxurious quarters, usually a Miami Beach oceanfront hotel, far from the grim, cold factory cities where the members, whose dues paid the bills, toiled at their jobs. Official functions occupied part of the day, but there was plenty of time to lounge around the swimming pool, at the race track, at the card table, and in night clubs. Reuther was miserably uncomfortable in such settings. During the Miami conclave that concluded the merger agreement, he refused to use the large hotel suite reserved for him as the AFL-CIO's second-in-command, insisting on moving to smaller, less expensive quarters. James Carey, a Reuther ally and president of the International Union of Electrical Workers, moved into the vacated suite and poked fun at Reuther's scruples, telling newsmen seeking Reuther for an interview that he was down the hall in a linen closet squeezing his own orange juice. Reuther saw the council's meetings as a harmful indulgence, a symbol, even a cause, of a labor movement retreat from its high calling that had contributed to resentment and cynicism within the ranks and among the public. His quixotic attempts to shame the labor barons out of their fondness for luxury were neither appreciated nor successful.[23]

Reuther's outlook and lifestyle, ascetic and self-righteous to a fault in the view of some, were in character. With an annual salary of $31,000 when he died in 1970 (Meany then received over $90,000), his pay was among the lowest for presidents of major unions, and he lived frugally. He did not smoke, had little interest in food, and none in drink. His UAW expense account was small and scrupulously accounted for. When attending AFL-CIO council meetings he accepted the generous expense allowance the federation provided and then turned it over to the UAW, paying his expenses out of the smaller amount provided by his union. A favorite recreation, cabinetmaking, drew upon his training as a die maker and reflected the tastes, habits, and skills of a craftsman.[24]

One strand in the dispute between Meany and Reuther comprised their conflicting ambitions. Each aspired to be the voice of a united labor movement, and each believed he had earned that right. Reuther saw himself as proven in all dimensions of union leadership: strikes, negotiations, administering a large and complex union, and initiating and generating support for progressive positions on a broad range of public issues. Meany's experience, confined to state and national labor bodies, was narrower. He even boasted that he had never walked a picket line. But Meany was a shrewd bureaucratic politician who carefully guarded his prerogatives as head of the labor federation and cultivated the support of the AFL-CIO's council members, whose expectations of a federation president he by and large met. Although understandably never making a public statement of his intentions, Reuther probably expected Meany, who was thirteen years his senior and turned sixty-five in 1959, to retire at a normal age, clearing the way for Reuther's succession. He misread the man. Meany resented

Reuther's presence (he told an interviewer that Reuther was only waiting for him to die), lived for his position, and clung to it until almost the day of his death in 1980 at the age of eighty-five, ten years after the accident that took Reuther's life. Frank Winn, Reuther's friend and close associate for more than thirty years, thought that Meany was the only adversary that Reuther, blinded perhaps by his own high-mindedness, had ever underestimated.[25]

One of the first issues on which the two men's views diverged concerned organizing unorganized workers, a campaign needed to revitalize the labor movement. By the end of the 1960s union membership had increased from 16 million at the time of the merger in 1955 to 19 million, but the fraction of union members in an expanding workforce had dropped from approximately one-third to one-fourth. Reuther favored an aggressive, well-financed effort under the central direction of the AFL-CIO, whereas Meany took the traditional position that organizing should be carried out by the affiliates within their jurisdictions. Dissatisfied with the AFL-CIO's refusal to support the kind of organizing drive he favored, Reuther, as president of the AFL-CIO's Industrial Union Department (IUD), launched a separate effort that enjoyed modest success. In any case, the failure of organizing to keep pace with the growth of the workforce remained the Achilles' heel of labor.[26]

On its own, the UAW supported unionization efforts of workers at the bottom of the pay scale, providing critical assistance to the drive of Cesar Chavez to bring the ill-paid laborers in California's fields and vineyards into the United Farm Workers, a crusade that recaptured the vitality and idealism of the 1930s. Urged on by his brother Roy and by Paul Schrade, Reuther was the first union president to enlist in the farmworkers' cause. The UAW and the IUD provided key financial aid and cooperated with liberal and religious groups in organizing support for a national boycott of nonunion grapes, a crucial element in Chavez's strategy. In December 1965, Reuther visited striking grape pickers in Delano, California, and met Chavez. Declaring, "I haven't felt anything like this since the old days," he led a farmworkers' demonstration, urged the growers in a personal conference to recognize and bargain with the union, and pledged a $5,000-a-month contribution to the strikers, half from the IUD and half from the UAW; he impulsively added another $5,000 as a Christmas present. Chavez recalled Reuther's visit as "a very significant day" because of the moral and financial support it produced and the favorable national publicity it generated. A delegation from the Farm Workers union sang their strike song and marched on to the floor and platform of the UAW's 1966 convention and heard Reuther pledge that "as long as we have a dollar in our strike fund, they are going to have our support to win their strike." Eventually, Reuther hoped, farmworker organizing would spread from California to Texas and Florida, creating a national union under Chavez's leadership. The UAW encouraged the effort with donations of funds and organizing staff. After Chavez's convention speech, UAW members joined a picket line at a nearby grocery store where nonunion grapes were sold.[27]

Using its political connections, the UAW helped expand Chavez's base. In 1966 Reuther, along with Jack Conway, persuaded Senator Robert F. Kennedy, a member of the Senate's Migratory Labor Subcommittee, to attend hearings in California, where the senator gained firsthand information on the exploitation of agricultural workers, met Chavez, and became the farmworkers' leading champion in Congress. Reuther had less success with Meany, whom he urged to go beyond the limited financial aid the AFL-CIO had by then extended by traveling to California to personally endorse the farmworkers' movement. Meany, who thought public gestures of support ineffective or even counterproductive, refused. Earlier he had excluded Reuther from membership on an AFL-CIO committee set up to assist the farmworkers, despite the fact that the suggestion for such a committee had come from Reuther, the only member of the AFL-CIO council who had visited the farmworkers' headquarters to give them assistance.[28]

In another effort in support of low-paid workers, Reuther and a large delegation of UAW officers and staff members, including many UAW African Americans, marched in support of striking black sanitation workers in Memphis, Tennessee, only a few days after Martin Luther King's assassination there. (King, who had shifted the focus of his crusade from obtaining equal rights to obtaining jobs and an improving standard of living, went to Memphis in order to support the strikers.) Following the march, the UAW announced a gift of $50,000 for the strikers and their union.[29]

Reuther suffered a series of personal slights at Meany's hands, some merely petty, others designed to guard the AFL-CIO president's position and prerogatives from what he saw as Reuther's encroachments. For example, Meany denied Reuther the routine honor of serving as an escort for President John F. Kennedy at an AFL-CIO convention, although Reuther was far better acquainted with the new president than any other labor leader and the UAW had poured resources into Kennedy's campaign. He refused to allow Reuther to represent the AFL-CIO in a meeting with President Kennedy on tax policy even though Reuther was chair of the council's Economic Policy Committee. He blocked several government appointments Reuther favored, including one of Reuther himself to the United States delegation to the United Nations. Adlai E. Stevenson, Kennedy's U.N. ambassador, had requested that Reuther be named, and Reuther was eager to serve because he believed American labor should be represented there and he was a fervent supporter of the international organization. Meany, however, refused to endorse the appointment, and Kennedy would not proceed without his consent. Since no one else was acceptable to Stevenson, no labor representative was appointed. Similarly, Meany blocked the appointment of Reuther protégé Jack Conway as undersecretary of labor. Reuther had written Kennedy recommending the appointment. Meany resented Reuther's direct approach to the president and later claimed that a mere phone call to him would have cleared the way, but Reuther suspected that no one with a UAW connection would have been acceptable. These and other slights poisoned the relationship between the two, with Reuther complaining bitterly in private of Meany's lack of respect for him, his ideas, and for the UAW. Once in a private discussion with Reuther, President Kennedy said he could well understand Reuther's frustration in dealing with George Meany because he had similar problems with another elderly, egotistical man, Charles de Gaulle.[30]

Reuther and Meany fought a running battle, with Reuther usually the loser, over the terms of American participation in international labor organizations, episodes that undermined trust and respect on both sides. Speaking to the UAW executive board, Reuther complained "it is really a great tragedy what [Meany] has done to the international labor movement." Meany attacked the AFL-CIO's membership in the International Confederation of Trade Unions (ICFTU) and wanted it to withdraw, an action Reuther viewed "as unthinkable . . . as for the US to withdraw from the UN." Although the AFL-CIO remained within ICFTU, its financial contributions, which provided a substantial part of the organization's budget, were so reduced at Meany's direction as to cripple its activities. The two differed over the control and organization of U.S. labor's support for trade union development in Latin America, with Reuther charging that the American Institute for Free Labor Development was too closely tied to reactionary business and political interests to serve as a valid trade union representative. The two leaders clashed again over American participation in the International Labor Organization (ILO) when it chose, following its established procedure of rotating officers on a regular basis, a Polish Communist as its presiding officer. UAW convention resolutions had repeatedly urged more contacts between West and East, including contacts of trade unionists, and Reuther pragmatically argued that the advantages of maintaining contact with labor organizations throughout the world and supporting the fact-gathering work of the ILO justified U.S. participation. Meany, who refused on principle to acknowledge Communists as legitimate representatives of workers, insisted on a U.S. boycott of ILO, and he won the support of a divided AFL-CIO executive council for his position.[31]

Foreign policy questions divided Reuther and Meany almost from the moment of the AFL-CIO merger. A rigid anticommunist, Meany relied upon the advice and organizational skills of Jay Lovestone, Homer Martin's advisor in the UAW's factional battles of the 1930s, in directing the AFL-

CIO's extensive overseas operations and formulating its foreign policy positions. Reuther tried without success to have Lovestone removed from his influential AFL-CIO post. There was no question that Meany would vigorously support the Johnson administration's military policy in Vietnam. Reuther consistently tried to soften the AFL-CIO's strongly worded resolutions but had little to show for his efforts. At the AFL-CIO's convention in December 1965, Meany proposed a resolution, authored by Lovestone, offering "our unstinting support for all measures the administration might deem necessary" in opposing "Communist aggression in Vietnam." In this blank-check endorsement of military action no mention was made of the administration's stated willingness to negotiate, and Reuther insisted that the inflammatory rhetoric, which risked goading the Chinese and the Russians into more active roles in the war, be toned down and that clauses favoring negotiations and programs of economic and social development be included. Threatened with a public fight on the convention floor, which both Meany and President Johnson wished to avoid, Meany offered and Reuther accepted a compromise that mentioned negotiation as a method the administration might use to secure peace and deemphasized the threat of further escalation contained in the original proposal. In a speech to the convention and in later press conference comments, Reuther put his gloss on the resolution, attempting to distance himself from its hawkish thrust by saying that although it was "acceptable, it was not written the way I would have written it"; he insisted that the statement took a "position that stands midpoint between two extreme[s]" of unilateral withdrawal and unlimited escalation.[32]

A year later the differences, which had been kept largely concealed, were brought into the open. In August 1966, the AFL-CIO executive council adopted a statement lauding Johnson's Vietnam policy and condemning all opposition to the war as "aiding the Communist enemy of our country." Reuther attacked the statement, reporting that he had opposed it in council sessions and denouncing it as "intemperate, hysterical, jingoistic, and unworthy of . . . a free labor movement." In November Reuther boycotted and then publicly criticized an executive council session where that body unanimously endorsed the AFL-CIO's foreign policy positions. In a long administrative letter sent to all UAW locals in December 1966, Reuther laid out his case against Meany's leadership, taking pains to show that the UAW's concerns encompassed a broad range of philosophical and political issues, domestic and internal as well as foreign. Pointing to "very fundamental trade union differences," he lamented the federation's failure to fulfill its original promise, a "cause for grave concern." Echoing the critique of many labor intellectuals and journalists, the statement charged that the AFL-CIO had become a "complacent custodian of the status quo" that lacked "the social vision, the dynamic thrust, the crusading spirit that should characterize the progressive, modern labor movement." The statement prescribed new policy positions and structural reforms for the federation, including a recommendation that it develop stronger ties to the "liberal intellectual and academic community and among America's young people." The most severe strictures were reserved for the federation's "narrow and negative" anticommunism, which, the UAW charged, "has not strengthened but rather weakened the free world's efforts to resist Communism and all forms of tyranny." Repeating a favorite Reuther refrain, the letter continued: "The most effective way to fight Communism is to make democracy work. We believe that anticommunism in and of itself is not enough." Clearly, the UAW had set out on an independent course.[33]

Soon after the issuance of this statement, ties between the UAW and the AFL-CIO began to break. Reuther resigned from the council and its committees, retaining only the presidency of the Industrial Union Department, and other UAW officers followed suit. Close observers believed the UAW's secession was inevitable. Yet Reuther moved slowly. Not until April 1967, when a UAW special convention conferred authority on the board to withdraw from the federation, did he publicly threaten to leave. He aimed to renew the labor movement, he said, but "this thing called labor unity is not a museum piece." If necessary, labor unity would be placed second to social commitment. "If we can get them all marching, so much the better. If we can't then we may have to make a decision to march alone, because," he told the cheering delegates, "we are determined to march one way or the other."[34]

Meany, securely in control of the federation's council and deeply resentful of the public charges of failure to fulfill the federation's mission, was in no mood to confess errors or make concessions. Disdainful of Reuther and his concerns, he pointedly told reporters that discussion at a council meeting Reuther had not attended had been "very very productive," and "on a very high level with practically nothing getting heated up or anything else." Dismissing Reuther's charges against his leadership as "baloney," he maintained that the trade union movement was "a more vital, a more vigorous and a more effective force for progress today than ever before in its history." The thrust of his defense pointed to the workers' share of national prosperity: "Wages are higher, the fringe benefits are better, the contracts are better, the welfare and pension plans are better for the entire trade union movement."[35]

All hope of reconciliation was gone. Reuther had lost faith in the ability of the federation, under Meany's direction, to reform itself. "What is wrong with the American Labor Movement," he told the UAW's executive board, "is it has no soul. It has wealth. It has power. It has no soul." To the UAW leadership, the AFL-CIO had abandoned the labor movement's

"How Long Has It Been Since You Walked Around Outside?"

"How Long Has It Been Since You Walked Around Outside?" From *The Herblock Gallery* (Simon & Schuster, 1968).

mission. "I joined the labor movement," Reuther added, "because I
wanted to be part of the continuing struggle to do something about the
status quo. Not to shore it up, not to dig its trenches deeper, but to change
it . . . and that I think is what motivated all of us." When Reuther asked
for a special AFL-CIO convention to consider his proposed reforms of the
federation's structure and operations, Meany agreed, with the proviso that
Reuther unconditionally promise in advance to accept its outcome.
Reuther would not bind himself to accept an unsatisfactory result. The
deadlock was broken in the spring of 1968 when the UAW refused to pay
the per capita tax on its membership owed to the AFL-CIO, a sum of $1
million, about 10 percent of AFL-CIO revenues. Reuther, who did not
want to disrupt organized labor's political effort in the midst of a crucial
national election, hoped that the UAW would be allowed to remain in
limbo, neither in nor out of the federation, until after the November elections, but the council voted for suspension, and thereupon the UAW
board, acting on authority granted at a recent convention, disaffiliated. By
then Reuther had come to see the "American labor movement" under
Meany as "the most irresponsible, the most conservative, social economic
and political force when measured against its relative power to do good—
and that's the way to measure it." In the private quarters of UAW board
meetings, he referred to the AFL-CIO council as "the mausoleum." The
time for a divorce had come.[36]

When the UAW left the AFL-CIO, it went alone. Reuther's failure to
enlist any of the former CIO unions in his crusade for the labor movement's
revitalization was a serious setback. The UAW's isolation made it easy to
dismiss his protest against Meany's leadership as a personal quarrel, and the
credibility of his charges was diminished when other unions, including
some that once were close to the UAW, failed to respond. Some labor leaders took exception to Reuther's public attacks, believing that criticisms
should have been aired only in private. Others were annoyed with a lack of
follow-through after charges were brought. Doubtless many were simply
content with Meany's direction of the federation, or at any rate were unprepared to challenge it. More significant than any of Meany's countermeasures was Reuther's failure to build support. In a lapse from his usual careful
study of a situation and preparation of an effective response, he seems to
have assumed that his critique of Meany's leadership was so clearly valid
that liberal labor leaders would be compelled by the force of the evidence
alone to rally to the cause. The isolation into which he maneuvered himself and the UAW was costly to the reform measures he supported.

A CRISIS AT LEAST EQUAL to those of the war and the UAW's quarrel with
the AFL-CIO stemmed from deepening racial divisions within American

society and within the ranks of auto workers. When racial upheavals swept American ghettos in the second half of the 1960s, the UAW's generally positive record on racial relations, the high average incomes of black auto workers, and the presence of a large, black middle class in Detroit tempted many to believe that the city, under progressive mayor Jerome B. Cavanagh, would be spared. In July 1967, a riot of unprecedented proportions shattered that illusion. During the disturbance, which took forty-three lives, caused millions of dollars in property damage, and had to be suppressed by soldiers of the Michigan National Guard and the United States Army, there was no disorder in the factories, but the impact of rising racial tension and black militancy was soon felt there. Reuther, at Mayor Cavanagh's urging, phoned President Johnson to recommend that federal troops be immediately dispatched to Detroit, and he pledged the volunteer help of 60,000 UAW members to clean up the mess left by the riot; like most of the well-intentioned reactions to the disturbance, performance fell far short of the promise. The riot accelerated the flight of the city's white residents to surrounding suburbs, a movement that began years earlier and would continue long afterward, driving deep spatial divisions between the region's different racial populations.[37]

In the aftermath, better job opportunities for minorities became a high prioity issue. Since employers were legally responsible for hiring, the major responsibility fell on them. On two occasions before the riot the auto companies had rejected proposals from the Michigan Civil Rights Commission to launch a minority affirmative action hiring program backed by funding from the federal government's Equal Employment Opportunity Commission; their objections in part were owing to the requirement of UAW participation. With the union and the car makers now in agreement that cooperation was necessary, various methods were tried to increase black employment, particularly among ghetto youth and the "hard-core" unemployed, and to recruit candidates for apprenticeships in the skilled trades. When Ford announced its hiring program, more than 1,500 mostly African American job seekers jammed Detroit antipoverty centers to apply for work. By the end of 1967 General Motors had hired 5,000 African Americans for its Detroit area plants out of a total of 12,000 new hires. By 1969 Ford had hired 13,000 of the formerly "hard-core" unemployed, and GM over 20,000. Retention rates matched those for other new employees. Chrysler, in cooperation with the UAW, established a training program for skilled trades workers that brought in over 4,000 blacks in two years. More than one-third of those Chrysler production workers who were upgraded to skilled trades as the decade ended were African Americans. According to one study, "the most substantial improvements . . . in the country for black blue-collar workers" were made in Chrysler's Detroit-area plants.[38]

Still, the programs' results were less than hoped for. Douglas Fraser noted at the end of 1969 that "after all this effort, we only had a miserable percentage of 4.4 percent blacks in [the] skilled trades." Chrysler, which relied partly on federal funds for its program, lost the bulk of them during the Nixon administration. When demand for cars fell in 1969, Ford and Chrysler laid off many recently hired workers under their contracts' seniority rules. For black workers the old adage of "last hired, first fired" still ruled. Appalled at the injustice and waste involved, UAW leaders proposed a "juniority" or "inverse seniority" plan whereby workers with high seniority, eligible for SUB payments and unemployment compensation benefits, could volunteer for layoff, thereby protecting the jobs of recently hired black and white workers. The plan was rejected by the companies, which claimed that the increase in labor costs resulting from the replacement of trained, disciplined, and reliable older workers with younger ones suspected of lacking those qualities made it uneconomical. Already disadvantaged on costs in competition with foreign-made cars, whose market share was growing, the companies refused to add to their financial problems. Blacks continued to be hired for auto jobs, but their employment was due more to labor shortages than to hiring programs.[39]

THE RIOT ALSO BROUGHT to the surface avowed revolutionary organizations among militant blacks, particularly in Chrysler's Detroit plants, where ancient, decrepit, dirty factories (the worst in the industry) and outmoded machinery created dangerous, disagreeable working conditions. Strong demand for the company's products in the late 1960s led to speedups and excessive mandatory overtime, sparking shop floor discontent. A white ethnic supervisory force and local union officer corps further aggravated racial tensions and black dissatisfaction. It was no coincidence that protest by African American auto workers was centered on Chrysler, a company that drew heavily on Detroit's black population for its workforce. An incident that focused a blazing light on the tensions springing from racial injustice and harsh working conditions occurred when James Johnson, Jr., an African American migrant from Mississippi employed at Chrysler's Eldon Avenue Gear and Axle plant on Detroit's East Side, believing that he had been unfairly treated and harassed because of his race, shot and killed three persons in the plant, including two foremen, one of them black. At the end of a widely-publicized trial, a Detroit jury acquitted Johnson of a murder charge owing to insanity stemming from the circumstances of his upbringing and employment in an oppressive, racist society.[40]

In 1968 the Dodge Revolutionary Union Movement (DRUM), the first of several quasi-Marxist, black nationalist, workers' organizations, emerged in the vast Dodge Main plant in Hamtramck, Michigan, where more than half of the 7,000 employees were blacks, to claim credit for a two-day wildcat strike, involving (by different estimates) between 2,000 and 4,000 workers. DRUM was followed by the Eldon Avenue Revolutionary Union Movement (ELRUM) and about a dozen similar organizations in other plants, all loosely allied in the League of Revolutionary Black Workers (LRBW). They published leaflets and papers attacking the racist practices of employers and the union; denounced the moderate black "Uncle Toms" and "sell outs" who were loyal to the UAW; brought up job grievances over unsafe and harmful working conditions that the companies and, they charged, the union had ignored; condemned the speedup of assembly lines; held rallies; and fomented wildcat strikes. Their fire was directed equally at the companies and at the UAW, which they charged conspired together against the interests of ordinary workers. DRUM and ELRUM picketed Solidarity House, denouncing Reuther as "a pig you pay . . . 25,000 a year to keep you in slavery." They accused local union officers and the "cheap gang of cut throat thugs, bureaucrats, crooks and sellout politicians" who held International Union positions of racism, urged that Reuther be fired and that half of the UAW's board and staff positions be designated for blacks, and asserted that only a militant black-led and controlled union, formed once the UAW had been decertified as bargaining agent, could adequately represent Chrysler's black employees. "Behead the Redhead," urged one anti-Reuther leaflet (no doubt rhetorically), and another asked that if Reuther is for integration as he claims, "why in the hell is it that he has never integrated the U.A.W.?" Answering their own question, the authors charged that Reuther was afraid to move against racism within the UAW because to do so would jeopardize his reelection as president and he feared the union's "honkies" might assassinate him. Among the demands directed at Chrysler, DRUM insisted that the corporation promote fifty blacks to foremen's posts at Dodge Main and name blacks as the plant's manager and as chairman of the corporation's board of directors.[41]

Both the corporation and the union reacted to the militants' challenge with a combination of concession and repression that curbed DRUM's appeal. Although DRUM attracted few members, there was a wider circle, amounting to perhaps as much as one-third of Dodge Main's workforce, who were supportive of its specific complaints about harsh working conditions and responsive to charges of bigotry lodged against some supervisors and union officers. Attempts to move into union electoral politics by running candidates and slates in local elections provoked a powerful UAW reaction and produced few victories. DRUM candidates lost races in Local 3 at Dodge Main for union offices including president, vice president, board members, and trustees. In several instances the organization's candidate achieved a place in a runoff but failed to carry a majority. In DRUM's most serious challenge, Local 3's white president running for reelection headed a "United Membership" slate, balanced with four blacks and six whites, that won all the local's top offices and executive board positions. In several of the disputed elections, the union mobilized a large bloc of the local's retirees, virtually all of them white, to vote—a maneuver that was legal under the UAW's constitution but naturally was resented and ridiculed by the militants. DRUM's condemnation of the procedure stated in a handout that "the UAW bigots . . . went around the entire city [of Hamtramck] . . . scraping the back streets and searching the cracks in the walls for old retired Polish pigs." Although a few of the militants subsequently were elected to union office—most notably Jordan Sims, who was a strong critic of Chrysler and UAW officialdom but not a DRUM member, at the Eldon Avenue plant (Local 961)—from the standpoint of electoral politics, black moderates were the main beneficiaries of LRBW agitation, winning elections in the coming months in a number of key Chrysler locals over both black militant and white opponents. Within a year of the Dodge Main wildcat, blacks had been chosen for four of the six full-time offices in Local 3 and 56 percent of the elected shop steward positions. DRUM's failure to gain a strong permanent political presence in the plant was partly self-inflicted, the consequence of rhetorical overkill, insults and threats to black workers who withheld their support, the rejection of any association with white "honkies," extreme ideological positions, and flirtation with violence (a DRUM fund-raiser raffle offered an M-1 rifle as first prize). The International sought to counter the militant movement by adding a moderate black, Marcellius Ivory, to its executive board and increasing the number of black International representatives on its staff, which stood at only 7.5 percent of the total as late as June 1968. Chrysler responded by blaming the discontent on "outside agitators" and firing the more outspoken members of DRUM for wildcatting, but it added moderate blacks in appreciable numbers to its plant-level supervisory force.[42]

In a sharply worded letter sent to all UAW members in the Detroit metropolitan area, the International executive board issued an ultimatum that warned of the consequences of further wildcats and affirmed the union's traditional integrationist stance on racial relations. "The UAW," the statement read, "will not protect workers who resort to violence and intimidation with the conscious purpose of dividing our Union along racial lines. . . . We believe there can be no separate answers. . . . There are no white answers to the problems; there are no black answers; there are only common answers that we must plan together in the solidarity of our common humanity." Thanks in part to their own tactics and internal divisions, combined with the repression of the militants and concessions to the moderates as engineered by the company and the union, the revolutionary black unions disappeared.[43]

Although the militant outburst was centered in Detroit, black wildcat strikes occurred at plants in other areas with large percentages of African American workers. Ford's Mahwah, New Jersey, assembly plant, where about 50 percent of the employees were African Americans, many of them residents of the Newark ghetto, experienced a series of brief wildcats mostly sparked by racial slurs from supervisors and fellow employees. The United Black Brotherhood, Black Panthers, and Students for a Democratic Society—the latter organization having been recently involved in a massive sit-in at Columbia University—appeared on the scene to support the wildcatters and vie for control of the uprising. They picketed the local's hall, accusing the union of inadequately representing black workers. The company discharged two strike leaders. The Tarrytown, New York, General Motors assembly plant was closed by a wildcat protesting disciplinary actions taken against absentees who failed to report for work on January 15, 1969, in honor of the fortieth anniversary of the birth of Martin Luther King, Jr. About one-fourth of the plant's 5,500 workers were absent, and African Americans made up about one-half of the hourly employees.[44]

Even before the racial wildcats occurred, a white backlash had set in, targeted more on politics than the workplace, a development that threatened to undermine the UAW's political effectiveness. Throughout the latter half of the 1960s, some white blue-collar workers were drifting to the right, driven by a compound of race and class anger. By 1965, a third of white auto workers thought the civil rights movement was pushing ahead too fast. A 1967 independent poll, commissioned by the UAW, showed that half the white rank and file, fearful that black advance would be at their expense, opposed further integration. Anger aimed at African American civil rights advances merged with resentment over the taxes imposed to fund the social programs of the Johnson Administration (seen as primarily benefiting an impoverished black population); together with hatred of extreme antiwar protestors, the tactics of the New Left, and the practices and emblems of the counterculture, these formed an explosive mixture. The riots and outbursts of black racial militancy in the plants heightened these fears and drove these resentments to new extremes.[45]

Although the racial fracture within the workforce and the union was more serious than at any time since World War II, the extent of racial divisions should not be overdrawn. By the end of the 1960s, with a tense racial situation in most of the nation, whites and blacks normally worked side by side in the auto plants without overt friction and cooperated in many union matters with little or no regard to race. The refusal of most black

UAW Local 7's softball team, c. 1965. Walter P. Reuther Library, Wayne State University

auto workers to respond positively to the leadership claims of the revolutionary black nationalist militants was as significant as the support that DRUM and similar organizations received. Although racial considerations and tensions were obviously present in some UAW locals and elsewhere in the organization, by the time of Reuther's death in 1970 the UAW was one of the largest and most powerful, genuinely if imperfectly, racially integrated private or public organizations in the United States. Even on some social issues, as distinguished from the economic and political, UAW blue-collar workers and their families could be found in advance of much of the population. The *New York Times* reported in 1968 that Flint, Michigan, with a dense concentration of mostly white UAW members and their families, became the first city in the United States to adopt, if only by a thirty-one vote margin, "the first open housing measure ever approved by a popular referendum." Pontiac, Michigan, another auto city with many UAW members, including many blacks, also adopted a fair housing ordinance. A year later residents of the affluent Detroit suburb of Grosse Pointe

Farms, home to few if any UAW members, rejected a fair housing measure in a referendum.[46]

THE POLITICAL, SOCIAL, AND CULTURAL CONFLICTS of the 1960s came to a tumultuous climax in the presidential election of 1968. The importance the UAW attached to the election was indicated by the resources the union committed to it. Sixty International representatives were assigned full-time to political activity for an entire year before the election, and as election day approached at least one thousand were working half-time or more. There had been disturbing signs of a weakening of the UAW's unity on political issues, and the leadership feared the reduced impact a fragmented union body politic would have on elections. Frustrations with the failure to end the war in Vietnam, dissatisfaction with the Johnson administration's championing of civil rights and its economic programs for the benefit of the poor, and a backlash against the decay of law and order wore away at white rank-and-file commitment to modern liberalism. The disaffection of some UAW voters first emerged in the 1966 midterm congressional elections when a survey showed that the Democrats' share of the UAW vote dropped by approximately 10 percent from the 1964 total. In Michigan the UAW-endorsed Democratic candidate for the United States Senate, the popular former governor G. Mennen Williams, failed to be elected to a seat previously held by a Democrat, following a bruising primary battle with Detroit mayor Jerome B. Cavanagh. In the primary Williams supported the Johnson administration's Vietnam policy, while Cavanagh ran as a moderate dove. In the general election Williams lost to GOP congressman Robert Griffin, a coauthor of the reviled Landrum-Griffin union regulatory act. In Illinois, another state with a strong UAW contingent, and where in 1964 Johnson had received 72 percent of the UAW vote, Senator Paul Douglas, a stalwart liberal, supporter of the president, and UAW-endorsed candidate, received only 48 percent of the UAW vote, the decline contributing to his defeat. In California, where 77 percent of UAW members had voted for Johnson in 1964, 49 percent voted for Republican Ronald Reagan, running for governor on a law-and-order, anti-protestor platform. This new voting trend threatened to undermine the UAW's commitment to its political goals and convinced the union's leadership that it must direct its efforts at persuading its members to keep the faith.[47]

Confidential surveys of UAW members revealed the erosion of support for the union's political objectives. A division by race within the ranks was apparent. According to the 1967 Quayle survey of UAW voting and opinion, 68 percent of African American auto workers approved of President Johnson's job performance but only 46 percent of whites did so—with only 38 percent of white auto workers in Flint. Eighty-five percent of all

auto workers voted for Johnson in 1964 but only 56 percent said they would
vote for him in 1968; 27 percent said they would vote for Nixon. When
Alabama Governor George C. Wallace entered the race as an independent,
20 percent of white auto workers, including some Nixon supporters, indicated they would vote for him. Although these findings expressed only a
nonbinding preference and overstated the support from UAW voters that
Nixon and Wallace would finally receive in the election, as a gesture of
protest they revealed the shaky, even shattered, commitment of many
members to the union's traditional Democratic liberalism. When asked in
the same survey to rank current issues about which they felt concern, taxes
and government spending programs placed first. The Vietnam War was the
next issue of greatest concern. Feelings were divided and the questions
ambiguous, but antiwar sentiment was strong. Of those who considered
Vietnam a concern, 46 percent thought the United States should fight to
win, but, if it became evident that the will or the means to victory was
lacking, the U.S. should withdraw. Thirty-seven percent of respondents
favored negotiations to end the war and 17 percent favored immediate
withdrawal by the U.S. More than half the respondents, it would appear,
aligned themselves with a more or less dovish position. Other issues of
concern were civil rights, with respondents equally divided between pro-
integration and anti-integration positions, followed by crime and juvenile
delinquency, inflation and the cost of living, and a long list of lesser concerns—all the way down to the proposition that Communism was an internal threat within the United States, volunteered as a concern by 1 percent
of the respondents. As one historian appraised the results, "in combination
with the deep-seated racism of many white auto workers, . . . the mounting tax burden dramatically weakened their thirty-year perception of the
Democratic Party as the party of the 'common man.' "[48]

REELING UNDER THE IMPACT of popular disillusion with the war, the
Democratic Party seemed on the verge of disintegration, creating for the
UAW leadership the most difficult political decisions it had ever faced. Senator Eugene McCarthy rocked the party by attacking Johnson's war policy
and announcing his candidacy for its presidential nomination. His strong
showing in the New Hampshire Democratic primary demonstrated the
depths of popular frustration with a war that apparently could neither be
won at an acceptable price nor from which the country could disengage.
There was little support within the UAW leadership for McCarthy, whose
ties to the labor movement were perfunctory, whose campaign behavior
was erratic, and who directed his appeal primarily to the college-educated
middle and upper classes. When invited to address the UAW convention,
along with other candidates Hubert H. Humphrey and Robert F. Kennedy,

he declined to show up. The spotlight now was on Reuther, for years the guiding force in determining the UAW's official political positions. He vacillated through the late winter and spring, publicly stating that he expected to vote for President Johnson's reelection but maintaining ties with the doves. When the board of Americans for Democratic Action endorsed McCarthy, a number of labor leaders, at the White House's request, resigned in protest; Reuther, who thought the endorsement a mistake, nevertheless stayed on rather than sever his links with the ADA liberals who supported the endorsement. Within the UAW, Reuther's reluctance to criticize the war policy provoked strong protests from associates he respected, including his brother Victor, head of the union's International Affairs Department. Nat Weinberg, who had been feeding Reuther antiwar material for months, submitted among many other items a *Wall Street Journal* editorial that questioned the war (how it must have pained Reuther to see the nation's leading conservative newspaper take a position more liberal than his own!). In a memorandum accompanying the editorial, Weinberg scored the "nightmarish, destructive and dangerous futility of U.S. policy throughout East Asia" that had led Americans to "kill, maim, uproot, incarcerate in concentration camps, and demoralize and degrade the men, women, and children we claim to be defending." Paul Schrade, the executive board's leading dove and an activist in the antiwar movement, charged that the UAW was now nearly as detached from and as ineffectual in helping to resolve the great moral issue of the times as the scorned AFL-CIO. At a special board session in March, he charged: "I think the UAW is bound up in inaction, not as great as the AFL-CIO [is], but to a degree that to me is a threat as well. . . . [R]ather than just focusing on what the AFL-CIO is doing or not doing . . . we should begin deciding what kind of union we are going to be."[49]

The UAW leadership's logjam on Vietnam began to break up following Senator Robert F. Kennedy's announcement of his candidacy for the presidency on March 16, followed two weeks later by President Johnson's astonishing pledge that he would neither seek nor accept the Democratic Party's nomination for another term. Vice President Hubert H. Humphrey inherited Johnson's tattered standard on Vietnam, along with the president's half-hearted support for his nomination. Humphrey's long if occasionally erratic devotion to social-democratic liberalism had won him many friends in the UAW, and he was clearly the favorite of a third or more of the executive board's members. Kennedy, now in closer agreement with the UAW leadership's views on policy than either his brother Jack or President Johnson had been, was the rival candidate for the UAW's support. Neither Humphrey nor Kennedy stirred much applause or enthusiasm in speaking appearances before the UAW's convention, a reflection perhaps of the delegates' confusion or disgust with the course of national politics. Battle lines

were drawn. Johnson pressed both Humphrey and Reuther to toe the administration's line on Vietnam, while Kennedy proposed a conditional bombing halt and the establishment of a coalition government in South Vietnam
that could be expanded to include the Viet Cong. The UAW leadership's dispute centered on West Coast regional director Paul Schrade. Before Johnson's withdrawal, Schrade had announced his support for Kennedy and said
he would join the slate of convention delegates pledged to Kennedy in the
California primary. Challenging an incumbent Democratic president was
not something UAW officers did lightly. At an off-the-record board session
on March 19, Reuther, furious with Schrade for breaking ranks, demanded
that he withdraw from the slate. "It was," Schrade recalled, "really a terrible session." Despite some board members' threats to oppose his reelection
as regional director, Schrade told the board that he stood by his endorsement of Kennedy and that he would become a member of RFK's convention
delegation. Then came the bombshell. In Schrade's account, "Leonard
Woodcock," who was sitting next to Schrade, "turned and said, 'I agree with
Paul,' and 'if I were in California I would do the same thing. I will not support Lyndon Johnson.' So this . . . put him in the anti-Johnson camp, and for
Robert Kennedy . . . which was the shock of our life." Reuther, Schrade continued, "was shocked too. Because here was Leonard, the super hawk on the
board, shifting ground rapidly all of a sudden. . . . " The next day Reuther
tried and failed again to talk Schrade out of his decision. In fact, a powerful
contingent of social-democratic board members, including Woodcock,
Doug Fraser, Ken Bannon, Ray Berndt, Martin Gerber, and Ray Ross,
informed Reuther that, like Schrade, they would support Kennedy regardless of the union's official position. According to a *New York Times* reporter,
the UAW's upper ranks now contained the largest number of Kennedy supporters of any union. Reuther had no choice but to recognize the depth and
passion of the Kennedy commitment among his colleagues. After Johnson's
withdrawal relieved him of the need to stand by the president, he conceded
that union officers and regional directors could support any candidate they
wished, but the UAW International itself would remain neutral, reserving
its official endorsement until after the Democratic convention, a tactic the
board had used in previous elections.[50]

It seems likely, as Victor Reuther and others close to Walter avowed,
that he eventually would have supported Kennedy for the nomination, but
for the moment he withheld an endorsement. Some board members, including Pat Greathouse, George Merrelli, and Nelson Jack Edwards, endorsed
Humphrey. The board remained "deeply divided" until the California primary. Schrade, asked by Reuther just before the primary how the board division broke down, replied that about one-third were with Kennedy, one-third
were with Humphrey, and one-third would do whatever Reuther wanted

them to do. "You're going to decide this question," he said. Reuther chuckled, but Schrade thought he was not amused by this unsolicited tribute to the sway he exercised with many board members. Schrade believed that Kennedy, who had already defeated McCarthy in primaries in Indiana and Nebraska while losing to him in Oregon (Humphrey entered the race too late to qualify for any primaries), would swing Reuther to his side with a victory in California. In the California and Indiana primaries—two states with substantial numbers of UAW members—the union, under the direction of the respective regional directors, was very active in Kennedy's behalf. Kennedy's assassination on June 4, 1968, the day of his victory in California's primary (Paul Schrade, campaigning with Kennedy in Los Angeles, was also shot in the attack but not fatally), foreclosed the need for a choice. Some 2,400 UAW members walked out of General Motors' Fremont, California, plant because a foreman allegedly told a worker that Senator Kennedy "got what he deserved."[51]

After Kennedy's assassination, it was certain that the UAW would support Humphrey but try to nudge him toward a moderately dovish position on the war. At the invitation of Clark Kerr, Reuther agreed to become a co-chair of the National Committee for a Political Settlement in Vietnam or Negotiation Now!—an organization of churchmen, academics, writers, and business leaders that hoped to start the process of winding down American participation in the war with agreements obtained between the two sides in talks getting underway in Paris. Negotiation Now! advocated an immediate, standstill cease fire, including a bombing halt; positioning of an international peacekeeping corps in Vietnam, consisting of forces from several Asian countries, to monitor the cease fire; fully free elections in South Vietnam, including protected participation by the National Liberation Front (Viet Cong), whose victory in an election Reuther was prepared to risk although he thought it unlikely; and land reform. The key item was the call to end the bombing of North Vietnam unilaterally, with the "expectation" that North Vietnam would suspend its military action in the south. The door to a resumption of bombing remained open if North Vietnam did not respond. To the UAW's executive board, Reuther made his new position clear. He and others from Negotiation Now! would meet with the candidate "and see if we cannot help Hubert Humphrey try to get himself straightened out on this foreign policy because I think he has been the prisoner of the Administration's policy. I think this is the big millstone that he carries," words that could have been as aptly applied to himself. Reuther met privately with Humphrey on June 16 and 24. Humphrey, sympathetic but noncommittal, asked for a draft of a speech reflecting Negotiation Now!'s platform, which Reuther, drawing on work by UAW assistants Irving Bluestone and Guy Nunn, sent to him on July 28. Still fearing to alienate Johnson, whose support for the nomination he thought essential to his success, Humphrey never delivered it.[52]

At the disorderly, strife-ridden Democratic convention, Reuther tried to obtain a compromise plank on Vietnam, based on the Negotiation Now! agenda, that would lay the foundation for a peaceful settlement, draw back into the party those followers of McCarthy and Kennedy who were drifting away, and give Humphrey a better shot at winning the election. Humphrey was prepared to accept the program with one crucial exception: the bombing of North Vietnam should continue until that country ended its military action, as President Johnson, who saw a unilateral bombing halt as a repudiation of his presidency, insisted. The proposal to end the bombing split the UAW leadership. At the convention, UAW board members Pat Greathouse and George Merrelli, supporters of Humphrey, voted against it, while others, including Douglas Fraser, voted for it and helped swing the Michigan delegation, which cast its votes as a block, into line in its favor when it came to a vote on the floor. There the proposal died. Another effort to reinvent Humphrey as a dove occurred when Reuther and Irving Bluestone, at Humphrey's invitation, traveled to Minnesota to meet with the candidate. Humphrey seemed to want to make the Negotiation Now! proposals a part of his campaign. Reuther told him he would have to break with Johnson on the war in order to win, but Humphrey retorted that if he crossed Johnson the president's opposition would cost him the support of some southern states. Again Humphrey asked for a draft statement, which was supplied but never used.[53]

When the executive board met in September to endorse a presidential candidate, all, with the exception of Schrade, agreed that it had to be Humphrey. Reuther, who introduced the endorsement resolution, insisted on a unanimous endorsement as the only kind that carried weight. At first Schrade argued that the UAW should make no presidential endorsement, concentrating its efforts instead on congressional and state elections. Reuther responded harshly: "Your position is a position of total abdication of responsibility," because it would contribute to the defeat of Humphrey and the election of Nixon and other reactionaries. The progress that had been made since 1961, he feared, would be lost under a Republican president. If everyone took Schrade's position, the Republicans would be back in power and "it would be a catastrophe for our Union." After further exchanges, Schrade was willing to change his position because he now saw some grounds for hope that Humphrey, endorsed (as Reuther pointed out) by antiwar Senators Edward Kennedy and George McGovern, would disassociate himself from a war policy. The resolution recommending a vote for Humphrey to the membership was unanimous. More than 2,600 delegates from UAW locals, the largest non-party gathering to endorse a candidate in the 1968 election, met in regional conferences to act on the board's recommendation. Humphrey won the support of 88 percent of the delegates, Republican candidate Richard M. Nixon one percent, and Alabama Governor George C. Wallace, running on an independent party ticket, received ten percent.[54]

REUTHER WAS CONFIDENT there would be no significant Nixon vote among auto workers, but there was reason to fear that Wallace's campaign, aimed in part at exploiting the fears and frustrations of white, northern, blue-collar workers, would make inroads among UAW voters. The proportion of southern-born whites in the auto workforce was still significant. In Indiana and Ohio 17 percent of all auto workers were whites born in the South. In Michigan, where the representation of southern whites in the general population was 5 percent, 11 percent of auto workers, concentrated in Flint, were white southerners. As Reuther reminded the executive board, "we all know that Flint is always considered to be the largest southern style town north of the Mason-Dixon line." The union predicted Wallace would take as much as 23 percent of the members' votes in Flint, 25 percent in Oakland County, and perhaps 75 percent in southern Macomb County, heavily populated by white-flight migrants, union and otherwise, from Detroit. A local UAW official stated "I wouldn't be surprised if 33 percent of the white votes in the plant[s] went for Wallace. There is deep sentiment among the white suburbanites for Wallace." In a straw poll taken in a Nashville local, Wallace got 62 percent of the vote. Other scattered evidence gave cause for alarm. At the Indianapolis Ford plant, the UAW's political action drive brought in $699 in voluntary contributions, while the Wallace campaign received $1,900 from the night shift alone. A photograph reproduced in the *New York Times* showed a $1,000 check from UAW local members made out to the Wallace campaign. Bumper stickers bearing the message "U.A.W. Members Support Wallace for President" appeared in Detroit and other auto cities. Many journalists and pundits were predicting that Wallace would take a large minority of auto workers' votes with his thinly disguised racist appeal, tough position on the war (calling for outright victory), antigovernment, antitax, anti-intellectual rhetoric, contempt for the long-haired, protesting acolytes of the counterculture, and, perhaps not least, the sly melding of a racist message with an assertion of masculine sexuality. A flyer circulated in some plants featured a picture of Humphrey kissing a black, female child alongside another of a smirking Wallace being hugged by a grinning blond in a miniskirt. The caption asked: "Which Do You Prefer?"[55]

Although no one would question that Wallace had supporters among the auto workers, the claims for the extent and depth of that support, which were subject to manipulation, vote rigging, and faulty reporting, were often overstated, particularly in the early stages of the campaign. UAW Local 326 in Flint voted to endorse Wallace at a meeting attended by only 200 of the local's 4,500 members. At a much better attended later meeting, the local shifted its endorsement to Humphrey. A poll of members of the huge Buick Local 599 in Flint showed Wallace with 49 percent, Humphrey with 39 percent, and Nixon with 12 percent. However, a later poll—conducted as the election approached and in conjunction with a strike authorization vote that brought out a much larger proportion of the local's membership—saw Wallace's support shrink to 14 percent. A reporter who "interviewed" several auto workers at a Ford plant by shouting questions at them from a distance as they walked to their cars in a parking lot wrote that voters' were moving in Wallace's favor. A *New York Times* headline that contributed to the stereotype that lasted through the campaign and beyond read "White U.A.W. Men Turn to Wallace: Michigan Sampling Shows Evidence of Shift." Not the media's best day.[56]

When Reuther appeared to speak at a meeting of perhaps 300 leadership people in St. Louis, he was heckled by about fifty Wallace supporters, who were accompanied by a sound truck and hats, flyers, and other campaign paraphernalia. As they tried to prevent him from speaking, he responded "look, get it off your chest, because I've been heckled by professionals, and I'm going to say what I came here to say." After spending forty-five minutes trying to break up the meeting, they paraded out. As they left one of the Wallaceites told a reporter that UAW Local 25 is "90 percent pro-Wallace," a figure later reduced by the local's president to 20 percent.[57]

With some estimates placing Wallace's support among the entire electorate as high as 25 percent, a vote that would have prevented either major party candidate from gaining an electoral college majority and thrown the election into the House of Representatives, the UAW launched the strongest political campaign in its history, targeting its efforts in states with concentrations of auto workers. The UAW attack appealed largely to self-interest. In speech and in print the Alabama governor's antilabor and anti-worker records were recited. Auto workers were reminded that Wallace had raised "soak the poor" taxes, especially those on beer and tobacco; that Alabama's rates for workers' and unemployment compensation were among the nation's lowest; that Wallace had refused to support repeal of the state's right-to-work law, which hampered union organizing and other activities; and that despite strident appeals for "law and order" and sneers at "bleeding heart" liberals, Alabama had one of the country's highest crime rates. Reuther warned that Wallace would push the nation into a "police state." In an address to the political activists attending a UAW Community Action Conference in September, he remarked, "George Wallace said the other day . . . if the police could run America for two years, they would straighten things out. . . . I saw the hatred in the faces of the state police in Selma, Alabama. You saw the hatred of the police dogs of Bull Conner's in Birmingham, Alabama. And I say pray to God that that kind of police mentality will not be given the job of straightening out America because that kind of mentality will destroy America."[58]

Practical measures built upon the union's rhetorical assault. The UAW donated $100,000 to a voter registration drive conducted in Michigan by the Democratic Party, the largest single sum received out of a total of $250,000 contributed. By election day the UAW had approximately 15,000 volunteers pledged to work in a get-out-the-vote drive in the state. Despite the UAW's recent disaffiliation from the AFL-CIO, their political arms cooperated effectively in the election effort, forming the core of the coalition that carried Michigan for Humphrey. On September 30, the Democratic candidate announced that if elected he would declare an immediate halt to bombing, and on October 31, President Johnson ordered a less sweeping bombing pause—shifts of position that contributed to a Humphrey surge as election day approached. With the UAW hammering home the message that a Wallace vote was a wasted vote, old habits among auto workers reasserted themselves. Humphrey, whose chances had been written off when the disastrous Democratic convention ended, cut deeply into Wallace's support in the northern states and nearly closed the gap on Nixon. In Michigan, where the union's effort was led by Douglas Fraser, Humphrey prevailed by two hundred thousand votes. Nationally, however, Nixon eked out a narrow victory.[59]

UAW officers took pride in the union's 1968 electoral showing. With the Democratic Party apparently self-destructing at its nominating convention only two months before the election, it was remarkable and even heartening that the race had drawn so tight by the end. Many pundits opined that an earlier embrace of the bombing halt proposal would have been sufficient to put Humphrey over the top. The vote, however, if closely examined, provided little ground for optimism; seen with the benefit of hindsight, the election marked a turning point in the union leadership's ability to mobilize and direct the rank and file as a political force. Although voting statistics for UAW members in 1968 are not available, returns from Michigan counties in which many auto workers resided throw some light on the emerging trends (the figures are for all voters in a county, not only blue-collar and UAW workers). Despite the data's limitations, they suggest that many white auto workers abandoned the Democratic Party's presidential candidate for the first time since the union's origins in the heyday of the New Deal. In Macomb County, Humphrey won 55.4 percent of the vote, 9 percentage points below Kennedy's total in 1960 and a whopping 19 points below Johnson's 1964 showing. In Genessee County, which includes the city of Flint, Humphrey got only 45.8 percent of the vote, 22 points under Johnson's 1964 total. Richard Nixon received 30.4 percent of the Macomb County vote and 38.8 percent in Genessee, while George Wallace received 14.2 percent in Macomb and 15.4 in Genessee. Although both of these counties contained rural, small-town, business, and professional elements that would not support Democratic Party candidates under any circumstances, they were centers of UAW membership and the focus of the union's political effort. Half the voters in these two counties, at least some of them formerly Democratic Party supporters, had voted for conservative candidates. The migration of those who would become Reagan Democrats had begun.[60]

ONLY WEEKS AFTER LEAVING the AFL-CIO Reuther tried to break out of the UAW's isolation by constructing a new platform for advancing a labor position on public issues. He denied that the new organization, the Alliance for Labor Action (ALA) was intended to be a rival labor federation, although Meany branded it a dual union and threatened to expel AFL-CIO affiliates that joined. In all probability, if the experiment had succeeded in attracting many affiliates it would have become a rival to the AFL-CIO. For the time being the alliance was limited to coordination of organizing campaigns and of political positions and activities. The unlikely partner for the UAW in this venture was the International Brotherhood of Teamsters (IBT), whose president, Jimmy Hoffa, was then in prison. Although it seemed odd for the ethically pure Reuther to align the UAW with an organization whose expulsion for corruption from the AFL-CIO he had helped bring about (and there were astonished gasps when the alliance's formation was announced), the cooperation between auto workers and teamsters was neither farfetched nor, for the short time it lasted, ineffective. Reuther had long known fellow Detroiters Hoffa and Frank Fitzsimmons, the latter now the Teamsters' acting president. Locally the two unions had erratic, sometimes friendly sometimes hostile, relations. Both presented a dynamic contrast to the lethargic AFL-CIO and were committed to recruiting unorganized workers; moreover, in a key concession from Reuther's standpoint, the Teamsters' leadership agreed to follow his lead on the political and other public questions that meant so much to him. Although membership in the alliance was open to any union, only the Chemical Workers' Union and one other small organization joined, but even alone the auto workers and the Teamsters formed a potentially powerful combination. With nearly 2 million members, the Teamsters were the largest union in the nation, and the 1.5 million member UAW was not far behind.[61]

Released by Nixon's victory from his imprisonment while a Democrat occupied the White House, Reuther escalated his criticism of America's Vietnam policy. In June 1969 he called on the United States to eventually withdraw from Vietnam, unilaterally if necessary. In October the UAW board supported the massive, peaceful, antiwar demonstrations of the Vietnam Moratorium Day with full-page ads in major newspapers and contributions of funds, and, for the first time, Reuther endorsed complete and early American withdrawal from the war. An ALA statement called on "our Government to face up to the reality that there is nothing to be won in Vietnam that is worth one more drop of American blood." ALA, the statement added, takes its stand "with those who are for getting out quickly and completely." Reuther also paid tribute to Emil Mazey's pioneering role in initiating UAW board opposition to the war. At a testimonial dinner he said: "On the overriding question of war and peace—which transcends everything—Emil's voice, more than that of any other leader in the UAW, has been heard."[62]

At the UAW convention in the spring of 1970, the last he was to attend, Reuther condemned the war on moral grounds for dividing the nation, wasting its resources, and tarnishing its credentials. He did not condone illegal acts of protest or anti-American radicalism. "I want to make it clear," he said, that "we condemn those Americans who burn the American flag and march behind the Viet Cong flag. We reject the concept that says in order to be antiwar you have to be anti-American; that kind of reckless attitude . . . is destructive and counterproductive." A few days later, when Nixon's invasion of Cambodia provoked massive demonstrations, resulting in the deaths of four young persons at Kent State University, Reuther set out to organize a national coalition against violence, an effort cut short by his death. He strongly criticized Nixon's expansion of the war in a telegram to the president: "Your decision to invade the territory of Cambodia can only increase the enormity of the tragedy in which our nation is already deeply and unfortunately involved in that region. . . . You pledged to bring America together, yet . . . you have driven the wedge of division deeper."[63]

After Reuther's death his successor as UAW president, Leonard Woodcock, together with Emil Mazey, Douglas Fraser, Irving Bluestone, and other colleagues, kept the UAW in the forefront of the union antiwar movement. UAW representatives took a leading role in the Labor for Peace movement, with 220 of the 985 delegates at its June 1972 conference coming from the UAW. They called for an immediate end to the war but rejected a resolution for a one-day protest strike. The proposal for a strike would split the peace movement and was undemocratic to boot, since the workers who would be expected to go on strike had been given no opportunity to express their views. In 1972 the UAW endorsed Democrat George McGovern for president as the candidate most likely to conclude the war immediately.[64]

The UAW and the ALA were also early opponents of the Nixon administration's plan for an immensely expensive anti-ballistic missile system, which the UAW executive board denounced as "a costly folly that would reduce security [and] add to the arms race," and Reuther endorsed proposals urging Nixon to begin negotiations to prevent the spread of nuclear weapons. The UAW's withdrawal from the AFL-CIO broke the united front of labor's support for the war and huge military expenditures, and began the renewal of labor's fragmented ties with other elements of the liberal community.[65]

AS THE WAR WOUND DOWN and as arms reduction and limitation agreements with the U.S.S.R. seemed in the offing, Reuther, mindful of a botched reconversion after World War II, became concerned about the economic consequences of peace and a thaw in the cold war. Since some Vietnam military contractors had little experience with production for civilian markets, he feared that their reluctance to test those hazardous waters might perpetuate the military-industrial complex. This was also a practical problem for the UAW leadership, since a substantial portion of current and prospective aerospace production was in the hands of UAW members who would be concerned about their jobs if military production was cut back. Reuther's plan was published as a pamphlet entitled, "Swords into Plowshares: A Proposal to Promote Orderly Conversion from Defense to Civilian Production . . . December 1, 1969." In testimony before the Senate Labor and Public Welfare Committee, he proposed that military contractors be required to put one-quarter of their after-tax profits from war production into a government trust fund. The money would be used to finance retraining and family benefits for workers displaced by cancellation of military contracts. As an incentive to encourage companies to plan for the transition to peacetime production, any amounts remaining in the fund would be returned to them as profits. When Senator Thomas Eagleton (Democrat, Missouri) asked Reuther whether persuasion rather than the threat of withheld profits would not be adequate to secure cooperation, Reuther replied that thirty years at the bargaining table had convinced him that "only the threat to their profits moves them." Although seven Democratic senators on the committee endorsed the plan in varying degrees, and the *New York Times* commended Reuther for trying to goad government, business, and labor into constructive thinking on the postwar economy, little was heard of it in Congress and nothing from the Nixon administration. Several of the proposals were incorporated in Senator George McGovern's National Economic Conversion Bill of 1969, which targeted conversion on socially useful objectives in low-cost housing, educational and health facilities, and pollution controls. The bill failed to pass.[66]

THE UAW HAD SUPPORTED the civil rights movement, antipoverty legislation, and full-employment policies to get at the roots of the racial and class strife that convulsed Harlem, Watts, Newark, Detroit, and other cities between 1965 and the end of the decade. The possibility of applying the union concept directly as a social model for ghetto rejuvenation seemed worth pursuing. The eruptions stemmed in part from social fragmentation and the frustrations of powerlessness, a situation with parallels to the industrial workplace before the formation of unions. Working with Jack Conway, Reuther's former assistant and a long-time associate in social and political causes, and through the Industrial Union Department of the AFL-CIO and the ALA, the UAW helped launch several experiments in the development of community unions, an adaptation of the trade union for purposes of community improvement. In 1967 Reuther wrote:

> A new concept of union organization has been developing in areas such as Delano and Watts, California. Properly nurtured and motivated, it can spread across the face of the nation, changing the social character of the inner city structure and uplifting the lives of millions of slum dwellers. This new organizing effort is "the community union." It is designed to provide the poor with their own self-sufficient economic organization . . . and cuts across many areas of social and economic need . . . health care, schools, public transportation, sanitation, building maintenance etc.

Conway added: "We believe that just as the auto worker and the steel worker . . . gained self-respect and dignity through organization, so, too, can the poor gain self-respect and dignity by the same methods." Community unions would be part union and part community organization, bringing residents together to bargain with landlords, the police, and other providers of services. They could initiate and then administer educational and retraining programs and engage in political activity. As usual, the UAW backed its initiative with significant funding.[67]

Characterized by two social scientists as "one of the most imaginative ideas to emerge from organized labor in the postwar period," community unions were established in ghettos in Chicago, Newark, and Watts. They faced serious challenges. Reliable and skillful leadership was difficult to find and develop, except in Watts, where a UAW steward, African American Ted Watkins, was energetic and resourceful. The community unions became entangled in rivalries with civil rights, ethnic, and political organizations in competition for community support and funds. They were resented by some ghetto residents and organizations as another attempt by "whitey" to impose a structure under his control on the ghetto. If they succeeded in attracting government or foundation money, their functions as manager and disburser of funds tended to overshadow community organization and other kinds of services. Although none of the experimental groups fulfilled the high hopes of Reuther and Conway by becoming permanent organizations of community residents, they did succeed for a time in drawing together a portion of the urban underclass in pursuit of common goals of betterment.[68]

When the ALA became involved, much of its effort went into these self-help organizations or was integrated into STEP, the Social, Technical and Educational Program. STEP was a joint UAW-Teamsters initiative for collecting supplies and equipment for use in medical, social, and educational work in developing countries and in deprived areas of the United States. Union members volunteered to repair and upgrade donated x-ray machines and other equipment in their free time. During the first year of the program the union transferred $1 million worth of such equipment overseas—to hospitals and clinics in India, Chile, Brazil, and Lebanon—as well as to rural areas in the southern part of the United States. Although the ALA could point to such good works and a record of advocacy in behalf of peace and arms control, areas in which the Teamsters' Union had not been previously active, after Reuther's death the ALA rapidly decomposed. Few in the UAW leadership would later defend it.[69]

THE UAW HAD SOUGHT TO BUILD a majority coalition of like-minded elements dedicated to social-democratic ends, a goal that was predicated on a party realignment into more clearly delineated conservative and liberal divisions. By the mid-1960s the future seemed promising with the coming together of unions, civil rights organizations, liberal religious groups, student reform societies, and a president in the White House whose progressive measures enjoyed majority support in Congress. The vanguard role in social, economic, and political reform that the UAW had aspired to for years was producing results, and more were expected. Although there were significant accomplishments, especially in securing equal rights, the UAW's expansive vision was never realized. Overtaken by events largely beyond its ability to control, but also victimized by the unintended consequences of some of its own actions, the union fell well short of achieving the full measure of its public agenda.[70]

CHAPTER 13

"A whole new middle class"

End of an Era, 1960–70

THE MIDDLE CLASS THAT THE UAW WAS BRINGING TO BIRTH WAS a middle class with a difference. Although auto wages and the material standard of living approximated historic middle-class averages, the work itself was manual, hard, and, for many, intrinsically unrewarding; the factory culture was rough and crude. A *Wall Street Journal* reporter, employed incognito for a week in 1967 on a Ford assembly line, found the work "grueling and frustrating, and while it may be repetitious, it's not simple. I learned how tough it can be." Hired as a summer replacement, the temporary employee's foreman knew and referred to him only by the last four digits of his social security number: "9616." A *Newsweek* reporter who spent four days of grinding labor on a Chevrolet assembly line in 1970 wrote "the single most important bond uniting auto workers is the never-ending physical agony of it all." With less than a minute to install shackles on the rear suspension system of Novas he fell behind on the first unit and never caught up.[1]

Harvey Swados, a radical essayist who put in several factory stints, described his auto workmates as "not merely indifferent . . . [but] actively hostile to their surroundings and what they did with their own hands. Their talk was continually seasoned with contemptuous references to the factory, to their work, and to the lives they led. Almost everybody . . . hated their work and admitted frankly that the only incentive to return from one day to the next was the pay check." Comments made to investigators, such as "the only reason a man works is to make a living" and "the things I like about my job are quitting time, pay day, days off, and vacations," suggest the dimensions of a culture of estrangement. Alienation from one's daily task was not, of course, confined to auto workers nor to those who worked with their hands. It could be found throughout the job hierarchy and across a range of occupations. Auto factory work, however, had become the most frequently studied, publicized, and invoked instance of modern workers' mental and emotional divorce from work.[2]

Not all auto workers, it must be remembered, were as hostile as some of these comments suggest. Auto work still provided, as it had since its earliest days, a significant and valued improvement in wages and working conditions for many, particularly those coming to the factory directly from rural and small-town settings. Jobs in the skilled trades and even in production work afforded pride and self-respect. Workers in a postwar California auto plant, most of whose families came to the state as "Oakies" or "Arkies" in the migrations of the 1930s and after, were well-aware of the collective and individual gains they now enjoyed in their jobs and lives. Blue-collar employees at a new General Motors assembly plant found the line-paced work unappealing compared to their previous jobs, but they valued the better pay and greater economic security.[3]

Some employers did little to encourage among their employees a creative attachment to their jobs. The hierarchical structure of the factory's social order and the prospect of a good wage were relied upon to maintain production, with little concern for enlisting deeper motivations. Someone who took the initiative to make the job more interesting and improve performance could meet with disapproval. When Irving Bluestone worked as a bearing grinder at a General Motors plant in New Jersey, he decided to learn something about high carbon steel, thinking the knowledge might make the job more interesting. Borrowing a book on the subject from a public library, he placed it on a bench next to his grinder, intending to read it during his lunch break. The foreman passed by, thumbed through the book, and asked, "What the hell are you doing with this?" When Bluestone explained, the foreman replied, "Look here, you don't need a book to do your job. Just do the job as you've been told and grind the damned races to spec. That's all I want you to do."[4]

Many auto workers, like other middle-class Americans, dreamed of rising in the social/economic scale but realistically saw that their prospects for improvement were dim. As a sociologist noted after an investigation and survey of an autoworker community, their "range of possibility" was constricted. Their idea of "self-improvement" or "getting ahead" could mean a change as modest as a different job classification within the factory, perhaps a transfer to less demanding or less unpleasant work, say from assembler to forklift operator, with only minor differences, if any, in pay. Mobility was also construed as the acquisition of property, such as a house and other consumer goods, objectives within reach for steadily employed workers. There was little opportunity for production workers to rise within the company. Few were promoted to assistant foreman or foreman. In the Oldsmobile factory in Lansing, Michigan, with more than 6,000 employees, there were normally only ten or twelve openings for assistant foremen in a year and most were filled by outsiders. Some workers, uncomfortable exercising the skills necessary for success as a foreman, did not covet a supervisory position. As one told an interviewer, "the foreman is rode to get out production and so he's got to ride his men. I couldn't do that." Occasionally a company might offer union officers supervisory positions, either in recognition of their qualifications or to destabilize a local's leadership. In John Anderson's union, Local 22 at Cadillac, "three of our local presidents have gone over to the company and gone on supervision," an action resented (with perhaps a touch of envy) as a betrayal of class loyalty. To move into engineering or any technical field was impossible without the requisite education. To advance to a skilled trade was difficult without the required apprenticeship, although "upgraders," taught a single skill or to operate a single machine and both scorned and feared by the apprenticed tradesmen, were a partial exception to the rule. Although many auto workers dreamed of an escape from the factory to a farm or small business of their own, the number who could acquire the capital and had the business skill to accomplish the feat was infinitely small.[5]

Advancement within the union was only a little less unlikely, although the attractions of union positions made them coveted by many. Shop floor union officials received their normal pay for the time union duties kept them from their jobs. In a General Motors plant surveyed shortly after World War II, stewards had two hours off each day at company expense to deal with grievances ("lost time" in the company's phrase); committeemen got five hours free each day for negotiations; and the chairman of the shop committee could take as much time as needed to present the union's case in grievances and participate in other negotiations. In addition to escape from the assembly line or the press room, union positions offered opportunities for social and personal contact with other workers and supervisors, and the satisfaction of providing services deemed valuable by one's fellows. For many workers, the steward or committeeman who negotiated settlements over speedups, favoritism, layoffs, disciplinary actions, unsafe or unhealthy conditions, transfers, and reclassifications simply "is the union," their only personal contact with the massive organization to which they belonged. The released time from auto work, with the addition of "super seniority," which guaranteed that as long as there was a job in the plant the union official would have it, and the occasional "perk," such as attending a union convention or conference at the local's expense, were the tangible rewards of these positions. With the necessary political and personal skills and connections, one might win election to one of the full-time, dues-funded local offices—of which (in locals of average size) there were usually only two, those of president and financial secretary. The large locals could afford additional full- or part-time positions as recording secretary, newspaper editor, and so on. Even more desirable was a full-time position on the union's regional or International staff as a "rep"; these "porkchoppers," in worker parlance, earned about one and a half to two times that of the average auto worker. Since competition was stiff and exceptional skills—political and otherwise—were required for success, few could expect to rise that far. Most workers realized, as one told an interviewer, "we don't have anything to look forward to except working [in the factory] the rest of our lives." In an assembly-line worker survey, 60 percent of the younger workers and 80 percent of the older ones stated that they did not believe they would ever have a chance for a better job. As with many other working Americans, dreams of personal advance were often projected onto the coming generation. By 1970 a college education for a worker's sons and daughters was a practical goal, given the increases in earnings and the greater opportunities for higher education afforded by the growth in number and size of colleges and universities.[6]

In 1967 the union leadership obtained a statistical portrait of the membership utilizing the services of the Oliver Quayle survey organization. The Quayle group questioned 2,103 union members, who were randomly drawn from auto, agricultural implement, and aerospace firms. Although the sample excluded employees of independent parts companies and Canadian auto workers, in other respects it was representative of the union's membership. One purpose was to tap sentiment on collective bargaining issues in preparation for the 1967 negotiations, but respondents were also questioned on many other matters, including attitudes toward the UAW and its activities.[7]

By length of membership in the UAW, the respondents divided into three groups of roughly equal size. One-third had been members ten years or less; one-third from ten years to less than twenty; and one-third for more than twenty years. With regard to religious affiliation, 68 percent reported they were Protestants and 27 percent Catholic; the remainder either did not respond or gave a different answer. Age distribution showed a gradually aging workforce. Thirty-four percent were under age thirty-five, 52 percent were between thirty-five and fifty-five, and 14 percent were fifty-five or over. The workforce was predominantly male, comprising 92 percent, with the heaviest male concentration at Ford (98 percent) and the largest female representation at General Motors. (Inclusion of the independent parts firms in the survey would have increased the female percentage.) By race, 79 percent were white and 20 percent black, with Detroit having the highest black representation of the areas surveyed (24 percent) and Flint the lowest (12 percent). In racial composition by employer, 87 percent of GM's employees were white and 12 percent black, while at Chrysler, whose facilities were concentrated in the Detroit metropolitan area, 63 percent were white and 37 percent black. Ford occupied a middle ground with 77 percent white and 23 percent black.[8]

The interviewers, who met with respondents in their homes, evaluated the household living standards of each respondent based on answers to questions and the observer's personal assessment. They reported that 10 percent met an upper- or upper-middle-class standard, 85 percent were in the lower middle class, and 5 percent were in the lower class; interviewers noted that the upper- and upper-middle-class group consisted almost entirely of families with no dependent children and two working adults. Although these ratings were partly subjective, they were based on direct observation by trained interviewers, and they confirmed the general impression that the great majority of UAW members had attained a lower-middle-class standard of living, a category that included about 60 percent of the American population at that time.[9]

Respondents were asked to rate the International Union and its operations as "excellent," "pretty good," "only fair," "poor," or "not sure." Among production workers—with the undecided omitted—67 percent of ratings were favorable (combining the first two responses) and 33 percent were unfavorable (combining the third and fourth responses). Among skilled workers there was a slight difference, with 63 percent favorable and 37 percent unfavorable, suggesting that the "skilled trades belly-ache" had either been blunted by this time or was confined to a relatively small element in the trades. Breakdowns of attitudes toward the union by age, race, gender, and place of employment showed some significant and perhaps surprising differences. In the age categories, workers under age twenty-five, of whom 75 percent approved of the union, were the most favorable of all age cohorts (so much for the youth rebellion of the late sixties at least among working youth!). By contrast, the ratings among the oldest group (those fifty-five and over) were one of the two least favorable, at 63 percent. By race, blacks' ratings were 72 percent favorable and whites' were 65 percent. This finding suggests recognition by African Americans that the union contributed to a superior workplace and good wages, and it also throws light on the lack of response to the attacks on the union by black radicals. By gender, males' ratings were 66 percent favorable and females' 74 percent, paralleling the breakdown by race. In general, these results suggest that the groups—blacks, women, and the young—that were historically most vulnerable to job insecurity and discrimination placed a high value on the union's accomplishments and benefits. By place of employment, 69 percent of Ford workers had a favorable opinion of the International Union; 67 percent of those at General Motors shared this view, but only 56 percent of those at Chrysler did so. In explaining their favorable ratings, members pointed to the union's success in obtaining material benefits in higher wages and fringe benefits, like pensions and medical insurance, but they also favorably rated the union's fights for workers' rights within the factories.[10]

With respect to attitudes toward their local union, respondents ratings were markedly lower, although still favorable. The overall favorable rating of locals was 54 percent, with Chrysler locals receiving negative (less than 50 percent favorable) ratings, the lowest among the Big Three. When asked to explain the unfavorable ratings, respondents responded, in order of importance, that grievances were handled poorly, they did not like the local officials, members had little voice in the local's actions, skilled workers were not fairly treated, and there were too many strikes over local issues. In general, in the view of the membership the UAW had been successful in negotiating the company-wide contracts that pertained to wages, benefits, protections of seniority and other workers' rights, but less so in satisfactorily resolving day-to-day shop floor grievances and creating a fully participatory climate among all workers in particular plants. One measure of participation, attendance at local meetings, showed that 18 percent of respondents had attended a meeting within the past month, an additional 35 percent within the past six months (for a combined total of 53 percent), 32 percent more than six months ago (for a combined total of 85 percent), and 15 percent had never attended a meeting. Not surprisingly, younger and more recently hired workers were less likely to have attended meetings than older ones.[11]

In judging whether strikes were justified, there was a clear priority given to strikes over local issues, such as production standards, health and safety concerns, and other working conditions matters, with 85 percent saying such strikes were justified. Strikes over national issues, such as compensation, general contract provisions on seniority and the like, were justified in the view of 66 percent of the respondents. In any event, in general, strikes in support of union goals at both levels had strong backing among the membership, with many members clearly most concerned about their daily working situation and its problems.[12]

SOMEWHAT AT ODDS with the survey results, some observers claimed that a dilution of worker attachment to the union had occurred. Reuther contrasted the 1930s, when "most of the guys . . . got their philosophy . . . where you were a part of a kind of a struggle for the right to be," with the present, "where you are operating on a high economic plateau of relative prosperity and some of the early elements of struggle are not there." "In the early periods . . . of this Union," he added, "we were motivated by the fact that we were the victims, like other workers, of exploitation and insecurity and low living standards. We are now getting into a period where the affluence of our technology and our society is going to give all these things to workers, and no questions will be asked." In large part the new attitudes could be traced to the union's success in achieving for its members a "consumer-oriented Americanism" (in a historian's phrase). Auto workers had acquired property and comfortable homes in good neighborhoods, and their jobs and income were more secure than ever. As union members' standard of living approached that of the middle class, their bonds with expressions and instruments of working-class culture weakened. A journalist's article on Flint auto workers was typical of the comments made by many. In contrast to the accepted wisdom on auto workers, those he spoke to were politically more conservative, younger, owned homes and other property, and tended to eschew some of the union's traditional liberal goals. They considered the sit-down strike of 1937, if they thought about it at all, as "simply a moment in history."[13]

The UAW sought to attack the problem of worker detachment and indifference through a new concept and structure of workers' education. The new approach rested on the premise that the development of union leadership and of members committed to the organization required the allegiance and support of both the worker and the worker's family. Reuther's own family, and those of some of his closest associates, including those of his two brothers, testified to the support and loyalty that dedicated families built on shared values could engender. May Reuther, who deserves some of the credit for the union's adoption of a family-centered approach to education, was as committed to the union and its mission as her husband. A pragmatic assessment of pressures and needs within the modern family also figured in the new strategy. As Reuther remarked to the executive board, "We can't get them [to participate] if we compete with their families, so we are going to get them with their families." The 1966 convention mandated that locals set up new member initiation-orientation programs designed to reach not only the workers themselves but also spouses and other family members. The convention debate revealed a concern among local officers that many new members credited the corporations for the gains the union had struggled for years to win. A new approach to education, it was hoped, would correct the error. Turning as he often did to the social-democratic Scandinavian nations for inspiration, Reuther used a new training school that the Swedish metalworkers' union had constructed in a country setting as a model. Although the original plan called for three or four training centers located in different regions—ideally situated within a day's drive for the union's scattered membership—the board eventually authorized an expenditure of $5 million (only a down payment in the event, since costs ultimately soared to more than $20 million) for a family education center at Black Lake in the woods of remote northern Michigan. It was a beautifully situated and constructed educational and vacation center, built for the ages to the highest standards, fully equipped with housing and dining accommodations, and recreational, educational, and conference

The Walter and May Reuther Education Center, Black Lake, Michigan. Walter P.
Reuther Library, Wayne State University

facilities. UAW members and their families would be brought to the center
on a rotating basis to study and discuss the labor movement and its social
and economic practices and goals, and there would be opportunities for
many leisure activities. As a living experience, the center would be predicated on values of community and democracy. Despite some doubts both
in the leadership and the rank and file about the concept and the balloon-
ing expense, Reuther moved ahead with the Black Lake project, devoting
much of his time and attention in the last years of his life to its construction, down to the smallest details. Black Lake was the last project of "the
man with a plan," and he was dedicated to it, even obsessed some thought.[14]

EXCEPT FOR THE DISPUTE with Local 600 in the 1950s and the skilled
trades storm (both now in the past) and the more recent upsurge of black
nationalism (intense but confined to a relatively small contingent in the
factories), Reuther and the Administration caucus had faced little organized
internal opposition. The COLA cap agreed to in 1967 and other complaints,
however, sparked the emergence of an opposition movement. A group organized in Local 600, took the name "Committee for Militant Unionism,"

under the direction of Art Fox, a skilled tradesman with leftist connections. Fox argued for the direct election of International Union officers by the members and cast doubt on the leadership's motives and accomplishments, saying "the men . . . wonder which side the present union leadership is really on, ours or the company." At the 1968 convention the method of electing officers was the subject of a long debate. Critics contended that election by the membership was a more democratic method. Defenders of selection by delegates argued that the system in place was vindicated by results and that nationwide political campaigns would be prohibitively expensive and cumbersome. By a large margin on a voice vote, the convention resolved to continue the election of officers by vote of the convention delegates. The motion for a roll call fell far short of the required support. Reuther had, according to a reporter, "roundly defeated" his few opponents. The "tests of strength," had "proved no tests at all."[15]

A more substantial opposition movement materialized with the formation of the United National caucus (UNC), spurred in large part by disgust over the failure to protect COLA; initially it was heavily represented by skilled workers, with a sprinkling of Trotskyists. Over time it became somewhat multiracial and politically diverse, but it failed to establish cooperative relations with the union's black militants because of the latter's racial separatism. Members of forty-two locals in Detroit, Flint, Windsor, Grand Rapids, New York, Chicago, and Milwaukee attended a conference in Detroit, adopted a resolution calling for direct election of union officers by the rank and file, and put together a slate of candidates to oppose Reuther and other Administration caucus candidates in the 1970 elections.[16]

At the 1970 convention, Art Fox, the United National caucus candidate for president, ran against Reuther, the first presidential election challenge since a weak effort in 1949. The showing was unimpressive, with Fox receiving only 1.6 percent of the roll-call vote (230 to 14,203). Even on his home ground, Fox had little support. The only vote he received from the sixty-two delegates representing Local 600 was his own. A challenge to Emil Mazey for secretary-treasurer by Pete Kelly of Local 160, the chair and one of the founders of UNC, produced a similar result. Important additions of new officers, reflecting a new political balance within the union, included abolishing the position of board member-at-large in favor of creating five new vice presidencies. Ken Bannon, Nelson Jack Edwards (the first African American officer), Doug Fraser (who was being positioned by Reuther for a run as his successor), Olga Madar (the first woman to serve as an officer), and Dennis McDermott, (regional director for Canada), were elected to fill these new positions, joining the existing vice presidents, Leonard Woodcock and Pat Greathouse. Each was opposed by a nominee from the UNC, but the results were as one-sided as in the previous elections for president and secretary-treasurer. Only three locals produced a significant number of votes for UNC candidates: Local 25, at a GM facility in St. Louis; Local 160, the local of skilled and technical employees at the GM Technical Center in Warren, Michigan; and Local 588 at the Ford stamping plant in Chicago Heights, Illinois, a local with a record of strong disagreements with the International leadership. Reuther boastfully made light of the opposition in a letter to Senator Edward M. Kennedy: "I told my colleagues that we ought to encourage the opposition to run a full slate since I think it is good for the soul and UAW democracy, plus the fact I have never felt quite good about being re-elected by acclamation. I believe that one ought to encourage enough opposition to make it interesting but never so much as to make it dangerous." Given the efficient operation of the Administration caucus and the general satisfaction with the regime the results are not surprising.[17]

To some historians, the opposition's potential has appeared more serious than Reuther's comment allowed. There were more challenges, it is true, for the regional directors' positions than was normally the case, with contests in nine regions, but nearly all the incumbents associated with and endorsed by the Administration caucus were easily reelected. None of the challengers campaigned as an anti-Reuther candidate. Only one incumbent backed by the Reuther organization was defeated, in a close vote, but the issues there were unconnected with the UNC and its criticisms. A *New York Times* reporter noted a civil tone to the proceedings, with an acceptance of "open competition without name-calling or rancor." Competition for union posts was more open and accepted than in the past, with little fear of negative consequences if the union's internal unity was subjected to pressure. Although the opposition was certainly not an immediate threat to the Reuther leadership, the fact that there was an organized opposition after so many years without one was of some significance.[18]

REUTHER DID NOT LIVE to see the Black Lake Family Education Center completed. On the night of May 9, 1970, Reuther, his wife May, Oscar Stonorov, the project's architect, and Billy Wolfman, Reuther's nephew and bodyguard, left Detroit for Black Lake in a chartered jet with two experienced pilots for a final inspection. As the plane approached the Pellston, Michigan, airport, beneath an 800-foot ceiling in a light rain, it clipped the top of a stand of trees at the end of the runway and crashed in flames. All those aboard were killed instantly, their bodies burned beyond recognition. A government investigation pointed to a faulty altimeter, which registered the plane's altitude at 1600 feet at the time of the crash when it actually was at 880 feet, as the accident's most likely cause.[19]

Reuther's unexpected death sent a shock wave through the UAW. When the memorial service began a few days later in Detroit, the nation's many auto factories fell silent as assembly lines and presses were shut down. For three minutes workers and machines stood motionless. Tributes poured in from both the "high and mighty" and the lowly. Ordinary auto workers contributed their thoughts, some in simple verses:

"He was loved by many, respected by all
among the world's great leaders, he stands ten feet tall.
I'll never forget him, for each time I falter,
I'll be driven even harder by the memory of Walter."[20]

Reuther was the leading American advocate and practitioner of social unionism, the idea that a union's responsibility to serve its membership takes place in harmony with and in the context of service to the public interest through an active pursuit of political, social, and economic betterment for all. As the *New York Times* wrote in an editorial entitled "Pioneer in Social Creativity," Reuther was "the most zealous union proponent of the concept that labor must go forward with the community and not at the expense of the community." His place as a labor leader, it continued, would be hard to fill (two years earlier the newspaper had reported the results of a poll of forty-eight labor journalists that rated Reuther the greatest living U.S. labor leader), but "the void will be greater still in the realms of idealism and social inventiveness." As a foundation for both the union movement and the nation, Reuther and his colleagues, supported by the UAW rank and file, wove together strands of the American progressive tradition and European social democracy. Although falling short of achieving their visionary goals, the UAW under his leadership won as much perhaps as was possible from a resistant and powerful corporate and political establishment.[21]

WITH REUTHER'S DEATH THE UAW confronted a decision it had not faced in twenty-five years: the selection of a new president. The union's constitution provided that in case of a vacancy occurring during a presidential term a successor would be chosen by majority vote of the members of the International executive board (the union's officers and regional directors). Following the funeral the board met to begin the process. Secretary-treasurer Emil Mazey presided, announcing that he would privately consult with and poll each board member. A second meeting was scheduled for May 22 to elect Reuther's successor.[22]

Mazey's poll of the twenty-five board members showed the two candidates, Leonard Woodcock, vice president and director of the General

Motors and Aerospace departments, and the popular, outgoing Douglas Fraser, vice president and director of the Chrysler Department, in almost a dead heat. The officers' preference was divided: Mazey and vice president Pat Greathouse supported Woodcock, while vice presidents Ken Bannon, Nelson Jack Edwards, Olga Madar, and Dennis McDermott favored Fraser. Among the regional directors the balance shifted in Woodcock's favor, reflecting his support from directors whose regions included one or more of GM's many factories, while Fraser had much support in the Detroit area, reflecting the presence there of Chrysler locals. Woodcock's board supporters represented a larger proportion of the union's membership than did Fraser's. The initial count was thirteen to twelve in favor of Fraser, but one regional director switched his vote to Woodcock, giving him the narrowest of majorities.[23]

Both men, Reuther's closest associates among the union officers, were superbly qualified by experience and outlook to lead the UAW. Both were reared in Detroit in immigrant, working-class families where industrial employment, union membership, and a progressive political orientation were taken for granted and formed the foundation for a life pattern. Fraser, who was born in Glasgow, Scotland, in 1916, where his father was an active union member, was brought to Detroit when six years of age. After graduation from high school, he followed his father into Chrysler's DeSoto plant on Detroit's west side. Outgoing and bright, he was soon elected a shop steward and when chosen as president of Local 227, he was one of the youngest local presidents in the UAW. In the union's internal divisions, he was allied with Dick Leonard, a previous president of that local, but when Leonard and his coalition partners were bested by Reuther in 1947, Fraser, like many others who had been in opposition to the Reutherites, made an easy transition to the other side. He first worked closely with Reuther during the 1950 Chrysler strike, winning the president's respect, trust, and friendship. As a Reuther protégé, he proved his negotiating and political skills. His ascent was steady: Reuther's administrative assistant, regional director, board member at large, Chrysler Department director, and vice president. He forged a strong bond with the rank and file and local officers, and his affection for the union and its members was deep and lasting.[24]

Although the week-long election campaign was conducted with civility by the principals, feelings were intense. Many board members were close to both candidates and recognized the outstanding, though different, leadership qualities of each. Some staff members, including Victor Reuther and Brendan Sexton, became embroiled, leaving scars that never healed. Woodcock, relying on his support in the numerous and large GM locals, threatened to demand a special convention as the final arbiter to reconsider the board's decision if he lost by a narrow margin of one or two votes—a constitutional procedure he was confident would result in his election. Convinced that Woodcock had a one-vote margin on the board, and unwilling to prolong the contest on the eve of negotiations with the Big Three, Fraser withdrew. Woodcock maintained, and events confirmed, that the rivalry in no way soured the two men's relationship. They worked together harmoniously and effectively during Woodcock's two terms in office (1970–77), and Woodcock, his second term completed when he reached the UAW's customary retirement age for officers, nominated Fraser as his successor. At the union's 1977 convention Fraser was named president without a contest.[25]

At the board's May 22, 1970 meeting Woodcock was elected unanimously as president of the United Automobile Workers. Fraser nominated Woodcock and paid tribute to Mazey for his handling of the election, saying that bringing the board through a difficult and unprecedented process without delay and without rancor was one of his greatest contributions to the UAW. In accepting the position, Woodcock seconded the praise bestowed on Mazey and promised to work closely with him and heed his advice, since "when I look back and realize how wrong I was on the question of the Indo-China War and how right he was over a period of time, . . . I will pay careful attention to his opinions." As soon as the vote was taken, Woodcock plunged into a whirlwind of activity in order to show the union's members and the public that his social commitments and energy were a match for Reuther's. On the day he became president, he appeared before the National Ford Council to discuss bargaining issues, held a press conference at Solidarity House, attended the General Motors stockholders' annual meeting—where he voted the UAW's seven shares in favor of a proposal in support of corporate responsibility to the public (it failed to pass)— and left that night by plane for Atlanta to lead a UAW delegation in a "March Against Repression" sponsored by the Southern Christian Leadership Conference.[26]

Ernest Woodcock, Leonard's father, was an English-born and trained skilled machinist who emigrated to the United States to work at his trade. Leonard was born in Providence, Rhode Island, February 15, 1911, where his father was employed by a machinery manufacturing firm. When the family returned to England for a time, Leonard received his schooling there. In the 1920s they relocated to Detroit, where Leonard attended classes at City College of Detroit (now Wayne State University) and Walsh Institute (now College) of Accounting. He found employment as a machine assembler at the Detroit Gear and Machine Division of the Borg-Warner Corporation, a supplier of transmissions and other drive train components, initially, during the depression's worst years, on a schedule of seven days a week, twelve hours a day, at 45 cents an hour. When the American Federation of Labor chartered a federal local at the plant, Woodcock immediately joined, and by 1936, when the UAW held its convention at South Bend, Indiana, Amalgamated Local 42, with four hundred dues-paying members, was the largest Michigan local represented there.[27]

Woodcock volunteered for action in the unionization surge in southeastern Michigan's auto industry, marching on picket lines and rendering service and support wherever needed. Sidelined by an illness, he missed the sit-down strikes but returned to take up educational work for the Wayne County CIO Council and other union organizations. His gaze, however, was fixed on the UAW and the Reuther brothers. His first close association was with Roy Reuther, who, like Woodcock, was an active member of the Socialist Party and vitally involved in union organizing in Flint and Detroit. Walter and Victor Reuther soon became his comrades. Throughout the UAW's internal ideological and power struggles from 1938 to 1947, Woodcock was one of the most loyal, active, and effective members of the Reuther caucus.

In the 1940s Woodcock began union organizing in western Michigan, concentrating on the Fisher Body plant in Grand Rapids, at the time the only major GM facility remaining unorganized. Success there sparked a series of closely contested organizing drives, most under Woodcock's direction, at automotive facilities throughout western and central Michigan. Organized as UAW Region 1D, the area became the foundation of Woodcock's union support. By the end of the war, he was widely acknowledged to be a skillful and courageous organizer. In 1944 Woodcock secured employment in the Muskegon, Michigan, plant of Continental Motors and transferred his union membership to that plant's local as a first step in a campaign for election as regional director. He was a principal organizer of Reuther's 1946 election to the presidency, serving as the "score keeper" for the Reuther caucus, keeping track of and soliciting votes. One close to the scene noted that it was no exaggeration to say that Woodcock "was the organizing genius in that campaign." After serving briefly as one of Reuther's administrative assistants, Woodcock easily won election in 1947 as Region 1D's director and with it a seat on the executive board. For thirty years, until he retired in 1977, he held elected leadership positions in the UAW. When two vice presidencies were created in 1955, Woodcock was elected to one of them and assigned to direct the Agricultural Implements Department, the Aerospace and Aircraft Department, and, most importantly (following in Reuther's footsteps), the General Motors Department. He continued to head the GM and Aerospace departments until the end of Reuther's presidency, always at Reuther's right hand when negotiations with the auto giant were underway.[28]

Woodcock was a leading UAW political activist, more directly involved in daily political operations than Reuther. Moving from the Socialist Party into the Democratic Party's left-of-center wing was a frequently followed path, taken by Woodcock when President Roosevelt decided to render military aid to Great Britain in the crisis of 1940–41. In the election of 1944, when the CIO unions mounted a major campaign for Roosevelt and supportive congressional candidates, Woodcock plunged into party activity in Muskegon and Grand Rapids. Selected as a delegate to the Democratic National Convention in 1952, he supported Governor Adlai E. Stevenson of Illinois, the party's presidential nominee, over significant opposition within the Michigan delegation. By 1960 he favored Senator John F. Kennedy, impressed by the Massachusetts' senator's efforts in behalf of labor during Congress's consideration of the Landrum-Griffin Act and by his straightforward handling of the political questions raised concerning his Roman Catholic faith. Woodcock was a key figure in galvanizing support for Kennedy within the Michigan delegation at the 1960 Democratic convention and in defusing strong opposition there to Kennedy's choice of Senator Lyndon B. Johnson as his vice presidential running mate.

Given Woodcock's record and demonstrated competence, it was not surprising that Kennedy should have considered him for several posts. When Reuther, who had already lost Jack Conway, his leading administrative assistant, to the new Kennedy administration, was informed of a feeler to Woodcock, he exploded, "My God! We can't decapitate the union for Kennedy!" Later Kennedy approached Woodcock about appointment as ambassador to the Republic of China on Taiwan. Reuther exclaimed: "Jack Kennedy's out of his mind, asking you to do that," to which Woodcock calmly replied, "Well, you're not very flattering." Reuther explained that he meant the appointment required someone in sympathy with Chiang Kai-shek's Taiwan regime, a qualification that excluded Woodcock. As Woodcock later noted, had he accepted the Taiwan appointment he would have been ruled out of consideration during the Carter presidency for the post of U.S. representative to the Peoples' Republic of China.[29]

Originally a strong supporter of President Johnson's Vietnam War policy, by 1968, with the country turning against the war and the Democratic Party tearing itself apart over the issue, Woodcock, with many other board members, turned to Senator Robert F. Kennedy. Although he was selected as a Kennedy delegate to the national convention in Chicago, the senator's assassination in June forced him to turn to Senator Eugene McCarthy, the other antiwar candidate. A careless and irresponsible performance by McCarthy before the Michigan delegation disillusioned Woodcock; unable to support either the senator or Vice President Hubert Humphrey, he resigned from the delegation prior to the convention.

As early as 1955, when he was elected vice president and appointed head of the General Motors Department, Woodcock had become Reuther's heir apparent. With only four years' difference in age between them, Wood-cock and Reuther were of the same generation. If Reuther remained in office until the UAW's mandatory retirement age of sixty-five, Woodcock, who could expect to serve only one three-year presidential term, could easily be passed over. As it became clear that Reuther would neither leave for a gov-erment post nor move to the AFL-CIO presidency, what had once seemed a natural progression in Woodcock's career was blocked. Moreover, it appeared that Doug Fraser, five years younger than Woodcock, was being groomed as Reuther's successor, perhaps with the president's support, although Reuther gave no public indication of his preference. Continuing his loyal service, Woodcock became reconciled to the prospect that the UAW presidency was not in the cards for him. Reuther's unexpected death suddenly reopened the possibility.

IMMEDIATELY FOLLOWING HIS ELECTION, Woodcock plunged into the turmoil of major negotiations. Owing mainly to the cap on COLA, the 1967 settlement had sparked serious discontent. As Woodcock later remarked, "we had considerable internal difficulties." For years pressure had been building within the UAW for a challenge to General Motors. The union had not confronted GM as the pattern-setter in any of the triennial rounds of negotiations (1955, 1958, 1961, 1964, and 1967) that occurred while Wood-cock was head of the GM Department. The conventional wisdom held that GM was too powerful, too rich, and too unyielding to confront directly. Bet-ter to go first to Ford or Chrysler with the union's demands, then face GM with an agreement in hand whose monetary terms GM could meet more easily than either of its competitors. Another practical consideration for avoiding GM was that a strike by the corporation's hundreds of thousands of employees would quickly exhaust the union's strike fund, possibly undermining support for the strike and even bankrupting the union. But Ford and Chrysler workers were asking why they should always be the first to risk a strike and their paychecks, and media observers and even repre-sentatives of Ford and Chrysler management taunted the UAW leadership for its timidity in the face of GM's formidable presence. The pressure on Woodcock to make GM the target was greater than would have been the case with Reuther. The new president, in command for the first time, could not afford to look weak or show a lack of confidence, although it is likely that Reuther too would have felt compelled to challenge GM in 1970. GM workers were restless, militant, and ready to strike, in part as a climax to the extraordinary increase in local strikes at the corporation's plants during the 1960s. GM lost 13.3 million worker hours in stoppages of one kind or another in 1969 alone. As Woodcock pointed out, there had been more authorized local strikes at GM plants in recent years than at the other two major companies combined. Absenteeism, another sign of discontent, had risen to 5 percent of the workforce each day, and in some plants to as much as 15 percent on Mondays and Fridays.[30]

In 1970 the UAW's goals were both traditional and innovative. The two items at the top of the agenda were an improved early retirement program and restoration of the uncapped COLA escalator. Closely related was a COLA "catch-up" to restore what had been lost during the three years the cap was in place.

Adopting the slogan "30 and Out," an element centered in UAW locals in Flint and Saginaw claimed support from 1,200 local union officers nation-wide and agitated for a plan to provide retirement pay of $500 a month after thirty years in the plant regardless of age. Workers who entered the plant in their twenties would be eligible for full retirement benefits in their fifties. The UAW leadership embraced the cause. In November 1969, Reuther, although previously reluctant to pledge firm support because he thought it a tactical error to make a hard-and-fast commitment before negotiations opened, told a "30 and Out" rally that he agreed with their goal. "Carry on your missionary program," he said. "Keep fighting. If you generate enough support, it will be recognized as a demand, and I certainly am not unsym-pathetic." During his keynote convention speech he, along with most of the delegates, wore the red, white, and blue "30-and-out" button, and remarked, "You do not have to be a social psychologist to know why it is that there is a deep human urge on the part of a worker who has been buck-ing a line for 30 years . . . to get out of the rat race in the plant." Again, there were multiple benefits from early retirement which broadened the pro-gram's constituency within the union and generated the support necessary to move it forward. An attractive plan would provide not only an earlier escape for the aging from the factory but also open up places for others, cre-ating opportunities for transfers and alleviating unemployment. The same reasoning defended demands for longer vacations with pay, additional paid holidays, and added relief time. All would create a need for additional employees while improving the lives of the current workforce.[31]

Other items on a long list that included something for everyone were basic wage hikes, COLA protection for retirees' pensions, a year-end cash bonus (a form of profit sharing modeled on the bonuses executives received, although lagging far behind in amount), improved SUB for low-seniority workers, payment of family dental care and out-of-hospital physicians' ser-vices, improved working conditions, better health and safety protections, an end to compulsory overtime, limits on subconctracting and establishing a right to strike during the contract term when subcontracting abuses occurred (important to skilled tradesmen, the principal victims of subcontracting), an orientation for new hires to introduce them to the union's achievements, and, finally, the elimination of pollution in and out of the plants. No realistic observer, of course, expected that all these items would be won. The bargaining agenda was in part a political document that acknowledged the wishes of different rank-and-file elements, in part a road map to the future (no matter how distant), and in part a bargaining device that gave negotiators items to trade or drop off the table in the rush to settle. With a strike fund of $120 million, the largest in the union's history and said to be larger than the combined strike funds of all U.S. and Canadian unions, the UAW seemed well-prepared for any contingency. An even more sweeping set of proposals, with greater emphasis on improving working conditions, was put forward by the United National caucus both before and during the strike.[32]

Bargaining with the auto corporations held no terrors for Woodcock. His experience at Reuther's side went back over many years. Woodcock's conduct of negotiations, however, was different. There were fewer emotional outbursts, fewer tactical innovations, and perhaps less creativity, but greater reliance on rational analysis and sober argument. Woodcock was not given to Reutherite oratorical didacticism, a change that was appreciated by the other side. As one industry participant told a reporter, "It's nice not to be lectured to all the time." Woodcock, whose analytical intellect and ability to absorb, master, and deploy large quantities of complex data were unmatched in the UAW's upper reaches, was a no-nonsense, cut-to-the-heart of the issue bargainer. An aide remarked that when bargaining "he makes his points so well, he just demolishes anybody on the other side." A hot temper and a sarcastic wit that sometimes exploded at the expense of colleagues and subordinates were kept under wraps at the negotiating table.[33]

Preliminary negotiations followed a well-worn script and throughout pointed toward a strike. The UAW submitted its proposals in mid-July. Six weeks later, on September 1, two weeks before the expiration of the contracts, the union received the companies' first offers. All, as usual, were virtually identical and, in the union's view, "woefully inadequate and unresponsive to the needs of our members." They included "take-aways"— demands that the union surrender gains it had previously won. "Take-away" items were ordinarily a bargaining device introduced by the companies that disappeared as negotiations went forward, but the fact that the companies had succeeded in "taking away" the uncapped COLA in 1967 made the takeaway threat more ominous, even frightening, than usual. On September 10, GM and Chrysler submitted second offers. (Ford, repeatedy targeted over the years, had been dropped from the list.) Although GM's offer moved some distance toward meeting the UAW's demands, since it

The UAW's Leonard Woodcock and General Motor's Earl Bramblett shake hands to open negotiations, July 15, 1970. Walter P. Reuther Library, Wayne State University

included a 9.8 percent wage increase and a restricted "thirty-and-out" retirement plan, it left COLA under a cap and ignored many other UAW proposals. These offers were also quickly rejected, and, with GM the agreed-upon target, the strike began at midnight on September 14. More than 350,000 GM workers walked out in history's largest and most costly auto strike. Not all of GM's blue-collar employees went on strike. Using a tactic previously employed to maximize pressure for a settlement, 75,000 UAW members remained at work in twenty-eight GM plants, of which sixteen were producing parts for sale to Ford, Chrysler, and American Motors in order that these GM rivals could maintain production and capture sales. The other non-striking plants were manufacturing non-automotive products and therefore not covered by the automotive contract. Negotiation of local agreements at GM's 164 bargaining units had already begun and were to continue throughout the national negotiations, and in some instances beyond the national settlement.[34]

Despite its large strike fund, the UAW was ill-prepared to financially support such a massive walkout. Skyrocketing expenditures at Black Lake had already put the union's finances under pressure. Thanks to cutbacks in car and aerospace production, the union lost over 140,000 members between May 1969 and May 1970, reducing dues income. With a deficit in the general fund of over $900,000 for the month of May 1970, union expenses were being temporarily met from the reserves in the strike fund, obviously poor preparation for massive outlays in strike benefits. Economizing and sharing the burden became the order of the day. In the most severe cost reduction measures taken by the UAW, 125 International representatives and other staff were laid off, along with 10 percent of clerical and maintenance personnel, at union headquarters. When the strike began UAW International officers and staff members took a 50 percent reduction in pay, and those officers who dealt directly with General Motors, including Woodcock and GM Department director Irving Bluestone, went entirely off the payroll. Further, Woodcock pledged that should the strike fund be exhausted, no one working for the International Union would draw a salary until the strike ended.[35]

With the strike costing the UAW nearly $20 million a week, these measures did not suffice. In addition to strike benefits, the fund was committed to reimburse General Motors for the medical and life insurance premiums of the strikers, a sum that eventually totaled $30 million. By mid-October the strike fund was in danger of drying up. Already the union had borrowed nearly $50 million from other organizations, including $25 million from the Teamsters (at a market-rate 8 percent interest, the loan secured by a pledge of the Black Lake property) and lesser amounts, mostly interest free, from other unions. A special convention of delegates from UAW locals called for October 24 authorized an emergency dues increase from two hours to four hours pay per month for all UAW members for the duration of the strike by a near unanimous vote; while this would sustain strike benefits at their current level only until November 30, it would assure payment of the insurance premiums. By demonstrating the membership's determination and ability to prolong the strike, the convention's decision may have affected General Motors' willingness to settle. As financial expenditures from the strike and Black Lake continued to mount, returning the union's general operating fund to a positive balance and repaying the Teamsters' loan was not completed until the spring of 1973.[36]

Within a week of the convention the long-stalled negotiations resumed, with the two sides edging toward a settlement. The major stumbling block was removal of the COLA cap, an issue on which it seemed an irresistible force had collided with an immovable object. Woodcock reiterated the UAW's argument that the escalator was counterinflationary because it raised wages only after rather than before price increases, and he discomfited the GM team by quoting the praise bestowed on the COLA approach by General Motors' former board chairman and father figure, Alfred P. Sloan, Jr., in his memoir *My Years With General Motors*. When negotiations dragged, Woodcock would reach for his copy of Sloan's book,

UAW retirees and officers support the General Motors strike, 1970. *Front row, left to right:* President Leonard Woodcock; Dave Miller, head of the UAW retirees organization; Vice President Olga Madar; General Motors department head Irving Bluestone. Walter P. Reuther Library, Wayne State University

prompting those on the other side of the table to cry, "Oh Leonard, not again!" Eventually, Woodcock became convinced that the chief GM negotiator, vice president Earl Bramblett, did not have the authority to conclude an agreement. He feared that the corporation's chief executive officer, chairman James Roche—not a direct participant in the negotiations—did not appreciate the lasting bitterness that would ensue if the strike were carried on through the holidays and into the new year, which seemed likely unless a settlement was reached soon. In an unprecedented move, Woodcock arranged a personal, private meeting with Roche in which he carefully explained that a prolongation of the strike would inflict serious, perhaps irreparable harm on the corporation, its employees, and the union. As Ford Department director Ken Bannon recalled, GM now realized there would be costly, turbulent "guerrilla warfare" in the plants when production resumed (as someday it must) if the strike went on much longer. Roche, whose career at GM had included stints in labor relations (an unusual occupational track at the corporation whose top officers ordinarily came up through finance or engineering) was a sympathetic listener. Furthermore, although GM's resources were vast and financially it could sustain a longer strike, it was feeling the pinch. With the strike now almost two months old, the corporation was losing $90 million a day in sales, its dealers' inventories were nearly exhausted, the expense of maintaining a white-collar workforce of more than 100,000 that had no production to manage and little to sell was burdensome, and the corporation was soon to report its first third-quarter loss since 1946. Within hours GM put forward a revised offer that formed the basis for a negotiated settlement, and a tentative agreement was reached on November 11.[37]

As in almost all negotiations, last-minute compromises made a settlement possible. The UAW gained the removal of the COLA cap—its major objective— but had to accept a delay of a year in its full implementation. And, after all, as critics pointed out, an uncapped COLA was not a new benefit. A "catch-up" for the missed cost-of-living increases was included in the wage package. An across-the-board "30-and-out" was not achieved, but a compromise version was incorporated in the new contract. The corporation had agreed to "30-and-out" for those who had reached fifty-eight years of age; the union held out for fifty-six as the age of eligibility but had to agree that the full benefit would be phased in. The immediate wage increase undoubtedly did much to insure the agreement's popularity and ratification. Workers in assembly and other basic production jobs received wage increases of 50 cents an hour (a figure both substantive and symbolic that Woodcock had intimated to Roche and the GM negotiators was necessary to get the agreement ratified). Although the figure included the COLA catch-up, it was nevertheless impressive. Other important provisions included an increase in the pensions of those already retired, health care improvements, higher sickness and accident benefits, added vacation time for workers with high seniority, a Christmas week holiday for all with the plants shut down, and improved SUB funding and pay-outs. A few days after the strike ended, GM announced raises for its salaried personnel that matched the increases won by its production workers. It also increased the prices of its cars, placing the blame on the settlement.[38]

Over some opposition, the GM council ratified the agreement and recommended its acceptance by the membership. The ratification was overwhelming, a landslide vote of 367,533 in favor and only 11,546 opposed. With strike funds running out and the holiday season's spending spree rapidly approaching, workers were eager to return to their jobs and their paychecks. Officially, the strike ended on November 20 after sixty-seven days (the second longest GM national strike), and production resumed on the 23rd, although failure to secure local agreements kept some workers out for several more weeks. Agreement was reached with Ford on essentially the same terms, but with the "frosting on the cake" of a dental insurance

UAW bargainers present General Motors with a "Regardless of Age, 30 and Out Now" cake during negotiations, 1970. Walter P. Reuther Library, Wayne State University. © 1970 JunebugClark.com.

plan in which the company agreed to "check-off" the premium from workers' wages, an instance of "the foot in the door" approach that would soon lead to company-paid dental coverage. Chrysler, where negotiations were complicated and delayed by the need to reach agreements for both U.S. and Canadian workers in the same contract, did not settle until January of the new year.[39]

Neither side fully realized its aims. General Motors, which had proclaimed that its goal was to contain labor costs, failed to do so, a failure that disappointed the business press and corporate leaders elsewhere. GM agreed to a wage package that was worth about 40 cents an hour more than its final pre-strike offer but fell about 40 cents or more short of the UAW's pre-strike demands. The corporation had also sought productivity gains through a crackdown on absenteeism and limitations on grievances, but it got nothing except a lower pay rate temporarily in place for presumably less efficient new employees. The big winner in the strike was Leonard Woodcock, who, by taking on GM for a pattern settlement and arguably winning, earned a distinction Reuther had never been able to claim. The challenge to the nation's largest and one of its richest corporations was judged sufficiently successful to solidify Woodcock's position as president and confirm the alle-

giance of the rank and file to the UAW. There were complaints about the
concessions made in delaying implementation of COLA and "30-and-out,"
and the United National caucus termed the settlement a "disaster." Yet the
great majority of auto workers were clearly relieved to see the strike end.
They were convinced that, in the circumstances, as much had been won as
was possible.[40]

THE GENERAL MOTORS SETTLEMENT was emblematic of the relationship
the UAW and the auto manufacturers had forged over the years. It moved
the members forward with improved living standards and working conditions (the latter achieved more as an expanded opportunity for escape from
the factory through earlier retirement with full pension benefits than in better conditions as such). Through the negotiated compromises, it acknowledged that the corporation must be profitable and demonstrated that the
union, its leadership stable despite the disruption of a presidential succession, was securely in place as the workers' representative. The "new middle class" created by the union in the favorable context of the industry's
prosperity was a hybrid, neither fully absorbed into the established middle
class nor part of a conventional working class. The auto workers, whose
weekly wages in stable dollars rose from $56.51 to $249.53 between 1947
and 1975, were the best paid blue-collar workforce in the world, solidly middle class in economic standing, able to support middle-class levels and
habits of consumption. Although Reuther, perhaps somewhat out-of-touch
with modern social and cultural trends, warned against the hazards of unrestrained consumerism—for example, telling the 1970 convention delegates
that "we have been brainwashed by the Madison Avenue hucksters and
they have gotten our values all mixed up"—most workers had embraced
consumerism as a personal and family goal. Supplementary unemployment
benefits and seniority protections gave them something akin to salary recip-
ients' status; in fact, with its mix of compensations and protections, auto
workers' income was more secure than that of many white-collar employees. But life in the auto factories remained separate and distinct. Its goals
were pursued collectively through an organization that, relying on the solidarity of the workforce, periodically confronted an adversary in tests of
strength that, while serious and hard fought, fell short of life-or-death struggles. Everyday work routines were different. Although much of the brutal
physical exertions and strains of preunion days had been drained from the
work process, there still was, as Harvey Swados observed, "one thing that
the worker doesn't do like the middle-class; he works like a worker."[41]

The strike also reflected the compromise that had been reached on control and regulation of the shop floor. The autocratic management control of
preunion days had passed away, but it had not been replaced by workers' con-

trol. Although management had resisted attempts to shift control to favor the workers, they defended and advanced their interests with weapons of their own. The grievance procedure, slow and cumbersome as it sometimes was, was an effective means of defending contractual shop floor rights. The right of local unions to negotiate contracts on shop floor and other matters, given teeth by the authorization to remain on strike beyond the settlement of a national agreement, gave locals a weapon to improve working conditions that they regularly employed. Strikes over unilateral changes in production standards and over threats to health and safety were not rare. Despite the disapproval of the International leadership, occasionally wildcat strikes were a weapon of last resort. Although the degree of workers' control fell well short of the shop floor domination favored by some elements on the left, a power-sharing relationship had been established.[42]

A similar pattern of partial victory, partial defeat, and compromise prevailed in the UAW's pursuit of a social-democratic society. The civil rights revolution of the mid-1960s, to which the UAW made a major contribution, took the nation far along the road to a more genuinely democratic society. Although cut short of fulfillment by the Vietnam War, the drive toward enhanced citizen entitlements in education, health, housing, and urban renewal produced significant results. To the end, Reuther preached to the membership the necessity, even priority, of reaching beyond the paycheck and the workplace to meet the challenges of an imperfect problem-plagued world. Questioning the delegates to the union's 1968 convention, he asked, "What good is a large wage increase if the world goes up in smoke and is reduced to a heap of atomic ash? What good is a guaranteed annual wage if your city and your neighborhood are burning down? What good is a better pension if the streets in your neighborhood are not safe to walk upon? What good is a longer vacation if the air you breathe is poisoned and the water is polluted and the highways are strangled with traffic so you can't move?"[43]

Perhaps the UAW's greatest achievement was internal solidarity, the necessary condition for success in any sphere. The centrifugal forces generated by cultural values of individualism had been contained to the extent necessary to create a sense of common purpose and destiny. Internal ideological and factional differences and rivalries had been ironed out to create a united front. Threats of secession by one or another element had been repulsed. Ethnic and racial tensions, once so evident and divisive, had been muted, even suppressed, in the course of working together for common ends and in the name of brotherhood and solidarity. In simple but heartfelt words a recently retired ordinary workman told Reuther what mattered most to him: "I want to thank you for all the things that the union did for me. You raised my wages, I live in a better house, I was able to give my children a better education. Those things are important, but most important of all, for eighteen years I worked in the Kelsey-Hayes foundry before the union came in, and for eighteen years the . . . workers called me 'dumb Polack.' Now they call me 'brother.' " Struggles in common had forged lasting bonds and brought about greater acceptance of each by all; this was also a vanguard union's victory.[44]

"Things that we had to do, we did"

WITH THE END OF THE 1960S THE UNITED AUTO WORKERS reached a major turning point. Since Leonard Woodcock and Douglas Fraser, the union's presidents in succession from 1970 until 1983, were experienced and effective leaders, fully committed to the UAW's mission and its historic social and political outlook, the loss of president Reuther meant less for the union's future than the seismic shifts in impersonal forces and circumstances that were occurring. A set of problems emerged whose specifics, not fully anticipated and in part beyond the union's control, threatened to curtail its impact and reduce its membership.

The UAW was by no means alone in facing challenges. The entire American labor movement suffered a wrenching contraction in the last quarter of the twentieth century, and the UAW survived as well as any industrial union. Nevertheless, an organization that had proudly claimed a place in the vanguard of progress had to redirect its forces to defend its gains and confront threats to its existence.[1]

THE MAJOR SOURCE OF SWEEPING CHANGE was the globalization of auto manufacturing and marketing. Already American manufacturers of optical products, consumer electronics, and some other goods had seen their markets shrink and their factories idled by their inability to compete with products manufactured abroad by lower cost labor. The same process made its way more slowly in car manufacturing and marketing because time and money were needed to work out engineering and styling problems, amass the capital required for investments in plant and machinery, and establish a distribution and servicing network. Although American manufacturers had long built and sold cars in European and South American countries, they had not historically faced significant competition from foreign manufacturers within the United States. What had been a domestic monopoly shared by three American producers (including their workers) became a market open to any manufacturer from elsewhere who dared to enter it.

Consumers benefited from the more vigorous competition through a wider selection of vehicles and features, better quality, product innovations, and a restraining hand on price increases. The costs were borne by those who relied on the American-owned industry for their livelihoods. By 1970 sales of cars manufactured by foreign firms (then consisting entirely of imports) amounted to approximately 15 percent of the American market, 33 percent in bellwether California. Over the next three decades, the numbers continued to climb. For the UAW this meant that its members, whose high wages made them vulnerable to competition from those willing to perform the same work for a lower price, no longer supplied the labor for a significant and growing portion of the cars Americans bought.

The popularity of foreign-built cars received a massive boost when gasoline shortages followed an embargo on oil shipments after the Arab-Israeli war of 1973. Consumers rushed to purchase small, fuel-efficient cars. Despite the introduction of compact cars by Ford and General Motors (the Pinto and the Vega, both plagued by problems), domestic manufacturers were largely unprepared for the radical shift in demand. To this, the UAW might have said "we told you so"; the union had urged the manufacturers to offer small, economical models since the end of World War II. Domestic car sales collapsed while foreign makers' sales rose to over 25 percent of the market. Plant closings resulting in layoffs of more than 100,000 created the worst unemployment situation in the domestic industry since the Great Depression. The UAW hedged without abandoning its traditional free-trade position, asking Congress to restrict imports temporarily in order to give American manufacturers time to redesign and retool to meet the new market demand. Congress took no action, but the threat moved Toyota, the leading importer, to agree "voluntarily" to keep its imports at existing levels. A second oil crisis at the end of the decade caused another rush to fuel-efficient cars and even more staggering unemployment at domestic firms, sparking consideration of import quotas. Again no action was taken by Congress, but some form of voluntary restraints on Japanese imports remained in place until the agreement was ended in 1985 by President Ronald Reagan. Depressed conditions in the domestic industry stretched into the 1980s, with plant closings, abandoned factories, and layoffs. At one point in 1982 more than one-third of UAW members in the auto industry and more than half in agricultural implement firms were unemployed. Average employment at the Big Three in 1983 was more than one-third below the 1978 average. By the end of the decade, Japanese and German firms, fearful of legislation requiring "domestic content" in cars sold in the United States as advocated by the UAW, and with an infrastructure of dealers and parts warehouses now in place, were ready to manufacture cars on American soil.[2]

The demolition of Dodge Main, 1981. Walter P. Reuther Library, Wayne State University

A parade of foreign-owned firms entered the country, led by Honda and Volkswagen (the latter purchased an unused, partly completed Chrysler facility in western Pennsylvania), followed by Nissan, Toyota, and other Japanese manufacturers. With the exception of Volkswagen, whose workers readily joined the UAW, avoiding union labor was an important consideration in siting these "transplants." Factories were placed in rural and small-town locations in Ohio, Kentucky, and Tennessee, where many residents (including the potential labor force) lacked experience with and enthusiasm for unions. Several years later, when the German firms Daimler-Benz and BMW decided to manufacture in the United States they located their plants in South Carolina and Alabama. Worker recruitment was systematically slanted to discourage formation of a union-represented workforce. Young persons from families without union connections or a union history were sought. The companies utilized employment questionnaires, interviews, and training programs (some supported by public funds) to determine attitudes toward unions among prospective employees and winnowed their hiring offers accordingly. They drew on a Japanese workplace culture that emphasized the common interests of workers and managers and portrayed the company as a caring family, a culture that merged easily with the historic paternalistic industrial ethos in the American South. Perhaps most importantly the companies promised attractive material rewards, thereby reducing incentives to unionize. The wages they offered were only marginally less than those paid in unionized plants and usually were the best factory wages available in the area (they realized savings by offering less in fringe benefits, such as pensions and medical insurance, that were of small interest to a young, relatively healthy workforce still many years from retirement), and they promised secure employment in an environment undisturbed by strikes or wrangling over grievances. It was somewhat ironic that the good wages enjoyed by nonunion transplant employees ("hitchhikers" in union parlance) were put in place to keep the union at bay, another instance in which the actions of unionized workers were of tangible benefit to others.[3]

The UAW leadership had publicly urged Japanese capital investment in the United States and Canada and welcomed the foreign manufacturers, confident that successful organizing would bring their employees into the union. With high expectations, the UAW launched campaigns, concentrating on Honda and Nissan, but the campaigns failed. The effort at Honda was aborted when it became evident it would not succeed; at Nissan, where the company waged a high-pressure antiunion campaign, a representation election conducted by the National Labor Relations Board, the first in a Japanese-owned plant, ended in a UAW defeat by a seventy to thirty margin. The only UAW successes were in plants jointly operated by Japanese and American manufacturers at Fremont, California (General Motors and Toyota), Bloomington, Illinois (Chrysler and Mitsubishi), and Flat Rock, Michigan (Ford and Mazda). In these plants the operating agreement specified recruitment of a UAW-represented workforce, put the operation primarily under Japanese management with Japanese-inspired work organization and routines, and provided that the output would be shared between the participants. In other words, the UAW could draw on its positions of strength in the American companies to establish its presence where those companies were involved in new or reorganized plants but nowhere else. The end result was that approximately one-third of the new vehicles purchased by Americans since the establishment of the transplants were made by non-UAW labor, a serious undermining of the union's position in the industry and a consequent weakening of its bargaining strength. It is impossible to say how changing circumstances (for example, the aging of the workforce) may alter transplant workers' outlook toward the union in the future.[4]

Over the years the UAW's membership was cut in half, from hovering at or just below 1.5 million to approximately 750,000, with most of the decline representing lost auto employment. The loss had a negative impact on dues income, staffing, lobbying activity, and possibly on political impact. In part, union jobs were lost to imports and transplants, in part to the continuing automation of production at domestic manufacturers, and in part to the independent parts producers, a segment of the industry which had never been completely organized and was now more difficult than ever for the union to enter. Jobs and union members were also lost in aerospace as the government reduced military spending and mergers led to layoffs. The departure of the Canadian contingent in the 1980s resulted in a loss of more than 100,000 members. In response to the problem, the UAW, like a number of other unions in similar circumstances, sought to organize workers outside its traditional industrial fields. In fact, the UAW had previously organized workers who made baby cradles, cigarette lighters, fire extinguishers, fishing rods and reels, dental and hospital equipment, and a host of other nonautomotive products. Its appeal to nontraditional workers was three-fold: its record of liberal activism and effectiveness drew some; its political influence in several states, particularly in Michigan, was attractive to workers there; and it offered experienced guidance in devising contract language and conducting negotiations. Although some successes resulted from these organizing efforts, they did not come close to compensating for the loss of autoworker members. One victory was the unionization of white-collar employees of the State of Michigan, whose local, with its 21,000 members—80 percent of whom were women—astonishingly became the largest in the UAW. A similar success was scored in Indiana when several thousand state employees signed up with a unity coalition of the UAW and the American Federation of Teachers. The affiliation of District 65 of the Distributive Workers of America, a 35,000-member organization centered in New York City that represented office workers, retail store employees, university employees, and others, was another addition. Secretarial and technical employees at several colleges, graduate teaching assistants at several universities, and employees of Blue Cross/Blue Shield of Michigan were brought into the UAW fold.[5]

DESPITE ALL THE CHANGES in the auto manufacturing environment, the UAW's relationship with the Big Three American manufacturers still comprised the core of its mission and activity. In this arena there was a decided shift in bargaining objectives toward a greater emphasis on security of income and of jobs. The 1973 contracts were the last to incorporate substantial improvements of the conventional nature. With Chrysler setting the pattern, the UAW won a major wage increase, company-paid dental care, "30 and out" retirement at any age, limited curbs on mandatory overtime, additional paid holidays, and, in a breakthrough on working conditions and worker empowerment, the establishment of joint union-management committees in each plant to investigate and remedy health and safety problems. In 1976 the focus shifted to job creation, sought primarily

Local 3's delegation to the UAW's 1974 convention. Walter P. Reuther Library, Wayne State University

through so-called Paid Personal Holidays (PPH's), which gave each worker ten additional days off each year to be taken when the worker desired but no more often than once a month. The PPH's were designed to stimulate hiring without encouraging "moonlighting" by current employees and to minimize disruption of production. New contract entitlements in income and job protections went well beyond those available to most Americans. These contract provisions created dilemmas for the companies by making it difficult and costly, but not impossible, for them to lay off workers and close plants.[6]

The strike weapon continued to be used, but with some differences. General Motors had the most troubled union relationship of any of the companies. The most widely-noticed strike of the period was that at the Lordstown, Ohio, Vega plant, operated by the General Motors Assembly Division. Although treated in some accounts as a rebellion of youthful, 1960s counterculturalists against factory work—"blue collar blues" was the tag—it was in fact an old-fashioned uprising against a company speedup. The Vega line, producing one hundred cars an hour, was the fastest in the world. The strike occurred after management cut the workforce by several hundred and installed robots to weld sheet-metal panels that were programmed to work at speeds their attending workers could not match. The successful strike resulted in a restoration of the workforce to its previous numbers. In order to avoid a general strike, which could bankrupt the union, but still put pressure on the corporation, the UAW devised its "Operation Apache" tactic, which consisted of short-lived strikes at key component plants. In the future the UAW would rely on selective strikes rather than a general strike at GM.[7]

GM launched a "southern strategy" (the UAW's term) of placing new plants in southern states, presumably in the hope that the union would be unable to follow. Parts plants were established in Louisiana, Alabama, Georgia, and Mississippi, and a large assembly plant in Oklahoma City. The UAW responded by negotiating transfer rights that gave preferential consideration for hiring in the new plants to those who were laid off from northern GM plants (which inserted a core of union loyalists within the workforce); moreover, after a struggle it obtained a pledge of "neutrality" from GM management when an organizing drive and representation election were to take place. Although top GM officials proclaimed their sincerity in agreeing to a neutrality pledge, in some southern plants local managers, in cooperation with community representatives, left few stones unturned in thwarting organization, including, in one instance, circulating among a plant's black employees a phony KKK membership card with the forged signature of a UAW organizer. The key election occurred at the Oklahoma City plant in 1979 with a UAW victory by a substantial margin. Resistance elsewhere was broken through the use of card checks to authorize a union, a device that blunted antiunion tactics. Eventually, all but one small southern plant were unionized.[8]

Flexing muscle through targeted strikes and aggressive organizing campaigns were not the UAW's only response to the new conditions it faced. In some UAW circles there was interest in exploring avenues of cooperation and joint determination of plant operations. Irving Bluestone, vice president and head of the General Motors Department after Reuther's death, was the principal UAW champion of "job enrichment," quality circles," "quality of worklife" (QWL), "employee involvement," or "joint action" as the programs, which differed from plant to plant in concept and application, were variously called. Working conditions, it was hoped, would be transformed, with beneficial results for workers' self-esteem and attitudes toward the job and improvements in productivity and product quality. By involving workers directly in the plant's decision-making processes, and utilizing teams consisting of workers and supervisors, work would become more satisfying and meaningful. The programs were not intended or permitted to displace collective bargaining on wages, benefits, and other material considerations, which would be handled as in the past, nor would they encroach on the contractual grievance procedure. The new jointly determined rules focused on ways of working, the breakdown and distribution of jobs, production planning, and worker feedback on design and manufacturing problems as they became evident on the shop floor. Although not all programs were cut to the same pattern, all the companies agreed to the union's proposals to implement the new approach. The results were, as Bluestone conceded, a "mixed bag." Although there was considerable enthusiasm in some quarters, where a good faith effort was made, elsewhere there was indifference and opposition on one or the other or both sides of the aisle. Even the union's executive board was of two minds, and there were heated debates at high levels. Some plant managers and other supervisory personnel and some rank-and-file workers and local union officers never accepted the program. There were those on both sides who argued that the sacrifices were one-sided, demanding more of them than they were given. This is not to say that the programs had no impact, but the impact varied widely from plant to plant. In an ironic twist, some non-union employers introduced QWL programs (or at least their rhetoric) as a way to reduce their employees' interest in unionizing.[9]

The concept of "jointness" was enormously enlarged and institutionalized when General Motors decided to launch a new manufacturing subsidiary, the Saturn Corporation, to build and market a compact, fuel-efficient vehicle in a new plant in Tennessee. Most of the Saturn workers were recruited among UAW members whose plants were being shut down. The contract between Saturn and the UAW was unlike any the union and General Motors had entered into. Joint determination was extended beyond the shop floor to include many functions in which workers and supervisors shared a common interest, from designing the car to selecting advertising material and dealers, functions that had previously been an exclusive and guarded prerogative of management. A consensus principle of decision-making (either side could veto a proposal under consideration) was implemented throughout the plant with the stated aim of transcending the contentious adversarial relationship of the past with a new co-determination. The contract required the company to provide permanent employment, with layoffs occurring only when conditions were "catastrophic." The union retained its right to strike.[10]

Later attempts by some companies to implement "modern," Japanese-inspired operating agreements were more controversial. So-called "lean production" meant reducing and consolidating job classifications, shifting workers from job to job, and utilizing teams. This was perceived by some workers as a sophisticated stratagem to impose speedups, motivated on the management's side by a desire to curtail union influence and worker protections.[11]

A CRISIS AT CHRYSLER and its resolution constituted the most dramatic and highly publicized event of the era. The company, hard hit by shifts in demand and always financially weak compared to General Motors and Ford, reported losses in 1979 of more than $1 billion as it lurched toward bankruptcy. The UAW violated its pattern-bargaining principle—wages at all of the manufacturers should be the same—by granting $203 million in wage concessions to Chrysler, but they were not sufficient to save the company. A coalition of Chrysler stakeholders that included blue- and white-collar employees, the UAW, company officers, Chrysler's banks, its dealers, and those state and municipal governments where Chrysler facilities were located sought guarantees for new bank loans from the federal government. Prying the loan guarantees out of a reluctant United States Congress was a joint effort, with the UAW supplying much of the lobbying muscle in lining up Democratic senators, who were crucial to the success of the effort. Arguably, obtaining the loan guarantees was the UAW's most important achievement in these years, and its role in saving Chrysler validated the union's decades-long pursuit of political influence. After intense and prolonged consideration, Congress passed a bill providing $1.5 billion in loan guarantees. The conditions included further concessions by Chrysler workers in wages and benefits of nearly $500 million (including a sacrifice of the PPH's, the most promising device for increasing employment), the largest single contribution to Chrysler's survival. Under pressure from the government, further wage concessions were granted in 1981 and 1982 after one proposed contract failed of ratification by a distressed membership. The average Chrysler worker lost an additional $200 a month in wages for three years. The joint effort to save Chrysler did not lead to perfectly harmonious relationships. Many Chrysler workers were incensed at management's failure to honor its "equality of sacrifice" pledge; among other things, they objected to bonuses for executives, the corporation's footing the bill for a dealers' and sales personnel's junket to Monte Carlo, and paying its executives' membership dues at the exclusive Bloomfield Hills Country Club. Such "business as usual" expenditures may have been more symbolic than substantive, but negative symbols can undermine morale as much as substantive losses. With a new lease on life, Chrysler began to recover, thanks to new products (the K-car and later the minivan) that sold well enough to return the company to profitability. As it turned out, with Chrysler on the mend, not all the loan guarantee amounts had to be drawn down. In the end, the federal government, which had received warrants for the purchase of Chrysler stock at a fixed, below-market price as part of the deal, made money. Not until December 1982 did a new contract with Chrysler begin to restore the cuts made during the bankruptcy crisis, and full parity for

Announcing the Chrysler loan guarantee agreement, 1980. *Left to right, front row:* Congressman James Blanchard, Senator Don Riegle, President Jimmy Carter, UAW President Douglas Fraser. *Foreground:* Chrysler Chief Executive Officer Lee Iacocca. Walter P. Reuther Library, Wayne State University

Chrysler workers with their counterparts at Ford and General Motors was not reached until 1985. In the view of many, Doug Fraser, owing to his long association with and great popularity among Chrysler workers, was the only UAW leader who could have persuaded them to make the concessions that saved the company, "the only person that could have done it."[12]

The joint effort, with Chrysler workers doing the heaviest lifting, had saved the jobs. As part of the negotiations, the UAW obtained representation on the Chrysler board of directors with the election of president Fraser to the governing body. Fraser made it clear he would be a voice for Chrysler workers on the board (not surprisingly none of the other board members, including chief executive officer Lee Iacocca, had actually worked in an auto plant); he absented himself from board discussions of collective bargaining strategy while fully participating in and voting on all other matters affecting the workforce. Although charges of a conflict of interest emanated from both management and worker sources, whatever their merit the presence of the UAW's top officer on the company's board, where he had access to company records and decision-making, was of value to the union. Fraser and Owen Bieber, his successor as president of the UAW and as a member of the Chrysler board, were able to delay some plant closings and to argue successfully against Chrysler's sale of its Acustar parts division. But the arrangement did not lead to a more sweeping restructuring of authority within the company. After Fraser retired, Bieber joined the board for a time, but the practice of making such an appointment, which had not been formalized, was then discontinued.[13]

Concession bargaining spread to other automotive and agricultural implement firms. In 1982, with the industry in a severe slump, the UAW agreed, despite threatening internal opposition, to reopen its contracts with Ford and GM. This was pattern bargaining in reverse, although the two auto makers would not receive anything like the full measure of concessions the UAW had made to beleaguered Chrysler. The new contracts froze wages, restricted COLA payments, and eliminated PPH's, saving Ford more than a billion dollars and GM more than three billion dollars in labor costs. In return the union obtained the strongest job security guarantees in its history: a "guaranteed income stream" for long-term employees, company-funded training programs, some restrictions on outsourcing of work, a profit-sharing plan, and a moratorium on plant closings. The provisions restricting outsourcing and plant closings were only partially effective; both issues remained on the table in future negotiations. From its historic pursuit of higher living standards for its members the UAW shifted emphasis to a defense of the gains workers had already won by preserving their jobs and guaranteeing their income. Later contracts gave workers access to a "Jobs Bank"; this allowed them to continue drawing pay and benefits while retraining for other jobs or performing nonautomotive work. The opposition to the 1982 contracts was formidable, especially at GM, where ratification carried by a mere 52 percent.[14]

In 1984 nearly all of the UAW's Canadian members, increasingly responsive to nationalistic sentiment, eager for autonomy, and disgusted with the concession contracts imposed by the United States government on Chrysler and now being extended to other companies by the UAW, withdrew from the UAW. The union lost 120,000 members, a costly and unfortunate loss that detracted from (in fact nearly eliminated) the substance of UAW's claim to be an "international union."[15]

POLITICALLY, THE UAW CONFRONTED a conservative national trend that had set in by 1968. The union maintained its historic tie to the Democratic Party, and its members continued to support Democratic candidates by substantial if somewhat shrinking margins, but it could not reverse that party's gradual decline in popular support and its loss of effectiveness in the federal and many state governments. The union endorsed every Democratic presidential candidate from Senator George McGovern in 1972 (although

Woodcock had favored Senator Edmund Muskie before he dropped out of the race), to Jimmy Carter in 1976 and 1980 (in 1976 the union played a pivotal role in obtaining the nomination for Carter in the Florida and Michigan primaries), to Walter Mondale in 1984 (a UAW favorite for his record of support for labor and socially progressive causes and for his assistance while vice president in obtaining the Chrysler loan guarantees), to Michael Dukakis in 1988, and Bill Clinton in 1992. To publicize peanut farmer Carter's candidacy among the rank and file in 1976, union political activists passed out at factory gates and in union halls 10 million peanuts packaged in 400,000 red, white, and blue bags each bag inscribed with the names of UAW-endorsed candidates. Doug Fraser called it "one of the nuttiest gimmicks ever dreamed up, but one of the best." After Woodcock's retirement from the UAW in 1977, Carter tapped him for important diplomatic missions, first to Vietnam to obtain information on Americans missing in action, and then to the Peoples' Republic of China to establish normal diplomatic relations between the United States and that country. At the conclusion of challenging and finally successful negotiations, Woodcock was appointed American ambassador there. Although the union ultimately supported Carter's reelection in 1980, its relationship with him soured during his presidency, and Doug Fraser personally endorsed Senator Edward M. Kennedy before the Democratic primaries. President Carter, UAW officers and members thought, had failed to support adequately the union's position on an issue of great concern: a comprehensive, universal, national health insurance plan. On the UAW's "number one priority," labor law reform legislation primarily aimed at ending the long delays in reaching NLRB decisions that had proved such a bar to union effectiveness, the House passed a satisfactory bill only to see it fall to a filibuster in the Senate despite the UAW's efforts and Carter's support. Fraser sought to revitalize political action by bringing together representatives of more than one hundred civil rights, women's rights, labor, and other reform-minded organizations in a Progressive Alliance, but in the conservative climate of the times it accomplished little. Exit polls in the 1980 election showed that 60 percent of UAW members voted for Carter and 40 percent for Reagan, the strongest showing for a Republican presidential candidate to that time.[16]

The gradual contraction of the union's political effectiveness was due in part to polarizing issues that divided the UAW's membership against itself and created a division between the leadership and elements of the rank and file. Most notably this was the case with the explosive question of busing school children in order to obtain a racial balance in public schools. Acting on a leadership recommendation, the 1972 UAW convention endorsed court-ordered busing by a large margin, despite some outspoken opposition. The endorsement was not supported by some rank-and-file members, many

President Owen Bieber welcomes Nelson Mandela to the UAW, 1990. Walter P. Reuther Library, Wayne State University

of whom expressed their views in letters to President Woodcock. The most extreme opposition emerged in Pontiac, Michigan, a center of GM car and truck production, where an organization called NAG (National Action Group) set up picket lines in an attempt to close down several Pontiac plants. For a few days violent action threatened, but the union condemned the picketing (most of the pickets were not union members), the plants continued to operate, and conditions eventually returned to normal. The busing controversy, which lost some of its force after the courts refused to order cross-district busing, contributed to a perception among some members that the union's leadership was one-sided in supporting public policies that favored blacks—was even, so some charged, anti-white. A similar, if considerably less explosive, reaction greeted the leadership's support of handgun control legislation, again prompting the claim that the position did not represent the views of ordinary members. On the other hand, the union's active enlistment in the cause of equal rights, both at home and abroad, continued to merit and receive the support of most UAW men and women. The union's long and substantial record of support for equal rights and its effective opposition to South African apartheid was warmly acknowledged by Nelson Mandela, the head of the African National Congress, when he toured the United States in 1990 following his release from a long imprisonment. His first stop in Detroit was at the Ford Rouge plant, where he praised the UAW for its leadership in the fight to impose economic sanctions on apartheid South Africa and announced to the cheering masses of assembled Ford workers, "The man who is speaking is not a stranger here. . . . I am your comrade."[17]

BY AND LARGE THE AUTO WORKFORCE continued to evolve along well-established lines. The percentage of blacks in the ranks gradually increased. By 1975 it was probably around 23 percent in the plants of the Big Three, and 18 percent in the UAW as a whole. The numbers are hard to determine exactly because the UAW kept no records by its members' race and company records were flawed. A significantly greater number of blacks became officers in locals and held offices and staff positions in the International Union, including those of regional director and vice president. By 1980, 17 percent of the "top UAW jobs"—that is, International officers and representatives—were held by African Americans, only a little less than their presence among the union's membership. Such advances toward equity reduced the likelihood of but did not entirely dispel disruptive incidents centered on racial concerns.[18]

The auto industry, including the workforce, remained a predominantly masculine world and culture ("no woman's land" as was sometimes said), and sexual discrimination and harassment were continuing problems, but the percentage of auto workers who were women gradually increased. By the mid-1970s there were about 300,000 women employed in the industry, or 21 percent of the total membership of 1,400,000, the highest proportion since World War II. Seniority rules determined that the most recent hires were most vulnerable to losing their jobs when downturns and layoffs occurred. Slowly women gained a wider range of occupational opportunities both in production work and the skilled trades. By 1977 a handful of women, including a black woman, had completed skilled trades apprenticeships and received journeymen cards. They had joined the factory's

Wildcat strikers walk out of a Chrysler plant, 1973. Walter P. Reuther Library, Wayne State University

elite. More women reached positions of union responsibility. By 1978, of the UAW's more than 1,600 locals, more than 120 had women presidents, and almost 5,000 women were serving as local officers and on local committees. In 1977 Doug Fraser named Carolyn Forrest as one of his administrative assistants, the first woman to hold that position. The number of women delegates to conventions and other gatherings slowly increased.

The UAW asserted women workers' equal rights in the plants, filing and eventually winning a suit against General Motors and Ford for refusing to treat pregnancy like other temporary disabilities. UAW women were active in national women's organizations. They were instrumental in founding the Coalition of Labor Union Women (CLUW) in 1974, and Olga Madar, formerly a UAW vice president, became its first chairperson. The UAW continued to support adoption of an equal rights amendment to the United States Constitution and agreed not to hold union conventions in states, such as Illinois, which had failed to ratify the amendment.[19]

The UAW remained a diverse organization with a national presence. In 1980 its 1,589 locals had contracts with 2,236 corporations and corporate entities. There were UAW units in thirty-seven states, Puerto Rico, and the two Canadian provinces of Ontario and Quebec. The membership was still auto-dominated but gradually spreading into nonautomotive, nonindustrial occupations. In 1980, 54 percent of the members were employed in core auto and truck manufacturing, 11 percent in auto parts manufacturing, 10 percent in agricultural implements, 4 percent in aerospace, and 21 percent in "other," a category containing a remarkable variety of manufacturing and service occupations. The occupational distribution of auto workers had changed some but not dramatically since the early days. In 1974 General Motors employed 415,448 blue-collar workers in the United States. Of this number, 89,091 (21 percent) were in skilled classifications; the increase since earlier days reflected the corporation's investment in automated production machinery that required the installation and maintenance services of skilled workers. The largest classification consisted of "operatives," the semiskilled, at 294,402, or 71 percent. Of their number about 100,000 (34 percent of semiskilled and 24 percent of the blue-collar total) were assembly line workers; most of the rest were engaged in parts manufacture. An additional 31,955 (8 percent) were classified as unskilled laborers and service workers. As always, one should be cautious in basing auto worker generalizations solely on those employed on the assembly lines.[20]

By both U.S. and international standards, American auto workers remained well-paid. A 1980 study under the auspices of the International Metalworkers' Federation of twenty-two industrialized nations with auto manufacturing (assembly or parts) capability—expressed in terms of the amount of time a worker had to spend at the job in order to purchase standard consumer items, including food, household goods, clothing, and durable goods—showed American workers in first place in nearly every category. In some categories U.S. workers were not first, reflecting a peculiar feature of a local economy. A Spanish auto worker, for example, need put in only five minutes of labor in order to purchase one kilo of oranges while an American worker had to be on the job for seven and a half minutes to make

A black worker on the assembly line, 1977. Walter P. Reuther Library, Wayne State University

the same purchase. On the other hand (and far more representative of the overall relationship), the Spanish worker had to work 1,882 hours in order to buy a car of the kind that a workingman might buy, while an American worked only 538 hours to make a similar purchase. Such figures were both cause for congratulation, in showing how relatively well-off American auto workers were, and disturbing, in that the differential in labor costs could well mean a loss of jobs in the future.[21]

Attitudes toward the job and the union had not changed as much as one might expect. An extensive 1979 survey of UAW members provided some evidence of worker malaise, but attitudes toward the job were generally positive. In politics, while there was significant alienation from the political process in general, in political affiliation tradition ruled, with Democrats far outnumbering Republicans and independents. Unions received very high marks, over 80 percent of respondents judging them favorably. But workers were less tolerant of the disagreeable aspects of the job than the depression-bred earlier generations had been. In fact, a division between older and younger, between veterans and recent hires, was discernible on many questions, with the latter less political and less likely to be active in the union. Absenteeism was a serious problem, with the

Building engines at Chrysler's Warren, Michigan, truck plant, July 1982. Walter P. Reuther Library, Wayne State University. Photograph by Earl Dotter.

daily rate running at about 6–8 percent. Not surprisingly (and for more than one reason), the absentee rate declined during periods of layoffs.[22]

DESPITE THE EXTERNAL FORCES pressing against it, the UAW was characterized more by continuity than change in the two decades after Reuther's death. The leadership was steeped in the Reuther tradition. Two future presidents, Owen Bieber and Steve Yokich, were elected regional directors (Region 1D and 1) at the same 1977 convention and elected vice presidents in 1980 by acclamation. Although neither was personally a part of the Reuther entourage, both held similar values and commitments. Bieber became president in 1983, Yokich in 1995. Internal opposition to the leadership was present during this period but relatively feeble. The concession contracts provided soil in which an opposition could grow, and they provoked strong criticism, but a formidable opposition force did not materialize. "Jointness" (as its opponents sometimes termed it), and which, it was charged, involved too close a collaboration with the companies, was also controversial and a focus of opposition. In the late 1980s a New Directions movement emerged, primarily in the plants of General Motors, which attacked joint action programs, concessions, and the related issues of outsourcing and whipsawing, the latter GM's practice of pitting one local against another in a competition for jobs. Although strong in a number of

Workers in the Buick foundry, Flint, Michigan, c. 1980. Walter P. Reuther Library, Wayne State University. Photograph by Earl Dotter.

locals (and certainly the most serious opposition movement since World War II), New Directions had relatively little support in the constitutional conventions, probably never exceeding 10 percent of the delegates. It contested several regional director elections, with little to show in the way of results, and proposed direct election of the president by the membership, which was voted down in conventions by wide margins. Given the scope and complexity of the problems, the disappointments and the losses that were incurred, it may seem remarkable that there was not a stronger opposition movement. Perhaps the failure of an opposition to mount a more serious challenge was a sign that most members were convinced the leadership was doing about as good a job in difficult circumstances as could be done.[23]

IT NATURALLY OCCURS AT THE CONCLUSION of a historical account of an institution's past to ask: does it have a future? Without knowing what will happen to the industry and to labor as a whole, both now deeply embedded in international settings, it is impossible to say. There is no ignoring the fact that the post-Reuther years have brought threats to the union's existence as its membership has declined and its influence has been constrained

UAW officers of the 1970s. *Left to right:* Douglas Fraser, Ken Bannon, Leonard
Woodcock, Irving Bluestone. Walter P. Reuther Library, Wayne State University.

and put under pressure. But perhaps there is a new vanguard role for the
UAW. The union's future may lie in becoming truly international—not only
in name as is now the case. As president Owen Bieber asserted at a meeting in Barcelona, Spain, of the World Auto Congress of the International
Metalworkers' Federation in 1990, "In the long run, there is only one
answer to the international power of corporations, and that is the international power of unions." Creating an effective international structure of
auto labor is a large order, but the UAW may be better equipped by experience and historic aspiration to undertake the task than any other organization. Success will require the creation of new bonds of affiliation and
collaboration reaching across the divisive boundaries of nationality, race,
gender, language, culture, and differing living standards. Much of the
UAW's history has revolved around bringing together in solidarity a fractious and diverse assemblage in order to identify and pursue a common
interest with mutual support and respect. A future as full of challenge as
the UAW's past lies before it.[24]

NOTES

Introduction

1. Leonard Woodcock, UAW, International Executive Board, Minutes, June 5, 1970, p. 290.

Chapter 1

"Hurry up!": William S. Knudsen, production chief at the Ford Motor Company's Highland Park, Michigan, plant, could shout "hurry up!" in fifteen languages. Ford R. Bryan, *Henry's Lieutenants* (Detroit: Wayne State University Press, 1993), 155.

1. The union's formal name has occasionally changed. Currently it is International Union, United Automobile, Aerospace and Agricultural Implement Workers of America, UAW.

2. Irving Bernstein, *Turbulent Years: A History of the American Worker, 1933–1941* (Boston: Houghton Mifflin, 1970), 16–125; Melvyn Dubofsky and Warren Van Tine, *John L. Lewis: A Biography* (New York: Quadrangle/New York Times Book Company, 1977), 181–221. Four recent introductions to the history of American workers and their unions in the twentieth century include Steve Babson, *The Unfinished Struggle: Turning-Points in American Labor, 1877–Present* (Lanham, MD: Rowman and Littlefield, 1999); James R. Green, *The World of the Worker: Labor in Twentieth-Century America* (Urbana: University of Illinois Press, 1998); Nelson Lichtenstein, *State of the Union: A Century of American Labor* (Princeton: Princeton University Press, 2002); and Robert H. Zieger and Gilbert J. Gall, *American Workers, American Unions: The Twentieth Century*, 3d ed. (Baltimore: Johns Hopkins University Press, 2002).

3. Robert H. Zieger, *The CIO, 1935–1955* (Chapel Hill: University of North Carolina Press, 1995), 1–41; Walter Galenson, *The CIO Challenge to the AFL: A History of the American Labor Movement, 1935–1941* (Cambridge, MA: Harvard University Press, 1960), 3–28, 123–34.

4. UAW, *Proceedings of the Second Constitutional Convention* [1936], 69. Titles of convention proceedings vary. All will be cited in this form.

5. Surveys of the auto industry's history include John B. Rae, *The American Automobile* (Chicago: University of Chicago Press, 1965), *The Road and the Car in American Life* (Cambridge, MA: MIT Press, 1971), and *The American Automobile Industry* (Boston: Twayne, 1984); David L. Lewis, *The Public Image of Henry Ford: An American Folk Hero and His Company* (Detroit: Wayne State University Press,

1976), 43; working conditions and working-class communities in pre- and early auto Detroit and Flint, destined to be the two major centers of production, are analyzed in Richard J. Oestreicher, *Solidarity and Fragmentation: Working People and Class Consciousness in Detroit, 1875–1900* (Urbana: University of Illinois Press, 1986); Steve Babson with Ron Alpern, Dave Elsila, and John Revitte, *Working Detroit: The Making of a Union Town* (New York: Adama Books, 1984; reprinted by Wayne State University Press, 1986), 2–50; Kevin Boyle and Victoria Getis, *Muddy Boots and Ragged Aprons: Images of Working-Class Detroit, 1900–1930* (Detroit: Wayne State University Press, 1997); Ronald Edsforth, *Class Conflict and Cultural Consensus: The Making of a Mass Consumer Society in Flint, Michigan* (New Brunswick: Rutgers University Press, 1987), 13–126. See also William H. McPherson, *Labor Relations in the Automobile Industry* (Washington, D.C.: Brookings Institution, 1940); and Joyce Shaw Peterson, *American Automobile Workers, 1900–1935* (Albany: State University of New York Press, 1987). Far more has been written about the Ford Motor Company and its idiosyncratic and immensely wealthy founder, Henry Ford, than any other car company. A scholarly study is Allan Nevins et al., a work in three volumes, respectively entitled: *Ford: The Times, the Man, the Company* (New York: Charles Scribner's Sons, 1954); *Ford: Expansion and Challenge, 1915–1933* (New York: Charles Scribner's Sons, 1957); and *Ford: Decline and Rebirth, 1933–1962* (New York: Charles Scribner's Sons, 1962). A critical assessment of Ford and his company is in Keith Sward, *The Legend of Henry Ford* (New York: Atheneum, 1968). A popular history of General Motors is Ed Cray, *Chrome Colossus: General Motors and Its Times* (New York: McGraw-Hill, 1980). Sinclair Lewis, *Dodsworth* (New York: Grosset and Dunlap, 1929), 20–21. A bibliographical essay on Detroit's industries is in Charles K. Hyde, "'Detroit the Dynamic': The Industrial History of Detroit from Cigars to Cars," *Michigan Historical Review*, XXVII, No. 1 (Spring 2001), 57–73. A similar essay on workers and labor in Detroit is Mike Smith, "'Let's Make Detroit a Union Town': The History of Labor and the Working Class in the Motor City," *Michigan Historical Review*, XXVII, No. 2 (Fall 2001), 157–73.

6. Peterson, *American Automobile Workers*, 30–31, and passim. For other accounts of the development of Ford's production system, see David Hounshell, *From the American System to Mass Production, 1800–1932* (Baltimore: Johns Hopkins University Press, 1984), 217–330; Robert Asher and Ronald Edsforth, "A Half Century of Struggle: Auto Workers Fighting for Justice," in Robert Asher and Ronald Edsforth, eds., *Autowork* (Albany: State University of New York Press, 1995), 6–9; Stephen Meyer III, *The Five Dollar Day: Labor, Management and Social Control in the Ford Motor Company, 1908–1921* (Albany: State University of New York Press, 1981), 1–65; David Gartman, *Auto Slavery: The Labor Process in the American Automobile Industry, 1897–1950* (New Brunswick: Rutgers University Press, 1986), 22–40; Nevins, *Ford: The Times, the Man, the Company*.

7. Gartman, *Auto Slavery*, 39–49; Lindy Biggs, *The Rational Factory: Architecture, Technology and Work in the American Age of Mass Production* (Baltimore: Johns Hopkins University Press, 1996), 89–169; Edsforth, *Class Conflict and Cultural Consensus*, 51–52. A detailed description of the different stages in the manu-

facturing process at the Ford Highland Park factory is in Clarence Hooker, *Life in the Shadows of the Crystal Palace, 1910–1927: Ford Workers in the Model T Era* (Bowling Green, OH: Bowling Green State University Popular Press, 1997), 28–42.

8. Gartman, *Auto Slavery*, 84–86; Meyer, *Five Dollar Day*, 32–33; Hooker, *Life in the Shadows*, 35.

9. See Henry Ford, in collaboration with Samuel Crowther, *My Life and Work* (Garden City, New York: Garden City Publishing, 1922), 80–84; Peterson, *American Automobile Workers*, 30–35; and Nevins, *Ford: The Times, the Man, the Company*, 466–76; Hooker, *Life in the Shadows*, 40; Gartman, *Auto Slavery*, 87–89.

10. Peterson, *American Automobile Workers*, 36–37; Edsforth, *Class Conflict and Cultural Consensus*, 21–22.

11. Robert W. Dunn, *Labor and Automobiles* (New York: International Publishers, 1929), 61.

12. Ford, *My Life*, 110.

13. Meyer, *Five Dollar Day*, 37–41; Charles K. Hyde, "The Dodge Brothers, the Automobile Industry, and Detroit Society in the Early Twentieth Century," *Michigan Historical Review*, XXII, No. 2 (Fall 1996), 68–70; Charles A. Madison, "My Seven Years of Automobile Servitude," *Michigan Quarterly Review*, XIX, No. 4, XX, No. 1 (Fall 1980, Winter 1981), 452–55.

14. Frank Marquart, *An Auto Worker's Journal: The UAW from Crusade to One-Party Union* (University Park: Pennsylvania State University Press, 1975), 30; Philip P. Mason, *Rumrunning and the Roaring Twenties: Prohibition on the Michigan-Ontario Waterway* (Detroit: Wayne State University Press, 1995), 73, 76; Babson et al., *Working Detroit*, 24–25; Stephen Meyer, "Work, Play, and Power; Masculine Culture on the Automotive Shop Floor, 1930–1960," in Roger Horowitz, ed., *Boys and Their Toys: Masculinity, Technology, and Class in America* (New York: Routledge, 2001), 22.

15. Peterson, *American Automobile Workers*, 96; Meyer, *Five Dollar Day*, 83–85; Gartman, *Auto Slavery*, 151–55; Thomas Klug, "Employers' Strategies in the Detroit Labor Market, 1900–1929," in Nelson Lichtenstein and Stephen Meyer, eds., *On the Line: Essays in the History of Auto Work* (Urbana: University of Illinois Press, 1989), 54; Sidney Fine, *The Automobile under the Blue Eagle* (Ann Arbor: University of Michigan Press, 1963), 2; Asher and Edsforth, eds., *Autowork*, 7–8. Autobiographical accounts by young Detroit auto workers in the 1910s and 1920s include Marquart, *Auto Worker's Journal*, 5–39; Clayton W. Fountain, *Union Guy* (New York: Viking Press, 1949), 16–30; and John W. Anderson, "How I Became Part of the Labor Movement," in Alice and Staughton Lynd, eds., *Rank and File: Personal Histories by Working-Class Organizers* (Boston: Beacon Press, 1973), 35–66. In addition, many of the oral history interviews with autoworker union activists conducted by Jack W. Skeels in the late 1950s and early 1960s—available at the Archives of Labor and Urban Affairs, Walter P. Reuther Library, Wayne State University—contain vivid and often detailed recollections of working conditions in the preunion auto factories. Unless noted otherwise, all interviews cited in this study are available at the Archives of Labor and Urban Affairs. See also Kenneth B. West, "'On the Line:' Rank and File Reminiscences of Working Conditions and the

General Motors Sit-Down Strike of 1936–37," *Michigan Historical Review*, XII, No. 1 (Spring 1986), 57–82.

16. Meyer, *Five Dollar Day*, 83–85; Peterson, *American Automobile Workers*, 95–96.

17. Peterson, *American Automobile Workers*, 9–29; the comparable census figures for all auto workers, in and out of Detroit, in 1930 are:

Total:	285, 674
Native-born white:	61% (includes children of immigrants)
Foreign-born white:	30%
Black:	7%

Peterson, *American Automobile Workers*, 15; Alan Clive, *State of War: Michigan in World War II* (Ann Arbor: University of Michigan Press, 1979), 8; Lois Rankin, "Detroit Nationality Groups," *Michigan History Magazine*, XXIII (Spring 1939), 129–205; Douglas Fraser interview with John Barnard, May–June, 1990, p. 2. An illuminating account with text and photographs of Detroit immigrant working-class family, community, and work life is in Boyle and Getis *Muddy Boots and Ragged Aprons;* Detroit's working-class neighborhoods are analyzed in Olivier Zunz, *The Changing Face of Inequality: Urbanization, Industrial Development, and Immigrants in Detroit, 1890–1920* (Chicago: University of Chicago Press, 1982), 332–84; Hooker, *Life in the Shadows*, 46–47, 50.

18. Clive, *State of War*, 9; Larry Lankton, *Cradle to Grave: Life, Work, and Death at the Lake Superior Copper Mines* (New York: Oxford University Press, 1991), 240–41. Chad Berry, *Southern Migrants, Northern Exiles* (Urbana: University of Illinois Press, 2000), is a social history of southern white migration to the North throughout the twentieth century. See also Edsforth, *Class Conflict and Cultural Consensus*, 39–126; Lloyd Jones interview with Jack W. Skeels, March 10, 1960, pp. 8–12; Kenneth T. Jackson, *The Ku Klux Klan in the City, 1915–1930* (New York: Oxford University Press, 1967), 127–43; Marquart, *Auto Worker's Journal*, 38–39.

19. Klug, "Employers' Strategies," 63–66; Marquart, *Auto Worker's Journal*, 31.

20. Louis Adamic, "The Hill-Billies Come to Detroit," *Nation*, February 13, 1934, p. 177; Judith Stepan-Norris and Maurice Zeitlin, *Talking Union* (Urbana: University of Illinois Press, 1996), 48–51.

21. Clive, *State of War*, 8; Peterson, *American Automobile Workers*, 26; Gartman, *Auto Slavery*, 139–40; Bob Campbell, "Starvation Farm Blues," Vocalion 02798, c. 1934, quoted in Paul Oliver, *The Meaning of the Blues* (New York: Collier Books, 1963), 54.

22. Joe Louis with Edna and Art Rust, Jr., *Joe Louis: My Life* (New York: Harcourt Brace Jovanovich, 1978), 11, 12, 14; Boyle and Getis, *Muddy Boots and Ragged Aprons*, 15–17; Stearns quoted in Richard Bak, *Cobb Would Have Caught It* (Detroit: Wayne State University Press, 1991), 96.

23. Peterson, *American Automobile Workers*, 25–27; August Meier and Elliott Rudwick, *Black Detroit and the Rise of the UAW* (New York: Oxford University Press, 1979), 5–22; Richard W. Thomas, *Life for Us Is What We Make It: Building Black Community in Detroit* (Bloomington: Indiana University Press, 1992), 25–26,

29–30, 42–45, 56, 106–7, 273; Shelton Tappes interview with Herbert Hill, #1, Part 1, October 27, 1967, pp. 1–2; Irving Howe and B. J. Widick, *The UAW and Walter Reuther* (New York: Da Capo Press, 1973; originally published in 1949), 209; Hodges E. Mason, "Discussion on the Labor Movement," in Elaine L. Moon, ed, *Untold Tales, Unsung Heroes: An Oral History of Detroit's African American Community, 1918–1967* (Detroit: Wayne State University Press, 1994), 131; Michael Honey, "Black Workers Remember: Industrial Unionism in the Era of Jim Crow," in Gary Fink and Merl E. Reed, eds., *Race, Class, and Community in Southern Labor History* (Tuscaloosa: University of Alabama Press, 1994), 124.

24. Edsforth, *Class Conflict and Cultural Consensus*, 114–21; Zaragosa Vargas, *Proletarians of the North: A History of Mexican Industrial Workers in Detroit and the Midwest, 1917–1933* (Berkeley: University of California Press, 1993), 52, 94–95, 205–7; Juan R. Garcia, *Mexicans in the Midwest, 1900–1932* (Tucson: University of Arizona Press, 1996), 40, 65–69. On the basis of a comparative study of auto workers in plants in four different countries (the United States, Italy, Argentina, and India), William H. Form concluded that the first generation of workers in these plants typically liked their jobs because they represented upward social and economic mobility from their rural origins; the monotony, routine, and physical exertion were certainly no worse than what they had known before. *Blue-Collar Stratification: Autoworkers in Four Countries* (Princeton: Princeton University Press, 1976), 15–19.

25. Clive, *State of War*, 8; Boyle and Getis, *Muddy Boots and Ragged Aprons*, 13–15; Steve Babson, "Living in Two Worlds: The Immigrant Experience in Detroit," *Michigan Quarterly Review*, XXV, No. 2 (Spring 1986), 370.

26. Some aspects of masculine shop floor culture are analyzed in Meyer, *Boys and Their Toys*, 19–30; Howe and Widick, *UAW and Walter Reuther*, 12; Gartman, *Auto Slavery*, 246–57; Madison, "My Seven Years," 447–49; Detroit executive quoted in Clive, *State of War*, 8.

27. William Stevenson interview with Jack W. Skeels, July 6, 1961, p. 6; UAW, *Proceedings of the Twenty-third Constitutional Convention* [1972], 223. For a history of skilled immigrant auto workers see Steve Babson, *Building the Union: Skilled Workers and Anglo-Gaelic Immigrants in the Rise of the UAW* (New Brunswick: Rutgers University Press, 1991).

28. Two other Reuther siblings, an older brother Ted and a younger sister Christine, were not active in the labor movement. Reuther's family origins, youth, and years as a Ford employee are treated in lesser or greater detail in these biographical accounts: John Barnard, *Walter Reuther and the Rise of the Auto Workers* (Boston: Little, Brown, 1983), 1–9; Nelson Lichtenstein, *The Most Dangerous Man in Detroit: Walter Reuther and the Fate of American Labor* (New York: Basic Books, 1995), 1–24; Victor G. Reuther, *The Brothers Reuther and the Story of the UAW: A Memoir* (Boston: Houghton Mifflin, 1976), 1–69; Anthony Carew, *Walter Reuther* (Manchester: Manchester University Press, 1993), 1–13; Frank Cormier and William J. Eaton, *Reuther* (Englewood Cliffs, NJ: Prentice-Hall, 1970), 1–20.

29. Ford, *My Life*, 87, 103, 106, 280; Peterson, *American Automobile Workers*, 45. For a fictionalized version of an encounter in 1926 between the French

intellectual, Louis-Ferdinand Celine, and Ford hiring officials—in which Celine claimed he was told that the car company preferred chimpanzees to humans for its workers—see Louis-Ferdinand Celine, *Journey to the End of the Night* (Boston: Little, Brown, 1934), 222–25; and Patrick McCarthy, *Celine* (New York: Viking Press, 1975), 35.

30. Robert G. Valentine, "The Progressive Relation between Efficiency and Consent," *Bulletin of the Society to Promote Scientific Management*, 1 (October 1915), 26, quoted in Lindy Biggs, "Building for Mass Production: Factory Design and Work Process at the Ford Motor Company," in Asher and Edsforth, eds., *Autowork*, 52–53; anonymous letter to *Ford Worker*, I, No. 3 (1926), 3, quoted in Meyer, *Five Dollar Day*, 40–41; Norman G. Shidle, "Practical Application of Education to Industry," *Automotive Industries*, 42 (June 1920), 1413, quoted in Gartman, *Auto Slavery*, 150; Matthew Josephson, "Detroit: City of Tomorrow," *Outlook*, February 13, 1929, quoted in Melvin G. Holli, ed., *Detroit* (New York: New Viewpoints, 1976), 164; Linda B. Downs, *Diego Rivera: The Detroit Industry Murals* (New York: Detroit Institute of Arts in association with W. W. Norton, 1999), 140–45.

31. *Detroit News*, January 5–7, 1914; *New York Times*, January 6, 1914; Meyer, *Five Dollar Day*, 108–114; Nevins, *Ford: The Times, the Man, the Company*, 512–41; Sward, *Legend*, 50–63; Lewis, *Public Image of Henry Ford*, 69–73; Marquart, *Auto Worker's Journal*, 5–9; Gartman, *Auto Slavery*, 209–11; Madison, "My Seven Years," 453–54.

32. Ford Motor Company press release, January 1914, copy in Ken Bannon Collection, Box 25, f. 1; "Report on Wages, Hours of Work, Standard of Living, August 1929," 4, Socialist Party of America Collection, State and Local File, Michigan, Duke University Library.

33. Tracy Doll interview with Jack W. Skeels, April 21, 1961, pp. 2–4; Gartman, *Auto Slavery*, 214–18; Hyde, "Dodge Brothers," 68–70.

34. George Addes interview with John Herling, October 16, 1978, pp. 2–3; George Addes interview with Jack W. Skeels, June 25, 1960, p. 3; Shelton Tappes interview with Herbert Hill, #1, Part 1, October 27, 1967, p. 6; William Stevenson interview with Jack W. Skeels, July 6, 1961, p. 9; Owen Bieber interview with John Barnard, April 10–11, 1997, p. 10.

35. Peterson, *American Automobile Workers*, 46–47; Edsforth. *Class Conflict and Cultural Consensus*, 83–84.

36. Meyer, *Five Dollar Day*, 123–47. For reproductions of photographs of some Ford and other Detroit workers' homes in this period, see Boyle and Getis, *Muddy Boots and Ragged Aprons*, 30–201.

37. Meyer, *Five Dollar Day*, 15.

38. Meyer, *Five Dollar Day*, 114–47, 173–200; Nevins and Hill, *Ford: Expansion and Challenge*, 324–54, 508–40, 591–93; Stephen Norwood, "Ford's Brass Knuckles: Harry Bennett, the Cult of Muscularity, and Anti-Labor Terror, 1920–1945," *Labor History*, XXXVII, No. 3 (Summer 1996), 365–91.

39. For Ford's "Americanization" program, see Meyer, *Five Dollar Day*, 149–68; Zunz, *Changing Face of Inequality*, 311–18; Hooker, *Life in the Shadows*,

113–17; Babson, "Living in Two Worlds," 379; Gartman, *Auto Slavery*, 224–27; Klug, "Employers' Strategies," 55–57. For similar programs in Flint, see Edsforth, *Class Conflict and Cultural Consensus*, 102–4.

40. Gartman, *Auto Slavery*, 218–28; for the Studebaker Corporation's version of welfare capitalism, see Donald T. Critchlow, *Studebaker: The Life and Death of an American Corporation* (Bloomington: Indiana University Press, 1996), 88–89.

41. Edsforth, *Class Conflict and Cultural Consensus*, 71–126; Sidney Fine, *Sit Down: The General Motors Strike of 1936–1937* (Ann Arbor: University of Michigan Press, 1969), 27.

42. Ruth Milkman, *Gender at Work: The Dynamics of Job Segregation by Sex during World War II* (Urbana: University of Illinois Press, 1987), 17–19; McPherson, *Labor Relations*, 8; Dunn, *Labor and Automobiles*, 72–77; Edsforth, *Class Conflict and Cultural Consensus*, 92, 238, n. 19.

43. Dunn, *Labor and Automobiles*, 76; Edsforth, *Class Conflict and Cultural Consensus*, 91–92; Gartman, *Auto Slavery*, 256–57; Milkman, *Gender at Work*, 30–31; Ruth Milkman, "Rosie the Riveter Revisited: Management's Postwar Purge of Women Automobile Workers," in Lichtenstein and Meyer, eds., *On the Line*, 132–35.

44. Fountain, *Union Guy*, 28; Nancy F. Gabin, *Feminism in the Labor Movement: Women and the United Auto Workers, 1935–1975* (Ithaca: Cornell University Press, 1990), 12, 28, 83, 175; Marquart, *Auto Worker's Journal*, 72.

45. For vivid recollections of health hazards encountered by workers in the Graham Paige foundry and other auto factories in the 1920s, see Charles Denby, *Indignant Heart: A Black Worker's Journal* (Detroit: Wayne State University Press, 1989), 24–36; John W. Anderson interview with Jack W. Skeels, February 17, 1960–May 21, 1960, p. 4; Daniel Nelson, *Managers and Workers: Origins of the New Factory System in the United States, 1880–1920* (Madison: University of Wisconsin Press, 1975), 24; Hooker, *Life in the Shadows*, 117–22.

46. West, "'On the Line,'" 72; UAW, *Proceedings of the Seventeenth Constitutional Convention* [1959], 149.

47. Peterson, *American Automobile Workers*, 60–70.

48. Zieger and Gall, *American Workers, American Unions*, 47; "Average Budgets of 100 Ford Workers, 1929," in Peterson, *American Automobile Workers*, 82; Edsforth, *Class Conflict and Cultural Consensus*, 84–85.

49. David Brody, *Workers in Industrial America: Essays on the Twentieth Century Struggle*, 2d ed. (New York: Oxford University Press, 1993), 63–64; Peterson, *American Automobile Workers*, 71–84; Edsforth, *Class Conflict and Cultural Consensus*, 90–96.

50. Peterson, *American Automobile Workers*, 90.

51. Walter P. Reuther, "Introduction," in Edward Levinson, *Labor on the March*, reprint ed. (New York: University Books, 1956), xiv; Bert Foster interview with Jack W. Skeels, July 26, 1961, pp. 1–2; Tracy Doll interview with Jack W. Skeels, April 21, 1961, p. 5; Walter Quillico interview with Jack W. Skeels, February 24, 1960, p. 2; Stepan-Norris and Zeitlin, *Talking Union*, 54–55; Bob Stinson in Studs Terkel, *Hard Times* (New York: Avon Books, 1971), 156; Gartman, *Auto Slavery*, 188–93; Nelson Lichtenstein, "'The Man in the Middle': A Social History of

Automobile Industry Foremen," in Lichtenstein and Meyer, eds, *On the Line*, 155; Nelson Lichtenstein, "Life at the Rouge: A Cycle of Workers' Control," in Charles Stephenson and Robert Asher, eds., *Life and Labor: Dimensions of American Working-Class History* (Albany: State University of New York Press, 1986), 239.

52. Marquart, *Auto Worker's Journal*, 30–31; Lichtenstein, "Man in the Middle," 157–58.

53. Stanley B. Mathewson, *Restriction of Output among Unorganized Workers* (New York: Viking Press, 1931), 59. Mathewson worked for a time at the Ford Motor Company and interviewed workers there and elsewhere. For instances of output reduction in auto plants, see Mathewson, 36, 37–38, 40, 43–45, 55, 59, 62, 65–67, 70, 78–79, 80, 86–88, 89–90, 114, 118–19, 123–24, 124–25, 125–26. Also Meyer, *Five Dollar Day*, 86–89; Marquart, *Auto Worker's Journal*, 11, 24; Walter Ulrich, "On the Belt," League for Industrial Democracy Leaflet No. 6 (1929), 8, quoted in Peterson, *American Automobile Workers*, 99; William Chalmers, "Labor in the Automobile Industry: A Study of Personnel Policies, Workers' Attitudes, and Attempts at Unionism" (Ph.D. diss., University of Wisconsin, 1932), 160; Gartman, *Auto Slavery*, 155–61; Hodges Mason interview with Herbert Hill, November 28, 1967, p. 5; and Lichtenstein, "Man in the Middle," 161–63.

54. Peterson, *American Automobile Workers*, 99–102, 109–10, 116–18, 120, 124, 126–27, 139–49, 151–52, 156; Edsforth, *Class Conflict and Cultural Consensus*, 114–21.

55. John W. Anderson, "How I Became Part of the Labor Movement," 44; John W. Anderson interview with Jack W. Skeels, February 17–May 21, 1960, pp. 1–2; Fountain, *Union Guy*, 29.

56. Nevins, *Ford: The Times, the Man, the Company*, 376–78, 380–84; Klug, "Employers' Strategies," 42–72; Gartman, *Auto Slavery*, 36–37.

57. Reinhold Niebuhr, *Leaves from the Notebook of a Tamed Cynic* (New York: Meridian Books, 1957), 132, (originally published in 1929).

58. Peterson, *American Automobile Workers*, 102–7; Edsforth, *Class Conflict and Cultural Consensus*, 80–83; Mason, *Rumrunning and the Roaring Twenties*, 74.

59. Nick DiGaetano interview with William A. Sullivan, April 29, May 7, 1959, pp. 23, 44–45.

60. *Detroit News*, June 17–22, 1913; Peterson, *American Automobile Workers*, 108–11; Melvyn Dubofsky, *We Shall Be All: A History of the Industrial Workers of the World* (Chicago: Quadrangle Books, 1969), 287.

61. Peterson, *American Automobile Workers*, 108–18.

62. Marquart, *Auto Worker's Journal*, 33–35; Frank Marquart interview with Herbert Hill, July 24, 1968, p. 3; Peterson, *American Automobile Workers*, 124–29; Roger Keeran, *The Communist Party and the Auto Workers Unions* (Bloomington: Indiana University Press, 1980), 28–59; for Flint, see Edsforth, *Class Conflict and Cultural Consensus*, 121–24.

63. Philip Taft, *The A.F. of L. from the Death of Gompers to the Merger* (New York: Harper and Brothers, 1959), 95–98; Peterson, *American Automobile Workers*, 121–24; Keeran, *Communist Party*, 48–51.

64. Douglas Fraser interview with John Barnard, May–June, 1990, p. 10.

65. Frank Marquart interview with Herbert Hill, July 24, 1968, p. 8; Mr. and Mrs. Joseph Billups interview with Roberta McBride, September 9, 1967, pp. 14–15; Marquart, *Auto Worker's Journal*, 15–20.

66. Peterson, *American Automobile Workers*, 82–83, 147, 150–56; Meyer, *Five Dollar Day*, 199–200; Edsforth, *Class Conflict and Cultural Consensus*, 83–91.

Chapter 2

"The genie is out of the bottle": George Edwards interview with John Herling, May 15, 1978, p. 33.

1. A volume that recaptures the uncertainties, sense of possibility, and achievements of workers during the Great Depression is Irving Bernstein, *Turbulent Years: A History of the American Worker, 1933–1941* (Boston: Houghton Mifflin, 1970). For a recent study of the era, see David M. Kennedy, *Freedom from Fear: The American People in Depression and War* (New York: Oxford University Press, 1999).

2. Joyce Shaw Peterson, *American Automobile Workers, 1900–1933* (Albany: State University of New York Press, 1987), 130–37; Sidney Fine, *The Automobile under the Blue Eagle: Labor, Management, and the Automobile Manufacturing Code* (Ann Arbor: University of Michigan Press, 1963), 17–20; James J. Lorence, *Organizing the Unemployed: Community and Union Activists in the Industrial Heartland* (Albany: State University of New York Press, 1996), 2–8; John B. Rae, *The American Automobile Industry* (Boston: Twayne, 1984), 73–86, 180; Ronald Edsforth, *Class Conflict and Cultural Consensus: The Making of a Mass Consumer Society in Flint, Michigan* (New Brunswick: Rutgers University Press, 1987), 136–42; Allan Nevins and Frank Ernest Hill, *Ford: Expansion and Challenge, 1915–1933* (New York: Charles Scribner's Sons, 1957), 570–96.

3. Nelson Lichtenstein, "Conflict over Workers' Control: The Automobile Industry in World War II," in Michael H. Frisch and Daniel J. Walkowitz, eds., *Working-Class America: Essays on Labor, Community and American Society* (Urbana: University of Illinois Press, 1983), 285–86; Steve Babson, *The Unfinished Struggle: Turning Points in American Labor, 1877–Present* (Lanham, MD: Rowman & Littlefield, 1999), 55. For a similar transition among Chicago industrial workers, see Lizabeth Cohen, *Making a New Deal: Industrial Workers in Chicago, 1919–1939* (Cambridge: Cambridge University Press, 1990), 213–49, 323–68.

4. Frank Lombardo interview with Frank Cormier and William J. Eaton, May 4, 1968, p. 1; Fine, *Automobile under the Blue Eagle*, 14; Art Vega interview with Jack W. Skeels, April 20, 1961, p. 7; Edsforth, *Class Conflict and Cultural Consensus*, 139–40, 160–61; Nick DiGaetano interview with William A. Sullivan, April 29, May 7, 1959, pp. 23–24; Joe Louis with Edna and Art Rust, Jr., *Joe Louis: My Life* (New York: Harcourt Brace and Jovanovich, 1978), 26–27. For discussions of the Great Depression's impact on working conditions, see Peterson, *American Automobile Workers*, 56, 132–33; also Ronald Edsforth and Robert Asher, with the assistance of Raymond Boryczka, "The Speedup: The Focal Point of Workers' Grievances, 1919–1941," in Robert Asher and Ronald Edsforth, eds., *Autowork* (Albany: State University of New York Press, 1995), 73–75, 81–88.

5. Art Vega interview with Jack W. Skeels, April 20, 1961, p. 8; Jess Ferrazza interview with Jack W. Skeels, May 26, 1961, p. 3.

6. Depression era working conditions are vividly recalled in John W. Anderson, "How I Became Part of the Labor Movement," in Alice and Staughton Lynd, *Rank and File: Personal Histories by Working-Class Organizers* (Boston: Beacon Press, 1973), 50–54; Raymond H. Berndt interview with Jack W. Skeels, May 3, 1963, p. 2.

7. Asher and Edsforth, eds., *Autowork,* 77; Leonard Woodcock interview with John Herling, June 21, October 1, 1982, p. 5. See Lew Michener interview with Jack W. Skeels, June 21, 1960, pp. 2–4, for similar conditions in the Ford assembly plant in Richmond, California.

8. Edsforth, *Class Conflict and Cultural Consensus,* 127–36.

9. Lorence, *Organizing the Unemployed,* 15–37; Roger Keeran, *The Communist Party and the Auto Workers Unions* (Bloomington: Indiana University Press, 1980), 69–71.

10. Anne O'Hare McCormick, "Ford Seeks a New Deal for Industry," *New York Times,* May 29, 1932, quoted in Allan Nevins and Frank Ernest Hill, *Ford: Decline and Rebirth, 1933–1962* (New York: Charles Scribner's Sons, 1962), 7; Keeran, *Communist Party,* 71–74; Peterson, *American Automobile Workers,* 130–31, 138–39; Alex Baskin, "The Ford Hunger March—1932," *Labor History,* XIII, No. 3 (Summer 1972), 331–60. A brief study of the march and its aftermath, by an attorney enlisted to defend the marchers, is Maurice Sugar, *The Ford Hunger March* (Berkeley: Meiklejohn Civil Liberties Institute, 1980).

11. *Detroit News,* March 8–13, 1932; Lorence, *Organizing the Unemployed,* 37–44; Steve Babson et al., *Working Detroit: The Making of a Union Town* (New York: Adama Books, 1984), 58–60; Judith Stepan-Norris and Maurice Zeitlin, *Talking Union* (Urbana: University of Illinois Press, 1996), 61.

12. Edsforth, *Class Conflict and Cultural Consensus,* 149; B. J. Widick, *Detroit: City of Race and Class Violence,* rev. ed. (Detroit: Wayne State University Press, 1989), 38, 53–54; Kennedy, *Freedom from Fear,* 98–103; for parallel developments in Chicago, see Cohen, *Making a New Deal,* 251–89.

13. Interview of Josephine Gomon, December 22, 1959, p. 7, Michigan Historical Collections, quoted in Fine, *Automobile under the Blue Eagle,* 27; Edsforth, *Class Conflict and Cultural Consensus,* 157–59.

14. Leonard Woodcock interview with John Herling, June 21, October 1, 1982, pp. 12–14.

15. *New York Times,* January 27–April 1, 1933; *Detroit News,* January 24–March 31, 1933; Peterson, *American Automobile Workers,* 139–40; Ken Morris interview with Jack W. Skeels, June 28, 1963, p. 9; Jess Ferrazza interview with Jack W. Skeels, May 26, 1961, p. 4; John W. Anderson interview with Jack W. Skeels, February 17, 1960–May 21, 1960, pp. 5–19; Anderson, "How I Became Part of the Labor Movement," 54–66; Fine, *Automobile under the Blue Eagle,* 27–29; Keeran, *Communist Party,* 87–95; Lorence, *Organizing the Unemployed,* 47–50. A contemporary account of these strikes by Walter P. Reuther was published as "Auto Workers Strike," in *Student Outlook,* II (March 1933), 15–16.

16. Bernstein, *Turbulent Years*, 34.

17. Leonard Woodcock interview with John Herling, June 21, October 1, 1982, pp. 4–5; Melvyn Dubofsky, *The State and Labor in Modern America* (Chapel Hill: University of North Carolina Press, 1994), 111–28; Fine, *Automobile under the Blue Eagle*, 30–38.

18. Bernstein, *Turbulent Years*, 37–91.

19. The Collins characterization is quoted in Fine, *Automobile under the Blue Eagle*, 39; Raymond H. Berndt interview with Jack W. Skeels, May 3, 1963, p. 10; Alan Strachan interview with John Herling, March 27, 1978, p. 7. The AFL official is quoted in Wyndham Mortimer, *Organize! My Life as a Union Man*, ed. Leo Fenster (Boston: Beacon Press, 1972), 54.

20. Bernstein, *Turbulent Years*, 94–96; Fine, *Automobile under the Blue Eagle*, passim; Edsforth, *Class Conflict and Cultural Consensus*, 161–62; Babson et al., *Working Detroit*, 65.

21. Fine, *Automobile under the Blue Eagle*, 38–40, 142–43.

22. Collins is quoted in ibid., 148. For the federal locals' strikes, see ibid., 85–95, 187–88; Henry Kraus, *Heroes of Unwritten Story: The UAW, 1934–39* (Urbana: University of Illinois Press, 1993), 83ff; Edsforth, *Class Conflict and Cultural Consensus*, 162.

23. William Stevenson interview with Jack W. Skeels, July 6, 1961, p. 4. For a scholarly analysis and interpretation of the role of "Anglo-Gaelic" skilled workers, see Steve Babson, *Building the Union: Skilled Workers and Anglo-Gaelic Immigrants in the Rise of the UAW* (New Brunswick: Rutgers University Press, 1991).

24. *New York Times*, September 23–November 7, 1933; *Detroit News*, September 23–November 7, 1933. For MESA's activities in 1933–34, see Babson, *Building the Union*, 163–68; Fine, *Automobile under the Blue Eagle*, 163–75; Keeran, *Communist Party*, 103–7; Frank Marquart, *An Auto Worker's Journal: The UAW from Crusade to One-Party Union* (University Park: Pennsylvania State University Press, 1975), 56–58; Edsforth, *Class Conflict and Cultural Consensus*, 159–60.

25. Babson, *Building the Union*, 111–12.

26. Fine, *Automobile under the Blue Eagle*, 155–63; Edsforth, *Class Conflict and Cultural Consensus*, 163; David Brody, "Workplace Contractualism: A Historical/Comparative Analysis," in *In Labor's Cause: Main Themes on the History of American Workers* (New York: Oxford University Press, 1993), 232–34.

27. Edsforth, *Class Conflict and Cultural Consensus*, 163–64.

28. Walter P. Reuther interview with Frank Cormier and William J. Eaton, July 1, 1968, p. 9; Fruehauf Trailer Co., NLRB 68 (1935); NLRB *v.* Fruehauf Trailer Co., 301 U.S. 49 (1937).

29. Fine, *Automobile under the Blue Eagle*, 151–54; Jerold S. Auerbach, *Labor and Liberty: The La Follette Committee and the New Deal* (Indianapolis: Bobbs-Merrill, 1966), 99, 109–14; Sidney Fine, *Sit-Down: The General Motors Strike of 1936–1937* (Ann Arbor: University of Michigan Press, 1969), 36–42; Robert H. Zieger, *The CIO: 1935–1955* (Chapel Hill: University of North Carolina Press, 1995), 48; Ed

Cray, *Chrome Colossus: General Motors and Its Times* (New York: McGraw-Hill, 1980), 288–90; Edsforth, *Class Conflict and Cultural Consensus,* 165–66.

30. Steve Jefferys, *Management and Managed: Fifty Years of Crisis at Chrysler* (Cambridge: Cambridge University Press, 1986), 56–66; Steve Jefferys, "'Matters of Mutual Interest': The Unionization Process at Dodge Main, 1933–1939," in Nelson Lichtenstein and Stephen Meyer, eds., *On the Line: Essays in the History of Auto Work* (Urbana: University of Illinois Press, 1989), 100–12; Fine, *Automobile under the Blue Eagle,* 337–41.

31. Leonard Woodcock interview with John Herling, June 21, October 1, 1982, p. 11; Richard Frankensteen interview with Jack W. Skeels, October 10, 1959–December 7, 1961, p. 15; Jefferys, *Management and Managed,* 61–66.

32. *New York Times,* May 24–June 5, 1934; Fine, *Automobile under the Blue Eagle,* 250–83; Keeran, *Communist Party,* 111–14. For recollections by participants and observers, see Philip A. Korth and Margaret R. Beegle, *I Remember Like Today: The Auto-Lite Strike of 1934* (East Lansing: Michigan State University Press, 1988); Raymond Boryczka and Lorin Lee Cary, *No Strength Without Union: An Illustrated History of Ohio Workers, 1803–1980* (Columbus: Ohio Historical Society, 1982), 195–96; Sol Dollinger and Genora Johnson Dollinger, *Not Automatic: Women and the Left in the Forging of the Auto Workers' Union* (New York: Monthly Review Press, 2000), 3–15.

33. *New York Times,* April 23–May 19, 1935; Fine, *Automobile under the Blue Eagle,* 387–403; Fine, *Sit-Down,* 48–49; Kraus, *Heroes of Unwritten Story,* 97–106; Dollinger and Dollinger, *Not Automatic,* 16–26.

34. Tracy Doll interview with Jack W. Skeels, April 21, 1961, p. 18.

35. Alan Clive, *State of War: Michigan in World War II* (Ann Arbor: University of Michigan Press, 1979), 13; Robert H. Zieger, and Gilbert J. Gall, *American Workers, American Unions: The Twentieth Century,* 3d ed. (Baltimore: Johns Hopkins University Press, 2002), 78–79; Fine, *Automobile under the Blue Eagle,* 386, 407.

36. Larry Carlstrom interview with John Barnard, March 7, 1997, pp. 2–17, 21; Nelson Lichtenstein, *The Most Dangerous Man in Detroit: Walter Reuther and the Fate of American Labor* (New York: Basic Books, 1995), 57.

37. Raymond H. Berndt interview with Jack W. Skeels, May 3, 1963, pp. 3–11; Fine, *Automobile under the Blue Eagle,* 407–8; Zieger, *CIO,* 30–31; Alan Raucher, *Paul G. Hoffman: Architect of Foreign Aid* (Lexington: University Press of Kentucky, 1985), 25–27; Ray Boryczka, "Seasons of Discontent: Auto Union Factionalism and the Motor Products Strike of 1935–1936," *Michigan History,* LXI, No. 1 (Spring 1977), 3–32.

38. Bernstein, *Turbulent Years,* 318–51.

39. Dubofsky, *State and Labor,* 128–31; NLRB *v.* Jones and Laughlin Steel Corp., 301 U.S. 1 (1937), and the Supreme Court case involving auto workers, NLRB *v.* Fruehauf Trailer Co., 301 U.S. 49 (1937).

40. Quoted in Zieger, *CIO,* 30.

41. Ibid., 22–24.

42. UAW, *Proceedings of the First Constitutional Convention* [1935], 7–19; Fine, *Automobile under the Blue Eagle,* 416–21.

43. UAW, *Proceedings of the First Constitutional Convention* [1935], 68–74; Fine, *Automobile under the Blue Eagle*, 416–19; Keeran, *Communist Party*, 134–37; Kraus, *Heroes of Unwritten Story*, 107–29; Edward Levinson, *Labor on the March* (New York: Harper and Brothers, 1938), 88–93.

44. UAW, *Proceedings of the Second Constitutional Convention* [1936], 69; a participant's account of the South Bend convention is in Kraus, *Heroes of Unwritten Story*, 161–81; *United Automobile Worker*, May 1936, Special Convention Number; *Detroit News*, April 27–May 3, 1936.

45. There is no biography of Martin. A sketch is in John Barnard, "Homer Martin," in George S. May, ed., *Encyclopedia of American Business History and Biography: The Automobile Industry, 1920–1980* (New York: Facts on File, 1989), 313–16. See also Homer Martin interview with Jack W. Skeels, November 11, 1959; Frank Winn interview with Frank Cormier and William J. Eaton, November 14, 1967, p. 4.

46. Kraus, *Heroes of Unwritten Story*, 127; Dick Coleman interview with Jack W. Skeels, June 23, 1960, p. 6.

47. Larry Carlstrom interview with John Barnard, March 7, 1997, p. 4.

48. George Addes interview with Jack W. Skeels, June 25, 1960, pp. 19–21; UAW, International Executive Board, Minutes, November 30–December 5, 1936, p. 7; an eyewitness account of the Eddystone Hotel confrontation by the labor reporter of the *Detroit News* is in Archie Robinson interview with John Herling, October 11, 1979, pp. 15–17; Walter P. Reuther Collection, Box 10, ff. 21–22.

49. Mortimer, *Organize!*, passim.

50. Harvey Klehr and John E. Haynes, "Communists and the CIO: From the Soviet Archives," *Labor History*, XXXV, No. 3 (Summer 1994), 444; Wyndham Mortimer, "Reflections of a Labor Organizer," prepared from taped interviews by the Oral History Program, University of California, Los Angeles, 1967, pp. 136–37, 150; in a posthumously published autobiography, edited by Leo Fenster and written with assistance from Henry Kraus, Mortimer made no mention of Communist Party membership (Mortimer, *Organize!*); Harvey A. Levenstein, *Communism, Anticommunism, and the CIO* (Westport, CT: Greenwood Press, 1981), 53, n. 68, 69.

51. Keeran, *Communist Party*, 121, 128; Bert Cochran, *Labor and Communism: The Conflict that Shaped American Unions* (Princeton: Princeton University Press, 1977), 108–9.

52. Anderson, Ganley, and McKie are discussed in Keeran, *Communist Party*, passim; there is a Nat Ganley collection and an oral history interview in the Archives of Labor and Urban Affairs; McKie is cast in a hero's role in Philip Bonosky, *Brother Bill McKie: Building the Union at Ford* (New York: International Publishers, 1953).

53. Keeran, *Communist Party*, passim; Frank Winn interview with Frank Cormier and William J. Eaton, November 14, 1967, p. 16.

54. Levenstein, *Communism*, 54; Stepan-Norris and Zeitlin, *Talking Union*, 180.

55. George F. Addes interview with Jack W. Skeels, June 25, 1960.

56. Kraus, *Heroes of Unwritten Story*, 158–59.

57. UAW, *Proceedings of the Second Constitutional Convention* [1936], passim; *Daily Worker*, April 27, May 2, May 4, 1936.

58. There is no biography of Thomas. See John Barnard, "Roland Jay Thomas," in May, ed., *Encyclopedia*, 439–50; *Daily Worker*, April 29, 1936; UAW, *Proceedings of the Second Constitutional Convention* [1936], 190; Richard Frankensteen interview with Jack W. Skeels, October 10, 1959–December 7, 1961, pp. 8–9, 24.

59. A brief account of Reuther's life is in John Barnard, "Walter Philip Reuther," in May, ed., *Encyclopedia*, 357–73. More detailed accounts include Lichtenstein, *Most Dangerous Man*; John Barnard, *Walter Reuther and the Rise of the Auto Workers* (Boston: Little, Brown, 1983); Victor G. Reuther, *The Brothers Reuther and the Story of the UAW: A Memoir* (Boston: Houghton Mifflin, 1976); Frank Cormier and William J. Eaton, *Reuther* (Englewood Cliffs, NJ: Prentice-Hall, 1970); Irving Howe and B. J. Widick, *The UAW and Walter Reuther* (New York: Da Capo Press, 1973), originally published in 1949; Anthony Carew, *Walter Reuther* (Manchester: Manchester University Press, 1993).

60. Lichtenstein, *Most Dangerous Man*, 25–46.

61. Cochran, *Labor and Communism*, 110–11; Lichtenstein, *Most Dangerous Man*, 56–58.

62. The case that Reuther was for a time in the 1930s a dues-paying member of the Communist Party is made in Martin Glaberman, "A Note on Walter Reuther," *Radical America*, November–December 1973, pp. 113–17. For some of the Socialist connections in the early UAW, see Cochran, *Labor and Communism*, 112–13, Kevin Boyle, *The UAW and the Heyday of American Liberalism, 1945–1968* (Ithaca: Cornell University Press, 1995), 41–43, and Lichtenstein, *Most Dangerous Man*, 50–56. George Edwards's UAW activities are related in Mary M. Stolberg, *Bridging the River of Hatred: The Pioneering Efforts of Detroit Police Commissioner George Edwards* (Detroit: Wayne State University Press, 1998), 38–62.

63. Jack Stieber, *Governing the UAW* (New York: John Wiley and Sons, 1962); *United Automobile Worker*, May 1936, Special Convention Number.

64. UAW, *Proceedings of the Second Constitutional Convention* [1936], 124–35, 232; *Detroit News*, April 27–May 3, 1936.

65. UAW, *Proceedings of the Second Constitutional Convention* [1936], 162, 253–55, 265; Keeran, *Communist Party*, 141–47; Archie Robinson interview with William J. Eaton, February 23, 1968, pp. 1–2; Steven Fraser, *Labor Will Rule: Sidney Hillman and the Rise of American Labor* (Ithaca: Cornell University Press, 1993), 347; *New York Times*, May 4, 1936; Howe and Widick, *UAW and Walter Reuther*, 52–53.

66. Walter Galenson, *The CIO Challenge to the AFL* (Cambridge, MA: Harvard University Press, 1960), 130–33. The CIO's influence is emphasized in Ed Hall interview with Jack W. Skeels, October 26, 1959, pp. 11–12; *New York Times*, August 4, 1936.

67. *United Automobile Worker*, August–December 1936.

68. Douglas Fraser interview with John Barnard, May–June 1990, p. 23; Carl Haessler interview with Jack W. Skeels, November 27, 1959–October 24, 1960, p. 261.

Chapter 3

"Storming the stronghold of the open shop": "I am fortunate to have been elected to a position where I can take a leading part in the historical task of storming the stronghold of the open shop." Walter Reuther to Victor and Roy Reuther, April 22–May 2, 1936, following his election to the UAW's International Executive Board. Reprinted in Kevin Boyle, "Building the Vanguard: Walter Reuther and Radical Politics in 1936," *Labor History,* XXX, No. 3 (Summer 1989), 442.

1. Harvey Kitzman interview with Jack W. Skeels, March 4, 1963, p. 14. The UAW position that it had jurisdiction over anything powered by an internal combustion engine was the basis of its claim to organize agricultural implement, aircraft, and aerospace workers. Stinson quoted in Studs Terkel, *Hard Times* (New York: Avon Books, 1971), 161. See also George Edwards interview with John Herling, May 15, 1978, p. 19.

2. Martin Gerber interview with John Herling, March 31, 1980, pp. 1–3; Mundale quoted in Sidney Fine, *Sit-Down: The General Motors Strike of 1936–1937* (Ann Arbor: University of Michigan Press, 1969), 57; see also Ronald Edsforth and Robert Asher, with the assistance of Raymond Boryczka, "The Speedup: The Focal Point of Workers' Grievances, 1919–1941," in Robert Asher and Ronald Edsforth, eds., *Autowork* (Albany: State University of New York Press, 1995), 87–97; George Merrelli interview with Jack W. Skeels, February 21, 1963, pp. 1–2; Bert Foster interview with Jack W. Skeels, July 28, 1961, pp. 13–14; Kenneth B. West, "'On the Line': Rank and File Reminiscences of Working Conditions and the General Motors Sit-Down Strike of 1936–37," *Michigan Historical Review,* XII, No. 1 (Spring 1986), 57–82.

3. *Detroit News,* October 16–17, 1936; Ronald Edsforth, *Class Consciousness and Cultural Conflict: The Making of a Mass Consumer Society in Flint, Michigan* (New Brunswick: Rutgers University Press, 1987), 151; Sloan quoted in Ed Cray, *Chrome Colossus: General Motors and Its Times* (New York: McGraw-Hill, 1980), 283; Nelson Lichtenstein, *The Most Dangerous Man in Detroit: Walter Reuther and the Fate of American Labor* (New York: Basic Books, 1995), 61–63. Murphy's election is covered in Sidney Fine, *Frank Murphy: The New Deal Years* (Chicago: University of Chicago Press, 1979), 229–53.

4. Larry Carlstrom interview with John Barnard, March 7, 1997, pp. 2–17, 21; Robert H. Zieger, *The CIO, 1935–1955* (Chapel Hill: University of North Carolina Press, 1995), 34–39.

5. Walter Galenson, *The CIO Challenge to the AFL* (Cambridge, MA: Harvard University Press, 1960), 133–34.

6. Frank Winn interview with Frank Cormier and William J. Eaton, October 13, 1967, p. 8; West, "'On the Line,' " 57, 59.

7. 306 U.S. 240; Fine, *Sit-Down,* 230, 332; Cray, *Chrome Colossus,* 304.

8. Frances Perkins, *The Roosevelt I Knew* (New York: Viking Press, 1946), 321–22.

9. *United Automobile Worker,* December 10, 1936; Henry Kraus, *Heroes of Unwritten Story: The UAW, 1934–39* (Urbana: University of Illinois Press, 1993), 212–13. Excerpts from a Bendix sit-downer's diary were published in Dave Elsila,

ed., *We Make Our Own History: A Portrait of the UAW* (Detroit: UAW Education and Publication Departments, 1986), 28.

10. *United Automobile Worker,* December 10, 1936; Steve Babson, *Building the Union: Skilled Workers and Anglo-Gaelic Immigrants in the Rise of the UAW* (New Brunswick: Rutgers University Press, 1991), 171–78; Kraus, *Heroes of Unwritten Story,* 215–25.

11. Merlin Bishop interview with Jack W. Skeels, March 29, 1963, pp. 17, 44; list in Henry Kraus Papers, Box 7, folder marked "Kelsey-Hayes Strike"; *United Automobile Worker,* December 1936, January 22, 1937; James J. Lorence, *Organizing the Unemployed: Community and Union Activists in the Industrial Heartland* (Albany: State University of New York Press, 1996), 136; Mary M. Stolberg, *Bridging the River of Hatred: The Pioneering Efforts of Detroit Police Commissioner George Edwards* (Detroit: Wayne State University Press, 1998), 51–53.

12. *Detroit News,* December 16, 1936.

13. A detailed account of events inside the plant is in a typescript entitled "The Kelsey Hayes Sit-In Strike," by Merlin D. Bishop, dictated immediately after the settlement in 1936, copy in Merlin D. Bishop Collection, Box 1, folder marked "Sit-Down Strikes." See also Richard T. Frankensteen interview with Jack W. Skeels, October 10, 1959–December 7, 1961, pp. 34–36; Victor Reuther, *The Brothers Reuther and the Story of the UAW: A Memoir* (Boston: Houghton Mifflin, 1976), 133–42; Lichtenstein, *Most Dangerous Man,* 63–73.

14. Victor Reuther interview with John Herling, December 13, 1977, p. 11; UAW press release, December 28, 1936; George Edwards interview with John Herling, May 15, 1978, pp. 32–33.

15. Walter P. Reuther interview with Frank Cormier and William J. Eaton, July 1, 1968, p. 7; Henry Kraus, *The Many and the Few: A Chronicle of the Dynamic Auto Workers* (Los Angeles: Plantin Press, 1947), 61. See also Kraus, *Heroes of Unwritten Story,* 226–35, and Frank Boles, "Walter Reuther and the Kelsey-Hayes Strike of 1936," *Detroit in Perspective* 4 (Winter, 1980), 74–90. Reuther was president of Local 174 until 1939, when the UAW's constitution was amended to prohibit executive board members from concurrently holding local presidencies. His leadership of this key local is analyzed in Lichtenstein, *Most Dangerous Man,* 91–98.

16. For all aspects of Flint and the sit-down strike there, see Fine, *Sit-Down;* a discussion of General Motors' labor relations, personnel, and welfare capitalist policies prior to the sit-down is on pages 22–53. For Flint's auto workers before the sit-down strike, see Edsforth, *Class Conflict and Cultural Consensus.*

17. In 1936 GM had approximately 170,000 hourly employees who received an average hourly wage of 75.6 cents, compared with an hourly rate of 55.6 cents for production workers in all of American manufacturing. Fine, *Sit-Down,* 22. The GM official is quoted in ibid., 38. *United Automobile Worker,* November 1936; West, "'On the Line,'" 65.

18. Wyndham Mortimer, *Organize! My Life as a Union Man* (Boston: Beacon Press, 1971), 104; Roger Keeran, *The Communist Party and the Auto Workers Unions* (Bloomington: Indiana University Press, 1980), 150–51.

19. Henry Kraus's book *The Many and the Few* is a vivid participants' account of organizing in Flint and of the sit-down strike. A second edition was published under the same title by the University of Illinois Press in 1985. An abbreviated version is chapter 13, "The Great General Motors Sitdown," in Kraus, *Heroes of Unwritten Story*, 236–73. The Kraus Papers in the Archives of Labor and Urban Affairs contain primary materials for this period of the UAW's history; see also Keeran, *Communist Party*, 150–55; Edsforth, *Class Conflict and Cultural Consensus*, 145–46.

20. Kraus, *Many and Few*, 55; Zieger, *CIO*, 50; Lenz quoted in Fine, *Sit-Down*, 119; Fania Reuther interview with John Herling, January 14, 1980, p. 27; Edsforth, *Class Conflict and Cultural Consensus*, 168–70.

21. *United Automobile Worker*, November–December, 1936; Galenson, *CIO Challenge*, 135; Keeran, *Communist Party*, 158.

22. The strike was covered in detail by the *New York Times*, the *Detroit News*, the *Flint Journal* (often with a company slant), and, from the union's point of view, by the *United Automobile Worker*; Lichtenstein, *Most Dangerous Man*, 74–79; Nelson Lichtenstein, "Auto Worker Militancy and the Structure of Factory Life, 1937–1955," *Journal of American History*, LXVII, No. 2 (September 1980), 336–38; Nelson Lichtenstein, "Conflict over Workers' Control: The Automobile Industry in World War II," in Michael H. Frisch and Daniel J. Walkowitz, eds., *Working-Class America: Essays on Labor, Community, and American Society* (Urbana: University of Illinois Press, 1983), 286–87.

23. Fine, *Sit-Down*, 156–77.

24. "Sit Down! Sit Down!" words and music by Maurice Sugar, composed in January 1937, printed in the *United Automobile Worker*, January 22, 1937; Timothy P. Lynch, "'Sit Down! Sit Down!': Songs of the General Motors Sit-Down Strike, 1936–1937," *Michigan Historical Review*, XXII, No. 2 (Fall 1996), 1–47; Christopher H. Johnson, *Maurice Sugar: Law, Labor, and the Left in Detroit, 1912–1950* (Detroit: Wayne State University Press, 1988), 212–13.

25. Fine, *Sit-Down*, 1–13.

26. For a participant's account of the bitter strike at two GM plants in Anderson, Indiana, see Claude E. Hoffman, *Sit-Down in Anderson: UAW Local 663, Anderson, Indiana* (Detroit: Wayne State University Press, 1968), 35–67; Sophie Reuther interview with John Herling, November 29, 1980, pp. 26–53. For Canada, see George Burt interview with Jack W. Skeels, April 23, 1963, pp. 2–6; Kraus, *Many and Few*, 159, 183–84. Stuart Strachan interview with John Herling, June 5, 1980, pp. 8–10, has an account of the Cadillac sit-down; only about 300 of a Cadillac workforce of 4,500 participated.

27. The seizure of Chevy 4, a legendary event in American labor history, has been recounted many times. See Fine, *Sit-Down*, 266–71, and passim. For accounts by participants see Kraus, *Many and Few*, 189–226, and Sol Dollinger and Genora Johnson Dollinger, *Not Automatic: Women and the Left in the Forging of the Auto Workers' Union* (New York: Monthly Review Press, 2000), 138–42.

28. Fine, *Sit-Down*, 266–74.

29. Carl Haessler interview with Jack W. Skeels, November 27, 1959–October

24, 1960, p. 18; Ed Hall interview with Jack W. Skeels, October 26, 1959, pp. 25–26; Wyndham Mortimer interview with Jack W. Skeels, June 20, 1960, p. 47.

30. Fine, *Sit-Down*, 285–92.

31. Copies of the one-page agreement and of the letter from William S. Knudsen to Governor Frank Murphy containing the pledge to conduct no negotiations with other organizations are in Walter P. Reuther Collection, Box 18, folder marked "Agreements, 1937–1947"; the agreement was printed in the *New York Times*, February 12, 1937; Fine, *Sit-Down*, 274–312; Walter P. Reuther, "The United Automobile Workers: Past, Present, Future," *Virginia Law Review*, 50, No. 1 (1964), 86.

32. Doug Reynolds, "We Exploit Tools, Not Men: The Speed-Up and Militance at General Motors, 1930–1941," in Martin H. Blatt and Martha K. Norkunas, eds., *Work, Recreation, and Culture: Essays in American Labor History* (New York: Garland, 1996), 242; William H. McPherson, *Labor Relations in the Automobile Industry* (Washington, D.C.: Brookings Institution, 1940), 9.

33. Russell Leach interview with Jack W. Skeels, July 27, 1961, p. 19; Al Leggatt interview with Jack W. Skeels, December 4, 1959, p. 17; Fine, *Sit-Down*, 228; Edsforth, *Class Conflict and Cultural Consensus*, 176.

34. Dollinger and Dollinger, *Not Automatic*, 130–38; Genora Johnson Dollinger interview with John Herling, September 24, 1979, pp. 36, 67–93; *United Automobile Worker*, February 25, 1937; Lorence, *Organizing the Unemployed*, 136–37; Philip S. Foner, *Women and the American Labor Movement from World War I to the Present* (New York: Free Press, 1980), 304–10. The documentary film *With Babies and Banners* recounts the Women's' Emergency Brigade's activities.

35. Emil Mazey interview with John Herling, May 1, 1978, p. 16; Jess Ferrazza interview with Jack W. Skeels, May 26, 1961, p. 28; Carl Haessler interview with Jack W. Skeels, November 27, 1959–October 24, 1960, pp. 180–81; Lichtenstein, *Most Dangerous Man*, 100–101; Richard T. Frankensteen interview with Frank Cormier and William F. Eaton, June 22, 1968, p. 3.

36. *New York Times*, January 24, 1937.

37. Sidney Fine, *Frank Murphy: The New Deal Years* (Chicago: University of Chicago Press, 1979), 326; *Detroit News*, March 14, 1937; Steve Babson et al., *Working Detroit: The Making of a Union Town* (New York: Adama Books, 1984), 76–83; Steve Babson, *The Unfinished Struggle: Turning Points in American Labor, 1877–Present* (Lanham, MD.: Rowman & Littlefield, 1999), 98–100; Lichtenstein, *Most Dangerous Man*, 80; Edsforth, *Class Conflict and Cultural Consensus*, 180–83.

38. *Detroit News*, March 9–April 7, 1937; Steve Jefferys, *Management and Managed: Fifty Years of Crisis at Chrysler* (Cambridge: Cambridge University Press, 1986), 72.

39. Mimeo sheet, copy in Walter P. Reuther Collection, Box 3, folder marked "Education Department"; R. J. Thomas interview with Jack W. Skeels, March 26, 1963, pp. 10–11; Arthur Hughes interview with Jack W. Skeels, March 12, 1963, p. 9.

40. Arthur Hughes interview with Jack W. Skeels, March 12, 1963, p. 4.

41. *United Automobile Worker*, April 7, 1937; Douglas Fraser interview with John Barnard, May–June, 1990, p. 18; Kraus, *Heroes of Unwritten Story*, 290; Fine, *Frank Murphy*, 326–41; Babson et al., *Working Detroit*, 80–90; Galenson, *CIO Chal-*

lenge, 148–50; Bernstein, *Turbulent Years*, 551–54; Steve Jefferys, "'Matters of Mutual Interest': The Unionization Process at Dodge Main, 1933–1939," in Nelson Lichtenstein and Stephen Meyer, eds., *On the Line: Essays in the History of Auto Work* (Urbana: University of Illinois Press, 1989), 112–16.

42. Clayton Fountain interview with John Herling, December 9, 1977, p. 12; Edward F. Gray interview with John Herling, July 20, 1983, p. 14; Arthur Case interview with Jack W. Skeels, August 4, 1960, pp. 22–23; Nat Ganley interview with Jack W. Skeels, April 16, 1960, p. 63.

43. *United Automobile Worker*, April 7–May 7, 1937; *Detroit News*, March 8–April 9, 1937; Tracy Doll interview with Jack W. Skeels, April 21, 1961, pp. 22–23; Lloyd Jones interview with Jack W. Skeels, March 10, 1960, pp. 55, 56–61; Russell Leach interview with John Herling, December 5, 1978, pp. 5–8; Donald T. Critchlow, *Studebaker: The Life and Death of an American Corporation* (Bloomington: Indiana University Press, 1996), 113–14; John Bodnar, "Power and Memory in Oral History: Workers and Managers at Studebaker," *Journal of American History*, LXXV, No. 4 (March 1989), 1027–28.

44. Emil Mazey interview with John Herling, May 1, 1978, pp. 12–16; Jess Ferrazza interview with Jack W. Skeels, May 26, 1961, p. 6; Ken Morris interview with John Barnard, December 12, 1996, pp. 24–25; McPherson, *Labor Relations*, 29–30.

45. Richard T. Frankensteen interview with Jack W. Skeels, October 10, 1959–December 7, 1961, pp. 71–73; Frank Winn interview with John Herling, April 16, 1978, p. 50; Lloyd Jones interview with Jack W. Skeels, March 10, 1960, p. 51.

46. Information on this local is drawn from Peter Friedlander, *The Emergence of a UAW Local, 1936–1939: A Study in Class and Culture* (Pittsburgh: University of Pittsburgh Press, 1975); see also David Brody, *Workers in Industrial America: Essays on the 20th Century Struggle*, 2d ed., (New York: Oxford University Press, 1993), 143–45. The firm and the UAW local in question are not identified in Friedlander's study, which is based largely on an extended oral history provided by a single participant.

47. Friedlander, *Emergence of a UAW Local*, passim; Douglas Fraser interview with John Barnard, May–June, 1990, pp. 24–25.

48. Larry Carlstrom, "Hits and Misses," p. 2, copy in possession of author, courtesy of Irving Bluestone. For a study of UAW membership and the formation of new locals in this period, see Daniel Nelson, "How the UAW Grew," *Labor History*, XXXV, No. 1 (Winter 1994), 5–24; Zieger, *CIO*, 334–35.

49. One woman activist tells her story in Catherine Gelles interview with Jack W. Skeels, July 7, 1961. Gelles, employed at Bohn Aluminum, was head of the Womens' Auxiliary of Local 174 during Reuther's presidency of that local.

50. Fine, *Sit-Down*, 200–201; Nancy Gabin, *Feminism in the Labor Movement: Women and the United Auto Workers, 1935–1975* (Ithaca: Cornell University Press, 1990), 8–46.

51. Catherine Gelles interview with Jack W. Skeels, July 7, 1961, pp. 1–3; Edward Levinson, *Labor on the March* (New York: Harper and Brothers, 1938), 176; Ruth Milkman, *Gender at Work: The Dynamics of Job Segregation during World War II* (Urbana: University of Illinois Press, 1987), 38–39.

52. Gabin, *Feminism in the Labor Movement*, 19–21; Ruth Meyerowitz, "Organizing the United Automobile Workers: Women Workers at the Ternstedt General Motors Parts Plant," in Ruth Milkman, ed., *Women, Work and Protest: A Century of U.S. Women's Labor History* (Boston: Routledge & Kegan Paul, 1985), 235–58. Stanley Nowak's story is told in Margaret C. Nowak, *Two Who Were There: A Biography of Stanley Nowak* (Detroit: Wayne State University Press, 1989); Judith Stepan-Norris and Maurice Zeitlin, *Talking Union* (Urbana: University of Illinois Press, 1996), 113–14.

53. *New York Times*, April 11, 1937; Warner Pflug, *The UAW in Pictures* (Detroit: Wayne State University Press, 1971), 62; Lichtenstein, *Most Dangerous Man*, 81–87.

54. Untitled narrative by Robert L. (Bob) Kanter [1976], pp. 1–5, copy in John Herling Collection, Box 5; Lichtenstein, *Most Dangerous Man*, 86; Ken Bannon interview with Frank Cormier and William F. Eaton, June 18, 1968, n.p.

55. Pat Greathouse interview with Jack W. Skeels, May 14, 1963, pp. 1–3.

56. Reuther, "United Automobile Workers," 199–205; Pat Greathouse interview with Jack W. Skeels, May 14, 1963, pp. 3–6.

57. *Detroit News*, May 27, 1937.

58. Press release, May 26, 1937, copy in Walter P. Reuther Collection, Box 8, f. 7; *Detroit News*, May 27, 1937; Frankensteen's account is in Richard T. Frankensteen interview with Jack W. Skeels, October 10, 1959–December 7, 1961, pp. 59–65; Catherine Gelles interview with Jack W. Skeels, July 7, 1961, pp. 7–8; *New York Times*, May 27–July 3, 1937; David L. Lewis, *The Public Image of Henry Ford: An American Folk Hero and His Company* (Detroit: Wayne State University Press, 1976), 250–51.

59. Michael K. Honey, *Southern Labor and Black Civil Rights* (Urbana: University of Illinois Press, 1993), 87–90; Allan Nevins and Frank Ernest Hill, *Ford: Decline and Rebirth, 1933–1962* (New York: Charles Scribner's Sons, 1962), 142–46.

60. Kraus, *Heroes of Unwritten Story*, 320–21; UAW, *Proceedings of the Third Constitutional Convention* [1937], 66; *Report to the Second Annual Convention. . . . August 1937*, p. 23; *Report of President R. J. Thomas . . . March 27, 1939*, pp. 7–8; McPherson, *Labor Relations*, 18; Ray Boryczka, "Militancy and Factionalism in the United Auto Workers Union, 1937–1941," *Maryland Historian*, VIII, No. 2 (Fall 1977), 14–15.

61. Frank Winn interview with John Herling, April 16, 1978, p. 63; George Edwards interview with John Herling, May 15, 1978, pp. 49–50; Stepan-Norris and Zeitlin, *Talking Union*, 115; Stuart Strachan interview with John Herling, June 5, 1980, p. 6.

Chapter 4

"An insecure person who happened on historic times": George Edwards interview with John Herling, May 15, 1978, p. 54. Edwards's statement on Homer Martin continued: "but [he] didn't have the capability to rise to an historic occasion."

1. John W. Anderson interview with Jack W. Skeels, February 17–May 21, 1960, p. 222; Bert Cochran, *Labor and Communism: The Conflict that Shaped American Unions* (Princeton: Princeton University Press, 1977), 127–28.

2. Walter Galenson, *The CIO Challenge to the AFL: A History of the American Labor Movement, 1935–1941* (Cambridge, MA: Harvard University Press, 1960), 157; William H. McPherson, *Labor Relations in the Automobile Industry* (Washington, D.C.: Brookings Institution, 1940), 9, 25–26; James J. Lorence, *Organizing the Unemployed: Community and Union Activists in the Industrial Heartland* (Albany: State University of New York Press, 1996), 159–294; Mary M. Stolberg, *Bridging the River of Hatred: The Pioneering Efforts of Detroit Police Commissioner George Edwards* (Detroit: Wayne State University Press, 1998), 60–62.

3. David M. Kennedy, *Freedom from Fear: The American People in Depression and War, 1929–1945* (New York: Oxford University Press, 1999), 346–51; William E. Leuchtenberg, *Franklin Roosevelt and the New Deal, 1932–1940* (New York: Harper and Row, 1963), 231–84; Alan Brinkley, *The End of Reform: New Deal Liberalism in Recession and War* (New York: Knopf, 1995), 15–30. For the Dies committee's investigation of communism and communists in the union, see United States Congress, House, Special Committee on Un-American Activities (1938–1944), Volume One. *Hearings*, August 12–23, 1938; Volume Two. *Hearings*, September 15–October 22, 1938; Volume Three. *Hearings*, October 24–November 21, 1938.

4. Frank Winn interview with Frank Cormier and William J. Eaton, November 14, 1967, p. 5; Homer Martin interview with Jack W. Skeels, November 11, 1959, p. 24; *New York Times*, April 19–20, May 2, August 3, September 9, 26, 30, 1937; Victor Reuther, *The Brothers Reuther and the Story of the UAW: A Memoir* (Boston: Houghton Mifflin, 1976), 184–85.

5. Lovestone quoted in Frank Marquart, *An Auto Worker's Journal: The UAW from Crusade to One-Party Union* (University Park: Pennsylvania State University Press, 1975), 79; Jay Lovestone interview with William J. Eaton, February 23, 1968, pp. 1–2; Cochran, *Labor and Communism*, 131–34.

6. Galenson, *CIO Challenge*, 151; Anthony Carew, *Walter Reuther* (Manchester: University of Manchester Press, 1993), 21; Ted Morgan, *A Covert Life: Jay Lovestone, Communist, Anti-Communist, and Spymaster* (New York: Random House, 1999), 125–26.

7. William Genske interview with Jack W. Skeels, July 23, 1960, p. 9; Bert Foster interview with Jack W. Skeels, July 26, 1961, p. 13; Ronald Edsforth, *Class Conflict and Cultural Consensus: The Making of a Mass Consumer Society in Flint, Michigan* (New Brunswick: Rutgers University Press, 1987), 176–77; Douglas A. Fraser interview with John Barnard, May–June, 1990, p. 20; Tracy Doll interview with Jack W. Skeels, April 21, 1961, p. 27; Roger Keeran, *The Communist Party and the Auto Workers Unions* (Bloomington: Indiana University Press, 1980), 189; McPherson, *Labor Relations*, 61–64.

8. Richard Edwards, *Contested Terrain: The Transformation of the Workplace in the Twentieth Century* (New York: Basic Books, 1979); Russell Leach interview

with John Herling, December 5, 1978, p. 8; Edsforth, *Class Conflict and Cultural Consensus*, 176–77; Nelson Lichtenstein, *The Most Dangerous Man in Detroit: Walter Reuther and the Fate of American Labor* (New York: Basic Books, 1995), 107–10; Nelson Lichtenstein, "Auto Worker Militancy and the Structure of Factory Life, 1937–1955," *Journal of American History*, LXVII, No. 2 (September 1980), 338–40; David Gartman, *Auto Slavery: The Labor Process in the American Automobile Industry, 1897–1950* (New Brunswick: Rutgers University Press, 1986), 263–64.

9. Copies of the early agreements with General Motors are in the Walter P. Reuther Collection, Box 18, ff. 1, 2. See also Sidney Fine, *Sit-Down: The General Motors Strike of 1936–1937* (Ann Arbor: University of Michigan Press, 1969), 323–27; Henry Kraus, *Heroes of Unwritten Story: The UAW, 1934–39* (Urbana: University of Illinois Press, 1993), 297–98; Stephen Amberg, *The Union Inspiration in American Politics: The Autoworkers and the Making of a Liberal Industrial Order* (Philadelphia: Temple University Press, 1994), 93–94; Ruth Milkman, *Gender at Work: The Dynamics of Job Segregation by Sex during World War II* (Urbana: University of Illinois Press, 1987), 40; Doug Reynolds, "We Exploit Tools, Not Men': The Speed-Up and Militance at General Motors, 1930–1941," in Martin H. Blatt and Martha K. Norkumas, eds., *Work, Recreation, and Culture: Essays in American Labor History* (New York: Garland, 1966), 232–42; Irving Bernstein, *Turbulent Years: A History of American Workers, 1933–1941* (Boston: Houghton Mifflin, 1970), 550; McPherson, *Labor Relations*, 49–52.

10. *UAW Solidarity*, March 1969; Lichtenstein, "Auto Worker Militancy," 340; Nelson Lichtenstein, *Labor's War at Home: The CIO in World War II* (Cambridge: Cambridge University Press, 1982), 14–16; Stephen Tolliday and Jonathan Zeitlin, "Shop-Floor Bargaining, Contract Unionism and Job Control: An Anglo-American Comparison," in Steven Tolliday and Jonathan Zeitlin, eds., *Between Fordism and Flexibility: The Automobile Industry and Its Workers* (Oxford: Berg, 1992), 107–8.

11. Nelson Lichtenstein, "Conflict over Workers' Control: The Automobile Industry in World War II," in Michael H. Frisch and Daniel J. Walkowitz, eds., *Working-Class America: Essays on Labor, Community, and American Society* (Urbana: University of Illinois Press, 1983), 287–88; Lichtenstein, *Most Dangerous Man*, 107–111, DuBrul is quoted on p. 110.

12. Lichtenstein, *Most Dangerous Man*, 111.

13. David Brody, "Workplace Contractualism: A Historical/Comparative Analysis," in *In Labor's Cause: Main Themes on the History of the American Worker* (New York: Oxford University Press, 1993), 221–50; Kevin Boyle, *The UAW and the Heyday of American Liberalism* (Ithaca: Cornell University Press, 1995), 13; Robert Asher and Ronald Edsforth, "A Half Century of Struggle: Auto Workers Fighting for Justice," in Robert Asher and Ronald Edsforth, eds., *Autowork* (Albany: State University of New York Press, 1995), 11; Kraus, *Heroes of Unwritten Story*, 297–306; Fine, *Sit-Down*, 323–28; Nelson Lichtenstein, "'The Man in the Middle': A Social History of Automobile Industry Foremen," in Nelson Lichtenstein and Stephen Meyer, eds., *On the Line: Essays in the History of Auto Work* (Urbana: University of Illinois Press, 1989), 163–64; McPherson, *Labor Relations*, 43–44.

14. Cochran, *Labor and Communism*, 128–31.

15. Edsforth, *Class Conflict and Cultural Consensus*, 185; Ken Morris interview with John Barnard, December 17, 1996, p. 29; Galenson, *CIO Challenge*, 151; Lichtenstein, *Most Dangerous Man*, 112–14; Kraus, *Heroes of Unwritten Story*, 318–19; Steve Fraser, "The 'Labor Question,' " in Steve Fraser and Gary Gerstle, eds., *The Rise and Fall of the New Deal Order, 1930–1980* (Princeton: Princeton University Press, 1989), 72–73.

16. Victor Reuther quoted in Judith Stepan-Norris and Maurice Zeitlin, *Talking Union* (Urbana: University of Illinois Press, 1996), 178; Galenson, *CIO Challenge*, 151; Lichtenstein, *Most Dangerous Man*, 115; John Barnard, *Walter Reuther and the Rise of the Auto Workers* (Boston: Little, Brown, 1983), 55–57.

17. Keeran, *Communist Party*, 185.

18. Ibid., 16–17.

19. Stepan-Norris and Zeitlin, *Talking Union*, 178; Kraus, *Heroes of Unwritten Story*, 319–20; *New York Times*, July 19, 1937; Victor Reuther interview with John Herling, November 29, 1977, p. 4.

20. Lloyd Jones interview with Jack W. Skeels, March 10, 1960, pp. 74, 76; Lichtenstein, *Most Dangerous Man*, 114.

21. Emil Mazey interview with John Herling, May 1, 1978, p. 30; Lloyd Jones interview with Jack W. Skeels, March 10, 1960, p. 77; UAW, *Proceedings of the Third Constitutional Convention* [1937], 29. A detailed account of the convention is in Kraus, *Heroes of Unwritten Story*, 324–46. Clayton Fountain, a delegate from Local 235, Chevrolet Gear and Axle in Detroit/Hamtramck, provided a participant's view in *Union Guy* (New York: Viking Press, 1949), 71–75.

22. UAW, *Proceedings of the Third Constitutional Convention* [1937], 138–41, 172–74, 218, 224 ff.; Kraus, *Heroes of Unwritten Story*, 333; UAW, International Executive Board, Minutes, August 30–September 13, 1937, pp. 31–32, 33; *West Side Conveyor*, November 9, 1937.

23. Lloyd Jones interview with Jack W. Skeels, March 10, 1960, p. 78; Ed Hall interview with Jack W. Skeels, October 24, 1959, pp. 33–35; Kraus, *Heroes of Unwritten Story*, 333–39; Morgan, *Covert Life*, 126; Lichtenstein, *Most Dangerous Man*, 116.

24. Galenson, *CIO Challenge*, 156.

25. Fountain, *Union Guy*, 72–74; Arthur Case interview with Jack W. Skeels, August 4, 1960, p. 11; Kraus, *Heroes of Unwritten Story*, 327; UAW, *Proceedings of the Third Constitutional Convention* [1937], 281–85; George Edwards interview with John Herling, May 15, 1978, pp. 3–4; Victor Reuther interview with John Herling, November 29, 1977, pp. 1–7.

26. UAW, *Proceedings of the Third Constitutional Convention* [1937], 94, 106–9, 257–61, 274–85; Stuart Strachan interview with John Herling, June 5, 1980, pp. 13–14; *New York Times*, August 22–31, 1937.

27. UAW, *Proceedings of the Third Constitutional Convention* [1937], 285–86; Kraus, *Heroes of Unwritten Story*, 340–46; Lichtenstein, *Most Dangerous Man*, 117.

28. A copy of the "letter of responsibility" is in Walter P. Reuther Collection, Box 18, f. 1; Lichtenstein, *Most Dangerous Man*, 117.

29. Kraus, *Heroes of Unwritten Story*, 350–58; Stuart Strachan interview with John Herling, June 5, 1980, pp. 15–19; Lichtenstein, *Most Dangerous Man*, 118–19.

30. Lichtenstein, *Most Dangerous Man*, 119–21; Cochran, *Labor and Communism*, 138–39.

31. *Socialist Call*, October 2, 1937; Charles E. Wilson to Robert T. Wilson, November 3, 1937, Charles E. Wilson Collection, Box 31, folder marked "W," Anderson University, Anderson, IN; *Vote Labor: The Voice of the United Labor Political Action Committee*, September 20, October 4, November 1, 1937, Henry Kraus Collection, oversize folder 1; radio addresses of Walter P. Reuther, "The Public Wants Service," and "Will the Labor Slate Bankrupt Detroit, If Elected?" October–November, 1937, Walter P. Reuther Collection, Box 539, f. 11; Bruce Nelson, "Autoworkers, Electoral Politics, and the Convergence of Class and Race: Detroit, 1937–1945," in Kevin Boyle, ed., *Organized Labor and American Politics, 1894–1994: The Liberal-Labor Alliance* (Albany: State University of New York Press, 1998), 121–56; Christopher H. Johnson, *Maurice Sugar: Law, Labor, and the Left in Detroit, 1912–1950* (Detroit: Wayne State University Press, 1988), 228–30; Lichtenstein, *Most Dangerous Man*, 87–91; Dudley W. Buffa, *Union Power and American Democracy: The UAW and the Democratic Party, 1935–72* (Ann Arbor: University of Michigan Press, 1984), 134.

32. Galenson, *CIO Challenge*, 157; Lichtenstein, *Most Dangerous Man*, 121–22; Ray Boryczka, "Militancy and Factionalism in the United Auto Workers Union, 1937–1941," *Maryland Historian*, VIII, No. 2 (Fall 1977), 16.

33. UAW, International Executive Board, Minutes, January 12–23, 1938, pp. 26–27; *New York Times*, January 18, 1938; "Review of the Situation in General Motors," copy in Walter P. Reuther Collection, Box 4, f. 12. Probably written by Reuther, this account was prepared for distribution at the UAW's convention in Cleveland, Ohio, in 1939. William E. Dowell to executive board members, March 5, 1938, UAW-GM Collection, Series I, Box 1, folder marked "Letters to Locals, March 5, 1938–January 4, 1939"; William E. Dowell to General Motors Locals, April 19, 1938, UAW-GM Collection, Series I, Box 1, folder marked "Letters to Locals, March 10, 1938–March 4, 1940."

34. Walter P. Reuther to Homer Martin, March 10, 1938, UAW-GM Collection, Series I, Box 1, folder marked "Correspondence UAW and GM, March 10, 1938–March 4, 1940"; Kraus, *Heroes of Unwritten Story*, 359–66.

35. *Detroit News*, April 1, 1938; *United Automobile Worker*, April 2, 1938; *West Side Conveyor*, April 5, 12, 1938.

36. Wyndham Mortimer interview with Jack W. Skeels, June 20, 1960, p. 211; Catherine Gelles interview with Jack W. Skeels, July 7, 1961, pp. 14–15; Sophie Reuther interview with John Herling, November 29, 1980, p. 25.

37. West Side Local 174 press releases, March 29, 30, 31, 1938, Walter P. Reuther Collection, Box 1, ff. 22, 44, Box 7, f. 4; Carl Haessler interview with Jack W. Skeels, November 1959–October 1960, pp. 44–49; Margaret C. Nowak, *Two Who Were There: A Biography of Stanley Nowak* (Detroit: Wayne State University Press, 1989), 120–29; Fountain, *Union Guy*, 80–81; George Edwards interview with John Herling, May 15, 1978, pp. 22–23; Lichtenstein, *Most Dangerous Man*, 98–101.

38. *Report of R. J. Thomas, President . . . Submitted [to the] 1940 Convention,* 19–20; George Edwards, Jr., to his family, November 7, 1937, George Edwards, Sr. papers, quoted in Stolberg, *Bridging the River,* 59.

Chapter 5

"A fight for the survival of the union": Leonard Woodcock interview with Jack W. Skeels, April 30, 1963, p. 14.

1. Walter P. Reuther, "Radio Address for Friday, March 3 [,1939]," p. 4, Walter P. Reuther Collection, Box 1, f. 21.

2. *United Automobile Worker,* March 5, 1938; *Detroit News,* March 2–8, 1938; Steve Jefferys, *Management and Managed: Fifty Years of Crisis at Chrysler* (Cambridge: Cambridge University Press, 1986), 79–80; Henry Kraus, *Heroes of Unwritten Story: The UAW, 1934–39* (Urbana: University of Illinois Press, 1993), 370–72.

3. Jack Conway interview with Frank Cormier and William J. Eaton, October 2, 1967, p. 6; Kraus, *Heroes of Unwritten Story,* 373–75; Roger Keeran, *The Communist Party and the Autoworkers Unions* (Bloomington: Indiana University Press, 1980), 196–97.

4. Frank Winn interview with Frank Cormier and William J. Eaton, October 2, 1967, p. 6; Anthony Carew, *Walter Reuther* (Manchester: Manchester University Press, 1993), 25–28.

5. Walter Goodman, *The Committee* (New York: Farrar, Straus and Giroux, 1964), 48–51; Ben Fischer to Michael Patane, February 17, 1939, Socialist Party of America Collection, National Correspondence, 1939, Box 171, Duke University. U. S. Congress, House of Representatives, Special Committee on Un-American Propaganda Activities in the United States, *Hearings,* I, 116, 125, 248, 250, 1532, 1560, 1607, 1626, 1653, 1654, 1659–61; III, 2188, 2221, 2322, 2333. *New York Times,* August 14–16, October 2, 19–22, 26–7, November 4, 15, 17, 1938; *Detroit News,* August 16, 1938; on Reuther's connection with the Communist Party, see Carew, *Reuther,* 23, for a review of the evidence. The fake version of the letter was circulated over the years in many forms. Among the earliest was a version contained in a handbill put out during the sit-down strike by the Flint Alliance, an organization of loyal General Motors employees. Victor Reuther interview with Frank Cormier and William J. Eaton, October 2, 1967, p. 18. A printed pamphlet containing the forged statements was simultaneously given national distribution: Joseph P. Kamp, *Join the C.I.O.—And Help Build a Soviet America* (n.p., 1937). According to Harvey Levenstein, the National Association of Manufacturers supplied over two million copies of this pamphlet to employers; Harvey A. Levenstein, *Communism, Anticommunism, and the CIO* (Westport, CT: Greenwood Press, 1981), 101. The original letter, written by Victor and Walter Reuther from the U.S.S.R. in January 1934 to friends in the United States, has disappeared. The earliest printed version, which lacks the controversial, forged, closing line, "Yours for a Soviet America," appeared in July 1934 in the *Challenge,* a publication of the Young People's Socialist League of America. A copy of the letter was placed in Reuther's FBI file and circulated among

government officials by director Hoover on the several occasions when Reuther was under consideration for a federal post. Henry Morganthau, Jr., Diary, Book 264, p. 328, Book 265, pp. 297–303, Franklin D. Roosevelt Library.

6. Clayton Fountain, *Union Guy* (New York: Viking Press, 1949), 84–85. A few months later Fountain left the party. Walter P. Reuther interview with Frank Cormier and William J. Eaton, July 1, 1968, p. 8. Whatever the actual words Reuther used, there is no question that an acrimonious exchange accompanied the split. For an account of this episode that makes no mention of the Communist Party's role, see Kraus, *Heroes of Unwritten Story,* 390–91. Lorin L. Cary, "Institutional Conservatism in the Early C.I.O.: Adolph Germer, A Case Study," *Labor History,* XIII, No. 4 (Fall 1972), 501–2; Nelson Lichtenstein, *The Most Dangerous Man in Detroit: Walter Reuther and the Fate of American Labor* (New York: Basic Books, 1995), 122–25.

7. Frank Marquart, *An Auto Worker's Journal: The UAW from Crusade to One-Party Union* (University Park: Pennsylvania State University Press, 1975), 123–24; Sidney Fine, *Frank Murphy: The New Deal Years* (Chicago: University of Chicago Press, 1979), 490–93. For an analysis of Reuther's departure from the Socialist Party with a different emphasis, see Lichtenstein, *Most Dangerous Man,* 126–28.

8. Tucker Smith to "Dear Paul," January 3, 1939; Arthur G. McDowell to Paul Porter, January 17, 1939; Arthur G. McDowell to "Dear Norman," January 21 [,1939], Socialist Party of America Collection, National Correspondence, 1939, Box 171, Duke University. Lichtenstein, *Most Dangerous Man,* 123–25. The ACTU publications *Michigan Labor Leader* and *The Wage Earner* give its views and activities. See also Leslie W. Tentler, *Seasons of Grace: A History of the Catholic Archdiocese of Detroit* (Detroit: Wayne State University Press, 1990), 342–46; Levenstein, *Communism,* 112–14.

9. The continuing controversy within the union was extensively covered in the *New York Times* and the *Detroit News,* January 1938–April 1939. See also Kraus, *Heroes of Unwritten Story,* 375–80; Walter Galenson, *The CIO Challenge to the AFL: A History of the American Labor Movement, 1935–1941* (Cambridge, MA: Harvard University Press, 1960), 160–61.

10. UAW, International Executive Board, Minutes, August 6, 1938, pp. 1–2; Galenson, *CIO Challenge,* 161–62; Kraus, *Heroes of Unwritten Story,* 380–86; Christopher H. Johnson, *Maurice Sugar: Law, Labor and the Left in Detroit, 1912–1950* (Detroit: Wayne State University Press), 231–32; Ted Morgan, *A Covert Life: Jay Lovestone, Communist, Anti-Communist, and Spymaster* (New York: Random House, 1999), 128–30; Lichtenstein, *Most Dangerous Man,* 125–26, 128–29.

11. Galenson, *CIO Challenge,* 163–65.

12. Kraus, *Heroes of Unwritten Story,* 393–98; Morgan, *Covert Life,* 130.

13. The most detailed secondary account of the entire course of events is Kraus, *Heroes of Unwritten Story,* 375–401. The *Detroit News* and the *New York Times* carried almost daily reports from the UAW battlefield, January 1938–April 1939. See also Ben Fischer, "Auto Report #2" [June 16, 1938], Socialist Party of America Collection, National Correspondence, 1938, Box 169, Duke University; Walter P. Reuther to John L. Lewis, July 26, 28, 29, 1938, Victor G. Reuther Collec-

tion, Box 4, f. ll; Galenson, *CIO Challenge*, 160–64; Lichtenstein, *Most Dangerous Man*, 129.

14. Arthur G. McDowell to J. A. Mattson, January 26, 1939, Socialist Party of America Collection, National Correspondence, 1939, Box 171, Duke University; *New York Times*, January 7, 13, 18, 21, 23, 24, 25, 26, February 22, 1939; Arthur G. McDowell to Norman [Thomas], January 21, 1939, Socialist Party of America Collection, National Correspondence, 1939, Box 171, Duke University; Ben Fischer, "Auto Report" [January 23, 1939], Socialist Party of America Collection, National Correspondence, 1939, Box 171, Duke University; Lichtenstein, *Most Dangerous Man*, 129.

15. Norman Bully interview with Jack W. Skeels, October 12, 1961, p. 11; Ken Morris interview with Jack W. Skeels, June 28, 1963, pp. 32–33; *United Automobile Worker*, January 21–April 8, 1939; *New York Times*, January 30, February 12, 13, 1939; George D. Blackwood, "The United Automobile Workers of America, 1935–1951" (Ph. D diss., University of Chicago, 1952), 119; for a vivid account of Homer Martin's appearance before a hostile audience at Local 235, see Fountain, *Union Guy*, 95–99; Paul Miley interview with Jack W. Skeels, July 24, 1961, pp. 36–37; Raymond H. Berndt interview with Jack W. Skeels, May 3, 1963, p. 12.

16. *United Automobile Worker*, West Side Conveyor Edition, June 28, 1939; Jess Ferrazza interview with Jack W. Skeels, May 26, 1961, p. 12; Emil Mazey interview with John Herling, May 1, 1978, pp. 53–55; Raymond Vess interview with Jack W. Skeels, October 12, 1961, p. 9; *New York Times*, January 26, 31, February 23, March 12, 26, 1939; *Detroit News*, June 9, 1939.

17. *New York Times*, March 5–8, 10, 1939; Blackwood, "United Automobile Workers," 119; *Detroit News*, June 22, 1939.

18. Blackwood, "United Automobile Workers," 127; *Detroit News*, March 27–April 7, 1939; *United Automobile Worker*, April 8, 1939; *New York Times*, March 28–April 6, 1939; Levenstein, *Communism*, 82–83; Kraus, *Heroes of Untold Story*, 404–16; an account of the convention is in Martin Halpern, "The 1939 UAW Convention: Turning Point for Communist Power in the Auto Union?" *Labor History*, XXXIII, No. 2 (Spring 1992), 190–216.

19. George Addes interview with Jack W. Skeels, June 25, 1960, pp. 30–31.

20. Mazey quoted in *Automotive News*, Prologue to the Future issue, 1975, p. 25, copy in Douglas A. Fraser Collection (II), Box 13, folder marked "Douglas A. Fraser Personal 1973–1976"; Leonard Woodcock interview with John Barnard, January 18, 30, 1991, pp. 11–12; Ken Morris interview with John Barnard, June 3, 1994, in author's possession.

21. Lloyd Jones interview with Jack W. Skeels, March 10, 1960, pp. 85–86; Richard Frankensteen interview with Jack W. Skeels, October 10, 1959–December 7, 1961, pp. 48–49; R. J. Thomas interview with Jack W. Skeels, March 26, 1963, p. 16.

22. Hillman quoted in Steven Fraser, *Labor Will Rule: Sidney Hillman and the Rise of American Labor* (Ithaca: Cornell University Press, 1993), 420.

23. Irving Bernstein, *Turbulent Years: A History of the American Worker, 1933–1941* (Boston: Houghton Mifflin, 1970), 569; for a biographical sketch, see John Barnard, "Roland Jay Thomas," in George S. May, ed., *The Automobile Indus-*

try, 1920–1980: Encyclopedia of American Business History and Biography (New York: Facts on File, 1989), 439–50.

24. For a different version, see George Edwards interview with John Herling, May 15, 1978, pp. 35–42; Wyndham Mortimer interview with Jack W. Skeels, June 20, 1960, p. 60.

25. Keeran, *Communist Party,* 199–200; Tracy Doll interview with Jack W. Skeels, April 21, 1961, pp. 31–32; *New York Times,* April 6, 1939; *Detroit News,* April 6–7, 1939.

26. Jack Stieber, *Governing the UAW* (New York: John Wiley and Sons, 1962), 6; Galenson, *CIO Challenge,* 171–72.

27. *Report of R. J. Thomas, President . . . Submitted [to the] . . . 1940 Convention,* 19–20; "History of the General Motors Department," undated typescript in Walter P. Reuther Collection, Pre-Presidential Papers, Box 20, f. 4.

28. "History of the General Motors Department," undated typescript in Walter P. Reuther Collection, Pre-Presidential Papers, Box 20, f. 4; UAW, International Executive Board, Minutes, April 24–30, 1939, pp. 11–13, 19, 31; *United Automobile Worker,* April 22, May 13, 20, June 14, 28, 1939; Carl Haessler interview with Jack W. Skeels, November 27, 1959–October 24, 1960, pp. 43–44; Walter P. Reuther, Report to the National GM Council, June 10, 1939, Walter P. Reuther Collection, Pre-Presidential Papers, Box 26, f. 7. A copy of the minutes of the first GM council meeting is in the Reuther Collection, Box 26, f. 7.

29. Walter P. Reuther, Report to the National GM Council, June 10, 1939, Walter P. Reuther Collection, Box 26, f. 7.

30. Frank Winn interview with Frank Cormier and William J. Eaton, November 14, 1967, p. 14; Lichtenstein, *Most Dangerous Man,* 135.

31. The 1939 strike may have been inspired by a successful strike of 600 tool and die makers at the Waterloo plant of the Briggs Corporation in January 1933. In a contemporary account, written as he prepared to depart for Europe, a youthful Reuther wrote, "A strategic moment had been selected . . . as the tools and dies for the new Ford car were about seventy-five percent complete and production could not begin on schedule without their completion." Walter P. Reuther, "Auto Workers Strike," *Student Outlook,* II (March 1933), 15. For extended accounts of the strike and additional documentation, see John Barnard, "Rebirth of the United Automobile Workers: The General Motors Tool and Diemakers' Strike of 1939," *Labor History,* XXVII, No. 2 (Spring 1986), 165–87; Kevin Boyle, "Rite of Passage: The General Motors Tool and Die Strike," ibid., 188–203; and Steve Babson, *Building the Union: Skilled Workers and Anglo-Gaelic Immigrants in the Rise of the UAW* (New Brunswick: Rutgers University Press, 1991), 219–26.

32. *United Automobile Worker,* June 12, 14, 21, 1939; *New York Times,* June 14, 15, 18, 1939; *Detroit News,* June 13, 14, 15, 1939; Ronald Edsforth, *Class Conflict and Cultural Consensus: The Making of a Mass Consumer Society in Flint, Michigan* (New Brunswick: Rutgers University Press, 1987), 186–87.

33. Walter P. Reuther interview with Frank Cormier and William J. Eaton, July 1, 1968, p. 9. A UAW "documentary" film on the strike, "United Action," produced under communist auspices for distribution to UAW locals, belied its title by omit-

ting all mention of Reuther; Leonard Woodcock interview with Frank Cormier and William J. Eaton, May 5, 1968.

34. *Time*, XXXIV, July 17, 1939; the strike received detailed coverage in the *New York Times* and the *Detroit News*, July 1–August 6, 1939.

35. *G.M. Picket*, No. 1, July 8, 1939.

36. Barnard, *Labor History*, 181.

37. Courtesy of Irving Bluestone; *G.M. Strike Bulletin*, No. 4, July 13, 1939.

38. John McGill interview with Jack W. Skeels, July 27, 1960, pp. 11–12; leaflet prepared for pickets, copy in Walter P. Reuther Collection, Box 5, folder marked "Tool and Die Strike, July 5–Aug. 12, 1939."

39. GM-UAW Agreement, August 3, 1939, copy in Walter P. Reuther Collection, Box 18, f. 1; Emil Mazey interview with John Herling, January 16, 1979, p. 8.

40. Howell J. Harris, *The Right to Manage: Industrial Relations Policies of American Business in the 1940s* (Madison: University of Wisconsin Press, 1982), 28–32.

41. *United Automobile Worker*, July 19, August 2, 1939; "Region No. 1–C Report, By Arthur L. Case, Regional Director, to the Executive Board Members, UAW-CIO" [August 1939], p. 1; "Report of Region No. 1–C, Presented by Arthur L. Case to International Executive Board, December 4, 1939," pp. 1–2; "Region No. 1–B Report, by William McAulay, Regional Director, to the International Executive Board, December 9, 1939."

42. "Report of R. J. Thomas, President, UAW-CIO, to International Executive Board, December 4, 1939," p. 2; *New York Times*, August 18–19, September 16, 29, 1939.

43. Jefferys, *Management*, 83–85.

44. Ibid., 85–87.

45. John McGill to Walter P. Reuther, February 8, 1940, Walter P. Reuther Collection, Box 25, f. 10; a copy of the mimeographed handout is in ibid., Box 7, folder marked "UAW-AFL Maintenance Jurisdiction Dispute."

46. Speech to Local 14 (Chevrolet, Toledo), press release, March 2, 1940, Walter P. Reuther Collection, Box 5, folder marked "Publicity"; Roy Reuther to "Dear Walt," undated [Spring 1940], Walter P. Reuther Collection, Box 25, f. 6; *New York Times*, April 8–15, 1940.

47. Terrell Thompson to Paul Copeland, March 28, 1940, copy in Walter P. Reuther Collection, Box 25, f. 28.

48. Votes cast in NLRB conducted elections at General Motors plants during all of 1940:

Total eligible	146,821
Total cast	134,474 (92 percent of eligible)
UAW-CIO	91,318 (68 percent)
UAW-AFL	26,052 (19 percent)
Independent union	1,376 (1 percent)
No union	1,010 (1 percent)
Neither CIO nor AFL	14,111 (10 percent)
Voided ballots	(1 percent)

Report of R. J. Thomas, President . . . submitted [to the] 1940 Convention, 19–20; *New York Times,* April 18–19, 1940; *Detroit News,* April 17–19, 1940; *United Automobile Worker,* April 24, 1940; Walter P. Reuther, "The United Automobile Workers: Past, Present, Future," *Virginia Law Review,* 50, No. 1 (1964), 86.

49. Lichtenstein, *Most Dangerous Man,* 140–41.

50. Lichtenstein, *Most Dangerous Man,* 141–47, 149–53; Nelson Lichtenstein, "Great Expectations: The Promise of Industrial Jurisprudence and Its Demise, 1930–1960," in Nelson Lichtenstein and Howell J. Harris, eds., *Industrial Democracy in America: The Ambiguous Promise* (Cambridge: Cambridge University Press and Woodrow Wilson Center Press, 1993), 129–33; Robert M. Macdonald, *Collective Bargaining in the Automobile Industry: A Study of Wage Structure and Competitive Relations* (New Haven: Yale University Press, 1963), 94; Jefferys, *Management,* passim; David Brody, "Workplace Contractualism: A Historical/Comparative Analysis," in *In Labor's Cause: Main Themes on the History of American Workers* (New York: Oxford University Press, 1993), 224; Steve Babson, *The Unfinished Struggle: Turning Points in American Labor, 1877–Present* (Lanham, MD: Rowman & Littlefield,1994), 116–18.

51. General Motors Agreement, June 24, 1940, UAW-GM Collection, Box 1, folder marked "May–April 1940"; Walter P. Reuther to officers and members of GM plants and locals, June 18, 1940, UAW-GM Collection, Series 1, Box 1, folder marked "Letters to Locals"; "History of the G. M. Department of the UAWA CIO," Walter P. Reuther Collection, Box 9, folder marked "Press Releases, 1941–1944"; Brody, "Workplace Contractualism," 236; Lichtenstein, *Most Dangerous Man,* 147–49; Reuther quoted in Ronald Edsforth and Robert Asher with the assistance of Raymond Boryczka, "The Speedup: The Focal Point of Workers' Grievances, 1919–1941," in Robert Asher and Ronald Edsforth, eds., *Autowork* (Albany: State University of New York Press, 1995), 96–97; Ray Boryczka, "Militancy and Factionalism in the United Auto Workers Union, 1937–1941," *Maryland Historian,* VIII, No. 2 (Fall 1977), 17–19; *New York Times,* June 16–25, 1940.

52. *Report of R. J. Thomas, President . . . Submitted [to the] . . . 1940 Convention,* 5–7; Jefferys, *Management,* 82; William H. McPherson, *Labor Relations in the Automobile Industry* (Washington, D.C.: Brookings Institution, 1940), 114–17.

53. Ibid., 69–73.

54. Ibid., 74–79, 98, 168–69.

55. Ibid., 79–97.

56. Ibid., 118–41, 148–50; Nick DiGaetano interview with William A. Sullivan, April 29, May 7, 1959, pp. 73–75; Brody, "Workplace Contractualism," 243–45; Jefferys, *Management,* 85–87; Steve Jefferys, "'Matters of Mutual Interest': The Unionization Process at Dodge Main, 1933–1939," in Nelson Lichtenstein and Stephen Meyer, eds., *On the Line: Essays in the History of Auto Work* (Urbana: University of Illinois Press, 1989), 119–21; Edsforth, *Class Conflict and Cultural Consensus,* 187–89; Nelson Lichtenstein, "Autoworker Militancy and the Structure of Factory Life," *Journal of American History,* LXVII. No. 2 (September 1980), 335–53.

57. Quoted in Marquart, *Auto Worker's Journal,* 72.

58. Judith Stepan-Norris and Maurice Zeitlin, *Talking Union* (Urbana: University of Illinois Press, 1996), 3; Ken Bannon interview with John Herling, June 3, 1980, pp. 6–8; Allan Nevins and Frank Ernest Hill, *Ford: Decline and Rebirth, 1933–1962* (New York: Charles Scribner's Sons, 1962), 133–67.

59. The Ford strike is the subject of numerous accounts. An overview is in an unpublished paper by Martin Halpern, "The 1941 Strike at the Ford Motor Company." A printed account of the strike and the events leading to it is in Nevins and Hill, *Ford*, 133–67; Nelson Lichtenstein, "Life at the Rouge: A Cycle of Workers' Control," in Charles Stephenson and Robert Asher, eds., *Life and Labor: Dimensions of American Working-Class History* (Albany: State University of New York Press, 1986), 204; Stepan-Norris and Zeitlin, *Talking Union*, 86, 90; Robert H. Zieger, *The CIO, 1935–1955* (Chapel Hill: University of North Carolina Press, 1995), 119; David L. Lewis, *The Public Image of Henry Ford: An American Folk Hero and His Company* (Detroit: Wayne State University Press, 1976), 252–61; Margaret C. Nowak, *Two Who Were There: A Biography of Stanley Nowak* (Detroit: Wayne State University Press, 1989), 161–66; Walter Quillico interview with Jack W. Skeels, February 24, 1960, p. 13; two scrapbooks of newspaper clippings on the strike are in the Ken Bannon Collection, Box 67.

60. Stepan-Norris and Zeitlin, *Talking Union*, 5, 105–6; Shelton Tappes interview with Herbert Hill, No. 1, Pt. 1, October 27, 1967, p. 35; Ken Bannon interview with Frank Cormier and William J. Eaton, June 18, 1968, p. 1; Richard W. Thomas, *Life for Us Is What We Make It: Building Black Community in Detroit, 1915–1945* (Bloomington: Indiana University Press, 1992), 277–304.

61. August Meier and Elliott Rudwick, *Black Detroit and the Rise of the UAW* (New York: Oxford University Press, 1979), 34–45; David Gartman, *Auto Slavery: The Labor Process in the American Automobile Industry, 1897–1950* (New Brunswick: Rutgers University Press, 1986), 250–51.

62. *New York Times*, November 25–28, 1939; *United Automobile Worker*, November 29, December 6, 1939; *Detroit News*, November 25–29, 1939; Marquart, *Auto Worker's Journal*, 89; Meier and Rudwick, *Black Detroit*, 67–71; Jefferys, *Management*, 84–85; Gartman, *Auto Slavery*, 251–52.

63. Ken Bannon interview with Jack W. Skeels, February 28, 1963, p. 7; Ken Bannon interview with John Herling, June 3, 1980, pp. 6–12; Lewis, *Public Image*, 264; Shelton Tappes interview with Herbert Hill, No. 1, Pt. 1, October 27, 1967, p. 43; *New York Times*, April 1–11, 1941; *Detroit News*, April 2–11, 1941; *United Automobile Worker*, April 15, 1941; Meier and Rudwick, *Black Detroit*, 87–107.

64. Lewis, *Public Image*, 265–66; *New York Times*, May 9–22, 1941; *Detroit News*, May 21–23, 1941; *United Automobile Worker*, May 15, June 1, 1941; Charles E. Sorensen with Samuel T. Williamson, *My Forty Years with Ford* (New York: W. W. Norton, 1956), 268.

65. *New York Times*, June 21–23, 1941; *United Automobile Worker*, May 15, July 1, 1941; Nevins and Hill, *Ford*, 166.

66. Stepan-Norris and Zeitlin, *Talking Union*, 121; Lewis, *Public Image*, 267; Lichtenstein, "Life at the Rouge," 243, 246–47.

67. Lewis, *Public Image*, 266–68; Sorensen, *Forty Years*, 269–71.

Chapter 6

"UAW-CIO, makes the army roll and go": from the wartime song, "UAW-CIO," written by Baldwin "Butch" Hawes in 1942 for the Almanac Singers. Two of the verses are:

> I was standing round a defense town one day
> When I thought I overheard a soldier say:
> "Ev'ry tank in our camp has that UAW stamp,
> And I'm UAW too, I'm proud to say."

> There'll be a union label in Berlin
> When those union boys in uniform march in
> And rolling in those ranks there'll be UAW tanks;
> To roll Hitler out and roll the union in!

> *Chorus*
> It's the UAW-CIO, makes the army roll and go;
> Turning out the jeeps and tanks and airplanes ev'ry day.
> It's the UAW-CIO, makes the army roll and go,
> Puts wheels on the U.S.A.

Baldwin Hawes, "UAW-CIO," People's Song Library Collection, Box 17, cited in Alan Clive, *State of War: Michigan in World War II* (Ann Arbor: University of Michigan Press, 1979), 60–61.

1. CIO, *Proceedings of the Fourth Constitutional Convention* [1941], 146–47.

2. John B. Rae, *The American Automobile Industry* (Boston: Twayne, 1984), 91–96; Martin Halpern, *UAW Politics in the Cold War Era* (Albany: State University of New York Press, 1988), 7.

3. Wartime membership in the union trended upward from 1941 to late 1943 then leveled off and moved slightly downward as the war's end approached, but there were many fluctuations. UAW, *Proceedings of the Eighth Constitutional Convention* [1943], p. 8; *Automobile Unionism (1943), Report of R. J. Thomas, President . . . October 4, 1943*, p. 1; *Automobile Unionism (1944) by R. J. Thomas, President . . . September 11, 1944*, p. 2; Robert H. Zieger, *The CIO, 1935–1955* (Chapel Hill: University of North Carolina Press, 1995), 153; Clive, *State of War*, 190.

4. Lowell J. Carr and James E. Stermer, *Willow Run: A Study of Industrialization and Cultural Inadequacy* (New York: Harper & Brothers, 1952), 73–74.

5. For a sensitive portrayal of a Kentucky family's plunge into the maelstrom of wartime Detroit, see Harriette Arnow's novel, *The Dollmaker* (New York: Macmillan, 1954).

6. Nelson Lichtenstein, *Labor's War at Home: The CIO in World War II* (Cambridge: Cambridge University Press, 1982).

7. Maurice Isserman, *Which Side Were You On? The American Communist Party during the Second World War* (Urbana: University of Illinois Press, 1993), 34–38.

8. Bert Cochran, *Labor and Communism: The Conflict that Shaped American Unions* (Princeton: Princeton University Press, 1977), 143–47.

9. UAW, *Proceedings of the Fifth Constitutional Convention* [1940], 293, 295–97; *New York Times*, July 28–August 7, 1940; *United Automobile Worker*, August 1, 1940; *Detroit News*, July 28–August 7, 1940; Isserman, *Which Side*, 44–45, 77.

10. UAW, *Proceedings of the Fifth Constitutional Convention* [1940], 296–98, 301–3; Roger Keeran, *The Communist Party and the Auto Workers Unions* (Bloomington: Indiana University Press, 1980), 210–11; Cochran, *Labor and Communism*, 151–53.

11. UAW, *Proceedings of the Fifth Constitutional Convention* [1940], 425–40; *United Automobile Worker*, August 1, 15, 1940; Keeran, *Communist Party*, 211; Victor Reuther to "Dear Norman," September 5, 1940, Socialist Party of America Collection, National Correspondence, 1940, Box 200, Duke University Library; Cochran, *Labor and Communism*, 151–53; Walter Galenson, *The CIO Challenge to the AFL: A History of the American Labor Movement, 1935–1941* (Cambridge, MA: Harvard University Press, 1960), 177–78.

12. UAW, *Proceedings of the Fifth Constitutional Convention* [1940], 592–94; Leonard Woodcock interview with Frank Cormier and Robert J. Eaton, May 5, 1968, p. 2; UAW, International Executive Board, Minutes, September 13–19, 1940, p. 72; George D. Blackwood, "The United Automobile Workers of America, 1935–1951" (Ph.D. diss., University of Chicago, 1950), p. 146.

13. Walter P. Reuther, radio address of October 30, 1940, Walter P. Reuther Collection, Box 539, f. 13.

14. *United Automobile Worker*, December 15, 1940; John Barnard, *Walter Reuther and the Rise of the Auto Workers* (Boston: Little, Brown, 1983), 77–79; Nelson Lichtenstein, *The Most Dangerous Man in Detroit: Walter Reuther and the Fate of American Labor* (New York: Basic Books, 1995), 160–66; Alan Brinkley, *The End of Reform: New Deal Liberalism in Recession and War* (New York: Knopf, 1995), 205–9; portions of the proposal are reprinted in Henry P. Christman, ed., *Walter P. Reuther: Selected Papers* (New York: Macmillan, 1961), 1–12.

15. David Brody, "The New Deal, Labor and World War II," in *In Labor's Cause: Main Themes on the History of the American Worker* (New York: Oxford University Press, 1993), 189–96; Anthony Carew, *Walter Reuther* (Manchester: Manchester University Press, 1993), 33–35; Barnard, *Walter Reuther*, 77–79.

16. Stephen Meyer, *"Stalin Over Wisconsin": The Making and Unmaking of Militant Unionism, 1900–1950* (New Brunswick: Rutgers University Press, 1992), 88–104; Zieger, *CIO*, 126–27; Cochran, *Labor and Communism*, 166–76.

17. Wyndham Mortimer, *Organize! My Life as a Union Man* (Boston: Beacon Press, 1972), 166–69; Cyril O'Halloran interview with Jack W. Skeels, June 20, 1960, p. 22; *Report of R. J. Thomas, President . . .* [1939], pp. 29–30; *Automobile Unionism (1939–1940), By R. J. Thomas, President . . .* [1940], pp. 44–46; *Automobile Unionism (1940–41) By R. J. Thomas . . .* [1941], pp. 38–46; *Automobile Unionism (1942) Report of R. J. Thomas* [1942], pp. 28–30; *Automobile Unionism (1943) Report of R. J. Thomas* [1943], pp. 2, 92–94; *Automobile Unionism (1944) Report of R. J. Thomas* [1944], 69–72; Cochran, *Labor and Communism*, 158–59.

18. Lew Michener interview with Jack W. Skeels, June 21, 1960, p. 23; Mortimer, *Organize!* 166–73; Lichtenstein, *Labor's War*, 56–57; Zieger, *CIO*, 127–30.

19. *United Automobile Worker*, June 1, 15, 1941; *Detroit News*, June 5–10, 1941; *New York Times*, June 6–10, 1941.

20. UAW, *Proceedings of the Sixth Constitutional Convention* [1941], 434; *United Automobile Worker*, June 15, 1941; Lichtenstein, *Labor's War*, 60–66; Richard Frankensteen interview with Jack W. Skeels, October 10, 1959–December 7, 1961, pp. 54–55; Mortimer, *Organize!* 174–86; Isserman, *Which Side*, 96–100; Cochran, *Labor and Communism*, 176–81.

21. *Detroit News*, June 6, 1941; *United Automobile Worker*, June 15, 1941; Kevin Boyle, "Auto Workers at War: Patriotism and Shop Floor Militancy in the American Auto Industry, 1941–1945," pp. 24–25 (unpublished paper in author's possession), a published version is in Kevin Boyle, "Auto Workers at War: Patriotism and Protest in the American Automobile Industry, 1939–1945," in Robert Asher and Ronald Edsforth, eds., *Autowork* (Albany: State University of New York Press, 1995), 99–126; Zieger, *CIO*, 127–30.

22. Nelson Lichtenstein, "Life at the Rouge: A Cycle of Workers' Control," in Charles Stephenson and Robert Asher, eds., *Life and Labor: Dimensions of American Working-Class History* (Albany: State University of New York Press, 1986), 244–46; Keeran, *Communist Party*, 226–49.

23. Victor Reuther interview with John Herling, November 29, 1977, p. 26; Tracy Doll interview with Jack W. Skeels, April 21, 1961, pp. 39–40; Douglas Fraser interview with John Barnard, May 15–June 22, 1990, pp. 32–33.

24. UAW, *Proceedings of the Sixth Constitutional Convention* [1941], 401–57; Carl Haessler interview with Jack W. Skeels, November 27, 1959–Octber 24, 1960, pp. 83–101; *New York Times*, August 3–17, 1941; *Detroit News*, August 3–17, 1941; Cochran, *Labor and Communism*, 184–95; Lichtenstein, *Most Dangerous Man*, 189–92.

25. UAW, *Proceedings of the Sixth Constitutional Convention* [1941], 688–711, 723–24; *United Automobile Worker*, August 1, 15, 1941; press release, April 30, 1941, copy in Walter P. Reuther Collection, Box 4, f. 16.

26. UAW, *Proceedings of the Twenty-Sixth Constitutional Convention* [1980], 155.

27. Richard T. Frankensteen interview with Frank Cormier and William J. Eaton, June 22, 1968, p. 5; UAW, *Proceedings of the Sixth Constitutional Convention* [1941], 613, 742.

28. "Address of Walter P. Reuther . . . over National Broadcasting Company," December 28, 1940, copy in Walter P. Reuther Collection, Box 539, f. 14; *United Automobile Worker*, February 1, 1941.

29. International Executive Board, Minutes, December 8, 1941, pp. 4–5; Nelson Lichtenstein, "Conflict over Workers' Control: The Automobile Industry in World War II," in Michael H. Frisch and Daniel J. Walkowitz, eds., *Working-Class America: Essays on Labor, Community, and American Society* (Urbana: University of Illinois Press, 1983), 289; UAW Research Department postcard survey, February 1943, UAW Research Department Collection, Box 14, quoted in Boyle, "Auto Workers at War," 27. For the view that the UAW's decision to cooperate with the government during the war through the no-strike pledge, and in other ways,

represented a "Faustian bargain" that ceded "much freedom and legitimacy to the warfare state," see Lichtenstein, *Most Dangerous Man,* 175–93.

30. The premium pay issue was the main topic of debate at the 1942 convention. UAW, *Proceedings of the Seventh Constitutional Convention* [1942], 91–109; Zieger, *CIO,* 167; Carl Haessler interview with Jack W. Skeels, November 27–October 24, 1960, pp. 106–27; *United Automobile Worker,* August 1, 15, 1942; *New York Times,* August 3–10, 1942; *Detroit News,* August 3–10, 1942; Clive, *State of War,* 64; Lichtenstein, *Most Dangerous Man,* 197–98.

31. Quoted in Clive, *State of War,* 27–29.

32. *Ford Facts,* December 17, 1941, quoted in Boyle, "Auto Workers at War," 26; UAW, *Proceedings of the Seventh Constitutional Convention* [1942], 18; Lichtenstein, *Most Dangerous Man,* 196–97.

33. Jack Conway interview with Frank Cormier and William F. Eaton, October 2, 1967, p. 2; Leonard Woodcock interview with John Barnard, January 18, 30, February 7, 1991, p. 17; Richard Frankensteen interview with Jack W. Skeels, October 10, 1959–December 7, 1961, pp. 51–52; UAW, *Proceedings of the Eighth Constitutional Convention* [1943], 174–231; *Detroit News,* October 4–11, 1943; *New York Times,* October 5–11, 1943; *United Automobile Worker,* October 1, 15, 1943; Isserman, *Which Side,* 163–64; Cochran, *Labor and Communism,* 214–18; Lichtenstein, *Most Dangerous Man,* 203–6.

34. Clayton Fountain, *Union Guy* (New York: Viking Press, 1949), 163; Carl Haessler interview with Jack W. Skeels, November 27, 1959–October 24, 1960, pp. 127–58; *New York Times,* October 5–11, 1943; *Detroit News,* October 4, 8, 1943; Cochran, *Labor and Communism,* 218–20.

35. Melvyn Dubofsky, *The State and Labor in Modern America* (Chapel Hill: University of North Carolina Press, 1994), 182–88; conditions in wartime plants are analyzed in Lichtenstein, "Conflict over Workers' Control," 289–304.

36. Sam Sage interview with Jack W. Skeels, July 18, 1960, pp. 30, 37–38; Jess Ferrazza interview with Jack W. Skeels, May 26, 1961, p. 15; John W. Anderson interview with Jack W. Skeels, February 17– May 21, 1960, pp. 200–201; Clive, *State of War,* 36; Lichtenstein, "Conflict over Workers' Control," 289–92.

37. Clive, *State of War,* 39–40, 66–67.

38. Ibid., 68; Lichtenstein, *Labor's War at Home,* 73; UAW Research Department postcard survey, February 1943, UAW Research Department Collection, Box 14, quoted in Boyle, "Auto Workers at War," 34; Arthur Hughes interview with Jack W. Skeels, March 13, 1963, pp. 18–20; Jess Ferrazza interview with Jack W. Skeels, May 26, 1961, p. 16; Donald T. Critchlow, *Studebaker: The Life and Death of an American Corporation* (Bloomington: Indiana University Press, 1996), 119; Martin Glaberman, *Wartime Strikes: The Struggle Against the No-Strike Pledge in the UAW During World War II* (Detroit: Bewick /Editions, 1980), 37–61.

39. Clive, *State of War,* 70–71; Boyle, "Auto Workers at War," 2; Lichtenstein, "Life at the Rouge: A Cycle of Workers' Control," 243; Arthur Hughes interview with Jack W. Skeels, March 13, 1963, p. 22; Jess Ferrazza interview with Jack W. Skeels, May 26, 1961, p. 16.

40. Sam Sage interview with Jack W. Skeels, July 18, 1960, p. 30; Lloyd Jones

interview with Jack W. Skeels, March 10, 1960, p. 105; Leonard Woodcock interview with Jack W. Skeels, April 30, 1963, p. 27; Boyle, "Auto Workers at War," 37–38; Lichtenstein, "Conflict over Workers' Control," 295–97.

41. Douglas Fraser interview with John Barnard, May–June, 1990, pp. 53–54; Jess Ferrazza interview with Jack W. Skeels, May 26, 1961, p. 17; George Lipsitz, *Rainbow at Midnight: Labor and Culture in the 1940s* (Urbana: University of Illinois Press, 1994), 22; Glaberman, *Wartime Strikes*, 51–60; Larry Carlstrom interview with John Barnard, March 7, 1997, p. 49.

42. Ken Bannon interview with John Herling, June 3, 1980, p. 28; Joshua Freeman, "Delivering the Goods: Industrial Unionism during World War II," *Labor History*, XIX, No. 4 (Fall 1978), 581–93. For interpretations that see the wartime strike wave as the "reemergence of a syndicalist movement," see Lichtenstein, *Most Dangerous Man*, 201–2; Lichtenstein, *Labor's War at Home*, 189–94; and, in the greatest detail, Glaberman, *Wartime Strikes*, passim.

43. Douglas Fraser interview with John Barnard, May 15–June 22, 1990, pp. 53–54; John B. Rae, *The American Automobile Industry* (Boston: Twayne, 1984), 90; Lichtenstein, *Most Dangerous Man*, 211.

44. UAW, *Proceedings of the Eighth Constitutional Convention* [1943], 410–14; Boyle, "Auto Workers at War," 41; *United Automobile Worker*, October 15, 1943.

45. Clive, *State of War*, 80; Zieger, *CIO*, 172; *Detroit News*, July 28–August 7, 1944; *New York Times*, July 29–August 2, 1944; Steven Tolliday and Jonathan Zeitlin, "Shop-Floor Bargaining, Contract Unionism and Job Control: An Anglo-American Comparison," in Steven Tolliday and Jonathan Zeitlin, eds., *Between Fordism and Flexibility: The Automobile Industry and Its Workers* (Oxford: Berg, 1992), 109.

46. UAW, *Proceedings of the Ninth Constitutional Convention* [1944], 168, 171–72; Carl Haessler interview with Jack W. Skeels, November 27, 1959–October 24, 1960, pp. 162–69; *Detroit News*, September 11–18, 1944; *New York Times*, September 11–17, 1944; *United Automobile Worker*, September 15, October 1, 1944; Irving Howe and B. J. Widick, *The UAW and Walter Reuther* (New York: DaCapo Press, 1973, orig. pub. 1949), 120–25.

47. UAW, *Proceedings of the Ninth Constitutional Convention* [1944], 147–55, 171, 172, 176–77, 193, 194, 215, 235; *New York Times*, September 12, 1944; *United Automobile Worker*, September 15, 1944; Barnard, *Walter Reuther*, 87–88; Lichtenstein, *Labor's War at Home*, 194–97, 214–15; Zieger, *CIO*, 162; Clive, *State of War*, 84–86; Glaberman, *Wartime Strikes*, 104–19; Lichtenstein, *Most Dangerous Man*, 211–19.

48. Marc Stepp interview with John Barnard, June 10–25, 1993, p. 3; Zieger, *CIO*, 153.

49. *Detroit News*, June 21–24, 1943; *New York Times*, June 22–24, 1943; *United Automobile Worker*, July 1, 1943; August Meier and Elliott Rudwick, *Black Detroit and the Rise of the UAW* (New York: Oxford University Press, 1979), 175–87, 192–97; Thomas J. Sugrue, *The Origins of the Urban Crisis: Race and Inequality in Postwar Detroit* (Princeton: Princeton University Press, 1996), 17–47,

57–81; Richard W. Thomas, *Life for Us Is What We Make It: Building Black Community in Detroit, 1915–1945* (Bloomington: Indiana University Press, 1992), 147–48, 168; Clive, *State of War*, 157–62.

50. CIO, *Proceedings of the Sixth Constitutional Convention* [1943], 279; Sidney Fine, *"Expanding the Frontiers of Civil Rights": Michigan, 1948–1968* (Detroit: Wayne State University Press, 2000), 12–13; George W. Crockett, Jr., interview with Herbert Hill and Roberta McBride, March 2, 1968, pp. 21–22.

51. Meier and Rudwick, *Black Detroit*, 73; Judith Stepan-Norris and Maurice Zeitlin, *Talking Union* (Urbana: University of Illinois Press, 1996), 143–44; Douglas Fraser interview with John Barnard, May–June, 1990, pp. 44–46.

52. Stepan-Norris and Zeitlin, *Talking Union*, 154–55, 157.

53. Meier and Rudwick, *Black Detroit*, 120–21, 154–56, 163–64, 167, 173, 214; Zieger, *CIO*, 154; Lipsitz, *Rainbow at Midnight*, 74–79, 81; Thomas, *Life for Us*, 244–46.

54. Richard Frankensteen interview with Jack W. Skeels, October 10, 1959–December 7, 1961, pp. 77–81; David Gartman, *Auto Slavery: The Labor Process in the American Automobile Industry, 1897–1950* (New Brunswick: Rutgers University Press, 1986), 284–87.

55. *Detroit News*, June 3–7, 1943; *United Automobile Worker*, June 15, 1943; *New York Times*, June 4–6, 1943; Meier and Rudwick, *Black Detroit*, 125–34; Dominic J. Capeci, Jr., *Race Relations in Wartime Detroit: The Sojourner Truth Housing Controversy of 1942* (Philadelphia: Temple University Press, 1984), 70–74; Clive, *State of War*, 138–39.

56. Meier and Rudwick, *Black Detroit*, 162–74; Thomas, *Life for Us*, 154.

57. Thomas, *Life for Us*, 165–72, 214; Joseph Billups interview with Herbert Hill, Shelton Tappes, and Roberta McBride, October 27, 1967, #3, pp. 2–5 [Tappes speaking].

58. Carl Shier interview with John Herling, February 23, 1980, pp. 20–22; Lichtenstein, "Conflict over Workers' Control," 293–94.

59. Meier and Rudwick, *Black Detroit*, 134, 208, 212.

60. Ibid., 53, 73–76, 77–78.

61. Ibid., 65–66; Hodges Mason interview with Herbert Hill, November 28, 1967, p. 27; Shelton Tappes interview with Herbert Hill, #1, Pt. 2, October 27, 1967, pp. 55–56.

62. UAW, *Proceedings of the Eighth Constitutional Convention* [1943], 373; Shelton Tappes interview with Herbert Hill, #1, Pt. 2, October 27, 1967, pp. 62–66; Jack Stieber, *Governing the UAW* (New York: Wiley, 1962), 41–45; Lichtenstein, *Most Dangerous Man*, 210–11.

63. *Detroit News*, October 10, 1943; *United Automobile Worker*, October 15, 1943; Shelton Tappes interview with Herbert Hill, #1, Pt. 2, October 27, 1967, pp. 67–68; Brendan Sexton interview with John Herling, February 24, 1979, p. 21; Meier and Rudwick, *Black Detroit*, 208–12.

64. Meier and Rudwick, *Black Detroit*, 212–13; George W. Crockett, Jr., interview with Herbert Hill and Roberta McBride, March 2, 1968, pp. 18–31; UAW, *Proceedings of the Tenth Constitutional Convention* [1946], 103–17; Lichtenstein,

Most Dangerous Man, 207–11; William B. Gould, *Black Workers in White Unions: Job Discrimination in the United States* (Ithaca: Cornell University Press, 1977), 371.

65. Meier and Rudwick, *Black Detroit,* 213–15.

66. Ibid., 136–37, 147–56; Karen T. Anderson, "Last Hired, First Fired: Black Women Workers during World War II," *Journal of American History,* LXIX, No. 1 (June 1982), 84–87; Fine, *"Expanding the Frontiers,"* 13.

67. Nancy F. Gabin, *Feminism in the Labor Movement: Women and the United Auto Workers, 1935–1975* (Ithaca: Cornell University Press, 1990), 78–79; Shelton Tappes interview with Herbert Hill, #1, Pt. 2, October 27, 1963, pp. 79–81.

68. Gabin, *Feminism in the Labor Movement,* 79, 88–89; Hodges Mason interview with Roberta McBride, February 2, 1968, pp. 3–7; Meier and Rudwick, *Black Detroit,* 162–63; Frank Marquart interview with Herbert Hill, July 24, 1968, pp. 14–15; Jess Ferrazza interview with Jack W. Skeels, May 26, 1961, pp. 181–82; *UAW Solidarity* March 1975.

69. Gabin, *Feminism in the Labor Movement,* 89–90, 140.

70. Ibid., 47–48; Ruth Milkman, *Gender at Work: The Dynamics of Job Segregation by Sex during World War II* (Urbana: University of Illinois Press, 1987), 53–54; Lichtenstein, "Conflict over Workers' Control," 292–93.

71. Glaberman, *Wartime Strikes,* 23; Lichtenstein, "Conflict over Workers' Control," 292–93.

72. Gabin, *Feminism in the Labor Movement,* 57, 59; Milkman, *Gender at Work,* 50.

73. Milkman, *Gender at Work,* 56–58.

74. Gabin, *Feminism in the Labor Movement,* 63, 65–69; Milkman, *Gender at Work,* 74–77; Ruth Milkman, "Rosie the Riveter Revisited: Management's Postwar Purge of Women Automobile Workers," in Nelson Lichtenstein and Stephen Meyer, eds., *On the Line: Essays in the History of Auto Work* (Urbana: University of Illinois Press, 1989), 136; Philip S. Foner, *Women and the American Labor Movement from World War I to the Present* (New York: Free Press, 1980), 354–56; Lichtenstein, *Most Dangerous Man,* 199–200.

75. Milkman, "Rosie the Riveter Revisited," 140; John Bodnar, "Power and Memory in Oral History: Workers and Managers at Studebaker," *Journal of American History,* LXXV, No. 4 (March 1989), 1211–12.

76. Gabin, *Feminism in the Labor Movement,* 78. For example, Walter Reuther outlined a day care funding program in the *Washington Post,* August 14, 1942; Catherine Gelles interview with Jack W. Skeels, July 7, 1961, p. 18; Foner, *Women and the Labor Movement,* 379–80.

77. Douglas Fraser interview with John Barnard, May–June, 1990, p. 47; Gabin, *Feminism in the Labor Movement,* 86–87; Milkman, *Gender at Work,* 89–96.

78. Mildred Jeffrey interview with Ruth Meyerowitz, August 13, 1976.

79. Gabin, *Feminism in the Labor Movement,* 95, 112–13; Walter P. Reuther to Alan Cranston, July 25, 1969, Walter P. Reuther Collection, Box 409, f. 4; Milkman, *Gender at Work,* 101–2.

80. *United Automobile Worker,* October 1945; Gabin, 114–15.

81. Mildred Jeffrey interview with Ruth Meyerowitz, August 13, 1976, pp.

63–64; Milkman, *Gender at Work*, 104–18, 130–44; Gabin, *Feminism in the Labor Movement*, 118–33; Milkman, "Rosie the Riveter Revisited," 129–52.

82. CIO, *Proceedings of the Seventh Constitutional Convention* [1944], 274; The Challenge of Peace, speech by Walter P. Reuther, March 16, 1944, copy in Walter P. Reuther Papers, Box 540, f. 14.

83. Walter P. Reuther, *Are War Plants Expendable? A Program for the Conversion of Government-Owned Plants to the Mass Production of Modern Railroad Equipment and Low-Cost Housing* (Ypsilanti, MI: Willow Run Local 50, UAW-CIO, 1945); *Detroit News*, May 10, 15, 1945; *Detroit Free Press*, May 22, 1945.

84. Alan Brinkley, *The End of Reform: New Deal Liberalism in Recession and War* (New York: Knopf, 1995), 201–26; Lichtenstein, "Conflict over Workers' Control," 304.

Chapter 7

"Teamwork in the leadership and solidarity in the ranks": The Reuther forces' battle cry in the postwar UAW internal struggle. See, for example, Walter P. Reuther, "Report to the Membership," September 1947.

1. William E. Leuchtenberg, *Franklin D. Roosevelt and the New Deal, 1932–1940* (New York: Harper & Row, 1963), 231–74; James MacGregor Burns, *Roosevelt: The Lion and the Fox* (New York: Harcourt, Brace, 1956), 291–380. A wide-ranging work on postwar America is James T. Patterson, *Grand Expectations: The United States, 1945–1974* (New York: Oxford University Press, 1996).

2. Reuther quoted in *New York Times*, December 30, 1945; Martin Halpern, *UAW Politics in the Cold War Era* (Albany: State University of New York Press, 1988), 37–49.

3. For analyses of labor's postwar political situation, see Nelson Lichtenstein, "Labor in the Truman Era: Origins of the Private Welfare State," in Michael Lacey, ed., *The Truman Presidency* (Cambridge: Woodrow Wilson International Center for Scholars and Cambridge University Press, 1989), 128–55; John Barnard, "Workers, the Labor Movement, and the Cold War, 1945–1960," in Robert H. Bremner and Gary W. Reichard, eds., *Reshaping America: Society and Institutions, 1945–1960* (Columbus: Ohio State University Press, 1982), 115–45; James C. Foster, *The Union Politic: The CIO Political Action Committee* (Columbia: University of Missouri Press, 1975), 54–56, 62–70.

4. Arthur M. Schlesinger, Jr., *The Vital Center: The Politics of Freedom* (Boston: Houghton Mifflin, 1949); *United Automobile Worker*, August 15, 1945.

5. John B. Rae, *The American Automobile Industry* (Boston: Twayne, 1984), 99–115; Halpern, *UAW Politics*, 7–11; Franklin D. Roosevelt, "Annual Message to the Congress," January 6, 1941, in *The Public Papers and Addresses of Franklin D. Roosevelt* (New York: Macmillan, 1941), IX, 672; on the political stalemate, see Patterson, *Grand Expectations*, 55–60.

6. For accounts of Reuther's early life, see John Barnard, *Walter Reuther and the Rise of the Auto Workers* (Boston: Little, Brown, 1983), 1–90; Nelson Lichtenstein, *The Most Dangerous Man in Detroit: Walter Reuther and the Fate of American Labor*

(New York: Basic Books, 1995), 1–219; Victor G. Reuther, *The Brothers Reuther and the Story of the UAW: A Memoir* (Boston: Houghton Mifflin, 1976), 1–245; Frank Cormier and William J. Eaton, *Reuther* (Englewood Cliffs, NJ: Prentice-Hall, 1970), 1–217; Nat Ganley interview with Jack W. Skeels, April 16, 1960, pp. 33–34.

7. Kevin Boyle, *The UAW and the Heyday of American Liberalism, 1945–1968* (Ithaca: Cornell University Press, 1995), 39–44.

8. An older brother, Ted, and a younger sister, Christine, constituted the rest of the Reuther siblings. Neither was active in the labor movement. Elizabeth Reuther Dickmeyer, *Reuther: A Daughter Strikes* (Southfield, MI: Spelman Publishers, 1989), 37, 218; *United Automobile Worker*, September 1954; Boyle, *UAW and the Heyday*, 22–27.

9. *United Automobile Worker*, August 1945; Lichtenstein, *Most Dangerous Man*, 134; Edward Levinson, *Labor on the March* (New York: Harper & Brothers, 1938).

10. Lichtenstein, *Most Dangerous Man*, 222–24; Boyle, *UAW and the Heyday*, 40–44.

11. Frank Marquart, *An Auto Worker's Journal: The UAW from Crusade to One-Party Union* (University Park: Pennsylvania State University Press, 1975), 98; Halpern, *UAW Politics*, 121–31.

12. *New York Times*, September 17, 1945; Howell J. Harris, *The Right to Manage: Industrial Relations Policies of American Business in the 1940s* (Madison: University of Wisconsin Press, 1982); Elizabeth A. Fones-Wolf, *Selling Free Enterprise: The Business Assault on Labor and Liberalism, 1945–1960* (Urbana: University of Illinois Press, 1994); Robert H. Zieger and Gilbert J. Gall, *American Workers, American Unions: The Twentieth Century*, 3d ed.(Baltimore: Johns Hopkins University Press, 2002), 148–49.

13. An early version of Reuther's wage-price proposal, prepared for presentation to the UAW's executive board, is contained in "A Wage and Price Program for Reconversion," May 24, 1945 (mimeo), copy in Walter P. Reuther Collection, Box 12, f. 7; Reuther also submitted a pamphlet, *How to Raise Wages without Increasing Prices*, 32 pp., to the Office of War Mobilization and Reconversion and other government agencies in June 1945. Other material is in Walter P. Reuther Collection, Box 21, ff. 6–9; Walter P. Reuther to Charles E. Wilson, August 18, 1945, reprinted in *New York Times*, September 16, 1945. See also *United Automobile Worker*, September 1, 1945; *Purchasing Power for Prosperity: The Case of the General Motors Workers for Maintaining Take-Home Pay* (Detroit: International Union, UAW-CIO, GM Department, October 1945); this seventy-plus page pamphlet, the most detailed statement of the union's economic case, was prepared by Donald E. Montgomery; Barton J. Bernstein, "Walter Reuther and the General Motors Strike of 1945–1946," *Michigan History*, 49 (1965), 260–77; Lichtenstein, *Most Dangerous Man*, 220–47; Halpern, *UAW Politics*, 51–55, 61. The historian quoted is Robert H. Zieger, *The CIO, 1935–1955* (Chapel Hill: University of North Carolina Press, 1995), 219–22.

14. Walter P. Reuther, "Our Fear of Abundance," *New York Times Magazine*, September 16, 1945; reprinted in Henry P. Christman, ed., *Walter P. Reuther:*

Selected Papers (New York: Macmillan, 1961), 13–21; *New York Times*, October 27, 1945; *Nation*, December 1, 1945; *New Republic*, December 31, 1945; Lichtenstein, *Most Dangerous Man*, 220–24.

15. "Transcript of Negotiations between General Motors and UAW," pp. 185–90; *New York Times*, October 21, 29, 1945; *Detroit News*, October 28, 1945.

16. *New York Times*, October 20, 1945; General Motors Vice President H. W. Anderson, quoted in *United Automobile Worker*, November 1945; *Detroit News*, October 20, December 30, 1945; General Motors press release, December 30, 1945; *The Wage Earner*, October 26, 1945, quoted in Irving Howe and B. J. Widick, *The UAW and Walter Reuther* (New York: Da Capo Press, 1973; orig. pub., 1949), 147.

17. *Business Week* quoted in *New York Times*, December 2, 1945; Halpern, *UAW Politics*, 56–60.

18. *New York Times*, September 23, 25, October 26, November 4, 20, 21, 22, 1945; negotiations in the General Motors and Ford strikes were covered in the *United Automobile Worker*, November 1945–April 1946; interview with Victor Reuther quoted in Nelson Lichtenstein, "Conflict over Workers' Control: The Automobile Industry in World War II," in Michael H. Frisch and Daniel J. Walkowitz, eds., *Working-Class America: Essays on Labor, Community, and American Society* (Urbana: University of Illinois Press, 1983), 303.

19. Halpern, *UAW Politics*, 63–64.

20. "Report of the National Citizens Committee, December 1945," Walter P. Reuther Collection, Box 24, f. 2; Walter P. Reuther to "All GM Local Unions," November 29, 1945, Walter P. Reuther Collection, Box 21, f. 7.

21. Lewis as quoted in *New York Times*, December 11, 1945.

22. *New York Times*, December 21, 22, 1945; "General Motors Statement before the Fact-Finding Board, January 21, 1946," copy in General Motors Corporation, Vertical File, Archives of Labor and Urban Affairs; Halpern, *UAW Politics*, 68–69.

23. *Detroit News*, January 10, 12, 1946; Cormier and Eaton, *Reuther*, 226; Halpern, *UAW Politics*, 71–72.

24. David L. Lewis, *The Public Image of Henry Ford: An American Folk Hero and His Company* (Detroit: Wayne State University Press, 1976), 433–34; *Wage Earner*, February 15, 1946; Lichtenstein, *Most Dangerous Man*, 242–43; Cormier and Eaton, *Reuther*, 227–29; Halpern, *UAW Politics*, 75–77, 79–81.

25. *United Automobile Worker*, January–March, 1946; *Detroit News*, March 13, 14, 1946; Lichtenstein, *Most Dangerous Man*, 243–46; Walter P. Reuther, "The United Automobile Workers: Past, Present, Future," *Virginia Law Review*, 50, No. 1 (1964), 86; Halpern, *UAW Politics*, 87–89.

26. Bernstein, "Walter Reuther," 276–77; Boyle, *UAW and the Heyday*, 31; Anthony Carew, *Walter Reuther* (Manchester: University of Manchester Press, 1993), 45–49; Lichtenstein, "Labor in the Truman Era," 138–40; Halpern, *UAW Politics*, 89–92.

27. Lichtenstein, *Most Dangerous Man*, 246; Laurence J. White, *The Automobile Industry since 1945* (Cambridge, MA: Harvard University Press, 1971), 251.

28. Howe and Widick, *UAW and Reuther*, 155–60; Halpern, *UAW Politics*, 92–93.

29. There is no biography of Thomas. See John Barnard, "Roland Jay Thomas," in George S. May, ed., *Encyclopedia of American Business History and Biography: The Automobile Industry, 1920–1980* (New York: Facts on File, 1989), 439–50; *Detroit Free Press*, June 20, 1946; "Memorandum on R. J. Thomas" [1946], Walter P. Reuther Collection, Box 5, f. 8; Louis Seaton interview with Frank Cormier and William J. Eaton, June 20, 1968, p. 4.

30. James M. Cleveland interview with Jack W. Skeels, October 3, 1961, p. 21; Paul Weber in *Wage Earner*, March 29, 1946; *Ternstedt Flash*, 1937, quoted in Francis Danowski, president, Local 51, "The State of the Union" [1946], copy in Walter P. Reuther Collection, Box 565, f. 1; Bill Dodds interview with John Herling, February 18, 1976, p. 31; Martin Gerber interview with John Herling, March 31, 1980, pp. 23, 28–30; Abe Zwerdling interview with John Herling, November 2, 1977, p. 5.

31. Leonard Woodcock interview with John Barnard, January 18, 30, February 7, 1991, pp. 24–25; George Addes interview with John Herling, October 16, 1978, p. 41; Carl Haessler interview with Jack W. Skeels, November 27, 1959–October 24, 1960, p. 173; *Detroit News*, March 10, 1946; *New York Times*, March 6, 10, 12, 15, 1946; Clayton Fountain, *Union Guy* (New York: Viking Press, 1949), 187–89; Halpern, *UAW Politics*, 85.

32. UAW, *Proceedings of the Tenth Constitutional Convention* [1946], 101, 282–83; Leonard Woodcock interview with John Herling, June 20, 1982, pp. 91–93; Fountain, *Union Guy*, 193; *United Automobile Worker*, April 1946; Bill Goode, *Infighting in the UAW: The 1946 Election and the Ascendency of Walter Reuther* (Westport, CT: Greenwood Press, 1994), 83; Halpern, *UAW Politics*, 95–97.

33. Brendan Sexton interview with John Herling, August 1, 1978, pp. 33–34; Bill Dodds interview with John Herling, February 18, 1976, p. 13; *New York Times*, March 26–28, 1946; Howe and Widick, *UAW and Reuther*, 159–61.

34. *Detroit News*, March 14, 1946; Cormier and Eaton, *Reuther*, 232–33; Howe and Widick, *UAW and Reuther*, 161–62; Fountain, *Union Guy*, 194–96; Keeran, *Communist Party*, 256; Goode, *Infighting in the UAW*, 83–85; Halpern, *UAW Politics*, 95–106.

35. Douglas Fraser interview with John Herling, January 20, 1983, pp. 28–29; *Michigan Labor Leader*, March 15, May 10, 1940; John W. Anderson interview with Jack W. Skeels, February 17, 1960–May 21, 1960, pp. 114–15; Howe and Widick, *UAW and Reuther*, 152–58; Goode, *Infighting in the UAW*, 84–87. An analysis of the socialist and ACTU components of the Reuther caucus is in Lichtenstein, *Most Dangerous Man*, 186–89.

36. The count given is the corrected official roll call vote. The teller's count, taken when the votes were cast, gave Reuther a slightly higher margin of 124.388. In any event, the vote was close. Shelton Tappes interview with Herbert Hill, #1, Pt. 2, October 27, 1967, p. 49; Jack Palmer interview with Jack W. Skeels, July 23, 1960, p. 40; Leonard Woodcock interview with John Barnard, January 18, 30, February 7, 1991, pp. 20–21; UAW, *Proceedings of the Tenth Constitutional Convention* [1946], 225, 336–463; *Detroit News*, March 28, 1946; Halpern, *UAW Politics*, 106; Goode, *Infighting in the UAW*, 87–88. Major GM locals that supported Reuther:

15. Fleetwood, Detroit
22. Cadillac, Detroit
235. Chevrolet Gear and Axle, Detroit
424. Fisher Body, Buffalo
434. Saginaw Steering Gear, Saginaw
594. Yellow Truck and Coach, Pontiac
595. Assembly, Linden, New Jersey
596. Fisher Body, Pontiac
626. New Departure, New Jersey
651. AC Spark Plug, Flint
652. Olds, Lansing
662. Delco-Remy, Anderson, Indiana
674. Assembly, Norwood, Ohio
719. Electro-Motive, LaGrange, Illinois
731. Fisher Body, Trenton, New Jersey
774. Chevrolet Gear, Buffalo

Major GM locals that split their vote with an edge to Thomas:
599. Buick, Flint
659. Chevrolet, Flint

Major GM locals that supported Thomas:
45. Fisher Body, Cleveland
686. Harrison Radiator, New York
933. Allison, Indianapolis, Indiana

37. The following is a breakdown of the vote by region and regional director.

Region	Vote to Reuther (%)	Regional director prior to election	Director's affiliation
1 Detroit (east)	51	Matthews/Bishop	Split
1A Detroit (west)	49.5	Leonard/Llewellyn	ATL
1B Pontiac	78.8	McAulay	ATL
1C E. Michigan	56.6	Swanson	ATL
1D W. Michigan	61.1	Forbes	R
2 Cleveland	23.5	Miley	ATL
2A Cleveland	6.3	Reisinger	ATL
2B Toledo	84.1	Gosser	R
3 Indiana	39.4	Atwood	ATL
4 Illinois/Wisconsin	40.3	Mattson	ATL
5 Southwest	53.5	Livingston	R
6 California	23.4	O'Halloran	ATL
7 Canada	35.8	Burt	ATL
8 Southeast	64.4	Starling	R
9 Northeast	78.0	Gerber	R
9A Northeast	50.2	Kerrigan	ATL

Source: Goode, *Infighting in the UAW*, 89.

38. *New York Times*, March 29–30, 1946; Halpern, *UAW Politics*, 108–111; Howe and Widick, *UAW and Reuther*, 162; Bert Cochran, *Labor and Communism: The Conflict that Shaped American Unions* (Princeton: Princeton University Press, 1977), 255–59.

39. Reuther, "United Automobile Workers: Past, Present, Future," 259; Jack Conway interview with John Herling, May 25, 1978; July 15, 1979, pp. 38–39; Nat Weinberg interview with John Herling, November 3, 1977, p. 5; *United Automobile Worker*, May 1946; *New York Times*, April 19–20, 1946; Carew, *Reuther*, 51–52; Halpern, *UAW Politics*, 113–19; Jack Stieber, *Governing the UAW* (New York: John Wiley and Sons, 1962), 112–13.

40. Leonard Woodcock interview with Jack W. Skeels, April 30, 1963, passim; Leonard Woodcock interview with John Barnard, January 18, 30, February 7, 1991, passim.

41. Jack W. Conway interview with John Herling, May 25, 1978; July 15, 1979, pp. 1–10.

42. Jack Conway interview with Jack W. Skeels, March 27, 1963, pp. 20–21; an analysis of the UAW's political structure at this time is in Halpern, *UAW Politics*, 121–22.

43. Walter P. Reuther to "All Local Unions, UAW-CIO," January 25, 1947, February 13, 1947, Walter P. Reuther Collection, Box 36, f. 13, Box 86, f. 10; UAW, International Executive Board, Minutes, March 17–26, 1947, pp. 159–61; Halpern, *UAW Politics*, 142, 173–83, 225; *Wage Earner*, May 2, 1947; Goode, *Infighting in the UAW*, 93–101; Cochran, *Labor and Communism*, 263–65, 272–75; Stephen Meyer, *"Stalin over Wisconsin": The Making and Unmaking of Militant Unionism, 1900–1950* (New Brunswick: Rutgers University Press, 1992), 186–99; Howe and Widick, *UAW and Reuther*, 165–66.

44. Carl Haessler interview with Jack W. Skeels, November 27, 1959–October 24, 1960, pp. 199–200; Roger Keeran, *The Communist Party and the Auto Workers Unions* (Bloomington: Indiana University Press, 1980), 281; Irving Richter, *Labor's Struggles: A Participant's View of 1945–1947* (New York: Cambridge University Press, 1994), 88, n. 24; Committee for UAW-CIO Progress and Unity, "To the Editors of All UAW-CIO Local Papers (Suggestions for Editorial)"; Walter Reuther, press release October 12, 1947, Walter P. Reuther Collection, Box 542, f. 10; George F. Addes to local unions, September 24, 1947, Walter P. Reuther Collection, Box 81, f. 1; Walter P. Reuther to George F. Addes, October 6, 1947, Walter P. Reuther Collection, Box 81, f. 2; Walter P. Reuther press release, October 10, 1947, Walter P. Reuther Collection, Box 64, f. 7; Halpern, *UAW Politics*, 198–99; *United Automobile Worker*, September 1947; Goode, *Infighting in the UAW*, 106–110, 116–21.

45. *United Automobile Worker*, May 1946; International Executive Board, Minutes, March 17–26, 1947, p. 161; Walter P. Reuther to Richard T. Leonard, March 14, 1947, Walter P. Reuther Collection, Box 83, f. 9; Richter, *Labor's Struggles*, 140; Walter P. Reuther to all members of the International Executive Board, April 11, 1947, Walter P. Reuther Collection, Box 579, f. 2.

46. *Chicago Daily News*, April 18, 1946; Walter P. Reuther, "Report to the Membership," September 1947; *United Automobile Worker*, September, October

1947; *New York Times*, April 23, 25, 28, 1946; *Wage Earner*, September 19, 1947; Goode, *Infighting in the UAW*, 112–15.

47. Brendan Sexton interview with John Herling, August 11, 1978, p. 40; Jack Conway interview with John Herling, May 25, 1978, July 15, 1979, pp. 1–2; Kenneth (Ken) Bannon interview with Warner Pflug, April 30, 1985, p. 10; Frank Winn interview with John Herling, October 22, 1983, pp. 4–7.

48. *Automobile Unionism, 1939–40, Report of President R. J. Thomas*, July 29, 1940, p. 46; *Automobile Unionism, 1940–41, Report of President R. J. Thomas*, August 4, 1941, p. 51; Nat Ganley interview with Jack W. Skeels, April 16, 1960, p. 34; Robert Ozanne, *A Century of Labor-Management Relations at McCormick and International Harvester* (Madison: University of Wisconsin Press, 1967), 196, 207, 209; Goode, *Infighting in the UAW*, 101–4; Fountain, *Union Guy*, 205–7; Halpern, *UAW Politics*, 205–6.

49. John Livingston interview with William J. Eaton, February 13, 1969, p. 4; Jack Conway interview with Frank Cormier and William J. Eaton, October 2, 1967, p. 13; Jack Conway interview with John Herling, May 25, 1978; July 15, 1979, pp. 43–44; *Detroit Free Press*, July 12, 1947; Fountain, *Union Guy*, 205–7; Walter P. Reuther to all local unions, June 23, 30, 1947, Walter P. Reuther Collection, Box 80, f. 12, Box 93, f. 13; Leonard Woodcock interview with John Herling, June 21, October 1, 1982, pp. 102–3; *United Automobile Worker*, August 1947; Cochran, *Labor and Communism*, 275–79.

50. *Detroit News*, March 8, 1947; Russell Leach interview with John Herling, December 5, 1978, pp. 34–40; Halpern, *UAW Politics*, 240–41.

51. *United Automobile Worker*, May 1947; Halpern, *UAW Politics*, 201–3; Keeran, *Communist Party*, 272–80; Richter, *Labor's Struggles*, 72; Meyer, *"Stalin over Wisconsin,"* 199–207; Lichtenstein, *Most Dangerous Man*, 260–66; Nelson Lichtenstein, "From Corporatism to Collective Bargaining: Organized Labor and the Eclipse of Social Democracy in the Postwar Era," in Steve Fraser and Gary Gerstle, eds., *The Rise and Fall of the New Deal Order, 1930–1980* (Princeton: Princeton University Press, 1989), 133–34; Fred A. Hartley, *Our New National Labor Policy: The Taft-Hartley Act and the Next Step* (New York: Funk & Wagnalls, 1948), 39–40; Ellen Schrecker, *Many Are the Crimes: McCarthyism in America* (Boston: Little, Brown, 1998), 184–87.

52. *United Automobile Worker*, December 1947; Melvyn Dubofsky, *The State and Labor in Modern America* (Chapel Hill: University of North Carolina Press, 1994), 201–8; Christopher L. Tomlins, *The State and the Unions: Labor Relations, Law, and the Organized Labor Movement in America, 1880–1960* (Cambridge: Cambridge University Press, 1985), 247–316; American Communication Association *v.* Douds, 339 U.S. 94 (1950); United States *v.* Brown, 381 U.S. 437 (1965).

53. UAW, International Executive Board, Minutes, September 8–12, 1947, pp. 173 ff.; UAW, *Proceedings of the Eleventh Constitutional Convention* [1947], 76–110; *United Automobile Worker*, November, December 1947; *Detroit News*, November 15, 1947; Halpern, *UAW Politics*, 207–9, 229; Goode, *Infighting in the UAW*, 104–6.

54. *New York Times*, September 28, 1946; Halpern, *UAW Politics*, 208–9; Foster, *Union Politic*, 64–69; David Caute, *The Great Fear: The Anti-Communist Purge under Truman and Eisenhower* (New York: Simon and Schuster, 1978).

55. UAW, *Proceedings of the Eleventh Constitutional Convention* [1947], 13, 17; *Detroit News*, November 9–15, 1947; Halpern, *UAW Politics*, 223–35.

56. George F. Addes interview with Jack W. Skeels, June 25, 1960, p. 39; *United Automobile Worker*, December 1947; UAW, *Proceedings of the Eleventh Constitutional Convention* [1947], 135; Halpern, *UAW Politics*, 231.

57. Boyle, *UAW and the Heyday*, 33; Halpern, *UAW Politics*, 231; Lichtenstein, *Most Dangerous Man*, 186–87.

58. Halpern, *UAW Politics*, 231–35. The following is a list of members of the International Executive Board after the 1947 UAW convention, with office or region and year of first election to the board. An asterisk (*) indicates a supporter of the Reuther caucus.

Walter Reuther*	President	1936
Paul Miley	2A (Ohio)	1937
Richard Reisinger	2 (Ohio)	1937
George Burt	7 (Canada)	1939
William McAulay*	1B (Pontiac, Michigan)	1939
Thomas Starling*	8 (Southeast)	1941
Charles Kerrigan*	9A (Northeast)	1941
Richard Gosser*	Vice President	1942
John Livingston*	Vice President	1942
Martin Gerber*	9 (New York, New Jersey)	1944
Norman Matthews*	1 (East Detroit)	1944
Cyril V. O'Halloran	6 (West Coast)	1944
Emil Mazey*	Secretary-Treasurer	1946
Mike Lacy*	1 (East Detroit)	1947
Edward J. Cote*	1A (West Detroit)	1947
Joseph McCusker*	1A (West Detroit)	1947
Donnel Chapman*	1C (Flint)	1947
Leonard Woodcock*	1D (Western Michigan)	1947
Charles Ballard*	2B (Ohio)	1947
Raymond H. Berndt*	3 (Indiana)	1947
Pat Greathouse*	4 (Wisconsin, Illinois)	1947
Russell Letner*	5 (Missouri, Southwest)	1947

59. UAW, *Proceedings of the Eleventh Constitutional Convention* [1947], 129–36, 174–75, 202; *Detroit Free Press*, November 15, 1947; Schlesinger, *Vital Center*, 148, 187; Halpern, *UAW Politics*, 265–70.

60. UAW, *Proceedings of the Eleventh Constitutional Convention* [1947], 203–4, 205; *United Automobile Worker*, December 1947.

61. *Detroit News*, November 13, 1947; Cochran, *Labor and Communism*, 263; George Addes interview with John Herling, October 16, 1978, p. 53; Halpern, 237–38; untitled paper on how to deal with Reuther, May 23, 1946, Maurice Sugar

Collection, Box 1, f. 24; Christopher H. Johnson, *Maurice Sugar: Law, Labor and the Left in Detroit, 1912–1950* (Detroit: Wayne State University Press, 1988), 290–91, 296–98.

62. Jack Conway interview with John Herling, May 25, 1978, pp. 5–6, July 15, 1979, pp. 12–13; Nat Weinberg interview with John Herling, November 3, 1977, p. 10; George Burt interview with John Herling, April 17, 1979, pp. 38–39; Martin Gerber interview with John Herling, March 31, 1980, p. 38; Irving Bluestone interview with John Herling, March 28, 1978, p. 37; Ken Morris interview with John Barnard, December 17, 1996, pp. 74–75; Victor Reuther in Judith Stepan-Norris and Maurice Zeitlin, *Talking Union* (Urbana: University of Illinois Press, 1996), 191; Victor Reuther quoted in Seth M. Wigderson, "The UAW in the 1950's" (Ph.D. diss., Wayne State University, 1989), 332; Boyle, *UAW and the Heyday*, 39–44; Keeran, *Communist Party*, 283–85; Halpern, *UAW Politics*, 237–38; Cormier and Eaton, *Reuther*, 252.

63. Marquart, *Auto Worker's Journal*, 132; Ethel Polk interview with John Herling, September 5, 1978, p. 28; William Kemsley to Walter P. Reuther, January 6, 1948, Walter P. Reuther Collection, Box 60, f. 2.

64. *United Automobile Worker*, December 1947; Boyle, *UAW and the Heyday*, 40–41; Lichtenstein, *Most Dangerous Man*, 222–24.

65. Shelton Tappes interview with Herbert Hill and Roberta McBride, February 10, 1968, #2, pp. 1–8; Stepan-Norris and Zeitlin, *Talking Union*, 75, 146–47, 190; Boyle, *UAW and the Heyday*, 43.

66. Shelton Tappes interview with Herbert Hill and Roberta McBride, February 10, 1968, #2, pp. 22–24; Wigderson, "UAW in the 1950's," 319–20, 335–40; Boyle, *UAW and the Heyday*, 44–45.

67. Maurice Isserman, *If I Had a Hammer: The Death of the Old Left and the Birth of the New Left* (Urbana: University of Illinois Press, 1987), 6–7; UAW, *Proceedings of the Twelfth Constitutional Convention* [1949], 70–82; Zieger, *CIO*, 253–93; Barnard, "Workers, the Labor Movement, and the Cold War," 128–35; Steve Rosswurm, ed., *The CIO's Left-Led Unions* (New Brunswick: Rutgers University Press, 1992), 2.

68. *New York Times*, March 20, 25, April 2, August 5, October 7, December 11, 1948, October 21, 1949; Harvey A. Levenstein, *Communism, Anticommunism, and the CIO* (Westport, CT: Greenwood Press, 1981), 269–71; Larry Carlstrom interview with John Barnard, March 7, 1997, p. 32; Zieger, *CIO*, 280–81.

69. *Report of Walter P. Reuther. . . . 1949*, pp. 108, 109–110; *United Automobile Worker*. May, June 1948; Fountain, *Union Guy*, 220–23; Larry Carlstrom interview with John Barnard, March 7, 1997, pp. 33–35; Zieger, *CIO*, 280; Levenstein, *Communism*, 271.

70. UAW, *Proceedings of the Twelfth Constitutional Convention* [1949], 85 ff.; CIO, International Executive Board, Minutes, November 17, 20, 27, 1948, pp. 79, 318–29, May 18, 1949; *United Automobile Worker*, August 1948, February–December 1949, February 1950, September 1953, June 1954, January–May 1955; *New York Times*, November 28, 1948, February 11, November 3, 1949; Pat Greathouse interview with Jack Skeels, May 14, 1963, pp. 16–19, 25; *Report of Walter P. Reuther. . . . 1955*, 13–D—14–D; *Report of Walter P. Reuther. . . . 1957*, 19–D—

24–D; Zieger, *CIO*, 250, 289–90; Lichtenstein, *Most Dangerous Man,* 310, 325; Rosswurm, ed., *CIO's Left-Led Unions*, 2; F. S. O'Brien, "Communist Dominated Unions," *Labor History*, IX, No. 2 (Spring 1968), 184–209; Mary S. McAuliffe, *Crisis on the Left: Cold War Politics and American Liberals, 1947–1954* (Amherst: University of Massachusetts Press, 1978), 53–54; Ozanne,*Century of Labor-Management Relations*, 216–21.

71. *Report of Walter P. Reuther. . . . 1951*, 159–63; *Report of Walter P. Reuther. . . . 1953*, 128–32; *Report of Walter P. Reuther. . . . 1957*, 19–D—24–D; *Report of Walter P. Reuther. . . . 1959*, 19–D—26–D; *Report of Walter P. Reuther. . . . 1962*, 26–34; Ozanne, *Century of Labor-Management Relations*, 221–24, 228–35.

72. *New York Times*, July 10, August 14, October 8, 1950, January 15, March 17, April 16, 1951; Stepan-Norris and Zeitlin, *Talking Union*, 19–20, 20–25; Nelson Lichtenstein, "Life at the Rouge: A Cycle of Workers' Control," in Charles Stephenson and Robert Asher, eds., *Life and Labor: Dimensions of American Working-Class History* (Albany: State University of New York Press, 1986), 255–57; Wigderson, "UAW in the 1950's," 367–72.

73. *United Automobile Worker*, August 1950; *New York Times*, August 6, 1950, March 12, 13, 14, 15, 1952, February 28, March 1, 25, May 13, 15, June 26, 1954; Resolution on HUAC, February 19, 1952, copy in Walter P. Reuther Collection, Box 249, f. 23; Stepan-Norris and Zeitlin, *Talking Union*, 202–3, 206–7. Signers of the Communist Party backed Stockholm peace petition were attacked at the Milwaukee plant of Seaman Body. James T. Selcraig, *The Red Scare in the Midwest, 1945–1955: A State and Local Study* (Ann Arbor: UMI Research Press, 1982), 89; Boyle, *UAW and the Heyday*, 73; B. J. Widick, *Detroit: City of Race and Class Violence*, rev. ed. (Detroit: Wayne State University Press, 1989), 130–34; Wigderson, "UAW in the 1950's," 133–34, 364–66, 424–27; *Detroit News*, March 4, 1952.

74. Walter P. Reuther and Emil Mazey to Executive Board, Local 595, Linden, New Jersey, Walter P. Reuther Collection, Box 248, f. 41; Walter P. Reuther to Local 200, Windsor, Ontario, Walter P. Reuther Collection, Box 236, f. 28; Halpern, *UAW Politics*, 262–63.

75. Lichtenstein, *Most Dangerous Man*, 313–19; Widick, *Detroit*, 127–36; *United Automobile Worker*, March–April, 1952; *Detroit News*, February 25–March 11, 18, 1952; Walter Goodman, *The Committee* (New York: Farrar, Straus and Giroux, 1968), 317–18; UAW, International Executive Board, Minutes, March 12, 1952, pp. 26–49, Minutes, March 14, 1952, pp. 8, 18–19, 29 ff.; UAW press release, March 15, 1952, Walter P. Reuther Collection, Box 249, f. 24; *Detroit Free Press*, March 18, 1952; *Detroit Times*, March 18, 1952; files on the expelled officers in Walter P. Reuther Collection, Box 278, ff. 2–3; William D. Andrew, "Factionalism and Anti-Communism: Ford Local 600," *Labor History*, XX, No. 2 (Spring 1979), 227–55; Stepan-Norris and Zeitlin, *Talking Union*, 19–20, 216. Walter P. Reuther, "The United Automobile Workers: Past, Present, Future," *Virginia Law Review*, 50, No. 1 (1964), 92–98; Reuther summarized his case against Local 600 in *Report of Walter P. Reuther. . . . 1953*, 100–104. Kenneth (Ken) Bannon interview with Warner Pflug, April 30, 1985, p. 42. A recent work, Judith Stepan-Norris and Maurice

Zeitlin, *Left Out: Reds and America's Industrial Unions* (Cambridge: Cambridge University Press, 2003), contains, among much else, a study of the controversy between Reuther and Local 600. See pp. 95–120, 272–73. The analysis marshals evidence critical of Reuther's actions.

76. UAW, International Executive Board, Minutes, May 3, 1954, pp. 67–77; "Statement by UAW-CIO on House Committee on Un-American Activities," Walter P. Reuther Collection, Box 579, f. 8; *New York Times*, April 30, 1954, May 28, 1955; Ralph S. Brown, Jr., *Loyalty and Security: Employment Tests in the United States* (New Haven: Yale University Press, 1958), 138–39.

77. *New York Times*, January 27, February 21, April 24, June 6, 18, 1957; Watkins *v.* U.S., 354 U.S. 178 (1957); Reuther, "The United Automobile Workers: Past, Present, Future," 93–96; Joseph Rauh, Jr., interview with John Herling, November 12, 1979, pp. 39–42.

78. Walter P. Reuther, "How to Beat the Communists," *Collier's*, February 28, 1948, pp. 11, 44, reprinted in Christman, ed., *Walter P. Reuther*, 22–35; Zieger, *CIO*, 260–61.

79. Reuther, "How to Beat the Communists," p. 44; UAW, *Report of the President . . . November 9, 1947*, Part 1, p. 44; David M. Oshinsky, *Senator Joseph McCarthy and the American Labor Movement* (Columbia: University of Missouri Press, 1976), 104–5.

80. Ken Morris interview with John Barnard, May 27, 1994, p. 11; Jack Conway interview with Jack W. Skeels, March 27, 1963, p. 12; Howe and Widick, *UAW and Reuther*, 235–43; David Gartman, *Auto Slavery: The Labor Process in the American Automobile Industry* (New Brunswick: Rutgers University Press, 1986), 275–77; Nelson Lichtenstein, "Conflict over Workers' Control: The Automobile Industry in World War II," in Michael H. Frisch and Daniel J. Walkowitz, eds., *Working-Class America: Essays on Labor, Community, and American Society* (Urbana: University of Illinois Press, 1983), 302–4.

81. Jack Conway interview with Jack W. Skeels, March 27, 1963, p. 12.

82. Ethel Polk interview with John Herling, September 5, 1978, p. 45; Boyle, *UAW and the Heyday*, 34; Ken Morris interview with John Barnard, May 27, 1994, p. 1; Howe and Widick, *UAW and Reuther*, 238–43; Lichtenstein, "Conflict over Workers' Control," 302–4.

83. Frank Wallick interview with John Herling, September 22, 1980, p. 37.

84. UAW, *Constitution of the International Union*, Article 12, Section 3; Reuther, "The United Automobile Workers: Past, Present, and Future," 89–90.

85. Jack Conway interview with John Herling, May 25, 1978, pp. 39–43; Irving Bluestone interview with John Barnard, October 1988–November 1992, p. 92; Carew, *Reuther*, 73–75; Stieber, *Governing*, 67–73; Tony Connole to Douglas Fraser, June 19, 1968, Douglas Fraser Collection (II), Box 13, folder marked "Personal 1968–1969."

86. Jack Conway interview with John Herling, May 25, 1978, pp. 39–43; Carl Shier interview with John Herling, February 23, 1980, pp. 45–46; UAW, *Proceedings of the Twelfth Constitutional Convention* [1949], 216–25; *New York Times*, July 10–16, 1949; Stieber, *Governing*, 67–68.

87. Bill Dodds interview with John Herling, February 18, 1976, p. 31; Douglas Fraser interview with John Herling, February 21, 1983, pp. 41–42; Nat Weinberg interview with John Herling, November 3, 1977, p. 25.

88. *UAW Solidarity*, Special Edition, January 1960; UAW, *Proceedings of the Fourteenth Constitutional Convention* [1953], 298–99; *United Automobile Worker*, April 1953; Stieber, *Governing*, 31–34.

89. For critical accounts and assessments, see Marquart, *Auto Worker's Journal*, 102–61; Cochran, *Labor and Communism*, 279, 324–30. For the contradictory pressures exerted on unions, see Melvyn Dubofsky, "The Past and Future Contradictions and Challenges of Labor Leadership," *Working USA: The Journal of Labor and Society*, III, No. 5 (January–February 2000), 25–26.

90. Marquart, *Auto Worker's Journal*, 102–6; John Anderson interview with Jack W. Skeels, February 17–May 21, 1960, pp. 175–76; Carl Haessler interview with Jack W. Skeels, November 27, 1959–October 24, 1960, pp. 174–75; Stieber, *Governing*, 54–58, 63–66, 132–39, 141–43; material on the Local 659 case is in Walter P. Reuther Collection, Box 253, ff. 18–32; for a statement of the charges against the local, see Emil Mazey to Dean Eagen, July 18, 1957, Walter P. Reuther Collection, Box 253, f. 18; *United Automobile Worker*, May 1954; the Local 659 History Committee, *We Make Our Own History: The History of UAW Local 659* (n.p., 1993), 45–48.

91. Jack Conway interview with John Herling, May 25, 1978, pp. 39–43; Nat Weinberg interview with John Herling, November 22, 1977, pp. 54–55; Irving Bluestone interview with John Barnard, October 1988–November 1992, p. 92; Stieber, *Governing*, 25, 30–31, 54.

92. Stieber, *Governing*, 54–58, 158–70; Mazey quoted in *UAW Solidarity*, October 1965; Douglas Fraser interview with John Barnard, May–June, 1990, pp. 82–83.

93. Jack Stieber, Walter E. Oberer, and Michael Harrington, *Democracy and Public Review: An Analysis of the UAW Public Review Board* (Santa Barbara: Center for the Study of Democratic Institutions, 1960), 7, 12–22, 51; Leonard Woodcock interview with John Barnard, January 18, 30, February 7, 1991, p. 133; *New York Times*, March 6, 24, April 6, 9, December 27, 1957; Stieber, *Governing*, 77–83.

94. Stieber, *Governing*, 153 ff.; Nat Weinberg interview with John Herling, November 22, 1977, p. 55; Paul Schrade interview with Frank Cormier and William J. Eaton, May 3, 1968, p. 2; Lichtenstein, *Most Dangerous Man*, 308–13; Cochran, *Labor and Communism*, 328–30; Ronald Edsforth, "Affluence, Anti-Communism, and the Transformation of Industrial Unionism among Automobile Workers, 1933–1973," in Ronald Edsforth and Larry Bennett, eds., *Popular Culture and Political Change in Modern America* (Albany: State University of New York Press, 1991), 118–23; Carew, *Reuther*, 74–75; *United Automobile Worker*, May 1962. For Reuther's initial opposition to a cost-of-living escalator, which he falsely branded a communist proposal to defeat its proponents, see Ronald Edsforth, *Class Conflict and Cultural Consensus: The Making of a Mass Consumer Society in Flint, Michigan* (New Brunswick: Rutgers University Press, 1987), 207–9; also, Sol Dollinger and Genora Johnson Dollinger, *Not Automatic: Women and the Left in*

the Forging of the Auto Workers' Union (New York: Monthly Review Press, 2000), 114–20.

95. Billie Sunday Farnum interview with Frank Cormier and William J. Eaton, October 14, 1967, n.p.; Irving Howe and B. J. Widick, *The UAW and Walter Reuther* (New York: Da Capo Press, 1973, orig. published 1949), 16; Stephen Meyer, "Work, Play, and Power: Masculine Culture on the Automotive Shop Floor, 1930–1960," in Roger Horowitz, ed., *Boys and Their Toys? Masculinity, Technology, and Class in America* (New York: Routledge, 2001), 19–21.

96. *United Automobile Worker,* March 1951, July 1953; Russell Leach interview with John Herling, December 5, 1978, pp. 59–60; Martin Gerber interview with John Herling, March 31, 1980, p. 40.

97. Jack Conway interview with Frank Cormier and William J. Eaton, October 2, 1967, pp. 18–23; Jack Conway interview with John Herling, May 25, 1978, p. 21; *United Automobile Worker,* June 1957.

98. *United Automobile Worker,* June 1946, June 1949; *Detroit News,* April 21, 1948; Ken Morris interview with John Barnard, December 17, 1996, pp. 62–69; Dollinger and Dollinger, *Not Automatic,* 85–97; Dickmeyer, *Reuther: A Daughter Strikes,* 3–12; Victor Reuther, *The Brothers Reuther and the Story of the UAW: A Memoir* (Boston: Houghton Mifflin, 1976), 270–81, 283–303; Widick, *Detroit,* 115–23; Lichtenstein, *Most Dangerous Man,* 271–72.

99. Hoover's statement is the version given by Joseph L. Rauh, Jr., who was associate Washington counsel for the UAW at the time of Victor's shooting. He went to see Attorney-General Tom Clark about getting the FBI involved. Clark reported, "Edgar says no. He's not going into the South every time some nigger gets [obscenity deleted]." Then Rauh added: "And this is exactly what the attorney general said to me on sending the FBI into Walter's and Victor's shooting. . . .It happened. . . . I heard it." Joseph L. Rauh, Jr., interview with William J. Eaton, December 11, 1967, p. 3; *United Automobile Worker,* May 1948; Irving Bluestone interview with John Barnard, October 1988–November 1992, p. 31; V. Reuther, *Brothers Reuther,* 269–303; Lichtenstein, *Most Dangerous Man,* 272–73.

100. Brendan Sexton interview with John Herling, August 1, 1978, p. 56; Martin Gerber interview with John Herling, March 31, 1980, p. 48; Jack Conway interview with Frank Cormier and William J. Eaton, October 2, 1967, pp. 18–23; *United Automobile Worker,* January 1954; *Detroit News,* May 30, 1948; Lichtenstein, *Most Dangerous Man,* 273–75.

101. Irving Bluestone interview with John Barnard, October 1988–November 1992, pp. 69–70.

102. *United Automobile Worker,* June 1951; *UAW Solidarity,* May 1962.

Chapter 8

"The glory days of growth and rich settlements": Don Ephlin interview with John Barnard, June 25, July 12, 1993, p. 21.

1. For a summary of fringe benefits in the industry from the late 1930s to the early 1960s, see Robert M. Macdonald, *Collective Bargaining in the Automobile*

Industry: A Study of Wage Structure and Competitive Relations (New Haven: Yale University Press, 1963), 29–39.

2. Ronald Edsforth, "Affluence, Anti-Communism, and the Transformation of Industrial Unionism among Automobile Workers, 1933–1973," in Ronald Edsforth and Larry Bennett, eds., *Popular Culture and Political Change in Modern America* (Albany: State University of New York Press, 1991), 107–9; Anthony Carew, *Walter Reuther* (Manchester: Manchester University Press, 1993), 56–57; Macdonald, *Collective Bargaining,* 4–5.

3. Figures cited in Nelson Lichtenstein, "From Corporatism to Collective Bargaining: Organized Labor and the Eclipse of Social Democracy in the Postwar Era," in Steve Fraser and Gary Gerstle, eds., *The Rise and Fall of the New Deal Order, 1930–1980* (Princeton: Princeton University Press, 1989), 145; *UAW Solidarity,* September 1966.

4. Nelson Lichtensetein, "Labor in the Truman Era: Origins of the Private Welfare State," in Michael Lacey, ed., *The Truman Presidency* (Cambridge: Woodrow Wilson International Center for Scholars and Cambridge University Press, 1989), 148–55.

5. Nancy Gabin, *Feminism in the Labor Movement: Women and the United Auto Workers, 1935–1975* (Ithaca: Cornell University Press, 1990), 144; *UAW Solidarity,* January 19, 1959.

6. John B. Rae, *The American Automobile Industry* (Boston: Twayne, 1984), 99–115; *Ward's Automotive Yearbook,* 46th ed. (Detroit: Ward's Communications, 1984), 59.

7. Lawrence J. White, *The Automobile Industry Since 1945* (Cambridge, MA: Harvard University Press, 1971), 251.

8. Walter P. Reuther interview with Frank Cormier and William J. Eaton, undated transcript; Louis Seaton interview with Frank Cormier and William J. Eaton, June 20, 1968, p. 5; anecdote courtesy of Irving Bluestone; Nelson Lichtenstein, *The Most Dangerous Man in Detroit: Walter Reuther and the Fate of American Labor* (New York: Basic Books, 1995), 277–78; GM executive quoted in William Serrin, *The Company and the Union* (New York: Knopf, 1973), 20.

9. Allan Nevins and Frank Ernest Hill, *Ford: Decline and Rebirth, 1933–1962* (New York: Charles Scribner's Sons, 1962), 294–388, 427–42.

10. UAW, *Proceedings of the Eighteenth Constitutional Convention* [1962], 57; William Genske interview with Jack W. Skeels, July 23, 1960, p. 42; UAW, International Executive Board, Minutes, May 7–11, 1951, p. 361; January 31–February 3, 1967, pp. 130–32, 134–35; *New York Times,* September 8, 1963. Two contemporary works on the labor movement that analyze its accomplishments and problems are Paul Jacobs, *The State of the Unions* (New York: Atheneum, 1963); and Sidney Lens, *The Crisis of American Labor* (New York: A. S. Barnes & Company, 1959).

11. Frank Marquart interview with Herbert Hill, July 24, 1968, p. 16; Frank Marquart, *An Auto Worker's Journal: The UAW from Crusade to One-Party Union* (University Park: Pennsylvania State University Press, 1975), 106–27.

12. Walter P. Reuther interview with William J. Eaton, August 20, 1969, pp. 3–4; Leonard Woodcock interview with Frank Cormier and William J. Eaton, June

20, 1968, p. 2; Joe Walsh interview with John Herling, August 16, 1978, pp. 35–36; *New York Times*, June 3, 1958.

13. Sam Sage interview with Jack W. Skeels, July 18, 1960, pp. 24, 41–42; Alan Strachan memoir, copy in Victor G. Reuther Collection, Box 16, f. 22; Carl Shier interview with John Herling, February 23, 1980, pp. 59–60.

14. For the postwar campaign to limit labor's gains see Howell J. Harris, *The Right to Manage: Industrial Relations Policies of American Business in the 1940s* (Madison: University of Wisconsin Press, 1982); and Elizabeth A. Fones-Wolf, *Selling Free Enterprise: The Business Assault on Labor and Liberalism, 1945–60* (Urbana: University of Illinois Press, 1994).

15. *UAW Solidarity*, February 1960; Lichtenstein, *Most Dangerous Man*, 302.

16. *United Automobile Worker*, April 4, 1951, August, 1956; Carew, *Reuther*, 57; Fones-Wolf, *Selling Free Enterprise*, 118; *UAW Solidarity*, March 1961, February 1962.

17. *United Automobile Worker*, June, September 1951, December 1956; Fones-Wolf, *Selling Free Enterprise*, 119; *UAW Solidarity*, March 1961, February 1962.

18. *United Automobile Worker*, March, April 1948; Walter P. Reuther to Eastern Cooperative League, October 29, 1946, Walter P. Reuther Collection, Box 72, f. 8; Walter P. Reuther to International Executive Board, UAW-CIO, March 17, 1947, Walter P. Reuther Collection, Box 72, f. 9; Mildred Jeffrey interview with Ruth Meyerowitz, August 13, 1976, p. 76, copy in John Herling Collection.

19. *UAW Solidarity*, June 1960; Fones-Wolf, *Selling Free Enterprise*, 126–27.

20. Fones-Wolf, *Selling Free Enterprise*, 80; Alan Raucher, "Employee Relations at General Motors: The 'My Job Contest,' 1947," *Labor History*, XXVIII, No. 2 (Spring 1987), 221–32; Walter P. Reuther to "All Local Unions and Plants," September 18, 1947, Walter P. Reuther Collection, Box 101, f. 12; Edsforth, "Affluence, Anti-Communism, and the Transformation of Industrial Unionism," in Edsforth and Bennett, eds., *Popular Culture*, 108–9.

21. Fones-Wolf, *Selling Free Enterprise*, 109–11.

22. Carew, *Reuther*, 58–60; Steven Tolliday and Jonathan Zeitlin, "Shop-Floor Bargaining, Contract Unionism, and Job Control: An Anglo-American Comparison," in Steven Tolliday and Jonathan Zeitlin, eds., *Between Fordism and Flexibility: The Automobile Industry and Its Workers* (Oxford: Berg, 1992), 108; Macdonald, *Collective Bargaining*, 5–6.

23. UAW-CIO press release, December 12, 1946, copy in Walter P. Reuther Collection, Box 80, f. 9; *Detroit Free Press*, April 25, 1947; *Detroit News*, May 11, 1947; *United Automobile Worker*, May, 1947; *UAW Solidarity*, March 1971; GM Department correspondence, 1947, Walter P. Reuther Collection, Box 101, ff. 8–13; Lichtenstein, *Most Dangerous Man*, 276; Macdonald, *Collective Bargaining*, 73–74.

24. Nat Weinberg interview with Jack W. Skeels, March 20, April 30, 1963, pp. 28–29; *New York Times*, May 30, 1948; *Detroit News*, May 25–26, 1948; Lichtenstein, *Most Dangerous Man*, 276–79.

25. GM Department correspondence, 1948, Walter P. Reuther Collection, Box 101, ff. 13–15; *Detroit News*, May 25, 1948; *New York Times*, May 26–30, 1948;

United Automobile Worker, June 1948; Carew, *Reuther*, 60–61; Irving Bluestone interview with John Barnard, October 1988–November 1992, p. 30; Barry Bluestone and Irving Bluestone, *Negotiating the Future* (New York: Basic Books, 1992), 272. Privately, GM President C. E. Wilson acknowledged that the union's demands in the 1945–46 strike for a wage increase without a price increase stimulated his thinking on COLA and AIF schemes. Walter P. Reuther interview with Frank Cormier and William J. Eaton, undated transcript.

26. Stephen Amberg, *The Union Inspiration in American Politics: The Autoworkers and the Making of a Liberal Industrial Order* (Philadelphia: Temple University Press, 1994), 156–59; *Daily Worker*, May 28, 1948.

27. *New York Times*, August 25, 1948, May 24, 1949; *UAW Solidarity*, July 1968.

28. Charles E. Wilson, "'Progress-Sharing' Can Mean Industrial Peace," *Readers' Digest*, September 1952, pp. 27–28.

29. Nelson Lichtenstein, "Reutherism on the Shop Floor: Union Strategy and Shop-Floor Conflict in the USA, 1946–70," in Tolliday and Zeitlin, eds., *Fordism and Flexibility*, 129–31.

30. Amberg, *Union Inspiration*, 156–59; Lichtenstein, *Most Dangerous Man*, 277–80; Lichtenstein, "Reutherism on the Shop Floor," 129–31.

31. Nat Weinberg interview with Jack W. Skeels, March 20, April 30, 1963, p. 9; Ken Bannon interview with Jack W. Skeels, February 28, 1963, p. 23; Ken Bannon interview with John Herling, June 3, 1980, pp. 34–35; *Detroit News*, December 17, 1948; *Detroit Free Press*, January 16, 1949; *New York Times*, January 16, 1949; Walter P. Reuther, "Announcement of UAW-CIO Social Security Program," November 15, 1946, quoted in Alan Derickson, "Health Security for All? Social Unionism and Universal Health Insurance, 1935–1958," *Journal of American History*, LXXX, No. 4 (March 1994), 1344; Walter P. Reuther, "Too Old to Work, Too Young to Die," portions reprinted in Henry M. Christman, ed., *Walter Reuther: Selected Papers* (New York: Macmillan, 1961), 39–41; Lichtenstein, "Reutherism on the Shop Floor," 126–27; Seth M. Wigderson, "The UAW in the 1950's," (Ph.D diss., Wayne State University, 1989), pp. 33–61.

32. UAW, *Proceedings of the Twelfth Constitutional Convention* [1949], 9–17.

33. Walter P. Reuther interview with William J. Eaton, August 20, 1969, p. 5; Ken Bannon interview with Jack W. Skeels, February 28, 1963, pp. 23–24; Ford 1949 Negotiations, Walter P. Reuther Collection, Box 121, f. 16; *United Automobile Worker*, July–November 1949; *Detroit News*, September 27–29, 1949; *New York Times*, September 29, 1949; UAW, *Proceedings of the Twelfth Constitutional Convention* [1949], 13, portions of Reuther's address reprinted in Christman, ed., *Walter Reuther*, 39–41; Joe Glazer, "Too Old to Work, Too Young to Die," reprinted in Sam Gindin, *The Canadian Auto Workers: The Birth and Transformation of a Union* (Toronto: James Lorimer, 1995), 110; Carew, *Reuther*, 62; Lichtenstein, *Most Dangerous Man*, 282–83.

34. Norman R. Matthews interview with Jack W. Skeels, March 8, 1963, pp. 8–9; Douglas Fraser interview with John Barnard, May 15–June 22, 1990, p. 60; Arthur Hughes interview with Jack W. Skeels, March 13, 1963, pp. 29–30; *Detroit*

News, May 4, 7, 1950; *New York Times,* January 26, April 18, May 5, 7, 14, 1950; *United Automobile Worker,* October 1949–May 1950; Lichtenstein, *Most Dangerous Man,* 283–84.

35. Walter P. Reuther speech at rally for the Forand bill, March 27, 1960; *UAW Solidarity,* June 1960, April 1970.

36. Carew, *Reuther,* 64; Nat Weinberg interview with Jack W. Skeels, March 20, April 30, 1963, pp. 23–27; Kenneth (Ken) Bannon interview with Warner Pflug, April 30, 1985, pp. 24–30.

37. *Detroit News,* May 23, 1950; *New York Times,* May 24, 1950; Lichtenstein, *Most Dangerous Man,* 279–81.

38. Leonard Woodcock interview with John Barnard, January 18, 30, February 7, 1991, p. 30; Leonard Woodcock interview with Frank Cormier and William J. Eaton, May 5, 1968, p. 5 and June 20, 1968, p. 2; Negotiations, 1950–51, Walter P. Reuther Collection, Box 121, f. 17; *United Automobile Worker,* December 1949–June 1950; Walter P. Reuther, "The United Automobile Workers: Past, Present, Future," *Virginia Law Review,* 50, No. 1 (1964), 86; Lichtenstein, *Most Dangerous Man,* 287–88.

39. *Fortune,* XLII, No. 1 (July 1950), 53; *United Automobile Worker,* March–July, 1950; *New York Times,* August 17, 29,– September 5, 24, December 12, 16, 1950; *Fortune,* XLIV, No. 1 (July 1951), 41; Wigderson, *UAW in the 1950's,* 61–65.

40. Reuther's statement in Proceedings of National Conference, General Motors Council, UAW-CIO, May 28, 1953, Walter P. Reuther Collection, Box 544, f. ll; Leonard Woodcock interview with John Barnard, January 18, 30, February 7, 1991, pp. 31–32; Jack Conway interview with Frank Cormier and William J. Eaton, November 20, 1967, p. 4; *New York Times,* August 13, 31, 1950, May 21–27, September 1, 1953; *Detroit News,* May 21–27, 1953; Lichtenstein, *Most Dangerous Man,* 294.

41. David Brody, *Workers in Industrial America: Essays on the Twentieth Century Struggle,* 2d ed. (New York: Oxford University Press, 1993), 169–72; Lichtenstein, "Reutherism on the Shop Floor," 133; Nelson Lichtenstein, "UAW Bargaining Strategy and Shop-Floor Conflict, 1946–1970," *Industrial Relations,* XXIV, No. 3 (Fall 1985), 372–73. For an interpretation that sees the 1950 GM contract as marking "the end of the era in which Reuther . . . could hope for a serious transformation in the governing structure of American industry," see Lichtenstein, *Most Dangerous Man,* 279–82; Serrin, *Company and Union,* 156.

42. *Detroit News,* March 19, 1955. See also the illustrated article on a laid-off auto worker in *Life,* June 13, 1955.

43. Franklin D. Roosevelt, *The Public Papers and Addresses of Franklin D. Roosevelt* (New York: Random House, 1938), V, 498–99; UAW, *Proceedings of the Thirteenth Constitutional Convention* [1951], 10–11, 273–74; *New York Times,* January 24, 1951; Carew, *Reuther,* 78; Lichtenstein, *Most Dangerous Man,* 284–85; Wigderson, *UAW in the 1950's,* 65–97.

44. Sumner Slichter quoted in Lichtenstein, "Reutherism on the Shop Floor," 128; UAW, *Proceedings of the Thirteenth Constitutional Convention* [1951], 172.

45. Nat Weinberg interview with Jack W. Skeels, March 20, April 30, 1963, pp. 8–12; Nat Weinberg interview with Frank Cormier and William J. Eaton, July 1,

1968, p. 2; Don Ephlin interview with John Barnard, June 25, July 12, 1993, p. 7; *United Automobile Worker,* April 1951; UAW, *Proceedings of the Thirteenth Constitutional Convention* [1951], 273–74; UAW, *Proceedings of the Fourteenth Constitutional Convention* [1953], 143–49.

46. Walter P. Reuther, Address to the Economic Club of New York, January 17, 1955, printed in the *Commercial and Financial Chronicle,* February 3, 1955, p. 18; UAW, *Proceedings of the Fifteenth Constitutional Convention* [1955], 15–17, 218–22, 239–41; *New York Times,* March 26–31, April 1–2, 1955; Rae, *American Automobile Industry,* 108; Wigderson, *UAW in the 1950's,* 70; Carew, *Reuther,* 78–79.

47. Leonard Woodcock interview with John Barnard, January 18, 30, February 7, 1991, p. 36; Louis Seaton interview with Frank Cormier and William J. Eaton, June 20, 1968, p. 3; Nat Weinberg interview with Jack W. Skeels, March 20, April 30, 1963, p. 16; Negotiations, 1955, Walter P. Reuther Collection, Box 122, ff. 1–9.

48. Frank Cormier and William J Eaton, *Reuther* (Englewood Cliffs, N.J.: Prentice Hall, 1970), 332; Walter P. Reuther interview with Frank Cormier and William J. Eaton, August 20, 1969, pp. 1–2; Jack Conway interview with Frank Cormier and William J. Eaton, November 20, 1967, p. 5; Kenneth (Ken) Bannon interview with Warner Pflug, April 30, 1985, p. 36.

49. Cormier and Eaton, *Reuther,* p. 333; Walter P. Reuther to Henry Ford II, May 30, 1955, Walter P. Reuther Collection, Box 96, f. 6; *New York Times,* May 31, 1955.

50. *New York Times,* April 30, May 1, 10, 22, 28–31, June 5–7, 1955; *United Automobile Worker,* June 1955; Nevins and Hill, *Ford,* 432–34; Lichtenstein, *Most Dangerous Man,* 284–86.

51. *New York Times,* June 13, 1955; Walter P. Reuther interview with William J. Eaton, August 20, 1969, p. 2; Kevin Boyle, *The UAW and the Heyday of American Liberalism, 1945–1968* (Ithaca: Cornell University Press, 1995), 95; Leonard Woodcock interview with John Barnard, January 18, 30, February 7, 1991, pp. 31–32.

52. *Report of UAW President Walter P. Reuther, 1959,* 66–68; *UAW Solidarity,* November 1966.

53. *New York Times,* August 9–September 20, November 10, December 22, 1955; *United Automobile Worker,* July–December, 1955; Owen Bieber interview with John Barnard, April 10–11, 1997, pp. 63–64; *UAW Solidarity,* November 1966; William Haber and Merrill G. Murray, *Unemployment Insurance in the American Economy* (Homewood, Ill.: R. D. Irwin, 1966), 464–66; Joseph M. Becker, *Guaranteed Income for the Unemployed: The Story of SUB* (Baltimore: Johns Hopkins University Press, 1968), 3–49; Carew, *Reuther,* 80; Lichtenstein, *Most Dangerous Man,* 286–87.

54. Derickson, "Health Security," 1333–56; Paul Starr, *The Social Transformation of American Medicine* (New York: Basic Books, 1982), 280–82, 315, 382; "Cast me not off . . . ," Walter P. Reuther transcript of testimony in support of the Forand bill, July 1959, Walter P. Reuther Collection, Box 422, f. 7; "Medical Care for the Aged," Statement to the House Committee on Ways and Means, Washington D.C., July 16, 1959, in Christman, ed., *Walter Reuther,* 283–98.

55. Walter P. Reuther, "Announcement of UAW-CIO Social Security Program," November 15, 1946, in Derickson, "Health Security," 1344; Brody, *Workers in Industrial America*, 176–77; Nelson Lichtenstein, "From Corporatism to Collective Bargaining: Organized Labor and the Eclipse of Social Democracy in the Postwar Era," in Steve Fraser and Gary Gerstle, eds., *The Rise and Fall of the New Deal Order, 1930–1980* (Princeton: Princeton University Press, 1989), 142–44. For the claim that the achievement of medical benefits undermined the drive for a national health program, see Derickson.

56. UAW, *Proceedings of the Twelfth Constitutional Convention* [1949], 14; reprinted in Christman, ed., *Walter Reuther*, 41–43.

57. *Report of Walter P. Reuther, President . . . July 10, 1949*, pp. 175–77.

58. UAW, International Executive Board, Minutes, September 10–14, 1956, pp. 24–29; *New York Times*, December 23, 1956, October 11, 1959, May 7, 1961; Jack Stieber, *Governing the UAW* (New York: John Wiley and Sons, 1962), 116–17; "Community Health Association (CHA), 1956," Walter P. Reuther Collection, Box 479, ff. 13–15, Boxes 480–86.

59. *New York Times*, April 19, 25, 27–29, May 1, 18, June 3, September 18, October 2–3, 1958. The 1958 negotiations are reviewed from the leadership's point of view in *Report of Walter P. Reuther, President . . . October 9–16, 1959*, pp. 9–35. See also Walter P. Reuther Collection, Box 122, ff. 13–14, Box 123, ff. 1–4; Wigderson, "UAW in the 1950's," 107–12, 115.

60. Joe Walsh interview with John Herling, August 16, 1978, pp. 29, 74; Nat Weinberg interview with Jack W. Skeels, March 20, April 30, 1963, p. 36; Jack Conway interview with Frank Cormier and William J. Eaton, November 20, 1967, pp. 1–2; Macdonald, *Collective Bargaining*, 7–9.

61. Stephen Schlossberg interview with John Herling, June 2, 1983, n.p.; UAW, *Proceedings of the Special Constitutional Convention . . . January 22–24, 1958.*

62. Jack Conway interview with Frank Cormier and William J. Eaton, November 20, 1967, pp. 1–2; Louis Seaton interview with Frank Cormier and William J. Eaton, June 20, 1968, pp. 1–3.

63. Jack Conway interview with Frank Cormier and William J. Eaton, November 20, 1967, p. 2; Irving Bluestone interview with John Barnard, October 1988–November 1992, pp. 76–77.

64. Walter P. Reuther interview with William J. Eaton, August 20, 1969, p. 7; Henry Santiestevan quoting Joe Walsh, interview with John Herling, January 27, 1981, pp. 22–23; Leonard Woodcock interview with Frank Cormier and William J. Eaton, June 20, 1968, p. 3.

65. Macdonald, *Collective Bargaining*, 206–36, 259–306; David Gartman, *Auto Slavery: The Labor Process in the American Automobile Industry, 1897–1950* (New Brunswick: Rutgers University Press, 1986), 280–84.

66. Reuther's statement to the committee of February 9, 1959, "Policies for Economic Growth," is reprinted in Christman, ed., *Walter Reuther*, 237–38; a 1958 statement before the Antitrust and Monopoly Subcommittee of the Senate Committee on the Judiciary, "Administered Prices in the Automobile Industry," is in

ibid., 216–36; Boyle, *UAW and the Heyday,* 47–48, 65, 136–37, 148–54; Lichtenstein, *Most Dangerous Man,* 221–25, 363–65.

67. Thomas J. Sugrue, "'Forget about Your Inalienable Right to Work': Deindustrialization and Its Discontents at Ford, 1950–1953," *International Labor and Working-Class History,* No. 48 (Fall 1995), 112–30; Steve Babson et al., *Working Detroit* (New York: Adama Books, 1984), 113–34; Thomas J. Sugrue, *The Origins of the Urban Crisis: Race and Inequality in Postwar Detroit* (Princeton: Princeton University Press, 1996), 125–52; Nevins and Hill, *Ford,* 319, 340–41, 352–61, 375–76; *United Automobile Worker,* November 1957. A review and critique of the historical literature on the deindustrialization of Detroit is available in Kevin Boyle, "The Ruins of Detroit: Exploring the Urban Crisis in the Motor City," *Michigan Historical Review,* XXVII, No. 1 (Spring 2001), 109–27.

68. Charles K. Hyde, *Detroit: An Industrial History Guide* (Detroit: Detroit Historical Society, 1980), 27; Sugrue, "'Forget about Your Inalienable Right to Work,'" 125–30; Amberg, *Union Inspiration,* 207–27; Harold L. Sheppard, Louis A. Ferman, and Seymour Faber, *Too Old to Work—Too Young to Retire: A Case Study of a Permanent Plant Shutdown* (Washington, D.C.: United States Government Printing Office, 1960), 8–31.

69. *UAW Solidarity,* January, July 1964, January 1965; *New York Times,* December 25, 1963, March 13, August 10, 1964; Stephen Amberg, "Triumph of Industrial Orthodoxy: The Collapse of Studebaker-Packard Corporation," in Nelson Lichtenstein and Stephen Meyer, eds., *On the Line: Essays in the History of Auto Work* (Urbana: University of Illinois Press, 1989), 190–218; John Bodnar, "Power and Memory in Oral History: Workers and Managers at Studebaker," *Journal of American History,* LXXV, No. 4 (March 1989), 1216–19; Donald T. Critchlow, *Studebaker: The Life and Death of an American Corporation* (Bloomington: Indiana University Press, 1996), 148–51, 183–84.

70. Sugrue, "'Forget about Your Inalienable Right to Work,'" 112–30; Ken Morris interview with John Barnard, January 29, 1997, pp. 18–19; John W. Dorsey, "The Mack Case: A Study in Unemployment," in Otto Eckstein, ed., *Studies in the Economics of Income Maintenance* (Washington, D.C.: Brookings Institution, 1967), 175–233; Barry Bluestone and Bennett Harrison, *The Deindustrialization of America: Plant Closings, Community Abandonment, and the Dismantling of Basic Industry* (New York: Basic Books, 1982), 71–72; *UAW Solidarity,* June 1961.

71. Judith Stepan-Norris and Maurice Zeitlin, *Talking Union* (Urbana: University of Illinois Press, 1996), 20–25, 127–28; *New York Times,* November 13, 15, 1951; Sugrue, *Origins,* 125–27, 132, 157–63; Sugrue, "'Forget about Your Inalienable Right to Work,'" 112–30; *UAW Solidarity,* April, July 1961; Nelson Lichtenstein, "Life at the Rouge: A Cycle of Workers' Control," in Charles Stephenson and Robert Asher, eds., *Life and Labor: Dimensions of American Working-Class History* (Albany: State University of New York Press, 1986), 251–52.

72. UAW, International Executive Board, Minutes, May 1–4, 1956, pp. 146–47, 150; Bluestone and Harrison, *Deindustrialization,* 52, 62.

73. Bluestone and Harrison, *Deindustrialization,* 71–72; Boyle, *UAW and the Heyday,* 94.

74. *UAW Solidarity*, West Side Conveyor Edition, December 20, 1960; Sugrue, *Origins*, 137–38.

75. Reuther, "United Automobile Workers," 63; *UAW Solidarity*, February 1957, October 1961, August 1963, April, July 1966, February 1967, July–August 1977; *New York Times*, July 25, 1964; Owen Bieber interview with John Barnard, April 10–11, 1997, pp. 35–37; Douglas Fraser interview with John Herling, February 21, 1983, pp. 10–11.

76. Sanford M. Jacoby, *Modern Manors: Welfare Capitalism Since the New Deal* (Princeton: Princeton University Press, 1997), 143–83.

77. *New York Times*, November 13, 15, 1951; *Detroit News*, November 13, 15, 1951; Local Union No. 600 *v.* Ford Motor Company (1951), plaintiff's brief, Carl Stellato to Walter P. Reuther, October 30, 1951, Harold A. Cranefield to Walter P. Reuther, November 8, 1951, Walter P. Reuther Collection, Box 249, f. 23; Sugrue, *Origins*, 153–63; Sugrue, "'Forget about Your Inalienable Right to Work,' " 1–21; UAW, International Executive Board, Minutes, May 1–4, 1956, pp. 146–47, 150; Lichtenstein, *Most Dangerous Man*, 290; *UAW Solidarity*, January 1959, May 1964. For an account that perceives greater potential in the Local 600 suit, see Judith Stepan-Norris and Maurice Zeitlin, *Left Out: Reds and American Industrial Unions* (Cambridge: Cambridge University Press, 2003), 122–26.

78. Reuther, "United Automobile Workers," 73–74.

79. Ibid., 74; Walter P. Reuther, "'The Impact of Automation,' testimony before the Sub-Committee on Economic Stabilization of the Joint Committee on the Economic Report," copy in Walter P. Reuther Collection, Box 56, f. 7, reprinted in Christman, ed., *Walter Reuther*, 67–100; *UAW Solidarity*, November 1966.

80. Reuther quoted in Lichtenstein, *Most Dangerous Man*, 290; Reuther, "Impact of Automation"; Ronald Edsforth, "Why Automation Didn't Shorten the Work Week: The Politics of Work Time in the Automobile Industry," in Robert Asher and Ronald Edsforth, eds., *Autowork* (Albany: State University of New York Press, 1995), 172–73; Walter P. Reuther interview with Henry Brandon in the *Sunday Times* [London], June 29, 1958.

81. Reuther quoted in Lichtenstein, *Most Dangerous Man*, 291; Cormier and Eaton, *Reuther*, 309–10; *Washington Post*, February 23, 1955; Christman, ed., *Walter Reuther*, 77, 91–95, 180. Reuther repeated the anecdote concerning automation in the Ford engine plant on many occasions, not always using the same wording.

82. Reuther's testimony before the Joint Committee on the Economic Report, as reported in the *Washington Post*, February 11, 1955; Amberg, *Union Inspiration*, 223–34.

83. Leonard Woodcock interview with Frank Cormier and William J. Eaton, June 20, 1968, p. 2; Edsforth, "Automation," in Asher and Edsforth, eds., *Autowork*, 155–79; Jack Stieber, *Governing the UAW*, 43–53; *United Automobile Worker*, May 1957; Wigderson, "UAW in the 1950's," 33, 98–99, 104–5; UAW, International Executive Board, Minutes, March 5–7, 1963, pp. 262–64; a copy of the proposal is in Walter P. Reuther Collection, Box 78, f. 13; Walter P. Reuther to John F. Dykstra, President, Ford Motor Company, March 23, 1962, Walter P. Reuther Collection, Box 96, f. 8; *New York Times*, March 25, 29, 1962.

84. Walter P. Reuther interview with William J. Eaton, August 20, 1969, pp. 8–9; UAW, *Proceedings of the Eighteenth Constitutional Convention* [1962], 60, 194; *UAW Solidarity*, February 1962, January 1963.

85. Marquart, *Auto Worker's Journal*, 137–40. For other expressions of this argument, see Lichtenstein, *Most Dangerous Man*, 276–98; Ronald Edsforth, *Class Conflict and Cultural Consensus: The Making of a Mass Consumer Society in Flint, Michigan* (New Brunswick: Rutgers University Press, 1987), 191–219; and Gartman, *Auto Slavery*, 268–91.

86. David Brody, "Workplace Contractualism: A Historical/Comparative Analysis," in *In Labor's Cause: Main Themes on the History of American Workers* (New York: Oxford University Press, 1993), 221–50; Lichtenstein, "Reutherism on the Shop Floor," 134–36; Lichtenstein, *Most Dangerous Man*, 291–92.

87. Irving Bluestone interview with John Barnard, October 1988–November 1992, pp. 58–59; *Report of Walter P. Reuther. . . .* [1949], 64–65; David Brody, "The Uses of Power I: Industrial Background," in *Workers in Industrial America: Essays on the Twentieth Century Struggle*, 2d ed. (New York: Oxford University Press, 1993), 187; Carew, *Reuther*, 62–64; Lichtenstein, *Most Dangerous Man*, 289.

88. *New York Times*, April 11, 16, May 6–31, July 10, 1949; *Detroit News*, May 1–5, June 1, 1949; Walter P. Reuther to Henry Ford II, May 9, 1949, Walter P. Reuther Collection, Box 96, f. 4; *United Automobile Worker*, January–June, 1949; Ken Bannon Collection, Boxes 40, 41, 67; Bannon's account, as director of the UAW's Ford Department, is in *Report of Walter P. Reuther. . . .* [1949], 78–80; Robert Asher, "The 1949 Speedup Strike and the Post War Social Compact, 1946–1961," in Asher and Edsforth, eds., *Autowork*, 127–54; see also Lichtenstein, *Most Dangerous Man*, 292–93, and Lichtenstein, "Life at the Rouge," 250–51, 253–55.

89. Don Ephlin interview with John Barnard, June 25, July 12, 1993, p. 7; Carew, *Reuther*, 83–84; Edsforth, "Affluence . . . " 114; Ronald Edsforth and Robert Asher, with the assistance of Raymond Boryczka, "The Speedup: The Focal Point of Workers' Grievances, 1919–1941," in Asher and Edsforth, *Autowork*, 97.

90. *New York Times*, August 2–3, September 1, 1951; James R. Zetka, Jr., "Work Organization and Wildcat Strikes in the U.S. Automobile Industry, 1946 to 1963," *American Sociological Review*, 57 (April 1992), 214–26; Ken Bannon to Douglas Fraser, June 5, 1952, Bannon Collection, Box 42, f. 11; John S. Bugas to Ken Bannon, January 27, 1954, Bannon Collection, Box 42, f. 11; Boyle, *UAW and the Heyday*, 135–36; Steve Jefferys, *Management and Managed: Fifty Years of Crisis at Chrysler* (Cambridge: Cambridge University Press, 1986), 139–45; Wigderson, "UAW in the 1950's," 113; Edsforth, "Affluence," 114–15; Steve Babson, *The Unfinished Struggle: Turning Points in American Labor, 1877–Present* (Lanham, MD: Rowman & Littlefield, 1999), 148–49.

91. Copies of the surveys, commissioned by the International Executive Board, are available in several collections. See, for example, the Ken Bannon Collection, Box 10 for the Harris survey, and the Walter P. Reuther Collection, Boxes 147 and 148 for the Quayle survey. Edsforth, "Affluence," 109–10; Lichtenstein, *Most Dangerous Man*, 287–88.

92. *Automobile Unionism, Report of R. J. Thomas* [1946], 71–72; *Report of the President . . .* [1947], 14.

93. *Report of Walter P. Reuther. . . .* [1949], 90–92; *Report of Walter P. Reuther. . . .* [1951], 189–99; *Report of Walter P. Reuther. . . .* [1953], 132–38; *Report of Walter P. Reuther. . . .* [1955], 16–D—17–D; Leonard Woodcock interview with John Barnard, January 18, 30, February 7, 1991, pp. 55–56; Irving Bluestone interview with John Barnard, October 24, 1988–November 23, 1992, pp. 46–48.

94. Stieber, *Governing the UAW*, 52–53; Leonard Woodcock interview with John Barnard, January 18, 30, February 7, 1991, pp. 48, 52–54; Irving Bluestone interview with John Barnard, October 24, 1988–November 23, 1992, pp. 48, 51; *Report of Walter P. Reuther. . . .* [1951], 193; *Report of Walter P. Reuther. . . .* [1955], 15–D—22–D; *Report of Walter P. Reuther. . . .* [1957], 24–D—28–D; *Report of Walter P. Reuther. . . .* [1959], 28–D—31–D; *Report of Walter P. Reuther. . . .* [1962], Pt. I, 37–41.

95. Carl D. Snyder, *White-Collar Workers and the UAW* (Urbana: University of Illinois Press, 1973), 6–19.

96. UAW Technical, Office, Professional (TOP) Department Collection, Box 1, f. 10, Box 2, ff. 6, 24–25; Snyder, *White-Collar Workers*, 30–56; *New York Times*, March 15, April 3, 27, 1966; Kenneth R. Bailey to Walter P. Reuther, December 15, 1967, copy in UAW Chrysler Collection, Box 74, f. 10.

97. Snyder, *White-Collar Workers*, 63.

98. Ibid., 78–112,

99. Brody, *Workers in Industrial America*, 179; Carew, *Reuther*, 64–65; Tolliday and Zeitlin, "Shop-Floor Bargaining," 113.

100. For an interpretation of the UAW's collective bargaining experience in the 1950s that emphasizes the limitations on its outreach into the wider economy and society, see Lichtenstein, *Most Dangerous Man*, 296–98.

Chapter 9

"Give 'em hell, Harry!": Steve Despot, financial secretary of UAW Local 212, so exhorted President Harry S. Truman during his opening campaign speech on Labor Day, 1948, in Detroit. Taken up by others there and elsewhere, the slogan became the battle cry of the Truman campaign. Ken Morris interview with John Barnard, June 19, 1992. The *Detroit News*, September 6–7, 1948, a family newspaper, primly reported shouts from the crowd of "Give it to em, Harry!"

1. UAW, *Proceedings of the Eleventh Constitutional Convention* [1947], 13; Nelson Lichtenstein, *The Most Dangerous Man in Detroit: Walter Reuther and the Fate of American Labor* (New York: Basic Books, 1995), 300. For politics and government from 1945 to 1960 see James T. Patterson, *Grand Expectations: The United States, 1945–1974* (New York: Oxford University Press, 1996), 10–441.

2. Kevin Boyle, *The UAW and the Heyday of American Liberalism, 1945–1968* (Ithaca: Cornell University Press, 1995), 5–6; Anthony Carew, *Walter Reuther* (Manchester: University of Manchester Press, 1993), 85; Irving Howe and B. J. Widick, *The*

UAW and Walter Reuther (New York: Da Capo Press, 1973, orig. pub. 1949), 273–74; Jack Stieber, *Governing the UAW* (New York: John Wiley and Sons, 1962), 37–40.

3. CIO, *Proceedings of the Sixteenth Constitutional Convention* [1954], 483–88; "Trade Unions without Socialism: Walter Reuther Talks about American Labour to Henry Brandon," the *Sunday [London] Times,* June 22, 1958. For the argument that labor received little in return for its support of the Democratic Party, see Nelson Lichtenstein, "From Corporatism to Collective Bargaining: Organized Labor and the Eclipse of Social Democracy in the Postwar Era," in Steve Fraser and Gary Gerstle, eds., *The Rise and Fall of the New Deal Order* (Princeton: Princeton University Press, 1989), 140; and Mike Davis, *Prisoners of the American Dream* (New York: Verso, 1986), 97–101.

4. Herbert S. Parmet, *The Democrats: The Years After FDR* (New York: Oxford University Press, 1976), 60–92; Alonzo L. Hamby, *Beyond the New Deal: Harry S. Truman and American Liberalism* (New York: Columbia University Press, 1973), 53–274; Dudley W. Buffa, *Union Power and American Democracy: The UAW and the Democratic Party, 1935–72* (Ann Arbor: University of Michigan Press, 1984), 6–7; Lichtenstein, *Most Dangerous Man,* 303–5.

5. Boyle, *UAW and the Heyday,* 48–49; Steven M. Gillon, *Politics and Vision: The ADA and American Liberalism, 1947–1985* (New York: Oxford University Press, 1987), 3–24, 36, 41; James C. Foster, *The Union Politic: The CIO Political Action Committee* (Columbia: University of Missouri Press, 1975), 54–56, 62–70.

6. Boyle, *UAW and the Heyday,* 23–27, 61–67; Gillon, *Politics and Vision,* 21, 27, 29–30.

7. Boyle, *UAW and the Heyday,* 39–41.

8. *United Automobile Worker,* July 1948; *New York Times,* July 8, 1948; Boyle, *UAW and the Heyday,* 54; Gillon, *Politics and Vision,* 42–47; Lichtenstein, *Most Dangerous Man,* 304–5.

9. Boyle, *UAW and the Heyday,* 54–55; *United Automobile Worker,* September 1948; *New York Times,* August 15, November 1, 1948; *Detroit News,* September 6–7, 1948; Walter P. Reuther, radio address, October 31, 1948, Walter P. Reuther Collection, Box 142, f. 11.

10. John C. Culver and John Hyde, *American Dreamer: The Life and Times of Henry A. Wallace* (New York: W. W. Norton, 2000), 452–65; Curtis D. MacDougall, *Gideon's Army* (New York: Marzani and Munsell, 1965), I, 248–83, II, 413–34, 484–506; Hamby, *Beyond the New Deal,* 195–246.

11. Boyle, *UAW and the Heyday,* 51–52; Reuther quoted in *Detroit News,* December 19, 1947; a slightly different version is given in *New York Times,* December 19, 1947; McDougall, *Gideon's Army,* II, 619.

12. *United Automobile Worker,* May 1948, May 1956; *New York Times,* November 4, 1948; Boyle, *UAW and the Heyday,* 3, 59–60; *Report of Walter P. Reuther. . . .* [1949], 46–47.

13. *Report of Walter P. Reuther. . . .* [1949] 48–49.

14. Foster, *Union Politic,* 155–56; *Report of Walter P. Reuther. . . .* [1953], 217; Buffa, *Union Power,* 14–15; Seth M. Wigderson, "The UAW in the 1950's" (Ph.D. diss., Wayne State University, 1989), 237–38; Arthur Kornhauser, Harold L. Shep-

pard, and Albert J. Meyer, *When Labor Votes: A Study of Auto Workers* (New York: University Books, 1956), 262.

15. Leonard Woodcock interview with John Barnard, January 18, 30, February 7, 1991, pp. 79–80; Fay Calkins, *The CIO and the Democratic Party* (Chicago: University of Chicago Press, 1952), 112–46; Buffa, *Union Power*, 13–19; Thaddeus Russell, *Out of the Jungle: Jimmy Hoffa and the Remaking of the American Working Class* (New York: Knopf, 2002), 155–70; Sidney Fine, *"Expanding the Frontiers of Civil Rights": Michigan 1948–1968* (Detroit: Wayne State University Press, 2000), 24–25.

16. Boyle, *UAW and the Heyday*, 3, 53; Fine, *"Expanding the Frontiers,"* 25; Stieber, *Governing the UAW*, 110–11.

17. Jack Conway interview with John Herling, May 25, 1978, p. 8; Buffa, 19–21, 35, 40–44.

18. Walter P. Reuther and George Addes to "All Local Unions," August 26, 1946, Walter P. Reuther Collection, Box 80, f. 6; Foster, *Union Politic*, 11–15, 24–25, 40–41, 108–11, 186–87; Buffa, *Union Power*, 45; Wigderson, "UAW in the 1950's," 239–45; Walter P. Reuther, "The United Automobile Workers: Past, Present, and Future," *Virginia Law Review*, 50, No. 1 (1964), 78–80; *Report of Walter P. Reuther. . . .* [1957], 183; Walter P. Reuther, testimony before Subcommittee on Privileges and Elections, Transcript, October 9, 1956, Walter P. Reuther Collection, Box 423, f. 7, portions reprinted in Henry P. Christman, ed., *Walter P. Reuther: Selected Papers* (New York: Macmillan, 1961), 143–75.

19. Boyle, *UAW and the Heyday*, 57–59; Kornhauser et al., *When Labor Votes*, 31–2, 38, 40–53, 69.

20. Foster, *Union Politic*, 59–60; Howe and Widick, *UAW and Walter Reuther*, 274–75; B. J. Widick, *Detroit: City of Race and Class Violence*, rev. ed. (Detroit: Wayne State University Press 1989), 153–54; Thomas J. Sugrue, *The Origins of the Urban Crisis: Race and Inequality in Postwar Detroit* (Princeton: Princeton University Press, 1996), 80–81.

21. Mary M. Stolberg, *Bridging the River of Hatred: The Pioneering Efforts of Detroit Police Commissioner George Edwards* (Detroit: Wayne State University Press, 1998), 87–93; Sugrue, *Origins*, 82–84; Widick, *Detroit*, 154; Lichtenstein, *Most Dangerous Man*, 306–8.

22. *Report of Walter P. Reuther. . . .* [1955], 111–D—115–D.

23. Sugrue, *Origins*, 222–24.

24. Kevin Boyle, "'There are No Union Sorrows that the Union Can't Heal': The Struggle for Racial Equality in the United Automobile Workers, 1940–1960," *Labor History*, XXXVI, No. 1 (Winter 1995), 8–14.

25. Boyle, *UAW and the Heyday*, 113–20; Sugrue, *Origins*, 100–102; *Wall Street Journal*, October 24, 1957; Wigderson, "UAW in the 1950's," 325, 404–6.

26. *New York Times*, November 16, 1951; Reuther, "The United Automobile Workers: Past, Present, Future," 99; Lichtenstein, *Most Dangerous Man*, 373; Wigderson, "UAW in the 1950's," 336.

27. Alan Draper, *Conflict of Interest: Organized Labor and the Civil Rights Movement in the South, 1954–1968* (Ithaca: ILR Press, 1994), 28; Boyle, *UAW and*

the Heyday, 126–27; Lichtenstein, *Most Dangerous Man*, 373–74; Wigderson, "UAW in the 1950's," 406–9.

28. Boyle, *UAW and the Heyday*, 107.

29. Boyle, *UAW and the Heyday*, 297, n. 50; *United Automobile Worker*, May 1953; Wigderson, "UAW in the 1950's," 411–23.

30. UAW, International Executive Board, Minutes, January 18–21, 1960, pp. 257–68; materials on Local 988 in Walter P. Reuther Collection, Box 277, f. 14; Michael Honey, "Black Workers Remember: Industrial Unionism in the Era of Jim Crow," in Gary Fink and Merl E. Reed, eds., *Race, Class, and Community in Southern Labor History* (Tuscaloosa: University of Alabama Press, 1994), 129–35; *New York Times*, August 16, 1960; Boyle, *UAW and the Heyday*, 126–29; Lichtenstein, *Most Dangerous Man*, 373–74.

31. Boyle, *UAW and the Heyday*, 117, 212–13; Sugrue, *Origins*, 100–101, 109–10; Widick, *Detroit*, 126–27; Fine, *"Expanding the Frontiers,"* 93–94.

32. Howe and Widick, *UAW and Reuther*, 228–30; Steve Babson, *The Unfinished Struggle: Turning Points in American Labor, 1877–Present* (Lanham, MD: Rowman & Littlefield, 1999), 138.

33. Howe and Widick, *UAW and Reuther*, 228–30; Kevin Boyle, "The Kiss: Racial and Gender Conflict in a 1950s Automobile Factory," *Journal of American History*, LXXXIV, No. 2 (September 1997), 496–523.

34. Local 7 souvenir program, 1940, copy in Nick DiGaetano Collection, Box 1, f. 10; *United Automobile Worker*, January, April, 1947; letter to Walter P. Reuther from thirty-two UAW members, April 16, 1948, Walter P. Reuther Collection, Box 20; *UAW Solidarity*, January–February, 1995; Olga Madar interview with John Herling, May 16, 1983, pp. 20–25; Walter P. Reuther and Richard T. Leonard to Elmer Baumgarten, January 6, 1947, Walter P. Reuther Collection, Box 19, f. 2; Walter Reuther, "To Foster Fair Employment in Our Own Industries and to Act Vigorously in the Public Arena," in *Equal Opportunity Is Good Labor Practice* (National Conference of Christians and Jews, 1960–1970), 29; Howe and Widick, *UAW and Reuther*, 229–30; Fine, *"Expanding the Frontiers,"* 106.

35. Boyle, *UAW and the Heyday*, 113–20.

36. Boyle, *UAW and the Heyday*, 85–91; *New York Times*, August 26, 1952; Kornhauser et al., *When Labor Votes*, 31–32; Gillon, *Politics and Vision*, 85–88, 100–101; Lichtenstein, *Most Dangerous Man*, 319–22; Walter P. Reuther, Statement to Democratic Party convention platform committee, August 11, 1956, Paul and Claire Sifton Collection, Box 30.

37. Boyle, *UAW and the Heyday*, 64–65; Robert H. Zieger, *The CIO, 1935–1955* (Chapel Hill: University of North Carolina Press, 1995), 313–16; Walter P. Reuther, Administered prices in the automobile industry, transcript, January 28, 1958, Walter P. Reuther Collection, Box 567, f. 4; Walter P. Reuther, "The Future of American Education—A Labor View," Address before the National Council for Social Studies of the National Education Association, November 23, 1956, excerpt in Christman, ed., *Walter Reuther*, 176–90; William C. Berman, *The Politics of Civil Rights in the Truman Administration* (Columbus: Ohio State University Press, 1970), 137–81.

38. Boyle, *UAW and the Heyday*, 61–63, 68–69.

39. *New York Times*, January 6, 1953; Boyle, *UAW and the Heyday*, 108–13.

40. UAW, International Executive Board, Minutes, April 11–14, 1960, pp. 56–63; Boyle, *UAW and the Heyday*, 120–26, 133–35; Lichtenstein, *Most Dangerous Man*, 372; Wigderson, "UAW in the 1950's," 372–76, 381–85.

41. Fine, *"Expanding the Frontiers,"* 16–19, 35–62; Buffa, *Union Power*, 82–84, 86–88; Wigderson, "UAW in the 1950's, 346–47, 385–87.

42. Boyle, *UAW and the Heyday*, 65–67, 69.

43. Carew, *Reuther*, 88–89; Anthony Carew, *Labour under the Marshall Plan* (Detroit: Wayne State University Press, 1987), 120; Lichtenstein, *Most Dangerous Man*, 327–30.

44. Carew, *Reuther*, 89–92; Lichtenstein, *Most Dangerous Man*, 330.

45. Carew, *Reuther*, 89; Victor G. Reuther, *The Brothers Reuther and the Story of the UAW: A Memoir* (Boston: Houghton Mifflin, 1976), 423–27; Lichtenstein, *Most Dangerous Man*, 330–31.

46. Walter P. Reuther, "How to Beat the Communists," *Collier's*, February 28, 1948; CIO, *Proceedings of the Twelfth Constitutional Convention* [1950], 297.

47. Boyle, *UAW and the Heyday*, 100–102; Robert H. Zieger and Gilbert J. Gall, *American Workers, American Unions: The Twentieth Century*, 3d ed. (Baltimore: Johns Hopkins University Press, 2002), 203–9; Zieger, *CIO*, 357–71.

48. Boyle, *UAW and the Heyday*, 102–4; Lichtenstein, *Most Dangerous Man*, 322–23.

49. Boyle, *UAW and the Heyday*, 103; Joseph Goulden, *Meany* (New York: Atheneum, 1972), 195, 200–206; *New York Times*, June 3, 1953.

50. CIO, *Proceedings of the Seventeenth Constitutional Convention* [1955], 17. Critiques of the mid-century labor movement include Daniel Bell, "The Capitalism of the Proletariat: A Theory of American Trade-Unionism," in *The End of Ideology*, rev. ed. (New York: Collier Books, 1961), 211–26; Paul Jacobs, *The State of the Unions* (New York: Atheneum, 1963); Sidney Lens, *The Crisis of American Labor* (New York: A. S. Barnes, 1961); C. Wright Mills, *The New Men of Power* (New York: Harcourt, Brace, 1948).

51. Lichtenstein, *Most Dangerous Man*, 333–34.

52. Goulden, *Meany*, 271–75; on Lovestone, see Ted Morgan, *A Covert Life: Jay Lovestone, Communist, Anti-Communist, and Spymaster* (New York: Random House, 1999), 141–339; "India, the United States, and the Free World," Address before the Indian Council on World Affairs, New Delhi, India, April 5, 1956, in Christman, ed., *Walter Reuther*, 129–42; Walter P. Reuther, "An American Looks at Asia," Address to Sixth National Conference of the United States Commission for UNESCO, November 6–9, 1957, Walter P. Reuther Collection, Box 548, f. 8; *New York Times*, April 3, 15, 17, 1956; Carew, *Reuther*, 95–96; Boyle, *UAW and the Heyday*, 104–6; Lichtenstein, *Most Dangerous Man*, 332–33, 340–42.

53. "India, the United States, and the Free World," in Christman, ed., *Walter Reuther*, 134–37; "Future of American Education—A Labor View," in Christman, ed., *Walter Reuther*, 188; Walter P. Reuther, "A Proposal for . . . A Total Peace Offensive," July 15, 1950, Walter P. Reuther Collection, Box 568, f. 9; Speech to the First

National Conference on International and Social Development, April 8, 1952, Walter P. Reuther Collection, Box 417, f. 9; UAW press release, November 14, 1956, Walter P. Reuther Collection, Box 547, f. 10.

54. "Free Labor Meets Khrushchev," text of interview with Premier Nikita S. Khrushchev, San Francisco, California, September 29, 1959, in Christman, ed., *Walter Reuther*, 299–315; *New York Times*, September 21, 22, October 30, 31, 1959; Carew, *Reuther*, 97–99; Arthur M. Schlesinger, Jr., *A Thousand Days* (New York: Fawcett World Library, 1967), 348; Lichtenstein, *Most Dangerous Man*, 343–45.

55. Goulden, *Meany*, 263–71; Babson, *Unfinished Struggle*, 164; UAW, International Executive Board, Minutes, September 8–11, 1959, pp. 56–58.

56. Robert F. Kennedy, *The Enemy Within* (New York: Harper and Brothers, 1960), 266–99; Carew, *Reuther*, 85–86; "Racketeering and Corruption in the Labor Movement," section of the opening address of the sixteenth constitutional convention of the United Automobile, Aircraft and Agricultural Implement Workers of America, Atlantic City, New Jersey, April 7, 1957, in Christman, ed., *Walter Reuther*, 191–94; *United Automobile Worker*, December 1957; *New York Times*, April 12, 1958; a copy of Reuther's testimony before the committee, March 27–29, 1958, is in Walter P. Reuther Collection, Box 418, f. 8; Lichtenstein, *Most Dangerous Man*, 346–48.

57. *United Automobile Worker*, April 1954–December 1955; *New York Times*, December 18, 19, 1965; Walter H. Uphoff, *Kohler on Strike: Thirty Years of Conflict* (Boston: Beacon Press, 1966), 413–21; Arthur M. Schlesinger, Jr., *Robert Kennedy and His Times* (Boston: Houghton Mifflin, 1978), I, 296–97.

58. Walter P. Reuther to Senator Barry Goldwater, March 7, 1958, Walter P. Reuther Collection, Box 418, f. 5; Schlesinger, *Robert Kennedy*, I, 181–88; *New York Times*, March 30, 1958; *Detroit Times*, January 21, 1958; *Detroit News*, January 22, 1958; "The Mike Wallace Interview," text of television interview, New York, New York, October 17 and 18, 1960, p. 17, Walter P. Reuther Collection, Box 564, f. 9; Carew, *Reuther*, 87–88.

59. *Wall Street Journal*, September 22, 1958; *New York Times*, September 17, October 5, 1958; *Detroit Free Press*, November 2, 1958; UAW, International Executive Board, Minutes, October 7, 1958, pp. 37–55; Carew, *Reuther*, 86–87; Lichtenstein, *Most Dangerous Man*, 348–49.

60. Carew, *Reuther*, 96–97; *London Daily Express*, September 3, 1957; *UAW Solidarity*, May 1959; "Address before the Berlin Freedom Rally," West Berlin, Germany, May 1, 1959, in Christman, ed., *Walter Reuther*, 279–82; Lichtenstein, *Most Dangerous Man*, 336–37, 344.

61. The *Sunday [London] Times*, June 22, 1958; Boyle, *UAW and the Heyday*, 5–8, 106; Carew, *Reuther*, 85–86.

Chapter 10

"Some frosting on the Chrysler birthday cake:" Walter P. Reuther referring to a Christmas bonus plan won from Ford following the settlement with Chrysler in 1964. Reuther told reporters he hoped to get the "à la mode" from General Motors.

Detroit Daily Press, September 19, 1964; *UAW Solidarity*, September 1964; *New York Times*, September 19, 1964.

1. John B. Rae, *The American Automobile Industry* (Boston: Twayne, 1984), 117–29; *New York Times*, March 13, 1970.

2. Nelson Lichtenstein, "Reutherism on the Shop Floor: Union Strategy and Shop-Floor Conflict in the USA, 1946–70," in Steven Tolliday and Jonathan Zeitlin, eds., *Between Fordism and Flexibility: The Automobile Industry and Its Workers* (Oxford: Berg, 1992), 131, 134–36; Jim Ellis, president of Local 228, to Ken Bannon, August 25, 1964, Ken Bannon Collection, Box 20, f. 6.

3. "General Motors Corporation 1979 Bargaining Fact Sheet," 16, copy in Douglas Fraser Collection, Box 12, folder marked "GM(2)"; Nelson Lichtenstein, "UAW Bargaining Strategy and Shop-FLoor Conflict: 1946–1970," *Industrial Relations*, XXIV, No. 3 (Fall 1985), 376–77; *New York Times*, October 17, December 18, 1969; Lichtenstein, "Reutherism on the Shop Floor," 136–38; Walter P. Reuther, "The United Automobile Workers: Past, Present, and Future," *Virginia Law Review*, 50, No. 1 (1964), 64.

4. Ed Cray, *Chrome Colossus: General Motors and Its Times* (New York: McGraw-Hill, 1980), 448–49, 461; *UAW Solidarity*, June 1969; *New York Times*, December 7, 23, 1965, February 11, May 1, July 14, 1969.

5. Kenneth (Ken) Bannon interview with Warner Pflug, April 30, 1985, p. 22. See Reuther's statements on a resolution affirming the use of strikes to combat speedups and opposing a proposal to give locals more autonomy in calling local strikes; UAW, *Proceedings of the Eighteenth Constitutional Convention* [1962], 216–17, 519–22. Steven Tolliday and Jonathan Zeitlin, "Shop Floor Bargaining, Contract Unionism, and Job Control: An Anglo-American Comparison," in Tolliday and Zeitlin, eds., *Fordism and Flexibility*, 112; *New York Times*, March 21, April 4, May 12, June 19, July 7, 8, 9, 12, October 4, 6, 8, 9, November 2, 14, 1966.

6. Ken Bannon Collection, Boxes 45–46; *New York Times*, August 17, 19, 24, November 14–December 12, 1963; *Wall Street Journal*, September 23, 1963; "Investigation of alleged charges regarding violation of Article 30, Section 24 . . . against President Bernard Fox of Local 588," October 16, 1963, Walter P. Reuther Collection, Box 248, f. 31.

7. Walter P. Reuther Collection, Box 247, f. 24; *New York Times*, March 9, 10, 12, 14, 1967.

8. Show Cause Hearing on Local 1264, April 7, 1969, Walter P. Reuther Collection, Box 271, f. 46; *New York Times*, January 29, 30, February 5, 1966, November 14–15, 1967, April 9, 1969; *Detroit News*, April 7–10, 1969.

9. Walter P. Reuther, "The United Automobile Workers: Past, Present, and Future," 71. Louis Harris and Associates, "The Mandate of the UAW Rank and File for Contract Negotiations in 1961," May 1961, 1, 4–7; this is a summary version of a longer report: Louis Harris and Associates, "A Study in Depth of the Rank and File of the United Automobile Workers (AFL-CIO)"; copy in Walter P. Reuther Collection, Box 103, f. 7–12. Nelson Lichtenstein, *The Most Dangerous Man in Detroit: Walter Reuther and the Fate of American Labor* (New York: Basic Books, 1995), 360–61.

10. UAW, *Proceedings of Special Bargaining Convention* [1961], 15, 17.

11. *UAW Solidarity*, March 1963; UAW, *Proceedings of the Eighteenth Constitutional Convention* [1962], 60; *New York Times*, April 16, 29, 30, June 26, 1961.

12. William Serrin, *The Company and the Union* (New York: Alfred A. Knopf, 1973), 176; *UAW Solidarity*, September 1961, February 1963; *New York Times*, June 29, August 27, 1961.

13. *Detroit News*, October 3–5, 1961; material on the Ford negotiations is in the Ken Bannon Collection, Box 11, ff. 19–20; *UAW Solidarity*, October 1961; *New York Times*, October 4, 12, 15, 20, 1961.

14. Walter P. Reuther to Louis G. Seaton, September 2, 1961, Walter P. Reuther Collection, Box 102, f. 6; *New York Times*, February 7, 1962.

15. Leonard Woodcock interview with Frank Cormier and William J. Eaton, June 20, 1968, p. 2; *UAW Solidarity*, September 1961; *Detroit News*, September 7–20, 1961; *New York Times*, September 7, 12, 21, 27, 1961; *Time*, September 21, 1961, pp. 110–11; material on the strike in Walter P. Reuther Collection, Box 127, ff. 1–8.

16. *UAW Solidarity*, September 1961.

17. UAW, *Proceedings of the Nineteenth Constitutional Convention* [1964], 41; *Report of Walter P. Reuther . . . Part One: UAW in Action, March 20–27, 1964*, pp. 13–35; Walter Heller in UAW, International Executive Board, Minutes, March 22, 1979, p. 6.

18. Lichtenstein, *Most Dangerous Man*, 398.

19. "Collective Bargaining Resolution," adopted at UAW, *Proceedings of the Nineteenth Constitutional Convention* [1964]; *Detroit Daily Press*, September 25, 1964; *New York Times*, March 21, May 2, 1964.

20. UAW, International Executive Board, Minutes, August 20, 1964, pp. 21 ff., September 9, 1964, pp. 55–58; *Report of President Walter P. Reuther . . . Part One: UAW in Action, May 16–21, 1966*, pp. 8–15, *Part Three*, pp. 101–11; Walter P. Reuther Collection, Box 129, ff. 15–18, Box 130, ff. 1–6; *UAW Solidarity*, September 1964, January 1965, April 1967, December 1969; Douglas Fraser interview with John Barnard, May–June, 1990, p. 70; Anthony Carew, *Walter Reuther* (Manchester: University of Manchester Press, 1993), 106; *New York Times*, July 3–September 10, 1964, December 4, 1966; Walter P. Reuther, "The Worker and His Mental Health," *Industrial Medicine and Surgery*, XXXIV (October 1965), 777–80; Lichtenstein, *Most Dangerous Man*, 399–400.

21. *Detroit Daily Press*, September 17–19, 1964; *UAW Solidarity*, September 1964, January 1966; UAW, International Executive Board, Minutes, January 15–16, 1968, p. 40; *Report of President Walter P. Reuther . . . Part One: UAW in Action, May 16–21, 1966*, pp. 19, 24–34.

22. *Report of President Walter P. Reuther . . . Part One: UAW in Action, May 16–21, 1966*, p. 24, *Part Three*, pp. 84–86; *Detroit Daily Press*, September 17–19, 1964; *New York Times*, September 19, November 24, 1964.

23. *Report of President Walter P. Reuther . . . Part One: UAW in Action, May 16–21, 1966*, pp. 21–24, *Part Three*, pp. 88–93; B. J. Widick, "GM Strike: Prototype of More Conflict," *Nation*, November 16, 1964; Walter P. Reuther to Louis J. Seaton, September 24, 1964, UAW-Vice President Leonard Woodcock Collection, Box 48, f.

16; "UAW-General Motors Local Leadership Newsletter," October 9, 1964, copy in UAW-Vice President Leonard Woodcock Collection, Box 48, f. 12; Lichtenstein, *Most Dangerous Man*, 400.

24. *Detroit Daily Press*, September 26–October 1, 1964; *New York Times*, September 26, 30, November 9, 1964; Lichtenstein, "UAW Bargaining Strategy and Shop-Floor Conflict," 377–78; newspaper clippings and other material on these negotiations and this strike are in the Ken Bannon Collection, Boxes 17–18; *UAW Solidarity*, September, October 1964; Seaton quoted in Lichtenstein, *Most Dangerous Man*, 401.

25. UAW, *Proceedings of the Thirteenth Constitutional Convention* [1951], 255–57; UAW, *Proceedings of the Sixteenth Constitutional Convention* [1957], 332; UAW, *Proceedings of the Twentieth Constitutional Convention* [1966], 157–58; Richard Korn, *A Union and Its Retired Workers: A Case Study of the UAW* (Ithaca: New York State School of Industrial and Labor Relations, Cornell University, 1976), 3–6.

26. UAW, *Proceedings of the Seventeenth Constitutional Convention* [1959], 116; UAW, International Executive Board, Minutes, March 2–6, 1970, pp. 241–44; Korn, *A Union and Its Retired Workers*, 10–13.

27. Raymond H. Berndt interview with Jack W. Skeels, May 3, 1963, pp. 26–27; *UAW Solidarity*, July, August 1961, July 1964, September 1966, February 1969; Korn, *A Union and Its Retired Workers*, 19–38.

28. UAW, International Executive Board, Minutes, January 31–February 3, 1967, pp. 96–97.

29. Lichtenstein, *Most Dangerous Man*, 415–19; UAW, International Executive Board, Minutes, January 15–16, 1968, pp. 41–42; *New York Times*, January 28, 1966, April 16–18, June 29, July 3, 1967.

30. Oliver Quayle and Company, "A Study in Depth of the Rank and File of the United Automobile Workers (AFL-CIO)," May 1967, pp. 69–71, 108, 115.

31. Leonard Woodcock interview with John Barnard, January 18, 30, February 7, 1991, p. 40; Douglas Fraser interview with John Barnard, May–June, 1990, pp. 100–101, 104–7; Kenneth (Ken) Bannon interview with Warner Pflug, April 30, 1985, p. 43; Lichtenstein, *Most Dangerous Man*, 414–16; Amberg, *Union Inspiration*, 179–206; Seth M. Wigderson, "The UAW in the 1950's" (Ph.D. diss., Wayne State University, 1989), pp. 162–64; Robert M. Macdonald, *Collective Bargaining in the Automobile Industry* (New Haven: Yale University Press, 1963), 134–205.

32. Leonard Woodcock interview with John Barnard, January 18, 30, February 7, 1991, pp. 58–59; Douglas Fraser interview with John Barnard, May–June, 1990, p. 99; Macdonald, *Collective Bargaining*, 190–91; Reuther, "The United Automobile Workers: Past, Present, Future," 71; Wigderson, "UAW in the 1950's," 447–72; Jack Stieber, *Governing the UAW* (New York: John Wiley and Sons, 1962), 47–48.

33. UAW, *Proceedings of the Twentieth Constitutional Convention* [1966], 404–13; Kenneth (Ken) Bannon interview with Warner Pflug, April 30, 1985, p. 43; *New York Times*, July 3, 17, August 18, 21, 23, 25, 28, September 19, 1966; Douglas Fraser interview with John Barnard, May–June, 1990, pp. 100–101; Lichtenstein, *Most Dangerous Man*, 414–16.

34. UAW, International Executive Board, Minutes, February 22, 1967, pp. 15–19; Lichtenstein, *Most Dangerous Man*, 414–16; Leonard Woodcock interview with John Barnard, January 18, 30, February 7, 1991, pp. 73–74; Douglas Fraser interview with John Barnard, May–June, 1990, p. 99; *UAW Solidarity*, April 1967.

35. Walter Reuther, "To Foster Fair Employment in Our Own Industries and to Act Vigorously in the Public Arena," in *Equal Opportunity Is Good Labor Practice* (National Conference of Christians and Jews, 1968–70), 26; UAW, International Executive Board, Minutes, October 6–9, 1969, p. 208; B. J. Widick, *Detroit: City of Race and Class Violence*, rev. ed. (Detroit: Wayne State University Press, 1989), 148; Thomas J. Sugrue, *The Origins of the Urban Crisis: Race and Inequality in Postwar Detroit* (Princeton: Princeton University Press, 1996), 100, 102–5; William B. Gould, *Black Workers in White Unions: Job Discrimination in the United States* (Ithaca: Cornell University Press, 1977), 371–84.

36. UAW, *Proceedings of Special Collective Bargaining Convention* [1967], 21–33; *New York Times*, May 30, 1966, March 15, 17, April 21–22, 1967; *UAW Solidarity*, June 1966, March, May 1967; *Report of Walter P. Reuther . . . Part One: UAW in Action, May 4–10, 1968*, pp. 10–15.

37. UAW, *Proceedings of Special Collective Bargaining Convention* [1967], 20–30; *Detroit News*, September 6–October 23, 1967; *Report of Walter P. Reuther . . . Part One: UAW in Action, May 4–10, 1968*, pp. 5–28; *New York Times*, May 15, July 9, 11, 16, 20, August 13, 26, 31, September 2, 7, October 8, 9, 1967; Kenneth (Ken) Bannon interview with Warner Pflug, April 30, 1985, p. 43.

38. Leonard Woodcock interview with John Barnard, January 18, 30, February 7, 1991, pp. 73–74; *UAW Solidarity*, December 1967; *Report of Walter P. Reuther . . . Part One: UAW in Action, May 4–10, 1968*, pp. 28–33; *New York Times*, October 22, 1967; Lichtenstein, *Most Dangerous Man*, 418.

39. Ken Bannon Collection, Boxes 22–28 for the Ford negotiations and strike; Kenneth (Ken) Bannon interview with Warner Pflug, April 30, 1985, pp. 44–47; Leonard Woodcock interview with John Barnard, January 18, 30, February 7, 1991, p. 40; *New York Times*, June 1, 1969; Lichtenstein, *Most Dangerous Man*, 419.

40. *Report of Walter P. Reuther . . . Part One: UAW in Action, May 4–10, 1968*, pp. 33–41; UAW Chrysler Department Collection, Box 75, ff. 9, 10, 11, 16; *UAW Solidarity*, December 1967; *New York Times*, November 9, 10, 18, 1967.

41. *Report of Walter P. Reuther . . . Part One: UAW in Action, May 4–10, 1968*, pp. 41–44; *UAW Solidarity*, December 1967–March 1968; *New York Times*, December 16, 30, 1967, January–April 1968.

42. *Report of Walter P. Reuther . . . Part One: UAW in Action, May 4–10, 1968*, pp. 72–75; *Section Two-Part Two, Departmental Reports*, pp. 8–14; *UAW Solidarity*, December 1967, *New York Times*, October 3, 24, November 19, December 22, 1967.

43. *Report of Walter P. Reuther . . . Part One: UAW in Action, May 4–10, 1968*, pp. 79–83; *Report of Walter P. Reuther . . . Part One: UAW in Action, April 20–25, 1970*, pp. 30–32; *UAW Solidarity*, March–September, 1968; *New York Times*, August 31, October 8, November 2, 1968.

44. Sam Gindin, *The Canadian Auto Workers: The Birth and Transformation of a Union* (Toronto: James Lorimer, 1995), 1–137.

45. UAW Administrative Letter for US-Canada free trade agreement, Walter P. Reuther Collection, Box 49, f. 7; *Report of Walter P. Reuther . . . Part One: UAW in Action, May 4–10, 1968*, pp. 75–78; Gindin, *Canadian Auto Workers*, 145–59.

46. Carew, *Reuther*, 92–94.

47. Frank Cormier and William J. Eaton, *Reuther* (Englewood Cliffs, NJ: Prentice-Hall, 1970), 367–68; Lichtenstein, *Most Dangerous Man*, 338–40.

48. *UAW Solidarity*, May 1959; *New York Times*, May 2, 1959.

49. Walter P. Reuther, "Declaration at Detroit," in *Free Labour World*, July–August 1966, pp. 9–14; Carew, *Reuther*, 95.

50. *New York Times*, May 6, 8, November 25, December 2, 1962, November 17, 1964; Carew, *Reuther*, 117–25; *Tribune*, June 6, 1969; Reuther reported on his trip to Japan in UAW, International Executive Board, Minutes, December 4–6, 1962, pp. 161–88.

Chapter 11

"Something short of perfect": Walter P. Reuther, July 30, 1960, to his staff. "In politics you arrive at that point you arrive at in collective bargaining. You exert all your influence, fight as hard as you can, and then you have to make a decision. . . . You wind up doing something short of perfect and that is where we are in the political struggle." "Special Meeting," July 30, 1960, Box 11, f. 17, UAW Citizenship Department Collection. Quoted in Nelson Lichtenstein, *The Most Dangerous Man in Detroit: Walter Reuther and the Fate of American Labor* (New York: Basic Books, 1995), 356.

1. UAW, International Executive Board, Minutes, December 13, 1960, quoted in Kevin Boyle, *The UAW and the Heyday of American Liberalism, 1945–1968* (Ithaca: Cornell University Press, 1995), 147. Among the many studies of the Kennedy presidency and politics in the 1960s are: James T. Patterson, *Grand Expectations: The United States, 1945–1974* (New York: Oxford University Press, 1996), 442–709; David Burner, *Making Peace with the 60s* (Princeton: Princeton University Press, 1996); Arthur M. Schlesinger, Jr., *A Thousand Days: John F. Kennedy in the White House* (Boston: Houghton Mifflin, 1965); Carl M. Brauer, *John F. Kennedy and the Second Reconstruction* (New York: Columbia University Press, 1977); Richard Reeves, *President Kennedy: Profile of Power* (New York: Simon and Schuster, 1993); Allen J. Matusow, *The Unraveling of America: A History of Liberalism in the 1960s* (New York: Harper & Row, 1984); Jim F. Heath, *Decade of Disillusionment: The Kennedy-Johnson Years* (Bloomington: Indiana University Press, 1975).

2. Boyle, *UAW and the Heyday*, 140–43; Eleanor Roosevelt to "Dear Walter," May 25 [1960], Eleanor Roosevelt Collection, Container 4429, Franklin D. Roosevelt Library; Theodore H. White, *The Making of the President 1960* (New York: Atheneum, 1961), 78–149; Lichtenstein, *Most Dangerous Man*, 354–55.

3. Jack Conway interview with Frank Cormier and William J. Eaton, January 10, 1968, pp. 4–6; Joseph L. Rauh, Jr., interview with Frank Cormier and William J. Eaton, December 18, 1967, p. 3; Boyle, *UAW and the Heyday*, 143–44; Lichtenstein, *Most Dangerous Man*, 355–56.

4. Boyle, *UAW and the Heyday*, 144–47; *Detroit News*, September 5, 1960; *UAW Solidarity*, September 12, 1960; Lichtenstein, *Most Dangerous Man*, 356–57; Oliver Quayle and Company, "A Study in Depth of the Rank and File of the United Automobile Workers (AFL-CIO)," June 1967, Vol. VI, Pt. I, pp. 1–6; Theodore C. Sorensen, *Kennedy* (New York: Harper & Row, 1965), 439; UAW, *Proceedings of the Eighteenth Constitutional Convention* [1962], 372.

5. Boyle, *UAW and the Heyday*, 147–54; Anthony Carew, *Walter Reuther* (Manchester: University of Manchester Press, 1993), 101–3; Lichtenstein, *Most Dangerous Man*, 361–66; see *UAW Solidarity*, September–December 1962, for a series of articles lauding social democracy in European nations presented as an inspiration for U.S. policy makers; Walter P. Reuther to John F. Kennedy, June 19, 1962, Walter P. Reuther Collection, Box 367, f. 10; UAW, International Executive Board, Minutes, June 18–20, 1962, pp. 84–90, March 5–7, 1963, pp. 149–56; *New York Times*, February 16, November 20, 1963.

6. Boyle, *UAW and the Heyday*, 152; Carew, *Reuther*, 103; *New York Times*, November 20, 1963; UAW, International Executive Board, Minutes, January 8–11, 1962, p. 110.

7. *UAW Solidarity*, March 1962; Walter P. Reuther, "A Proposal for . . . A Total Peace Offensive . . . A Positive Program to Defeat Communism," p. 19, copy in Walter P. Reuther Collection, Box 420, f. 7; Walter P. Reuther to John F. Kennedy, telegram, March 14, 1961, Walter P. Reuther Collection, Box 367, f. 8; statement before the House Ways and Means Committee on the Trade Expansion Act of 1962, Walter P. Reuther Collection, Box 425, f. 8; Walter P. Reuther to John F. Kennedy, October 23, 1962, Walter P. Reuther Collection, Box 367, f. 10; Walter P. Reuther to John F. Kennedy, telegram, July 26, 1963, Walter P. Reuther Collection, Box 367, f. 11; Walter P. Reuther, "We *Can* Make the Russians Disarm," *Saturday Evening Post*, December 7, 1963; Boyle, *UAW and the Heyday*, 72, 144; Lichtenstein, *Most Dangerous Man*, 357.

8. Lichtenstein, *Most Dangerous Man*, 358.

9. August Meier and Elliott Rudwick, *Black Detroit and the Rise of the UAW* (New York: Oxford University Press, 1979), 208; UAW, International Executive Board, Minutes, September 24–26, 1963, p. 48; Boyle, *UAW and the Heyday*, 167–68, 171.

10. Walter P. Reuther, Testimony before the Democratic Platform Committee, July 7, 1960, Walter P. Reuther Collection, Box 550, f. 3; *New York Times*, July 8, 1960; Walter P. Reuther to John F. Kennedy, November 21, 1961, Walter P. Reuther Collection, Box 367, f. 8. For the Kennedys and the civil rights movement, see Taylor Branch, *Parting the Waters: America in the King Years, 1954–1963* (New York: Simon and Schuster, 1988), 351–922; Brauer, *John F. Kennedy*, 1–320; Matusow, *Unraveling of America*, 60–96.

11. Arthur M. Schlesinger, Jr., *Robert Kennedy and His Times* (Boston: Houghton Mifflin, 1978), I, 349; undated memo, Douglas Fraser Collection, Box 28, folder marked "Mazey, Emil"; UAW, International Executive Board, Minutes, May 23, 1961, pp. 64–67; Kevin Boyle, "Little More than Ashes; The UAW and American Reform in the 1960s," in Kevin Boyle, ed., *Organized Labor and American Pol-*

itics, 1894–1994: The Labor-Liberal Alliance (Albany: State University of New York Press, 1998), 222; *New York Times*, August 1963; Irving Bluestone interview with John Barnard, October 1988–November 1992, p. 86; Walter P. Reuther, "The United Automobile Workers: Past, Present, and Future," *Virginia Law Review*, 50, No. 1 (1964), p. 100; Boyle, *UAW and the Heyday*, 169–70; Irving Bernstein, *Promises Kept: John F. Kennedy's New Frontier* (New York: Oxford University Press, 1991), 92.

12. Walter P. Reuther, Transcript of testimony before the House Judiciary Committee, July 19, 1963, Walter P. Reuther Collection, Box 415, f. 13; *New York Times*, July 20, 31, 1963; Boyle, *UAW and the Heyday*, 170–71.

13. Boyle, *UAW and the Heyday*, 172–76, 181.

14. *Detroit News*, June 24, 1963; *New York Times*, June 24, 1963; Carew, *Reuther*, 103; Lichtenstein, *Most Dangerous Man*, 382–83; Branch, *Parting the Waters*, 842–43.

15. Boyle, *UAW and the Heyday*, 176–77; Lichtenstein, *Most Dangerous Man*, 382–85; Schlesinger, *Robert Kennedy*, I, 364.

16. Joseph Goulden, *Meany* (New York: Atheneum, 1972), 322–23; *New York Times*, August 13–14, 1963; UAW, International Executive Board, Minutes, September 24–26, 1963, pp. 48–50; Walter P. Reuther, Note for George Meany File, August 9, 1963, Walter P. Reuther Collection, Box 302, f. 6; Lichtenstein, *Most Dangerous Man*, 385; Irving Bluestone interview with John Barnard, October 1988–November 1992, pp. 146–48.

17. UAW, International Executive Board, Minutes, September 24–26, 1963, pp. 56–63; Boyle, *UAW and the Heyday*, 177–80; Lichtenstein, *Most Dangerous Man*, 385–86.

18. *New York Times*, August 29, 1963; Walter P. Reuther, Transcript of Remarks, August 28, 1963, Walter P. Reuther Collection, Box 552, f. 3; Irving Bluestone interview with John Barnard, October 1988–November 1992, p. 84; Lichtenstein, *Most Dangerous Man*, 386–87; Branch, *Parting the Waters*, 883.

19. Walter P. Reuther to Mrs. John F. Kennedy, May 8, 1964, Walter P. Reuther Collection, Box 368, f. 5; a copy of Robert F. Kennedy's remarks is in the UAW Vice President's Office—Leonard Woodcock Files, Box 46, f. 10.

20. Herbert R. Northrup et al., *Negro Employment in Basic Industry: A Study of Racial Policies in Six Industries* (Philadelphia: Wharton School, University of Pennsylvania, 1970), I, 76–80; Jack Stieber, *Governing the UAW* (New York: John Wiley and Sons, 1962), 41; Thomas J. Sugrue, *The Origins of the Urban Crisis: Race and Inequality in Postwar Detroit* (Princeton: Princeton University Press, 1996), 97.

21. Sugrue, *Origins*, 103–5; Seth M. Wigderson, "The UAW in the 1950's," (Ph.D. diss., Wayne State University, 1989), 390.

22. Marc Stepp interview with John Barnard, June 10, 18, 25, 1993, pp. 11–12; UAW, International Executive Board, June 24–26, 1968, p. 196.

23. Marc Stepp interview with John Barnard, June 10, 18, 25, 1993, p. 11–12; *New York Times*, May 12, 1968.

24. Marc Stepp interview with John Barnard, June 10, 18, 25, 1993, p. 14; B. J. Widick, *Detroit: City of Race and Class Violence*, rev. ed. (Detroit: Wayne State

University Press, 1989), 149–50, 159–61; Steve Babson, "Living in Two Worlds: The Immigrant Experience in Detroit," *Michigan Quarterly Review*, XXV, No. 2 (Spring 1986), 378; Lichtenstein, *Most Dangerous Man*, 375–76; Heather Ann Thompson, *Whose Detroit? Politics, Labor, and Race in a Modern American City* (Ithaca: Cornell University Press, 2001), 49–54.

25. Stieber, *Governing the UAW*, 42–45; Horace Sheffield interview with John Herling, October 14, 1983, pp. 13–14; Boyle, *UAW and the Heyday*, 129–31; UAW, *Proceedings of the Seventeenth Constitutional Convention* [1959], 362–63.

26. Jack Conway interview with John Herling, July 15, 1979, pp. 50–52; Horace Sheffield interview with John Herling, October 14, 1983, p. 18; Horace Sheffield interview with Herbert Hill, July 24, 1968, pp. 18–23; Douglas Fraser interview with John Barnard, May–June, 1990, p. 89; Douglas Fraser interview with John Herling, February 21, 1983, pp. 20–21; UAW, *Proceedings of the Eighteenth Constitutional Convention* [1962], 432–35, 506–11; *New York Times*, May 9, 10, 1962, August 1, 1968; Lichtenstein, *Most Dangerous Man*, 378–81; William B. Gould, *Black Workers in White Unions: Job Discrimination in the United States* (Ithaca: Cornell University Press, 1977), 387–88.

27. Shelton Tappes interview with Herbert Hill and Roberta McBride, February 10, 1968, p. 38; a copy of the department's summary report for 1970 is in the Leonard Woodcock Collection, Box 22, f. 5.

28. Sidney Fine, *"Expanding the Frontiers of Civil Rights": Michigan, 1948–1968* (Detroit: Wayne State University Press, 2000), 130, 327–30; Reuther, "The United Automobile Workers: Past, Present, Future," 101; *New York Times*, June 28, 1961; *Report of Walter P. Reuther . . . October 9–16, 1959*, p. 356; *Report of Walter P. Reuther . . . May 4–10, 1962. Part Three: Departmental Reports*, pp. 127–28. Bennet M. Berger examines the Milpitas, California community in *Working-Class Suburb: A Study of Auto Workers in Suburbia* (Berkeley: University of California Press, 1960).

29. Nancy F. Gabin, *Feminism in the Labor Movement: Women and the United Auto Workers, 1935–1975* (Ithaca: Cornell University Press, 1990), 144, 146–47, 160–64; *United Automobile Worker*, January 1956; *UAW Solidarity*, December 1969.

30. Gabin, *Feminism in the Labor Movement*, 167–68, 190–91.

31. Ibid., 200; Philip S. Foner, *Women and the American Labor Movement from World War I to the Present* (New York: Free Press, 1980), 482–83. For the somewhat tangled history of repeal of protective legislation in Michigan, see Sidney Fine, *"Expanding the Frontiers of Civil Rights": Michigan, 1948–1968* (Detroit: Wayne State University Press, 2000), 275–77; *Detroit Free Press*, April 24, 25, 1970; *UAW Solidarity*, May 1970.

32. For Reuther's convention speech endorsing the proposal, see UAW, *Proceedings of the Twentieth Constitutional Convention* [1966], 144–45; Olga Madar interview with John Herling, October 20, 1984, pp. 5–12; Gabin, *Feminism in the Labor Movement*, 216–18; Douglas Fraser interview with John Herling, February 21, 1983, pp. 14–18; Irving Bluestone interview with John Barnard, October 1988–November 1992, pp. 88–89; *UAW Solidarity*, June 1966; *Wall Street Journal*, July 24, 1967; Foner, *Women and the Labor Movement*, 497.

33. Victor G. Reuther, *The Brothers Reuther and the Story of the UAW: A Memoir* (Boston: Houghton Mifflin, 1976), 447; Walter P. Reuther to Lyndon B. Johnson, March 16, 1965, June 25, 1965, October 18, 1965, Walter P. Reuther Collection, Box 368, ff. 12, 13; Boyle, *Organized Labor and American Politics,* 223–24.

34. Memo and enclosures, Walter P. Reuther to Lyndon B. Johnson, January [2], 1964, Walter P. Reuther Collection, Box 368, f. 9; UAW press release, "UAW Executive Board Urges Prompt Senate Passage of House-Approved Civil Rights Bill," May 6, 1964, Walter P. Reuther Collection, Box 578, f. 1; Boyle, *UAW and the Heyday,* 181–84; Lichtenstein, *Most Dangerous Man,* 389; Taylor E. Dark, *The Unions and the Democrats: An Enduring Alliance* (Ithaca: Cornell University Press 1999), 55, 61.

35. *New York Times,* May 10, 1963, October 15, 1964; *UAW Solidarity,* January 1965; Quayle et al., "A Study in Depth," Vol. VI, Pt. II, pp. 15–18; Boyle, *UAW and the Heyday,* 197–98.

36. Stephen Schlossberg tape interview with John Herling, June 21, 1983; Boyle, *UAW and the Heyday,* 193–94.

37. Carew, *Reuther,* 104–5; Joseph L. Rauh, Jr. interview with John Herling, n.d., II, 17–33; Joseph L. Rauh, Jr., interview with William J. Eaton, December 18, 1967, pp. 5–11; Stephen Schlossberg tape interview with John Herling, June 21, 1983; Boyle, *UAW and the Heyday,* 195–96; Lichtenstein, *Most Dangerous Man,* 392–95.

38. *UAW Solidarity,* November 1965; UAW, International Executive Board, Minutes, March 23–26, 1965, p. 103.

39. *New York Times,* March 3, 1965; Walter P. Reuther to Lyndon B. Johnson, March 9, 1965, Walter P. Reuther Collection, Box 368, f. 12; Walter P. Reuther to National Coalition of Conscience members, March 1965, Walter P. Reuther Collection, Box 377, f. 13; Walter P. Reuther to Willie G. Brooks, president UAW Local 453, April 13, 1965, Walter P. Reuther Collection, Box 578, f. 3; Boyle, *UAW and the Heyday,* 198–99.

40. UAW, International Executive Board, Minutes, March 23–26, 1965, p. 103; Walter P. Reuther to Willy Brandt, June 18, 1965, Walter P. Reuther Collection, Box 463, f. 6; Boyle, *UAW and the Heyday,* 199–201.

41. King quoted in Boyle, *UAW and the Heyday,* 201.

42. Walter P. Reuther, Statement in support of an Anti-Poverty Program before the House Committee on Labor and Education, April 9, 1964, Walter P. Reuther Collection, Box 417, f. 11; *New York Times,* May 29, 1964; Walter P. Reuther to Lyndon B. Johnson, March 19, June 26, 1964, Walter P. Reuther Collection, Box 368, f. 9; Boyle, *UAW and the Heyday,* 187–88; Lichtenstein, *Most Dangerous Man,* 391–92.

43. *New York Times,* April 26, 1964, May 27, November 7, 1965, August 22, 1966; Walter P. Reuther to Hubert H. Humphrey, March 2, 1965, Walter P. Reuther Collection, Box 370, f. 1; Walter P. Reuther to Lyndon B. Johnson, June 26, 1964, Walter P. Reuther Collection, Box 368, f. 9; Boyle, *UAW and the Heyday,* 213–16; Lichtenstein, *Most Dangerous Man,* 389–92.

44. *New York Times,* April 14, 15, September 14, October 6, 11, 14, 19, 1966, March 11, 1968.

45. *New York Times*, June 5, 15, 20, 1968; a copy of Reuther's speech is in Walter P. Reuther Collection, Box 517, f. 22 and of a press release, June 19, 1968, in Walter P. Reuther Collection, Box 559, f. 1; UAW, International Executive Board, Minutes, June 24–26, 1968, pp. 45–48; Boyle, *UAW and the Heyday*, 242–43, 245–46.

46. Walter P. Reuther to Lyndon B. Johnson, May 13, 1965, Walter P. Reuther Collection, Box 46, f. 4; UAW, International Executive Board, Minutes, January 10–13, 1966, pp. 187–90; Walter P. Reuther to Mayor Jerome Cavanaugh, January 26, 1966, Walter P. Reuther Collection, Box 428, f. 11; *New York Times*, November 15, 1965, December 2, 1966, June 4, 12, 1967; Boyle, *UAW and the Heyday*, 202–5; Lichtenstein, *Most Dangerous Man*, 402–4.

47. *New York Times*, November 7, 1965, March 11, 1966, April 22, July 12, 1970; Walter P. Reuther statement before the Select Subcommittee on Labor of the House Committee on Education and Labor on Proposals to Amend the Fair Labor Standards Act, June 24, 1965, Walter P. Reuther Collection, Box 422, f. 13; Walter P. Reuther Collection, Box 417, ff. 2–4; UAW, International Executive Board, Minutes, January 10–13, 1966, pp. 184–85, June 24–26, 1968, pp., 173–74; Walter P. Reuther to Lyndon B. Johnson, February 11, 1966, February 2, 1967, June 26, 1968, Walter P. Reuther Collection, Box 369, ff. 1, 3, 7.

48. Walter P. Reuther, "America's Challenge: A National System to Organize and Finance Personal Health Service to Meet the Nation's Health Needs," October 14, 1969, copy in Walter P. Reuther Collection, Box 562, f.1; *New York Times*, November 7, 1965, November 15, 1968, January 31, September 28, October 15, 1969, January 27, 1970.

49. Walter P. Reuther Collection, Box 417, ff. 2–4; UAW, International Executive Board, Minutes, June 24–26, 1968, pp. 173–74; Irving Bluestone interview with John Barnard, October 1988–November 1992, pp. 168–71.

Chapter 12

"A stressful time": Douglas Fraser referring to the divisions within the UAW leadership over the Vietnam War, interview with John Barnard, May–June 1990, p. 116.

1. Kevin Boyle, *The UAW and the Heyday of American Liberalism, 1945–1968* (Ithaca: Cornell University Press, 1995), 207; James T. Patterson, *Grand Expectations: The United States, 1945–1974* (New York: Oxford University Press, 1996), 593–709; Allen J. Matusow, *The Unraveling of America: A History of Liberalism in the 1960s* (New York: Harper & Row, 1984), 275–439; Robert Dallek, *Flawed Giant: Lyndon Johnson and His Times, 1961–1973* (New York: Oxford University Press, 1998).

2. Boyle, *UAW and the Heyday*, 207.

3. Joseph L. Rauh, Jr., interview, May 7, 1987, quoted in Boyle, *UAW and the Heyday*, 211; interview with Irving Bluestone in Frank F. Koscielski, "Divided Loyalties: American Unions and the Vietnam War" (Ph.D. diss., Wayne State University, 1997), 81–82; Frank Winn interview with John Herling, October 22, 1983, pp.

51–52; Douglas Fraser interview with John Barnard, May–June 1990, p. 119; Paul Schrade interview with John Herling, December 10, 1977, p. 4

4. *UAW Solidarity*, 1960–1965; UAW, International Executive Board, Minutes, March 23–26, 1965, pp. 116–18; Walter P. Reuther to Lyndon B. Johnson, March 30, 1965, Walter P. Reuther Collection, Box 368, f. 12; Emil Mazey to all officers and board members, March 4, 1965, Walter P. Reuther Collection, Box 597, f. 1; *New York Times*, April 4, 1965; Boyle, *UAW and the Heyday*, 208–9.

5. UAW, International Executive Board, Minutes, March 23–26, 1965, pp. 116–18; Nat Weinberg to Walter P. Reuther, January 28, 1966, Walter P. Reuther Collection, Box 165, f. 6; Koscielski, "Divided Loyalties," 82 ff.; Boyle, *UAW and the Heyday*, 207–11.

6. Paul Schrade interview with John Herling, December 10, 1977, pp. 47–48; Mazey speeches to different audiences, May 15, August 7, September 17, 1965, in Emil L. Mazey Collection, Box 3, ff. 2, 9; Koscielski, "Divided Loyalties," 82; Philip S. Foner, *U.S. Labor and the Vietnam War* (New York: International Publishers, 1989), 23; Boyle, *UAW and the Heyday*, 207–11, Nelson Lichtenstein, *The Most Dangerous Man in Detroit: Walter Reuther and the Fate of American Labor* (New York: Basic Books, 1995), 404–6.

7. UAW, International Executive Board, Minutes, October 12–14, 1965, pp. 181–94; *New York Times*, October 22, 1965; Boyle, *UAW and the Heyday*, 211.

8. UAW, *Proceedings of the Twentieth Constitutional Convention* [1966], 372–73, 474; *New York Times*, May 21–22, 1966; Douglas Fraser interview with John Barnard, May–June 1990, p. 117.

9. AFL-CIO, *Proceedings of the Sixth Constitutional Convention* [1965], 133, 563–64; Foner, *U.S. Labor*, 30–31.

10. Edward F. Gray interview with John Herling, July 20, 1983, p. 63; Foner, *U.S. Labor*, 42.

11. *Labor Today*, VI, No. 6 (Winter 1967–68), 5–12, 13–14; Foner, *U.S. Labor*, 51–53, 60–61, 65; Koscielski, "Divided Loyalties," 61–62, 98–100; see also "Emil Mazey Writes a Letter to George Meany," *Dissent*, 15 (May–June 1968), 205; *New York Times*, September 25, November 13, December 12, 1967; *Business Week*, November 18, 1967.

12. *Meet the Press*, 11, No. 39 (Millwood New Jersey, 1973), 5–8; Jack Conway interview with Frank Cormier and William J. Eaton, December 27, 1968, p. 1; Paul Schrade interview with John Herling, December 10, 1977, p. 4; Frank Winn interview with John Herling, October 22, 1983, p. 48; Koscielski, "Divided Loyalties," 87–91; Elizabeth Reuther Dickmeyer, *A Daughter Strikes* (Southfield, MI: Spelman, 1989); UAW, International Executive Board, Minutes, March 1–2, 1968, p. 59; *New York Times*, September 25, 1967.

13. Douglas Fraser interview with John Barnard, May–June 1990, pp. 117, 120; Boyle, *UAW and the Heyday*, 221–22; Koscielski, "Divided Loyalties," 94; Oliver Quayle and Company, "A Study in Depth of the Rank and File of the United Automobile Workers (AFL-CIO)," (June 1967), pp. 67–71, 78; Harlan Hahn, "Dove Sentiments among Blue-Collar Workers," *Dissent* 17 (May–June 1970), 202–5; Henry Berger, "Organized Labor and American Foreign Policy," in Irving Louis Horowitz

et al., eds., *The American Working Class: Prospects for the 1980's* (New Brunswick: Transaction Books, 1979), 193–211; Andrew Levison, *The Working-Class Majority* (New York: Penguin Books, 1975), 158–63; Brendan and Patricia Sexton, *Blue Collars and Hard Hats* (New York: Random House, 1971), 52–53, 102.

14. Koscielski, "Divided Loyalties," 138.

15. Boyle, *UAW and the Heyday,* 221; Sexton and Sexton, *Blue Collars,* 52–53; UAW, *Proceedings of the Twentieth Constitutional Convention* [1966], 372–73, 470. When a UAW political publication, *UAW Washington Report,* criticized the Chicago police for their forceful suppression of street demonstrations during the 1968 Democratic convention, the paper's editor and Reuther received letters from rank-and-file members upholding the police action and criticizing the demonstrators; Walter P. Reuther Collection, Box 52, f. 13; Koscielski, "Divided Loyalties," 215; *New York Times,* May 16, 1970.

16. Leonard Woodcock interview with John Herling, June 21, 1982, p. 124.

17. Lichtenstein, *Most Dangerous Man,* 391; Boyle, *UAW and the Heyday,* 158–60, 208; Peter B. Levy, "The New Left and Labor: The Early Years (1960–1963)," *Labor History,* XXXI, No. 3 (Summer 1990), 298–300; Peter B. Levy, *The New Left and Labor in the 1960s* (Urbana: University of Illinois Press, 1994), 11–15.

18. Levy, *New Left and Labor,* 14–15; Boyle, *UAW and the Heyday,* 181, 200.

19. Boyle, *UAW and the Heyday,* 212.

20. Douglas Fraser interview with John Herling, February 21, 1983, pp. 42–43; Koscielski, "Divided Loyalties," 97; Boyle, *UAW and the Heyday,* 227; Lichtenstein, *Most Dangerous Man,* 420–21.

21. *New York Times,* April 21, 1970; Walter P. Reuther interview with William J. Eaton, August 20, 1969, p. 10.

22. *Factory,* April 1967, quoted in Carew, *Reuther,* 134.

23. Frank Cormier and William J. Eaton, *Reuther* (Englewood Cliffs, NJ: Prentice-Hall, 1970), 325; Steve Babson, *The Unfinished Struggle: Turning Points in American Labor, 1877–Present* (Lanham, MD: Rowman & Littlefield, 1999), 164.

24. Walter P. Reuther to Emil Mazey, November 15, 1957, Walter P. Reuther Collection, Box 303, f. 6; John Barnard, *Walter Reuther and the Rise of the Auto Workers* (Boston: Little, Brown, 1983), 178–80; Victor Reuther, *The Brothers Reuther and the Story of the UAW: A Memoir* (Boston: Houghton Mifflin, 1976), 325–27, 364–77.

25. Carew, *Reuther,* 110, 134.

26. *New York Times,* December 14, 1962, November 6, 1963, April 6, 1967; Walter P. Reuther, "Proposal for a Comprehensive, Cooperative, Coordinated Organizational Drive," February 1961, Walter P. Reuther Collection, Box 567, f. 7; UAW, International Executive Board, Minutes, July 11–14, 1961, pp. 145–46; Carew, *Reuther,* 110–11.

27. *UAW Solidarity,* July 1966; *New York Times,* December 16, 17, 18, 1965, October 2, 1967, September 15, 1969; Paul Schrade interview with John Herling, December 10, 1977, pp. 39–46; Walter P. Reuther speech at Delano, California, December 16, 1965, Walter P. Reuther Collection, Box 555, f. 4; Walter P. Reuther to Cesar Chavez, March 5, 1968, Walter P. Reuther Collection, Box 345, f. 3; UAW,

Proceedings of the Twentieth Constitutional Convention [1966], 225, 232; UAW, International Executive Board, Minutes, January 31–February 3, 1967, pp. 63–67; Jacques E. Levy, *Cesar Chavez: Autobiography of La Causa* (New York: Norton, 1975), 202–4.

28. Arthur M. Schlesinger, Jr., *Robert Kennedy and His Times* (Boston: Houghton Mifflin, 1978), II, 825.

29. *New York Times*, April 9, 1968.

30. *New York Times*, December 7, 1961, August 16, November 13, 14, 18, December 9, 1962. Walter P. Reuther Collection, Boxes 301 and 302, contain many Reuther dictated memos for a George Meany file identifying and describing his clashes with Meany. UAW, International Executive Board, Minutes, January 15–16, 1968, pp. 42–48; Walter P. Reuther to Mrs. Eleanor Roosevelt, April 18, 1961, Eleanor Roosevelt Collection, Container 4486, Franklin D. Roosevelt Library; Carew, *Reuther*, 109–10.

31. Walter P. Reuther to George Meany, February 14, 1961, Walter P. Reuther Collection, Box 301, f. 12; "WPR Note," March 8, 1961, Walter P. Reuther Collection, Box 301, f. 12; UAW, International Executive Board, Minutes, March 23–26, 1965, pp. 120–23; UAW, International Executive Board, Minutes, June 8, 1966, pp. 21–27; Walter P. Reuther to George Meany, telegram, June 9, 1966, Walter P. Reuther Collection, Box 303, f. 13; Statement to AFL-CIO Executive Council, June 16, 1966, Walter P. Reuther Collection, Box 38, f. 8, *New York Times*, June 11, 14, 17, 19, 20, 1966; Carew, *Reuther*, 108, 111 ff.; Lichtenstein, *Most Dangerous Man*, 406–9.

32. Carew, *Reuther*, 107–9, 125–27; Ted Morgan, *A Covert Life: Jay Lovestone, Communist, Anti-Communist, and Spymaster* (New York: Random House, 1999), 288–89; *John Herling's Labor Letter*, December 25, 1965; *New York Times*, December 14, 16, 1965; Boyle, *UAW and the Heyday*, 219–20; Foner, *U.S. Labor*, 32.

33. UAW, *Administrative Letters*, Vol. 18, Letter No. 16, December 29, 1966, pp. 1441–44; *New York Times*, June 17, August 25, 27, November 12, 15, 17, 18, 20, 23, December 6, 16, 30, 31, 1966, February 10, 1967; Foner, *U.S. Labor*, 41–42.

34. *New York Times*, February 4, 10, April 23, 1967; Walter P. Reuther et al. to George Meany and William Schnitzler, telegram, February 3, 1967, Walter P. Reuther Collection, Box 303, f. 1.

35. Meany quoted in *New York Times*, February 25, December 8, 1967, March 26, 1968.

36. *New York Times*, March 3, 13, 14, May 3, 17, July 4, 1968; UAW, International Executive Board, Minutes, January 15–16, 1968, p. 32, April 10, 25, May 2, 23, 1968, pp. 124–33, 137, November 20–21, 1968, p. 36; Walter P. Reuther to George Meany, July 1, 1968, Walter P. Reuther Collection, Box 303, f. 3; George Meany to Walter P. Reuther et al., July 10, 1968, Walter P. Reuther Collection, Box 303, f. 3; Carew, *Reuther*, 132–33.

37. Sidney Fine, *Violence in the Model City: The Cavanaugh Administration, Race Relations, and the Detroit Riot of 1967* (Ann Arbor: University of Michigan Press, 1989); Widick, *Detroit*, 166–86; *New York Times*, July 28, October 29, 1967; Walter P. Reuther, Memorandum to the file, July 31, 1967, Walter P. Reuther Collection, Box 369, f. 5.

38. Sidney Fine, *"Expanding the Frontiers of Civil Rights": Michigan, 1948–1968* (Detroit: Wayne State University Press, 2000), 239; *UAW Solidarity,* March 1968; Widick, *Detroit,* 192–93; *New York Times,* October 27, 31, November 19, 1967, March 24, October 31, 1968, January 7, 19, May 15, 1969; Douglas Fraser to Walter P. Reuther, December 19, 1969, Walter P. Reuther Collection, Box 5, f. 4; William B. Gould, *Black Workers in White Unions: Job Discrimination in the United States* (Ithaca: Cornell University Press, 1977), 391.

39. Fraser quoted in Heather Ann Thompson, *Whose Detroit? Politics, Labor, and Race in a Modern American City* (Ithaca: Cornell University Press, 2001), 105; *UAW Solidarity,* May 1969; Widick, *Detroit,* 193; Walter P. Reuther interview with William J. Eaton, August 20, 1969, pp. 5–6; *New York Times,* March 12, April 12, 1969, February 15, April 11, 1970.

40. Conditions in Chrysler plants, including industrial accidents (some fatal) and incidents of shop-floor violence, are discussed in Thompson, *Whose Detroit?* 58–70, 105–7; James Johnson's tragic story, including an account of his trial, is woven throughout Thompson's study.

41. *New York Times,* July 13, 16, October 22, 1968, February 11, 1969; ELRUM, "The History of an Opportunist: Walter Reuther," p. 1; DRUM handout, November 1968, Walter P. Reuther Collection, Box 74, f. 4; Bill Beckham to Walter P. Reuther, February 13, 1969, Walter P. Reuther Collection, Box 74, f. 4; League of Revolutionary Black Workers handout, November 1969, copy in Walter P. Reuther Collection, Box 74, f. 4. The RUM's have attracted considerable comment. See Steve Jefferys, *Management and Managed: Fifty Years of Crisis at Chrysler* (Cambridge: Cambridge University Press, 1968), 162–87; Thompson, *Whose Detroit?* 109–24; James A. Geschwander, *Class, Race, and Worker Insurgency: The League of Revolutionary Black Workers* (Cambridge: Cambridge University Press, 1977); Dan Georgakas and Marvin Surkin, *Detroit: I Do Mind Dying,* updated edition (Cambridge, MA: South End Press, 1998), 19–41, 69–83, 85–102; Boyle, *UAW and the Heyday,* 251–52.

42. In addition to the accounts cited above, see Horace Sheffield interview with Herbert Hill, July 24, 1968, p. 32; Thompson, *Whose Detroit?* 111–24; 159–73; *New York Times,* March 13, 1969, April 20, 21, 1970; *Detroit News,* May 28, 1969; UAW, International Executive Board, Minutes, June 24–26, 1968, p. 196; Widick, *Detroit,* 196–98; Boyle, *UAW and the Heyday,* 253–54; Jefferys, *Management and Managed,* 176, 180–81.

43. Statement of UAW International Executive Board, March 10, 1969, Walter P. Reuther Collection, Box 80, f. 3; UAW, *Proceedings of the Twenty-Second Constitutional Convention* [1970], 22.

44. *New York Times,* January 18, 20, April 24–May 1, June 29, 1969.

45. Boyle, *UAW and the Heyday,* 220–21.

46. *New York Times,* May 12, 1968; *UAW Solidarity,* April 1968; Sidney Fine, "Michigan and Housing Discrimination, 1949–1968," *Michigan Historical Review,* XXIII, No. 2 (Fall 1997), 108; Fine, "Expanding the Frontiers," 327.

47. For the 1968 election, see Matusow, *Unraveling of America,* 395–439; Lewis Chester, Godfrey Hodgson, and Bruce Page, *An American Melodrama: The*

Presidential Campaign of 1968 (New York: Viking, 1969); Theodore H. White, *The Making of the President, 1968* (New York: Atheneum, 1969); Seth M. Wigderson, "The UAW in the 1950's" (Ph.D. diss., Wayne State University, 1989), 236; Quayle et al., "A Study in Depth," Vol. 1, Pt. 1, 39; Boyle, *UAW and the Heyday,* 221–22.

48. Quayle et al., "A Study in Depth," Vol. 1, Pt. 1, 67–71, 128, 178; Boyle, *UAW and the Heyday,* 221–22.

49. Weinberg and Shrade quoted in Boyle, *UAW and the Heyday,* 237; *New York Times,* May 10, 1968; Steven M. Gillon, *Politics and Vision: The ADA and American Liberalism, 1947–1985* (New York: Oxford University Press, 1987), 209–13.

50. Paul Schrade interview with John Herling, December 10, 1977, pp. 1, 14–15; UAW, International Executive Board, Minutes, April 10, 25, May 2, 23, 1968, pp. 48–50; *New York Times,* March 24, May 9, 10, 1968; Boyle, *UAW and the Heyday,* 238–39.

51. Schlesinger, *Robert Kennedy,* II, 911; Douglas Fraser interview with John Barnard, May–June 1990, p. 125; Paul Schrade interview with John Herling, December 20, 1977, p. 18; *New York Times,* June 7, 1968.

52. UAW, International Executive Board, Minutes, June 24–26, 1968, p. 69; Boyle, *UAW and the Heyday,* 241.

53. "Statement Presented to Democratic Party Platform Committee by Walter P. Reuther . . . August 20, 1968," copy in Walter P. Reuther Collection, Box 559, f. 3; Douglas Fraser interview with John Barnard, May–June 1990, p. 118; Irving Bluestone interview with John Barnard, October 1988–November 1992, pp. 158–59; Boyle, *UAW and the Heyday,* 249–50; Koscielski, "Divided Loyalties," 110.

54. UAW, International Executive Board, Minutes, September 10–12, 1968, pp. 9–16, 29–31, 63–67; *New York Times,* September 24, 1968; *UAW Solidarity,* October 1968; Boyle, *UAW and the Heyday,* 250–51.

55. James N. Gregory, "Southernizing the American Working Class: Post-War Episodes of Regional and Class Transformation," *Labor History,* XXXIX, No. 2 (May 1998), 142; UAW, International Executive Board, Minutes, November 20–21, 1968, p. 37; *New York Times,* October 27, 1968; Boyle, *UAW and the Heyday,* 253; Gillon, *Politics and Vision,* 221.

56. *New York Times,* September 10, 12, October 6, 21, 1968; UAW, International Executive Board, Minutes, November 20–21, pp. 36–37; Foner, *U.S. Labor,* 67; White, *Making of the President,* 453; Koscielski, "Divided Loyalties," 162–63; Chester et al., *American Melodrama,* 707–9.

57. *St. Louis Globe-Democrat,* September 30, 1968; Walter P. Reuther, Hemsley Lecture Series, Brandeis University, October 29, 1968, copy in Walter P. Reuther Collection, Box 560, f. 1.

58. A copy of Reuther's speech, September 22, 1968, is in Walter P. Reuther Collection, Box 53, f. 2; *New York Times,* September 23, 1968.

59. Boyle, *UAW and the Heyday,* 254; Buffa, *Union Power,* 110–11, 215; Douglas Fraser interview with John Barnard, May–June, 1990, p. 85; Bill Dodds to Walter P. Reuther, October 31, 1968, Walter P. Reuther Collection, Box 52, f. 13; Carew, *Reuther,* 129.

60. For Reuther's optimistic reading of the union's effectiveness in reducing the Wallace vote, see UAW, International Executive Board, Minutes, March 20–21, 1968, pp. 34–38; Boyle, *UAW and the Heyday*, 255–56.

61. UAW, International Executive Board, Minutes, June 24–26, 1968, pp. 35–39; *UAW Solidarity*, July 1969; *New York Times*, July 24, 1968, May 27, 1969; Carew, *Reuther*, 136.

62. UAW, International Executive Board, Minutes, October 6–9, 1969, pp. 433–41, November 7–9, 1969, pp. 7–12; *UAW Solidarity*, November, December, 1969; *New York Times*, October 14, 1969; Foner, *U.S. Labor*, 87–89.

63. *New York Times*, April 21, 1970; UAW, *Proceedings of the Twenty-Second Constitutional Convention* [1970], 22; Walter P. Reuther to Richard M. Nixon, telegram, quoted in Koscielski, "Divided Loyalties," 22; Victor Reuther, *Brothers Reuther*, 462.

64. Koscielski, "Divided Loyalties," 120, 201–2; Foner, *U.S. Labor*, 134–43, 148–50.

65. Frank Fitzsimmons and Walter Reuther to "Dear Senator" [sent to all United States senators], July 11, 1969, Walter P. Reuther Collection, Box 409, f. 4; *New York Times*, July 2, 1969; *UAW Solidarity*, March 1969.

66. UAW, International Executive Board, Minutes, June 23–26, 1969, pp. 95–96; a copy of "Swords into Plowshares" is in the Walter P. Reuther Collection, Box 423, f. 11; Walter P. Reuther to Senator Edward Kennedy, July 11, July 25, 1969, Walter P. Reuther Collection, Box 410, f. 10; *New York Times*, December 2, 4, 1969; Carew, *Reuther*, 130–31.

67. Victor Reuther, *Brothers Reuther*, 380; Carew, *Reuther*, 137; Conway quoted in Derek C. Bok and John T. Dunlop, *Labor and the American Community* (New York: Simon and Schuster, 1970), 441.

68. Bok and Dunlop, *Labor and the American Community*, 441–50; for a critique, see Boyle, *UAW and the Heyday*, 213–17.

69. Carew, *Reuther*, 137.

70. An account and assessment that credits the UAW with a pioneering political vision during the Reuther era, although realized only in part, is in Boyle, *UAW and the Heyday*, passim (see pp. 259–61 for a summary statement). An interpretation, covering much the same ground, that places more emphasis on the internal contradictions and compromises in the UAW's message and actions is in Lichtenstein, *Most Dangerous Man*, passim.

Chapter 13

"A whole new middle class": Walter P. Reuther, "The labor movement in America is developing a whole new middle class," in an interview with Henry Brandon, Washington correspondent of the *Sunday Times* [London], June 22, 1958.

1. Roger Rapoport, *Wall Street Journal*, July 24, 1967; *Newsweek*, September 14, 1970, p. 81.

2. Harvey Swados, with an introduction by Nelson Lichtenstein, *On the Line* (Urbana: University of Illinois Press, 1990); 28, originally published in 1957. Ques-

tioned about the Swados book by TV interviewer Mike Wallace, Reuther replied that while he did not share Swados's point of view, he conceded that "the workers' identity" suffers in a mechanized production system, "his sense of creative expression is almost completely wiped out." Transcript of "The Mike Wallace Interview," January 25, 1958, p. 8, copy in Walter P. Reuther Collection, Box 564, f. 5; Ely Chinoy, *Autoworkers and the American Dream*, 2d ed. (Urbana: University of Illinois Press, 1992), 85, originally published in 1955; Douglas Fraser, Robert L. Kanter Memorial Lecture, March 10, 1983, copy in Douglas Fraser Collection (II), Box 2; C. Wright Mills, *White Collar: The American Middle Classes* (New York: Oxford University Press, 1956), 215–38, first published in 1951; Robert Blauner, *Alienation and Freedom* (Chicago: University of Chicago Press, 1964), 89–121.

3. Bennett M. Berger, *Working-Class Suburb: A Study of Auto Workers in Suburbia* (Berkeley: University of California Press, 1960), ix, 23–85, 91–98; Charles R. Walker and Robert H. Guest, *The Man on the Assembly Line* (Cambridge, MA: Harvard University Press, 1952), 38–65, 81–91. A sociological study that qualifies to a degree the conventional dreary portrayal of auto factory work and life is William H. Form, *Blue-Collar Stratification: Autoworkers in Four Countries* (Princeton: Princeton University Press, 1976).

4. Barry Bluestone and Irving Bluestone, *Negotiating the Future: A Labor Perspective on American Business* (New York: Basic Books, 1992), xi.

5. Berger, *Working-Class Suburb*, 86, 89; Chinoy, *Autoworkers*, 44, 49, 57; John W. Anderson interview with Jack W. Skeels, February 17–May 21, 1960, p. 167.

6. Chinoy, *Autoworkers*, 97–109; Irving Howe and B. J. Widick, *The UAW and Walter Reuther* (New York: Da Capo Press, 1973), 235–43, 253–59, originally published in 1949; Gladys Palmer, "Attitudes toward Work in an Industrial Community," *American Journal of Sociology*, 63 (July 1957), 17, quoted in George Lipsitz, *Rainbow at Midnight: Labor and Culture in the 1940s* (Urbana: University of Illinois Press, 1994), 237–38; Robert Guest, "Work Careers and Aspirations of Auto Workers," *American Sociological Review*, XIX, No. 2 (April 1954), 319, cited in Lipsitz, *Rainbow at Midnight*, 237–38; Douglas Fraser interview with John Herling, January 20, 1983, pp. 43–44.

7. Oliver Quayle and Company, "A Study in Depth of the Rank and File of the United Automobile Workers (AFL-CIO)," May 1967. The survey was not given public distribution. Copy in Ken Bannon Collection, Boxes 27–28.

8. Ibid., 9–14.

9. Ibid., 10.

10. Ibid., 19–24, 48.

11. Ibid., 30–43, 48; Walker and Guest, *Man on the Assembly Line*, 123–34.

12. Quayle et al., "Study in Depth," 197.

13. UAW, International Executive Board, Minutes, December 4–6, 1962, pp. 137–38; UAW, International Executive Board, Minutes, June 26, 1969, pp. 262–85; Ronald Edsforth, "On the Decline of Rank-and-File Militance in the Postwar UAW," paper in author's possession, p. 15; *New York Times*, September 1, 1969; Reuther speech at UAW Local 600 dinner, March 27, 1965, p. 20, copy in Walter P.

Reuther Collection, Box 553, f. 10; UAW, *Proceedings of the Twentieth Constitutional Convention* [1966], 222.

14. UAW, *Proceedings of the Twentieth Constitutional Convention* [1966], 98–105, 217–22; UAW, International Executive Board, Minutes, June 14–16, 1967, pp. 58–73; UAW, International Executive Board, Minutes, June 26, 1969, pp. 262–85; Reuther described his hopes and dreams for the center in detail in a speech to a delegation of Chrysler workers meeting at Black Lake, March 20, 1970, Walter P. Reuther Collection, Box 563, f. 4; *UAW Solidarity*, September 1969; Pat Sexton, "Brendan's Voyage," *Labor Studies Journal*, XVI, No. 1 (Spring 1991), 35–43; Anthony Carew, *Walter Reuther* (Manchester: University of Manchester Press, 1993), 138–39; Lichtenstein, *Most Dangerous Man*, 436–37. Asked by Irving Bluestone "what do you think you've done best?" Reuther replied "I think I'm a good educator." Irving Bluestone interview with John Barnard, October 1988–November 1992, pp. 95–98.

15. "Committee for Militant Unionism," leaflets in the Walter P. Reuther Collection, Box 51, f. 4, Box 52, f. 10; UAW, *Proceedings of the Twenty-First Constitutional Convention* [1968], 94–126; Pete Kelly interview in Robert H. Mast, ed., *Detroit Lives* (Philadelphia: Temple University Press, 1994), 219; *New York Times*, May 7, 12, 1968.

16. Pete Kelly interview in Mast, ed., *Detroit Lives*, 219.

17. UAW, *Proceedings of the Twenty-Second Constitutional Convention* [1970], 308–28, 356–57, 424–875; *New York Times*, April 24, 1970; *Detroit News*, April 20–23, 1970; Walter P. Reuther to "Dear Ted" [Senator Edward M. Kennedy], May 7, 1970, Walter P. Reuther Collection, Box 410, f. 10; *UAW Solidarity*, May 1970.

18. UAW, *Proceedings of the Twenty-Second Constitutional Convention* [1970], 356–57; Lichtenstein, *Most Dangerous Man*, 435–36; *UAW Solidarity*, May 1970; *Detroit Free Press*, April 24, 1970; *New York Times*, April 21, 1970; *Detroit News*, April 24, 1970.

19. John Barnard, *Walter Reuther and the Rise of the Auto Workers* (Boston: Little, Brown, 1983), 212; Lichtenstein, *Most Dangerous Man*, 437; *New York Times*, July 16, 1970.

20. *New York Times*, May 15–16, 1970; Lichtenstein, *Most Dangerous Man*, 437–38. The quoted verses were composed by J. L. Swigart, Committeeman and Skilled Trades Chairman, UAW Local 1501. A mimeographed copy is in the Leonard Woodcock Collection, Box 41, f. 12.

21. *New York Times*, April 4, 1968, May 11, 14, 1970; Barnard, *Reuther*, 212–14. The best summary and assessment of Reuther's thought and activity as union leader and public figure is in Carew, *Reuther*, 140–49.

22. UAW, International Executive Board, Minutes, May 15, 1970, pp. 1–13; UAW, Constitution of the International Union, Art. 10, sec. 17.

23. UAW, International Executive Board, Minutes, May 22, 1970, pp. 2–7.

24. Douglas Fraser interview with John Barnard, May–June, 1990, pp. 1–13; *UAW Solidarity*, June 13, 1977.

25. Douglas Fraser interview with John Herling, January 20, 1983, pp. 55–56; Leonard Woodcock interview with John Herling, October 1, 1982, pp. 7–14; *Wall*

Street Journal, May 19, 1970; Don Ephlin interview with John Barnard, June 25, July 12, 1993, pp. 26–27; Kenneth (Ken) Bannon interview with Warner Pflug, April 30, 1985, pp. 51–58.

26. UAW, International Executive Board, Minutes, May 22, 1970, p. 22; *UAW Solidarity,* July 1970.

27. Biographical material on Woodcock drawn from John Barnard, *Leonard Woodcock: Unionist and Citizen* (Detroit: Walter P. Reuther Library, College of Urban, Labor and Metropolitan Affairs, Wayne State University, n.d.). Woodcock's account may be found in interviews with Jack W. Skeels, October 30, 1963; with John Herling, June 21, October 1, 1982; and with John Barnard, January 18, 30, February 7, 1991.

28. Brendan Sexton interview with John Herling, February 24, 1979, p. 49; Leonard Woodcock interview with Jack W. Skeels, April 30, 1963, p. 37.

29. Leonard F. Woodcock interview with John Barnard, January 18, 30, February 7, 1991, p. 92.

30. Leonard Woodcock interview with John Barnard, January 18, 30, February 7, 1991, pp. 40–43; Ed Cray, *Chrome Colossus: General Motors and Its Times* (New York: McGraw-Hill, 1980), 461–64.

31. Bargaining objectives for 1970 are listed and discussed in UAW, Administrative Letter, "Highlights of the UAW International Executive Board's Thoughts and Suggestions for the UAW 1970 Collective Bargaining Program," February 9, 1970, and in UAW, *Proceedings of the Twenty-Second Constitutional Convention* [1970], 29, 133–81; *UAW Solidarity,* March, May 1970; *Detroit Free Press,* April 20–21, 1970; *New York Times,* November 9, 1969, February 17, March 13, April 19, 21, 26, 1970; Carew, *Reuther,* 138; Lichtenstein, *Most Dangerous Man,* 435–36.

32. UAW, Administrative Letter, "Highlights of the UAW International Executive Board's Thoughts and Suggestions for the UAW 1970 Collective Bargaining Program," February 9, 1970; UAW, *Proceedings of the Twenty-Second Constitutional Convention* [1970], 29, 133–81; United National Caucus, March 1970, leaflet in UAW President's Office: Douglas Fraser Collection, Box 75, f. 6; Transcript of United National Caucus television panel broadcast, November 8, 1970, copy in Ken Bannon Collection, Box 65, f. 12.

33. *Nation's Business,* March 1971, p. 27; Brendan Sexton interview with John Herling, February 24, 1979, Part 2, p. 51; Donald Ephlin interview with John Barnard, June 25, July 12, 1993, pp. 24–25; Ralph Showalter interview with John Herling, January 10, 1980, pp. 20–22.

34. UAW, International Executive Board, Minutes, September 14, 1970, pp. 12–13; *UAW [19]70–[19]73: A Report on UAW-Auto Industry Negotiations* (n.p., n.d.), 1–5; Woodcock's notes on the negotiations are in Leonard Woodcock Collection, Box 61, ff. 11–12 and Box 62, ff. 1–11; William Serrin, *The Company and the Union* (New York: Alfred A. Knopf, 1973), 25–69; *UAW Solidarity,* October 1970.

35. UAW, International Executive Board, Minutes, July 29, 30, 1970, pp. 133–34; Materials for International Executive Board meeting of July 29–30, 1970, UAW International Executive Board Meetings Collection.

36. UAW, International Executive Board, Minutes, October 22, 1970, pp. 5–9, 12–14; *Proceedings UAW Special Convention,* October 24, 1970, pp. 32, 37, 43–54; *UAW Solidarity,* November, December 1970, May 1971; Serrin, *Company and Union,* 201–8.

37. Leonard Woodcock interview with John Barnard, January 18, 30, February 7, 1991, p. 43; Irving Bluestone interview with John Barnard, October 1988–November 1992, 118–19; Serrin, *Company and Union,* 243–85; Kenneth (Ken) Bannon interview with Warner Pflug, April 30, 1985, pp. 33–34; *Wall Street Journal,* November 20, 1970; *Detroit Free Press,* January 25, 1971.

38. Leonard Woodcock interview with John Barnard, January 18, 30, February 7, 1991, p. 43; *UAW [19]70–[19]73,* pp. 8–13; *UAW Solidarity,* December 1970; *Detroit Free Press,* November 27, 1970; *Detroit News,* November 24, 1970.

39. Woodcock reported on the conclusion of the negotiations in UAW, International Executive Board, Minutes, November 11–12, 1970, pp. 2–26; *UAW Solidarity,* January 1971; *Detroit Free Press,* November 21, December 8, 1970; *Detroit News,* November 23, December 10, 1970.

40. *Wall Street Journal,* November 20, 1970; United National Caucus leaflet, December 1970, copy in UAW President's Office: Douglas Fraser Collection, Box 75, f. 6; B. J. Widick, *Detroit: City of Race and Class Violence,* rev. ed. (Detroit: Wayne State University Press, 1989), 219–20.

41. Ronald Edsforth, "Affluence, Anti-Communism, and the Transformation of Industrial Unionism among Automobile Workers, 1933–1973," in Ronald Edsforth and Larry Bennett, eds., *Popular Culture and Political Change in Modern America* (Albany: State University of New York Press, 1991), 107–11; UAW, *Proceedings of the Twenty-Second Constitutional Convention* [1970], 21–23; Harvey Swados, "The Myth of the Happy Worker," reprinted in Swados, *On the Line,* 237; Sanford M. Jacoby, *Employing Bureaucracy: Managers, Unions, and the Transformation of Work in American Industry, 1900–1945* (New York: Columbia University Press, 1985), 278–80. A study that maintains the continuing working-class character of the lives of auto and other manual workers is Patricia C. and Brendan Sexton, *Blue Collars and Hard Hats* (New York: Random House, 1970).

42. Edsforth, "Affluence," 114–16.

43. UAW, *Proceedings of the Twenty-First Constitutional Convention* [1968], 27.

44. Reuther related the story of the Kelsey-Hayes foundry worker in a Labor Day address at St. Matthew's Methodist Church in Detroit on September 6, 1959. A copy of the address is in Walter P. Reuther Collection, Box 433, f. 2. A letter from Thaddeus Ogar to Reuther, June 15, 1961, copy in the Victor G. Reuther Collection, Box 29, f. 6, establishes the identity of the worker.

Epilogue

"Things that we had to do, we did": Owen Bieber interview with John Barnard, April 10–11, 1997, p. 55.

1. For an analysis both sweeping and penetrating of the labor movement's decline since the 1960s, see Nelson Lichtenstein, *State of the Union: A Century of American Labor* (Princeton: Princeton University Press, 2002), 140–245.

2. UAW press release, June 12, 1980, UAW President's Office: Douglas Fraser Collection, Box 23, folder marked "Trade"; UAW, International Executive Board, Minutes, June 8–9, 1981, pp. 9–14; *Report of Douglas A. Fraser, President . . . UAW, Part One: UAW in Action*, May 1983, p. 8; "Auto Employment Levels by Company (U. S. Hourly)," May 1983, copy in UAW President's Office: Douglas Fraser Collection, Box 21, folder marked "Research."

3. *UAW Solidarity*, June 1978; *Automotive News*, October 19, 1981; "Nissan Employees Handbook," September 1982; UAW, International Executive Board, Minutes, March 14–16, 1983, pp. 163–73, June 22–23, 1983, pp. 65–70.

4. Leonard Woodcock, transcript of press conference, October 19, 1972, copy in UAW President's Office: Leonard Woodcock Collection, Box 162, f. 2; Speech of Pat Greathouse to the North American-Japan IMF Conference, Tokyo, July 11, 1977, copy in UAW President's Office: Douglas Fraser Collection, Box 28, folder marked "Greathouse, Pat"; UAW, International Executive Board, Minutes, February 26–28, 1980, pp. 19–51.

5. *UAW Solidarity*, May 1973, September 15, 1978, July 2, 1979.

6. *UAW Solidarity*, October 1973, October 16–31, 1976; Douglas Fraser interview with John Barnard, May–June, 1990, pp. 138–39, 144–46; Leonard Woodcock interview with John Barnard, January 18, 30, February 7, 1991.

7. Irving Bluestone interview with John Barnard, October 1988–November 1992, pp. 121, 154–56; statement of Gary Bryner, president of Lordstown Local 1112, in UAW, *Proceedings of the Twenty-Third Constitutional Convention* [1972], 81–83; Irving Bluestone to International Executive Board Members, January 25, 1973, copy in UAW President's Office: Leonard Woodcock Collection, Box 25, f. 10; Emma Rothschild, *Paradise Lost: The Decline of the Auto-Industrial Age* (New York: Vintage Books, 1973).

8. *UAW Solidarity*, January 1977, September 15, 1978, July 23, 1979; UAW, International Executive Board, Minutes, September 10–13, 1978, pp. 16–21, December 15–17, 1980, pp. 327–29, September 20–22, 1982, pp. 44–50, 92–99; antiorganizing measures at GM's Saginaw Gear plant in Athens, Alabama, documented in UAW President's Office: Douglas Fraser Collection, Box 12, folder marked "General Motors" and Box 18, folder marked "Organizing."

9. Irving Bluestone interview with John Barnard, October 1988–November 1992, 123–39; for a general discussion of employee involvement see Barry Bluestone and Irving Bluestone, *Negotiating the Future: A Labor Perspective on American Business* (New York: Basic Books, 1992), 145–64; UAW, International Executive Board, Minutes, December 12–14, 1978, p. 162, December 2–5, 1985, pp. 191–99.

10. For a favorable assessment of the Saturn experiment, see Bluestone and Bluestone, *Negotiating the Future*, 191–201; Don Ephlin interview with John Barnard, June 24, July 12, 1993, pp. 46–48; UAW, International Executive Board, Minutes, July 1, 3, 1985, pp. 23–43, July 24, 1985, pp. 3–33.

11. Steve Babson, ed., *Lean Work: Empowerment and Exploitation in the Global Auto Industry* (Detroit: Wayne State University Press, 1995); James P. Womack, Daniel T. Jones, and Daniel Roos, *The Machine that Changed the World* (New York: Harper Perennial, 1991); Steve Babson, "Restructuring the Workplace: Post Fordism or Return of the Foreman?" in Robert Asher and Ronald Edsforth, eds., *Autowork* (Albany: State University of New York Press, 1995), 227–56.

12. *UAW Solidarity*, August 1979–February 1980; Douglas Fraser interview with John Barnard, May–June, 1990, pp. 168–203; Marc Stepp interview with John Barnard, June 10, 18, 25, 1993, pp. 42–50; UAW, International Executive Board, Minutes, November 12–14, 1979, pp. 14–16, October 24, 1985; *Report of Douglas A. Fraser . . . UAW, Part One: UAW in Action* [1980], 16–18; Ken Morris interview with John Barnard, January 29, 1997, p. 53; Robert B. Reich and John D. Donahue, *New Deals: The Chrysler Revival and the American System* (New York: Penguin Books, 1986).

13. Douglas Fraser interview with John Barnard, May–June, 1990, pp. 171–82; UAW press release, July 15, 1980, copy in UAW President's Office: Douglas Fraser Collection, Box 4, f. 9; Marc Stepp interview with John Barnard June 10, 18, 25, 1993, pp. 55–64.

14. UAW, International Executive Board, Minutes, January 22, 1982, February 14, 1982, pp. 44–59, June 7–9, 1982, pp. 44–65; Don Ephlin interview with John Barnard, June 25, July 12, 1993, pp. 37–39; Owen Bieber interview with John Barnard, April 10–11, 1997, pp. 65–66.

15. Bob White interview with John Herling, May 1983, pp. 27–38; UAW, International Executive Board, Minutes, December 8–10, 1981, pp. 84–154, December 10, 1984.

16. *UAW Solidarity*, July–November, 1972, September 1973, November-December 1976, October 15–30, 1978; Peter D. Hart Associates, "A Survey of the Voting Behavior and Attitudes of the United Auto Workers in the State of Michigan, December 1978," copy in UAW President's Office: Douglas Fraser Collection, Box 14; UAW, International Executive Board, Minutes, December 15–17, 1980, p. 29; Leonard Woodcock interview with John Barnard, January 18, 30, February 7, 1991, pp. 112–17; Douglas Fraser to all members of Congress, September 19, 1977, UAW President's Office: Douglas Fraser Collection, Box 15, folder marked "Labor Law Reform"; Fraser statement of January 15, 1980, copy in UAW President's Office: Douglas Fraser Collection, Box 19, folder marked "Presidential Campaign (3)."

17. UAW, *Proceedings of the Twenty-Third Constitutional Convention* [1972], 78–91; UAW President's Office: Leonard Woodcock Collection, Box 9, ff. 3–9; Ken Morris interview with John Barnard, January 5, 1997, pp. 36–42.

18. UAW, International Executive Board, Minutes, August 6–8, 1974, pp. 58–59; *Washington Post*, December 28, 1980; *Detroit News*, July 30, 1980.

19. *UAW Solidarity*, December 1971, May 1974, July–August 1974, January–February 1975, June 29, 1977, November 11, 1977, December 1977, May 15, 1978; UAW, International Executive Board, Minutes, December 10–12, 1984, pp. 168–74; Nancy F. Gabin, *Feminism in the Labor Movement: Women and the United Auto Workers, 1935–1975* (Ithaca: Cornell University Press, 1990), 222–28.

20. UAW Research Department memo, November 12, 1980, copy in UAW President's Office: Douglas Fraser Collection, Box 21, folder marked "President's Office—Staff"; B. J. Widick, ed., *Auto Work and Its Discontents* (Baltimore: Johns Hopkins University Press, 1976), 8.

21. "The Purchasing Power of Working Time; An International Comparison, 1981," 35–41, copy in UAW President's Office: Douglas Fraser Collection, Box 26, folder marked "Wages."

22. Marc Stepp to Douglas A. Fraser, July 14, 1980, Don Ephlin to Douglas A. Fraser, July 9, 1980, UAW President's Office: Douglas Fraser Collection, Box 1; Peter D. Hart Research Associates, "A Survey of Attitudes of Members of the United Auto Workers, November 1979, Report to the UAW National Executive Board, November 13, 1979," in UAW President's Office: Douglas Fraser Collection, Box 14, folder marked "Hart Research Associates." Auto workers continue to attract the attention of authors, academic and otherwise, who offer different evaluations and perspectives. Widick, ed., *Auto Work and Its Discontents*, is a compilation of essays by authors with both autoworker and academic credentials. Richard Feldman and Michael Betzold, eds., *End of the Line: Autoworkers and the American Dream* (Urbana: University of Illinois Press, 1990) is a valuable collection of interviews with workers at a Ford truck plant. Other works that portray auto workers either at their jobs or when they have been laid off include Ruth Milkman, *Farewell to the Factory: Auto Workers in the Late Twentieth Century* (Berkeley: University of California Press, 1997); Steven P. Dandaneau, *A Town Abandoned: Flint, Michigan, Confronts Deindustrialization* (Albany: State University of New York Press, 1996); Kathryn Marie Dudley, *The End of the Line: Lost Jobs, New Lives in Postindustrial America* (Chicago: University of Chicago Press, 1994); Josie Kearns, *Life after the Line* (Detroit: Wayne State University Press, 1990); Joseph J. Fucini and Suzy Fucini, *Working for the Japanese: Inside Mazda's American Auto Plant* (New York: Free Press, 1990); and Laurie Graham, *On the Line at Subaru-Isuzu: The Japanese Model and the American Worker* (Ithaca: Cornell University Press, 1995). A personal account that relates with amusing irreverence stories of absenteeism, drinking and drug use, dogging it on the job, and other factory rat vices is Ben Hamper, *Rivethead: Tales from the Assembly Line* (New York: Warner Books, 1986); the author's slurs on the company (GM), the union, and the great majority of workers who did their jobs and supported their families, refrained from drinking and drug use while working, and cared about the quality of the product must have infuriated the targets.

23. UAW, *Twenty-Ninth Constitutional Convention* [1989], 15.

24. *UAW Solidarity*, January–February 1990; for statements on the American labor movement's present condition and possible future, see Lichtenstein, *State of the Union*, 246–76; and Robert H. Zeiger and Gilbert J. Gall, *American Workers, American Unions: The Twentieth Century*, 3d ed. (Baltimore: Johns Hopkins University Press, 2002), 240–70.

BIBLIOGRAPHICAL NOTE

THERE IS NO GENERAL WORK BY A SINGLE AUTHOR ON THE history of the United Auto Workers, on the history of auto work, or on the history of the auto workers themselves. Several books, present from different perspectives, overall accounts. The union's Education Department produced *We Make Our Own History: A Portrait of the UAW* (Detroit: International Union, UAW, 1986), on the occasion of the union's fiftieth anniversary. This well-illustrated book was intended primarily for the union's members. More profusely illustrated is Warner Pflug, *The UAW in Pictures* (Detroit: Wayne State University Press, 1971). A third volume, with a substantial text as well as many illustrations, casts a wider net to include workers outside the automotive field but at its core contains an account of auto workers in Detroit: Steve Babson et al., *Working Detroit: The Making of a Union Town* (New York: Adama Books, 1984). Similarly, Mike Smith and Thomas Featherstone, *Labor in Detroit: Working in the Motor City* (Chicago: Arcadia Publishing, 2001), presents photographic reproductions with brief commentary.

Two volumes consisting of essays by different authors provide accounts of important topics and trends with little overlap between them. They are: Nelson Lichtenstein and Stephen Meyer, eds., *On the Line: Essays in the History of Auto Work* (Urbana: University of Illinois Press, 1989); and Robert Asher and Ronald Edsforth, eds., *Autowork* (Albany: State University of New York Press, 1995).

The work which more than any other offers an integrated analysis and interpretation of the union's history in satisfying factual depth is Nelson Lichtenstein, *The Most Dangerous Man in Detroit: Walter Reuther and the Fate of American Labor* (New York: Basic Books, 1995). Although a biography rather than a history, since Reuther was a major force in the union for the thirty-five years from its founding until his death, this study necessarily recounts, analyzes, and assesses many of the most significant events and trends in the union's story. Lichtenstein's vantage point on Reuther and the UAW is somewhat to the left of the subjects, which gives the interpretation a critical edge. The periodical *Labor History* (XXXVII, No. 3, 1996, pp. 365–91) published a symposium on this Reuther biography, with contributions by five historians and a rejoinder by Lichtenstein.

Other books on the UAW and the auto workers include:

Babson, Steve. *Building the Union: Skilled Workers and Anglo-Gaelic Immigrants in the Rise of the UAW.* New Brunswick: Rutgers University Press, 1991.

Boyle, Kevin G. *The UAW and the Heyday of American Liberalism, 1945–1968.* Ithaca: Cornell University Press, 1995.

Clive, Alan. *State of War: Michigan in World War II.* Ann Arbor: University of Michigan Press, 1979.

Edsforth, Ronald. *Class Conflict and Cultural Consensus: The Making of a Mass Consumer Society in Flint, Michigan.* New Brunswick: Rutgers University Press, 1987.

Fine, Sidney. *The Automobile under the Blue Eagle.* Ann Arbor: University of Michigan Press, 1963.

———. *Frank Murphy: The New Deal Years.* Chicago: University of Chicago Press, 1979.

———. *Sit-Down: The General Motors Strike of 1936–1937.* Ann Arbor: University of Michigan Press, 1969.

Gabin, Nancy F. *Feminism in the Labor Movement: Women and the United Auto Workers, 1935–1975.* Ithaca: Cornell University Press, 1990.

Gartman, David. *Auto Slavery: The Labor Process in the American Automobile Industry, 1897–1950.* New Brunswick: Rutgers University Press, 1986.

Halpern, Martin. *UAW Politics in the Cold War Era.* Albany: State University of New York Press, 1988.

Howe, Irving, and Widick, B. J. *The UAW and Walter Reuther.* New York: Da Capo Press, 1973.

Jefferys, Steve. *Management and Managed: Fifty Years of Crisis at Chrysler.* Cambridge: Cambridge University Press, 1986.

Keeran, Roger. *The Communist Party and the Auto Workers Unions.* Bloomington: Indiana University Press, 1988.

Lichtenstein, Nelson. *Labor's War at Home: The CIO in World War II.* Cambridge: Cambridge University Press, 1982.

Meier, August, and Rudwick, Elliott. *Black Detroit and the Rise of the UAW.* New York: Oxford University Press, 1979.

Meyer, Stephen. *The Five Dollar Day: Labor, Management and Social Control in the Ford Motor Company, 1908–1921.* Albany: State University of New York Press, 1981.

———. *"Stalin Over Wisconsin": The Making and Unmaking of Militant Unionism, 1900–1950.* New Brunswick: Rutgers University Press, 1992.

Peterson, Joyce Shaw. *American Automobile Workers, 1900–1933.* Albany: State University of New York Press, 1987.

Stieber, Jack. *Governing the UAW.* New York: John Wiley and Sons, 1962.

Sugrue, Thomas. *The Origins of the Urban Crisis: Race and Inequality in Postwar Detroit.* Princeton: Princeton University Press, 1996.

Thompson, Heather Ann. *Whose Detroit? Politics, Labor, and Race in a Modern American City.* Ithaca: Cornell University Press, 2001.

INDEX